C000244043

AIRPORTS

by
Martin Harrison & Alan Lord

4th Edition
ISBN 1 898779 14 7

16 colour photographs

Published and distributed by:

BUCHair (U.K.) Ltd
P.O. Box 89, Reigate, Surrey, RH2 7FG
Tel: +44 (0)1737 224747
Fax: +44 (0)1737 226777
E-mail: buchair_uk@compuserve.com
Website: http://www.buchair.rotor.com

Printed in Great Britain
Copyright © M S Harrison 1997

Where to get the products of BUCHair (U.K.) Ltd and Bucher & Co. Publikationen.?

If you cannot get our products at your local bookstore or if you need information about publication dates or prices, please contact the following organisations in, or nearest to, your country.

Australia

Mr James L Bell
BUCHER PUBLICATIONS (Australia)
PO Box 232
Riddell, Victoria 3431

Phone: (3) 54 28 63 12
Fax: (3) 93 79 07 67

Canada

Aviation World
195 Carlingview Drive
Rexdale
Ontario, M9W 5E8

Phone: (416) 674-5959
Fax: (416) 674-5915

http://www.interlog.com/~avworld
avworld@interlog.com

Denmark

NYBODER BOGHANDEL, ApS
114 Store Kongensgade
DK-1264 Copenhagen K

Phone: 33 32 33 20
Fax: 33 32 33 62

Deutschland

BUCHair (Deutschland)
PO Box 750210
D-60532 Frankfurt a.M.

Phone: (06105) 951 700
Fax: (06105) 951 701

http://www.photopart.com
buchair.d@photopart.com

Finland

AVIATION SHOP
Kajanuksenkatu 12
SF-00250 Helsinki

Phone: (09) 449 801
Fax: (09) 149 6163

France

LA MAISON DU LIVRE
76 Boulevard Malesherbes
F-75008 Paris

Phone: (1) 45 22 74 16
Fax: (1) 42 93 81 23

Great Britain

BUCHair (U.K.) Ltd
PO Box 89
Reigate
Surrey
RH2 7FG

Phone: (0) 1737 224 747
Fax: (0) 1737 226 777

http://www.buchair.rotor.com
buchair_uk@compuserve.com

Ireland

Irish Air Letter
20 Kempton Way
Navan Road
Dublin 7

Phone: (01) 838 06 29

Italy

LA BANCARELLA
AERONAUTICA S.A.S.
Corso Duca Degli Abruzzi 12
I-10128 Torino

Phone: (011) 53 13 41
Fax: (011) 562 93 59

Japan

NISHIYAMA YOSHO Co. Ltd
Takin Building 3F
12 4-7-11, Ginza, Chuo-ku
Tokyo 104

Phone: (03) 3562-0820
Fax: (03) 3562-0828

Netherlands

BOEKHANDEL VENSTRA B.V.
Binnenhof 50
Postbus 77
NL-1180 AB Amstelveen

Phone: (020) 641 98 80
Fax: (020) 640 02 52

Norway

Scanbook Norway
Automobilla, A/S
Automobilla Bookshop
Uranienborgveien 25
Postboks 7035, Homansbyen
N-0306 Oslo
Phone: 22 60 86 00
Fax: 22 60 86 02

Osterreich

BUCHER & CO., PUBLIKATIONEN
Postfach 44
CH-8058 Zurich-Flughafen
Schweiz

Phone: (01) 874 1 747
Fax: (01) 874 1 757

jp@buchair.ch

Schweiz
(Bestellungen)

BUCHER & CO., PUBLIKATIONEN
Postfach 44
CH-8058 Zurich-Flughafen

Phone: (01) 874 1 747
Fax: (01) 874 1 757

jp@buchair.ch

Schweiz
(Laden - Glattbrugg)

BUCHairSHOP
Bucher & Co., Publikationen
Schaffhauserstrasse 76
CH-8152 Glattbrugg

Phone: (01) 874 1 747
Fax: (01) 874 1 757

jp@buchair.ch

Schweiz
(Laden - Flughafen)

BUCHairSHOP
Bucher & Co., Publikationen
Terrasse, Terminal B
CH-8058 Zurich-Flughafen

Phone: (01) 874 1 747
Fax: (01) 874 1 757

jp@buchair.ch

South Africa

Mr Karel Zayman
SKY NEEDS
PO Box 1385
Kempton Park 1620

Phone: (011) 472 32 55
Fax: (011) 792 83 18

Spain

LA AERTOTECA
LIBRERIA MIGUEL CREUS
C/Congost, 11
E-08024 Barcelona

Phone: (93) 210 54 07
Fax: (93) 210 59 92

USA

BUCHair (USA), Inc.
PO Box 750515
Forest Hills
NY 11375-0515

Phone: (718) 263 8748
Fax: (718) 275 6190

Buchair@mail.idt.net

INTRODUCTION

This, the fourth Buchair book about the world's airports, is the seventh I have written on the subject. It started, a long time ago, as a hobby - something to do in the evenings and at weekends. It's now a full-time job for a few months, requiring three people. Over four hundred reports were received from all over the world, each containing information in one way or another.

Sometimes one report conflicts directly with another. A matter of weeks might separate the two, and both could be, by the time you read this book, long in the tooth. Times change with remarkable speed at airports. The nature of construction works at, say, Las Vegas and Manchester means that the book can't be completely accurate over two or three years. Some younger readers might fail to appreciate this. Parts of Africa (and even Europe) can explode into political unrest suddenly, with obvious implications for security arrangements.

Over the years readers will have noticed improvements - increased content, better presentation and so on. The most obvious change in this edition is that the maps have been generated electronically. There are new maps and there are updated maps - additional information about Denver and, once again, the layout of two airports that, at the time of printing, aren't in operation. Wherever possible, readers' wishes have been taken into consideration but many conflict with each other. You can't have *more* information, *more* maps and *more* everything else for *less* money, I'm afraid.

What I don't know at present is if I'll be able to write the next edition myself. My business now takes up much of my time and I have to be all over the country, working for one client or another. The days are long and I don't always feel like settling down to writing about airports in the evening. To put it another way, I don't usually feel like doing *anything* most evenings.

Each time this book comes out, I thank the many readers for their messages of support and for their suggestions. The book can sit on the bathroom window sill for use by readers who haven't the slightest intention of travelling to some of the far-flung places. Alternatively, it goes in some people's hand luggage as they set off on marathon spotting trips. The book is supposed to allow some readers to dream and others to plan. It can't do all the jobs for you. Part of the joy of world travel is doing things for yourself. I don't think it's *my* job to supply the names, addresses and phone/fax numbers of every airport manager in the world.

It becomes self-defeating after a while. As long as only one or two intrepid travellers turn up at some remote destination, they might find interest and assistance. A few years later, a bus-load turns up and the show's over . . . for everyone. Farmer's fields sometimes get treated as if they are common land, with spotters trampling all over crops. Farmers can get a bit funny about having their livelihood messed about. Spotters do all sorts of things that, in themselves, aren't really too bad. The roofs and bonnets of rental cars are often used as somewhere to stand, for a better view over a fence. This book can't actually recommend doing this, any more than it can countenance taking a pair of wire snippers to cut gaping holes in fences. In other words, some activities are just plain daft, and likely to lead to prosecution.

Apart from at one or two airports, spotters are a nuisance to managers, especially for anyone in charge of security. Heathrow's made that perfectly clear. If things are to get better, *everyone* who travels abroad is going to have to learn to behave sensibly. Some hope!

When the very first *International Airfield Guide* was published, it contained information about most of Europe and some of the more accessible parts of North America. There was nothing about South America, most of Africa nor the Far East, Australia or New Zealand. Adding information is easy, especially when it's about new destinations. What takes hard work is keeping it all up-to-date and, much of the time, it can't be done. People just don't go to Skardu, or Billings, or Ciudad Bolivar every couple of years.

Nevertheless, successive editions of this book have managed to paint a continually changing picture of what's happening where. I have merely put it all together. It's the four hundred or so reports that provide the actual information. The message is simple: if you want to see data revised, please drop me a line and I'll see it's put to good use. If the book is accurate, and of use to you, then it's done its job. If things change, as change they certainly will over the next two or three years, all it takes is a simple diagram and a few words explaining where the book has become out-of-date.

The book is about airports. It's not about general aviation fields and it's not about military airfields, aviation museums or wrecks and relics. I've been asked to include information about all these. It doesn't take too much imagination to work out what size the book would be, and how much it would cost, if I did include all this information. Consistency would, of course, be a major problem. I don't even want to think what the consequences might be of publishing information about a military airfield in, say, Senegal or Bosnia. Occasionally, there are details about the odd stored DC-8 or Caravelle, where they are relevant. Similarly, when there is a significant general aviation field near a far-flung airport (Lanseria or Essendon, for instance) they are included, to help plan an itinerary.

Maps take a lot of work and it's easy enough to take a photocopy and mark up changes. There are more than a hundred of them, now including Chep Lap Kok and the new Gardermoen. Others have been added so that we now have a map for just about every European capital city and something from all the world's major capitals.

There isn't much information about Libya, Iraq or a few of the other potential trouble-spots in the world. Not much point, really. Nobody's likely to fancy a trip to Sarajevo or Tehran because there's a reasonable chance it will end in tears.

So, here it is - what might be my last effort, after a long time. I've done my best to provide what you, the reader, have requested over the years. It can't be all things to all men but I sincerely hope it will provide hours of pleasure and information. It isn't perfect. Solid, and current, information was promised about one or two airports but, somehow, it never materialised. There are last minute changes that I'd like to add but the clock keeps ticking and it just has to go to the printers. If you want to help with information for the next edition, please do write to me at PMEditions, POBox 56, Crewe CW2 5FF, England.

ACKNOWLEDGMENTS

Lots of people have written lots of stuff, posted high-quality publicity material and generally gone out of their way to ensure that I was working with the best information. Jeremy Parkin has surfed the Net and down-loaded lots of good stuff from people who deserve a credit, if only they had posted their names with their data. Where names were supplied on the Internet, they are listed below. My personal thanks (and ditto on behalf of all readers) go to:

Andrew Abshier, Neil Arundel, Georges Van Belleghem, Piet Biesheuvel, Bill Blanchard, Kevin Bond, Andy Bowden, Rev. George Brigham, Jan Broe, Chris Busby, Lee Caulfield, Paul Chandler, John Chapman, Mark Checkley, Oto Chudy, Jonathan Clough, Michael Coad, Neal Cohen, Colman Corcoran, Milan Cvrkal, Luca Dall'Olio, Marco Finelli, Colin Fogwill, Billy Fullen, Claude-Patrick Giraud, Ian A. Gratton, Howard Griffin, Ian Grove, Lars-Inge Grundberg, Geraint Hayward, Ian J. Hiles, Harro Hofman, Dave Hose, Roger Jannsens, Ian Johnson, Jeff Katims, John Kelley, Steve Kinder, Matthias Kilian, Stephen J. King, Kimmo Koivula, Mickey Kopanski, Andrew Longdon, Phil Longdon, Takanori Maeda, Michel Magalhaes, Geert Marien, Peter May, Sean Meagher, Ken Milne, Huw Morris Jones, Tony Orr, Clemens Oude Meijers, Alistair Ness, John Palmer, Colin Parker, Jeremy Parkin, Ewan Partridge, R. Paulson, E. Graham Payne, Brian T. Richards, Brian Roffee, Vik Saini, Renato Salzinger, Dave Sheldon, David Shephard, Mick Smith, Steven Sowter, Christopher Swann, Henry Tenby, Mikko Tolonen, Lars Victoria, Chris Walker, Peter Watson, Thomas H Weidekamp, Simon Wills, Steve Wilson, D. Woodrow and Jim Woodrow.

Martin Harrison
30 October 1997

COVER PHOTOS

Front cover: Fairbanks International Airport, Alaska supplied by Mark Butler, Alaska International Airport System

Back cover: Miami International Airport, by kind permission of Hernando Vergara, Metro Dade County Aviation Department

AP = PAKISTAN

GILGIT
GIL   OPGT

On a motorway, driving 150 miles takes about two hours, only there aren't any motorways round here. By road, Skardu to Gilgit used to take about fifteen hours - and that was in summer! In winter, the trip took two days. It's a bit mountainous, so the jeep driver needs something to calm his nerves. Rather than resort to drink, a little (or, actually, quite a lot of) hashish is the best way. For some reason, the occasional jeep disappears off the road, tumbles a few hundred feet down to the river and, by the time anyone knows there's a problem, the crows have picked the bones clean. Now that the road has been surfaced, things have got a little better, and therefore quicker and safer. Air travel, in this part of the world, is hairy but it's the only way to travel.

Flights from Rawalpindi must be able to return, once they have taken off. Patience is therefore required. A twelve hour delay isn't anything to make a fuss about. It also gives you time to get used to the smell of the toilets . . . from the lounge, that is.

Sixteen thousand feet is no big deal in the average F.27 and it allows a reasonably good view of Nanga Parbat, a mountain some ten thousand feet higher. Subject to the weather, and plenty of other things, Pakistan is another world. If you want to see things that will take your breath away, this is where to go. Tourism is relatively new and, it has to be said, narcotic substances provide much of the attraction at a fraction of what they offer on a typical street corner in Amsterdam. Not just top-grade hash but heroin is plentiful in the bazaars.

The airport's delightful, colonial-style, passenger terminal is served by PIA F.27s but only when the weather is fair. A footpath, at the tree line, leads along the western perimeter of the field. Anyone who really must have a photograph of an F.27 can, in theory, take one here. There are no military aircraft based, so security precautions are not as strict as at other Pakistani airports.

This note applies to all airports in the country: Pakistan is surrounded by Iran, Afghanistan, China and India. The dispute over Kashmir means that a state of near-war exists with India. Little needs to be said about the perceived threat which its other neighbours pose. The people are extremely friendly and outgoing but they are held in an iron grip by the police and the military. Foreigners, under these circumstances, represent a genuine threat which must not be under-estimated. Aviation photography is therefore not something to be explained after the event. It will fall on deaf ears.

Where to stay in Gilgit? For a different experience, try the Jubilee Hotel. Price negotiable. Western commodities, such as soap, are worth a lot, in these parts. What makes the Jubilee slightly different is that it doesn't have en suite facilities. Well, to be honest, it might still have a communal latrine in the back yard. Interesting though. A final note for anyone bound for these parts: electricity is still considered a luxury.

ISLAMABAD
ISB   OPRN   Chaklala   5m/8km NW of Rawalpindi

Officially known as Islamabad, the airport complex is in fact closer to Rawalpindi, the two cities being very close to each other, and combines civil and military activity, both of some significance. To the left of the Islamabad Airport terminal and stands is Rawalpindi base, used by the Pakistani Air Force.

Islamabad has one feature which is almost unique in the country: a viewing balcony which is open to the public. Anyone wishing to record registrations, rather than take photos, will enjoy a couple of days here. All representative types of the PIA fleet can be seen, in the company of domestic carriers. The departure lounge is large and modern, and can also be used for watching the activity.

To the left are the numerous military C-130s and 707s, plus some trainers. Showing anything but passing interest will, almost certainly, be misunderstood. When security precautions are as tight as they are in Pakistan, it is sensible to take one or two of your own.

KARACHI
KHI   OPKC   Quaid-e-Azam International   10m/16km N

The main passenger terminal is modern, air conditioned and clean. It has three levels: arrivals on the lower, departures in the middle, the restaurant and viewing gallery on top. The external viewing gallery is, of course, permanently closed.

Projecting from the terminal are two rotunda satellites: one for international flights and the other for domestic. Once inside the departure area, it's possible to walk around, and see most of the aircraft, very much like Pier 3/the Satellite at Gatwick (which they closely resemble). With binoculars, all movements can be logged from either terminal but discretion is essential. Photography is to be considered as reckless.

Nothing will ever stop the local populus from going to the airport to meet and greet, or to wave off. The gallery might have been closed to them but the people congregate instead in large numbers on the elevated departure level road. It's possible to blend into the masses, without drawing attention to one's self. Anything other than casual note-taking is bound to draw attention. If anyone contemplates taking a camera out of the gadget bag, and locking a 200mm zoom lens onto the front of it, it's best to think of it like dropping your pants. The effect will be pretty much the same!

This is the country's principal international airport, so visiting airlines, a predictable assortment of Asian and European long-hauls, may not be as interesting as the chance to see most of the PIA fleet and the other domestic carriers. These include Aero Asia ROMBAC 1-11s, Bhoja Air and Shaheen Air 737s.

Karachi is also served by another (all-civil) field, called SHARA-E-FAISAL, of which nothing has been reported. Apart from a nominal military presence at Quaid-e-Azam, there are two other military fields in the area. Detailed exploration is not recommended!

LAHORE
LHE   OPLA   2m/3km NW

Probably best for the smaller airliners used by PIA and the other domestic carriers, Lahore has a pleasant passenger terminal. Its main problem is that larger aircraft use remote stands, about a mile away, where they are completely hidden by trees.

It is advisable to be content with reasonably good views of some of the aircraft on stands adjacent to the terminal, rather than be tempted to venture along the perimeter, by the runway, in the vain hope of logging all the movements.

The lack of any significant general aviation at this airport is probably explained by the existence of WALTON airfield, of which nothing has been reported.

PESHAWAR
PEW   OPPS   2m/3km NW

PIA operate domestic and international flights from this airport, though not in any great number. The runway is used by a mixture of fighters, trainers and strike/attack aircraft, so self-discipline could be the rule of the day. Leave the camera in the hotel room - that way there's more chance of returning there in the evening!

For anyone who wants to see the Pakistani Air Force, Peshawar's passenger terminal is probably the safest location in which to do it. Standing at a window for three hours, in full view, is not a good idea, though!

SKARDU
KDU   OPSD

Skardu is the regional capital of Baltistan (where balti curries come from). Like Gilgit, Skardu is a bit basic. Not only do you need to take your own towel, but soap is also a good idea.

Skardu means "starry place". See it at night. It's unforgettable, almost as unforgettable as arrival by air but departure is even worse - bloody terrifying! The PIA 737 descends to the airport through twisting mountain passes, and the captain is just earning a living. This is Living on The Edge. That's when the weather is good.

Set close to the River Indus, in the high desert, Skardu is surrounded by 20,000 feet high mountains and the war zone of Kashmir is only 80 miles away. As if that weren't enough, China is even closer. The scenery is, of course, breathtaking.

There is normally no active military presence at the airport but it is geared up to act as a forward operating point. The authorities are trained to be on constant alert for anyone who might be doing a spot of reconnaissance.

A40 = OMAN

MUSCAT
MCT   OOMS   Seeb International   25m/40km

The Sultanate of Oman has quite a lot to offer as a destination and the relaxing of visa restrictions is meant to encourage tourism, so entry is much easier than in the past. Anyone who visits is probably making a one-hour technical stop on their way to or from the Far East, under cover of darkness. Most of this traffic now uses alternatives to Muscat, such as Dubai, or is operated by B.747-400s which can fly direct.

Taxiing to the normal departure runway threshold means passing the hangars. Next to the terminal is the ramp for visiting military and general aviation movements, followed by the Sultan of Oman Air Force facility, with at least one Hercules close to the taxiway, a collection of helicopters, and probably a 1-11. The next apron is that of the Royal Flight but their aircraft are usually hangared, as well as being a fairly common sight at Heathrow. The last hangar is that of the para-military Royal Oman Police Air Wing, and one or two of their fleet may be outside.

Viewing is possible from the terminal, though only after passport control. The escalator which gives access to the Duty Free Shop also offers the rest of the upper floor for exploration. There is now a large seating area with windows overlooking the eastern end of the apron. On some occasions, security personnel can prevent anyone but passengers entering the terminal, probably due to local activities such as the arrival of a VIP. VIPs in the Gulf tend to be seen as rather more important than elsewhere in the world.

For the visitor staying in Muscat, it will be worth a short description of the facilities: to the right of the terminal is the OAS hangar and ramp with a collection of Twin Otters and F.27s. The limited amount of traffic handled at the main terminal is mostly Gulf Air, Air India and PIA, whose F.27s and 737s are among the more interesting. Ethiopian Boeings and Thai A300s supply the other notable arrivals. Much of the traffic passes through between 22:00 and midnight.

All the separate facilities here are individually accessed from entrances off the main road and each has its own security checkpoint. Some form of introduction to the company would lead past the Omani guard to a small, friendly group of British expatriots, particularly at ROPAW and Oman Air Services. Between those friendly expats, who would welcome talking to someone new, is the guard who probably welcomes talking to nobody, and certainly not in anything other than Arabic!

A5 = BHUTAN

PARO
PBH   VQPR

The capital city of Bhutan is Thimpu, served by Paro airport, into which Druk Air's BAe146s fly from various points in Asia. Photos of a Druk Air (Royal Bhutan Airlines) 146 are rare indeed. Photos at Paro are as rare as hens' teeth.

The government has limited foreign tourists to a maximum of 2,250 annually. The other restriction is that tourists must guarantee to spend a certain amount of money in the country. Bhutan, in travellers' terms, is very exclusive indeed - and very expensive. The airport is situated in a narrow valley, surrounded by extremely steep mountains. Approach, in poor weather conditions (it gets a lot of cloud at 7300 feet above sea level), is not exciting at all - it's terrifying!

The passenger terminal building is tiny, as it would be. It only has to accommodate the people who can fill a 146, not many. Stepping through one of the patio doors, there are small gardens, surrounded by fences.There is absolutely nothing to do except wander around and view the magnificent scenery. Taking a superb photo, once at the apron's edge, couldn't be easier. The trick is getting there in the first place. Anyone who makes the trip can see some of the most wonderful scenery and architecture in the entire world. Bhutan is, quite simply, the ultimate.

A6 = UNITED ARAB EMIRATES

DUBAI

DXB	OMDB	International	3m/5km SE

There's no doubt that the UAE has enough petro-dollars to flash it around. So, as you would expect, the airport's passenger terminal is rather ostentatious. Get used to seeing hexagons and columns that sprout like giant hogweed. After a while, it all gets a bit much. Unlike most other airports in the Gulf, Dubai handles many long-haul flights as well as the usual regional traffic. About forty scheduled passenger airlines use Dubai plus a growing number of cargo operators. The Duty Free Shop is quite famous but only cheap if you want cut-price Gucci etc.

Due to its location, halfway between Europe and the Far East, Dubai handles an interesting mixture: Thai and Singapore International Airbuses, Eva 747s, Air China 767s and Finnair DC-10s. Traditional links between Central Europe and the Middle East mean that Balkan A320s and 767s, LOT 737s and Tarom A310s are regular visitors but there are also Olympic 737s, Air Malta A320s and Turkish A340s. South African and Ethiopian 767s visit, and Federal Express use 747s and MD-11s. For daily up-to-date schedules, a copy of Emirates News, an English language newspaper, is recommended.

Passenger aircraft park on the main apron, facing away from the two parallel runways, aligned 12/30, with the terminal building at the western corner, closest to town. Next to the passenger terminal, and almost directly opposite the thresholds of Runways 12L/R, is the apron used for cargo and general aviation.

The main apron consists of 23 stands, with a planned extension of another 20. Unlike Sharjah and Abu Dhabi, Dubai's arrivals park nose-in, instead of at air bridges. The cargo apron is easily seen from the staff car park. The six bays, each big enough to take a 747, are planned to be doubled to twelve. Beyond the cargo area is the general aviation facility, which usually contains two or three corporate jets each day. Delivery flights, when passing through, also park here.

Between the cargo and GA facilities is the Emirates' maintenance area, comprising three hangars. One, capable of holding a couple of 747-400s, is used by the airline, while the others are mainly occupied by Air Force C-130s. Aerogulf Helicopter Services have their own hangar, usually with about a dozen Bell 212s to be seen, plus the occasional police MBB 105.

At the eastern end of the field is the royal hangar, where the sheik's aircraft can be seen, often in the company of visiting Gulfstreams and other private jets, owned by the privileged. Showing undue interest is obviously not wise.

Security precautions in the Middle East mean that viewing the movements from outside the passenger terminal can be fraught with difficulties. A pass is required from the airport authorities, just to stand near the car park and record the registrations. Getting one isn't as easy as it used to be. Permission to take photographs, without some good reason, is out of the question. High fences surround the field, and comprise two barriers, about 5 metres apart, making ground level photography impossible. There's no view from the terminai until after passport control, so spotters tend to use the perimeter instead. Photographers get in a hire car and drive to Sharjah (q.v.).

The airport road passes close to both the main apron and the royal hangar. Parking in a layby is not unusual, to watch movements on the taxiway, for instance. Staying there for four hours and using a camera or binoculars (worse still, a telescope), however, does invite attention.

The Four Points Hotel is operated by Marriott which means a room doesn't come cheap. They do their best to give value for money, however, and the rooftop swimming pool is very close to the flightpath, if not actually directly underneath it. Spotters could do worse than spend the day by the pool rather than look for other places. It's tempting to try and contact the Airport's Public Relations Department but it spends more time handling VIPs than dealing with the general public.

ABU DHABI

AUH   OMAA   International   23m/37km SW (bus 40 minutes)

This is the Emirates most modern airport, with a satellite pier in front of the arc-shaped passenger terminal. Movements are similar, in terms of colour schemes, to those visiting Dubai. Abu Dhabi is, however, the capital city, so there are more corporate jets to be seen. Most of these use the stands to the right of the satellite. An ornate state reception building, also to the right-hand side of the apron, is used to welcome the sort of people who expect to be welcomed by more than a chauffeur carrying a board with their name on it.

The terminal's cafe and seating area, from which the apron can be watched, are predictably to the left. The view is good, if not ideal: if anything moves, it can be seen. The runway is about half a mile away, at the far side of two taxiways, thus making photographs difficult. Security presence might be expected to make matters worse but this is not so. Negotiations to take photos through the glass are normally successful.

The airport is developing, with service roads to the different aprons. At the far end, towards the threshold of Runway 31, one apron is shared by Emirates Air Service and a small general aviation terminal. To see anything parked here, the occasional Cessna, Piper or jet, a walk is necessary but not necessarily recommended! The cargo apron, halfway between the passenger and GA terminals, is hidden from view by the cargo terminal.

In the opposite direction, the Gamco apron can be seen from a couple of vantage points at close quarters. Apart from the usual Gulf Air aircraft, the stored ADC Airlines TriStar 5N-BBB.

Abu Dhabi's first airport is now BATEEN Air Base (OMAD), passed on the road to the present airport. An unmarked ADAF Mirage guards the entrance but is unlikely to prevent a determined enthusiast gaining entry. Guards, standing in its shadow can, AND WILL, do that!

Close inspection of the resident UAE military aircraft and the Presidential Flight, barely visible from the road, is unlikely. The only hope of access is by negotiation with Abu Dhabi Aviation, whose extensive fleet of helicopters is based here. Even if access be arranged, permission to take photographs should be obtained separately from the security office.

SHARJAH

SHJ   OMSJ   International   15m/25km SE

Most enthusiasts, visiting Sharjah, do so in a car rented at Dubai, not much more than half an hour's drive away. Nobody knows for how long existing arrangements will apply but Sharjah airport has something to offer (albeit at a price) that few others can match. Hand over your money, wait for as long as it takes, and you get a pass to take photos on the ramp.

One of the conditions is that you supply a couple of passport-sized photos. These are taken before flying out since, in Sharjah, they cost about the same as a Ferrari. Well, 200 Dh, which is about US$50. And no, they're not taken by Lord Lichfield. Don't be in a hurry. Nobody else is. When you get your pass from the Airport Security Office (the door you need is marked PASS), after a decent wait - and a whole day is not unusual - you'll be 100 Dh the poorer but, for your money, you get the chance to take portraits of some fabulous aircraft.

This doesn't include Iran Air who are, to say the least, a bit funny about that sort of thing. Lest you be tempted by something taxiing toward you, try to imagine that a security officer is watching you from the aircraft. If he doesn't like what you're doing, there's no reason to assume he won't have the plane stopped, and pop down the airstairs with his little AK-47, and invite you to take a ride. This is not to be misunderstood to mean a pleasure flight or some sort of freebie.

Sharjah specialises in cheap electrical goods, which can be bought in some quantity and shipped back to Russia for sale at a profit. This means that as many as forty Russian aircraft can be seen in a single day, many of the flights no doubt officially sanctioned.

A typical day's haul at Sharjah can include movements by any of the following airlines: Armenian, Azerbaijan, Belarus, Estonian, Kazakhstan, Kyrgyzstan, Latvian, Lithuanian, Moldova, Moscow, Tajik, Tojikistan, Turkmenistan and Uzbekistan. Few of these movements park at the passenger terminal, however. A few people can arrive in a Yak-42, Tu-154, Il-62 or Il-86. Their purchases often require at least an additional Antonov of some kind, or even an Il-76. The Air Cess fleet is always ready.

The single runway, 12/30, is served by a taxiway, off which are four apron areas. Arriving by road from town, the clover-leaf flyover leads, via a roundabout, to the passenger terminal, at the far (eastern) end. In front of the terminal is the main apron, with air bridges, plus an additional stand, for use by the Royal Flight 737, A6-ESH. To the left are three more stands. A hangar to the right of the main terminal holds the sheik's 737.

Visiting scheduled traffic features a good range of operators, including all Gulf Air types, Kuwait A320s, Alyemda A310s, Algerian, Iranian and Syrian 727s (plus other types), as well as Uzbekistan and CSA A310s, and a variety of Air China aircraft. The main charter airlines are, predictably, Britannia (767s) and Condor (757s and 767s). Details (not to be taken too literally) of each day's aircraft movements are to be found in Emirates News.

A service road leads west from the roundabout. Along it are several vantage points. The first overlooks the passenger aprons and, beyond the fuel compound, another offers a view of the cargo apron. Lufthansa and German Cargo Airlines occupy the far building, where daily movements are regular. At least a couple of 747s can be expected, as well as up to four DC-8s.

At the far end of the service road are, respectively, the service and military aprons. Whilst security at Sharjah is not as strict as at Dubai, procedures are still necessary if confrontation is to be avoided. The perimeter road seems to allow views without red tape but, having travelled this far, it might be wise (and polite) to take a few minutes to observe the niceties. Arousing the interest of one of the army guards is certainly going to be more time-consuming in the long run, and parting as the best of friends is unlikely.

The perimeter fences are not in the best condition, and offer temptation to an ardent photographer. Crossing them, where they have fallen down, might look like a good idea. One minute, it feels like you're all alone. The next minute, your telephoto lens reveals a bayonet! Think about it. They are good enough to supply ramp passes, yet here is someone doing his own thing.

Sharjah really is worth a few days. Instead of a day pass, a weekly pass is certainly worth the extra money. After all, the flight cost plenty and it would be stupid to be there when something really extraordinary (such as an Indian Navy Il-18, for example) taxis in, only to find that you're not going to get a photo of it. Worth bearing in mind also is that hotels in Sharjah aren't cheap but they're cheaper than in Dubai.

AL AIN
AAN   OMAL   International   15m/24km SW

The Ruler of the Abu Dhabi Emirate (also the President of the UAE) needed access to this oasis, so Al Ain airport was built. The enormously long runway (2.5m/4km) is little-used, and rarely by traffic needing the full length.

The main terminal building, which has to be seen to be believed, is for the Ruler's own use. There is also a small general aviation centre, which houses the passenger terminal used by ordinary folk. Only a few resident Cessnas and Pipers are to be seen, unless the Ruler is visiting. In that event, security becomes proportionately strict.

Even the most dedicated aviation enthusiast may find more interest in the local camel market.

RAS AL KHAYMAH
RKT   OMRK   International   10m/16km SE

A Gulf Air 737 daily links this airport to Abu Dhabi. Occasional visitors can be seen but not enough for even the most serious enthusiast to plan a trip here. Thus the airport sleeps in the sun most of the time, while the local population goes about its business of trading.

The only unusual aspect of this airport results from local trade, predictably in cheap electrical goods, and therefore enough reason for the arrival of ad-hoc shopping flights from Russia and the CIS states. An-12s and Il-76s are therefore to be expected but possibly not in enough quantity to justify the drive.

A7 = QATAR
DOHA
DOH   OTBD   International   5m/8km SE

Almost all the scheduled services (about 90% in fact) are supplied by Gulf Air 737s, with the more interesting PIA A300s and Egyptair 767s passing through at night. The only residents of any note are the government's fleet of Boeings, a reasonably common sight at Heathrow.
From the town centre, the passenger terminal is at the end of Airport Road. Heading east from town instead, along Ras Abu Aboud Road, the northern end of Runway 16/34 is passed. This leads to the Qatar Air Force. Stopping and taking photos are not recommended!

A9C = BAHRAIN
BAHRAIN
BAH   OBBI   Muharraq International   46km NE of Manama

The only worthwhile airliners are the Gulf Air fleet, whose 747s and 737s don't visit the most of Europe, and one or two Saudia 737s each day. DHL have a package cargo service with (Saudi-registered) Metros and Merlins. A Saudia Citation flies nightly services into Bahrain for DHL, but the other visitors each day are probably fuel-stopping. Military movements are most likely to be USAF C-141s or Australian C-130s, and a US Navy C-12 is normally present.
Executive traffic is down to a trickle and only the Royal Flight 727 and Gulfstream are based. With the arrival of the fighter aircraft, operating from a base opposite the terminal, restrictions on photography increased.
At the ends of the runway are good vantage points, the better probably being that next to the sea and the military parking area, but guards here prevent any thoughts of using a camera. At the opposite end, just after the old and new roads meet, the other viewing point is close to the holding point and was never guarded, (but that was prior to the arrival of the fighters).

B = CHINA
BEIJING
BJS   ZBAA   Capital   16m/25km NE

Most of the enthusiasts visiting Beijing (and much of China) still take advantage of the excellent specialist tours. Because organised tours have more likelihood of gaining access to some of the airside areas of Chinese airports, the lone traveller will continue to be exceptional. His log and photo collection will certainly be thinner. It can be done . . .
The old passenger terminal is positioned at the end of a ceremonial way, in the best Soviet tradition. Beyond its apron lies the new terminal, used by international flights, and served by its own access highway. There is much construction activity around the new terminal - to the right of the international terminal, and it's scheduled for completion in 1999. Views from inside are minimal, so the upper (arrivals) approach road, to the right, is as good as anywhere to monitor the movements. If the weather is particularly wet, which it often is in summer, umbrellas are dirt-cheap at stalls in the terminal.
The ancient domestic terminal is worth a look, as it's from here that many of the Soviet types are seen at close quarters. After passing through a security check, windows offer good views for the spotter. (Note, incidentally, that JAL and ANA also use this terminal.) The glass, however, is not

up to modern western standards, making photos difficult. Anyone standing outside, and using binoculars or a camera, can be subject to individual interpretation. One day, a guard will smile and mutter something probably quite nice. Later, or the next day, someone else can tell you to stop. What might follow depends on your knowledge of Mandarin.

Having travelled this far, for the chance to see exotic Chinese airline movements, you can hardly decide to turn round and go somewhere else, just because things are a bit slow. Reports from Guangzhou say it's exciting and busy, yet some statistics say Beijing handles more traffic. A log containing more than a hundred aircraft, after a full day's spotting, is all that it's reasonable to expect . . . at most. There's a mixture of Western and Soviet types, the latter being what most enthusiasts seem to prefer. There might be, on the average day, no more than a couple of Tu-154s, Yak-42 and Y-7s (An-24s). More than three Il-86s is unlikely.

It's the out-of-the-ordinary movements that justify the effort. In Beijing, they really are something special - such as a China Flying Dragon Twin Otter, a MIAT 727 or an Air Koryu Tu-154. For a change of scenery, it might be worth seeking the PLA Museum at Datang Shan, Chiangping, about 40 km north of the city. With a little help at the hotel reception, a taxi can be negotiated for the day at a cost of about US$50.

Outside the gate sit a couple of Il-18s with another inside the main building. There are seven Li-2s and about forty MiGs to be seen. Reports of an eighth Li-2 are explained by the presence of a C-47 carrying the marks 4766. XT-115 is another C-47/DC-3, and there are two C-46s also. The rest of the airliners are all relatively humdrum, if you call an Il-62, two Il-12s, a Trident, a CV-240, a Viscount and an Il-14 humdrum! And lots, lots more besides. In all, about a hundred aircraft.

It's the People's Revolutionary Museum, in town, that contains another dozen or so inlcuding the U-2 and Trident B-2207.

GUANGZHOU

CAN   ZGGG   Baiyun   8m/13km SE

China Travel has offices in Hong Kong, where package tours are offered to Guangzhou, still better known as Canton. A more expensive option($250) is to book a day return flight with Southwest from Hong Kong. One of the problems is that Southwest have a monopoly on the route, which is popular with tourists and so a flight of less than twenty-five minutes costs rather more than is reasonable. Affordable, nonetheless, but beware of the overbooking, especially if hoping to catch the last evening flight home. The train takes three hours and costs about US$80 return. Be especially vigilant for almost anything at the station, as tourists are considered easy targets. And remember, no, you definitely do not want a taxi except from the official rank, thank you very much. Penalty for ignoring advice, and believing local smooth-talkers, is armed robbery or even death in some isolated location. This is a very serious warning.

The taxi ride from the railway station should cos no more than $3 and one of the best hotels is the Baiyun Airport Hotel (about $50 for a single room). Across the parking lot is the passenger terminal. For a reservation, fax them on 011-86-20-665-9006.

Now regarded as China's busiest airport, Baiyun has as much to offer, in its way, as Kai Tak. Anyone who doubts this fact can study a China Southern fleet list, as this is their base of operations. After a few days of seeing the same old Thai Airbuses at Kai Tak, Guangzhou offers China General Yak-42s, China Northwest and Southwest Tu-154s, China Xingjiang Il-86s, Sichuan and Air Great Wall Tu-154s plus plenty of 737s. If this desn't whet the appetite, there's Air Vietnam Tu-134s twice a week and a decent selection of carriers from elsewhere in Southeast Asia.

There are two separate passenger terminals, neither of which have viewing facilities. Between the terminals is a courtyard, complete with a few shops, where staff access the main ramp. Taking photos and spotting from here appear to be approved. However, it's probably best to ignore the terminal area. Instead, buy a city map from reception in the hotel and use it to point out, to your taxi driver, where you want to go. In the morning, when movements are often in a northerly direction, it will probably be the eastern perimeter side, a hundred metres or so from the threshold, and about a five-minute ride from the hotel. Photographers need about 135 mm focal length and there are plenty of items piled against the fence to help poke the lens over it. After lunchtime, move round to the western side. It's as easy as that!

At the extreme southern tip of the field is a busy road and a bus stop. Across the road from here is where everyone stands, on top of the wall. Expect attention - a lot of attention, some of it rather undesirable. The locals are naturally curious anyway, and the average westerner looks, to them, something like a Martian would in Trafalgar Square. So far so good. But then a bright little thing wants you to help her polish her English. Oh yeah, sure. Another warning coming up: it's best to tell her to sod off. Just say it again and again until she does. What happens if you don't? Your taxi will, surprisingly, be going in just the direction she wants to go. In other words, to your hotel room. If this gets your attention, and you feel frisky, go take a cold shower instead. In what you thought was the privacy of your room, police will demand you hand over HK$5,000, to avoid arrest.

GUILIN
KWL ZGKL   7m/11km SE

Many of the short trips from Hong Kong, organised by China Travel, involve a two night stay. Alternatively, fly there from Guangzhou for US$160 return. The flight, in a 737, takes less than an hour. Arrival by air is sometimes after dark and the Holiday Inn, probably the town's biggest building, is a likely resting place. Some rooms overlook a MiG-15 in what looks like a cabbage patch. After a memorable day on the river, and possibly a second night at the hotel, departure can mean the only chance to sample the airport.

Wandering about, outside the terminal area may not be a good idea but there is little to see. There may be another aircraft on the apron, such as a Y-7 or a Tu-154, but even this might be asking too much. The departure area offers the chance to see what little there is. However, at the end of the taxiway by the end of the runway are a couple of dozen assorted MiGs.

QINGDAO
TAO ZSQD   25km

Arrival by air a this airport means keeping the eyes peeled for a squadron of locally-based MiG-21s. These are the reason why venturing too far from the passenger terminal is unwise. There's not a lot of reason to do so, since movements can be seen after passing the security check. A long stay is not necessarily recommended as facilities are a bit basic. What's to be seen is mostly China Southern and Shandong A300s, MD-83s and SF340s. Cameras should be at the ready when boarding, because most passengers have to walk across the tarmac. To the right of the terminal is an apron-side restaurant which, if open, should offer a very good view indeed.

WUHAN
WUH ZHWT   Wangjiaddun   3m/5km

Wuhan is a major city, the capital of Hubei Province. It sits on the Yangtze River, which is now known as the Ch'ang Chiang. Chinese names are something of a problem for the average westerner, and even reference to official documents doesn't clarify the situation. Wangjiaddun is also known as Hsukiapeng and has an extremely interesting range of movements. Quantity is another matter, however. Anyone wishing to witness the action will need to be an early riser, as a good number of Guangzhou Regional An-24s and Yunshuji Y7s depart before 0800.

WUHAN
        ZHHH   Nanhu

Nanhou, or Nanhu, is the city's other airport, also quoted as being called Hankou, and there are reports of Air Wuhan/Wuhan Airlines Il-14s operating from here. It is certainly the airline's centre of operations but the airfield is also used as a military base. Visits here are therefore more likely to be by escorted tour parties, rather than the lone traveller trying to 'pole off' a few goodies!

XI'AN
XIY   ZLXY   Xianyang

Xi'an has become a major tourist destination, to be found in some holiday brochures and atlases as Hsian or Sian. To present the right image to the world, the new Xianyang airport has been built. Airline traffic is still modest, though interesting of course. The China Northwest base has a number of Tu-154s and An-24s to be seen.

All that remains at XIGUAN are a pair of old Ilyushins: an Il-14 and an Il-18, both of which could be moved to another location (or broken up) by now.

B = CHINA/TAIWAN

KAOSHIUNG
KHH   International

This is a city with a population of 2 million and it's growing fast. So is the airport! It has a large, new passenger terminal, which might mean the closure of the old one. International flights use the left-hand pier and domestic flights, most of which go to Taipei, the right. The new viewing facilities are still something of a mystery but what can be seen includes the occasional Vietnamese and Eva Air movement plus China Air Lines A300s and A320s.

TAIPEI
TPE   RCTP   Chiang Kai Shek International 25m/40km SW (bus 90 min)

Anyone who has visited Washington's Dulles International will see the resemblance with Taipei's main passenger terminal. Given that Taiwan has maintained, with strong political and economic support from the USA, that it is China, a visible link with Washington DC is easy to understand. Taipei is reported to be the world's Number One destination for hi-jacked aircraft - about twenty a year. No prizes for guessing where most of them come from.

Taipei's main airport is, from a spotter's point of view, best described as generally user-hostile. The airport layout is similar to Changi with an approach road between the parallel runways. The terminal and car parks are predictably placed.

The terminal is used for checking-in and inbound passport and customs clearance. It is linked to two ranks of departure lounges, again like Changi, with China Airlines on one side and everyone else on the other. There are no views from any part of the buildings. Access to a departure lounge, after entering passport control, allows views of two or three stands only. It is possible for departing pasengers to walk the length of the lounges and record what is parked on one side of the apron. It's tedious and it doesn't reveal anything that can't be seen just as well elsewhere around the Pacific.

Visitors to Changi will also recognize the similarity between the location of the Singapore Airlines maintenance base there and China Airlines' version here. Maybe the designs come cheaper by the dozen. Eva Air also have a maintenance base, beside Runway 06/24, inside which is normally housed a Falcon 900, the personal hack of Evergreen International's owner.

Located at the entrance to the terminal complex is the Airport Hotel, where a room costs about US$85 per night. It's good value in this part of the world, and much used by aircraft crews. The food is, quite literally, a matter of taste. Some upper level rooms allow views of both runways.

Close to the hotel is the air museum, open between 09:00 and 17:00. To get there, it's best to take the hotel bus and stroll across the grass. The reward for the effort is rather a lot of propaganda, such as: "the aviation industry was introduced to China in the late Ching Dynasty stemming from the far-sighted policy of Dr Sun Yat Sen in developing the Chinese Air Force." etc etc. Much of the information is in Chinese so it might not be understood by everyone. A lot of stuff about defectors from Communism and how well they're doing in the Free World. Among the exhibits are C-47 B-126 and fighters such as an F-100, RF-101A and F-104.

The larger exhibits are parked in the open. Immediately to the north, on the other side of the road, is a line of trees and a fence, beyond which is the taxiway to Runway 05L. Zoom lenses allow good photos from along the fence, especially in the mornings, when the sun can be most helpful. Opposite the museum entrance is a six-storey observation tower, which gives an impressive view over the airfield. Photos are a bit of a problem, not made any easier by the dirty glass from which observers are kept at a distance.

TAIPEI
TSA   RCSS   Sung Shan   3m/5km N

Failure to see anything at Chiang Kai Shek might encourage the spotter to try his luck at Sung Shan, the downtown domestic airport. High walls have been built to make things no easier here. Along the northern perimeter, Sun Yat Sen Freeway is hardly the place to walk in the hope of seeing something and the terminal area (departure lounges apart) is no better. Mintsu Road, parallel to the freeway, is believed to be one of the best places where aircraft can be seen on final approach. Anyone seeking directions should look for its intersection with Sungchiang Road.

Traffic, to western eyes, is undoubtedly good, offering a mixture of Far Eastern and China Airlines 737s, plus Fokker 100s and BAe 146s. Prop-driven traffic is very much in evidence, including Foshing ATR-42s and Formosa SF340s. Dash 8s and Do228s add extra variety. Three hours should yield about sixty airliners, after which the whole sequence repeats. Cameras and telescopes are not a problem here, remarkably when there are government 727s, Falcon 50s and quite a few Beech 1900s on the go.

C = CANADA

ABBOTSFORD BC
YXX   CYXX   8m/13km SW

Not an airport where many scheduled services are operated, but few visitors to the Vancouver and Seattle area would miss the opportunity to have a look. Apart from a moderate amount of general aviation, this airport is entirely dominated by one famous operator: Conair.

Fire-fighting is just as important in heavily-forested Canada as in the western United States, and Conair's headquarters at the airport demonstrates that it treats business seriously. The offices are modern, and the reception area is up the stairs. A request for a look at the aircraft causes few problems, so there is no excuse for walking around without permission. Depending on the time of year when a visit is made, the number of residents can vary, late summer being when fire risk is greatest, and inmates therefore at their lowest. The A-26s ended their useful life many years ago, and were stored here. The fleet is quite varied, and one or two representatives of each type, ranging from Grumman Firecats to DC-6s, plus the more modern CL-215s can be seen.

CALGARY AL
YYC   CYYC   International   7m/11km NE (bus 30 minutes)

For a complete picture of events here, travel southwards, towards the city, but this need not necessitate the use of a hire car, despite the distance. Two hotels, the Port o Call (expensive) and the Airliner (affordable), operate courtesy buses and both are within walking distance of the southern complex.

The Calgary International Airport which most visitors know about is the new, modern terminal, located well to the north of the field. The building is split into two: the northern annex being almost exclusively the preserve of Canadian Airlines and offering no views of the apron. The upper level of the main building is faced with smoked glass and offers a good view between the two main piers, international on the right and domestic on the left. A commuter airlines pier has been added to the north/right end of the passenger terminal.

Any airline traffic which doesn't park within sight of the glazed area of the main building will pass beyond the end of the right hand finger. Since this usually comprises most of the American operators, some of which (like Continental and American Trans Air 727s) can be interesting, it may be worth the walk to the glazed link between the two halves of the building. Photography is possible here but some skill is necessary to judge the critical moment when an incoming aircraft will be just at the right angle as it turns.

Catch the Number 57 bus, which runs along Air Services Way, the approach road to the passenger terminal, to 78 Avenue, where new facilities have been created. Canadian have a maintenance base next to the cargo area, there are CL-215s based, and there's a viewing area at the end of the road, close to the taxiway for Runway 28 - an excellent place for photos from sunrise to about 11:00. 727s need about 70 mm focal length. There are even dustbins, for standing on to clear the fence.

The real action at Calgary is at the southern end, though there can be more than one runway in use. Down at the 'old' end of the field, there are two centres of activity, at either side of the threshold of Runway 34. MacKnight Boulevard is the main road which links the two aprons, the western of which is shared by the executive customs ramp and Fields. A fairly steady trickle of biz-jets uses the customs ramp before dispersing, either to Fields or, across the runway, to Hudson General. What will be seen at Fields is strictly a matter of luck. They specialise in DHC aircraft, which can be anything from Buffaloes of the Mexican Navy and the NWC at China Lake, to a couple of CAF Twin Otters. The Amoco HS748 is also based here in the company of a good number of Citations.

The East Hangars comprise a selection of aprons worthy of a visit in their own right. Traffic to be seen here is extremely varied and can feature CAF F-5s and Tutors, and the Mobil Canada fleet (including the Dash Eight). Based here, apart from Federal Express, are a number of operators; Alpine Helicopters have an apron with at least one handsome Bell 212 present, whilst Highland Helicopters usually only have one or two JetRangers on their ramp. Next to Alpine Road is the museum with, among its exhibits, a DC-3 painted in Northwest colours.

The Kenn Borek hangar is large but can stay firmly closed, with nothing parked outside it. On the apron behind, however, should be at least one North Cariboo aircraft and a good selection of prop-jets and biz-jets, ranging from King Air 200s to the Esso 737. The viewing area (complete with picnic tables) close to the threshold of Runway 34 is accessible from McKnight Boulevard. Another short access road leads to the closest vantage point for the threshold of Runway 34. With the sun behind in the morning, this is a rewarding location for the photographer, subject to wind direction. In the afternoon, some vacant ground next to the customs ramp also faces the threshold but is probably too far away for good photographs. In the corner of the field, next to this spot, is a small helicopter compound/graveyard containing the wrecks of about twenty JetRangers; not much good to those in search of registrations but quite interesting.

Calgary is a large, busy airport with a range of vantage points and a commendable variety of traffic. To get the best out of what is there, it will be necessary to spend two or three days moving about between the different parts of the field.

CASTLEGAR BC
YCG   CYCG   Ralph West   3m/5km

The Crowsnest Highway from town offers a panoramaic view of the airport, though it disappears from view as you approach the perimeter. The field is on a plateau between the Columbia River and the mountains. A turn to the right leads to the passenger terminal, where scheduled activity consists of the usual commuters. Continuing past the terminal, the road leads past the general aviation ramp, used also by a few air taxi operators, to the control tower and an air tanker base.

CRANBROOK BC
YXC   CYXC   Kimberley   10m/16km N

Without doubt a scenic part of British Columbia, which is saying something, Cranbrook is a small community right in the heart of the Rockies. Actually, around these parts, they are the Selkirk

Mountains. It's only a few miles to the US border, and nearer to Calgary than to Vancouver. The town is served by a commuter airport. Scheduled services are operated, on a like-for-like competitive basis, by Canadian and Air Canada. Activity is minimal but there are air tanker bases, on the right of the approach road.

DAWSON CITY YT
YDA   CYDA   Municpal   11m/18km

The facilities comprise a gravel strip for the runway and a passenger terminal, plus customs facilities in a cabin, so this is an international airport. The scheduled link is with Alaska, operated by an Air North C-47, whose daily service goes to Fairbanks or Old Crow. The aircraft climbs out, then makes a 300 degree turn as it gains height at the same time as missing the surrounding hills. Make the most of it because that's all there is, apart from ten or so light aircraft.

EDMONTON AL
YEG   CYEG   International   21m/33km S (bus 45 minutes)

The closure of Edmonton Industrial Airport, on June 1st 1996, has meant that traffic at the International airport has increased. The few enthusiasts who have ventured the trip out to this airport have found a good roof top viewing deck. Traffic has grown in recent years with Air Canada using most of their fleet types, Canadian with 737s and A320s, and rather less frequent appearances by NWT and Westjet 737s. US carriers offer only the usual aircraft and international carriers are infrequent, to say the least. Any length of time spent here will seem very heavy going, despite the good facilities. The RAF often use this airport for VC-10s and Hercules movements, usually connected with activity at Cold Lake, to the east.
   A visit to Edmonton could be at the expense of some very good movements at nearby Calgary, which is in a different league for most types of aircraft. If searching for all the airfields in the area, SAINT ALBERT is worth the effort, despite being an airstrip. It usually has a couple of B-25 fire bombers based. Take Primary Highway 2 north from Edmonton, pass through the town, and the strip is about 5km further on, signposted to the left.

FORT SIMPSON NT
YFS   CYFS

The airfield is in a forest clearing beside the Mackenzie River, south of the road from town. The apron, beside the single runway, is used for the passenger terminal and an airborne fire-fighting base. As can be expected in this part of the wrold, security measures cost considerably more than the threat represents, so fences only tend to be erected if the moose or bears get too friendly. There is very little to see, apart from the occasional Ptarmigan or Buffalo Airways flight.

GATINEAU PQ
YND   CYND   16m/25km ENE of Hull

The Ottawa River divides the capital city, in Ontario, from Hull in Quebec. The divide is also a cultural one in many ways, as it forms the frontier of the French speaking Canadians. Some miles down river from Hull is a small airport which serves Hull and the scenic Gatineau area.
   As befits an airport in this location, its scheduled air links are mainly with French-speaking Canada, with a few commuter services being operated. The facilities are modern and well laid out, but not over-used. The glass fronted terminal overlooks the ramp, and vantage points at either side reveal alternative views of what few aircraft may be seen here. Since these aircraft are unlikely to be seen anywhere else on the average itinerary, other than considerably further east, it is worth the trip if seeking to fully cover the aviation scene in this part of Canada.

HALIFAX NS

YHZ   CYHZ   International   25m/40km NE (bus 50 minutes)

The return trip from town costs C$18 and the journey is worthwhile, because Halifax is a busy regional airport. The passenger terminal is located in the standard Canadian manner, at the intersection of the two runways, 15/33 and 06/24. It makes life a little difficult for the spotter, and almost impossible for the photographer, though there are alternatives. At the right hand end of the terminal is a limited view but it's worth the walk along the perimeter fence for photos of the movements on the taxiway. The various ramps and hangars used by the smaller operators are reached by walking from the terminal towards the threshold of Runway 06.

Air Canada DC-9s and CAI 737s dominate the arrivals board but regional services mean plenty of Air Atlantic Dash 8s and Air Nova BAe146s. The nearby Shearwater CAF base open house day can combine reasons to visit. The base is near Dartmouth, on the far side of the harbour. Simple headings, such as eight miles east, are misleading. The road from Halifax heads northeast, but the base itself is to the southeast of town.

Once across the bridge in Dartmouth, take a right onto Pleasant Street, Highway 322. The road passes the base entrance. It's mostly used by helicopter units. At any time other than when an airshow is being held, the only sure way to gain access to the base is to write (or possibly phone) beforehand. Even this cannot guarantee success, of course.

HAMILTON OT

YHM   CYHM   Civic   6m/9km SW

Airline traffic is mostly commuter schedules, a few charter flights and one or two package delivery services. Anyone driving between Toronto and Niagara Falls may consider a detour. The airport is well away from the direct road but the sign-posting is good. With so few scheduled services during the day, the main appeal is probably the Canadian Warbirds Museum, well stocked with a good variety of interesting aircraft. The field is also home for a considerable number of light aircraft.

HAY RIVER NT

YHY   CYHY

This is not a name that many of us recognize, and few would imagine that the airport had two runways. The town is on the southern shore of Great Slave Lake and it has a railroad link as well as being at the end of the Mackenzie Highway. The airport is about a thirty minute walk from the motels, in town, and well worth the effort. Just after the road and railway cross the river, the airport is on the left. The passenger terminal is located facing the main runway.

It is probably the aprons which face the cross runway which are of some interest, as they are occupied by the general aviation (half a dozen aircraft), Buffalo Airways and an air tanker base (often empty when aircraft are active elsewhere). Buffalo Airways' centre of operations provides somewhat more permanent consolation for enthusiasts of piston power: The C-47s stored in the open vary from complete to fuselage only.

Airline traffic is sparse, ranging from modern Dash 8s of Canadian to good old C-47s. Anyone with an interest in general aviation will need to investigate the nearby floatplane base, which explains the lack of light aircraft at the airport. Water is in far greater supply, in this part of the world, than runways.

KELOWNA BC

YLW   CYLW   Ellison Field   9m/15km NE

Scheduled commuter operations do include Westjet 737s and the usual Dash 8s, but most visitors will probably be seeking the Kelowna Flightcraft base. A service road runs between, and parallel to, the runway and Highway 97. At the far end of it, from town, are hangars and their resident general aviation, plus several Kelowna CV-580s in storage. The airline's building is at the other end of the road, next to the passenger terminal. Unlike Penticton, this is not the sort of place that will please the family on holiday, as it's located in a rather wide valley and surrounded mostly by farmland.

LONDON OT
YXU   CYXU   7m/11km NE

With the growth of STOLports, London has witnessed significant growth in the last few years. The small passenger terminal has an upper level observation deck, most of which is now closed. A hole, about four feet square, was the observation point in summer 1994!

Anyone staying in Ontario will nevertheless find that London does offer chances to get close to commuter airliners but it requires quick reflexes. The chain link fence at either side of the passenger terminal offers limited views of the ramp. Good photos of aircraft on the move are possible. Getting close to the other aircraft on the field necessitates a car or an awful lot of walking.

MONTREAL PQ
YUL   CYUL   Dorval International   14m/22km

All Montreal's scheduled flights now use Dorval. The passenger terminal is not new by any standards but it is light and pleasant, with a glass front overlooking most of the apron. There is an extensive observation deck along the front, but this has been closed for many years, and is falling into disrepair.

To accommodate the extra stands needed by a busy airport, a tunnel gives access to the satellite of departure lounges on the far side of the ramp. This is only accessible to passengers who present boarding cards. It is wise to delay passing through passpost control, if travelling to the USA, because the viewing facilities are not the best. Without recourse to exploration, nearly all the activity can be satisfactorily monitored from the seats in the main hall. A good proportion of the airliners taxi by on their way in or out. The installation of air jetties has made life more difficult and it can need skill to get an acceptable photograph of Air Canada 767s, which congregate at the right hand end of the terminal, out of sight. A temporary finger was opened in April 1997 to provide extra gates while the new international complex is being built.

On leaving the main terminal, a right turn leads to the maintenance area, where a variety of aircraft normally includes one or two of the Transport Canada fleet. Next to this apron are the cargo sheds and the Province of Quebec CL-215 facility. These are seen at close quarters from the cargo area, as is the Innotech ramp, where new Challengers are fitted out prior to delivery. A short drive round to this apron may result in the sight of a new aircraft rolled out of the hangar, in pristine condition; close scrutiny may be possible.

Backtracking to the Cote de Liesse, the main highway to Montreal, there are several roads which lead to a variety of aprons and facilities on the southern perimeter. It is extremely difficult to negotiate the turn to this area from the eastbound carriageway, so a visit on the way from the city would make life easier. There are two separate sections to the southern complex, reached respectively by 43rd and 55th Streets. The former reveals a quantity of operators and types, ranging from cargo and courier airlines to plenty of executive aircraft, with general aviation in quantity to swell the numbers.

Each apron has its own office/hangar and all can be seen at close quarters without needing access to the other side of the fence. At the northern end of 55th Street is a car park for employees, often frequented by local watchers, and the end of Jenkins Avenue has been a traditional place where traffic landing on Runway 28 or using 06R/24L can be watched.

16

MONTREAL PQ
YUL   CYUL   Mirabel International   33m/51km NW

Over thirty miles north of Montreal and this on a toll motorway, Mirabel comes as a great disappointment. Depressing, too, is the prospect of having to pay to drive back to Montreal with the camera unused. Those using only binoculars and logbooks can sit on the upper level of the terminal and wait. Almost all international flights have now pulled out, and carriers such as Ladeco, Alitalia and Lufthansa now operate into Dorval.

The facilities are modern and cater for passengers only, even the lounge area being nowhere near the glass overlooking the large apron. Mirabel will be promoted as a dedicated cargo and charter airport but, even if this happens, there may still be little reason to visit.

MONTREAL PQ
YHU   CYHU   Saint Hubert   12m/19km S

Also in the Montreal area and worthy of a short detour is St Hubert, close to the main highway link with New York State. St Hubert is a large airfield used by the Canadian Armed Forces, though the resident fighters left long ago. What remains is army activity, supported by the Caribous and Otters, with occasional weekend visitors of a more spectacular nature. Also to be seen are the Helicraft base, on the perimeter, and a good selection of the Canadian general aviation scene, on the south side.

For anyone who feels the need to log as many registrations as possible in the Montreal area, St Hubert is worth the trip. An interest in airliners is not repaid here nor, it has to be said, is the need to see something out of the ordinary. It is, of course, comments such as these which draw howls of protest from people who swear that the sight of a Jinsen PJ-2600 is special.

NANAIMO BC
YCD   CYCD   Cassidy   10m/16km S

When crossing by ferry to Vancouver Island, Nanaimo is the normal port of entry. On the way south, towards Victoria, is the community of Cassidy and at the eastern side of the road nearby is a small airport. Hardly likely to be the high spot of any trip to Canada, it does offer a chance of a portrait photograph of aircraft up to SD3.60 size, operating a regular shuttle to Vancouver.

Anyone heading north from Nanaimo (to Comox for example) would be well advised to seek out Sproat Lake, near PORT ALBERNI, where Forest Industries Flying Tankers still operate a pair of Martin Mars flying boats.

NORTH BAY ONT
YYB   CYYB   2m/3km E

The airport is east of the city, off Highway 11 to Airport Road. Scheduled traffic consists of Air Ontario Dash 8s, shuttling to Toronto several times a day, and Bearskin Airlines Metros to more remote destinations. Plans exist to replace the under-used passenger terminal, with building work starting in 1998.

The field also houses the NORAD HQ,so USAF and CAF visit fairly regularly. Other aircraft often make refuelling stops and it is not unusual to find the odd Tutor or Hornet present. The base has mounted Voodoo and CF-100 gate guardians whilst, downtown in Lees Park, are a pole-mounted Bomarc SAM and another CF-100. The Bomarc base, also off Highway 11 and about 6 miles north of the city, houses the helicopter flight training facility of the local university.

About two miles east at TROUT LAKE is the floatplane airport. North Bay Airways fly hunters and fishermen to remote lakes in Beavers and Otters, and some general aviation is usually present.

OSHAWA OT
YOO   4m/6km

Thirty miles or so east of Toronto, Oshawa airport is only a small diversion if motoring from Ottawa or Montreal. It is a pleasant airport to visit, especially at weekends, when activity is minimal. Since the local airline is primarily a commuter operation, it doesn't fly much at weekends, so its aircraft can be seen at leisure. An L-shaped ramp has most of the general aviation on one side and Skycraft on the other. Skycraft's fleet includes a few small twins as well as Bandeirantes. The ramp is open to all sensible folk, and the airliners to be seen undergoing servicing mingle with some other interesting types, including a Pembroke.

OTTAWA OT
YOW   CYOW   Macdonald-Cartier International   11m/17km SSE

Movements are dominated by Air Canada and Canadian Airlines, but other operators include First Air, Voyageur and Air Ontario. The many recent renovations have, effectively, created a much improved Macdonald-Cartier airport compared with the enthusiast-unfriendly Uplands. There is now a glazed observation area in the centre of the passenger terminal, offering views of all airport movements by being opposite the intersection of the two main runways.
 Transport Canada has a significant fleet based at Ottawa, ranging from Viscounts and JetStars to King Airs and Dakotas, all in perfect condition, and the CAF base, to the north of the terminal, offers additional interest. The Transport Canada hangar is only one part of the facilities which now line the north side of the taxiway to Runway 25. Next to it are two FBO's: Shell and Esso Avitat. First Air's hangar, at the far/eastern end, is reached from Thad Johnson Road, outside the terminal complex. To reach it, take the exit road (Airport Parkway) and pass under the taxiway before leaving at the first intersection, Alert Road. This can offer a golden opportunity to see at close quarters their 727s, showing off their rainbow livery. There are views from Alert Road of the hold for Runway 25 and, by passing the end of the runway, of traffic on the runway, though a long lens is needed for photographs.
 Anyone arriving by way of the Parkway could leave without ever knowing that there is another self-contained airfield at the northern end, beyond the CAF facilities. Riverside Drive in Ottawa leads to a separate and self-contained airfield, complete with its own runways, accessible from Hunt Club Road. The facilities at the northern end are excellent and a good number of light aircraft are based here. Also to be seen are the Department of Mining and Resources aircraft and one or two old DC-3s and Cansos.
 Ottawa's appeal is broad, with something to please everyone; old, rare types rub shoulders with a good selection of airliners, and CAF operations include Cosmopolitans, Falcons and Buffaloes with some regularity, plus the occasional Chinook and T-33. With the right runways in use, half a day spent in the either the terminal or Employee Parking Lot 3 can produce a delightful variety, though the pace can be unhurried. From this external vantage point the parked Delta Connection/Business Express Saab 340s can be seen and, on certain afternoons, Martinair's 767 is fully visible on its stand.
 The museum at ROCKCLIFFE is housed in a splendid new pyramid building, instead of the old hangars on the southern edge of the field. Some of the inmates are rotated occasionally, to the science or war museums, both in the city. The larger exhibits are stored externally, including the Trans Canada Airlines Viscount. Leaving Ottawa city centre north, Wellington and Rideau Streets ultimately become Montreal Road. A left turn at St. Laurent Boulevard leads to the airfield.
 A drive round the field, past the forces base, leads to the general aviation. There is surprisingly little action, especially during the week, and a stroll around the inmates is possible. Apart from a variety of home-produced hardware, there are floatplanes to be seen and a walk down the ramp to the Ottawa River may reveal more, tied up.
 For anyone relying on public transportation, Rockcliffe needs a little time and patience. The No95 bus operates from Ottawa to Blair, with a change to the No198 for Rockcliffe. The journey takes about an hour.

PENTICTON BC
YYF   CYYF   Municipal   4m/7km S

Most parts of British Columbia are scenic but Penticton is better than most. It is a resort in its own right, so motels are plentiful. The Skytel is one of the cheaper examples, with the bonus of overlooking the runway threshold. Aircraft noise is, however, rarely a problem! The town nestles in the beautiful Okanagan Mountains, with the lake and National Park to the north and Skaha Lake at the southern end of the runway.

Scheduled traffic comprises mostly Dash 8s and Jetstreams but there are other movements to be seen, including fire bombers and air tankers. A holiday stay of a few days will allow the family to enjoy Canada at its prettiest (which is saying something) including a day on the beach. This is to be recommended, as the beach is actually at the end of the runway, and just across the road from the Skytel. A canalside footpath runs parallel to the runway, offering photographers the chance of a different mountain backdrop. Whichever way the camera points, east or west, there's no getting away from the mountains!

QUEBEC CITY PQ
YQB   CYQB   Aeroport de Quebec   9m/15km W

The modern terminal is light and airy, with the domestic apron laid out in front of the windows. Most of the traffic is feeder-liners, though one or two Air Canada jets do appear. A need to see jet traffic means travelling west to Montreal. A modest amount of international traffic is supplied, predictably, from the United States. This can be seen to the left. Air Alliance (it helps to say Air Al-yonce) has a maintenance base, and their hangar usually has something inside.

Next to the approach road, at the threshold of the cross runway, is a generous general aviation ramp, with a reasonably good selection of residents, all seen with ease. It is always tempting to say that Quebec is good for logging, but lumberjacks normally do that!

A quarter of a mile from the main terminal is the Quebec Province Government fleet of CL-215s. There is a lot, most of them parked outside, together with the odd PBY and Conifair DC-4 or DC-6.

RED DEER AL
YQF   CYQF   Industrial

The relatively large passenger terminal invites optimism but there is next to nothing, in terms of scheduled airline activity, to be seen most of the day. This airport could, however, be an essential stop for propliner fans. The airfield is at the edge of a military area, and it stages an annual air show, of sorts. Beside the runway are aprons and hangars used by Buffalo Airways and Air Spray, either or both of which can contain something of interest. Apart from that, there are only a few twin-engined aircraft among the general aviation residents. When travelling by road, the field is off Primary Highway 2A, about half way between Red Deer and Penhold.

REGINA SA
YQR   CYQR   Municipal   3m/5km SW

Like many cities miles away from anywhere else in Canada, Regina is a regional aviation centre and thus somewhat self-supporting, but its scheduled links with the rest of the country are not very exciting. The terminal is red brick with glass brick panels to let in the light. Unfortunately, it doesn't allow views of the main apron. However, the occupants of this ramp are unlikely to be of particular interest, and some of the regional cargo operators can be seen from the fence, just to the right of the terminal. To the left is the general aviation visitors' terminal and ramp but it only handles a few light aircraft from across the border.

In front of the terminal is the only runway, 12/30 and, at right angles to it, and to the right of the cargo terminal, are the general aprons, hangars and quite a lot of aircraft. Anyone spending more than a day here will be in serious pursuit of a quantity of Canadian registrations, rather than interesting types which can be seen easier elsewhere. About forty miles west of Regina is MOOSE JAW, where the Canadian Armed Forces 2CFFTS is located.

ROCKY MOUNTAIN HOUSE AL
YRM   CYRM   80m/130km W of Red Deer

Anyone travelling across Canada in search of air tankers might care to make a telephone call before driving all the way to Rocky Mountain House, as the journey can be wasted at certain times in the season. Only when the fire risk increases are aircraft certain to be posted here, sometimes up to four A-26s. Their base is at the end of the runway, some distance away from the general aviation. You have to be dedicated to make the trip. It's about 130 kilometres west of Red Deer, along Highway 11. Having driven through town (blink and you'll miss it), head towards Nordegg. A turn to the north, onto a parallel road, leads to a signpost and a right turn. After about 5 km, make a left turn.

SAINT JEAN PQ
YJN   CYJN   2m/3km SW

Highway 10 is called the Autoroute des Cantons de l'Est, and heads out of Montreal across the St Lawrence River at Champlain Bridge. It links up with Interstate 91 in Upper New York State. Once over the river, St Hubert is to the north and, a few miles further, St Jean is to the south. Turn south off Exit 9 and the road is signposted to the town. It is better to leave at St Luc and by-pass the towns. The airfield is at the side of this road.

St Jean is quieter than St Hubert but it was famous for being an almost permanent residence for the Constellations of Conifair. Still to be seen are a few C-54s and Forestry Commission Cansos but visits should be made during normal working hours to ensure that hangars are not locked up, as their contents can yield some more interesting residents.

SASKATOON SA
YXE   CYXE   5m/8km NW

There are two runways, 14/32 and 08/26, and the terminal is near the intersection, facing 14/32. Whilst the building has a considerable amount of glass facing the apron, only passengers get to see the view, so no photos can be taken from the building. Like Regina, the general aviation terminal is to the left and normally has one or two small American visitors present.

Facing 08/26, and quite a walk from the terminal, are the main hangars and aprons. Anyone intent on walking here from the passenger terminal is advised to keep to the road, rather than attempt a short-cut across the grass. Since there is often a NWTAir aircraft parked by this fence, it is often tempting to head across the grass but the whole area is fenced off at its perimeter and the only way from one side of the fence into a different area is to crawl under it.

A considerable variety of aircraft can be seen in the hangar complex, including the provincial government fleet and one or two King Airs. A T-33 has been mounted on a pole at the entrance. A leisurely stroll around the ramps should be rewarded by plenty of interesting aircraft, most of which can be viewed at close quarters.

TORONTO OT
YYZ   CYYZ   Lester B Pearson International   18m/29km WNW

The multi-storey car park towering above the oldest of the main buildings, Terminal One, is still the best place for a view of the airline ramps, but is accessible only up to level 8. It should not be assumed that the top storey was the best, especially in winter, when it was often inaccessible to cars. Level 8 gives a slightly lower view of the aircraft, and is certainly better for photography. The rooftop (Level 9) is now occupied partly by Transport Canada's ground movement control tower.

Security has become tighter than previously but this doesn't mean that the authorities are heavy-handed. The patrolling officers know that spotters and photographers make much use of the car park and, as long as common sense prevails, nothing should spoil the fun. It is now widely accepted that, at an international airport, security is a modern requirement so the patrols are for everyone's protection.

Speculation about Toronto's new facilities included whether or not Terminal 3 would improve the lot of the enthusiast. To quote one publication on the subject, passengers who arrive at Terminal 3 really make a debut. Coming in at roof-top level of the glassed-in transfer corridor, they can survey airport activity and the surrounding landscape in full daylight . . . on the way to customs and immigration.

Thus, departing passengers and others can expect business as usual! This, at Toronto, means disappointment, as none of the passenger terminals offer any views at all to the general public, with all airside windows being monopolised by those awaiting embarkation.

Toronto ranks highly, compared with other international airports, as the quantity and variety of movements continues to grow. Canadian Airlines International occupy half of the new terminal. Additional operators like Air India, Cathay Pacific and Korean with 747s, Finnair and Vasp with MD-11s and Aerolineas Argentinas with A310s, ensure there is no shortage of interest. Cubana Il-62s, Varig 767s and Cargo Jumbos provide a supplement to the already significant string of European arrivals, and Aeroflot operate summer charters.

It should also be borne in mind that Toronto handles a large amount of domestic traffic: Air Ontario Dash 8s and Jetall Metros are still to be seen but commuter operators do seem to come and go with surprising rapidity. Names which are taken for granted one year are frequently replaced by others, suggesting that operating profits are, at the best, low.

To handle the increase in traffic, particularly commuter carriers, Terminal 2 has a new pier which screens much of the apron from the link road to the south side. This road continues past the threshold of Runway 24L but the parking area has now been blocked off and a variety of tow away zones have sprouted. The former Worldways hangar, on the south side, is now occupied by Skyservice/Esso Avitat and handles a variety of general aviation including biz jets and, next to it, is a large Canadian Airlines hangar. Both can be reached via Convair Drive.

To the north, the picture is just as interesting and lively. On the way along Airport Road to Derry Road and the general aviation area, it is worth making a turn at Orlando, where the road passes very close to Air Canada's maintenance ramp. Just to the west of Air Canada's hangar is Cargo Corner, used mostly by parcel carriers.

For executive aircraft enthusiasts who still wish to keep an eye on the airline traffic, the East Service Road in the general aviation area is extremely popular, being close to the thresholds of 10, 24R and 15 (Left and Right). The parking area/waste ground opposite the Met Office is close to the taxiway used by bizjets and, with luck, the occasional propliner on the move.

A small aircraft, the size of a Citation, would need a 200mm lens, so airliners are well within reach. Afternoons and summer evenings offer the best lighting conditions, due to the southerly aspect. For those in search of cargo operators in action, some disappointment awaits, as they tend to move mostly at night, along with the other numerous courier-related aircraft which fly from Toronto, so action shots are less likely than static ones, taken through the fence.

The car parks servicing the McDonnell-Douglas plant still offer a good vantage point for landing shots, and it is either here or by the Met Office that Toronto's small, but growing, enthusiast population can usually be found. Security personnel are keen to deter use of the McDonnell-Douglas car park, however. The general aviation area, off Derry Road, is totally fenced in and, for the most part, generally inaccessible. The occasional friendly security guard has been known to allow entry to Skycharter and Tornoto Jet Centre hangars.

Fields' apron is always that most likely to contain an interesting visitor. Apart from the part of the apron visible from the approach road, a service road leads round the hangar, revealing the rest, and other aircraft parked on it. The staff at Fields have earned a reputation for being hostile to the enthusiast. They actively pursue camera-carrying enthusiasts who show an interest in aircraft. A request for a look round is definitely a waste of breath!

With the increase in traffic at Pearson, the use of runways has started to follow the American model: aircraft can often be seen on approach to both parallel runways at the same time. Thus, unlike Heathrow, there are no designated runways for arrivals and departures. To relieve pressure on slots, a new runway is currently under construction, parallel to the existing 15/33.

Propliner fans associated YYZ for many years with Millardair. Carl Millard's fleet of immaculate (mostly) C-117Ds and C-54s was accessible and extremely photogenic. Times changed but, it seems, Millardair didn't. All but two of the C-117Ds have gone.

TORONTO OT
YTZ   CYTZ   City Centre   1m/1.5km SW

A new control tower and passenger terminal have recently been opened at what used to be called Toronto Island. A little ferry called Maple City crosses the narrow channel, on what is reputed to be the world's shortest ferry ride, to the airport, which has no shortage of runways or hangars. Permission has recently been granted for the construction of a tunnel to replace the ferry, so those intent on a visit should ride it while it remains. Fortunately, this is still an informal place where a request at the control office, to the left of the terminal, should result in access to the hangars being gained.

The CN Tower dominates the backdrop and can be fitted somehow into a souvenir photograph, while the view from the top gives a very good idea of the airport's layout and the considerable number of its residents. Ontario Place, also on the lakeshore in downtown Toronto, hosts major exhibitions in summer. Kiowas and Tutors have been noted and, not to be missed close by, there is a Lancaster permanently mounted on a pole.

TORONTO OT
YZD   CYZD   Downsview   8m/13km N

Downsview may not handle scheduled traffic, nor have many residents but it is nevertheless worth a visit. This was once the home of Boeing Canada's DHC-7 and DHC-8 production plant, but these have been replaced by the Bombadier group, which has meant the arrival of Canadair Regional Jets at the old de Havilland plant for painting. The vast field is shared with a small CAF base. Reached from Exit 364 off the Macdonald-Cartier Freeway (Hwy 401), Dufferin Street crosses Wilson Avenue and leads to the employee car parks at the edge of the ramps. There is normally very little activity to watch here but there should always be one or two aircraft which have been rolled out of the paintshops, awaiting delivery to some exotic customer.

TORONTO OT
YKZ   CYKZ   Buttonville   20m/32km

East of Downsview on the MCF/401, Exit 367/Woodbine Road (Hwy 8) leads north to Markham. For anyone travelling to Buttonville from downtown Toronto, it should be borne in mind that Woodbine is the continuation of the Don Valley Parkway.

Buttonville is a busy field with a smart little terminal and a nice aviator's book store. There are several operators, especially those with helicopters, so interesting photos are always possible.

TRENTON OT
YTR   CYTR

Not to be confused with its more famous namesake in New Jersey, this is a major base of the Canadian Armed Forces. The quantity of personnel generate some demand for civilian air transport, and Voyageur Airways provide links with Kingston and Toronto, with King Air 100s. The short detour off the highway would not be worthwhile for most, except for the presence of the CAF transports also to be seen. Since these include Buffaloes as well as the more common Hercules, and their ramp is next to an accessible road, it may be considered as a stop, even for those in a hurry, between Montreal or Ottawa and Toronto. Airline activity, such as it is, is largely curtailed at weekends, which applies also to military business. A visit during the week is therefore more likely to yield results.

VANCOUVER BC
YVR   CYVR   International   9m/15km SW (bus 30 minutes)

Sea Island is shared by the airport and the small, quiet community of Burkeville, with two arms of the Fraser River to the north and south and, to the west, the great expanse of Georgia Strait. The southern half of the island is occupied by the airfield. Runway 08/26, extending west into the bay, splits the field in two, with the main passenger terminal and cargo to the north and the general aviation and marine terminals to the south.

The diagonal Runway 12/30 is remote from all accessible parts, a shame since it handles a lot of commuter (and therefore smaller) traffic. The busy main terminal is centrally located, reached by a long highway with only the CAI maintenance hangar on the right/north. A new runway, on the north side, was scheduled for completion about the same time as the new international terminal. It takes much of the departing traffic, leaving the diagonal 12/30 for commuters.

A service road to the south gives access to rather more facilities but vantage points aren't numerous. Next to the cargo terminal is the Air Canada maintenance hangar, where the occasional foreign military visitor parks. Off Miller road, to the south, is a road leading to this maintenance area. Turn right at the end, where there is an old hangar now used for storage of various vehicles. The fence between this Transoprt hangar and the AC facility is probably as good as anywhere on the field for watching the action.

By continuing down Miller Road to the traffic lights and turning right (a right turn on red is permitted in Canada) Russ Barker Way leads to the end of the runway, and another right turn, posted to Burkeville, reveals the holding point and a different view of Hudson General's apron. This long hangar is also used by Transport Canada, and a proportion of their fleet is towed out in the morning; this is the best place to identify them. For anyone who enjoys watching and logging, this large expanse of grass offers an ideal location, as many aircraft land on Runway 26. The holding point is too far away for photos, however. Airport Road South offers no views of the Hudson General ramp but other large aprons are close at hand, on the other side of the road. Continuing down Russ Barker Way, a series of large aprons offers prospect after prospect of all sorts of aircraft: an Air Canada Viscount still with its engines, most of a CF-100 Canuck and a Sea-Bee in British Airways colours have been (and maybe still are) some of the more memorable. To the left is the river and the marine terminal with several Twin Otters, Beavers and Cessnas tied up at the water's edge.dunno

Sunny days are not particularly welcome at this point, as it faces south and the photographer will have to be up early in the morning and return in the evening to get acceptable shots. A light overcast sky is much to be preferred. Beyond the seaplane base are the Air BC apron and the Executive Air Craft terminal. There is also a short track which leads to the edge of the South Terminal apron. Air BC's fleet is a busy one, so few aircraft spend much time at the base during the day. Watching the South Terminal apron requires patience if the fine selection of Islanders, Navajos, Aztecs and even Apaches in airline service are sought after. Biz-jets are plentiful at Executive Air Craft and it is one of the few places where the Victoria-based British Columbia government fleet can be seen regularly at close quarters. Public transport visits all parts of the airport: a shuttle bus operates a link between this area and the main terminal.

After the bustle of the south side, the main terminal can seem tame. Traffic here includes the Air BC Jetstreams, Dash 8s and BAe 146s, plus a good selection of US airlines some of which can be too close for photographs. The nearby staff car park looks promising but usually a quantity of freight containers obstructs the view. Inside the terminal, the glazed front overlooks a wide expanse of ramp but, if a wide body parks close in, it completely obscures the view. Visitors to Vancouver will also have to travel to other airports in Canada if they are to get vaguely close to some of the traffic seen here: Victoria can be particularly good.

The overall verdict for Vancouver is mixed: for wide-bodies, 737s and the like, there are many better places to go but, for those in pursuit of local carriers and a different selection of executive traffic, it has few equals. Under these circumstances, it is difficult to make an objective assessment. In an area where scenery and aircraft abound, remembering that Seattle is not far away, Vancouver is a superb destination.

VANCOUVER BC
CXH   Harbor Heliport   1m/1.5km W

Anyone visiting this picturesque city will almost certainly see Stanley Park which projects into Burrard Inlet. From here, the distant movements of Helijet Airways S-76s can be seen. The base is on the site of the old Cold Harbour seaplane base, one and a half blocks east of the Bayshore Inn. Anyone trying to get there by public transport will be seeking the Seabus terminal, and car drivers will find parking very difficult. The action is only moderate, with a few helicopters on the ground at any one time.

Other fields which may be of interest to anyone staying in the area for a while: DELTA AIR PARK and BOUNDARY BAY are off Ladner Trunk Road. Further east, on the north side of the Fraser River, is PITT MEADOWS, another field used by general aviation. LANGLEY MUNICIPAL, 4km to the SE of Delta Air Park, also offers a wide variety of general aviation.

VICTORIA BC
YYJ   CYYJ   International   17m/27km NE

It's difficult to visualise Victoria as the capital of British Columbia, since it is totally overshadowed by Vancouver on the mainland. It can also be difficult to find the airport as it's almost in Sidney, rather than anywhere near Victoria. Patricia Bay Highway (17) passes close and a turning leads to the passenger terminal. To its left is a customs/baggage reclaim area, and a fence next to this keeps the apron safe from intruders but allows decent views of all visiting aircraft. Air BC Dash 8s, the odd Canadian Airlines 737 and a selection of commuter carriers can all be seen at quite close quarters from this corner. From here, the threshold of Runway 02, often used, is within reach of a 200mm lens. Continuing past the entrance to the main terminal, a dirt road leads to Butler Aviation but only for a handful of light aircraft.

From Highway 17, by following signs to the industrial area, the general aviation side of the field is reached, with fifty or so light aircraft, plus hangars for Flying Firemen and the British Columbia government. It is difficult to see the BC Government fleet well, even when they are out of the hangar, but permission for a closer inspection may be sought at the tower. The registrations of these official aircraft are placed very tastefully in the cheatline, so they are difficult to read. Note that the last letter is shown on the fin.

Because of the enormous amount of flights between Victoria and Vancouver, this airport offers a real chance for the photographer to obtain first class pictures of many smaller aircraft which remain out of reach at the larger airport.

VICTORIA BC
YWH   Inner Harbour   1m/1.5km SE

The city centre is perhaps a little quaint, especially to British eyes. It is a caricature of Britain, aimed at tourists from Seattle who arrive on the ferries. The grey stone buildings are, in the main, handsome as they surround the harbour, and close to the centre of things is the small jetty where the seaplanes operated. Helijet S-76s, rather than Twin Otters, are the modern mode of transport.

Victoria is a ferry terminal, and anyone travelling to Seattle will find that check-in can be very early indeed. If this necessitates an overnight stay, it is wise to shop around for hotel rooms, which can be ridiculously expensive downtown. Bed and breakfast accommodation, in private houses, sounds like a suitable alternative but not everyone likes getting up at 04:00 to cook breakfast for departing guests.

WHITEHORSE YT
YXY   CYXY   3m/5km E

Yukon Territory is not the sort of place one calls into, while passing. Whitehorse is a reasonably pleasant drive north from Skagway, in Alaska. Both take a lot of getting to! The Alaska Highway follows the Yukon River valley, and passes the airport, just after the turn into town and the C-47 weather vane. The field, on a plateau overlooking the town and the river, boasts no less than three runways.

Not much happens here. From the short approach road, the passenger terminal is directly in front, beyond the car park. To the right is the transport museum and to the left, Canadian's cargo shed. The museum mostly tells the story of how the highway and the oil pipeline were built. The car park is level with the terminal's upper floor, so it leads directly into the check-in area. Passengers then descend the stairs to the ramp. The main apron is likely to contain little or nothing of significant interest most of the day. Three Canadian flights are operated daily to Vancouver, there is an occasional Ptarmigan service to Yellowknife, and one or two Air North movements. Exploration of the rest of the field is therefore normal. Passing the cargo shed, the service road leads to a smoke jumper's base, where something might be parked. From their car park, the runway and main apron can be seen through the fence, but movements require a 300 mm zoom lens.

Unless there is something to be seen at the terminal, it is necessary to return to the highway and take the next exit, which leads around the threshold of the diagonal runway, to Air North, a tanker base and the air taxi ramp. The pace of life is normally slow enough for ramp tours to be possible. Normally, this should include an intimate relationship with at least one A-26. A car park next to Air North's base offers a view of the runway thresholds, but through a fence.

Lodging is affordable and tolerable: the Roadhouse Inn, for example, charges something like C$45 for a room but there are others to choose from. For a complete picture of Whitehorse aviation, the next turning off the Highway, South Access Road leads down to the town. Watch out for a right turn before reaching the river. This is Miles Canyon Road, which leads to the floatplane base on the edge of where the river widens enough to be called Schwatka Lake.

WINDSOR OT
YQG   CYQG   6m/9km NE

This is Canada's version of Detroit, with a car plant of its own and all the charm that goes with it. The airport is worth the small detour from the road between Toronto and Detroit, if only to get quite close to visiting Canadian Airlines 737s, Air Canada DC-9s and a growing selection of commuter operators. The terminal is not one of the finest in Canada but the car park to the right is close enough to the ramp for anyone standing on a car roof to be able to do some useful work with a camera. Anyone calling in after 15:00 should be rewarded with one or two movements but a protracted stay isn't likely. The general aviation hangars and aprons don't often contain much excitement but odd rarities pass through with some regularity.

WINNIPEG MN
YWG   CYWG   International   4m/6km W

Winnipeg's only shortcoming is the fact that the observation deck is closed, thereby rendering airline operations from the terminal out of sight. In fact, these movements amount to CAI 737s and a lot of Air Canada aircraft, all by far the least interesting of what can be seen here.

A car isn't essential to get around Winnipeg but it does save a lot of time. The general aviation and local operators' ramps are quite close to the main terminal but it is a circuitous route to get there. Ellice Avenue (not Sargeant) leads to the aprons and a right turn at Ferry Road reveals a delightful assortment of aircraft: the Hudson Bay Fur Trading Company, known in Canada as 'The Bay' (essentially a large chain of department stores) has a hangar where their aircraft are based.

Next door neighbours are Canada's Department of Transport with King Airs, a Beaver and a DC-3, next to which are two buildings used by Perimeter for their Beechcrafts and Metros.

At the end of the road is the Aero Centre, a general aviation terminal, and a left turn leads to the museum entrance and its car park. The view from here is tantalising, with C-46s and DC-3s and, across on the far side of the runway, the CAF base and ramp.

For those on foot, the rest is extremely frustrating, as all the aircraft seem so close but it takes time to get around to where they are. Early risers will find that a lot of the more interesting residents will all be leaving at the same time and it can be hard to decide where to go first. The museum's apron is shared by other operators and all of them are of interest to any enthusiast. The CL-215s normally spend more time on the apron than anywhere else and they sit side by side with Perimeter's fleet of ageing Barons and Queen Airs.

Air Manitoba's corner of the field features Curtiss Commandos and HS748s plus one or two smaller types, an engineless ex-Air Canada Viscount and, nestling in the long grass, the surprisingly complete remains of a few Bristol Bolingbrokes. These hulks are only a stone's throw from their birth-place, as the Bristol Aircraft Company built countless examples of these machines here during the war. Manitoba is littered with them!

The CAF base is active and training sorties are carried out in a variety of machinery. No recent reports have been received but regular visitors are known to include Canadair Tutors, T-33s, C-130s and the all-yellow Beech Debonairs. Together with a CC-137 visiting every afternoon and the odd Cosmopolitan and RAF Hercules or VC-10, there is plenty to delight the enthusiast.

The Western Canada Aviation Museum is quite famous in North America. The volunteers have done an incredible job with their relics, and the CF-101, Viscount and Bristol Freighter are in pristine condition. The WCAM justly claims to be one of Canada's largest and most complete aviation museums - a close and tangible link with their flying history. For a modest entrance fee, most visitors will find the boast to be well-founded but the closing time of 16:00 must be borne in mind when planning a visit.

Anyone in search of photographs of airline movements will probably be much better rewarded elsewhere in Canada but a drive north and a left turn along Notre Dame Avenue leads to a viewing point, good in the mornings when Runway 18 is in use, but photographers will get closer by heading a little further north. The road and runway converge and the holding point is opposite Logan Avenue, where the aircraft are within range of most cameras.

About fifty miles west of Winnipeg is PORTAGE LA PRAIRIE, home of CAF's 3CFFTS base and its CT-134 Musketeers.

YELLOWKNIFE NT
YZF   CYZF

The passenger terminal occupies its traditional Canadian spot, facing the intersection of the two runways, 09/27 and 15/33. Whilst the main ramp faces Runway 15, interest focuses very much along the northern side of Runway 27, for this is where the maintenance hangars are to be found.

The prime attraction of Yellowknife is its large, and thriving, population of propliners. Buffalo Airways' DC-3s, C-47s, Curtis C-46s and Canadair CL-215s are maintained in airworthy condition at the NWT Air hangar, often in the company of NWT's own L-100-30. Next door are the DND hangar, which houses several CAF Twin Otters, and Echo Bay where First Air look after their four locally based HS 748s. Add Air Tindi Beavers and Twin Otters, Ptarmigan Airways, Canadian North's 737s and Canadian Regional F.28s, and it's clear that a trip to Yellowknife is worth the journey. Whilst ramp access at the terminal isn't allowed officially, it is possible to walk across for a quick photo, with the help of staff at one of the maintenance bases.

The prevailing winds make Runway 33 the most used, and an early start is needed to catch airccarft on the move (from over the fence just north of the main terminal). Between early June and the end of August, a couple of government-operated CL-215s are based for the fire-risk season. These are regularly augmented by contract fire-fighters, such as Conair Trackers or DC-6s in the past. Between 1995 and 1999, the contract has been awarded to Buffalo Airways, whose DC-4s will be in evidence. Given that the main terminal is less interesting than the hangars, a view of the main apron is best from the cafeteria/bar. The windows are not tinted and aircraft park close enough for a standard lens to be used.

The OLD TOWN floatplane base is also worthy of inspection, as Ptarmigan and Air Tindi use it. During the summer, a dozen or so Twin Otters and Cessna 185s take off from the lake each day, best seen from a rocky hill at Air Tindi's base on Latham Island. It's a couple of kilometres from downtown and it's about the best place to take such photos in the whole of Canada. Downtown bonuses are the beautifully-restored Buffalo Norseman in the company of Max Ward's Twin Otter and usually a decent selection of Tindi's aircraft.

Yellowknife is not the sort of place to visit at the drop of a hat. Travelling this far requires some sort of arrangements. For about £550, Henry Tenby offers a round-trip from Edmonton or Calgary, plus accommodation and a round trip in a Buffalo DC-3 to either Hay River or Fort Simpson. Bearing in mind that a peak season return fare between Edmonton and Yellowknife costs £325, the package should be attractive to genuine propliner enthusiasts. Mr Tenby, who works for NWT Air, shares the enthusiasm and takes personal care with visitors. For further details, contact Mr Tenby at Postal Service 9000, Yellowknife, NT X1A 2R3, Canada. The fax number is (403) 873 4274 and the telephone (403) 920 4358.

CC = CHILE

SANTIAGO
SCL   SCEL   A. Merino Benitez   6m/10km

Reports from Chile are few and far between. References to Santiago tend to be annoyingly vague, since the city has two airports (the other being Los Cerillos ULC/SCTI) and a military airfield, known as el Bosque.

Benitez is where it all happens, as Los Cerillos is mainly used by general aviation, with one or two tasty movements thrown in for good measure. Only the international terminal has a purpose-built observation deck, accessed by glass doors on the second floor. Not surprisingly, it overlooks the international apron, though the runway is visible. LANChile's maintenance facility and storage areas are easily seen, with a few interesting aircraft in evidence. In May 1997, there were four ex-Ladeco 1-11s plus cargo types from South and Central America. International movements include Air France, American, KLM and United plus, of course, the LANChile long-haul 767s.

A short covered walkway leads from the international terminal to domestic. Views from it are limited but the roadway between the terminals allows some photos. Once inside the domestic perminal, next to nothing is visible without passing through the security check. Once airside, however, the apron is seen to contain plenty of LANChile, National and Ladeco. For the photographer, the Andean backdrop is a bonus.

Anyone arriving by air will be able to get their bearings from a window seat. There are many parked aircraft to be seen, including Alta Air B.1900s, Avant and National 737s, Fast Air Cargo DC-8s and an assortment of air taxi twins.

The end of the runway (unfortunately, the report doesn't say which end) is where the locals congregate, especially at weekends, and there is a picnic area with eatery stalls. Try a lightly-done guinea pig and coke! Traffic is steady without being either boring or too slow, and photographers usually come away from Santiago with a nice collection of shots.

PUNTA ARENAS
PUQ   SCCI   Carlos Ibanez del Campo

Go any further and you fall off the end. Next stop Antartica! Punta Arenas is the southernmost city in the world, with an airport used by both civil and military traffic. Spotting is a bit tricky because there's nowhere inside the passenger terminal and the road outside it is rather close to the Chilean Navy base. There is a T-33 gate guardian.

Not a lot happens during the course of the average day and it's best to arrive rather early in the morning to see something on the move. Aerovias DAP based their small operation here but it stopped (as did they) in May 97. Apart from Alta Air, most of the scheduled services are LANChile and National Boeings but there is a handful of light aircraft to be recorded.

CP = BOLIVIA

COCHABAMBA

CBB	SLCB	Jorge Wilstermann	2m/3km

At only 7000 feet above sea level, this is one of Bolivia's lower airports. To read the entry in ABC World Airways Guide, it would appear that there is little excitement at Cochabamba. Scheduled traffic is a slow procession of Lloyd 727s. What makes the airport interesting doesn't appear in ABC. Firstly, there is a B-25 (FAB-542) preserved, in the middle of a roundabout on the road from town. The approach road passes the threshold of the little-used cross runway and leads past the terminal to the hangars and aprons of Lloyd and Canedo. Lloyd's facility is surprisingly large but only one or two aircraft may be present.

After such a long journey, to such an exotic location, the first question could be: where is everything? The cargo apron, on the opposite side of the cross runway from the passenger terminal, invites inspection. Permission is needed. The reward for the effort is a selection of C-46s and DC-3s. Cochabamba's reputation has been built up so that reality can be a disappointment. An early arrival is one way to make the best use of the day. It is reported that many of the aircraft depart in the early morning and do not return until late afternoon. The word "many" should not be interpreted as a vast quantity. This is Bolivia, not O'Hare!

The small military base, round the corner from the cargo ramp, operates PC-7s, and is located so that it doesn't interfere with civil operations. This is a bonus for photographers, whose activities are therefore less likely to be misinterpreted.

LA PAZ

LPB	SADL	El Alto International	8m/13km NW (bus 40 minutes)

Perhaps one of the most exotic destinations any enthusiast can find in the world, everything about La Paz is truly memorable. 'El Alto' means 'the high one' and, at 13,000 feet (4,000 metres) above sea level, it is certainly an accurate name. The federal capital of Bolivia is Sucre but La Paz has always been the commercial heart of the nation, high on the Altiplano. The Trufi bus from Plaza Isobel la Catolica serves the airport.

Communications in this part of the world, thinly populated by a poor nation, dominated by the Andes and with sparse ground links, place a great dependance upon aircraft for many essentials. Cheap aircraft have found their way here and the DC-6 can be considered as being the latest word in luxury. Any piston engined airliner which can be pressed into service may find its way here, to operate the most unusual of cargo flights.

Meat is an essential food and it arrives at La Paz in these old airliners, ranging from C-46s and Martin 404s to DC-3s and DC-4s. This activity is not related to any scheduled passenger traffic, and the enthusiast can negotiate his way, with a smattering of Spanish, around the aprons. Piston engined aircraft, even in Bolivia, do have a limited lifespan, and several examples lie around the field in disrepair. They make a sad ?sight.

The airfield lies in a flat, open Altiplano landscape but with the Andes in sight. It is not busy, by any stretch of the imagination. The airport's essential appeal is the cargo ramp, and scheduled passenger airline flights are neither exciting nor frequent. They can be seen from the restaurant but photographers will experience problems with the glass, which is ?neither clean nor optically correct. The window at the top of the stairs also offers a view.

To the left of the terminal is the cargo area and, to the right, Fri Reyes is beyond the military compound. Arriving from town, the approach road to the terminal passes the entrance to the cargo apron, where a sentry is posted. A separate road leads past the military base to Fri Reyes. Old propliners are to be found on both the cargo ramps in some numbers, ranging in condition from serviceable to component parts. Don't expect concrete or tarmac - the surface is a mixture of dirt and oil. The buildings are generally in poor condition, though Fri Reyes has a more conventional appearance. Activity is, at best, moderatly paced, the busiest days being reported as Thursdays and Fridays.

Political activities in many parts of South America are sudden and unpredictable which can mean that military uniforms often represent power to the populus. This can have unfortunate consequences for an unsuspecting enthusiast who thinks that a souvenir photograph of a Lloyd 727 at the terminal is no big deal. When visiting the Fri Reyes area, the military compound can be seen, and its inmates are close enough to log. Instead of concentrating 100% on the aircraft at La Paz, it's also worth keeping an eye on the guards. They are keeping an eye on you! The use of cameras should be accompanied by exaggerated, even theatrical, displays so that it can be seen, from a distance that nothing suspicious is happening.

SANTA CRUZ
SRZ   SLCZ   El Trompillo

This is the city's old airport which, in this part of the world, suggests things will be interesting: less so than at other remote South American destinations, but there is a little action to see. Cargo aircraft are thin on the ground, and most of the residents are general aviation and the Air Force's T-33s. If half of these aircraft appeared at Frankfurt or Gatwick, there would be a stampede to see them. In Bolivia, they are slightly disappointing.

SANTA CRUZ
VVI   SLVR   Viru Viru International   10m/16km

The most interesting scheduled operations here are the occasional para-military, and incredibly cheap, TAM services. The rest of the traffic is virtually undiluted Lloyd 727s. Bolivia is an interesting country to visit, and it is tempting to want to see everything. Santa Cruz seems to offer, from fleet lists in JP, plenty of scope. The reality, even in this part of the world, is something of a let-down. There are about seven scheduled movements a day, and the quantity of aircraft on the cargo ramp can be disappointing.

Along one side of the runway are the passenger terminal and a US Government facility next door, outside which a twin-engined light aircraft is normally parked. At the other side of the terminal, beyond the fire station and control tower, is the cargo terminal and apron. Propliner fans travel the world, seeking quality, rather than quantity. The result is mouth-watering photographs of old aircraft with others in the background. What is often forgotten, by other aviation enthusiasts, is that all the other aircraft could be in the background. If the prospect of seeing six DC-3s on their home ground is appealing, then Bolivia might be the country to visit. This is not the land of Holiday Inns and Burger Kings on every street corner. It is South America: poor, often barely accessible and always thinly populated.

CS = PORTUGAL

FARO
FAO   LPFR   4m/6km W (bus 30 minutes)

Movements can be seen from the spectators terrace in the terminal. A 200mm lens is usually adequate but do note the view is southerly and therefore not much good during the middle of the day. Charter flights are operated in groups, each relating to the country of origin. The British arrive on Thursdays, the Dutch on Mondays and the Germans on Wednesdays. Weekends are a mixture, though British aircraft predominate.

Most of the arrivals are turned round between 09:00 and 13:00, though the evenings witness a repeat display. The airport information desk in the arrivals hall offers a schedule of the day's visitors, though registrations are not included. It should be assumed that sod's law applies: if an aircraft is small and/or rare, it could park at a remote stand, so it usually does!

Since the terrace offers a bar and TV monitors, showing flight information, alternative vantage points should not be necessary. However, for those who wish for something different, immediately after leaving the airport compound, a left turn to Praia de Faro leads to a causeway over a lagoon, directly under the flightpath to Runway 11. The fence is high enough to cause problems for photographers without something on which to stand. Parking places are lacking on the causeway, but they are to be found at both ends.

Most days start with a northerly cross wind and end with a south westerly breeze, which makes a change of runway at some point necessary. After a lot of walking, the intrepid photographer may find something different from the view in the terminal but, if the runway direction is changed, it can be hard, hot and thirsty work. When Runway 29 is in use, good photos can be taken as the aircraft line up for departure, especially early in the morning. Take the road, along the southern perimeter - in other words, facing north - towards Praia de Faro (the beach), when Runway 11 comes into use. Opposite the passenger terminal is a hill, from where excellent photos can be taken. The road is close enough to the runway for 100 mm focal length lenses to be perfectly adequate.

FUNCHAL
FNC   LPFU   Santa Cruz/Madeira   14m/22km NE

Madeira is a Portuguese-owned island out in the Atlantic. Like the Canaries, which are slightly further south, Madeira is not one island but a small archipelago. Also like the Canaries, Morocco is the nearest country. Islands that stick out of the Atlantic are rarely flat, as they are volcanic in origin. Experienced pilots are required for landings here.

At the end of the runway is a hill which makes approach decidedly tricky. It would help matters if the runway was flat. Accidents, however, don't happen too often so there's no reason to avoid a holiday here. The airport is small, with a passenger terminal and apron on the coastal side of the runway.

The observation deck has a cafe and offers an excellent view of the traffic. Anyone arriving in a hire car should prepared for a walk, as the car park is sometimes full. Like Faro, charter flights are rostered by country of origin, with Mondays and Thursdays the busiest. British arrivals are a feature, though Transavia and several Scandinavian carriers also visit. The German presence on a Thursday can include three LTU flights and four or five Condor. Aerocondor's Do228 operates local flights to Porto Santo, Madeira's other island some distance to the northeast.

For an alternative view of proceedings, without visiting the airport, the surrounding hills are very close indeed, offering opportunities for unusual photos of aircraft taking to the air. It can, however, be hard work on the feet. The Atlantis Madeira Hotel, in Machico, overlooks Discovery Bay from the hillside and offers a good view of the movements from the comfort of the swimming pool.

LISBON
LIS   LPPT   Portela de Sacavem   5m/8km N (bus 35 minutes)

Since the terminal complex offers little opportunity to see what is happening, it is normal to investigate other locations. There was a terrace and snack bar, above the domestic area, which might now be closed. It doesn't really matter because the extensions to the main terminal seriously interfered with the view.

A new ramp has been constructed, for A340s, near the threshold of Runway 35. Unfortunately, the bushes along the perimeter are virtually impenetrable but views are possible, if you keep walking. A right turn, after passing the end of Runway 03, leads off Avenida dea Amoreiras (Lovers' Lane in English) and a bridge over the road. This is where the local photographers gather, especially in the afternoon.

When Runway 21 is in use, photographers make for Charneca, near the northwest corner of the field, and close to Runways 21 and 17. Go down Estrada de Manique to the end, turn left. There is a trucking company called Lusitania, in front of which is a dump facing the airport. Because this spot is above the level of the runway, really good rotation photos are possible, usually after about 16:00. Recommended for somewhere to stay is the New Ibis Hotel, near the Novotel and the Praça de Espanha. A west-facing top floor room is best, from which can be seen everything on final approach.

OPORTO
OPO   LPPR   Francisco sa Carneiro   6m/9km N (bus 20 minutes)

Oporto is geographically remote and economically depressed. The airport is north of the city on the N107, about 10km from where it joins the A1. The N107 passes right along the southern perimeter, where there is ample room to pull off the road and watch aircraft on approach to Runway 36. Beyond this is a left turn, leading to the airfield and a fork some 100 metres after means bearing left again. On the right is a residencia where a bed for the night can be found at reasonable prices (food is a different matter). At the end of the approach road is a roundabout. To the right is a cargo building or hangar and the passenger terminal.

Accessible from inside the terminal is the open viewing deck from which all the action can be watched and photographed, particularly in the morning, due to the south westerly aspect.

It would be easy to underestimate this airport as just another charter destination. The majority of flights are domestic, most of them going to Lisbon, but any airport worthy of direct Varig connections to Brazil should be taken rather seriously.

CU = CUBA

HAVANA
HAV   MUHA   Jose Marti International

The international passenger terminal is on the south side of the runway, at the eastern end, with the domestic terminal on the north side. The large viewing area along the front of the international terminal? and both its glass front and open deck offer fine views. It's also possible to see most of the action from the restaurant/bar on the first floor. From here, the ramp, runway and remote parking area are all visible, with most aircraft taxiing past the terminal.

Photography is permitted officially but a 300mm lens is essential to capture anything which is on the runway. Times can change, and it would be prudent to seek official guidance before having a go. If permission is not going to be granted, it is better to find out politely, than to suffer a long interrogation, possibly risking the confiscation of some possessions.

The domestic terminal offers better facilities for the photographer. The observation deck is external and overlooks the action. Anyone spending a few days in Havana, with time to visit the airport, will no doubt take advantage of what is on offer on both sides of the runway, leaving with an impressive collection of photos. The logbook might lack variety but it will certainly contain a considerable quantity of Cuban registrations. The average day at Havana offers a really interesting selection of airliners, few of which are likely to be seen outside Cuba, except by well-travelled (and frequently lucky) spotters. Most of the common Soviet-built types are much in evidence, including Yak-40s and many Antonovs. The Aero Caribbean Britannia is stored and their active aircraft still include Il-18s and one remaining Il-14.

In the city are one or two sites worthy of exploration: Revolution Square has a Hawker Fury and a Vought Kingfisher, and Lenin Park has a selection including a couple of An-2s, a MiG-21 and a Yak-18T. No serious airliner enthusiast is likely to miss the chance of a visit to the Expo Cuba site, as it features Caravelle HI-499 in full, but rather fictitious, Cubana colours.

SANTIAGO DE CUBA
SCU   MUCU   Antonio Maceo

Santiago is on the south coast, not far from the US base at Guantanamo Bay. A visit here is normally only possible when staying on Cuba for a reasonable length of time. Preserved Il-14 CU-T816 wears Cubana colours, and it is here that most of the Volo Turistico An-2s are to be found. One or two of them sport Cubana colours. Most of the scheduled traffic is made up of Yak-40s but, as is to be expected in Cuba, there are always oldies and goodies to be seen.

VARADERO
VRA   MUVR   J G Gomez

This is becoming a significant charter airport but there still a few days when nothing at all is likely to be seen. Cubana have a maintenance base here, for work mostly on the Aerotaxi An-2s and their own An-26s, but it isn't visible from the passenger terminal. Photography is allowed, but most opportunities come from the departure lounge windows.

CX = URUGUAY

MONTEVIDEO
MVD   SUMU   Carrasco International   18m/27km S

The airport has a single passenger terminal with a restaurant on the first floor, overlooking the runway and most of the ramps. All aircraft pass in full view, allowing reasonable photographs. Movements tend to be rather slow, offering plenty of time to view the preserved Pluna Viscount, CX-BJA, which stands to the right of the terminal. A photograph may prove difficult because of the fencing but a request for access might be granted.
   To the right of the terminal is a cargo area and nearby are several stored FH-227s belonging to Air Uraguay. Exploration of the military ramp, which lies beyond these aircraft, is probably unwise, especially as its ramp can easily be seen from the terminal restaurant.

C5 = GAMBIA

BANJUL
BJL   GBYD   Yundum International   18m/27km S

A taxi from the town passes the main gate to the airport, some two miles from the terminal, with little to see on the way. No spectator facilities are provided but most of the apron is visible from the car park and departure hall. Once through the customs check, there is a good viewing area but the going is decidedly slow, with only two or three flights each day.
   Scheduled airlines visiting include Nigerian 737s and Ghana DC-9s, with charters becoming regular, attracted by the beaches and sunshine: Condor DC-10s accompany Premiair and Britannia. The flying club has one or two interesting aircraft, and its entrance is via the security post next to the terminal. Being close to the runway, it can be the best place on the airfield.

C9 = MOZAMBIQUE

MAPUTO
MPM   FQMA   International

Whilst this is a large country, its capital city is only 80 miles from the border with South Africa. Predictably, most of the international movements carry ZS- registrations, although TAP started the European influx with the occasional A340. The rest of the traffic is mostly SAExpress Dash 8s, with SAA and LAM shuttling back and forth to/from Joburg.
   The passenger terminal faces the main runway, with a shorter runway to the right, used mostly by the aero club which faces it. There is an observation area which overlooks almost everything apart from the aero club itself. Entrance is free and there is a cafe. The main reason photography isn't allowed is that, on the far side of the runway is the military base, with a few helicopters, An-26s and four derelict C-47s. To the left of the terminal are LAM's maintenance base and Aviation Services. Anyone walking round to the aero club, which isn't far, will see a small number of twins.

32

D = GERMANY

AUGSBURG
AGB   EDMA   Muhlhausen

Anyone travelling between Stuttgart and Munich will take a detour here, as the field is very close to Autobahn A8. The approach road reveals the airport on one side and the glider area on the other. To the left is Runway 07/25 and several hangars and, next to the central parking area, is the zuschauerbereich or spectator area. It's at the edge of the apron, positioned as if everything else is second in importance. Nice attitude! From here, the main general aviation apron is to the left and the pasenger terminal to the right. To what extent this stays a pleasant airfield, or develops into a small regional airport, remains to be seen but it's probably worth a stop. Augsburg Airlines (previously Interot) base their Dash 8s here, plus Beech 1900s. This is Germany's sales outlet for Beechcraft.

BAYREUTH
BYU   EDQD   Bindlacher-Berg   6m/9km

The smart modern terminal has a roof terrace, glazed at the front, which offers a very good view of the field. To the right of the terminal, from the landside, is a chainlink fence where an alternative ground level view is reasonable. To the left of the terminal are the main hangar and some general aviation hardstands. The general aviation terminal is to the right of the main terminal. Nobody would dream of spending nuch time at Bayreuth; traffic is much too slow. The only scheduled operations were Eurowings commuter flights which might continue.

BERLIN
SXF   EDBS   Schönefeld   12m/19km SE (bus/train 55 minutes)

The rooftop observation deck normally offers a comprehensive view of proceedings between 10:00 and 18:00. On the other hand, the proceedings amount to only a dozen or so daily movements. It can be a waste of time, so it might be best to consult a timetable. For advance information and anything else that can be elicited, contact: Berlin-Brandenburg Flughafen Holding GmbH, Flughafen Schönefeld, D-12529 Berlin.

When this was the capital of the DDR, it was the centre for Interflug's scheduled operations with, on the far side of the field, the maintenance base and many aircraft parked outside it. All there is to be seen these days is the occasional charter flight, operated by Condor, Aero-Lloyd or LTU, plus the occasional visitor from one of the former Eastern-bloc countries. Everything else has moved to Tegel or Tempelhof. It would be unwise to travel to the airport, in the belief that some exotic arrival, such as Air Koryo, Cubana or Vietnam Airlines was due. Such scheduled movements have a nasty habit of being cancelled or, just as likely, arriving a day or so late. Anyone with only a restricted amount of time would do well to forget about a trip out here, as it can be an extraordinary disappointment. Its reputation survives mostly because of the old DDR days, which are long gone.

BERLIN
TXL   EDBT   Tegel   5m/8km NW (bus 30 minutes)

Tegel Airport is modern, with a drum-shaped terminal, reminiscent of the Worldport at Kennedy, because car parking is in and on the terminal itself. Except in winter, the roof is almost completely accessible, with views of all the stands plus, in the distance, the two parallel runways and possibly one or two military aircraft parked at their own terminal on the far side. Before deciding to investigate the observation deck, beware the security check includes the requirement that cameras be opened up. Film should, if possible, therefore be loaded only after arrival.

This is going to cause problems for a few people, so it would be sensible to pack something which can be used to clean glass. The glass which will, almost certainly, need cleaning is at the top of the glazed stairwells which lead to various offices. One overlooks a part of the ramp, and can offer a glimpse of something photogenic. The other, which faces the taxiway, is better. That's the one that gets the smeared glass! Needless to say, the airport staff are quite used to seeing photographers, especially in winter, using this vantage point.

There is a small technical area, for maintenance and cargo but, on the average daytime visit, it is unlikely to yield anything of note. The number of airlines operating scheduled services into Tegel has grown but, realistically, there is still little to be seen here that can't be witnessed just as easily at many other European airports. However, for the intrepid, Tegel does offer the chance of good photography, though from on high.

BERLIN
| THF | EDBB | Tempelhof | 4m/6km SE (bus 40 minutes) |

The quadrant of enormous pre-war hangars, occupy the northwest corner of the field and once housed 60% of Germany's commercial aircraft. Times have indeed changed. Inside the passenger terminal, there are no views except from the departure area, so whatever can be seen is from the fence. Scheduled traffic is augmented by the occasional American military movement.

Templehof's name has a very nostalgic sound to it, by association with the blockade. One corner is occupied by the immense hangars used by the US Military base, and their segmental arrangement ensures that aircraft parked on the ramp are very difficult to see. The museum's C-54 is parked in the northeast corner, and so close to the fence that a good quality souvenir photo is difficult to take.

Tempelhof's fortunes have been revived by the introduction of scheduled traffic. Since there are no more Conti-Flug BAe146s, all commercial movements are prop driven, and include Lufthansa, Sabena, Crossair, Luxair, CSA, Eurowings and SAS among others. Being close to the city centre, it is popular with businessmen, who make use of the S-bahn (look for the big green S). Paradestrasse station is closest to the passenger terminal but spotters will find Tempelhof just as convenient. Between the two stations are the thresholds of Runways 09L and 09R. The perimeter fence at this, the western, side normally offers the best views.

When the 27 runways are in use, Leinestrasse station is nearest to the perimeter, a short walk down the street of that name. Frequent use of the S-bahn will make use of a block of five tickets, which can be the cheapest way to travel.

BRAUNSCHWEIG
BWE   EDVE

A magnificent old building, built to impress, the terminal has a huge upper level terrace plus another at the edge of the apron. This latter is ideal for photos of the occasional biz-jet, or to log the many parked aircraft. The flagpoles make some photos from the deck difficult, but they are unlikely to feature a scheduled airliner because it leaves early, very early, in the morning.

BREMEN
| BRE | EDDW | Neuenland | 2m/3km SSW (tram 15 minutes) |

Bremen is situated to the southwest of Hamburg and, as such, is a likely port of call for anyone passing. The airport is moderately busy, handling Lufthansa 737s and some regional commuter carriers. Muk Air and Cimber Air movements are much easier to see, and photograph, here than at Copenhagen, so Brehen has its appeal. At the end of 1996 there was quite a lot of reconstruction but little knowledge about how it would change things. To the right of the terminal is a ramp for executive visitors. To the left are the Roland Air hangar and Lutfthansa Flying Club. This is probably the main attraction of Bremen, with King Airs in the full Lufthansa scheme and the bright yellow Bonanzas. Over the field to the right is the remaining general aviation, and there are adequate places for viewing most of the residents from the perimeter of the main apron.

Towards the coast from Bremen is BREMERHAVEN (EDWB) which is trying to develop itself as a major cargo centre. For nayone touring in the area, it might be worth the journey to find out how things are going.

COLOGNE/BONN
CGN   EDDK   9m/15km S/ 12m/19km W (bus 30 minutes)

Because the view from inside the terminal is so good, it is disappointing to find that the windows have a slight colour tint, which does have a noticeable effect on photos. Scheduled for completion in 1999 is an eight-gate termianl extension, to the left of the existing complex.

The viewing deck appears to be in two distinct parts. Be sure to explore them both. They overlook the apron and the nearby runway threshold. The front of the deck is glazed in part, making photography a little tricky. There are only limited chances to use these side areas, but they do produce better results. Opening times in Germany are normally good, which is helpful, as the busiest times at Cologne/Bonn are between 07:30 and 10:00, with another spell from 16:00 to 19:30. The rest of the day can be very quiet. If runway 14L is being used, it can be an excellent airport to visit, as all traffic taxis past the main terminal, but other days can give a totally different impression of the place.

Occasional cargo flights by Affretair or Seagreen and Russian charters can make a visit an interesting one but, most of the day, there may be little to see, apart from the regular trickle of Lufthansa domestic flights plus the occasional Condor or LTU Sud charter. More variety is provided by the Luftwaffe transport fleet, which shares the runways. The base is to the right of the passenger terminal, and some distance away beyond the WDL F.27s, so that only aircraft on the move can be identified. These will include 707s, Challengers and Hansas during the week, plus occasional Transalls in the circuit and foreign VIP flights. Expectations should not be high, especially at weekends.

During the night, TNT's parcel hub operation is at its busiest, with as many as a dozen aicraft arriving from all over Europe around midnight. UPS have built a hangar in the expanding cargo area, and a 727 is usually parked on their apron during the day. Unfortunately, these parcel carriers are difficult (if not impossible) to identify from the passenger terminal, as they are generally parked so as to be seen nose-on.

To the right of the terminal is the ramp for light aircraft (many of which park on the grass), and Runway 14R/32L, which these smaller aircraft normally use. Executive movements use the Lufthansa Cityline terminal on the far side of the apron, where a selection of Fokker 50s share the ramp with some of the larger general aviation types.

Directly in front of the terminal is the cargo apron, some distance away, but any occasional visitors will need to be on the move if they are to come within range of a camera. At each side of the field are trees, giving a clear indication that the forest had to be cleared to build the airport.

Anyone planning a tour round Germany in summer, of which Cologne/Bonn would feature, might also need to know of Koblenz airfield, 60 km or so further south. It's near Winningen, 10 km west of the city. Some time around the end of June/early July, there is a Fly-In, usually good for over 400 reggies.

DORTMUND
DTM   EDLW   Wickede   6m/9km NE

This is a very quiet airport but it may be of interest to anyone wanting a good portrait of Eurowings aircraft. Metros, ATR-42s and Saab 340s all visit, and can be seen at close quarters from the ramp level viewing area. Access is free and there are a few light aircraft to be seen. Also worth watching out for are LGW's Cessna 404 and Islander. Far from being as busy airport, like Frankfurt or Dusseldorf, it is in the area and thus might make an interesting detour for anyone wanting one or two good-quality photos of some of Germany's smaller airliners.

DRESDEN

DRS EDDN Klotsche 6m/9km NE (bus 30 minutes)

Dresden will no doubt be an interesting and busy airport in the future, as the economy of what was East Germany strengthens. Meanwhile it can be rather tedious. The majority of movements are domestic services, and there is little action during the day. The spectator deck (flughafenterrasse) faces north . . . probably the only good news for the photographer. Entry costs DM2 and the facilities are rather basic but there is also a restaurant to the left.

An interest in general aviation from the DDR days is satisfied by what remains of the old Dresden aircraft factory. The apron is located, across the runway, directly opposite the terrace. A 300mm lens or a long walk are needed. From the terminal take the first turn past the hangars. At the end of the lane is the entrance gate, on the left. The apron can contain as many as a dozen An-26s. At the far end of the field, next to the threshold of Runway 22, is a military base which housed (and may still do so) An-2s and MiG-21s/23s.

DÜSSELDORF

DUS EDDL Rhein-Ruhr 5m/8km N (train 15 minutes)

The modernisation of Düsseldorf was effectively complete with the opening of an additional new runway, and passengers use one terminal with its three radiating piers. Many international flights arrive at the centrally placed Pier/Flugsteig B, and its roof forms the observation deck. To the right, Flugsteig A handles mostly Lufthansa and Air France whilst, to the left, charter traffic uses Flugsteig C. The disastrous terminal fire destroyed, amongst other things, the cafeteria.

Pressure for slots at Frankfurt has meant that Düsseldorf had to grow as a viable alternative, and the departure board shows that most European capital cities and many other international destinations are served direct.

Enthusiasts travelling around Europe often need a car to sample some of the better locations, but Düsseldorf can be enjoyed by anyone arriving by air or train. The S-bahn links the city with the airport, and the observation facilities have few equals in the world. The train costs DM8 and entry to the terrace another DM2.50. The ticket encourages a return visit, as it features a colour photo and technical details of an airliner. It might show an Olympic 737 or a CSA ATR, or many others. The tickets are, in other words, collectable.

Strict noise abatement regulations are enforced, with no flights being permitted between 23:00 and 06:00, and no departures after 21:00. Between midnight and 05:00, the terminal building is closed. Opening shortly after the airport, at 06:15, the observation terrace, (zuschauer- terrasse) has a commanding view of the airfield, with only aircraft parked on the far sides of the lateral piers being out of sight. An early start is essential, as the based LTU fleet leaves for holiday destinations soon after the airport opens. Unlike Frankfurt, there is no longer a security check before going onto the roof.

In front of the zuschauer-terrace are the parallel runways 06/24 (L and R), and to the left is Runway 15/33, used (if at all) only by general aviation which has its own terminal on the west side of the field. All movements can therefore be seen from the roof, and most airliners pass within range of the camera lens when taxiing. The photographer will find Düsseldorf the ideal airport for definitive portraits of a wide selection of airliners, both scheduled and charter. The LTU Sud 757s and 767s, despite being operated from Munich, do visit Düsseldorf. Rationflug, Sunways, Jaro, Viva Air and Istanbul Airlines are regular operators. Applications for slots from carriers such as Air Bosnia were turned down, so it looks like Cologne/Bonn might be getting this traffic.

It is sometimes assumed that Germans have a love for Turkey as a holiday destination. This may be so, but the majority of Turkish flights carry guest-workers (mostly employed in the more menial jobs, including working in car assembly plants) home to see their relatives.

Because the terrace faces north, the patient photographer is sure to leave with good results. Before leaving the airport, however, a little exploration may be worthwhile. Anyone using the terrace has probably parked the car in one of the three multi-storey car parks (Parkhaus 1-3). A complex circular road system surrounds this area, and a road at ground level (NOT Kalkumer Strasse) leads west. The hangar is at the western end of the apron is labelled Thyssen, and its

doors can be firmly shut some days. Just beyond, the free car parks P5 and P20 are located. Close to P20 is the general aviation terminal and its own apron. The aircraft parked here often include something unusual, and photographs are best taken in the afternoon. The three hangars are occupied by Rheinland Air Service, Krupp and Jet Aviation. SD3.60s are parked on the apron in the company of a few corporate and visiting executive aircraft.

It is a long walk west to the maintenance hangars at the opposite end of the field. From the road a few aircraft can be seen. Since these might reasonably include a few A330s and MD-11s, the journey is necessary for anyone who wants to check out everything on display. Even without these aircraft in the log book (they probably won't make good photos on the maintenance ramps) a day at Düsseldorf offers splendid variety and good quantity - certainly one of Europe's most interesting airports.

ERFURT
ERF   EDEF   3m/5km NW (bus 15 minutes)

The small, two storey terminal building overlooks the apron. At either side, the chainlink fences are doubled. This makes photography impossible because, although the lens can be poked through the first screen, the second is only a few metres away. Fortunately, there is rarely anything extraordinary to be seen. Apart from a handful of light aircraft, the main scheduled services are operated by Eurowings which can be seen better at many other airports in Germany.

FRANKFURT
FRA   EDDF   Main International   6m/9km SW (train 10 minutes)

Frankfurt has been a favourite airport with enthusiasts for many years, and its appeal continues, especially for spotters, though photographers are less likely to applaud all the recent changes. There are few airports in the world (except nearby Düsseldorf) which offer a complete package to match Frankfurt. If the whole complex could be rotated through 180 degrees, so that the sun shone from behind, it would probably be perfect!

Having arrived at the airport, it will be worth curbing enthusiasm to get onto the roof. Once in the terminal, a visit to the basement (Level 0) supermarket will ensure a good stock of drinks and snacks at moderate prices (by German standards). What is available at the sales kiosks on the roof is very expensive and has little variety. Not everyone is prepared to pay Dm3.50 for a coke, even on a hot day. Arrival at the airport for about 08:00 ensures time to stock up with food and drink before queuing for the baggage search. The deck opens at 08:00 and closes at 19:30, just before when a polite man on a bicycle tells you to put the binoculars away, forget about the 747 on approach and go home.

Access to the roof deck necessitates a security check, after which the payment of Dm7 allows a walk onto Pier B. There is much similarity in the layouts of Düsseldorf and Frankfurt, the main exception being that the central pier at Frankfurt has two diagonal extensions, only one of which is accessible. The entry ticket should be kept somewhere safe because it can be used for re-entry if, for example, making a quick trip to the supermarket. It also has another use.

Once through the security check to get onto the observation deck, even old hands will feel some excitement: the constantly widening vista of airliners as each corner is turned reveals a variety of operators as well as much of the Lufthansa fleet. On the far side of the runway is the USAF's Rhein-Main base, with one or two transports. Some of the aircraft on nearby stands will only be photogenic once they are on the move. Despite the deck having a southerly aspect, it is often possible to find somewhere for a good photo. The commuter carriers have been forced out of the central terminal area, so that these aircraft are now parked some distance to the east. This can sometimes make identification a problem, and photographs very difficult. There is a rule at Frankfurt which states that the more interesting the aircraft, the less likely it is to offer a good photograph. Immoderate language, in several languages, can be heard as a Mauritius A340 or a Tyrolean Dash 8 turns away at the last minute. It happens regularly, so get used to it.

Because almost all arrivals land in full view, on Runways 25L/R normally, it must not be assumed that they will all taxi out and take off in the same direction. Many departures use

Runway 18, at the western extremity of the field. Those wishing to log all the visitors would do well to remember this fact, and ensure that all incoming movements are logged.

Traffic to be seen from the deck is of the highest order, being a representative collection of airlines from all parts of the world. Heathrow no longer offers anything like the same opportunities to gain close access to such a variety of airliners, and the range of angles to take photos means that most of the shots will have a pleasant choice of backgrounds. On the distant north side of the field is the Ratioflug hangar and ramp, with its F.27s beyond the reach of most binoculars, and to the west are Lufthansa's enormous maintenance and cargo facilities. The cargo centre is already Europe's largest, and still growing.

At the western end of the field is Runway 18, used only in that direction, with a viewing area close by. Photographers with cars will have a very rewarding time here, particularly in the afternoons, when the sun has moved round. Those on foot must take the No.77 bus from the airport bus station to the cargo centre, and it is a fifteen minute walk around the perimeter. There is a small car park, and a slightly elevated platform ensures that photographers have a first class view. A 200mm zoom lens will ensure good photographs of aircraft down to about 737 size. The road passes through a tunnel below the runway, and Tor (Gate) 31 is the last accessible point to the perimeter. This faces south and might be of use to photographers with long lenses. Clearly seen from here is the DC-3, reportedly that which used to be on display on the roof terrace.

Linking Terminals 1 and 2 is a people mover called Sky Line. It's essential transport for spotters when Runways 07L/R are in use. The escalator leads to McDonalds and the viewing balcony. Opening times are the same as the main deck and the one ticket is good for both, so don't lose it. During most days, the spotting from here is excellent, though landing from the opposite direction are not unkown. Terminal 2 handles many of the morning transatlantic arrivals, so this may be a good place to start the day. At other times its apron might only hold a few commuters.

The guided airport tour (flugfahrt) parties meet on the Terminal 1 roof, by the front fuselage section of the DC-8 on Pier B. The DM9 is expensive and some say it's worth every pfennig. Not everyone agrees, however. The full tour takes about 45 minutes and includes Lufthansa Cargo and their maintenance hangars for 737s, 747s and A310s. The bus does not pass the general aviation ramp but offers a chance of photos as aircraft line up at the hold for Runway 18. Frankfurt Airport is constantly developing and the authorities are making every effort to accommodate the needs of the enthusiast. Sometimes compromises are necessary but nobody would deny that it is still one of Europe's finest airports. A day's stay here is over all too soon. Where to go in the evening? Try the InterCity Hotel near Frankfurt station. The room price of about DM100 a night includes a travel pass valid to/from the airport, thus saving DM11 a day.

Anyone who collects registrations, and needs another two hundred or so to round off the day, should make the short trip to EGELSBACH. Trains run from Frankfurt Hbf every hour and the flugplatz is a ten-minute walk from Egelsbach station.

HAMBURG
HAM   EDDH   Fuhlsbüttel   8m/13km N (bus 20 minutes)

Entry to the observation deck, between 07:00 and 20:00 (22:00 on Fridays), costs DM3 and there is a security check. In winter - November to March - between 08:00 and dusk. The authorities have done their best to make life as easy as possible for spotters, as they do in Germany.

The deck overlooks the threshold of Runway 23, where most arrivals land, and even moderate camera equipment allows some very good landing shots. Many of the movements pass the deck on their way to stands on other parts of the apron, many out of sight, and they may take off on Runway 33. When Runway 23 is being used for departures, everything is wonderful. All aircraft must pass very close to the deck, within reach of all cameras.

At the left-hand (southern) end of the main apron are the new terminal and the cargo area. Behind the new terminal is a circular multi-storey car park, eight floors high. For anyone who only wants to log the movements, the top of this car park attracts attention. Do note there are signs (in German only) at the entrance to the car park saying spotting is not allowed. No arguments, or complaints, if they chuck you off!

Beyond this terminal and car park, facing the threshold of Runway 33, is a hangar area for commuter airlines, occupied by Hamburg Airlines. Weg beim Jäger is the road that leads to alternative views but it's not as easy to find as it used to be. This road heads for the Lufthansa maintenance base and is where traffic landing on 33 (occasionally) can be seen at close quarters. From the fence, aircraft parked on the southern apron can be seen with ease. General aviation can be seen in the distance, in the centre of the field. From Terminal 4, follow the signs saying Centrum and turn right at the crossroads.

Without a car, that is probably all the average enthusiast needs to know about Hamburg. It is busy, it offers variety and the sun in the morning makes the photographer a very happy person. Local enthusiasts, who had to endure the lack of observation facilities for some time, made use of the many alternative viewpoints around the perimeter. A car is essential to reach most of them, especially if runway changes occur.

HAMBURG
XFW   EDHI   Finkenwerder   11m/17km NW (bus 35 min)

Crossing the River Elbe from the city, or from Fuhlsbüttel, by way of the tunnel, a drive north following the west bank leads to the village of Finkenwerder, with the airfield on the northern edge of the houses. The bus service No 150 leaves Altona station. A high bank/levee obscures the field from view but a walk to the top reveals the DASA plant where the Airbuses are fitted out. Visits at weekends are usually fruitless because everything is locked up. Since there are only four or five runway movements a day, photography of aircraft on the far side of it usually need a 300 mm lens. Guided tours (in English or German) are possible but they need organizing well in advance. For more details phone +40 7437 5322 or fax +40 7437 4194.

HANNOVER
HAJ   EDVV   7m/11km W (bus 20 minutes)

There are two runways, on opposite sides of the field and, between them, the terminal with a rooftop observation deck - bad news for photographers, as (a) the majority of the movements are small and, by the time they come within range of the camera, they are almost in plan view, and (b) the escalators are often not working, necessitating a long climb to the roof! There's an assortment of biz-jets during the week and scheduled traffic can include something out of the ordinary. In 1996, for example, there was a wekly flight from Barnaul by Sibaviatrans Tu-154.

Between the runways, beyond the passenger terminal, is a significant area for general aviation, though much of it is difficult to see. Although the multi-storey car park is not as high as the terminal, it does allow a different, and better, view of the many light aircraft.. Most of the general aviation can be seen from the fences.

Hannover will host World Expo in the year 2000, so work is under way to extend the airport's terminals. Terminal C will add another eight gates for charter operations. Terminal A will handle the scheduled traffic, and Terminal B a mixture. A railway connection is also proposed.

LEIPZIG
LEJ   EDLS   Halle   8m/13km WNW

This airport has the almost obligatory, by German standards, observation deck. It is a good airport. Everything which moves passes within range of a 200mm zoom lens. The only drawback is the southerly aspect. Behind the air traffic control building is an 'Aeropark' where some relics of Interflug have been moved. It is a comprehensive collection: apart from the Il-62 DDR-SEF and the Tu-134 DDR-SCF, there is an Il-18 DDR-STA and a couple of crop-sprayers. The Il-14 which completes the collection is by the ice rink in the town of Halle, 15 km to the west. Latest news from Leipzig is that the Interflug passenger aircraft serve as restaurants and the Il-14 is used as a travel agency, which should help their survival.

Outside the terminal area, another photo opportunity exists at the east end of the runway. By following the road towards Schkeuditz, there is a small village called Kursdorf, just north of the airport boundary. The runway is easy to find!

MANNHEIM
MHG   EDFM   Neuostheim   4m/6km E

What makes Mannheim airport worth a detour, when driving past, is the presence of Arcus-Air. Apart from their many smaller aircraft, the airline operates Do228 scheduled services to Erfurt, Dresden and Leipzig. These flights operate only occasionally, so reference to a timetable is important. On Sundays, the Dorniers might not be seen at all, as they are often confined to their hangar. The airport is more accurately described as an airfield (flugplatz rather than flughafen) and has a (free) car park from which the apron can be seen. The low hedge doesn't hamper the view but the sun can be a nuisance around midday. The best times to see the Dorniers on their home patch is before 08:00, so early starters might have less problems.

Finding the airfield can be difficult. When coming from the Karlsruhe - Frankurt autobahn (A5) take the A656 exit (Mannheim Neckarau) and follow the signs for Mannheim-Neuostheim or Mannheim-Flugplatz. From the city, head out in the direction of Heidelberg and turn left at the planetarium, following the signs for Neuostheim and Flugplatz. Take care not to follow the tram tracks. When they bear off to the left, go straight ahead or you'll finish up in the village.

MÖNCHENGLADBACH
          EDLN   Düsseldorf Express

Though still a light aircraft field, there is a growing number of scheduled traffic, operated by VLM, Debonair etc. It's one of those increasingly rare airports, where the staff are still very friendly and the occasional visiting enthusiast might be allowed to have a look around. From town, take the 010 bus.

MUNICH
MUC   EDDM   Franz-Josef Strauss   13m/20km NE (train 25 minutes)

Between the two parallel runways are all the main facilities, including the railway link. The airport has two stations; one for the passengers at the terminal area and another, reached before it, for spectators called Besucher-park. The airport shuttle train from the city's main station is service No. S8. In the southern part of Bavaria are the Alps, so people don't mind climbing. This is good, because the observation point is an enormous pyramid, and there are plenty of stairs to climb. From the station platform to the top - 271 in all. On the other hand, the station does have elevators to ground level, and there is a spiral ramp footpath instead of the steps. At the bottom is a DC-3, painted in Swissair colours. The view from the top is excellent but there is no shade. Like the central theme building at Los Angeles, everything can be seen, but from a distance. Photographers who don't have 300mm lenses will find that many of the movements aren't worth the effort. The kiosk which sells food and drink is at the bottom of the hill, so it's worth thinking ahead before the climb. Better still, take food and drink with you, before setting out, because there's no guarantee the kiosk will be open.

The movements include quite a selection of Turkish airliners, once again used mostly to take guest-workers home to their families for a few days.

MÜNSTER OSNABRUCK
FMO   EDLG   Greven   16m/26km SE

This is mainly a general aviation field. Its appeal to the enthusiast is the fleet of Hansa Luftbuild light aircraft known, because they are painted bright yellow, as Banana Airways.

NÜRNBURG
NUE   EDDN   4m/6km NE (bus 20 minutes)

The internal viewing facilities are spoiled by the tinted glass which makes colour photography a waste of time. However, anyone engaged in only logging movements can enjoy a visit here. The rooftop deck can be even more frustrating, particularly on a sunny day, as the reflections in the glass make photography of any worth almost impossible. The charter terminal is to the left of that used for scheduled flights and at either side are the cargo apron, to the right, and the hangars and general aviation, to the left. Aero Dienst and Eurowings occupy the two hangars closest to the passenger terminals, and light aircraft are housed in lock-up hangars out on the grass.
  Traffic during the week is slow, being restricted to a handful of Lufthansa 737s and the based Eurowings fleet. Summer weekends offer increased variety, with additional charter flights. Nearby military bases mean that British and American visitors are often seen, with C-130s making regular troop flights.

PADERBORN
PAD   EDLP   Lippstadt   11m/18km W

It's a dedicated enthusiast who will go far out of his way to visit Paderborn. It is extremely quiet, though the observation deck is free. What can be seen, and then only occasionally, is a Eurowings movement.

SAARBRÜCKEN
SCN   EDRS   Ensheim   8m/12km E

Apart from the occasional Hamburg Airlines Dash 8 and, less so, a Luxair Brasilia, there isn't much scheduled traffic to see. The cost of parking a car for a short while can seem poor value, but there are other places across the road which might be worth the effort. The terrace at the front of the terminal costs DM1 (sometimes) but the view is good, despite facing south.
  To see the Jet Aviation apron, the restaurant has windows, though the car park next to it is also close. This is at the western end of the apron, beyond which the lands slopes down from the end of Runway 09. The road in this direction is inaccessible but things are different to the west. Instead of heading out to the autobahn, a right turn passes Contact Air and a hangar, where one or two aircraft can be worth a stop. The road enters a deep valley, passing below the threshold of Runway 27, after which it continues around the perimeter towards Ensheim. At the top of the hill is a good view of the field, through the wire mesh fence.
  Weekend scheduled traffic is non-existant, so a visit during the week may be best. From the Mannheim - Saarbrücken autobahn (A6), leave at exit St Ingbert West and follow signs for the airport.

STUTTGART
STR   EDDS   Echterdingen   9m/15km S (bus 35 minutes)

The large apron is not dominated by the passenger terminal but by hangars and general aviation. The new terminal has been built, to the right of the existing one, in the corner of the apron. Parked well out into the middle are usually Condor/Lufthansa aircraft, many of which are wide-bodies, and the terminal is tucked away in the northwest corner. The viewing facilities are not really adequate, and enthusiasts have found other vantage points, though some ingenuity and effort is involved. Pink sector car parks are short-term, and can be used to pick up arriving passengers. The ticket allows 20 minutes of free parking, so it's possible to go into charter terminal 3, ask the security officer for the day's schedule (tagesflugplan) and drive off to Bernhausen. Taking longer than 20 minutes costs DM2.50.

Apart from most German operators, with a good variety of aircraft types, many European airlines are regular, so that while Stuttgart is not as busy as Frankfurt or Düsseldorf, it has does have plenty to choose from. Traffic has been bolstered by a host of charter flights, and there is no shortage of operators from abroad, such as Egyptair with anything from 737s to 767s and A300s, plus American Transair, Arkia and Pegasus, to name but a few. The US Military base on the south side of the field also attracts some sporadic visitors, including MAC charters.

The observation deck, which faces south, costs DM3 and many of the more interesting aircraft, such as charters, cargo carriers and general aviation, park a long way from it. The cheapest car parks are P9 and P0, which cost DM12 per day. The S-bahn rail connection, indicated by a green S, leaves from the city's main station and costs DM4 each way.

Guided tours of the airport are offered to parties, usually local, and it is possible to be added to the list. Advance notice can be obtained of tours, and bookings made, by ringing Public Relations on 0711-948-2326 but they need to know at least a day before, if a name is to be added. At peak times, two tours are operated each day, so there should be no problems.

The new approach road still passes commendably close to part of the apron but the occupants are shielded from view by a glazed wall. Anyone arriving by car can pass the main entrance and continue 200 metres or so beyond the last buildings. A track leads across the fields to the perimeter, and a very close view of the holding point for Runway 08. From here, all movements can normally be seen, though traffic on 26 turns off well before reaching this end. When Runway 26 is in use, the road at the opposite end of the field, leading into Bernhausen, has an alternative vantage point. At the southern end of the underpass, a walk up to the fence gets reasonably close to the runway.

The really energetic can also follow footpaths around the eastern perimeter for a view of the 08 holding point. Not only is there access from the north but the road out of Bernhausen towards Echterdingen passes the entrance to the USAF base. Parking the car around here means a walk to the perimeter fence. Neither the police nor the American security personnel mind spotting from this fence, but they can get upset if stepladders are used to see over it.

The last runway extension involved the realignment of part of Autobahn A8/E11 slightly to the north.

DQ = FIJI

NADI
NAN   NFFN   International   6m/9km S

The terminal is divided into two: international passengers use the right-hand side (viewed from landside) and domestic the left. The observation deck, on the roof of the domestic terminal, is reached by an unmarked staircase next to the snack bar, and faces the intersection of both runways. The deck lacks facilities (there aren't even any seats) but it is possible to go downstairs to the snack bar for a drink and a spell out of the sun. The wire mesh doesn't prevent photos using a standard lens - things do come that close. To the right, and out of sight from the deck, is the Air Pacific hangar which faces the international part of the terminal. The cargo area is to the left and also out of view.

What can be seen, however, is everything which moves. Traffic is fairly brisk, mostly due to the comings and goings of the small Sunflower movements. All their commuter aircraft can be seen in one day (or less!), as the airline's hangar is directly opposite the deck, on the far side of the cross runway. What remains to occupy the time is only about a dozen movements a day. It might not sound much but each one is likely to be of much interest: mostly 737s of Air Nauru, Air Marshall Islands, Air Vanuatu and so on, though Air New Zealand 767s call regularly.

Anyone staying on the island for a while should also bear in mind that Suva, on the eastern side of the island, also has an airport, called NAUSORI (codes SUV/NFSU) which is certain to be worth a visit.

EC = SPAIN

ALICANTE
ALC   LEAL   5m/8km S

Officially it's Alicante but most of the local road signs point to Alacant. Spanish is the second language round here, much as it is around Gerona (spelled Girona). The purpose of an airport, developed to handle charter flights to the exclusion of all else, is to cope with vast numbers of people. They pile into the terminal, airside, from their wide-body flights (and a lot of 757s) and onto their buses, once landside. Two weeks later the whole process happens in reverse, as far as holiday makers are concerned but the reality is that, as one lot arrives, others will take their seats to go home. There is no Executive, Club or First Class at Alicante. It's Cattle Class for everyone. Herd them in, ship them out. It's surprisingly civilised, under the circumstances. The traffic is national-specific from day to day. Germans one day, Danes another, Dutch . . . and lots of British.

Downstairs, there's nothing to see apart from check-in desks and thousands of people. Upstairs, the apron is visible through the glass. A glazed corridor, along which walk incoming passengers, divides the departure area from the tarmac. The perimeter is surrounded by a double fence, always bad news for photographers, and there's not much (if any) high ground on the coastal side of the field. To the right of the terminal is its predecessor and, next to that, the control tower. Very modern, if you like that sort of thing, but best described as: it will be nice when it's finished. To the left of the apron stand a couple of DC-3s, long past their prime and covered in a thin film of sand.

ALMERIA
LEI   LEAM   5m/8km N

Apart from a small number of 'alternative' holiday destinations, there is little to support this airport. Occasional Aviaco DC-9s and foreign charter flights visit, and these can be seen by passengers from the rampside patio. Landside visitors must content themselves with a view of the taxiway from the side of the terminal. Before lunchtime, the sun only offers the chance of improving a tan; it spoils photos.

BARCELONA
BCN   LEBL   Prat   9m/15km SW (train 20 minutes)

Anyone considering renting a car here should also consider taking up fishing, or growing roses, instead. The airport poses problems but nothing on the scale of driving round the city. Barcelona is probably as bad as it gets - anywhere in the world. For a start, they have toll motorways (autopistas) with intersections (nus) that make Spaghetti Junction look like a crossroads. Also, bear in mind that it seems they spent all the money on the roads and didn't have enough left over for the signs. If you know where you're going, they're quite handy (though sometimes a bit misleading). If you don't know where you're going, they're a nightmare. And that's when the roads are quiet. Imagine having seen, out of the corner of your eye, a sign saying that was your exit, as you passed at 110 kph, and having a sixteen-wheeler right up your backside. This is not funny. What makes matters worse is the intersections lead to more intersections so that, in the end, you can't even figure out (a) where you left the motorway or (b) which motorway it was. Then they sting you for another couple of quid to get back. If you are offered a Tabasa Totes Direccions map, tear it up. Don't even look at it. Barcelona has a ring road. Part of it is called Ronda de Dalt and the rest is Ronda Litoral. Quite where one becomes the other is something left to conjecture. According to the diagram for Junction 16, Nus Llobregat, the airport is south but it's actually to the west. Approaching the airport by any other road, other than the

Ronda or an autopista, signs for the airport are few and far between. They tell you you're on the right road, rather than where the right road is.

The problem is that a plane or a train gets you to the airport but there's nowhere to see things from, apart from a couple of windows on the first floor of Terminal C. To get to the end of the runways, you need a car, and that's not so bad if you pick it up at the airport. It's getting back to the airport that's the problem. That and getting into or across Barcelona.

This is Spain's second largest city, just as Milan is Italy's. It's a vast place - a significant commercial centre and a major industrial city - so it generates a lot of business traffic. The Pont Aeri shuttle flights to and from Madrid leave every fifteen minutes or so, and they have to compete with other airline operations to Madrid. Iberia 727s do the shuttle job. Apart from Madrid traffic, there are flights every day to no less than thirty Spanish destinations. Eurpoean destinations number about forty but transatlantic flights are mostly by feeders via Madrid.

Seen from the landside, it's easy to think you're at Orly Sud. Long terminals on one side of the seven lanes of road and parking on the other. The railway station is linked to the terminals by an elevated travelator, and the trains which run from Placa de Catalunya are very smart, even though the seats are hard enough to make your bum go numb after ten minutes. At the western end, reached first by car, Terminal A is for all non-Spanish airlines. Inside it, nothing can be seen from landside. Information desks have monitors listing flights, including their registrations. Ditto Terminal B, used by Spanish airlines (mostly Iberia). Terminal C is for the Madrid shuttle and some general aviation, though this might not amount to much. To its left, and seen from the road, is an apron containing a nice assortment of Spanish airliners of all types from A310s to ATRs. Fences rule out photos. The view from Terminal C does allow all the movements to be seen but many of them a long distance away.

This means the only option is to head for the end of the field. By car, it isn't so bad but getting back is another matter. Just after the car wash, take the first available exit, marked B-250 El Prat de Ll and Zona Franca. It leads to a T-junction and an obvious right turn. This goes past a rather awesome-looking housing estate (meaning that stopping for directions isn't recommended) and, to the right, a park. Follow the edge of the park and, sooner or later (if you still have wheels on the car), you come to its corner, where benches have been moved to some elevated ground. This is where local people sit and watch. It's very close to the end of the preferred departure runway but it does face into the sun. Keep going past the end of this runway and there is a left turn onto waste ground where the car can be parked. On one side are aircraft landing on Runway 25 (and ideal for photos in the afternoon) and, on the other, departures off Runway 20, looking at their best in the mornings.

BILBAO
BIO   LEBB   Sondica   6m/9km N

Perhaps one of the most scenic of all Spanish airports, the mountainous background could make the various vantage points extremely good for a photographer. The problem is the distinct lack of subject matter, with Iberia jets being the only regular visitors. Even the light aircraft appear regularly at other European airports.

FUERTAVENTURA
FUE   GCFV   Puerto del Rosario   7m/11km SW of Corralejo

The terminal area isn't as good as Coleta del Fuste for reading off registrations. The problem with this location is that many of the charter flights are German, mostly on Saturdays and Mondays - since they don't have underwing registrations. One of the quieter of the Canary Islands, neither the facilities nor the quantity of movements stand comparison with Gran Canaria, Tenerife or Lanzarote.

GERONA
GRO   LEGE   Costa Brava   5m/8km S

In Catalan, this is Girona, and the gateway to some extraordinary holiday resorts. Most extreme is Lloret de Mar which is as tacky as a resort gets, this side of the Atlantic - like Benidorm with less class. Calella and Tossa de Mar aren't so bad, and there are places like Llafranc and Tamariu, which really are rather special. The hotels, generally speaking, are past their best so packages to the Costa Brava are very affordable. In other (slightly snobbish) words, this is a bit bottom end of the market.

The airport has a single runway, to the east of which is the main apron and not much else. A range of European charter carriers fly in, reaching their peak in August. Outside peak times there is very little traffic. In October, for instance, the movements board for the entire day might feature five flights at the most. Britannia and Airtours plus something like Sobeliar or Hapag Lloyd. The rest of the apron might contain half a dozen or so light aircraft, usually parked at one end or the other.

The landside view from the terminal is non-existant but a road to the right of the terminal leads to a corner of the main apron where the airliners can be seen. The fence is expanded metal, rather than chain-link, so photos are all but impossible. Around the perimeter is a single fencebeyond which are fields and woodland. Accessible in theory but not really a very good idea . . . and not really worth the trouble. If this is te sort od stuff you're after, go to Palma instead and see more of it.

LAS PALMAS
LPA   GCLP   Gran Canaria   14m/22km SSE (bus 30 minutes)

The large terminal offers passengers a good view of almost every aircraft to visit, and the balcony is a bonus. Traffic is an extremely good mix, and anyone with a hire car could justify a couple of visits during a holiday. Transatlantic flights between Spain and South America often refuel at Las Palmas, though most of these movements take place after dark. Scheduled traffic includes inter-island services by the locally based Iberia subsidiary, Binter Canarias, and Royal Air Maroc operate ATRs and 737s. Charter traffic shows how popular the island is with the Scandinavians: almost all the charter airlines from that part of the world, and from Germany, are regular visitors, with wide-body movements being a regular occurrence.

On the far side of the field, though quite some distance away, is the military base, used by some CASA 212s, and a Search and Rescue facility. The Aviocars are seen at an oblique angle and can therefore be identified but the SAR F.27s usually park so that they are seen end-on, frustrating any attempts at identification, unless on the move . . . a rare occurrence!

At the southern end of the field, and hardly worth the effort if the observation deck is open, was a fine view of the end of the runway near Las Puntillas. This was where the wild dogs lived, though it's been converted into a football pitch, with a screen of palms to obscure the view. Even medium quality photos are no longer so easy because of the improvements. Continue round the edge of the field and photos can be obtained in the morning sunshine. There are reports of a DC-7 seen from the southern end of the field, and in somewhat better condition than its white-painted counterpart, to be found decaying on the hill at MASPALOMAS.

IBIZA
IBZ   LEIB   5m/8km SW

The new passenger terminal is large and modern, and good views are available at the right-hand side, through the tinted glass of the domestic departure area windows. Most of the apron can be seen but the general aviation ramp is out of sight. In the lounge area, the bar serves drinks and snacks at reasonable prices.

The original terminal is now used for general aviation. The adjacent wire fence to the left, near the control tower, offers a limited view of executive movements, which normally include several from various European countries. It is useful to contact someone in authority at the terminal, so that suspicions are not raised. At the opposite end of the new terminal are Iberia Cargo and a staff car park, where fences allow other views. At Ibiza, there are a few places to see most movements but no single spot allows everything to be seen on the ramp. To be able to monitor the situation better, there is a well-used track leading from the main road to the end of the runway, which may offer something more comprehensive for both watchers and photographers.

Playa d'en Bossa is fairly close to the airport, and lies under the flightpath of aircraft on finals. Anyone planning a visit may consider staying at the strategically placed Hotel Club Bahamas, and hiring a cycle from one of many shops, thereby reducing travelling time to the airport at a moderate cost. The quantity and variety of visitors are not in the same league as Palma but the facilities in the airport complex are better. As usual in Spain, most of the action takes place in the mornings or after dark.

LANZAROTE
ACE   GCRR   Arrecife   4m/6km

The passenger terminal is adequate for anyone noting registrations but photographers will make their way to Playa de Matagordo. A car is essential, however, and the road between Arrecife and Puerto de Carmen has a turning where it can be parked. From here, a five minute walk is all that is needed, even with the children. Anyone who must take holidays with the family will find Lanzarote a good destination.

The family can sit on the beach, facing the sea, and the enthusiast can turn round and see the threshold of Runway 03. From the tops of the sand dunes in the morning, it is possible to follow the angle of the sun so that, by about 16:00, the high ground on the west offers a splendid view of aircraft turning to line up for take off. Traffic is modest, but photographers will be rewarded by first class shots, rarely needing the full range of a 200mm zoom lens. Military activity is minimal, so the police take little interest in aviation enthusiasts.

MADRID
MAD   LEMD   Barajas   10m/16km ENE (bus 30 minutes)

Barajas is just ten miles out of the city, and is easily reached by a special bus service which operates every five minutes from the underground bus station at Colon, at a cost of about 200 pesetas. There are two crescent-shaped terminals side by side, for domestic and international flights respectively.

The upper level of the domestic terminal (at the extreme left-hand end) offers a reasonable and comfortable but limited view, overlooking both principal runways, 15/33 and 01/19, and the taxiing aircraft. It is officially forbidden to take photos (through glass) but the police do not seem to mind. This should not be taken as permission, of course. Discretion, and a 200mm zoom lens, will be useful. Large helpings of patience are also at a premium . . . this is a frustrating airport.

To the right, and beyond the international terminal, is the cargo ramp, an area of much activity. Aircraft parked here can be seen from outside the international terminal, some of which should be within range of the zoom lens. Cargosur, who operate Iberia cargo flights, still operate some DC-8s. In the far corner of the ramp, the Post Office CASA 212s and TNT BAe146 await their evening's work and beyond them are the Falcons and 707s of Grupo 45, the Spanish Air Force VIP Squadron.

The general aviation ramp, comprising mostly Falcon 20s and Corvettes which deliver packages at night, has moved to the cargo terminal, to make way for a passenger terminal extension. Identification of the biz-jets etc has been made much more difficult (if not impossible). Anyone leaving Madrid on an international flight can check in early and make use of the cafe in the departures lounge, from where these aircraft are best seen.

The steady stream of Iberia A320s, DC-9s and 727s dominates the activity, as much of the long-haul wide-body fleet generally leaves at night to arrive in South America at dawn. Domestic services are operated by Aviaco, so visits by other Spanish airlines are rare. Foreign operators are standard European fare, except for SAS MD-87s, though Spain's links with Latin America mean that more interesting visitors are regular. Avianca, Aeromexico, Varig, Cubana, LANChile, Aeronaves del Peru and Pluna can all be seen, often in the afternoon, though their movements can be weekly, rather than daily. The chances to enjoy Barajas are so limited, it must be stressed that it is not an airport to be considered as a destination in its own right, involving a long drive or an expensive flight.

The Spanish Air Force museum is at CUATRO VIENTOS (LEVS), containing among its exhibits a Do24, two CASA Azors and a British Rapide, G-ACYR. Admission is free, though photography is forbidden. Indeed it is forbidden (in theory) anywhere on the airfield, due to CASA and the active military presence. There are some 150 light aircraft and police/traffico helicopters based here.

From the city centre, take the Metro's Grey/Circle line to Canillejas-Aluche, from where the Green line goes to Carabanchel. Cost: about 130Ptas. From Carabanchel, a taxi to the control tower is necessary, the cost of which should be about £4 single.

The activity of SAR 403 Sqdn, and the security which accompanies it, occasionally leads to difficulties. Start at the tower and negotiate. Photos might be possible, subject to a levy (official or otherwise) but should not be attempted without agreement. Acitivity is likely to be monitored, through binoculars, even if you are walking along the fence. Take photos - expect problems, and this might even include those obtained on the ramp, with "permission" (okay by me, senor) on a private ramp.

Nobody starts out to be difficult. Approach things right, and Vientos is seriously interesting. Annoy people who think you should show a bit of respect, and they'll teach you how to show respect! It's always worth asking someone, at one of the offices visited, if they can phone for a taxi to take you back to the Metro station. No problem, senor. That's how it is - you be nice to them and they'll be nice to you. Madrid's other general aviation field is GETAFE, but little is known about it.

MAHON
MAH   LEMH   Menorca   4m/6km SW

Minorca is the quietest of the Balearic Islands but its popularity is increasing, with the airport expanding to handle the traffic. Most of the charter traffic is British and of interest to only a few enthusiasts but Aviaco do operate scheduled services to the mainland. Because the terminal area is poor for watching, and worse for photography, the perimeter fence is the only place to exercise serious interest. A hire car is useful as there are some very long walks otherwise.

To the right of the terminal, the view is across the apron, and from the car park, the main apron and light aircraft can be seen. Cameras should be used with discretion. Resorts are spread across the island, particularly on the northern coastline, so a visit to the airport will probably involve a taxi ride or the hire of a car.

Light aircraft from Europe are quite prominent here, though the local residents are based at the Mahon Aero Club airfield, some six miles away. As there is only one road across the island, the Aero Club grass strip is easy to find, and there is rarely any trouble gaining access, for some photos of unusual types.

MALAGA
AGP   LEMG   6m/9km SW (bus/train 10 minutes)

The view from inside the terminals is only possible once departing passengers have gone through passport control. Car parks at either side of the terminals allow good views of the aprons, and they are widely used by holidaymakers catching their last sunshine before departure. Anyone walking about taking an interest in the movements arouses little attention.

To the left of the international terminal are the Jet Aviation facility and aeroclub hangars. It is probable that a request for a close inspection will be refused: in this event, all except hangared aircraft can be identified from the main road, next to the threshold of Runway 32. On the opposite side of the runway, in the southwest corner of the field, is a military base which attracts a few visitors. Traffic, mostly charter operators, is generally brisk, though a couple of Iberia 747s call each week. The airport is served from resorts and Malaga city by buses and trains.

PALMA
PMI   LEPA   Son San Juan   6m/9km E (bus 30 minutes)

The only public transport to the airport is bus service No.17, which runs from the Plaza España in the centre of Palma every half hour. The twenty minute journey costs about 120 pesetas. What you see when you arrive is a new terminal, a bit like Changi in shape. Unlike Changi, there are no observation facilities. All is not gloom and doom, as at least the perimeter offers some hope.

The northern side of the field is probably best for a good view of proceedings. Take the motorway exit for Coll d'en Rabassa or, coming from C'an Pastilla, turn right at the lights (in the middle of Coll d'en Rabassa) towards San Ferriol. Straight across at two roundabouts, past the Continente Hypermarket and the windmill, tun into the industrial area, then take the only exit off the roundabout to a sharp bend in the road. Here is a track and a view of the apron, on te far side of Runway 06L. There's a bar an high ground, above the level of the double fence. This is the place to be. From here, 75% of the airport, and virtually all traffic, are visible, often at close quarters. The aspect is south-easterly so it's not ideal for morning photos - a pity since that's the busiest time. It is, however, great from tea-time until late evening, when traffic is quite brisk again.

The resort of C'an Pastilla is near the airport, and aircraft are close to touchdown as they pass overhead. There is a patch of undeveloped ground which allows a decent view of the end of the runway, and even photos of landing aircraft. Rooms facing traffic at the Helios Hotel are popular. The new runway, 06R/24L, is restricted (not least by local hostility) to landings on 24 and take-offs on 06.

The airport is moderately active all week, siesta time apart, but the weekends are busiest. Any enthusiast who records airline movements at major airports will probably witness only a small percentage of charter operators, so Palma offers a very real opportunity to see a range from all over Europe, including as many as three Premiair DC-10s on Saturdays.

The general aviation field of SON BONET is a 15 minute drive from Palma, and thirty or so aircraft are normally present. The local staff are bothered by lots visitors, particularly in the peak summer period. Most of what is there can be seen from the fence but anyone wishing to gain access should telephone the airfield on 264 670 beforehand.

TENERIFE
TFS   GCTS   Reina Sofia   37m/59km SW (bus 40 minutes)

The terminal's balcony is leased by a catering company, who provide refreshment for those who wish to catch the last of the sunshine before going home. It is, like Las Palmas, the best place to see the apron and get good photos of all the movements. Some of the aircraft which park out on the apron may require longer lenses. Whether this deck is only available after passport control is not certain.

A service road leads south past the Texaco filling station to the perimeter and Los Abrigos, where the needs of all photographers are met. Bushes next to the fence by the threshold of the runway mean that aircraft landing on 07 are easier to see than those on the ground, especially as distance and heat haze make life difficult. Runway 25, when in use, offers much better prospects, however. By going all the way round the south side of the field, all movements can be seen, and photographs are of a high quality, with the sun behind the camera and the hills behind the aircraft. The small beach east of El Medano has a cafe and offers good spotting.

Traffic is predictable, as with most Spanish resort airports: charters dominate the movements board, and weekends are particularly busy. Like Las Palmas, the island is popular with the Scandinavians, and their numbers supplement the German and British flights.

TENERIFE
TFN   GCXO   Los Rodeos   8m/13km NW (bus 30 minutes)

The airport is surrounded by fences, making it difficult to take photos on the left side. In front of the terminal is a small (free) car park and, inside, there is a cafe with lots of seats and views of the movements. Photography is good, but through glass, and subject to the limited amount of traffic. There are (still?) two ex-LAC Viscounts stored in the maintenance area.

At the perimeter, it's only by the Aero Club entrance that decent shots are possible, with the aid of a 200mm lens. For an elevated view, La Esperanza road offers the best opportunities, again with a 200mm lens, but the only scheduled traffic are the inter-island flights, operated by Aviaco F.27s and Binter Canarias CN-235s.

VALENCIA
VLC   LEVC   Menitses   10m/16km W

Tourists don't flock to Spain via Valencia. It's an airport used, on one side by the air force and, on the other, for mostly regional and some international communications. For travel by rail, take line C4 from Valencia's main station towards Riba-Roca, and alight at Aerodromo de Menitses.

The terminal building is a strange sight, a rather sombre sandstone building inside which are few views of the field. This is mostly due to the fighter squadron on the far side. What's on the ramp is easily seen from the approach road, especially at the left hand side, from where the Air Nostrum Fokker 50s can be seen, parked on the tarmac. One or two occasional visitors add interest but Valencia is one of those airports that quietly gets on with its business.

The southern side of the field is screened off from the road by a high concrete wall. What there is to be seen behind it amounts to twenty-odd light aircarft, parked by what must have been the original passenger terminal. It is possible there is also a small air museum but this wasn't confirmed. To the right-hand side of the terminal is Air Nostrum's modest maintenance facility, next to which a coastguard Sea King is normally present on its own pad. Beyond it are glimpses of one or two aircraft worthy of further exploration. A car is handy now, as it saves a lot of time. At the roundabout above the Menitses (not the airport) highway intersection, head west parallel to the railway line and follow the signs for the piscina municipal. By parking on the wasteland next to next to the sports ground, the airfield is in full view on the other side of the railway and a road. Apart from one or two light aircraft, there are the interesting remains of a few withdrawn aircraft, including an F.27.

EI = IRELAND

CORK
ORK   EICK   3m/5km S

A small airport, with the occasional scheduled visit by Aer Lingus F.50s, Shorts and 737s, the terminal's viewing area has quite heavily tinted glass. This is fine for spotting but photographers might do better to head for the rental car parking area. Things move at a leisurley pace in these parts but the occasional Easy Jet or Air South West arrival stirs things up a lttle. TNT and Hunting's aircraft operate nightly.

DUBLIN

DUB   EIDW   Collinstown   5m/8km N (bus 30 minutes)

Aer Rianta, who operate Dublin Airport, have achieved a balance between security and the needs of the many spotters. The viewing gallery on the third floor is fully enclosed and overlooks the apron between the main terminal and Pier A. Movements on Runways 10/28, 11/29 and 16/34 are also visible. In the distance, aircraft parked at Iona and the flying club can be identified. Runway 05/23 is no longer used, except for taxiing and some parking. Anyone listening on the radio might hear reference to Corcoran Boulevard - this is Taxiway P1, also part of what used to be the runway and now used for remote parking. The apron is visible but through glass that is not generally clean. Photographers really should take with them something to clean the glass.

At the far end of the gallery, the cargo ramp can be seen and, at the other end, by the lifts, is a partial view of the Team and Aer Lingus hangars. The daily flights bound for America mean the gallery gets busy for a while but, as soon as the aircraft depart, so do the people. The concourse between the terminals is now strictly for passengers only, due to the provision of additional shopping facilities. The Sky View Bar has a good view of the apron, especially facing towards Ryan Air but the purchase of an appropriate beverage is essential. This is Ireland, and it would be a foolish man who went near a bar without partaking of a bevy or two.

Outside the terminal, Car Park 4 overlooks the Ryan Air apron, with additional views of Aer Turas and any cargo aircraft which might be present. Hunting Cargo, DHL, TNT, Emerald and Heavylift are all regular daytime inmates. From the nearby roundabout, a link road passes the Aer Lingus headquarters, beyond which is a footbridge. Even from the top, only a part of the Team and general aviation area is visible. There is little reason to find somewhere out in the open to spend any amount of time and doing so can cause the security personnel to show undesirable, and probably unnecessary, interest. The advice is therefore to see whatever there is to be seen, keep moving, and get back into the terminal for a longer stay.

To get to the perimeter road, make a left turn at the roundabout onto the main road in the direction of Drogheda and Belfast. After another left turn at the next roundabout, posted Swords, the road passes close to the runway. There are lay-bys where it is possible to sit and enjoy life, a popular pastime in Ireland. Photos of aircraft landing, complete with tyre smoke, need only a 200mm zoom and departing traffic is just as easily seen, subject to runway in use, of course. Also seen from here is the giant TEAM Aer Lingus hangar and maintenance area and some general aviation. A left turn at the corner of the field, at the thresholds of Runways 11 and 16, the road continues to the Westlands site, used by some light aircraft and where Aer Lingus Commuter maintain their Fokker 50s and 146s. By following the road, the main runway (10/28) is reached, and there are views along both sides.

There's no reason not to visit Dublin in winter but it's much better, and busier, in summer when scheduled movements are accompanied by a range of charters. Thus it isn't unreasonable to expect Aer Lingus A340s rubbing shoulders with AmTrans 757s and smaller aircraft of Futura, Aero Lloyd, Lauda Air, Tyrolean and Royal Air Maroc. Not only do the Irish need to go on holiday but we must remember that the rest of the world has good reason to visit Ireland on holiday. Chuck in a couple of tasty Boeings on maintenance and a day at Dublin can be quite an experience.

Irish light aircraft are thinly spread so anyone with an interest in the country's civil register will want to visit to WESTON, on the N4, where a good proportion of all the nation's aircraft can be seen.

GALWAY

GWY   EICM   Carnmore   4m/6km E

This airport is tucked away on the western extremity of Europe. Anyone who visits will note that the people like it that way. The pace is, even by Irish standards, relaxed. Carnmore is somewhere to chat to people about aviation, rather than experience a lot of action.

50

SHANNON
SNN   EINN   16m/25km W of Limerick (bus 45 minutes)

Shannon is famous for its small number of quality movements, ranging from Aeroflot crew training and delivery flights to . . . almost anything.

Comparable in many ways to Prestwick, Shannon handles some trans-atlantic traffic, with the last chance of fuel before crossing the ocean, but the main runway, 06/24, is generally quiet enough, and long enough, to be of use for wide-bodies in the circuit.

The spectators' enclosure in the old terminal offered fine views of the traffic but it can remain closed for part, if not all, of the day. This may be due to the alternative facilities now on offer. The new terminal features an observation area, behind glass. The reflections can cause problems for photographers. Any visitor will need a large slice of luck, or prior warning, to leave Shannon with a photographic record of one of those really extraordinary movements. Anyone touring Ireland in a car will also be able to park at the appropriate end of the runway.

Between the passenger terminal and Runway 06/24 is a small Aer Lingus maintenance hangar. Most of the interest is generated by aircraft on the ground, seen by travelling in the opposite direction. A road leads past the cargo terminal and the Omega facility, round the end of Runway 31. Just beyond it are an Irish Air Corps base and Guinness Peat. A long walk (or short drive) through the industrial estate is worth the effort. After passing the threshold of Runway 24, the road leads to the massive Shannon Aerospace hangar.

WATERFORD
WAT   EIWF

From town, take the road for Cork and you can't miss the airport. This is another of those airports where driver and navigator might fall out . . . prematurely. The road really does dwindle into little more than a cart track. Just as you prepare to turn round, the airport appears on the right. Apart from the occasional BA Jetstream, traffic is general aviation but, for propliner fans, the ex-Aer Turas DC-7, EI-AWA, is still to be seen in a field nearby.

ES = ESTONIA
TALLINN
TLL   EETT   Ulemiste   2.5m/4km S

After so many years on the "wrong" side of the Iron Curtain, places like Tallinn have acquired an interest factor that they sometimes don't really warrant yet. Enthusiasts, trying to mop up registrations dating back to Soviet times, are drawn to the Baltic States, to record what's there while it's still there. At Tallin, it's mostly Tu-134s. The passenger terminal, at the western end of the field, looks modern. There are few views from landside, except for a dirty window downstairs.

Traffic seems to use Runway 27 for landings and 09 for departures, probably due to noise restrictions. From the southern side if the terminal, 09 landings and some taxiing aircraft can be seen. The alternative is to try between the terminal and the gate for cargo and maintenance.

Travel between town and the airport is by the No 2 municipal bus which operates every 20 minutes or so. The fare is EEK 4.

ET = ETHIOPIA
ADDIS ABABA
ADD   HAAB   Bole International

On the bright side, they can't stop you looking. That's about it, really. It might be tempting to take a few photos as the plane taxis in, but this means using an airline that isn't Ethiopian. Not only do the national airline cabin staff stop you, there is every chance they'll seize not only the flm but the camera too. Ingenuity might even be required to log aircraft. To be on the safe side, try writing them into the Daily Telegraph crossword or something similar. In other words, whatever you do, take precautions.

The terminal has no views except for airside. Since most flights are between 12:00 and 15:00, there's a chance of logging most of the Ethiopian fleet on the apron. The serious traveller can see it all, in due course, elsewhere, and get good photos.

F = FRANCE

Previous editions of this book have supplied a lot of information about airports in France. Most of it has been repetitious, boring and of little or no use to either the reader or the traveller. It's a large country and businessmen do have to get to Paris from out in the Sticks. Many airports operate commuter services to Paris and/or Lyon in the morning and evening. For the rest of the day, all most of them have on offer, apart from general aviation, is a withdrawn Caravelle and an Aeropostale F.27.

This applies to ANNECY Meythet, AVIGNON Caumont, BEAUVAIS Tille, BELFORT Fontaine, BEZIERS Vias, CARCASSONNE Salvaza, CHAMBERY/AIX LES BAINS Voglans, CHERBOURG Maupertus, CLERMONT-FERRAND Aulnat, COLMAR Houssen, DINARD Pleurtuit, GRENOBLE St Geoirs, LA ROCHELLE Laleur, LE HAVRE Octeville, LE TOUQUET Paris-Plage, LILLE Lesquin, MONTPELLIER Frejorgues, NIMES Garons, PAU, PERPIGNAN Rivesaltes, POITIERS Biard, ROANNE Renaison, STRASBOURG Entzheim, TARBES Ossun-Lourdes, TOURS St Symphorien and VALENCE Chabeuil. In return, there are whole new countries in this edition, such as Estonia, Latvia and Lithuania. A reasonable swap?

BORDEAUX
BOD   LFBD   Merignac   7m/11km W (bus 35 minutes)

As the regional capital of southwest France, Bordeaux handles quite a quantity of traffic, and a better variety than most other French airports have to offer. Many of the movements are Air Inter but they do include representatives of each type in the fleet. Apart from its many domestic flights, Bordeaux is important enough to warrant an en route stop by wide-body flights, including Air France 747s and Air Afrique Airbuses. Sadly, these most interesting visitors arrive in the early morning or late afternoon, so the middle of the day has little excitement.

The French Air Force base is quite active, with plenty of Mirages and Jaguars on the move during the week. Another presence here is that of GAM-Dassault and its Falcon production line. There is more chance of a customer despatching a Hercules, for example, to pick up spares, than that of a sporadic Falcon flight but both are bonuses to bear in mind.

Inside the passenger terminal is a lift which serves the spectators' terrace. Next to the lift button is a very permanent-looking sign which reads, "Closed Terrace". The first floor level restaurant offers the only real view, though it gets very warm in summer. The adjacent toilet windows face the ramp though, once again, the heat is a problem. One would have to be extremely dedicated to make the trip to Bordeaux for the chance to peer out of a toilet window for two or three hours!

CHATEAUROUX
CHR   LFLX   Deols   3m/5km NNE

Some way south of Paris, this airport has become worthy of a visit for anyone passing in the car. Aero Technique Espace is a company which carries out subcontract work for Airbus Industrie. Since some of the newly built aircraft are ferried here for painting, it is possible to see some surprisingly exotic colour schemes outside the hangar.

The airport owners are looking for an operator who needs to develop a cargo (probably parcels) hub in this part of France. If they succeed, a passing visit could be even more worthwhile.

LYON
LYS   LFLL   Satolas   15m/23km ESE (bus 45 minutes)

Perhaps on a par with Marseille, this is one of France's busier airports, outside Paris. The roof terrace, situated between the two terminal wings, is open on Sundays but the view is an elevated one. The car park beside the domestic terminal overlooks much of that apron and a similar view from the taxi stands, at the opposite end, allows the freight area to be inspected.

Traffic is made up mostly of flights by Air France and Air Inter. The only operator based at Satolas is Air Exel, whose Brasilias use the domestic terminal. When Runway 36 is in use, it is worth leaving the terminal area and following the signs for 'Fret et Fatton'. Two left turns lead past the fret/ freight sheds to Ets Fatton, where the taxiway and holding point can be seen at close quarters. Photography here is at its best in the afternoon, with the sun perfectly placed.

Development at Satolas seems to be nearing completion at last. The TGV station is open and work in both the passenger terminals and car park areas is complete . . . until the next phase, no doubt. Closer into town, and easily missed, is LYON Bron which is still believed to handle general aviation, including biz-jets.

MARSEILLE
MRS   LFML   Provence International   15m/23km NW (bus 30 minutes)

Summer means increased traffic and another chance for the observation deck in Marignane's international terminal to be open again. The entrance fee pays the cost of the security check but it is a very dedicated enthusiast who stays all day. The lack of shade means that the heat of the afternoon gets wearing, and there are no facilities for buying a much needed drink or, perhaps more important, for going to the toilet.

Opening hours are, reportedly, between 10:00 and 18:00 on weekends, public holidays and during the school holidays. Weekends, and Saturdays in particular, are rather quiet. Photos of movements on the apron suffer from having a sepia tint, imparted by the bronze coloured glass of the two metre high security screen.

Carriers are varied, though movements by the Securité Civile CL-215s are few and related mostly to fire-fighting emergencies in late summer. Since their compound, and that of Aerospatiale, are out of bounds and generally out of sight, it would be wise not to pin hopes on seeing anything of the inhabitants. Other vantage points include the top level of the multi-storey car park, P6, though some distance away from the ramp for photos, and the general aviation terminal to the northwest, where smaller aircraft can be seen at close quarters. The adjacent taxiway is rarely used, as the opposite direction runway is favoured due to the prevailing winds.

The dedicated and intrepid might be prepared to brave the summer heat and explore. From Merignac town the road to Le Jai passes the far end of the field, where an alternative view of the hangar areas allows most of the inmates and other residents to be seen.

NICE

NCE   LFMN   Cote d'Azur   4m/6km SW (bus 15 minutes)

Terminal 1 is light, airy, modern and pleasant for passengers. Casual visitors, such as spotters, have nowhere to go in this building, apart from the toilet. The construction of Terminal 2, next to the large general aviation ramp, has enabled a different view of the field to be opened up. The access roads and Zone 3 car park serving the new building are close to the taxiway, and photographs in the late afternoon make the most of sun. Much of the interest at Nice is generated by general aviation, and biz-jets from all over Europe can be seen. Saudi Arabian and American businessmen also feel the need for the occasional trip to Nice, especially when major events, such as the tennis or Formula One Grand Prix are taking place in Monte Carlo, or the Cannes International Film Festival.

Other interesting movements are regional ATR-72s and Securité Civile Firecats, as the jet airliners tend to be much as can be seen at any other major European airport. The cargo area usually contains, during the daytime, an Aeropostale F.27.

An alternative vantage point, also on the western side of the field, is very popular, as it is close to the taxiway between the apron and Runways 05L/R. This is the shopping centre with parking provision for 3,000 cars, hence the name CAP3000. Leaving the terminal on the busy main road in the direction of Antibes, it is only a ten minute walk to the far/western side of the river, where the car park overlooks the airport. The facilities include seats and a general view of the entire airport. Afternoons and evenings are the best times to visit.

At the end of the field, where the road passes close to the holding point for Runway 23R, aircraft landing and those on the taxiway are seen at close quarters. Again the sun can be a major problem to the photographer. The conifers, planted along the edge of the Boulevard des Anglais, were meant to provide an effective screen between the airport and the road. They are now mature enough to be doing their job rather well, and views through them are best described as glimpses.

PARIS

Those with a car will do best if they are accompanied also by two maps: Michelin produce Environs de Paris, No.96, and Plan de Paris, No.10. The former is essential to discover the various fields located on the outskirts, while the latter makes it possible to visit Issy without fights breaking out between driver and navigator. The latter also details all the one way streets, which ease the problem of passing some time in the city centre.

Travel by bus is more economical when carnets of tickets are pre-purchased for RATP journeys. To get to le Bourget and Charles de Gaulle, buses Nos. 350 and 351 leave from the Place de la Nation, Gare de l'Est and Gare du Nord, while the SNCF train serves Charles de Gaulle by line B.

Travel to Orly involves catching an Orlyrail train, from Quai d'Orsay, Pont St. Michel or Gare d'Austerlitz, to Pont de Rungis, where a bus connects with the airport. SNCF line B also serves Denfert-Rochereau and Antony, from where the Orlyval people mover (a two-car tram without a driver) completes the journey to Orly Ouest.

Light aircraft can be seen in number at several fields, all of which offer good opportunities for the enthusiast but travel will probably be by car. Close to Versailles, and not far from Orly, is TOUSSUS-LE-NOBLE with a large number of residents, with ST CYR L'ECOLE close by, on the edge of Versailles. To the west is the last field to complete the short tour, CHAVENAY, and a day's trip around these fields will make an impressive log, but no significant impact on the French register!

Aéroports de Paris (ADP) is the company which operates Orly and Charles de Gaulle. They prepare, for daily use, photostat documents entitled 'Prévisions des Mouvements'. It doesn't need a degree in French to know that these are the movement timetables. They are known to be available for Charles de Gaulle, with sheets coloured separately for CDG1 and CDG2. It is probable that similar sheets are also supplied for Orly Sud and Orly Ouest. The airport information desk is the obvious place to ask.

PARIS

CDG   LFPG   Charles de Gaulle   14m/22km NNE (bus/train 30 minutes)

Charles de Gaulle's traffic is shared between the two terminals and keeping track of both is a problem. Air France occupy Terminal 2, effectively four terminals: A, B, C and D (with two more nearing completion) and the views from here are minimal. Air France passengers in transit will say otherwise, pointing out that gate A40 offers a fine view of a large percentage of the arrivals and departures, as well as overlooking the domestic ATR/146 area and the 747Fs on the cargo apron. Between Terminal Areas 1 and 2 are a few other buildings of significance: the railway station, with a bus link for passengers, the splendidly located Ibis Hotel next to it, with some rooms offering restricted views of movements, and the control tower.

Terminal 1 is the original drum-shaped building, which handles non-Air France movements in some quantity, but has no views from within. The road at Arrivals Level 2 does allow a popular view of the proceedings. The battle between spotters and gendarmes has been won, it seems, by the spotters as there are no recent reports of conflict. Continued sensible behaviour on this road level of the terminal should ensure that the victory becomes permanent. Bus drivers in particular are keen to remind spotters that they do stand perilously close to such obects as passing wing mirrors - one false step can end in serious injury.

The roadside, particularly for spotters, isn't necessarily the best place to stand. The views from within the building through the full height windows beside, say, doors 8, 10 and 12 is equally good. Photographers will need to stand at the parapet. The same area, 8 to 12, is probably as good as anywhere. It overlooks Satellites 2 and 3 but allows views also of movements on the northern Runway 09/27, which means a few of the aircraft, mostly Air France, which can't be accommodated on 10/28. Beyond the taxiway is the apron for Terminal T9 (*neuf* means new as well as nine) the charter terminal, which features an increasingly good variety of visitors: Pegasus 737s, Air Jet 146s and Air Alfa A300s for instance. For the spotter, and many photographers, this is probably as good a place to take up temporary residence as any at CDG.

Having established that neither terminal offers comprehensive viewing possibilities, the alternatives have to be pursued. Bearing in mind that the road layout is quite confusing, alternative spots can be found and one of the best was, more or less, below the control tower. To screen off this vantage point, a row of tall conifers now obscures the view. Anyone who shins up the bank on the western side of the main approach road to Terminal 1 can get a portrait of one or two of the airliners parked nearby. At least one French government aircraft, often an A310, is normally parked within range of a camera. Extended stays at the fence are not a good idea! Out to the west is Entretien Nord, and the Air France hangars. There is usually something parked outside to justify the detour.

CDG is a modern airport, designed for the convenience of passengers. Air France has its own facilities, including effectively its own runway, and the competition gets everywere else. As is always the case, things are not quite that simple: Air France also plays host to a small number of foreign operators, such as Aeromexico. This can mean that an arriving star visitor, such as a 767, can go unidentified. Instead of cursing bad luck, anyone with some knowledge of flight numbers (gleaned from either a timetable or a radio) might care to contact the ADP Aéroports de Paris information desk. In most instances the aircraft's registration can be supplied.

PARIS

JDP   Issy les Moulineaux   5m/8km SW (bus/train 30 minutes)

Paris is ringed by the busy Boulevard Périphérique. In the southwest corner of the city, just east of the river, is the heliport, living in the shadow of this main artery but not easily found without a map. The Porte de Sèvres exit (NOT Quai d'Issy) leads to the front door. Metro users will alight at Balard and walk under the Périphérique overbridge.

Heli Union have a base here but the majority of their helicopters are away earning their living, so that only a few can be seen at any one time. Another operator is the Gendarmerie, usually with an Alouette on the ground. It is unwise to expect vast quantities of helicopters but a few examples will offer variety to a trip log otherwise dominated by light aircraft or airliners.

A footpath along the perimeter is marked 'no entry' to deter motor vehicles, so the sign can be (and is) ignored by pedestrians. Proof of this for the wary, who may be afraid to venture this way, is offered on the ground: there is sufficient squashy evidence left by dogs for walkers to divide their concentration between what they can see on the airfield and what they should see under their feet.

PARIS

LBG   LFPB   le Bourget   9m/15km N (bus 20 minutes)

During the Paris Air Salon, the ramps to the north are crammed with biz-jets, and many of them can be seen by anyone investigating all the nooks and crannies. Photos are being made more difficult by the erection of more and more temporary buildings, but it is possible to get up to many fences, and gates, for a chance to look at this spectacular array. Through the year, this part of the field is where the action is concentrated, and all roads between the buildings are worth exploring, as the different angles can yield one or two aircraft.

North of the old UTA hangars, FBO's handle plenty of traffic and the service road passes around Europe Falcon Service to a gate by the fence. There are several windows in the EFS hangar, revealing some exotically registered Falcons, but few aircraft pass on the taxiway, just beyond, during the day. Even the length of the grass, enough to spoil photos by obscuring wheels, conspires against the photographer. The EFS area is at the extreme northern end of the ramp area. Close to it is a quasi-military base. Restrictions imposed unilaterally by EFS on photos and spotting are often enforced by someone in a uniform. To what extent the law is on their side is debatable but it doesn't need a law degree to figure out who will have the last say. In several instances, 'the last say' means confiscation of log books and film. Try arguing that in a court of law during a weekend trip to Paris!

South of the main terminal area is the famous Musée de l'Air, with its many exhibits. Other aircraft are stored on the remote Dugny side of the field. As there may be someone with nothing better to do than take a couple of guys over there, it may be worth showing an interest.

PARIS

ORY   LFPO   Orly   9m/15km S (bus/train 35 minutes)

Despite the amount of traffic which uses Charles de Gaulle, there are enough interesting operators to ensure that Orly is still worth a visit, and often a lengthy stay. Many major international operators use Orly, though these are now mainly European, plus a good variety of North African traffic.

Because some of these more interesting visitors are sporadic, there are afternoons which seem interminable, with only a procession of domestic commuters to be seen. Reference to a timetable is therefore necessary to ensure that Orly repays the interest. The two terminals are Orly Ouest, mostly used by Air Inter and Orly Sud, effectively the centre of the action. The spotter can stand at the windows on the left hand side of Orly Ouest's Departures level and identify a fair number, but by no means all, of the Air Inter airliners. Once this is done, it's best to head to the northern end of the building and take the people mover shuttle to Orly Sud.

There are two platforms: that to the left is the Orlyval link which goes to Antony. It costs FFr76 for a ticket into central Paris. The free transfer to Orly Sud leaves from the right-hand platform.

For the spotter, there are windows on the first floor and mezzanine levels. The terrace is considerably higher, and it offers a much greater area from which to watch activities. A loose mesh is hung over the entire enclosure, which allows in the pleasant sunshine, and the glass is only a minor irritation to most photographers. Watching is good but work with a camera can be a little more difficult, especially due to facing south though, with care, good results can be obtained.

Any of the vantage points chosen in the terminal should follow a visit to the most important level of all: the basement, where a supermarket offers a good range of snacks and drinks at affordable prices. A shop at this level stocks aviation postcards, with a selection for those who seek souvenirs, or additions to the collection.

Elsewhere on the field, there are some other places worth a look. Just north of Orly Sud is the cargo terminal, handling a variety of operations, many of which are C-130s of foreign air arms. The guardians of the gate don't offer any assistance to those wishing to take photos, and ground clutter can compromise the quality of portraits. Further north are the Air Inter and Air France hangars and ramps, in which can be found a good selection of operators and types.

On the opposite side of the N7, and best reached from remote parking area P7, there are two areas which can yield plenty of interest. Close by the road is the VIP terminal, and a line-up of French Government Falcons is not uncommon. When foreign dignatories are expected, this area is at its best . . . and out of bounds. The best way to know if this is a likelihood is to look out for a proliferation of flags. The tall timber fence hides the taxiway to runway 25 but another, lower, fence abuts it, and can be scaled for good views of airliners taxiing. This is by far the best spot to obtain those ground level shots, without having recourse to telephoto lenses.

Photographs taken from the roof deck can become repetitive, despite the subject matter, because the rows of trees and buses appear so often. Another feature of Orly photos is the clock on the control tower; first time visitors may not notice these considerations through the viewfinder but they are very noticeable in the results. Time often goes quite slowly at Orly, especially in the afternoon. Attention then turns to the details. Directly opposite the Orly Sud terminal, on the southern edge of the field by the threshold of 02L, are the Concorde prototype painted in Air France colours, and an ex-Corse Air Caravelle. Out to the east are another two Caravelles (one ex-Catair and the other ex-Air Inter) plus 727 F-BPJU.

Much of the traffic is Air Inter which normally lands on the same arrivals runway as the other traffic, 26. Runway 25 is normally used for departure, so all incoming traffic should be logged and, if possible photographed. In many instances this is not possible from the deck. Corsair 747s and Alia A310s might taxi past to a stand but Air Outre Mer DC-10s and Egyptair 747s tend to use stands at the western end of the ramp. Blast screens between Orly Sud and Orly Ouest mean that many interesting visitors might not be photographed, without a visit to the fence opposite car park P5. This is only a two-storey building but the roof might offer the chance to take a photo of something exceptional as it taxis to the hold for Runway 25.

TOULOUSE

TLS LFBO   Blagnac   6m/9km NW (bus 35 minutes)

It should not be overlooked that Toulouse is an active airport, and not just the home of Airbus Industrie assembly. The passenger terminal handles a good number of charters, especially in summer, with such remarkable movements as Portugalia F.100s, Egyptair wide-bodies and Trans-Med 737s plus a good variety of aircraft from North Africa. In the absence of an observation deck, the upper level restaurant is the only place to see them, but the view is good. For nostalgia-freaks, the Air Toulouse International Caravelles offer a link with the past.

The increasingly wide range of products rolling off the Airbus Industrie lines do make this an interesting airport. The only guided tours of the plant are offered to parties, which must be pre-booked. There are two versions, French and English, and the latter must be booked at least four weeks in advance. About a week's notice is adequate for the French tours. The A330 and A340 production lines are included, as are the all-important flight lines and paint shops. For further details, telephone 61 154 400. Anyone with a real interest in Airbus Industrie, travelling to Toulouse by car, will no doubt pass Chateauroux (q.v.) on the way, as a company subcontracts some of the Airbus finishing work there.

Airbus Industrie do not go to extreme lengths to advertise their presence, and the approach is signposted in a rather low-key fashion. In other words, directions are necessary. Leaving the upper level of the terminal, a right turn and a walk down the ramp lead to a roundabout. Take the road marked 'Fret' which passes the cargo area, where a couple of interesting aircraft might be present. At the end of the road is another roundabout, and another right turn onto the bridge over the main highway. The dusty road down the near side of the highway leads to the No.66 bus stop. Where it goes, and how much use it is, nobody knows! At the far end of the bridge is another roundabout and a walk alongside the highway, past the Airbus building, to the far end of the airport. It is now time to get to the other side . . .

At the traffic lights, follow the sign which says St Martin. The D124 leads there and any turns from now on will be to the right. The high grassy bank inside the perimeter fence prevents views of the field. The first available right turn leads past the FedEx building to the Airbus factory. Here is the security gate and a large car park from where a selection of nearly finished wares can be seen, though a souvenir photograph will probably be less than ideal.

F-O = FRENCH OVERSEAS DEPTS and PROTECTORATES
GRAND CASE
SFG   Esperance

The Air Guadeloupe flights fly regularly to this, the 'other' part of the island of St Martin, owned by Guadeloupe, and French-speaking. Literally a few miles from Princes Juliana airport, Esperance is so small, it could best be described as a strip. As befits a place of this size, the three Do228 flights each day can be witnessed on the ramp, with a souvenir portrait easily obtained.

G = UNITED KINGDOM

This section has been divided into the countries and principalities. The first is England, followed by Scotland, Wales and Northern Ireland. The Isle of Man and the Channel Islands appear last. The UK is quite a small country to have so many airports competing with each other for business. Some of them, like those in France, don't really warrant an entry intheir own right as there is so little to say. They're probably all interesting *to visit*, for reggie chasers, but they don't necessarily make for interesting *reading*. Thus there are no separate entries for CARLISLE Crosby, EXETER, GLOUCESTER Staverton, PLYMOUTH Roborough, NEWQUAY St Mawgan, PENZANCE Heliport, and in Scotland DUNDEE Riverside, PERTH Scone and INVERNESS Dalcross.

BIGGIN HILL
EGKB   1m/1.5km N

This is probably one of Britain's, and possibly the world's, most famous airfields because of its World War II history. Now it houses Britain's largest collection of general aviation. The main road passes the western boundary, and many aircraft can be seen. The southern apron area has its own access and there are several hangars, all crammed full of light aircraft. At the far end of Runway 11 is a (restricted) access road across the threshold of Runway 29, to more aprons and hangars. Nowhere else in Britain is it possible to log so many aircraft at one go.

Interest in the larger visitors is centred further north along the main road. Passing the threshold of Runway 03, and the RAF base with its Spitfire, the general aviation terminal sits next to the western apron. It is here that the biz-jets arrive for customs clearance. The apron can be seen from the terminal windows and from the fence, where photos are possible, though both the view and content are often slightly limited.

BIRMINGHAM
BHX   EGBB   International   6m/9km SE (train 10 minutes)

England's second city boasts an airport to match the status but, even in summer, traffic is only moderate. The main passenger terminal, past British Airways Eurohub, has a viewing deck but there is all too little to see from it. The Eurohub terminal, on the south side of the apron, does not restrict the excellent view from the spectator's grassed area. Most, if not all, jet traffic passes this area as it taxis in or out. Some of the commuters tend to use the runway best suited to their destination, when prevailing winds blow across, rather than along, the field.

British Airways dominate the movements but, during the summer especially, there is a fair variety of charters, including some from across the Atlantic. But Birmingham offers some of the best opportunities to get portraits of smaller aircraft. Many of the business flights betwen Birmingham and Europe take place in the very early morning or late evening.

On the west side of the field, on the site of the original Elmdon Airport, are the domestic general aviation, cargo and Maersk Air facilities. A staircase at the corner of the old terminal is popular for a view over the wall, and it would appear that attempts to seal it off have not been entirely successful. At weekends, there can be one or two aircraft parked here, including the occasional interesting cargo carrier. The screen wall separating this ramp from the road has, next to the hangar, a gate: now the only vantage point, though it is normally possible to take a photo of one or two of the Maersk residents, parked close by.

BLACKBUSHE
BBS   EGLK   6m/9km NW of Farnborough

More a reasonably large airfield than an airport, Blackbushe is on the north side of the A30 trunk road, a few miles north of Farnborough. Most of the time, the only action is light aircraft in the circuit, most of which operate from the old terminal area, next to the main road. It is probable that every resident and visitor can be identified from the car park or from the perimeter fence.

On the north side of the field, some distance west, is a modern facility where the larger aircraft, including some Beech jets, are to be seen. The access road passes the western end of the runway and leads to car parking areas immediately next to the ramps. Those who wish to see inside the hangars will possibly find difficulty. Unlike the occasional visitor to a remote field in, say, a rural part of France, this is England, and close to London, so there is no shortage of spotters who could make a nuisance of themselves.

BLACKPOOL
BLK   EGNH   Squire's Gate   3m/5km S

In some ways, Squire's Gate can be considered to be two separate airports, functioning side by side. The main passenger terminal is used mostly by holidaymakers bound for the Isle of Man and Dublin with Manx, Brymon and Ryanair. To its left is a car park which also serves as the viewing area. This is convenient, as it is situated between the terminal and the gas rig heliport, where one or two Bond Dauphins might be seen.

Beyond the heliport are hangars and ramps used for general aviation, with Westair occupying the farthest one. Another viewing area here ensures that all the light aircraft are visible without any real need for ramp access. Bond's hangar can be seen in a separate area, reached by turning left at the

Vulcan, next to the Aero Club. By heading east, past the terminal, and then turning right a few times, there is a road leading to a new housing estate. This road runs parallel to the runway and aircraft using it are within range of a 200mm lens. Alternatively, stand in the corner of the supermarket car park. Plenty of others seem to.

BOURNEMOUTH
BOH   EGHH   Hurn   4m/6km NE

Hurn airport boasts an extremely pleasant modern terminal, and what could be described as a viewing garden next to the ramp. Movements not using the terminal may not be seen on the move from here as the runway is partially out of sight. Traffic is very slow but the runway does offer occasional movements of the Flight Refuelling (FR Aviation) Falcons and some additional rarities. Access to the far/north side of the field is restricted, due to FRA activity, and security measures are tight. Anyone intent on a visit to the north side should try to make formal arrangements beforehand.

The B3073 road, which runs along the southern perimeter, offers excellent views across the airfield. Taxiing aircraft, depending on the runway in use, pass very close to the low fence. A turning to the north at the roundabout in the southwest corner of the field leads to another vantage point which can be particularly good in the late afternoons.

BRISTOL
BRS   EGDD   Lulsgate   9m/15km SW

The airport is southwest of the city on the A38. Important road connections with the M5 motorway are tortuous, to say the least. The charter flights at summer weekends boost the movements total but a visit during the week in winter must be scheduled to coincide with one or two of the international commuter flights.

Bristol airport has the car parking sewn up, so that it's almost impossible to find anywhere that's free. The perimeter road to the south is good for ground level shots and the small observation deck is well-placed. As an alternative, a left turn onto the A38 followed by the first left and another left turn after about a mile, along Cooks Bridle Path, gains access to the runway's edge. Just before the road turns right, there is a track leading to the aero club where a few light aircraft are parked.

The service road to the east of the passenger terminal is posted as no access to unauthorized traffic. Pedestrians can (in theory?) walk along here for close-up views of the occasional JEA Fokker or Brymon Dash 8 which may be parked awaiting its next flight.

BRIZE NORTON
BZZ   EGVN   1m/1.5km S

It may come as a surprise to some readers to learn that scheduled services are indeed operated from Brize, but the RAF needs to maintain a constant link with its remote outpost in the Falkland Islands. This is where a TriStar departs for its long journey. Being a military base, access is restricted but the majority (if not all) the parked aircraft can be seen from the perimeter. TriStars are not the easiest of aircraft to hide among the relatively small buildings.

CAMBRIDGE
CBG   EGSC   2m/3km NE

All that can normally be seen from the main road are a few parked light aircraft. The dedicated follow a road at the western end of the field, between the A1303 and Sainsburys, and try to identify some of the visitors to Field's technical facility. The ramp beside the super hangar can be seen and there are places to see if something interesting, such as an LTU TriStar, is parked outside. Vantage points along the A1303 on the northeast side of the field, and around the village of Teversham allow the runway to be seen. Most of the time, the traffic amounts to little more than the occasional Cessna in the circuit, but Suckling Do228s operate scheduled services to Manchester and Amsterdam.

COVENTRY
CVT   EGBE   Baginton   4m/6km SSE

Coventry is so close to Birmingham International that any real hope of growth of its own airport is strictly limited. A few links are operated regularly but they are unlikely to be enough to draw serious interest. There are other features, however. The terminal area and its car park next to the taxiway are far less interesting than the Air Atlantique ramp, with its handful of Islanders, DC-3s and even a couple of DC-6s. Helicopter movements are also quite plentiful but not enough to warrant a prolonged stay. The road between the city and the airport passes the splendid aviation museum and the hulks of a few abandoned Daks can also be see through the trees. A playing field and a rugby pitch can be crossed for close access to the Air Atlantique facility, for those who can't be bothered to try the simple method of gaining entry: asking.

EAST MIDLANDS
EMA   EGNX   Castle Donington   9m/15km SE of Derby

The spectators terrace in the old terminal building is easily found, and well-placed, for a good view of the apron and anything using it. However, the mesh screen makes photography impossible. There are less scheduled services than charters to the sun. Britannia are almost as common as British Midland. The passenger terminal has an extension, best described as a big tin box. It offers no views out (in any direction). To the east of the terminal area is a separate viewing park which overlooks the threshold of the runway and is also the home of the aviation museum. Apart from the almost obligatory Vulcan, there is an Elan Argosy, still in good condition, and reasonably photogenic. Dotted around the field elsewhere are the remains of Vanguards which became Merchantmen, and ended their days here.

To the west of the terminal, things can be more interesting. Not only is there a BMA maintenance base but quite a few aircraft have been stored here. Fields have their own apron and hangar where aircraft up to VC-10 size are regularly seen. Jetstreams receive their paint here, and it is often possible to see something exotic on the ramp, prior to delivery.

As an alternative to the officially approved viewing park, which is on the south side of the runway, some people are still tempted to find other places at the perimeter. A footpath runs along the northern fence, and is reasonably close to the runway. Fortunately, the British climate means that the sun is not usually a problem.

HUMBERSIDE
HUY   EGNJ   6m/9km NE of Brigg

A modest regional airport but the ramp can be seen in part from the terminal. British International Helicopters base a Westland WG.30 here, seen at close range, if access to the service road is gained at the right time. Beyond their apron is a line of hangars used by the general aviation fraternity. Air UK have managed to keep services going for quite a while but other airlines seem to come and go. The City Air Bus Do228 service to London only lasted two months, and Euro Direct Belgie took over where Euro Direct left off.

LEEDS/BRADFORD
LBA   EGNM   8m/13km NW of Leeds

The passenger terminal is modern, the only view from which is at the first floor level, in the lounge/ cafeteria. Movements are not particularly lively but photographers may find consolation by having a closer look at the Northair facility on the far/south side. Bayton Lane leads to a hill which overlooks the airport. From here all movements including those of Northair are visible.

The main A658 road heads south towards Bradford. A left turn, towards Leeds, is followed by another, leading to the golf course. This is where photographers go, though some walking is involved. The footpath runs along the south side of the runway, accessible from a lane next to the golf course. Extremely good north-facing portraits can be taken from here.

LIVERPOOL
LPL   EGGP   Speke   8m/13km SE

The bar/cafeteria area on the first floor of the South Terminal offers a view of the apron and taxiway but ground floor extensions have not improved matters at all. For the best view, it might be better to walk along to the edge of the eastern part f the apron, where the visiting general aviation parks. Scheduled services operate to Dublin, Belfast, Isle of Man, Southampton, Aberdeen and, in summer, Jersey. A range of chartered services also operate in the peak summer months. Emerald Airways' fleet of HS 748s is based here and, during the day, several examples are parked on the apron, awaiting night freight services. Bond Helicopters also have a base for Irish Sea gas and oil exploration support services. The airport is particularly busy at night, being a hub for the Royal Mail Skynet first class letter post, freight and newspaper flights to Ireland and the Isle of Man, TNT and Ford Motor Co operations.

A large light aircraft resident fleet (private and flying schools) is still based at the old northern part of the airfield but all their movements can be seen from the new terminal.

LONDON

With the exception of the new Docklands airport, all are located well outside the city and the cost of getting from the City Centre to Heathrow or Gatwick will quickly give some indication of how far out the airports are. The British Airports Authority is responsible for the main airports, and they are taking very seriously indeed the IATA security recommendations. Both airports have formal viewing facilities, and much effort has been put into ensuring that only these are used by enthusiasts.

The use of alternative sites around both fields is deterred. Other airports close to London are Luton and Stansted, both of which have their attractions, but neither of which come close to the Big Two for the number, or variety, of movements. Total journey times for City (underground, Thames Light Railway and shuttle bus), Gatwick (via Waterloo), Heathrow (underground - Piccadilly Line) and Stansted (via Liverpool Street) are given from Charing Cross, rather than just the time taken by the train once leaving the station.

LONDON
LCY   EGLC   City   4m/6km E (train/bus 75 min)

London City airport continues to grow, in spite of pathetic integrated links with the city. Ask any British spotter where the airport is, and he'll tell you: it's under the "ers" of *Eastenders*.

Without a car, London City is a pain, though the authorities go to great lengths to stress otherwise. This is because London's businessmen can take a taxi from Plaistow tube station, and ask for a receipt. There is a shuttle bus link from the Docklands Light Railway station at Canary Wharf. British Rail's Silvertown station (reached from Liverpool Street) is the closest.

The runway and terminal area occupy a patch of land between the disused Royal Albert and King George V Docks. The airport sees little use at weekends, and could not be described as busy during the week. It is possible to watch the moderate action from the terminal area but the view is just as good from the perimeter. Just after crossing the bridge between Victoria and Albert Docks, the road passes the end of the runway. The roundabout here is only a few steps away from Silvertown station. As arrivals drop steeply onto Runway 28, they can be seen clearly, and the turn off to the apron is only 200 metres away.

Because it's a commuter airport, an early start is essential. First thing in the morning, the ramp can look quite full with a selection of 146s and Fokker 70s. The problem is that six aircraft make it look full and, when they've gone, it's . . . empty. Good for photos, though, and an hour's parking only costs a pound.

LONDON
LGW   EGKK   Gatwick   32m/50km S (train 60 minutes)

British Airports Authority surveyed 1,100 people before going ahead with their work to the rooftop spectators area at Gatwick. Of the people they spoke to, half were passengers and half lived locally. This, to BAA, is known as market research. Very strong interest was shown in airfield tours (surprise, surprise) so, for some reason, they stuck a Channel Express Herald (G-CEXP, c/n 195, originally 4X-AHO) on the roof - not quite the A310 they used in their publicity release. It would have looked nice in Arkia, or even British United Airlines, colours. The ramp tours were too much of a security risk, not like they are in Germany or Switzerland, of course.

Almost all alternative vantage points have now been closed to the enthusiast, in an attempt to control their movements. All that remains is the observation deck which does allow a very good general view of the proceedings but photographers may quickly tire of the limitations. There is the chance of shots of wide-bodies as they taxi to a stand, or as they push back, but a large percentage of movements never come within range. The deck is accessed by going to the north end of the departures level and climbing the stairs or taking an elevator.

The variety of traffic is excellent, as charter flights now form a much smaller proportion (though still a large number) of movements, which features many intercontinental, European and commuter services.

Most of the favourite haunts have now gone: the north side car park, for example, was replaced by British Airways' North Terminal. At the opposite side of the field, development and deterrents have put an end to the use of several spots on the south side of the runway. It may still be possible to witness landings from the road at either end of the field but that at the eastern (most frequently used) end is too distant for photos of any worth.

LONDON
LHR   EGLL   Heathrow   15m/23km W (train 75 minutes)

The entry for Heathrow in the last edition started with a statement from the Security Manager: "Heathrow Airport Ltd welcomes spotters and amateur photographers so long as they use the facilities provided on the Queens Building Roof." Spotters and amateur photographers are offered what the airport authorities are prepared to give them and, for an airport of this magnitude, it is not good enough. There's a visitor centre on the north side of the field, which might be interesting for dads and the kids on a Saturday afternoon. The trouble is it might generate further interest in aviation so, if it does its job, the problem gets worse.

The Security Manager has had to deal wth the occasional mortars fired, by the IRA, onto an active runway at an international airport, so he's rightly concerned about anyone driving slowly around the perimeter. He will be concerned about it for many years because it's not going to stop until three quarters of those cars have somewhere to go. Spotters want registrations and photographers want good shots. The "Queens Building" roof just about caters for spotters but portraits of Viva Air 737s and Iberia A320s aren't quite what photographers want, as 747-400s taxi past, tantalisingly, to the south on their way from Terminal 3 to line up on 27L.

The Terminal 2 roof (which used to be accessible from the Queen's Building) offers only a general view, with very few opportunities for the photographer. Compensation for restricting the size of the spectators' area is that (a) entry is free and (b) the opening hours have been extended.

Apart from aircraft taxiing onto the stands in front, used mostly by A320s of Iberia, Lufthansa and Air France, many other movements can be out of range for good photography (this is subjective, of course).

More frustrating still is the southeast corner of the deck. This is closest to the taxiway used normally by the long-hauls leaving Terminal 3. The gap between a lamp pole and Stand 12 is so narrow that when something (normally an Olympic A300) is parked, there is just too little room for photos. There are several multi-storey car parks in the central terminal area. The most popular was that serving Terminal 2, as it overlooked part of the Terminal 3 apron, and good photos were quite easy to take. Screening put an end to this on all floors, but viewing is still possible. Much the same applies to the other multi-storeys though none of the others have protective screens because distances are greater.

The area next to the enormous British Airways maintenance area, close to the threshold of Runway 27R has always attracted spotters as it is one of the few places that ensures all landings can be monitored. A lengthy stay here is unlikely, as parked cars are moved frequently. The alternative spot, by Hatton Cross tube station, for use when Runway 27L is used for landing, is off the airport complex, and the collection of parked cars in side roads on the south side of the A30 readily identifies the better spots.

The entire perimeter fence has now been enclosed by screening, the specific purpose of which is to deter viewing. The odd gap in these 'defences' comes under a lot of pressure from those wishing to take photos, particularly the access point next to the threshold of Runway 27L. Regular stops are made by the police, to ensure that anyone standing here is moved on, so most of the good vantage points can be disregarded.

Elsewhere around the perimeter, on roads accessible to the public, there are views of British Airways' maintenance areas, some of which reveal airliners in reasonably photogenic spots. The traffic lights where the taxiway and road cross has been used by photographers but airliners on the move in or out are very infrequent. The cargo and executive aprons on the south side are partially visible. There is a lay-by next to the main cargo ramp but blast screens and multiple layers of fencing are sure to prevent activities other than logging one or two aircraft.

LONDON
| LTN | EGGW | Luton | 2m/3km E of Luton (bus 15 minutes) |

Luton is a modern and often busy airport. Well placed relative to the M1 motorway, it handles a significant quantity of charter traffic, much of which is by British airlines. Monarch and Britannia Airways have their maintenance bases here but their operations are spread through the entire country, so few of their aircraft are in evidence on the average visit.

The international terminal offers no views at all. Beyond this terminal, where the taxiway enters the apron, there is a viewing area, very close indeed to passing aircraft, but the fence makes photography very difficult. Part of this viewing area has been developed to form a small domestic terminal.

Many enthusiasts visiting the field will make a tour of the perimeter and be on their way, as the central apron is large enough to contain a quantity of varied aircraft, including biz-jets and cargo carriers.

On the opposite side of the approach road from the main apron is the general aviation area, where quite a number of light aircraft are parked, all visible from the fence. Before this ramp is reached, there is a road to the right which leads round to a remote car park. This road is used as a direct link, and passes the Hotel Ibis. The fences on this side, around the McAlpine hangar, have been much strengthened, so that it is now difficult to see the aircraft, let alone note their registrations. What can be seen in there (with luck) can be very interesting indeed.

Instead of entering the airport complex by turning right at the roundabout, it might be worth driving on to the next roundabout and turning right. After the hotel, bear right and watch for a small turning to the right. The road, which winds past the end of the runway, leads ultimately to an emergency access gate. It might be necessary to walk part of the way but the sunlight and the view for photographers are good until the middle of the afternoon. This location can be accessed directly from the main road from the M1 by leaving it at a roundabout and passing under the new road. A series of left turns is necessary.

LONDON

STN	EGSS	Stansted	34m/46km N (train 110 min)

The passenger terminal is on the south side of the runway, beyond the cargo facility when arriving by road. The views around the terminal are minimal. The roundabout from which a road leads to the cargo area also has a sign for Self Storage. This road is a dead end but it overlooks the runway, albeit at some distance. The taxiway is, however, closer and many aircraft are within range of a 200mm lens. A prolonged stay here will, in the course of time, attract attention. The police may ask to see some form of identification, while they size you up. The private security personnel, however, tend to take a more direct approach. It may be counter-productive to argue that the police take a lenient view!

The "old" side of the field is worth exploration. Large, unoccupied car parks allow close access to a few aircraft parking areas where something exotic might be parked. Exotic, at Stansted, can mean very exotic. The business terminal and the CAA hangar will be of interest to any non-regular visitor to the airport. The road to Tye Green passes waste ground and a grass bank, both of which allow overall general views of the airfield and runway.

MANCHESTER

MAN	EGCC	International	11m/17km S (train 20 minutes)

Definitely Britain's busiest airport outside London, the traffic still includes a good number of international carriers linking the north of England with many business centres around the world. The additional number and variety of charters in summer can be as good as anywhere else in the country except for Gatwick. The airport is served by its own direct rail link from the city, the station being about halfway between Terminals 1 and 2. And it's getting another runway at last, on the south side of the field, so everything that used to apply, apart from Moss Lane, has changed.

What hasn't already changed will probably do so in the next couple of years. The Terminal 1 multi-storey car park always offered good views and Level 13 is probably the best place to go (at least in the second half of 1997). The car park overlooks the most interesting part of the airport. All the international traffic, of which there is plenty, can be seen and most of it photographed. Movements using Terminal 2 pass by and there is usually something interesting standing around the cargo and maintenance areas. In Manchester, "interesting" means *really* interesting.

The new cargo terminal, west of the central terminal area, is accessible but the continuous sheds do not allow the aircraft to be seen, except from the western corner of the ramp. Terminal 2 was not designed to improve matters for the enthusiast but is located in the northern corner of the terminal area, away from much of the activity. Try walking from Terminal 1 to Terminal 2 and see how long it takes, and all for no reward. The travelators, most of which work most of the time, help the journey feel more like a day than a week. And you get to see the building work, where a new hotel is being built. Not much else, though.

There's not much point in providing alternatives to the central terminals if people don't know about them. Not only is there observation from the car park, something at ground level is also available. In a car, make for The Romper, a pub on the northwest side of the field. Turn right and follow the rest of the traffic to the new viewing area. Very close to the taxiway for 06 but facing south. Given that the other side of the field has become a major building site, there's not much alternative. Less than ideal for photographers on a sunny day but as close as spotters are likely to get without being hauled off by the police or squashed under the wheels of a 747.

Prevailing winds mean that Runway 24 sees most use so the Airport Hotel, on the road to Wilmslow via Heald Green, is probably as good as anywhere. The car park and open ground mean that aircraft taxiing to the hold pass close enough for photography but, once again, the sun is not always at its most helpful from this angle.

The rail link from Manchester (and Crewe) is in a cutting, so there are no ground level views from the train. By the time the next edition of this book is published, the scene at Manchester will have changed greatly. If its history is anything to go by, the situation will not get worse but that's because the authorities here recognise that they have to take the needs of spotters into consideration. In the meantime, expect the A538 (to Wilmslow) road patterns to change regularly.

NEWCASTLE
NCL   EGNT   International   6m/9km NW (train 30 minutes)

England's most northerly airport handles a good number of airlines in the summer, when charter traffic peaks. It has, over the years, attracted extremely interesting services. The terminal has a roof deck, though quality photography is difficult once aircraft park. The aero club and GillAir facilities are visible, but distant, on the far side. Restrictions are imposed on access to the aero club, but not necessarily strictly enforced. A car park next to the club house overlooks the apron.
  Scheduled traffic is slow by most standards, but varied. Compensation may be provided by occasional military diversions and crew training flights. The nearby ranges mean that quite a few fighter pilots are tempted to make a short detour and carry out a 'practice diversion'. This often involves a short but impressive diplay to please the sightseers on the roof.
  Over the years, Newcastle has hosted plenty of airliners on delivery across the Atlantic, often to quite exotic operators. These movements are hardly to be considered daily (or even weekly) but the presence on the apron, in front of the tower, of something extraordinary shouldn't come as a surprise.

NORWICH
NWI   EGSH   Horsham St Faith   4m/km N

Norwich, which used to be called Horsham St Faith many years ago, now has a terminal bright enough to be seen from 20 miles out in Category 3 conditions. It handles Air UK and other airlines but most of the real interest is generated around the site of the old terminal area, for this is where Air UK carry out maintenance on F.27s. The industrial estate is reached from Hurricane Way and, from the road, a glimpse of something extraordinary is always possible.

SHEFFIELD

Brand new airports, like Denver and Osaka, appeared in the last edition. This time round there is news about Gardermoen, Hong Kong and Athens . . . and Sheffield. It's taken 75 years to build an airport for Sheffield. Just down the M1 motorway is East Midlands, and both Leeds/Bradford and Humberside are also quite close. Think of it as London City up north. The runway, 08/26, is only 1200 metres long, so operations are going to be mostly ATR-42/Dash 8 and Regional Jets.

SHOREHAM-BY-SEA ·
ESH   EGKA   2m/3km W

Quite the most delightful passenger terminal reminds visitors what Shoreham must have been like in its rather modest heyday. It is like a scene setting for a 1930s movie. The elevated railway line passes the airport, though there is no station. Parked on the grass and the small apron are plenty of light aircraft and there are, on either side of the terminal, enough hangars to contain plenty of registrations, plus some interesting aircraft. Permission for a closer look should be sought.

SOUTHAMPTON
SOU   EGHI   Eastleigh   4m/6km N (train 10 minutes)

Eastleigh's major refurbishment is complete. The moderate amount of cross channel flights continues all year round, but holiday traffic builds up during the summer. The Genavco facility carries out maintenance on executive jets, with some interesting examples often present. The largest scheduled movements are British Airways 737s (which actually look very impressive from the car park), though Air UK, Jersey European, Air France ATR-42s and Aurigny Trislanders make up much of the airline traffic. Beyond the passenger terminal, the road leads only to restricted areas and the long term car park and, at the southern edge, the car park around Genavco has been closed.

SOUTHEND

SEN   EGMC   Rochford   3m/5km N

Things were getting so bad at Southend, with most of the scheduled services withdrawn, that something drastic was needed. So they called it London (Southend)! Watch out, at this rate, for London (East Midlands) and London (Southampton). A small spectator area, in the gap between the tower and the terminal, allows a view of the ramp to be seen. There is a bar in the terminal which has an excellent view of the ramp, though there is often little on it to see on the move, apart from an Aurigny Trislander. To the left of the terminal is the base of British World Airlines who, at quieter times, allowed ramp access for photography of their Viscounts and 1-11s. Maintenance work for other carriers means that some interesting aircraft visit Southend. The ramp can be seen by driving past the terminal area, along a service road past the many parked cars and offices. A turning on the right reveals a small aero club and the maintenance ramp. On the far side of the runway, the tails (but, in most cases, not much more than the tails) of the stored 1-11s can (could?) be seen.

The railway bridge, on the road to Rochford, offers an elevated view of the main apron. Traditionally, one or two 707s have stood close to this road, in the company of the mortal remains of scrapped Belfasts.

The remote cargo and hangar area is not easily found, as access is not via the perimeter road. Although a manned security gate now prevents access to this area, there is a bank from where some of the withdrawn Viscounts and 1-11s can be seen and, to a very limited extent, photographed.

TEESSIDE

MME   EGNV   6m/9km E of Darlington (train 15 minutes)

Too close to Newcastle to become a major airport, as they compete for many of the passengers. Newcastle's inter city rail and Metro services ensure better connections for holidaymakers, many of whom can fly direct to America in summer. Teesside therefore handles mostly commuter links with Heathrow, Air UK and British Midland providing most of the scheduled traffic. In summer, there are a few charters to the sun. There is a south facing roof deck, which overlooks the apron but subject matter is often lacking for the casual visitor. To the left are several hangars and aprons, and ramp access is often possible.

ABERDEEN

ABZ   EGPD   Dyce   5m/8km N (bus 20 minutes)

The old terminal, in Dyce, was replaced by a modern building on the far/western side of the runway. The peak of oil-related movements is over but the helicopters based here are still numerous and active. Totally exposed to the elements is a viewing area to the south of the terminal/ramp, which looks down the length of the apron, faces north, and offers quite good opportunities for photographers, though only of the fixed wing movements. A notice on the wire fence states that it's in accordance with government standards and they realise it's a problem for photographers. It's a pity, but hardly surprising, that nobody has thought of finding a solution.

There are no real views from inside the building but, to its left/north, the grass bank is higher than the fence and an excellent place to watch, and photograph, the movements. What is to be seen from here is the Bristow apron, with half a dozen or so Super Pumas and S-61Ns in various stages of operation. Security personnel can be increasingly concerned about people standing for long periods on this bank, so any close encounters with officialdom should be treated politely.

The access road leading north from the terminal passes the hangars of Bristows and BIH, though glimpses of inmates are few. The photographer who is more anxious to get a good portrait than to log all the residents will be rewarded at Aberdeen, and the operators can be welcoming to parties of visitors, if trips are properly organised.

On the far side from here is the old airport, whose ramps still exist but are now occupied by Bond Helicopters and Business Air. Visits in summer allow the most to be made of the long daylight hours and there are plenty of vantage points next to fences to suit most needs. The concentration of so much specialist operation makes Aberdeen one of Britain's most interesting airports. For a close-up view of activity on both runways, head north from the old terminal area into a housing estate, where a grass mound on the edge of some wasteland offers a good view. It's almost directly opposite the control tower.

EDINBURGH

EDI   EGPH   Turnhouse   7m/11km W (bus 25 minutes)

Technically, Turnhouse is the name of the old facility on the north side of the field, where there was a small military base (it closed in March 97). The new terminal has a roof deck which is good for photographers; it overlooks the entire field but the capital city of Scotland generates a variety of scheduled traffic. British Airways 757 shuttle flights are augmented by British Midland, Loganair and Air UK, plus daily Crossair Saabs, Sabena 146s and Air France Fokkers/737s. Summer charters boost the log book with Aero Lloyd MD-80s and A320s being fairly frequent.. Cargo traffic is doing well, and it isn't unusual to see as many as six Electras side-by-side on the ramp.

The executive facility is separate and accessible only via a security gate, but the inmates can be identified (with some difficulty) from the north side. Leaving the main terminal and heading east towards the city, a left turn at the first roundabout leads to the old apron. Weekends can reveal a few commuter airliners parked but photos are difficult, as the aircraft park close to the fence. The aero club, by the railway line, is accessed from a gate on the north side of the field.

Driving towards the airport perimeter from Kirkliston leads to the north side of the field. There is, almost directly opposite where the two taxiways join (from cargo and the passenger terminal), an emergency access road leading to a grass bank. A 200mm lens in the late afternoon can provide some good photos.

GLASGOW

GLA   EGPF   International   9m/15km W (bus 25 minutes)

Once known as Abbotsinch, this is the premier airport for Scotland, and by far the busiest for fixed-wing aircraft. The central ramp can be seen from the terminal, and some photos through the glass can be of an acceptable quality.

The terminal extension is another of those from the Big Tin Shed school of architecture. To the west is one hangar occupied by Loganair. From the Loganiar hangar. a footpath (of sorts) leads to a grassy bank, close to the threshold of Runway 05 - okay when the wind's blowing from the "wrong" direction. The perimeter fence on the far side can be reached but a car is needed. Take the A726 exit for Erskine off the M8 and follow the perimeter. A turning to a couple of farms and the new Glasgow Flying Club location allows a view, if not photos.

Traffic is similar to other British airports plus ATPs. Brymon Dash 8s and British Regional SD3.60s and EMB145s add variety. Icelandair's 737s arrive in the afternoon during the week but, on Saturdays, the flight is operated by a Fokker 50. Most of the transatlantic flightshave deserted Prestwick - American, Air Canada, Air Transat and Canada 3000 being regular in summer.

PRESTWICK

PIK   EGPK   1m/1.5km NE

Prestwick is well-placed to receive transatlantic traffic, having a long runway, and being on the west coast of Scotland. However, the regular strong westerly breeze on this coast can make landing on the north-south runway an experience to remember. Occasional crew-training, transatlantic deliveries and military flights stopping for fuel make up a portion of the meagre traffic. The long runway and large terminal only serve to increase the impression of quietness.

A dedicated enthusiast could spend all day on the balcony but see few movements to record. The Sea King base on the eastern side often provide the only interest. A road on the eastern side of the field ends at the perimeter fence, almost directly opposite the main terminal. Also, an area of waste land in the south east corner, near the control tower, gives a good view of both the runway and taxiway. Finding something to see, or photograph, can be the problem.

CARDIFF
CWL   EGFF   Wales   12m/19km SW (bus 30 minutes)

A fairly small airport for a fairly small principality, the passenger terminal is pleasant and it has a roof deck. There is more to see on summer weekends, when charter flights operate, since scheduled movements are modest. During the week, an SF340 in Air France colours may be of interest. Also visible is the museum, with a significant collection in a very tight space. This has been shoe-horned into a tiny site, to make way for the new British Airways maintenance facility. Heathrow regulars will be used to the sight of several 747-400s parked at Terminal Four, but these aircraft have a more startling effect when they arrive at such a small airport.

On the far side, viewed from the observation deck, are the aero club aircraft and, to the left of the terminal, an apron is used occasionally by executive visitors but not in large numbers. Photography of aircraft on this ramp is difficult, as vantage points are limited.

Between the terminal and the aero club is the Cambrian Airways Viscount. By taking the road from the airport to Rhoose, a mile or so, the second right turn in the village leads to a playing field. At the far side is the perimeter fence and the Viscount. Also visible from here may be one or two light aircraft at the aero club which could not be seen from the terminal.

CHESTER
CEG   EGNR   Hawarden   5m/8km W

The city is very much in England but the airport is just across the border, such as it is, in Wales. No scheduled activity but this is quite a large field, the south side of which is occupied by British Aerospace. On the average weekday, there are one or two 125s (usually in primer) to be seen. Tucked away on the north side is SCA Hygiene Paper, whose security post allows access to Hawarden Air Services. From the car park, beyond the gate, can be seen a couple of Hind helicopters. Behind the hangars are several MiGs and An-2s. It's not too far from Liverpool for anyone who wants to see something just that little bit different.

BELFAST
BFS   EGAA   International   13m/20km NW (bus 40 minutes)

Investment to match the international tag has certainly brought Aldergrove, as it used to be known, up to date. There is a businesslike, though not necessarily brisk, air to the movements though, with such an enormous catchment area, summer charter flights include transatlantic carriers. At the mention of Belfast, considerations of security still come to mind, and it may be a surprise to find that it does not prevent viewing or photography.

The viewing area has lightly tinted glass through which all scheduled movements can be photographed. It's in its own little conservatory-type room and very well placed indeed. The traffic on Runway 07/25 is within range of a 200mm lens and an F.27 or HS748 on the apron my need 28mm as they park very close. There is usually an Air Belfast 1-11 to be seen, and photographed, from the observation room.

Traffic throughout the year is varied, though not busy. An enormous proportion of passengers travel to/from London, and there are some very busy days around Christmas, Easter and July. 5,000 passengers can be carried in just one day on the British Airways shuttle at Christmas, ferrying expats home to Northern Ireland. At such peak times BMA and BA will press any aircraft into service that is available. On these occasions, even 747s are to be seen.

The cargo and executive terminals handle a small amount of traffic, though nothing extraordinary. Access to the cargo ramp is extremely difficult, so its daytime residents might only be seen by someone landing or taxiing by. There is an RAF base on the far side. Fixed-wing visitors (from Beavers to TriStars) taxi past, and helicopters overfly within range of cameras and binoculars. There is a short cross-runway which necessitates listening to an airband radio, so as not to miss some movements.

BELFAST
BHD   EGAC   City   2m/3km E (bus 10 minutes)

Known generally as either Belfast Harbour or Sydenham, this is where Shorts' assembly plant is located. Completed SD3.60s parked outside are well beyond the range of even a 300mm lens. Heavylift Belfasts collect Fokker 100 wings for delivery, and scheduled airlines include Loganair, Manx, Capital and Jersey European (there being no charters).

The main car park fence is right beside the apron and taxiway. A standard lens is ideal for taxiing aircraft, and a 200mm zoom necessary for those on the runway. The terminal building is something that locals might feel the need to defend. To everyone else it's crude and basic.

ALDERNEY
ACI   EGJA   The Blaye   1m/1.5km S

The airport is known locally as Alderney International but the title is a little grandiose, even if there are customs and immigrations facilities. Anyone who has an interest in smaller airline operations will enjoy Alderney as the diet is undiluted Trislanders, those of Air Sarnia and Aurigny. A good airport for a classic landing shot of each colour scheme but, after half a day, a log book will yield no further surprises.

GUERNSEY
GCI   EGJB   4m/6km SW (bus 20 minutes)

As is to be expected of a holiday island, traffic is busiest in the summer, when it becomes (at best) moderately busy. To any British national, what visits is generally considered mundane but European enthusiasts often have a different perspective. Apart from the occasional German charter, most of what visits can be seen in greater volume, and better, at Jersey. The perimeter offers the photographer more than the free roof terrace. From here some stands are seen well but the runway is not.

JERSEY
JER   EGJJ   5m/8km W (bus 30 minutes)

This is the fifth busiest airport in Britain and much of the traffic only visits in summer. Consequently, July and August weekends are very busy times indeed. Afficianados of prop-liners (though not necessarily piston, of course) are sure to enjoy Jersey. F.27s, ATPs, HS748s, and SD3.30/60s in a good mixture of British colour schemes, plus occasional Maersk, Braathens and Luthanasa Cityline movements, and its appeal to European enthusiasts is obvious.

Additional jet traffic features a predictable mix of Britannia, BMA and BA, so a Saturday spent at Jersey has much to offer. It is common for such an interesting airport to lack some essential feature like, for example, an observation deck. Jersey has two: both excellent, with views across the stands and the west end of the runway. There is no charge for admission, and refreshments are available in the departure hall. Reports from Jersey always seem to say the same thing: the terminal is a perpetual building site. Maybe, in the next couple of years, things will improve.

Bus service No.15 runs past the airport, between St Aubin and St Helier, so a hire car is not necessary. Since the decks are preferred by most photographers, exploring the perimeter is not essential though this too offers further variety. Perhaps the most difficult aircraft to photograph are the Aurigny Trislanders, and their staff can be helpful in the occasional quiet moment.

Taking the road west to St Ouen's Bay, a track leads close to the perimeter where taxiing aircraft pass close on their way to Runway 09. A 70-200mm lens may be needed for aircraft landing, but movements on the taxiway pass much closer. East of the terminal, next to the aero club, taxiing aircraft still pass within range of the camera, but the bonus is a large quantity of light aircraft, including many foreign visitors. Walking further east, a footpath leads under the threshold between the approach lights, and photos of landing aircraft are also easy to take.

A long stay on the island, with many visits to the airport may be another matter. Most of the aircraft to be noted on the first day will be seen many times, as they shuttle back and forth between Jersey and various airports in Britain.

ISLE OF MAN

IOM   EGNS   Ronaldsway   14m/22km SW (bus 55 minutes)

A visit to the Isle of Man makes an enjoyable break, but the airport would not be the main reason. The Manx Airlines fleet operates most of the services, with occasional daytime appearances by the Business Air SD3.60. There is a bus service from Douglas and the steam train runs to nearby Castletown Station. On the northwest side of the field is the main terminal, and to the southwest, the coastline of Derbyhaven.

There are no views from the terminal, apart from through the restaurant windows, but low fences between the car parks and apron at each side of the building allow close encounters with arrivals. All three runways, 04/22, 09/27 and 18/36, have places where photos can be taken, though the best location is probably next to the aero club, in the northeast corner. Road A12 runs to the aero club from Castletown, between the perimeter and the coast, and the coastal footpath is ideal for photos until mid-afternoon.

The hangars, on the north side, are worthy of investigation as it is here that the world's only Percival Q6 is housed. Airliner enthusiasts may not show much interest but unique and historical craft are rare, and this one only leaves its hangar occasionally. Also to be noted is the Manx Airlines maintenance base, used also for work on Loganair and BMA ATPs.

By hiring a cycle in Castletown, one morning trip to the aero club could be combined, another day, with an afternoon trip to the terminal car park. To spend a full day at Ronaldsway would necessitate nice weather and a very good book.

HA = HUNGARY

BUDAPEST

BUD   LHBP   Ferihegy   10m/16km SE (bus 35 minutes)

It is possible to get to the airport by underground train and take a No. 93 BKV bus from Kobanya-Kispest but the express Volan bus from Engels Square is the simplest way and takes about the same time. Another reason to take the Volan bus is that tickets, costing about 70 pence, are paid for once on board. Using ordinary public transport, it must be remembered that tickets must be bought before travelling. With heavy penalties for anyone hitching a free ride, even by accident, a simple mistake can have unfortunate consequences.

Hungary has endured a miserable existence over the years, and one of the old rules was that talking on public transport was forbidden. As most foreign visitors are unlikely to speak much of the language, casual conversation would be rare. If the locals seem unfriendly, at least this information offers a reason. A car can be the most difficult means of transport, as direction signs aren't exactly numerous.

There are two terminals and, to all intents and purposes, two entirely separate airports. Ferihegy 1, the old terminal, is closest to the road and does have a spectating facility. It is covered and double glazed, which makes photography a little difficult. Without prior permission, photography can still be more than just difficult! Using this terminal are most of the international carriers, except for Air France, Alitalia, Delta and Lufthansa, plus general aviation.

To the right of the deck, and visible, are the maintenance hangars and, in the distance, the cargo apron. Further away, quite a long way, is the more modern Ferihegy 2 terminal. The main concourse has a striking resemblence to Frankfurt, though on a rather smaller scale. The observation deck is best described as a rooftop cafe, and it has the advantage, compared with Frankfurt, that entry costs next to nothing. It is relaxed and enjoyable place to sit, especially with Hungarian prices being so low, and the view is of Malev's Boeings (the Tupolevs being withdrawn from use) plus, rather more distant, some Yak 40s and Let 410s.

Budapest is strictly for the enthusiast who has seen everything at the usual European destinations, and needs something different. The journey to Hungary takes time and money. Excitement is not a word which readily springs to mind when describing Ferihegy.

The approach road to Ferihegy 2 has on display Il-18 HA-MOA plus an Il-14 and another aircraft. Scattered around the field are a few relics of the old days. Tu-134 HA-LBG is now used for fire practice and Il-18 HA-MOG is reported to be a ground instructional airframe. The museum compound repays interest, as it contains a number of unusual types, to western eyes.

To complete coverage of Budapest's aviation scene, it's necessary to visit BUDAORS, which is a major general aviation field. The old connections with the CIS will endure for a while, and such types as An-2s, Yak-18s and Zlins can all be seen in the company of one or two Turbolets and the ABKS Turbo Porters. North of the city, DUNAKESZI is the home of the Malev Flying Club, whose light aircraft all wear full airline colour schemes.

HB = SWITZERLAND

BASEL

| BSL | LFSB | EuroAirport | 7m/11km NW (bus 15 minutes) |

While operations are considerably less in number than Zurich or Geneva, this is still a very interesting airport. Arrival from the Swiss city of Basel/Basle ensures that the most interesting parts of the field can be visited, whilst anyone driving from the French side is faced with confusion.

Fences line both sides of the roads to form what must be the most complex international boundary in the world. After some time, it becomes apparent that access is not possible to the Swiss facilities. Having been so close, you might be tempted to give up, drive away and start again from the Swiss side, which takes a disheartening length of time. Try this instead: diagonally opposite from the car rental desks, on the arrivals level, is a door. It has no marking but, pass through it to the Swiss side. For obvious reasons, the Swiss police do control this door (it's a border crossing, after all), so take your passport, or prepare to be sent back.

Scheduled movements have increased in quantity and variety in recent years, with Crossair's fleet being regular visitors. The terrace to the left of the terminal is only open between 13:00 and 19:00, precisely the time when the sun shines from the wrong angle. The SFr1 admission fee is hardly money well spent but the adjacent cafeteria, where the view is little different, is very expensive indeed. Anyone visiting in a car will drive to the far end of the central complex for views of the general aviation. Jet Aviation has a large hangar, whose inmates normally include a varied selection of biz-jets. Maintenance work for small operators means that their ramp can contain some extremely unusual types, but the construction of the Crossair hangar has restricted viewing.

BERN

| BRN | LSZB | Belp | 5m/8km SE (bus 20 minutes) |

Switzerland's capital city nestles in the Bernese Oberland, the mountainous backdrop being most picturesque, but causing severe restrictions on movements, due to the steep approach. STOL airliners, such as the Air Engiadina fleet and some Crossair SF340s, operate the only scheduled services here.

The terminal is surrounded by several hangars, the contents of which are varied, and interesting, and the photographer can have a very rewarding hour or so, roaming around the residents. At the centre of things is a grass enclosure, and the entire proceedings can be witnessed from here. With the right weather, this can be a very enjoyable experience indeed.

The passenger terminal appears, from the outside, rather primitive. This is Switzerland, so it comes as no surprise to find it is very pleasant inside. Its next door neighbour is Air Engiadina's hangar. At weekends, when commuter flights are rare, this is where the fleet can be seen and photographed. Heliswiss, Alpar and Eagle Air are all based here, but anyone planning a visit may find that there is more action to be seen during business hours on a weekday, as the field is essentially devoted to general aviation at weekends - on one hand, the Heliswiss hangar is normally locked up but, on the other, there could be three Do328s and a Jetstream, all waiting to be photographed at closer range than anywhere else in Europe.

GENEVA

GVA   LSZB   International   3m/5km NW (bus 20 minutes)

Switzerland's second airport is better known to most people by its old name of Cointrin. Its variety of traffic, and the places from which to see it, mean that many photographers rate Zurich quite a long way behind Geneva.

The observation deck has been an essential feature of the airport for several years, offering a panoramic view of almost all the apron, the satellite terminals, and the runway beyond. It does not offer toilet facilities, however. Anyone parking in the undergound car park (costing SFr1 per hour) will note the position of the toilets before going through the security check and paying another Swiss Franc for admission to the deck. It opens at the relatively late time of 09:30.

The wide body movements park at the extreme right of the apron, so some of these movements must be captured whilst they are on the move. The deck stretches the full length of the passenger terminal but it doesn't quite reach the remote stands 14-19. Visible from the eastern end of the deck is DC-7C 45187 which used to carry fictional HB-SSA markings. It started life with KLM as PH-DSH and ended its days as VR-BCW and N9498.

There are three circular lounges for gates numbered accordingly: 20+, 30+ and 40+, where most of the scheduled airliners park, always passing so that a photo can be taken. On the far side of the runway are the general aviation ramps, offering mostly twi-engined aircraft, many of which are identifiable. To the left, the original passenger terminal is now used for charter traffic, especially in winter. Skiing holidays mean Britannia 767s, though there are visitors from other parts of Europe, notably Scandinavia. Beyond it, in the southwest corner of the field, is the apron occupied by Aeroleasing and Jet Aviation, but it is out of sight from the balcony. A walk is necessary. An access road off Route de Meyrin leads to the terminal/hangar and the fence where the parked biz-jets can be seen at reasonably close quarters. The access road to Aeroleasing reveals a cycle track. Take the short walk along it, as the view from here is good, overlooking the Aeroleasing ramp and the holding point for Runway 05. There is a grass bank, for an elevated view, and the fence has suffered damage, where holes have been enlarged for camera lenses.

Route de Meyrin heads north to the community of the same name. A right turn, after passing the end of Runway 05, is followed by a few more right turns as directed by the signs. The road leads to the general aviation facility. Opposite the army vehicle store is a high concrete wall, and things look bleak. Don't panic! In the corner is a gateway marked public access. It leads to an aero club which has its own viewing area. From here, all movements in and out of the complex pass very close, though not with any great regularity. The apron's residents can be identified, as can some of those in the hangar to the right. Nestling among the trees and the buildings beyond the hangar are the remains of an Italian Gulfstream 1. Some say it's I-GGGG, c/n 51.

Follow the concrete wall and more aircraft can be seen. The first hangar has windows so its inmates can be seen, and its car park allows another vantage point. The apron is part of the facility for hangars 2 and 3, both of which are inaccessible, beyond a gate. Normally parked in the corner, very close to the fence, is the strange-looking (Dewoitine?) C-552/HB-RBJ.

Because both the car park and the viewing area offer a broad view of the runway and the main terminal area, it is tempting to take photos of airliners on the move. Before doing so, it might be worth considering the angle of the sun and the background. Experienced photographers know that the quality of portraits from here, even in the afternoon, is not as good as they would wish and certainly not as good as can be taken from the terminal's observation deck.

Geneva handles an inspiring selection, many of which are rare at other European airports. Added to the international movements are the increasing commuter flights by Metros and Saabs, to give Geneva that rare combination of good movements and no shortage of vantage points from which to see them. It's likely that travellers with a European itinerary will wish to stay overnight at Geneva. Switzerland is not a cheap country in which to stay but France offers better value. The border is just north of the runway. Heading east from the terminal, one of the first exit roads passes under the runway on its way to the customs post and Ferney-Voltaire. At the roundabout, a left turn along the Route de Meyrin leads up the hill to another roundabout. Here are the Novotel and Formule 1 hotels, the latter offering basic accommodation (for up to three people in a room) for only FFr140 a night.

A return trip to the airport, next morning, involves passing through the same customs post, as it's the easiest route to take. The photographer's view of the taxiway from the southern side of the tunnel is excellent. Parking the car and walking all the way back to it is, however, something to be considered as the quality of photographs is of the highest order . . . by anyone's standards.

LUGANO
LUG   LSZA   Agno   5m/8km N (bus 10 minutes)

A twenty minute bus ride from the town, or less than an hour by car from Milan, taking motorway exit Lugano Nord. The airport is small, modern and pleasant, though car parking is expensive. As befits an Alpine resort, biz-jets are regular visitors, and scheduled services are offered by Crossair 146s and SF340s. Photography is easy, especially with the weather enjoyed by this area. For a view of the general aviation, continue past the terminal to a grassed area and some hangars.

SANKT MORITZ
SMV   LSZS   Samedan   3m/5km NE

This airport is in the very heart of world-famous, and rather exclusive, skiing country. Anything which needs to be purchased in this area is therefore expensive. Unless travelling overland to the airport by car, the only alternative means of getting there is by taxi. The relatively short journey from town is by no means cheap! At 5600 feet above sea level, this is Europe's highest airfield (comparable in height to Denver) and certainly one of the most spectacular for its surrounding scenery. Samedan's railway station is close to the airport, just a short walk away, past the Heliswiss hangar.

The airport is at its busiest between December and April, with many corporate aircraft, up to 1-11 and DC-9 size, visiting for part of the season. Some remain for the duration of the owners' holidays, sometimes flying away for a couple of hours, or days.

Samedan is linked to Zurich in winter by Air Engiadina, though Aeroleasing Lear Jets have offered competition on the routes. Close to the threshold of Runway 03, not far from the passenger terminal, is a level crossing with automatic barriers to warn of movements. Since the field is surrounded by a cross country skiing circuit, sporting and spotting can be enjoyed by a privileged few. Photography is not a problem at Samedan, and the terminal has a cafeteria, where one can meet the pilots or other aviation buffs. The added bonus is that, quite remarkably, car parking is free! To enjoy the threshold of Runway 21, a little energy or a car are needed. Places to take photos are obvious and easily found.

SION
SIR   LSGS

This is a small field, primarily serving a military purpose. The car park is free and viewing facilities are good. It is reasonable to expect several helicopters and plenty of general aviation. The Swiss Air Force presence during the week can mean that a variety of types are active.

ZÜRICH

ZRH   LSZH   Kloten   8m/13km N (train 10 minutes)

The view from Zürich's roof terrace, open in summer from 08:00 to 21:00 (cost: SFr2 entry before the security check), is restricted by Terminal A's pier extension. There are many stands out of sight is still extremely good.

This is all relative, as what can be seen from the deck does represent a broad picture of the proceedings, since most movements can be seen as they pass from one part of the field to another. Because the roof deck has its limitations, the various multi-storey car parks attract attention for alternative vantage points. Car Park B allows the stands for that terminal to be seen, and many of the others. Car Park F, to the right, is lower and overlooks the cargo and Crossair ramps, Terminal A, and the aircraft taxiing to Runway 28. With several runways in use, the office block in front of Car Park F means that not all movements to be seen.

Detailed advice about the observation deck will be of use. The SFr2 entry fee is paid into the turnstile, where change machines are provided. They even take banknotes. Each visitor is supposedly only allowed three items of luggage: one *fotoaparat*, for most people, might mean the Instamatic but it must also include a couple of single lens reflexes and a selection of lenses. One *handtasche* means a bag, which isn't necessarily just a ladies' handbag. A permissible *schirm* is an umbrella. If security personnel decide a visitor has too much baggage, there are left luggage lockers, but it would be wise to take only what is needed. Something to eat and drink might be wise. Paying SFr2.90 for a cup of coffee isn't everyone's idea of good value for money. The cafeteria is, however, the only place on the terrace where smoking is allowed.

Despite its shortcomings, the deck is excellent. Most of the residents on Swissair's maintenance ramp can be seen, if not identified. The remote stands, at the far side of the Flughafenbahn building, usually contain a number of charter airliners, and aircraft landing on Runway 14 can be seen with binoculars. Operators are identifiable but that's all. Many of the MD-80s and Fokker 100s only come into sight again when departing on 28, which is the annoying frustration. This also applies, of course, to virtually all the Crossair movements, and there are many.

Between Runway 16/34 and the taxiway is a remote general aviation parking area, probably about as secure as they get. The residents are beyond the reach of most binoculars and telescopes. Beside the threshold of Runway 16 is a DC-8 still wearing faded Air Afrique colours - c/n 45568, TU-TCP.

Swissair's maintenance area is usually worth close scrutiny. To reach it from Terminal B, walk to the main concourse, at the same level as the Pou-de-Ciel hanging from the roof. To the right is a door which leads straight into the Parkhaus. Stairs at the far side lead down to a short tunnel and the road to a ground level car park. The two Classic Wings C-47s are normally visible, plus anything else which may have taken up temporary residence.

Without recourse to time-consuming exploration, the movements can all be seen from somewhere in the central complex. One of the extra attractions is the tour bus (rundfahrten), which leaves from the observation deck pier, and costs SFr3. This offers a comprehensive look at the airport and a stop is often included at the intersection of Runways 28 and 16/34. This viewing area is ridiculously close to the aircraft and, after leaving the bus, some incredible opportunities exist for photographers. Between April and October, the tours operate hourly on Wednesdays (13:00 to 16:00) and at weekends (12:00 to 16:00). They are subject to the weather conditions, and at all other times they are only available for parties who have booked in advance.

For the energetic in search of light aircraft, the Wanderweg has much to offer. This is reached by walking to the eastern corner of the field, past the cargo terminal, and following the yellow signs. It takes twenty minutes to reach anywhere with a view but the reward should be some-thing in the region of a hundred registrations. When Runway 28 is in use, which is regularly, photographers can also obtain ground level portraits of a wide variety of departing aircraft.

With Runway 14 used mostly for landings and 28 for departures, the Wanderweg leads to one of the better spots but transport is essential for the other. A car park next to the thresholds of Runways 14 and 16 is used by most serious photographers. Reference to the photos in any recent JP Airline Fleets will demonstrate that the results are first class. Rümlang is a village worthy of note, as a road from it leads to another popular vantage point, complete with its own car park. It overlooks Terminal B, Runway 16/34 and the taxiway to Runway 10.

As long as the shortcomings are borne in mind, and the visit is combined with one to Geneva, the trip should result in the best of both airports producing a comprehensive cover of Swiss movements. While Geneva specialises in shorter range aircraft, Zürich has the Swissair widebody fleet on display (in the morning, prior to departure) and a varied assortment of Asian 747s and A340s rub shoulders with Gulf Air A320s, various Dash 8s, Saab 340s and 2000s: a unique combination. On summer Saturdays, there can be a good selection of Spanish charter flights. Display boards on the observation deck show the colour schemes of seventy-two operators. A prolonged stay will, almost certainly, allow most of them to be seen at close quarters and there aren't many airports in the world that claim that. Perfect it isn't, but it does come pretty close!

HC = ECUADOR
QUITO
UIO   SEQU   Mariscal Sucre   5m/8km N

The let-down and approach to Quito are, like Hong Kong, considered fun or terrifying. Arrival by White Knuckle Airways is an achievement which, to pacify the faint of heart, happens many times without incident every day. The airport is an anti-climax, as there are very few movements (sometimes three only) on the average day, so it takes dedication for Quito to be on an itinerary. There are some interesting aircaft parked around the tarmac, and there is also a military base with, it is reported, a small museum. Photos from the terminal windows seem to pose no problems. The Noratlases move only rarely, and the Caravelle hulks not at all. Quito is an airport to tell your friends about . . . it's more fun than being there!

HI = DOMINICAN REPUBLIC
PUERTO PLATA
POP   MDPP   La Union International   15m/23km W

On the north coast , Puerto Plata is a tourist area, with charters coming from the USA, Canada and Europe. The appeal is obvious: hot climate, exotic surroundings and gallons of cheap booze. Viewed from the other side, wages are so low that profits are astronomical. Most of the flights are mundane, coming from Miami and New York, but Turks and Ciacos Airways Islanders and Trislanders make it an airport with a difference. They are best seen from the edge of the apron.

SANTIAGO DE LOS CABALLEROS
STI   MDST   Cibao International

Less than 100 miles north of Santo Domingo is Santiago where Cibao is to be found. Like Herrera, sightings of g.a. and executive aircraft are more likely, though there are occasional scheduled operations to San Juan by LIAT Dash 8s. Reference to distances in this part of the world may mislead, as roads are generally in very poor condition: this is not a wealthy country.

SANTO DOMINGO
SDQ   MDSD   Las Americas   19m/30km E

The Dominican Republic is still good for two stored Super Constellations, HI-548CT and HI-583CT, and that, in these modern times, can be reason enough for propliner fanatics to visit. Las Americas has aprons on either side of the terminal but with little chance of viewing. The main terminal, although glass fronted, offers few good views of the aprons. Anyone planning to spend some time here should head instead for Wendy's on the first floor. For those who pass through passport control, the departure lounge also offers good photography. The authorities seem to have little interest in photographic activity in the terminal but have a far stricter view on anyone exploring the cargo area. The main apron is best seen from next to the Dominicana hangar, to the right. A separate access road leads to the cargo terminal, and the maintenance base of AMSA and Aerochago, where the Connies are stored. Scheduled traffic includes Copa B737s and ALM MD-80s, though Air Aruba's YS-11 often fails to keep its appointment.

The exotic assortment of piston types, including C-46s, Martin 404s, Convairs and DC-6s, make Las Americas unique, but many of the Dominican examples are grounded. A few quiet words with a worker may help gain admission to the cargo ramp. A few dollars may be a greater help, however, though it must be noted that photographers are becoming more commonplace, and therefore better understood.

SANTO DOMINGO
HEX   MDHE   Herrera   4m/6km SW

The reason that general aviation is lacking at Las Americas airport is because most of it uses Herrera, closer to the town. Most of the residents can be seen from the perimeter, and anyone with a reasonable amount of Spanish (or good sign-language) may try to negotiate access to some of the hangars, where many of the more interesting aircraft lurk, out of sight. US dollars, usually in tens, can be of great help.

HK = COLOMBIA

BOGOTA
BOG   SKBO   Eldorado   8m/13km E

A visit to Eldorado airport is exciting, and extremely exotic. With the jungle is all around, this is life on the edge, in more ways than one. Guns are numerous and very visible.

There are still C-46s and DC-3s flying cargo, and their numbers are swollen by a wide range of other propellor types: Twin Otters, Bandeirantes, F.27s HS748s and CASAs. There are plenty of colour schemes, too, including Satena who operate the el-cheapo domestic flights. Subject to availability, this is the way to see Colombia.

RIO NEGRO
MDE   SKRG   Jose Maria Cordova International   4m/6km S of Medellin

The passenger terminal at this new airport, formerly known as Medellin, has an excellent spectator's terrace. There is some jet traffic but lots of the flights are operated by propellor-driven aircraft, and all of them rather exotic. Twin Otters and Fairchild F-27s of ACES rub shoulders with Aries Bandeirantes and Satena HS748s. Every movement needs a photograph, or so it seems. Traffic is only moderately brisk, but each aircraft is something rather special, and very exotic.

MEDELLIN
MDE   SKMD   Olaya Herrera   23m/37km SE

The old airport is further down the valley, and this is where the old piston airliners are still to be found, and in reasonable numbers. Scheduled traffic offers a variety of prop commuter flights with Avianca Fokker 50s, Satena CASA 212s, AVES Otters and ATR-42s. The cargo area, about a quarter of a mile from the main terminal, offers DC-3s operating for a airlines such as Aero Vanguardia, LANC, and Sadelia - enough to make the average enthusiast swoon. This area also houses some general aviation and a C-54, HK 528, which was last reported as resting on its tail. For access to the cargo ramp, a reasonable knowledge of the Spanish language is useful, though there is always somebody around who wants to show off how well he speaks American English.

At the INTERNATIONAL airport, a recently-constructed terminal offers that paradise that makes the journey here worthwhile - a terrace overlooking all movements, and the luxury of a bar and restaurant. This is the home of Tampa, the local cargo carrier, whose services to Miami leave frequently, using 707s and DC-8s. Add to this a variety of scheduled movements by Avianca, ACES, and Aerorepublica, and you may wonder if you'll ever want to leave.

VILLAVICENCIO
VVC   SKVV   la Vanguardia   4m/6km

Colombia is a large country with a significant undeveloped region. The best way to get to Villavicenzio is by Satena, with their Aviocars and HS748s, at a ridiculously low cost by western standards. Anyone who has an interest in piston aircraft would do well to consider a $10 trip from Bogota to Villavicencio, where the small airport's traffic is free of the sound of jet engines.

Because the jungle was cleared to make this airport, photographs of old airliners with an equatorial background take on a truly exotic appearance, and there is no shortage of subject matter. The single storey passenger terminal is adequate for the purposes, and has a cafeteria and a few shops. More important, the security staff do allow photos to be taken, with access to the ramp. Many small airliners are based here, though operations tend to be ad-hoc, with little regard to timetables. Such operators as AVESCA, El Dorado and Transamazonica all base aircraft here, plus several others, and there are plenty of operators of Cessna/Piper fleets.

One edition of the British TV programme, *Pertpetual Motion*, featured the DC-3. Very much in evidence were the many DC-3s, C-46s and C-54s standing around at Villavicenzio. Few other airports in the entire world do as much maintence work on DC-3s. Anyone visiting might care to contact Aliansa, the airline which was featured. Also prominently featured was Nubia Alvarez Rodriguez, Jorge's sister. She might welcome the chance to talk to people who watched the programme.

HL = SOUTH KOREA
CHEJU
CJU   RKPC   International

This is a small island in the East China Sea, and close to the Sea of Japan, which has two airports and a few heliports. Scheduled services use International but most are domestic flights. Continental Micronesia 727s visit and Asiana fly to Fukuoka but, apart from that, it's mostly what can be seen at Seoul. In fact, the majority of flights, about a dozen per hour, are bound for Pusan or Seoul. Added interest is offered by a small detachment of (two) naval Tracers and a couple of helicopters. The passenger terminal is modern, with facilities for watching and photographing the movements. What exactly these facilities include was not made clear by the report.

SEOUL
SEL   RKSS   Kimp'o   16m/25km W

The magnificent passenger terminal created for Korean Air and Asiana has its own apron, in a corner a little remote from most of the action. Facing the runway is the old international passenger terminal, and between them is the small domestic building. The quantity of sky blue airliners is hardly surprising but there are numerous small aircraft to be seen in these colours: to the left of the new terminal, a pair of hangars house the Korean Air biz-jet fleet.

It's the domestic terminal that offers the facilities, and very good indeed they are, too - apart from the burgers at the cafe. The main (and probably only) problem is the lack of elevators, so it's hard work climbing to the eighth floor. A spacious indoor area overlooks the runway and, beyond it, the West Apron. Everything, apart from what's at the Korean/Asiana terminal, is visible through the glass. A door at the back of the gallery leads to an external area which faces the other terminal. Well, to be honest, it pretty much faces the back of it at an oblique angle, making it imposible to see some of the aircraft until they move. The deck is open from 08:00 to 20:00.

Assuming traffic uses Runway 32, which appears to be the norm, everything passes the observation deck sooner or later. The West Apron, on the far side, contains general aviation with a row of maintenance hangars at the back. Traffic is predominantly Korean Air and Asiana, their terminal being used also by Chinese carriers and other interesting airlines such as Vietnam and Continental Micronesia. All other carriers use the "other" international terminal, T2, including All Nippon, Uzbekistan and Vasp.

The airport and city are linked non-stop by six limousine bus services - fare Won2,500. Oridnary bus services operate to each side of the Han River: No.600 to the south side and No.601 to the railway station and most of the major hotels. The fare was last reported to be Won700.

HS = THAILAND

BANGKOK
BKK   VTBD   Don Muang International   15m/23km NNE (bus 20 minutes)

The cost of living in Thailand is, by western standards, low. Nevertheless one or two words of advice before arriving may be in order. There is a courtesy bus service into town but tickets must be purchased before leaving the Arrivals area. Failure to do this leaves a tired traveller at the mercy of extremely keen taxi drivers. Thai Airways no longer operate a courtesy bus between the International Terminal and the Asia Hotel (which is still excellent value for money). Taxis cost about 500 Baht (more than £10) to the city centre, or you can catch an air-conditioned bus from the domestic and T1 terminals for only 70 Baht

What used to be called the International Terminal is now two terminals. The original, now Terminal 1, is symmetrical, with viewing areas at the ends of the fourth floor. That to the left (north) is where spotters first got the hang of Bangkok. Good value meals and no hurry. A cup of decent coffee could be made to last a couple of hours, if necessary, and nobody would mind. The southern cafe is self-service, with coffee out of plastic cups but, being nearer to the domestic terminal, offered a fighting chance to read off registrations. Runway directions can change regularly, so you might get some exercise.

Adjoining Terminal 1 is, predictably, Terminal 2 where there are no views to speak of. Continuing south, sooner or later, you have to leave the air-conditioned comfort for the oven-like conditions outside. It comes as a shock. Forget the multi-storey car park. The glazed tube link to the domestic terminal is a good area to try logging, better than in the terminal itself if an A300 is parked in front of the cafe window. Being lower has its disadvantages, and that's one of them.

International traffic is good, though not always in daylight hours. Biman F.28s, Druk Air 146s, Yunnan 737s and Airbuses from Pakistan and India.

Beyond the apron is a view of the runway threshold, so inbound or outbound aircraft can be seen passing along one of the taxiways. On the far side of the field is the military base, though distance and heat haze conspire to ensure that serials can not be read, except in the early morning. This is probably a good thing, as the pleasant Thai temperament does not extend to the military personnel who patrol the airport.

The domestic terminal is not without its merits. For a start, its visitors are unlikely to be seen on the average day at Düsseldorf or Liverpool. Leaving the international terminal at ground level, turn left and walk along by the chain fence. Through it can be seen whatever is parked on one side of Pier 4 and on part of the domestic ramp. Once inside the domestic terminal, a security check is followed by a flight of stairs leading to a small snack bar. The view is excellent of both the domestic ramp and international movements on the taxiway.

At the southern end of the field, past several military hangars, is a storage compound which contains (presumably) the mortal remains of A300 HS-THO, which was declared a write-off. It is painted all-white.

Cameras in the hands of the average tourist excite no interest and it is possible for the security presence to be low-key. Low-key can be plain clothes, of course, and the use of a 300mm zoom for a close up of something exotic, even a civil airliner, could be risky. Also conspiring against the serious photographer is the cleanliness (or lack thereof) of the glass. Bangkok is an ideal airport for watching, and even noting, a fine variety of movements but any photographic record, other than tourist 'snaps', will be the result of luck, in more ways than one.

The good news: ramp access is possible! The bad news: it costs Bht 750 to take still photos for up to three hours (no problem) and another Bht 900 an hour for an 8-seater bus. In other words, this is for organized tour parties only. Further details from Wing Commander Tawatchai Rachawat, Airport Operations Department, Airports Authority of Thailand, Vibhavadi Rangsit Road, Bangkok 10210, or fax on (code plus) 531-5559. You must also submit written permission from each airline if wishing to take a photo of their aircraft. That really is the tricky bit! Imagine having paid your money and standing on the ramp when something extraordinarily exotic taxis into view. No piece of paper, no photo! Local contact with Ops might yield different results. Try 535-1650 or 535-1705 or, at weekends, the duty officer on 535-1566.

CHIANG MAI
CNX   VTCC   3m/5km

The best way to reach the airport from town, is to take a Tuk-tuk, a three-wheel motorbike. Depending on your abilities to bargain with the driver, the journey should cost about Bht 40 (about £1). On arrival at the passenger terminal, it's worth asking at the information desk for a timetable of the day's events. Don't expect too much. Traffic is only moderate, featuring mostly a few Thai A300s and ATR-72s. Kumming, Hong Kong and Bangkok Airways are all reported as regular visitors. In the evenings, a Silkair A310 could also be likely.

To the left of the terminal is a fence where it's possible to overlook the apron and the runway. The late afternoon sun makes things quite difficult for photography however. At the other side of the passenger terminal is the cargo building, and between them is a gate which offers another view of the apron. Visible from here are aircraft at the Thai Air Force's Chiang Mai Base. If any military aircraft are parked outside, the guard at the gate can make life difficult for anyone showing (unwelcome) interest.

This is northern Thailand, less than 100 miles from both Laos and Burma, neither of which might represent the best neighbours. It would be naive to pretend that westerners are always regarded as friendly and harmless.

CHIANG RAI
CEI   VTCR   Ban Du   5m/8km N

A visit to northern Thailand is not like a holiday jaunt to Bangkok or Phuket. This can seem quite hostile territory, unless you know what you're doing. This airport, probably the country's northernmost, is quite close to the border but is not a military base. A Thai A300 visits two or three times a day, and a photo is easily taken. Otherwise, the journey is hardly worthwhile, in civil aviation terms.

PHUKET
HKT   VTSP   International   18m/30km N

Several shuttle buses link the airport with the resort's different hotels. Patong Beach, about 20km to the south, is probably the best served. Officially, this is Thailand's second busiest airport but it comes a long way behind Bangkok. Anyone considering a day's spotting at the airport might do well to contact the airport's information desk by telephone before making the journey. The number is 327230-7 and, for public information, try extension 1111 or 1122.

Traffic is mostly Thai A300s, which park at the air jetties but there are also ATR-42s and 737s, which normally park out on the apron. Variety may be offered by the occasioal day-time Malaysian 737 or a Silkair A310.

The airfield has been built beside the coast, the 09 threshold being virtually on the beach. To the south of the runway are the aprons and the passenger terminal, which faces the coast. Parallel to the runway, and separating the passenger and cargo terminals, is a fence. This overlooks the apron used mostly by turboprops. At the side nearest a house and garage stands a group of trees, ideal for shade when staying any length of time. The view from the fence is excellent, as it also allows photos of aircraft on the runway. If extra height is needed, there are some old posts to stand on. They also make a good place to sit.

Jet aircraft taxi round and park at the other side of the passenger terminal, so are normally out of sight unless they move. When Runway 27 is in use for landing, incoming movements are hidden by a hill on top of which are the ATC aerials, so a radio is useful to ensure that the camera is ready for use.

As is to be expected in this part of the world, the airport is surrounded by lush vegetation. Palm trees abound. It is possible, for the adventurous and energetic, to explore other vantage points around the perimeter. The most obvious is the beach, reached by walking through the national park. There is no fence at this side of the field, so security officers keep watch for anyone trespassing near the runway. It is also worth noting that walking along the beach is hazardous, as the tide can cause one or two problems. Rather than run unnecessary risks, it might be best to take other people's word for it: the fence next to the apron faces north, has good views and isn't risky at all.

HZ = SAUDI ARABIA

DHAHRAN
DHA   OEDR   International   8m/13km SE

Apart from limited views from the departure lounges, there is little scope for observing the fairly busy traffic here. The upper levels of the Dhahran International Hotel (near the terminal area) provide panoramic but distant views of the 'civil' runway and taxiways. Good landing shots could be obtained from the airport - city road, just by the northern threshold but the aircraft normally land in the opposite direction!

Even in normal times, there is much fighter activity here, many visiting C-130Hs and the occasional USAF C-5 and C-141 but the military facilities are not visible from the civil side of the airport. Most long-stay executive movements park on the cargo ramp and others go in front of the main terminal. Airlines feature many of the usual European carriers but of note are Airbuses of Air India, PIA and, a long way from home, Korean Airlines. PAL and Thai International A300-600s are also regular visitors while Gulf Air 737s visit frequently on the 'Air Bridge' from nearby Bahrain, as does Yemenia's 737. Saudia are naturally busy and the ramp usually contains two or three A300s as well as a few 737s.

The international and domestic terminals face the 'civil' runway and all aircraft visiting park nose-in. Across the runway is the cargo and general aviation long-term parking and, to its right, the ARAMCO facility, with a good number of aircraft normally present. At the southern end of Runway 34R/16L, that most remote from Dhahran, is a large air force dump. Being close to a missile site, approach must be avoided. Anyone with the slightest interest in military aviation would be advised to make do with the consolation Lightning, Sabre and T-33 on poles by the main road. It would be unrealistic to imagine that Dhahran has returned to normal after the Gulf War, and it can be assumed that the military presence is always on a high level of alert, with activities and attitudes to match.

JEDDAH
JED   OEJN   King Abdulaziz International   11m/17km N

Jeddah is located on the Red Sea coast of Saudi Arabia and is the closest city with an airport to Mecca, the most important place in the world for muslims and one of pilgrimage (the Hadj) for any who can make the trip. The annual influx of aircraft to Jeddah has repercussions throughout the world for airlines, with short-leases being sought for almost anything which can carry lots of economy passengers. At these times, the Hadj terminal is the gateway to Mecca and close scrutiny by non-muslims is unwise.

A vast airport, with three parallel runways although one would easily be able to handle the amount of movements for most of the year. The civil operations take place on the western and central runway, with all the terminal facilities between them. Beyond, and to the east, is the military base, with its own runway. The RSAF base about half their C-130s here at any one time, with the rest at Riyadh's old airport. The two all-white VIP C-130Hs and various examples painted in Saudia colours are also often parked here, totalling about twenty, just visible in the heat haze, and otherwise inaccessible. Between the eastern and central runway is the King's 747 hangar, though there is rarely any activity to be seen around it.

The terminal and general aviation areas are situated between the western and centre runways, as is the impressive Hadj terminal. There is no viewing area in the Saudia terminal but, inside, one gets a good view of the airlines' aprons. All the Saudia aircraft are parked neatly in lines according to aircraft type and are served by (unpopular) mobile lounges from the terminal. Foreign airliners are parked along the western side and are served by mobile lounges from the 'Other Airlines' terminal, to the north. Photography is an extremely risky business and is probably best done from the aircraft as it taxis in or out.

The general aviation ramp is within walking distance from the Saudia terminal and is accessible to someone who has a plausible reason to get past the reception area at Arabasco (the Fixed Based Operator). Although most of these aircraft are regularly seen in Europe, they make an extremely impressive, and highly photogenic, sight in the constant sunshine and backed by the scenic hills in the distance. When Saudia's Special Flights fleet is taken into account, there can be few other places in the world where fifteen or more Gulfstreams are almost always present at any time. An interesting collection of local operators with hangars in this area are Petromin (with Twin Otters and F.27s) and Saudia Special Flights/Ministry of Resources (with Skyvans and JetRangers). At least forty executive jets could be expected here on a typical day.

Visiting airlines include all the major European carriers, several from Asia and a few from Africa. Many schedules are operated in the middle of the night and the more interesting aircraft to operate here are Ethiopian and Kuwaiti 727s, Yemenia and Gulf Air 737s, and PIA A300s.

RIYADH
RUH   OERK   King Khaled International   22m/34km N

The loop road from the city has the airline terminal, split into domestic and international, on one side and the VIP terminal on the other. In the middle is a mosque.

Foreign airlines are limited to a selection of major European national carriers. Gulf Air 737s do visit several days a week.

Viewing is good from the airside of the terminal, with the cargo ramp some distance to the left, and the general aviation terminal directly opposite, across one of the two runways. Unlike Jeddah, there are no hangars, and far less residents but the g.a. terminal is signposted clearly from the main airport highway. It is a long drive round the perimeter for perhaps twenty or so inmates, ranging in size from 727s to HS125s.

The large VIP terminal is impressive, to say the least. Its ramp hosts either nothing at all or, frequently, a fair number of Middle Eastern executive jets when there's a major ministerial gathering in town. Typical sightings include a Syrian Tu-134, Yemenia's VIP 727 and the usual array of Gulfstreams. The idea of going near this area with a camera would be ridiculous and using it even more so! Only small compensation, the Saudi TV channels diligently record all important arrivals and departures, so close-ups of various interesting executive aircraft appear almost nightly on the news.

Riyadh's old airport is now a military base, a couple of miles out of town. It is used by the RSAF and also very much by the USAF since the Gulf War. The views from the road are only distant and anyone who wants to find out more about the movements will check in at the Marriott Hotel. The upper floor rooms allow the E-3s, KC-10s and KC-135 movements to be seen, plus a selection of the local military aircraft in the circuit.

I = ITALY

ANCONA

AOI	LIPY	Falconara	6km N

Named after the village of Falconara, the airport has become strategically important since the United Nations became involved in Bosnia. The passenger terminal is on the west side of the field, and its observation balcony has been closed. UN movements apart, this is a sleepy airport, handling three or four flights a day to Milan and Rome. Avionova ATRs and Alitalia MD-82s, so there's precious little reason to make an effort. Summer charters tend to be more inbound than outbound, the local beaches offering the usual sun, sea and sand. As long as UN flights continue, there will be an interesting selection (though only occasionally) of carriers, including some from Russia. It would be reasonable to expect security arrangements have been stepped up a notch.

BERGAMO

BGY	LIME	Orio al Serio	3m/5km

The signposts give clear directions from the Milan to Verona Autostrada (A4). Scheduled passenger services amount to very little but cargo and charter activity are a little livelier. The car park, next to the passenger terminal, offers a good view of the cargo ramp though the aircraft can be parked head-on. On the far side of the field is the general aviation facility, with about thirty light aircraft to be seen from the fence.

BOLOGNA

BLQ	LIPE	Guglielmo Marconi	4m/6km NW (bus 20 minutes)

Better known locally as Borgo Panigale, Bologna offers the enthusiast everything that's required. The roof terrace in the brand new terminal is normally open from 08:00 to 21:00 and there is no glass to make life difficult for photographers. Even the car parking is free. There are two bus services from the railway station, No 91 being the cheaper (L1,300) and slower. The direct service costs L6,000 and operates every twenty minutes.

There is even better spotting by leaving the terminal and turning right at the traffic lights. Another right onto Via dell' Aeroporto leads past a wall behind which the army helicopters sit, and after another right turn, past the fire department with a couple of Agusta Bell 206s, to the Aeroclub, which also has a north-facing roof terrace, close to the taxiway. If this isn't enough, carry on west along Via della Fornace, which leads to Via della Salute. A side street leads to the perimeter, and even closer views of the taxiway, close to the holding point for Runway 12.

Alternatively, leave the terminal and head north on Via Triumvirato, where an embankment beside the river allows a view of the end of Runway 30. A series of left turns, into the community of Lippo, leads down the Via Surrogazione to the fence by the runway. The holes in the fence were apparently created by photographers but it would appear they used high explosives for the job. In other words, you can't go wrong. From here an Albanian A320 (for example) requires a 200 mm lens.

The airport is quite close to the city centre, on the far side of the Tangenziale Austostradale Kennedy (ring road). The passenger terminal is in the southwest corner of the field, close to the threshold of Runway 30. International flights are modest, but domestic traffic is good. In summer, the variety of foreign operators increases, and can include such visitors as Olympic 737s. The cargo apron, tucked away in the eastern corner of the apron normally receives only only a couple of regular visitors: a TNT BAe 146 which arrives at midnight and stays for a couple of hours, and another 146 which spends all day on the ramp during the week.

What used to be the flying club apron is now the West Apron used by commuter airliners, up to Fokker 100 size, everything else (146s upwards) uses the East Apron.

CATANIA
CTA   LICC   Fontana Rossa   4m/6km SSE

A modern airport, and one which may be of more interest to military fans. Less than a hundred miles north of Malta, affordable day return services allow seven hours ashore. This may be of interest to anyone who has negotiated a visit to Sigonella. To fill in the rest of the day, the No.24 bus runs regularly between the town and the airport. The large balcony allows views of only half of the two ramps, for scheduled services and general aviation. Opposite is the military base, with several helicopters and some CL-215s. As there is only the occasional Alitalia or Air Malta arrival, plus infrequent charters, it may be tempting to take a hike in search of the two withdrawn Trackers. The result should be a polite warning from a guard against such an activity.

FLORENCE
FLR   LIRQ   Peretola/Amerigo Vespucci   3m/5km

The best place for photos is by the fence, where the sun is at its best until about 15:00. Since this also coincides with most of the action, this can't be bad. The majority of the movements are on the small side, which means they can be very attractive subjects. Carriers such as Avianova, Air Dolomiti, Eurowings and Meridiana are all regular visitors and, with BAe146s being considered large, photographers can add some excellent portraits to their collection. There aren't many places in Europe where it's possible to get so close to these Dash 8s, ATRs and Do228s. Meridiana have a maintenance base here.

GENOA
GOA   LIMJ   Sestri/Cristoforo Columbo   4m/6km W

The coastline on the Gulf of Genoa slopes steeply to the sea, so this airport is packed very tightly into its space. From town, SS1 is the easiest road to take, but the Autostrada to Savona (A10) has an exit for the airport. The modern passenger terminal features a lot of glass and bright red steel. The single runway, 11/29, is built on reclaimed land in the bay so that movements cause the least noise nuisance to the local population, many of whom live very near.

    The observation area is on the upper level, next to the restaurant and bar. The whole area is behind glass and every movement on the runway can be seen. Behind the terminal is the aero club, with the general aviation and Piaggio plant next to it. Because most of the scheduled movements are operated by Alitalia, it is Piaggio which often provides the most interest. Because of the sun, afternoons are best for photographs, and it's worth remembering that the air jetties are usually only occupied by jet traffic. ATRs and Saab 340s need long lenses, and should be caught while on the move. It isn't always easy.

MILAN
LIN   LIML   Linate   6m/9km E

When Linate is busy, it is very busy. During the week, there can be a movement every two minutes, but it would be foolish to arrive after lunch and expect the pace to be brisk. Early mornings are best. The viewing gallery has been closed for some years, but none of the locals use the terminal area anyway. Apart from the predictable quantity of Alitalia movements, there is variety, provided by Meridiana and an increasing amount of third-level flights. Because the city centre is so close, business traffic is frequent, with several biz-jets being based, or operating from, the airport.

    Movements can still be witnessed from Canzo cemetery but the fence has been repaired. The holes in the wire mesh are now very small and will remain so for a few months until the regular visitors change the situation. Italian photographers have a way of winning their battles with fence-builders, but this one might take some time! From the terminal, a short way along Viale Forlanini is a turn to the right, to Rivolta, which leads to the Idroscalo. This artificial lake was once used as a seaplane base but now forms part of a public park. Keeping the Idroscalo on your right means following the sign for Idrascalo Est, then Crema. Follow the small blue direction signs for Canzo, travelling parallel to the perimeter fence. A small square leads to the cemetery, the fence, and a fine close-up view of the taxiway. On the far side is the town of Linate. With sun behind, it's best for the photographer in the mornings, when traffic is busier.

As the sun moves round, the photographer can do the same. A footpath follows the fence to the threshold of Runway 36R and, after a short walk along the road there is another footpath heading back north. The runway is now seen from the western side. By heading north into Linate, it's only a short distance to the general aviation area on the west side of the field. Whilst there is usually a lot of interesting aircraft, there are no places around the g.a.terminal (ATA) from which to see them. Runway 36L is used only by light aircraft, due to its length. Traffic using this is best seen from Viale Forlanini, but it means missing more exciting movements on the other side.

This information was accurate for 1997 but political moves are afoot for 1998. It is quite possible that much of Liante's more profitable services (the ones with the most passengers) will be transferred to Malpensa. This is not a prediction, because predictions don't always come true.

The general aviation field, BRESSO, is hemmed in by housing, and its single runway, again north/south, sees very few movements. The hangars and apron are on the western side, but there is little to see.

MILAN
MXP   LIMC   Malpensa   29m/47km NW

A long way out of the city, on Autostrada A7, Malpensa handles the larger movements, but is much less busy than Linate. For this reason, local knowledge makes use of the perimeter road essential for a short time. It passes commendably close to the hold for Runway 35R, with the opportunity to enjoy close encounters with a range of Alitalia movements, including the wide-bodies, mostly before lunchtime. Occasional tourist charter flights are operated, and the summer season is supplemented by a good variety of ski charters in winter. Interest rapidly turns to Linate, as it's busier and normally handles a wider variety.

Worth watching out for are military cargo flights which feature C-130s of many European air forces and, until sanctions, the odd Iraqi Il-76, the reason for their presence being the Agusta/SIAI production facility.

NAPLES
NAP   LIRN   Capodichino   4m/6km NE (bus 25 minutes)

A regular bus service is operated to the airport from the city centre. It leaves from the railway station and the Piazza Garibaldi. The passenger terminal has a glazed spectator's gallery. From it can be seen everything that moves. The majority of scheduled traffic is operated by Alitalia and ATI but there are some regional carriers to add a little spice. The far side of the field is reserved for non-civilian use. The US Navy has its own ramp, as do the police helicopters and the Italian Air Force, whose G222s are extremely difficult to identify, due to the distance and the heat haze.

PISA
PSA   LIRP   Galileo Galilei   2m/3km NW (train 5 minutes)

Pisa is an hour by train from Florence. Competition is fierce between the airports of Pisa and Florence to develop international services to Tuscany. The runway is used primarily by the Italian Air Force's San Giusto base, with plenty of G222s in evidence. There is a C-119 on the gate. Though its identity wasn't confirmed in the report, it could be MM61922/SM-26 which first saw service with Linee Aeree Italiane as I-LADY.

ROME
CIA   LIRA   Ciampino   10m/16km SE

Located in the city's southeastern suburbs, Ciampino has a large general aviation facility, a small terminal for inclusive tour charters, and a military base featuring VIP executive aircraft. There are different vantage points at the perimeter, one being in Ciampino itself, on the eastern side of the runway, remote from the terminal. The road to Ciampino passes round the northern edge of the field, and photos of landing aircraft are possible.

Whilst there is an extremely good selection of interesting types and operators to be logged, including civil biz-jets in number, photographers can expect frustration. No attempts should be made to take photos from the terminal area, inside or outside the building. Arrest is very likely, due to the security measures which result from the VIP movements. Any knowledge of Italy's turbulent politics, and massive corruption, means that precautions must be seen to be strict.

ROME
FCO   LIRF   Fiumicino   22m/34km SW   (train 40 minutes)

Also known by its official name of Leonardo da Vinci, the roof terrace extends across the front of both terminals and along the top of the linking pier, but it was closed permanently many years ago.

The international terminal allows no views at all, and the domestic terminal is only marginally better. The occasional tantalising glimpses through ground floor windows are supplemented by a slightly better view from the two first floor restaurants . . . but beware prices which are treble those in what is already an expensive city.

Much of Italy's domestic fleets can be seen, particularly in the evenings, in the company of the majority of Alitalia's European operations airliners, while some of the movements taxiing to/from the international terminal pass within range.

At various points outside the two terminals, there are more glimpses of aircraft, the upper level road overlooking the cargo apron. Other aircraft are visible from the road which passes Alitalia's maintenance area but not adequately so, from a photographer's point of view.

The airport is close to the coast, but there is a road between the sea and the perimeter. Signposted to Focene, it runs alongside 16R/34L where there is parking and an excellent view. To see most of the movements, it is best to settle close to the intersection between this runway and the threshold of 07, which heads away from the fence. A right turn at the end of the runway is marked 'Fregene'. A close-up view of aircraft at the hold for 16R is at its best in the early morning. As the sun moves round, photographers experience a range of problems. Beyond a bend in this road, where it heads north again, is a turning to the right. At the end of it is Runway 16L/34R and the holding point for Runway 25. A footpath across open ground leads there, though the aspect is better for spotters than photographers.

TURIN
TRN   LIMF   Caselle   10m/16km NW

Also known as Citta di Torino, the layout is similar to Bologna, with the passenger terminal in the southwest corner of the field and the single runway, 18/36. However there is far more activity along the western side of the field. Alitalia Cargo 747s are a regular sight, most of which are used to ferry Cadillac bodies to Detroit. Alenia (formerly Aeritalia) has a production plant where work is carried out on the AMX and Tornado. It was here that Italian F-104s were assembled.

Hangars contain an interesting assortment. Turin is famous all over the world for being the home of FIAT, so their fleet of biz-jets is based here. In an adjacent hangar are Euro-Fly's biz-jets, plus a few small helicopters and other aircraft. Euro-Fly's DC-9s are rarely seen here, as they normally operate from Malpensa or Bergamo.

Traffic is increasing, and there are places around the perimeter from where it can be seen at

86

close quarters. In the mornings, when things are quite brisk, it's best to leave the terminal area and make left turns, past Caselle cemetery and the Alenia plant, in the direction of Malanghero. Before reaching the village, a playing field with a football pitch is seen on the left. The footpath goes past the far side to the perimeter.

In the afternoon, coming out of the terminal area, take a right turn for San Maurizio. On the edge of town is a right turn at the ERG filling station. This leads to the airport perimeter, with a close view of the taxiway and, just beyond, the runway.

VENICE
VCE   LIPZ   Tessera   8m/13km NW (boat 20 minutes)

Even the most hardened enthusiast will make the airport only a secondary reason for a visit to Venice, such is the nature of the city, steeped in history and unique beauty. The most unusual feature at Tessera (or Marco Polo) is the boat service linking it with the city and Lido. The journey across the lagoon is the quickest way, and definitely the most scenic.

The airport follows the common Italian layout, with its terminal area at one end of the runway, in this case aligned 04/22. The passenger terminal has the bus station and harbour to its right, seen from the landside, and a terrace area to the left, where the best view is found. The passenger terminal occupies what was the car park area immediately in front of the old terminal.

The scheduled traffic includes Alitalia, Meridiana and Air Littoral, and these are complemented by a steady charter programme in the summer. A series of right turns from the terminal leads to the general aviation apron or, alternatively, a drive to the cargo area ensures that anything present can be seen with the bonus of being able to log all the landing aircraft.

VERONA
VRN   LIPX   Villafranca Veronese   7m/12km SW

Anyone touring Italy by road might consider a stop at Verona, as it is at the intersection of two major highways: Milan to Venice and Modena to Innsbruck. The civil scene is decidedly quiet for much of the day, with a handful of mostly Meridiana flights, though there are occasional visits by British Airways, Air France, Air Dolomiti and Lufthansa.

The passenger terminal does have an observation gallery but the glass is tinted. Photographers may therefore prefer to walk half a mile or so, parallel to the runway, where the view and the sunshine are at their best all day. The military presence means that caution really must be exercised.

Boscomantico is a separate military base, very close to town and looking unchanged since World War II. It's used by a flying club and comes in handy, occasionally, if general aviation has to divert from Villafranca.

JA = JAPAN
FUKUOKA
FUK   RJFF   Itazuke   6m/10km E

The southernmost main island of Japan is Kyushu, linked by both a causeway and Shinkansen (bullet train) to cities on Honshu. Fukuoka is a major city, with its own international airport. Apart from the regular wide-body visitors, like those of ANA and JAL, there are plenty of other movements which are of interest. They range from Japan Air Charter DC-10s to Nagasaki Koku Islanders. Most of the surrounding Pacific Rim countries operate wide-body services to Fukuoka.

The passenger terminal features an observation facility on level four. From it, all movements on Runway 16/34 are visible, the threshold of 16 being quite close. However, photographers will not be thrilled to read that the deck is fronted by an acrylic screen, which makes photos of any quality almost impossible to take.

KAGOSHIMA
KOJ   RJFK   18m/29km S

Whilst essentially a regional airport, it does handle some international flights. The vast majority are domestic though, in Japan, this represents an extremely interesting array. Access to the substantial roof terrace necessitates a small admission charge. Traffic is not brisk but each movement would be regarded by most to be of interest. During the course of the average afternoon, for example, all principle Japanese carriers are seen. A couple of dozen Japanese airliners in the space of two hours or so is probably adequate reward for the trip, but it must be remembered these include the complete range, from ANA 747s to a dozen or so YS-11s.

Add a Korean Air 727 and a Dragonair 737, and the fact that they can all be adequately photographed with, at most, a 135mm lens and Kagoshima becomes a significant airport. The most basic photographic equipment will achieve results for aircraft on the apron and those on the runway are within reach of the average telephoto lens. To ensure that the leisurely pace doesn't get too tedious, the terrace has vending facilities. The Maritime Safety Agency maintains a couple of King Air 200s here, and other light aircraft can be seen. A short walk from the terminal past the apron leads to some hangars where the photos can be taken.

KUMAMOTO
KMJ   RJFT   5m/8km E

Kumamoto has a deck and plenty to see from it. In return for a 50 Yen admission charge to the roof deck, the excellent view features mainly wide bodies. The choice of airlines and number of movements may be limited, relatively speaking, but all the domestic airlines are to be seen, including a number of local ANA YS-11s.

Although Kumamoto is not widely known in Europe, it is an expanding gateway to Japan, but only Korean Air calls regularly at present. Other foreign carriers are likely to be attracted here, to ensure that it can be regarded as a truly international airport. As a bonus, general aviation is also to be seen, with a dozen or so light aircraft on the apron, to the left of the domestic terminal.

MIYAZAKI
KMI   RJFM   2m/3km S (bus 10 minutes)

One of Kyushu's smaller airports, Miyazaki is on the east coast of the island, though arrival here leaves no doubt that plans are afoot. The ultra-modern terminal was opened in March 1990 and, unlike its counterparts in almost every other country, here is a new airport terminal with ideal facilities for the enthusiast.

The very reasonable admission charge to the first class observation deck allows easy photography of both the apron and movements on the runway. To be realistic, traffic is limited though, once again, wide body aircraft are featured. The opportunity to take perfect photos of ANA 767s and YS-11s sounds wonderful from a few thousand miles away. The reality, it has to be admitted, is perhaps not quite so exciting.

Variety is provided by the occasional Korean Air flight from Seoul, together with some general aviation movements: the helicopters which call in for refuelling include Maritime Safety Agency Bell 212s, and the circuit usually features one or two training Bonanzas.

NAGOYA
NGO   RJNN   Komaki   12m/19km N (bus 35 minutes)

Nagoya is Japan's third largest city so it generates a fair amount of airline traffic. From the railway station, there is a bus service which costs about 850 Yen each way. As expected, when you get there, the observation deck is first class, but do note the rather restricted open hours, by

Japanese standards - 10:00 and 18:00. There's a good view over the entire airfield though there is an admission fee of 150 Yen (about £1.50). At the entrance to the deck, on the roof of the domestic terminal, is a small museum display . . . nothing special but nice to see but you have to pay to get in.

JAL 767s and JAS DC-9-40s are the order of the day, with a few Nippon Airlines Fokker 50s, but the occasional Korean and China Eastern Airbus add some variety, as do the Air Micronesia 727s. Runway 34 sees most use, and its threshold is only about ten minutes' walk from the terminal. Photographers are strongly recommended to take the trip, as the light conditions are almost perfect.

Whilst traffic can be described as moderate at best, there are normally nine or ten Self-Defense Force C-130s to be seen opposite the terminal. Mitsubishi have a maintenance facility for military aircraft, as a bonus. A stay in Nagoya does not mean spending a fortune. This isn't Tokyo, and there is a good selection of inexpensive hotels around the station area in town.

OKINAWA

| OKA | ROAH | Naha | 2m/3km SW |

Two and a half hours' flying time southwest of the main islands which make up Japan are the Ryukyu Islands, the biggest of which is Okinawa. Naha, at the southern tip, is the biggest city. Whilst the airport is very much regional, the majority of its scheduled movements comprise JAL and ANA wide-bodies, the various Japan Transocean aircraft for which Okinawa is the main hub, plus a few international flights, such as Northwest 747s, Continental 727s and China Airlines 737s. In other words, Okinawa offers pretty much the same fare as can be seen at Tokyo or Osaka, apart from Ryukyu Commuter Islanders and Twin Otters. The cheapest way to visit is by means of a stopover on a Taipei-Okinawa-Japan ticket.

The new domestic terminal is operational and its observation deck (excellent as usual) is open between 08:00 and 22:00. The only drawback might be that Japan Transocean continue to use the old terminal.

OSAKA

| KIX | | Kansai International | 18m/30km SW (bus 60min train 25min) |

It took two mountains to build the island on which this airport stands. It cost something in the region of fifteen billion dollars to build. That money has to be repaid and airport tax is slightly on the high side. Stick a piece of plastic in a machine, pay it, and forget about it until the monthly payment slip arrives. A cup of coffee doesn't cost £5 - it actually costs £1.90, which isn't cheap, and a hot dog can set you back £2.20. So what if a burger and fries cost £5?

Kansai is the sort of place where normal standards are put aside. The terminal is something special. Instead of paying the taxi fare (£120 one way!) into Osaka, take a bus for £8.20. The Nankai Railways dark blue trains are a problem, if you are a nervous woman. At first glance, it appears they are called Rapists, but closer inspection reveals the word is actually Rapi:t.

If you like modern architecture, you'll love Kansai. A giant wing of a roof, with steel tubes, cables and huge nuts and bolts all over the place. There is more than enough glass to ensure the place feels light. Being inside Kansai is at least as good as travelling and, in many cases, better.

New airports usually mean bad news for the spotter, but not so in Japan. At one end of the airport complex is a purpose-built observation hall, open between 10:00 and 21:00. It's a short ride from either the Airport Hotel or the international arrivals area in a dark blue coach. The bus journey costs 800 Yen but the ticket includes admission and the return journey. The best way to find the bus stop is on the free Terminal Guide brochure. Leave the passenger terminal on level 1F, preferably by door F at the far end. To the left are the "group bus" stands, two of which are reserved for the observation hall buses.

Before leaving the passenger terminal, it might be worth a visit to the basement level, B1, where the convenience store is to be found. Snacks and cans aren't cheap here but they're cheaper than any of the alternatives.

The observation hall is in a five storey building, the top floor of which is completely open giving a view of the entire airfield and, on the floor below is a McDonalds-type fast food restaurant. It's best to be extremely hungry before going there, so that the prices don't hurt so much. All movements can be seen from the deck, though photography is only at its best in the mornings. Prevailing winds are also important, because not all runway movements are easily photographed.

To reach Osaka's other airport, Itami, the bus leaves from Stop No.8 on level 1F (outside door BC). Journey time is about an hour, depending on traffic, and the fare is 1800 Yen (about £10). Alternative transport into town, and several other nearby towns, is offered by high speed catamaran, which leaves from the airport's ferry terminal. Journey time is less than forty minutes. A regular jet-foil service also operates to Kobe, which takes only half an hour.

OSAKA
OSA   RJOO   Itami   10m/16km W

As Kansai opened, the international terminal at Itami was closed, and all flights transferred. The future of domestic movements through Itami is a matter for speculation, as all flights may one day be moved to the new airport. Land suitable for building is expensive in Japan, hence the need to move mountains into the bay. Flights over populated areas cause much local opposition, so Kansai is the logical airport for the future.

The observation deck is on the roof of the domestic (effectively the only) terminal, and offers views of all movements, between 07:00 and 21:00. Centrally located on the first floor (that immediately above the airline check in desks) is a staircase which leads to a turnstile. Pay the 50 Yen and have a nice day. For closer views of the JAS YS-11s and SF340s, it's worth investigating the departures area, as there are numerous windows which allow eye level photos, rather than looking down from the roof.

A day's spotting is still quite lively. General aviation is modest, as befits a modern airport. The occasional rotary movement by one of the residents can be seen, though somewhat remote from the deck. Anyone in search of closer encounters must walk past the cargo sheds for a view of the hangars. A left turn outside the terminal leads to several hangars at the corner of the field and, beyond, this walk ends at the access point to the fuel farm, served by many tankers during the day. From here, the end of the runway is close enough for the photographer in need of an alternative vantage point. While much has been said about the cost of almost anything in Japan, things at Itami are slightly more affordable. Many of the hotels, which are only a short walk from the airport, now charge about £70 a night. The inexperienced traveller is warned about the alternative type of accommodation: these are called "love hotels", where rooms are normally paid for by the hour. The decor is usually the quickest, and least embarrassing, way of telling the difference. If it's pink and fluffy, it might not be what you want.

TOKYO
RJTF   Chofu   18m/30km SW

This is Tokyo's executive airport, handling much of the air taxi and other business flights. Even the most ardent airliner fan will probably make the (difficult) journey to take a few photos of the various types to be seen here. The hundred or so light aircraft also feature a handful of helicopters and Saturday is probably the best day for a visit when, as befits a businessman's airfield, not much flying takes place.

Before leaving the hotel, it is wise to ask someone to write in Japanese characters 'Chofu Airport' as it will come in handy later. The underground train goes to Shinjuku and the Keisei private railway operates a service to Chofu. Normally, the booking clerk will be English-speaking but not so the taxi driver on your arrival. Here, the piece of paper will be of use and the fare should be about 800 Yen (£3). The journey takes ten minutes, and a request at the control tower for ramp access may result in an interrogation session. The permission which should follow the questions is best augmented by requests at the flying clubs around the apron. The Japanese are a very polite nation.

90

TOKYO
HND   RJTT   Haneda International   12m/19km S (train 20 minutes)

From Tokyo's main station, local trains take the traveller to Hamamatsu-cho and, from here, a monorail link goes to Haneda, on Tokyo Bay. The trip takes about half an hour and costs 480 Yen (less than £2), a small price to pay for getting to one of the more interesting airports in Asia, especially as the facilities for the enthusiast are of a high quality - six floors up is high enough. A complete new terminal, on the far side, is called "The Big Bird" and it's rather like an expensive shopping mall with an airport tacked on. The (free) observation deck sits on the terminal's top level, 6F, facing southwest. This means that top-quality photos are best taken before 11:00. Most of them, too, in all probability. When the airport opens (the deck, believe it or not, opens earlier!) at 06:30, the pace hots up quickly. Fifty or so departures before 08:00 is about standard for the average day and not all of them come back. A red eye special, in other words, for the spotter.
    Signs for the deck take some finding, especially first thing in the morning. From the All Nippon check-in desks, the Galleria (the expensive shopping mall) can be seen. Escalators and elevators go to Level 5, and stairs go to the top.
    The view is obstructed only by railings which don't seriously hamper photography. Cameras can be placed on top of the fence, or lenses can be placed between the polesso that they don't intrude. There are toilet, drinks machines and two separate cafeterias close by. Expect the deck to be crowded, especially on holidays. It's relatively quiet by 22:00 when it closes.
    All aircraft movements can be seen but anything by the old terminal can be a bit difficult to identify. China Airlines, the sole user of the old terminal, tend to use the distant Runway 04 for departures, for their three flights a day. It would appear that, already, the new terminal is lacking in sufficient stands. This means that many of the YS-11s, 737s and A320s park some way from the terminal, making photography almost impossible. The road to the new terminal passes under the runways and, at either side of the field are chain link fences. They are effective in keeping out intruders without making photography difficult. In te mornings, it's worth standing near the maintenance base and facing west. After lunch, try the other side, facing east.
    Traffic is domestic, except for China Airlines who operate one or two 747s a day. Japan Air System and All Nippon fleets dominate, but JAL's presence features aircraft unlikely to be seen in Europe: 747SRs and 767s as well as DC-10s. Most enthusiasts probably associate Haneda with YS-11s, though developments changed the situation for the worse.
    To get the most from Haneda, an early start is recommended. The new terminal deck doesn't open until 10:00, which is a pity, given the angle of the sun by that time. Counting up, a typical midweek day should yield the following: JAL - 15 747s, 5 DC-10s and 5 767s; JAS - 20 A300s, 15 MD80/87s and 3 YS11s; ANA - 15 747s, 30 767s, 5 737s 5 A320s and 2 YS-11s, making a total of over one hundred aircraft operated by the main carriers. Taking into consideration that there are several other operators, a full day at Haneda is indeed a full day!

TOKYO
NRT   RJAA   New Tokyo International   40m/64km E (train 55 minutes)

Japanese farmers continue to make life difficult at Narita. One tiny plot of land, close to the airport is owned by about four hundred farmers, making its aquisition virtually impossible. This doesn't help get the new runway built, which is exactly the farmers' intention. When the Japanese don't like what's going on they do something more positive than digging holes, getting dirty, and calling themselves Swampy. Terminal 2 is open. It cost $1.5 billion, and has observation decks at both ends of level 4, but close-wire fences make photographs impossible. Airlines using the new terminal are mostly JAL, JAS and ANA, with occasional visits by the likes of KLM, Aeroflot, Garuda and Thai. The departures area inside the new terminal can become extremely congested. A twenty minute queue is not unusual, after which access to the departure areas allows the chance to take photos and a clear sight of other parts of the airport. A shuttle train operates to the satellite, which contains gates C81 to D99.
    Until the new runway is opened, all movements to Terminal 2 are visible from the observation

deck on Terminal 1. Departures can be airborne before they pass which make photos tricky.

For the present, then, Terminal 1 is still the place to go, though frequent shuttle buses operate between the two arrivals levels. Below the main observation deck, there are windows with views of the aprons, so most of the action can be seen, and photographed, with some ease. The advantage of the Terminal 1 deck is that special holes have been provided, at about waist height, so that cameras can be used. Reports dated 1997 suggest that building work at Terminal has been making things difficult . . . but not impossible.

Being the country's main international gateway, the range of aircraft visiting is restricted largely to major operators, with a surprisingly large amount of Northwest Airlines activity. Most of the activity takes place in the afternoons and, disappointingly, evenings, although the Chinese movements in daylight hours offer ever-increasing variety. The Japan Asia and JAL wide body fleets operate from Narita, and the occasional Qantas 767 visits in the evening. Of the wide-bodies from other parts of the Far East, Korean MD-11s are probably most interesting, though Continental 727s are regular movements.

At the far (southern) end of the field are the large maintenance facilities of All Nippon and JAL. Located in this area is an aeronautical museum, open between 10:00 and 17:00. Admission is Y500 and among the smaller aircraft are a Puma and a YS11. The perimeter fence is worth detailed exploration, as the authorities have realised that photographers really do want to poke their lenses through the fence. Rather than allow acts of vandalism to take place, these holes are now formed properly and provided by the airport management for the job.

Ground transportation between the airport and the city is, for most folk, a choice between the cheaper On Liner bus, which takes two hours, the so-called Airport Limousine to/from Hakozaki-cho Air Terminal or the Japan Railways Narita Express (N'EX) for Y2900. Travel between Narita and Haneda is most straight-forward by taking the Limousine Bus.

A lot is said about Japan being expensive. Once outside Tokyo, it's no more expensive than most of Europe. A Japan Railpass, giving two weeks of unlimited travel for about £250, is good value for the tourist, and is valid on the Narita Express. In most cities, there are hotels downtown, used by businessmen, which cost around £40 a night - maybe £60 in Tokyo. Coke is sold in vending machines everywhere for the equivalent of 60 pence. A Big Mac meal costs about £3.50, about the same as "proper" Oriental food - stir fry and noodles, that sort of stuff.

JY = JORDAN

AMMAN
AMM   OJAI   Queen Alia International/QAIA   20m/32km S (bus 30 minutes)

An efficient airport for the traveller but not overwhelming for enthusiasts, the observation deck has been closed and only a mediocre view of the ramp is possible through the windows of the upper (landside) restaurant/bar in each terminal. There are runways on either side of the approach road and the two crescent-shaped terminals are for Royal Jordanair, on one side, and foreign airlines on the other. Also between the runways are the cargo terminal and Alia's maintenance base, though both are difficult to see from inside the terminal. Good landing shots, with a 200mm length zoom lens, can be taken from the airport approach road but only with caution.

Since Royal Jordanian developed a hub-and-spoke operation, several arrivals in the middle of the morning from points in the Middle East are followed by departures for Europe/USA shortly afterwards, with virtually nothing until the whole procedure follows in reverse in the evening. Apart from Royal Jordanian A310s, Saudia A300s and a few Gulf Air/Egyptair 737s, there is little here to stimulate the interest of the average enthusiast.

The proximity of the old MARKA airport to the city and the limited space were prime reasons to build QAIA. This is, however, a busy little airport with most of the activity being provided by Royal Jordanian Air Force C-130s and CASA 212s, all of which are resident. The government's aircraft are based here, plus the Gulfstreams and TriStar. Other aircraft to be found here include the Flight Academy Bulldogs and the Falcons' Pitts Specials, with the odd biz-jet and USAF Starlifter visiting. There are limited views from the perimeter but, once again, photography is not recommended.

LN = NORWAY

BERGEN
BGO   ENBR   Flesland   12m/19km S (bus 40 minutes)

A circular terminal has been constructed, complete with air bridges, close to the old terminal. The Scandinavian climate doesn't justify external observation decks but the military presence, with F-5s and F-16s, is such that watching aircraft at Bergen isn't actively encouraged, anyway.

The merger between Lufttransport and Helikopter Service had little effect on the operation of Super Pumas from Bergen. Their hangar is visible from the old terminal, whilst that of Norving is tucked away, out of sight. Airline operations are slow but the ramp can contain a Wideroes Dash 7, a Norving Dornier and a Norskair Brasilia, all at the same time!

BODO
BOO   ENBO   1m/1.5km SW

The uninviting and implacable wall which confronts the landside visitor is not a spotter-deterrant. On the other side of the road are the comfortable suburbs of the quiet town, and the screening deflects much of the noise. Norway, like the rest of Scandinavia, is extremely environment-conscious. Traffic is modest but interesting. Domestic services are mostly operated by propellor-driven aircraft, with only occasional 737s and MD-87s of Braathens and SAS to be seen. The semi-circular passenger terminal is modern, and even features air jetties. The cold winter is long, and passengers must be sheltered from the elements. Viewing is possible from the upper level gallery but most of what can be seen is the roof below! Photographers will need a long focus lens to capture one of the many Dash Sevens taxiing. Once on its stand, it is almost hidden from view.

The lack of flat ground on Norway's coasts means that maximum use is made of runways. This usually means sharing with a military base. Movements by helicopters and Twin Otters are rare but the Skv 331 F-16s make use of the runway for crew training and other exercises.

OSLO
FBU   ENFB   Fornebu   5m/8km SW (bus 20 minutes)

Only ten minutes' drive from the city centre along the E18, Drammensveien, the airport is on the left, on a peninsula between the city and the fjord. The approach road, Snaroyveien, passes the Park Royal Hotel, and the general aviation facility is reached by making a right turn here. The scheduled airlines terminal is straight on, at the far side of Runway 06/24. Next to the cafe is the entrance to the spectator's terrace (believed to be closed). The view from the windows is adequate and seats are provided so that, on the odd day when the weather isn't kind, it's still possible to watch the movements. The airlines using this terminal are European, and all operations, including those of SAS, are limited by the lengths of the two runways.

Anyone with a particular interest in the SAS fleet might have to stay here for a few days. It's the best place for clearing up Norlink Fokker 50s and those elusive domestic DC-9s and MD-82s.

Modernisation has been a major project, and one of the few which has made life easier for the photographer. The new multi-storey car park brings aircraft using Runways 06 and 24 comfortably within range of a 200mm zoom lens. Because the city is so close, 06 is preferred for landings and 24 for departures. The background, being densely forested hills, makes the most ordinary aircraft, such as SAS DC-9s, at Fornebu look good.

As an alternative, the fence next to the fire station can be good but the view is sometimes blocked by the parked snow-moving equipment. The sun is at its best after 17:00 but, in summer, good quality photos are possible until very late in the evening.

The general aviation terminal has its own ramp, where executive movements can be seen. To the right of this small terminal are the hangars of Braathens and Fred Olsen and, between them, the Oslo Aero Club overlooks most of the apron and Runway 01/19. For light aircraft, Fornebu is rewarding, even moreso in summer when the floatplanes are parked at the water's edge, but anyone with an interest in airliners will prefer the passenger terminal area. Movements worth bearing in mind are those of Air Stord, Teddy Air, Braathens, Danish visitors Muk Air and Sun-Air, the occasional Premiair charter and Wideroes Dash 8s, whose movements are not uncommon here. Much of what now happens at Fornebu is likely to be overtaken by events at . . .

OSLO
GEN   ENGM   Gardemoen   32m/50km NE

Quite some distance out of the city, this airport has a runway long enough to take wide-body movements, so it is the capital city's transatlantic gateway. The other civilian movements are charter flights, dominated by Braathens and Premiair, though there are based Air Force C-130s and Falcons as some compensation. The Norsk Teknisk Museum is dedicated to military history, although outside is Caravelle LN-KLH (c/n 3), painted in SAS colours.

Things are now changing, and in a very big way. Runway 01/19 becomes 01L/19R and between it and its new parallel neighbour is what amounts to a brand new airport. Apart from the architecture, which is quite individual, it all looks rather familiar. Like Singapore, Munich, Chep Lap Kok (and a few others) in fact. Brand new facilities were, in the second half of 1997, nearing fruition and it won't be too long before airlines are encouraged to move their operations to where the landing fees will recoup the investment costs.

STAVANGER
SVG   ENZV   Sola   9m/15km SW (bus 30 minutes)

The new terminal is even further from the runway than its predecessor, though it may contain similar facilities for seeing movements taxiing. The old terminal had a cafe with very adequate windows for this purpose. The far side of the runway is taken up by a military base of some significance, the F-5s being quite active, and can be seen on the runway. Also based here are Sea Kings and Lynxes but identifying any of these movements can be an extremely frustrating business. The pursuit of an interest in aviation is not an ideal pastime in Scandinavia, as the terminal facilities are designed to beat their winter climate. Any visitor engaged in watching aircraft will probably be in the country on business and the airport will be an item of interest on the trip.

LV = ARGENTINA

BUENOS AIRES
AEP   SABE   Aeroparque Jorge Newbery   5m/8km NE

This is Argentina's busiest airport, with over four hundred movements a day, and can be compared to New York La Guardia or Rio's Santos Dumont for its waterfront location, beside the Rio del Plata or River Plate. The important difference is that the perimeter is separated from the water by the Lugones Highway, which means that the entire airport is visible from one point or another, and there are even recommended observation points.

Facilities here are, by European standards, rather out of date and primitive. Seen from another perspective, Aeroparque has character. The single runway, 13/31, is shared by the commercial airport, the military air base (Base Aerea Militar) and a museum.

Commercial operations are handled in a complex of terminal buildings, linked by a covered walkway. Austral, Lapa and Dinar operate domestic flights, with Aerolineas Argentinas handling domestic and international flights with aircraft up to 757 size. A separate facility exists for cargo operations.

There are no special facilities as such for observation, and the roof terraces have been closed. Photographers should consider the restaurant in the Austral area, which allows a good view of the ramp and taxiway. Photographic opportunities are good, with quality shots being possible of most of the operations. What can't be seen close enough from the terminal will be better observed from the perimeter.

Access from the city centre by bus requires a short ride on either the No 33 or 56, from Retiro Railway station, some two miles to the south.

The roads surrounding the field are all close to the perimeter fance: Rafael Cantilo and Sarmiento Avenues are the links at each end, between la Pampa Street and Lugones Highway, and it is by making this circuit that almost everything to be found at Aeroparque can be seen. The northern end of the runway is close to the south side of Rafael Cantilo Avenue, and this is where the best ground level photos are to obtained.

The museum is worth a visit, since it houses such interesting pieces as a Viking and a Bristol Freighter among twenty or so other exhibits. It offers good views of the runway and taxiway and there are several grandstand type areas that provide the necessary height to allow photographers an unobsructed view over the fence. General aviation at Aeroparque, mostly biz-jets and larger twins, is concentrated on the opposite side of the runway from the terminals. Smaller aircraft use the nearby DON TURCUATO field, where up to three hundred can be seen without any trouble.

BUENOS AIRES
EZE   SAEZ   Ministre Pistarini   32m/50km SW (bus 45 minutes)

A much larger airport, reserved almost solely for international traffic, is the main gateway, known locally as Ezeiza. All Aerolineas Argentinas wide-body operations are to be seen here, in the company of almost all other flights from abroad. Excluded are Aerolineas Argentinas 727s, which operate a significant amount of international flights, and are the largest aircraft to be seen at Aeroparque. The blue bus service No 86, marked Fournier, serves the airport, but only if they are also marked 'Aeropuerto'.

The Aerolineas Argentinas terminal nestles between the other two, so the panoramic view from it is limited. To the left is Terminal 2 for international flights, and to the right is Terminal 1, for domestic. It doesn't take much imagination which is the better one to try. Aircraft on the cargo terminal ramp can be seen from the restaurant.

The gate guardian, seen from the approach road, is a C-47 in naval colours. The serial, reported as CTA-15, may be 5-T-15. The military base is at the north end of the field, beyond the Aerolineas Argentinas maintenance apron. Armada Argentina's transport wing is, by definition, purely military, but there are other semi-official operators which carry passengers to supplement the income and to help develop the country's economy in the regions. Many of the services are therefore scheduled to operate on a regular basis. To reach vantage points on the perimeter, a car is essential as distances are too great for walking.

CORDOBA
SACO COR   Pajas Biancas

Most of the traffic here comes from Buenos Airies and consists of Austral, Aerolineas, and Lapa, although Southern Winds, Alta and Andesmar have a small presence. The movement rate is slow with most taking place in the morning. The terminal offers views of the ramps and runways but faces east, making photography difficult during the busiest period of the day. General avaiation hangars are situated on either side of the terminal but seem to contain little of interest.

USHUAIA
USH SAWH

This one of the world's most remote destinations. Like many others in distant corners of the world, Tierra del Fuego is a remarkable place. The scenery is quite splendid but, with the stormy waters of Cape Horn close at hand, the weather can be unpleasant at times. With the Beagle Channel on the southern perimeter and mountainous scenery all around, photos at Ushuaia take on a magic all their own. Despite the naval air arm presence sharing the runway, it is a relaxed place and photos at the taxiway edge are easy to take. Aerolineas Argentinas 737s are the largest regular visitors and F.27s make one or two calls during the course of the average day.

LX = LUXEMBOURG
LUXEMBOURG
LUX   ELLX   Findel   3m/5km ENE (bus 20 minutes)

Findel's terminal has all the usual conveniences, including a roof observation deck. If this is not open, alternative views of the modest ramp can be had from the terrace at each side of the building. Indeed, for some photographers, the terraces may prove to be more suitable. Movements are decidedly slow, featuring the Luxair fleet, of course, occasional Icelandic 757s, and not much else.

Down Route de Treves is the old terminal building and the aero club hangar, situated on top of quite a steep bank, making it difficult to see any of the inmates. For anyone on foot, the long walk to this general aviation facility is hardly worth the effort, as any aircraft parked outside can be seen just as easily from the bus, which passes on its way between the city and the airport terminal. Without permission to have a look around, departure from Findel can be accompanied by some disappointment for lovers of smaller aircraft.

In the opposite direction, take a right at the motorway intersection (towards Trier) and watch out for an immediate exit to the new cargo centre. The turning might be posted to Sandweiler. It passes the end of Runway 24, at a higher level than the motorway, and is good for a view of almost anything that moves. If Runway 06 is in use, there are one or two vantage points beside the taxiway to the holding point. The best is an emergency access point, easily seen if you slow down and watch out for the sign for a Bank.

LY = LITHUANIA
VILNIUS
VNO   EYVI

Municipal buses, Nos 1 and 2, operate to the airport from the railway stations and city centre. On arrival at the passenger terminal, look for the information booth in the Arrivals hall and as for a copy of Vilnius in your Pocket. It's still early days, and Vilnius isn't Warsaw or Prague, so there may still be some official opposition to spotting around the perimeter or to photography. Official opposition doesn't necessarily mean it's illegal but differences of opinion are possible. Guess who will win, given that anyone in a uniform has had sixty years or so to get used to being obeyed.

The passenger terminal is new - functional, glossy and sterile, with large, tinted windows facing the apron. What you see is mostly Lithuanian Yak-42s and Tu-134s. This is a country that needs to get in touch with the rest of the world, which isn't the same as everyone else wanting to go there. Traffic is modest, and that's being polite. So there is plenty of time for someone with a car to explore the perimeter - but nort much point. Most of what can be seen in a day is probably sitting on the apron or on Lithuanian Airlines' maintenance ramp.

LZ = BULGARIA
BOURGAS
BOJ   LBBG   International   8m/13km NE (bus 20 minutes)

The passenger terminal is small, outdated and frequently overcrowded. It does, however, handle a good selection of mid-European carriers. As befits an old terminal, it has an observation deck on the roof and there can be much to see.

Naturally, the majority of movements are Balkan: An-12/24s and Il-18s supply prop power. A rather predictable procession of Tu-134/154s makes up the majority with some Yak-40s for variety. The political changes which have swept through Central Europe have not adversely affected old relationships, so visiting airlines will be dominated by Aeroflot, Malev and CSA for some time yet. Aeroflot visitors are mainly Tu-154s but An-12s are seen, and there can be as many as three Il-76s visiting per day. The local nature of Hemus Air operations means that their Yak-40s and Turbolets are rarely seen outside the country, though they are regular visitors to Bourgas. With beaches so close to the airport, it is possible to keep an eye on the traffic during the course of a holiday. Regular patrols are operated along the beach by various types of aircraft: the An-2s, Mi-8s and Ka-26s which are most frequently seen are based at the airport, on the far side of the field from the passenger terminal.

SOFIA
SOF   LBSF   International   6m/9km E (bus 20 minutes)

Organised package tours are probably the only way to visit Bulgaria, though they are very rare to Sofia. Enthusiasts tours are occasionally operated, and these undoubtedly allow much of the difficult paperwork to be sorted out by others, preferably beforehand. Hotels should be pre-booked but not pre-paid, as there can be severe complications if the money has not been received.

The No.84 bus leaves from the University, close to the city centre. The 0.30 lev fare is so cheap, it can barely be converted into most currencies. One of the sights en route is that of Il-18 LZ-BEV which is supposedly preserved in a residential area. Its state was so poor, by the end of 1991 that it may not exist for much longer.

The airport passenger terminal has an observation deck on the top floor but this is permanently closed. Other parts of the terminal offer only one alternative: the restaurant on the upper level of departures,which is inaccessible, except to passengers. To the left of the terminal, a wire fence separates the viewer from the VIP transport stands where interesting aircraft are normally parked. Inside the building, to the right, is a view of the main apron, at the side of the luggage deposit.

To the right of the terminal, a security gate at the end of the wall gives access to the facilities and, from this gate, aircraft parked in front of the hangars can be seen. The derelict remains of Il-18 LZ-BET are also visible, parked on the grass next to the taxiway. On the opposite side of the runway, effectively out of sight, are government aircraft. These include anything from An-2s and Mi-8s to Yak-40s and Tu-134s. The most interesting visitors, to western eyes, are almost certainly the Central European carriers and military movements. What is seriously lacking is a vantage point from which to see them.

VARNA
VAR   LBWN   International   5m/8km NW

Varna's place in the sun seemed assured, in more ways than one, ten years ago. With Black Sea resorts in summer and ski slopes in winter, Bulgaria made inroads into the tourist market but western tastes, it would seem, demanded something a little more sophisticated. The regular charter flights from all parts of Europe have shrunk back, and Varna now caters mostly for eastern Europeans.

The airport's passenger terminal is adequate for the purpose, and a small terrace overlooks the apron. Most of the movements in summer are charters, several of them by German airlines, plus a few scheduled services to nearby countries. The Bulgarian Navy has a small presence, mainly Mi-8s, but activity is rare.

N = UNITED STATES of AMERICA

This country occupies a significant amount of the book. To enable airports to be found with some ease, the entries have been placed according to their states, starting with Alaska and ending with Wyoming. The standard two-letter codes are used, so AK for Alaska means that it appears in front of AL for Alabama. Puerto Rico, whose aircraft use N registrations, appears at the end of the USA section. The alphabetical index, at the rear of the book, enables entries for airports to be found with ease.

ANCHORAGE AK
ANC   PANC   International   7m/11km SW

Alaska would rate as a large country if it were independent. Small communities are separated by bleak, though beautiful, scenery and roadbuilding is a difficult process under such climatic conditions. Since there are so many lakes throughout the state which can be used by floatplanes, roads are not essential for survival. They are needed for growth, of course.

Alaska is also one of the most misunderstood locations on earth as it is considered to be cold and remote. Anchorage is very close to the Pacific Ocean, so it does not suffer the climatic extremes associated with, say, Stockholm or Leningrad (both at similar latitude). It is no further north, in British terms, than the Shetland Isles but it does enjoy the benefits of a warm ocean current. In summer, the days are long and the temperatures very pleasant. The seeming remoteness arises mostly from the way we say a map of the world, with Alaska in the top left hand corner. Anchorage is actually about the same distance from Western Europe as Houston.

The enormous area which can loosely be termed Anchorage International Airport includes a number of features which would each offer very attractive prospects in their own right. The importance of the airport as an intercontinental staging post dwindled rapidly with the advent of 747-400s. The ability to fly non stop between Europe or America's East Coast and Eastern Asia has taken a fair slice out of Anchorage's economy. This is a shame. International movements still include a large quantity of cargo flights, and it will be some time before all these can operate non stop. The 747Fs of FedEx, UPS, Northwest and the Asian carriers grace the aprons as usual but the lunchtime rush, when up to two dozen Jumbos used to pass through, is over. What is left is still rewarding, especially since the movements are local, and therefore likely to be seen in normal circumstances nowhere else in the world. Two or three Asiana and Nippon Cargo 747s are par for the average day, plus ten or so FedEx flights, including MD-11s, DC-10s and Airbuses, with a couple of Korean and a Gemini. Not bad.

There are two main terminals at the the heart of the airport, for domestic and international traffic. Access is possible to the domestic building, though photography even through glass is often difficult. Some of the best vantage points are from lounge areas with glass on both sides, making bright reflections a major problem. Markair and Alaska Airlines, in that order, dominate the traffic, though Reeve Aleutian and ERA/Jet Alaska add variety.

Visible from the domestic terminal are, to the east, the various cargo aprons, each of which features some very interesting aircraft. On the opposite side of the field is the South Air Park, again with its own specialities. To the north, not visible from the centre of activity, are remote ramps used for parking some of the more exotic visitors. To the northeast, and almost to be considered as a separate airport, is the lakeside annex known as Lake Hood. A taxiway just north of the international ramp links this to the main field.

Between the two main terminals is an employees' car park which overlooks a large apron. Through the fence, photographs of the cargo 747s are taken, with completely uncluttered backgrounds. Taxiing jumbos also pass within range to and from the international terminal. Many pleasant lunchtimes can be spent here, often in the warm sunshine.

Without a car, the mile-long journey to the furthest apron needs time, especially with all the intermediate stops. A letter prior to a visit is normally met by appropriate enthusiasm. Reeve Aleutian's pioneering spirit is demonstrated by their downtown museum. Northern Air Cargo operate DC-6s, with the company's approach to business bringing back memories of how aviation used to be. An Argosy here, an Electra there: the aprons offer a string of interesting airliners. The various operators are Alaska Airlines, Reeve Aleutian, the FAA, Markair Cargo, Van Dusen FBO and Northern Air Cargo. Sadly, some of the museum-piece Packets associated with this area have been shipped away to more lucrative locations. Good quality food is to be found opposite the Delta/JAL etc cargo shed, at the Fly In Restaurant, similar in style to Denny's.

The drive round to South Air Park passes a C-123 on a pole, in front of Kulis ANG base. The C-130s on the ramp can be seen from the fence. The southern apron has operations at each side, many of the more interesting movements requiring an early start, if they are to be seen. On the eastern side of the ramp are the Era Aviation terminal, Alaska Helicopters and Air Logistics. The Era car park offers close views of the Convair and Twin Otter movements, though the helicopter fleets are generally based upstate, earning their keep. The most interesting operator on the other side of the ramp was Troy Air, with its small fleet. A casualty in 1989, Troy Air may have now disappeared without trace, but another casualty, the fire-blackened hulk of a 727 fuselage, was dumped here after an accident.

The current state of the TWA Starliner is unknown, so it may have been broken up. Its neighbour, in the training area, an ex-Reeve DC-6, was last known to be in an even worse state so this too might have gone. They are (probably were) only visible from the perimeter road, and access requires arrangement with the Airport Authority. From the main terminal area, travelling north, the road crosses the taxiway to Lake Hood on its way past the main Post Office. A C-119 and a couple of C-82 hulks occupy this corner, though the road offers views of other items of aviation history. The Cargomasters which are resident include one in airworthy condition. Its arrival on a runway is memorable!

The aprons further north have been developed and include a facility for UPS and Fed Ex, across the road from the Post Office. Beyond the new cargo ramp is an apron worth inspection, as it normally contains a couple of C-119s and a C-97. Postmark Drive, the public road which passes the aprons, ends at a T-junction. Two left turns in quick succession lead to a hill, ideal for taking photos of aircraft taxiing to the hold for Runway 14.

The road continues round the end of the runway and offers more elevated views on the other side. This is West Access Road, which leads to a right turn more or less opposite the end of Runway 6L. Look out for turnings, any of which could result in standing on banks, overlooking Runway 6R. In other words, if you want photos of aircraft on the runway, Anchorage offers plenty of alternatives.

Lake Hood, without a car, will occupy at least one full day. It is a mile long and almost half a mile wide at one point. With all the various jetties and docking areas, it has a very long coastline indeed. DHC Otters and Beavers abound, plus large numbers of Cessnas. Paint schemes tend to be as colourful as possible to attract custom and to aid visible location, if necessary. Salmon fishing from mid July is very big business, and movements are frequent. Without suggesting that aircraft are ever overloaded, some of them do labour to get off the lake!

Operators which come close to airline status at Lake Hood are Penair, with a servicing base in the southwest corner, and South Central Air, whose tiny freight shed is south of the taxiway link. Occasionally, the Islander can be seen scurrying across, and its irregular visits here represent the few opportunities to take its portrait.

On the southern edge of Lake Hood is the aviation museum, which pays homage to the part played by aircraft in developing Alaska. Opening times may not be regular, but a visit is recommended. Also close to the lake are the International Airport and Clarion Hotels, neither of which can be classed as inexpensive.

Accommodation is not to be treated lightly in these parts. Make reservations early and be prepared to say you're only staying one night. The cost could use up a week's allowance anywhere else. For $45, try the Midtown Lodge but don't expect en suite facilities. Access to an indoor toilet can be considered a luxury in Alaska.

ANCHORAGE AK
MRI   PAMR   Merrill Field   1/1.5km E

As befits a city on the edge of a vast and empty country, Anchorage has good air communications for light aircraft. The only significant operator at this field is Wilbur's, whose terminal supports the airline's activities at the main airport. Access by car, or foot, to the various ramps is easy. It should be noted that the Markair Express fleet undergoes servicing here, so a Twin Otter or Cessna Caravan may be seen. The small terminal next door to this maintenance hangar belongs to the optimistically-named Airlift Alaska whose Cessna Stationairs may perhaps prove too small for a real airlift. The An-2s are normally the largest residents. Nearby is the Red Ram Motel, cheap at $49 for a room.

ANCHORAGE AK
EDF   PAED   Elmendorf Air Force Base   8m/13km E

Elmendorf is a main diversion field for Anchorage when bad weather strikes. Anyone visiting Anchorage will be anxious to record as much of the aviation scene as possible, as frequent visits are few. Guided base tours are operated, normally from the Post Road gate. Post Road, from the city centre, passes through the evocative yards of the Alaska Railroad, beside the river. In July, many evenings are spent by local folk watching vast numbers of enormous salmon leaping on their way to their spawning grounds. Inside the base, the two flights of F-15s occupy separate ramps and hangars. A tour normally includes the C-130s and helicopters on the far side, but access to the interesting visitors ramp may not be possible.

FAIRBANKS AK
FAI   PAFA   International   5m/8km SW

It's a long drive north from Anchorage, and one which may be out of the question to many, even with a hire car, as mileage is normally charged separately in Alaska, as in Canada. The airport has passenger and cargo terminals, plus several hangars and ramps on one side of the main runway, 1L/19R, and the general aviation facility with its own runway, 1R/19L, on the other. Between them is a lake, accessible from the general aviation side, which is used by a considerable quantity of single-engined aircraft. Most of what can be seen on the move at Fairbanks can also be seen at Anchorage except on those rare occasions when Anchorage is closed. Fairbanks is the main diversion field, and the ramps can look extremely impressive, when occupied by a large quantity of wide-bodies. In summer, Fairbanks gets better summer weather than Anchorage but the sun sets quite early, 21:00 or so, due to the hills.

The facilities lined up west of the main runway are just across the road from the Golden North Motel. Expect to pay about $65 for a night but the standard of accommodation is worth the extra money, compared with what $38 buys. A service road leads to the Everts Air Fuel ramp at the north end, though their hangar is further down the road, beyond Brooks Air Fuel. Active aircraft include a number of DC-4s/6s and C-46s, though often only a small part of the fleet. Stored aircraft, by the UPS facility at the southern end, include some interesting hulks.

Markair and Northern Air Cargo have their own facilities, next to the terminal building, though nothing may be visible outside during the average day. Follow the road round the end of Runway 1L for access to the general aviation and, from it, the floatplane base. The main runway is visible from here but too distant for photography. For more light aircraft, it's worth investigating Metro

Field (MTX) on the south side of town. Exploration, it must be said, is likely because Fairbanks is the sort of place to visit, log and photograph what's there, then move on. Waiting for something on approach can, believe it or not, become quite tedious.

FAIRBANKS AK

FBK	PAFB	Fort Wainright	1.5m/2km SE

For some reason the entrance to this field is at the eastern end, that most remote from town. On weekends this military base can be "open post", without entry restrictions. Before attempting to inspect the resident aircraft, permission should be sought. The rampside dispatcher's building seems to be as good a place as any.

The Bureau of Land Management has a base here, with a few CASA 212 smoke jumpers and a civil OV-10 Bronco observation aircraft. The air tanker base amounts to nothing more than some wooden huts, behind which are stored spare engines. What air tankers are to be seen is obviously variable, though three or four could be a realistic expectation in summer. On the opposite side of the runway are the Army helicopters.

KENAI AK

ENA	PAEN	Municipal	1m/1.5km N

When driving from Anchorage, especially on a summer weekend, patience can be needed. The road is used by many RVs, and overtaking isn't easy. The first part of the journey, through the Chugach National Forest, offers views of the Kenai Mountains across the Turnagain Arm, and a stop at Portage Glacier is worth the sort detour. After that, it's great, if you like trees. The Kenai (pronounced keen-eye) Peninsula projects southwest from Anchorage, with Cook Inlet on its north side. The area is scenic with a capital S: tall fir trees forest the hills, mountains form much of the backdrop and, on clear days, Mt McKinley is visible, almost 200 miles away. It's a bit like being able to see Heathrow from Manchester, in terms of distance!

Salmon fishing is big business in these parts. The season starts in early July. DC-6s ferry huge quantities out of the airport and the floatplanes bring the fishermen. By the end of June, salmon fishing is not what everyone calls sport. Up river at this time of the year there are often more fish than water - they're probably glad to get out. They're all going to die after they've spawned anyway. More advice, about Alaska's national bird: mosquitoes round here grow to something about the size of a Cadillac. To kill them, take a baseball bat.

The airport has one runway, 1/19, at the south end of which is a cemetery. The residents are not likely to complain about aircraft noise. They are also unlikely to take exception to anyone standing around, camera in hand, awaiting the next aircraft moving up the taxiway. As they say in these parts, folks is less hassle when they're dead.

Markair and ERA operate hourly from Anchorage but scheduled air traffic is the least of the airport's attractions. On one side of the runway is the centrally placed main terminal and ramps for South Central, at the southern end, and the fish hauliers at the north. On the western side, accessible by a road junction immediately after passing the end of Runway 1, is the floatplane canal, with the take-off area at the north end. The canal is, in effect, a long stretch of water for the aircraft to park.

Accommodation is not cheap in Anchorage. Kenai is no different. The airport's information board suggested The Place might be a good bet. At $60 for a night, this was relatively inexpensive. A room in Soldotna starts at around $85.

PALMER AK

PAQ PAAQ   Municipal   1/1.5km SE

On the edge of town, 40 miles from Anchorage on Glenn Highway, is this small airport. Apart from one or two light aircraft in the circuit, not much happens. This is because almost any stretch of water is bounded by houses, many of them quite grand. At the bottom of the garden is the Cessna 185, as normal as a Ford Escort in Europe. Among the fifty or so residents are the Woods Air Service fleet, which includes C-47s and C-118s. From Glenn Highway, turn left before reaching the runway. Across the railroad track is Woods' hangar, almost big enough to hold one of their C-118s. Lots of zig-zagging leads to the rest of the field, with little in the way of reward.

SKAGWAY AK

SGY   Municipal   1m/1.5km S

Assuming there is no history of insanity in your family, you have to be a serious aviation enthusiast to visit Skagway. There is little to justify the trip. At one end of the runway is the fjord called Lynn Canal, with mountains on the opposite shore. All very scenic and all very historical. Unless you are particularly interested in Cherokee Sixes and the occasional Islander, there is nothing of any significance. The White Pass and Yukon Railroad might be more exciting, as it links historic downtown Skagway with Bennett, the gold rush ghost town. Great stuff, but not really in aviation terms.

SOLDOTNA AK

SXQ   1m/1.5km SE

From Anchorage, follow Highway 1 for Kenai, and Soldotna is just a little way down the road past Kenai. The airfield, on the far side of town is posted. Apart from fifty or so light aircraft, there is nothing to justify the effort, though it can be used as an air tanker base.

WASILLA AK

WWA

From Anchorage, Glenn Highway parts company with the road to Wasilla, George Parks Highway, before reaching Palmer. There are only fifty or so light aircraft to be seen but possibly worth the trip is the Museum of Alaska Transportation and Industry. Anyone who relishes rooting around relics will be rewarded by by an Alaska ANG C-47, 0-315200, C-123 N98 in FAA colours and H-21 Workhorse 34362, plus several other pieces of interest.

BIRMINGHAM AL

BHM KBHM   Municipal   5m/8km NE

Birmingham's passenger terminal is an excellent place to witness what happens on the runways. Driving around the perimeter is even better. On the far side of the runway are the Alabama ANG, using the main runway like the other traffic, only the jets deploy chutes for increased braking. To one side of the base are the hangars and fixed base operators where a good assortment of biz-jets is to be found, and on the other helicopters in some variety.

The cargo ramp is closer to the terminal, where the usual FedEx, UPS and Airborne Express aircarft can be seen. Beyond them, on the far side of the cross runways, is the general aviation apron where the light aircraft are housed. Among them are a few larger twins and biz-jets. PEMCO have their own separate ramp where work is carried out on C-135s amongst other types.

DOTHAN AL
DHN   KDHN   6m/9km NW

Birmingham-based PEMCO Engineers is one of America's largest companies to be involved with converting passenger airliners into cargo configuration. The facility at Dothan usually has several 727s waiting their turn, many of the most recent examples wear United colours.

MOBILE AL
MOB   KMOB   Pascagoula Regional   14m/22km W

Known locally as Bates Field, this airport is rather slow going but, in the afternoons, it offers the best opportunities for photographers. The low fence next to the old terminal allows standard lens shots of anything that passes on the taxiway. A small number of redundant airliners have found their way here in recent years but the current state of affairs is unknown. Mobile Aerospace is also a facility on the field, where airliners can often be seen either awaiting their turn for work or being made ready for delivery.

The US Coastguard have a major base, used for aviation training. The variety of aircraft, including Guardians and helicopters, makes it worthwhile seeking permission for a visit.

FAYETTEVILLE AR
FYV   KFYV   Drake Field/Municipal   5m/8km S

A pleasant little airport, with a surprising quantity of regional activity, including no less than five airlines. In the afternoon, a standard lens is required to take photos of the movements, the fence being only about four feet high. Ramp access isn't really necessary but, if morning photos are required because of tour itineraries, the staff are friendly and happy enough to accompany you out onto the apron. The autumnal colours of the leaves make this a very colourful location, as the tree-covered hills form a perfect backdrop.

An interest in biz-jets makes this an attractive airport. The Tyson Foods fleet is based and there are also many visitors during the week, due to the retail giant Wal-Mart being located in nearby Bentonville.

Admission to the small aviation museum costs a couple of dollars, though it covers mostly older general aviation. There is a display about Skyways Airlines, which was based in Fayetteville.

FORT SMITH AR
FSM   KFSM   Municipal   4m/6km SE

If you like Jetstreams, you'll love Fort Smith. Being only a modest regional airport, traffic is slow during the day but TW Express, Northwest Airlink and American Eagle all call. Photos of aircraft on the apron can be taken, over the fence, presenting no problems. The Arkansas ANG F-16s need the full extent of a 80-200mm lens, when being taken on the move. The base is guarded by a photogenic F-4D and access will be needed to log or take photos of the ramp.

LITTLE ROCK AR
LIT   KLIT   Adams Field   4m/6km SE

The main concourse of the passenger terminal is fine for spotters but the windows have tinted glass. Photographers will quickly discover that the perimeter offers little as an alternative. Airline traffic is mostly Air Midwest (USAir Express) Beech 1900s but one or two USAir F.28s and Conquest Metros do visit, along with American, Delta and Southwest. British Aerospace have a facility here, which always worth a look, and handles its fair share of visiting biz-jets. The Air Force have been known to use the field for training C-130 flight crews.

CHANDLER AZ
               Memorial   10m/16km SW

Heading south from Phoenix, on Interstate 10, bound for Marana and Tucson, it is worth watching the eastern horizon for the shimmering shapes of the aircraft parked at Chandler. The next exit, Queencreek Road, leads to the airfield along a signed Private Road, which becomes a track where the sign says: Pavement Ends - but the diversion will be worthwhile for any lover of piston power. Fences are unnecessary and free access is available to all the inmates, which include the Biegert Aviation DC-4s and T & G's selection of DC-7s, two of which once served with BOAC, as well as Privateers, Lodestars and C-119 Packets. Activity is usually restricted to a few men doing maintenance work, so a wander around the apron should result in a memorable collection of photos, and all in the Arizona sunshine.

Since the community of Chandler is due south of Mesa (q.v.), Country Club Road may be used as an alternate means of getting to the airfield. Beware signposts for the aerodrome, as these refer to the general aviation field Stellar Air Park, not a location for lovers of piston power.

STELLAR AIR PARK will no doubt have many fans, as general aviation fields are good for quantity. In this case, the quality is elsewhere. The road due south from Mesa is one to be avoided by some, and taken in anticipation of good logging by others.

FLAGSTAFF AZ
FLG   Pulliam   4m/6km SE

Anyone travelling by car to the Grand Canyon and other scenic places in the west may pass through Flagstaff and consider it to be a major town in the region. Its fame stems mostly from being on Route 66 (now effectively replaced by I-40) but its importance is not reflected in the size of its airport, nor the amount of traffic handled. In fact, the air links are quite local, with the majority of the flights being to Phoenix. These scheduled services are operated by Sky West Metros and the airfield has precious little other traffic. A small terminal is surrounded by plenty of vantage points, so that anyone in need of a photograph of the occasional visitor will be accommodated. It is unlikely that a diversion here will result in any great surprises, or reward of any kind.

GOODYEAR AZ
GYR   Municipal   25m/40km W of Phoenix

Known to most enthusiasts as Litchfield Park, Goodyear is worth a visit for anyone passing on the way to/from Luke Air Force Base. The field is used for major crew training programmes, due to its good weather all year round. One of the airlines to make the use of the field for this purpose has been Lufthansa, who used Debonairs and Barons. To see if anything is still stored at Litchfield, a bit of walking is necessary. In September 96, DC-7 N777EA was in storage.

GRAND CANYON AZ
GCN   National Park   7m/11km S

Located on the South Rim of the canyon, the airport handles twin engined aircraft (some of them jets) operating scheduled services, mainly from Las Vegas - Las Vegas Airlines, Air Vegas , Air Nevada, Arizona Pacific and Scenic offer mostly orgainsed tour parties. The pleasant terminal building is usually bustling with day trippers intent on sampling the awesome view of this natural spectacle. The ramp at either side of the terminal often contains some interesting aircraft but numbers are low. A redundant DC-4 is known to have been stored here. A request to stroll onto the apron for a photograph or two is normally successful, though few would consider the airport as being anything other than a very distant second placed feature of the trip. On the way through the village to the South Rim, the helipad is on the right-hand side, close to the road.

On the North Rim, another helicopter pad handles the occasional visitor, as the distance between the two communities by surface transport is enormous. It should be remembered that the South Rim is 8,000 ft above sea level (and the North Rim even higher) so it can be inaccessible due to snow for a prolonged winter period. Anyone intent on visiting the Canyon in April or November should check conditions before departure. In November, 90 degrees in Las Vegas or Phoenix can be matched by freezing temperatures at the Grand Canyon, despite the short distance between them. Next to the road leading to the rim of the canyon, in the middle of South Rim's spreadeagled village, the heliport is used for regular sightseeing trips over the canyon. Normally there are three of four helicopters, JetRangers and Ecureuils, to be seen.

KINGMAN AZ
IGM   Municipal   9m/15km NE

The airport still provides the town with a link to the outside world but its fame stems from its almost nil humidity and, as a result, its suitability for storing redundant airliners. The days when considerable numbers of 707s and DC-8s could be seen are over, Marana and Las Vegas being used these days, but the remains of the odd airframe are still present. At the last count, a number of Jetstreams kept company with a DC-4 and a C-123 Provider.

MARANA AZ
MZJ   Pinal Air Park   22m/34km NW of Tuscon

Few airports seem to attract so much subjective opinion as Marana. All reports are offered as definitive yet, over the years, there has been much conflicting information. Are spotters allowed in or not? Once upon a time, when it was a case of one or two visitors a month (or even a week), somebody from Evergreen had time to be sociable. And then it became famous. Visible from I-10 between Tucson and Phoenix are the shimmering airliners stored in quantity. There are two distinct storage areas: the apron, with many 'active' Evergreen aircraft among the hulks, and the central runway compound, where a large number of bigger airliners are parked. The range of colour schemes to be seen here is vast, more than could be expected at the average active airport. Movement isn't a feature of Marana, apart from the A-10s from Davis-Monthan crew training, but a proper tour of the stored aircraft needs prior arrangement with Evergreen.

Caution must be shown when compiling a book such as this, especially when suggesting that aviation enthusiasts can always expect a warm welcome at some airfields. The staff at Evergreen Air Center have jobs to do. Some days they might be very busy, which could mean having to turn even the most polite requests down. Anyone wishing to visit the Air Park is strongly advised to write beforehand (enclosing an international reply coupon) to the Marketing Department, Evergreen Air Center Inc, Pinal Air Park, Marana, Arizona 85653-9501. The standard reply should say that the museum aircraft have all been moved and that everything else that takes place on the field is Company Business. And not yours, in other words!

There is no doubt that many requests have been successful but, over the space of two years, the situation changes. What is printed in this book can cause unwelcome attention, to the point that staff find themselves spending too much time doing jobs they are not paid to do. For anyone who cannot understand the situation, it is suggested they read the entry for Hong Kong, where enthusiasts at the Aero Club have become so numerous that visitors cannot be made as welcome as might be wished.

Even if nothing more than a walk along the apron's edge results from a visit, this will yield a remarkable variety of interesting (to put it mildly) aircraft, though this will be overshadowed by the disappointment of not getting close to the main storage area.

MESA AZ

MSC	Falcon Field	12m/19km NE

East of Phoenix, this is the home of the Champlin Fighter Museum. For anyone in search of old aircraft, particularly well restored, there are Fokkers and Sopwiths, Wildcats and a MiG-17. The number of Confederate Air Force residents adds to the specialist interest. A few biz-jets and Air Response C-54s can be seen but S-1 Trackers are most numerous, awaiting conversion into water/borate bombers. The Hughes H-64 Apache assembly plant offers very little parked outside, to indicate what goes on inside the buildings.

PAGE AZ

PGA	Municipal	1m/1.5km E

The rapidly developing recreation area of Glen Canyon and Lake Powell is centred on the town of Page, which is still in its infancy. Civilisation has arrived, though Page Airport shares little of the growth, so far. This is probably because so many people arrive in campers and other recreational vehicles, usually towing boats. Aviation serves only a small proportion of the needs, and Lake Powell Air Service have a Twin Otter and some Cessna 207s, used most of the time for scenic overflying. Close by is Monument Valley, and the Twin Otter can often be seen next to the strip at Kayenta, waiting to take a party over some other very impressive scenery. Scheduled services, operated by Skywest Metros, are rarely seen in the daylight but they link the town with Phoenix, Flagstaff and St George.

PHOENIX AZ
PHX   KPHX   Sky Harbor International   4m/6km SE

America West's hub operation has ensured that Sky Harbor has become a busy airport, with two runways in use all day. The growth of traffic mirrors that of Phoenix/Scottsdale and the climate is the main reason. Apart from high summer, this part of Arizona has lovely weather and a trip in late autumn or early spring is very enjoyable.

The airport's passenger terminals are located between the two parallel runways and the best view of the proceedings is from the top of the multi-storey car park, though this can present some problems. Many of the airline movements will be seen to the south or southwest, so the sun does cause trouble to the serious photographer.

Despite Scottsdale being a leisure-oriented community, with its own general aviation field, Sky Harbor does have a very significant general aviation presence, mostly in the centre of the field. These aircraft include many executive types, and biz-jets are quite numerous. The access road from 24th Street passes the hangars and aprons, and it is possible to see most of the based aircraft on their ramps. This approach to the airport gives a better guide to the general layout than the 40th Street access, at the eastern end, with the cargo and commuter areas being visible on the way to the car parks. Expansion at Phoenix has revolved round the based airline, America West, who opened a new terminal and a maintenance hangar, both found to the east of the central complex. As the company continues to add a variety of color schemes, Sky Harbor provides the photograper with plenty of opportunities.

Access to the Arizona ANG is from 24th Street, just north of the I-10 intersection, after passing the threshold of Runway 8R. Apart from getting access to the F-104 on a pole, there is little point in going to the ANG base, as the KC-135s are all identifiable from the main terminal area. With its variety of domestic traffic, and the occasional foreign movement, Phoenix rates extremely highly and the added local attractions of Litchfield Park, Mesa, Scottsdale, Chandler Memorial, plus Tucson not far away, make this part of Arizona very attractive to the enthusiast.

SCOTTSDALE AZ
SCF   Municipal   9m/15km N

There is enough money in Scottsdale for its residents and business interests to consider themselves as a serious community in their own right, rather than as a suburb of Phoenix. The airport is small, though it bristles with large numbers of small aircraft plus a good selection of executive aircraft. There are many hangars and aprons to be explored.

The passenger terminal reflects a community on its way up in the world: it is rather elegant. However, the enthusiast is more likely to drive around the accessible part of the perimeter and make notes of the more interesting inmates, before passing on elsewhere.

SEDONA AZ
SDX   2m/3km SW

Travelling between Phoenix and the Grand Canyon means passing through the scenic Oak Creek Canyon. At the top (north) is Flagstaff and at the bottom (south) is Sedona. The airport is a modest affair, to be kind, but it may be worth a detour for anyone interested in saturation coverage of Arizona's aviation scene.

TUCSON AZ
TUS   KTUS   International   10m/16km S

Tucson is synonymous, in the aviation world, with Davis-Monthan. It is nevertheless a destination for civil enthusiasts as the airport has much appeal in its own right. Even here, the military presence extends its arms, with the north side of the field being occupied by the Arizona ANG, with an accent on training. The passenger terminal offers only limited viewing facilities but the movements are merely a diluted version of what can be seen better at Phoenix. Since few enthusiasts visit Tucson for the chance to stand around in the terminal and log scheduled airliners, it might be appropriate to concentrate on what can be seen elsewhere.

The perimeter holds delights which can't be sampled anywhere else. To enjoy them, a car is essential. Valencia Road, on the north side, has a few places where the ANG F-16 serials can be identified, and a little further west of the base is what was once one of the largest Viscount collections in the world. Jade Point owned this fleet, many of which provided spares for the others. One or two relics might yet survive.

Continuing west along Valencia to South Park Avenue, a left turn offers more delights for the lover of older airliners. Hamilton's work on 707s is slow, and many are parked, still bearing the colours of their last operator, awaiting conversion to turbine power and other rumoured modifications. This area bristles with interesting aircraft, a C-133 Cargomaster, several UH-1s and C-54s which have escaped from D-M, and a selection of types which have included in the past (and may still) an ex-Thai Air Force C-123 and a Stratocruiser whose rear end was removed, reportedly by mistake, plus many more. Star resident is the immaculate L-1049 (C-121) N109TW.

AMARC, the Aerospace Maintenance and Regeneration Center, at Davis-Monthan Air Force Base casts a long shadow across Tucson and the southeast sector of the city is almost totally occupied by the vast storage compound. Tours at the height of summer are best avoided, as the heat is excessive and, even in October, the heat is wearing by lunchtime. Tours of Davis-Monthan are now restricted to Wednesdays only, and booking ahead requires three months notice to avoid disappointment. Do note that no tour covers the entire vast aircraft disposal area, so further investigation may be required from the fence.

The main entrance to the base is at the southern end of Craycroft Road, and anyone assembling for a tour will probably come here from downtown Tucson, having seen nothing of the enormity of the place beforehand. A better idea can be gained when travelling to the Pima County Air Museum on the south side, down the Tucson-Benson Highway (I-10) as most of the compound can be seen, on the left, before the Wilmot Road exit is reached. A left turn, on Wilmot Road, leads to the southern edge of the field, to the museum, and to a collection of scrapyards. Lovers of airframes for their own sake have hours of pleasure, hunting through vast numbers of derelict helicopters etc.

The museum houses a superb collection of aircraft. Last admission is at 16:00, but an earlier arrival would be wise.

The perimeter of D-M provides hours of investigation, and obtaining a record of the serials will provide much hard, but extremely enjoyable, work. The eastern perimeter is easier to check, though many of the B-52s have had their tails removed, which makes life difficult.

TUCSON AZ
E14   Avra Valley   20m/32km NW of Tucson

A close neighbour to Marana, this field is nevertheless classified officially as Tucson. Off Interstate 10, drive through Marana village, then follow your nose through the maize and cotton fields. Eventually the airfield is signposted. The reason for making a detour on the way to/from Pinal Air Park is Mr Vern Raeburn's famed CV-240 and ex-MATS Connies. Permission should be sought to take photos but there should be no problem.

A dirt road, marked "Parachute Club" leads to their Beech 18 and a variety of stored piston types which, at the last report, included a P-2, a Mexican DC-3, a couple of C-54s, ex-Nantucket Marine Timber Company C-118 and three CV-440s. Well worth the detour, but do watch out for rattlesnakes.

Fifty bucks should be enough temptation for one of the pilots to take you up in a Cessna or Piper for half an hour or so. Take the camcorder and film a couple of good passes over Marana, then do all your identification work in the comfort of your own home. Hours of pleasure on those cold winter nights.

WILLIAMS AZ
	Gateway	20m/32km SE of Mesa

The former Williams Air Force Base is being developed as aprominent aviation centre, according to the public relations statement. Having inherited three parallel runways, there is certainly scope for development which Americans do rather well. Somewhat early in the day to be saying what will happen but it's worth making a detour to see if anything's happening, apart from some general aviation doing circuits.

YUMA AZ
YUM	KYUM	International	5m/8km S

The airport has customs facilities for the occasional movement from Mexico, which justifies the 'international' status, as the only scheduled services are occasional Metros. The terminal has a car park next to it, and photos of the ramp are possible here. What is also seen is the US Marine base, with considerable numbers of aircraft. On the opposite side of the runway is the small McDonnell-Douglas test facility. The extreme length of the runway, and the equally extreme temperatures endured by Yuma, made this an ideal testing place for prototypes, and the compound may contain the odd aircraft.

From the terminal, on the north side of the field, 32nd Street leads to a left turn and closer proximity to the runway and McD-D. A sandy track at the side of this compound allows any inmate to be identified and/or photographed but a reminder about the depth, and softness, of the sand next to this area should be heeded. It is easy to continue driving along the perimeter until it is too late. Beyond the McDonnell-Douglas area, the road passes close to the runway, and it's possible to take photos of aircraft on the move. Since the base is often used by Top Gun crews, there is some understandable concern over security and any casual watching of interesting F-5s or A-4s is often misunderstood. The units visiting from Miramar are a considerable attraction, though low-visibility schemes make serials difficult to read. Without access to the base, aircraft on the ramps are almost impossible to identify, due to distance and heat haze.

BAKERSFIELD CA
BFL	KBFL	Kern County/Meadows Field	6m/9km N

Meadows Field is easy to find, as long as it's borne in mind that it is also known as Bakersfield Municipal Airport and Kern County Airport. Getting out of the car is not compulsory. One or two commuters might be visible on the ramp at a busy time, all just as easy to see at LAX. Perhaps the rather ugly (but unique) XF-84H on a pole will justify the visit. The other airfield in the area is Shafter Airport, also known as Minster Field (!), where a selection of more light aircraft reside.

BURBANK CA
BUR   KBUR   Burbank-Glendale-Pasadena   3m/5km W

The existing passenger terminal has served for many years and is more pleasant inside than its exterior suggests. Airline traffic is mostly Southwest, American, United, Skywest and Alaskan, and there are windows within the terminal which allow photos of aircraft being pushed back.

The multi-storey car park offers views of runway activity but, to see the contents of the various ramps (Lockheed, Warner, Disney, MCA and Universal), a car is essential. For access to the perimeter, the airport operations department might be helpful.

CARLSBAD CA
CLD   Palomar   2m/3km E

On I-5, between LA and San Diego, this quiet airport may be worth a detour. There is a dozen or so difficult-to-photograph Air Resorts Convairs, rotting away in the sun. Flight International also base a part of their large fleet here. Apart from that, not much happens.

CHICO CA
CIC   KCIC   Municipal   6m/9km N

The journey takes some dedication, as it is a long drive northeast from San Francisco. Leaving I-5 at Orland, Chico is about 20 miles east. Aero Union's operation is separated from the main airport by a road, and the base is at the eastern end of the field. A high wire fence surrounds the facility, with signs saying that loitering, trespassing and photography are not permitted. This would not appear to be an inherently welcoming operator. Nevertheless, a request for ramp access still produces results, though it must be borne in mind that straying off the Aero Union patch is not permitted.

The chance to take photos of the DC-4 fleet may not be for much longer, as turboprop power is becoming affordable. This is generally in the shape of P-2s and P-3s at present. The rest of the field is also of interest, though not necessarily the scheduled traffic, which comprises mostly United Express Bandeirantes and Ameriflight Pipers. The museum is worth a visit, if only to see the delightful Viscount 700 parked there. There are, however, other exhibits worthy of interest.

CHINO CA
CNO   4m/6km E

It is not true that half the fun of Chino is finding it. The directions are simple . . . when you know. Pomona Freeway (Hwy 60) skirts the southern edge of Pomona and Ontario. The community of Chino is immediately south, but the airport exit is two or three miles east. Take Euclid (Hwy 83) south and the airport is difficult to miss, on the left side of the road. The Euclid exit was, and might still be, only accessible to eastbound traffic.

Arrival at Chino is confusing, as there are many ramps and hangars. Several compounds look inviting but may be no-go areas, due to the presence of a C-130 maintenance facility. The Planes of Fame Museum became famous as a centre of excellence for restoration, so more warbirds were attracted. The last reported visit, however, suggested that there was nothing to be seen. Evidence of the old fire-bomber days also seems to be consigned to the past.

CULVER CITY CA
CVR   Hughes   2m/3km N of LAX

___

The main road heading north from LAX, Sepulveda Boulevard, has a right turn, Lincoln Boulevard, which skirts the northern perimeter of the airport. It is also only a short drive along it, across Manchester Boulevard, to Hughes Airport. Passing the western threshold of the single runway, a right onto Jefferson reveals very quickly if there will be anything to see on the far side. Apart from one or two corporate visitors, there are usually a few Hughes helicopters to be seen on the ramp. Everything else is safely hidden behind closed doors.

FRESNO CA
FAT   KFAT   Air Terminal   5m/8km NE

___

The airline traffic here is not very brisk but the variety is adequate for most enthusiasts. Views from the terminal are restricted and photos are hard come by. The California Air National Guard has an almost road-side apron, in front of which stand a selection of older jets. Across on the far side is a base for TBM Tankers but only the occasional water bomber is present, close to a small Army UH-1 base. Interest in the TBM ramp can be misconstrued as prying into the Army area and there has been the occasional misunderstanding here. The rows of Trackers, visible from the passenger terminal, have been stored for many years.

Westair's maintenance base features United Express commuters undergoing checks. A trip to Fresno is more likely to be a quick recce of Westair and TBM than a prolonged stay.

FULLERTON CA
FUL   Municipal   24m/38km E of LAX

___

Leaving the noise and other splendours of Los Angeles International Airport for the joys of Fullerton is not many people's idea of a good time. The route is south on Sepulveda to Hermosa Beach, then left/east along Artesia. Fullerton Airport is at the end of the road. Its residents were once rudely described as being 150 spam cans. Access to the field is (sometimes grudgingly) offered, with a warning not to venture past the windsock, unless prepared to pay a $1000 fine!

HAWTHORNE CA
HHR   KHHR   Municipal   3m/5km E of LAX

___

At least it isn't far from LAX to Hawthorne. Take Imperial or El Segundo. Apart from a hundred or so light aircraft to see, there are helicopters and a small museum which includes a Sea-Bee and an A-4 Skyhawk. For access to the field, the Security Aviation building is on 120th Street, off Crenshaw, just north of its intersection with El Segundo.

For general aviation, try also Torrance. Sepulveda Boulevard runs due south, past Los Angeles Airport, and reaches the sea at Redondo Beach. Here it turns inland and becomes Pacific Coast Highway. After a couple of miles heading east, the airport is on the left, on Airport Drive (from Crenshaw). It is the spiritual home of all Robinson mini-helicopters. Robinson warn of danger from getting too close, mostly to satisfy their insurance underwriters. Access to the rest of the field is easy enough, via the desk in the building next to the control tower. What you get is numbers, in both senses of the word: a couple of hundred light aircraft can take about an hour and a half to log, for those who like that sort of thing.

INYOKERN CA
IYK   Kern County   1m/1.5km E

North of Edwards Air Force Base on Highway 395, the town of Inyokern can be seen from miles away. So can the airport. Directions are unnecessary. Metroliners operate regular links with Los Angeles, so it's usually possible to see one at close quarters on the little apron. Most of the time, Inyokern bakes in the sun and, even during the week, there is very little activity to witness.

LANCASTER CA
WJF   General William J Fox Field

A little way north of Palmdale, and visible from a long way off, this airfield may contain something worth the detour, most likely a couple of Aero Union DC-4s on duty. Some extremely unusual aircraft ended their days here, including the prototype F-111 (is it still there?) and an airworthy Argosy was noted on the last visit.

LONG BEACH CA
LGB   KLGB   Daugherty Field   3m/5km NNE

The airport's main tenant is McDonnell-Douglas, with its vast assembly plant for MD-80s, MD-11s and C-17s. The airline terminal handles a few America West 737s and TWA MD-80s, though traffic is modest. However, this is a useful alternative way of getting charter passengers into the Greater Los Angeles area, taking advantage of reduced landing fees. Anything at the terminal is therefore a bonus, as this is just one of the stops on a tour of the perimeter.

To the left of the terminal is the cargo apron where the usual parcels carriers can be seen, awaiting their evening departures and, at some distance from the C-17 facility, the Douglas Historical Foundation DC-2, NC1934D, is parked. The McD-D facility is large indeed and much of the airport's boundary is taken up by its buildings. There are several access gates and that most likely to yield results is Gate Four, with its car park behind the blast screen of the main ramp. Several visitors have attempted to find viewing points around the McDonnell-Douglas plant but given up, with little or nothing to show for their efforts. Every accessible road is worth investigation, as it could offer the one chance to see something out of the ordinary.

Photographers are not officially welcome at this ramp but hurried attempts to snap something interesting may not be as successful as asking for permission of the gatekeeper. At quiet times, it may be that his/her indifference on the matter may allow a better quality photograph to be taken, especially if it is pointed out that the picture will only form part of a personal collection.

Around the FAA control tower are business aircraft with the occasional military visitor to be seen. A parking space around here is usually hard to find but persistence will be rewarded by a good variety of interesting types. Also visible, near the terminal on the far side of the runway, is the AiResearch ramp, now used to complete assembly of Gulfstream 4s, and for servicing older models. A side road allows close inspection of this apron and hangar but access can be difficult, and Long Beach is acquiring a name for security measures. These are quite strict, and little attempt is made to be friendly, thereby increasing the deterrant. The Airport Operations office has

112

confirmed that logging registrations from the fence is not a problem but undue interest, especially with a camera, can lead to over-zealous action by their own security personnel.

LOS ANGELES CA
LAX   KLAX   International   15m/23km SW

Arriving by road at LAX, the third busiest airport in the world, the terminals are seen to be arranged in a U-shape, at the centre of which is the striking Theme Building, offering a panoramic, though distant, view of all movements. The restaurant in this building has been totally refurbished to create a James Bond meets Star Wars theme and, although prices have increased, it still offers good value. When the Theme Building is closed, the alternative vantage point is the multi-storey car park next to the Tom Bradley Terminal, which handles international flights.

The tunnels which give access to some of the terminals are still there and a security check is followed by quite long walks, some close encounters with the aircraft being the prize for the effort. Each of these terminals is served by a limited number of airlines, so any photographs will be at the expense of many movements being missed. Not all terminals offer views of the runways, with much internal modification having taken place in recent years. Terminal 1 offers good photographic possibilities of aircraft lining up on 24L. Leaving this terminal at the departures level, a gap between the buildings will allow good views of visitors to Terminal 2 which is now handling an increasing amount of international traffic. Runway views seem to have been blocked by construction of restaurants in Terminal 3. Access inside the Tom Bradley terminal is limited and offers little in the way of viewing. Occupants of this terminal can be viewed from either end of the arrivals level roadway, but photography is limited due to a screen of vegetation. Terminals 4, 5, 6, and 7 all offer views of the southern runways but internal refurbishment has put double glass screens at the end of Terminal 4. Airliners moving around adjacent terminals can be seen at close quarters, so a systematic circuit should result in a few areas where photos can be taken.

The Tom Bradley Terminal obscures from view the cross-field taxiways, which blocks the view enough to obscure the vision from the old control tower. This necessitated the building of the taller tower which dominates the airport.

To sum up the situation in the central complex, it is no longer possible to get within reach of many of the more interesting aircraft but those who are content to play the percentage game will do well. The end of Runway 24L was, for many years, a popular place to stand. An elevated roadway has now been constructed from Vicksburg Avenue which forms a bridge over Sepulveda Boulevard. Steps on both sides of Sepulveda give access to the bridge and the inclusion of a pavement makes this location a photographer's dream as aircraft arrive on 24R (200mm lens) and 24L (50mm lens). This position also allows all take offs on these runways to be monitored, but a collection of signposts and lampposts makes photographs of these aircraft impossible. Travel south on Sepulveda for a block and the West Los Angeles College offers several fuselages and an ex-Coastguard helicopter in a fenced compound.

Whilst it is quickest to get to the south side by way of Sepulveda, under the runways, at least one trip round the eastern end is recommended. Leaving the airport on Century Boulevard, and ignoring the direct Sepulveda route, a right turn after the Delta maintenance base, at Avion Drive, is followed by a relatively circuitous route, most of which is close to all the eastern cargo ramps. The range of aircraft to be seen around here is good, as it features mainly carriers who operate only occasional flights, as well as Emery Express and Evergreen International.

This road joins Aviation Boulevard at the threshold of 25R, and a right turn leads to Imperial Highway, where there are more busy aprons than many quite interesting airports could boast. Devoted mainly to cargo operations, there are many ramps to be explored, most of which can be seen from under-used car parks and emergency access roads. The nature of cargo operations at LAX means that these areas are busiest in the evening. The car park next to the Imperial Cargo Terminal offers a tremendous, and northerly, view to the thresholds of Runways 25L/R, regarded by many well-traveled enthusiasts as being one of the best photo-locations in the USA.

Before reaching Sepulveda Boulevard, Imperial Highway serves one large general aviation terminal, part of whose ramp is visible from the car park. There is a good number of biz-jets to be seen at close range but photographs are hard to obtain. West of Sepulveda are a few more aprons, including one for Federal Express, and the last area worthy of inspection is the Imperial Terminal, which handles very few aircraft these days, but anything there is liable to be interesting. The car park here, being quiet, offers good views of Runways 25L/R.

A right turn off Imperial onto Pershing will allow the remote stands south of the FedEx hangar to be seen. These often contain Mexicana 727's and the occasional El Al 747. Returning from the coast end of Imperial, a right on Hillcrest Street and then left turn leads onto Imperial *Avenue*. After a short drive there is an elevated vantage point looking north over the airport complex.

LAX is currently studying a variety of development plans all of which would create a series of new terminals west of the Tom Bradley Terminal. Almost all the options call for a reconfiguration of the north and south runways and one plan even joins a realigned runway for commuter flights at Hawthorne Airport to a dedicated roadway being built to LAX..

It is unlikely that even the serious photographer will leave Los Angeles with a portrait shot of every type of aircraft seen but patience and time spent around the perimeter should make it possible to record a fine selection, particularly when so many major airports seem to offer variety seriously reduced by hub operations.

LOS ANGELES CA

VNY	Van Nuys	24m/38km N of LAX

Van Nuys is some distance north of Los Angeles, just off San Diego Freeway. It is a very large general aviation field which offers no scheduled flights but is the home of a large number of biz-jets. It is split into two unequal parts by Sherman Way, and a look at the southern portion will reveal one or two items of interest, a drive round the entire perimeter should reveal everything present. The airfield has always featured something of interest, as well as playing host to the annual Aviation Expo where in 1996 the B-2 Stealth Bomber made its first Los Angeles appearance. The California Air National Guard unit has a separate little corner, where its C-130s sit, all close to the fence. The entrance to the base is on Rubio Avenue, where their F-104 gate guardian can be seen.

MADERA CA

MAE	Municipal	1m/1.5km S

Conveniently close to the highway, when driving between Los Angeles and San Francisco, Madera once provided the pleasant surprise of a few withdrawn piston airliners in storage. They have gone, and with them went any real reason for the detour. Traffic during the day is negligible.

MODESTO CA

MOD	Harry Sham Field	3m/5km E

The journey along I-99 can be broken by a stop at Modesto. It is a quiet little airport, which is used for commuter flights to San Francisco and San Jose. For the chance of a photo of a Metro or Jetstream, it may be worth the trouble, but there isn't much else of note.

MOJAVE CA

MHV	Kern County	5m/8km E

Another field worth a detailed look is not far from Edwards Air Force Base; Dick Rutan worked on his Vari-Eze and Long-Ez projects here and it was also the base for his around-the-world Voyager project. Stored aircraft and test facilities have always made a visit here an interesting proposition, usually with something extraordinary to be seen.

Itineraries which feature California and Nevada or Arizona could involve passing Mojave, but never without a stop. The far side of the runway became the storage area for ex-TWA CV-880s, and a pair of C-133 Cargomasters also became famous residents. The dry weather is ideal for storage, and also for flying: Canadair did much testing of the Challenger prototypes at Mojave, losing two in the process, and Flight Systems Inc. have many military aircraft for conversion to drones.

A walk round the apron reveals a selection of fighters converted to civilian use: T-33, F-104 - nothing is too extreme to be considered as recreational transport at Mojave! The stored aircraft are a different matter: a wide range of airliners destined for many carriers spend some time here before delivery. MDC Finance MD-80s can be seen from a distance, but the USAirways 146s have gone. A tour might be available on Sundays, for those who turn up at the admin. office. A caretaker will operate a van tour for $10. During the rest of the week, interest in the far side inmates can result in a checklist, if requested at the admin. office.

MONTEREY CA

MRY	Peninsula	5m/8km ESE

In Del Ray Oaks, and next to Highway 68, the airport has the Del Monte heights to the south. The name of Del Monte is famous to anyone who has ever bought canned fruit and it is here that the Del Monte Aviation fleet of business aircraft is based. The airport is best visited around lunchtime when a gathering of American Eagle, Trans States Jetstreams and Skywest Brasilias are present. There are also plenty of executive movements, but bear in mind the small passenger terminal no longer offers viewing facilities.

The executive ramps are east of the main terminal and the road is elevated above the level of the airfield, allowing good but distant views. To the north of the field is Fort Ord and a naval college, both of which justify a fair amount of military visitors. Anyone who intends to investigate this airport should consider doing so in the afternoon as it is prone to fog in the mornings.

NAPA CA

APC	County

A few miles north of San Francisco Bay, Napa is worth a detour for anyone interested in seeing something different. Several Beech 36s and King Airs are based here for use by Japan Air Lines' pilot training school.

OAKLAND CA

OAK	KOAK	International	10m/16km SW (bus 20 minutes)

On the opposite side of San Francisco Bay from its more prestigious neighbour, the site is effectively two separate airports. To the east of the field are the FBO's and general aviation whilst the scheduled passenger traffic and cargo operators occupy a terminal area nearer the bay.

A selection of scheduled flights can be viewed from the domestic terminal, but only by taking a walk down the long pier and looking out of the various windows at the gates. Scheduled operations are dominated by Southwest, with America West in second place. Horizon F.28s operate into Oakland several times a day to alleviate the boredom. The cargo terminal handles the usual operators, with FedEx having a mini hub here. Most of the cargo carriers can be seen from outside the passenger terminal, at the commuter gate. The main interest lies in the maintenance and general aviation aprons up the eastern side of the field. These should be visited in the morning, if serious attempts at photography are going to be made.

Once famous for being the main bases for World Airways and Transamerica, present day operations owe much to that history. This is still an active airport for MAC charters which, once upon a time, was how those two airlines earned much of their living.

The quantity of airliners has never been Oakland's main strength; its speciality lies in there usually being something present out of the ordinary. Maintenance bases carry out work for unusual operators, and it is along the eastern perimeter that a line of hangars and ramps can produce rarities. Identifying everything is a problem, so the photographer can suffer very real frustration. Large numbers of executive aircraft use the terminals here, and much more can be parked on the airside of the large hangars, out of sight from the road. It is quite normal for a morning at Oakland to result in a fascinating and varied collection, and what can be seen here is usually more interesting than San Francisco International.

The airport is located on Bay Farm Island, just a few miles from Nimitz Highway (I-880). A bridge at the north end of the island leads to Central Avenue and Alameda. At the northwest tip, overlooking San Francisco Bay, is Alameda Naval Air Station. Heading south on Nimitz, it's a short journey to HAYWARD Air Terminal (HWD), usually worth a look.

ONTARIO CA
ONT   KONT   International   3m/5km E

Promoted to some sort of international standing by being used as a West Coast version of Newark. Ontario's name is often synonymous with Red Eye Specials, where no-frills bargain flights operate. During the daytime, when cut-rate fares are not possible, the moderate traffic contains little out of the ordinary. The pleasant terminal building has a walkway next to part of the ramp, where airliners can be seen, though over the modest blast screens. Low walls permit enough height to be gained for photography. A massive building programme here will, by 1999, see the completion of two new domestic terminals giving the airport another 26 gates.

Lockheed have a C-130 service facility, to the right of the terminal when driving in. Due to the presence of foreign military aircraft, there is no shortage of posted notices warning against photography. To ensure that heed is taken, there should be more personnel to enforce it.

Ontario's largest operator is UPS, though their parcels traffic reaches its busy peak after dark. All types of their aircraft, including the elusive 747s, visit the parcels sorting facility here but the recent erection of huge blast screens has made viewing difficult. Continuing about a mile past the UPS cargo area on arrival at Archibald Avenue, a right turn leads to an area where both runways are visible. A low fence here allows photography. Union Flights are also to be seen, and anything from their Buffaloes to one or two Beech 18s are a common sight here.

OXNARD-VENTURA CA
OXR   County   1m/1.5km E

When travelling along Highway 101 between Los Angeles and San Francisco, this is one of the airports to be considered as a detour through the orange groves. Scheduled traffic through the neat little terminal is minimal, and strictly limited to commuters. However, Oxnard has been known as the last resting place of one or two airliners. The field is quite open, so there is no shortage of vantage points from which to see interesting aircraft.

PALMDALE CA
PMD   KPMD

Airline operations are negligible, with only United Express Beech 1900's visiting from LAX, and one or two charter operators making occasional appearances. Down a track, in a secluded corner, was the last resting place of the airframes built in the A-11/YF-12 project. Recent reports suggest at least one TriStar airframe has joined them.

PALM SPRINGS CA
PSP   KPSP   Regional   2m/3km E

Surrounded by thousands of square miles of desert and scrubland, Palm Springs is an emerald green cushion of golf courses, where enough water is sprinkled every day to supply a good-sized town. Literally a few paces east of City Hall, the municipal airport was essential to the growth of Palm Springs The airport handles upwards of sixty flights a day, two thirds of which are commuter services. After passing through security, the terminal offers the opportunity to savour a patio-like atmosphere, great for photos, although the subjects are invariably the American major airlines. On the opposite side of the airport from the terminal several FBO's are based along Gene Autry Blvd. A variety of biz jets and dozens of private aircraft can be seen on the ramps. Farther along this boulevard is the Skywest maintenance facility. Their parking lot offers the opportunity to photograph whatever is present. A mothballed F-14 Tomcat from the USS Theodore Roosevelt guards the entrance to a museum of World War II aircraft, which include a B-17, P-51 and a P-40.

BERMUDA DUNES is a new community (using the term loosely) and the residents enjoy a lavish lifestyle. Naturally the airport houses a fair number of corporate transports. Undue interest in them is not always welcomed.

RIVERSIDE CA
HMT   Hemet - Ryan Field

Hemet, home of Hemet Valley Flying Service, is officially called Riverside Hemet. It is not a major field and the distance between Riverside and this airport is over sixty miles. Leaving I-10 at Beaumont, Highway 79 winds it way south. For anyone interested in older transports it's worth the drive. The setting is lovely and the aircraft are interesting: plenty of tankers are to be seen, ranging from stored aircraft to the newly configured C-130s. Riverside's other tow airports, FLABOB (RIR) and MUNICIPAL (RAL), might be worth a detour for logging purposes but there is little airline activity at either. Also nearby is PERRIS, a small airfield but anyone who wishes to add a couple of Twin Otters to a day's log can find them here, used for para-dropping.

SACRAMENTO CA
SMF   KSMF   Metropolitan   10m/16km NW

Metropolitan airport is relatively disappointing, with no views from the terminals, and not much activity to see, apart from the occasional military aircraft in the circuit, having come from Beale, McClellan or Mather, all of which are nearby. Walkways along the edge of the apron are close to the aircraft, indeed too close when some of them are pushed back, but photography is not at its best here. The commuter terminal, on the right, does have a rampside observation area but this can be out of bounds when there is an aircraft to be seen!

Business movements use Sacramento EXECUTIVE (SAC) some 4 miles south of town where, during the week, good numbers can be seen from the fence on either side of the terminal. This airport's most important resident is Union Flight, for it is here that their operations base is found.

SAN DIEGO CA
SAN   KSAN   Lindbergh International   2m/3km NW (bus 15 minutes)

A huge building progamme continues to change the face of the airport considerably. The East Terminal has been renamed Terminal One after problems with passengers who couldn't tell their east from their west. Vantage points exist at gates 8 and 13 although airliner variety is strictly limited to the majors, with the exception of Aero Mexico. The West Terminal has now been renamed Terminal Two and a new extension has more than doubled its size. As operators move their gates to this terminal, views of aircraft on the ramp will greatly improve. Leaving Terminal One and heading east along North Harbor Drive, almost all viewpoints have been blocked by blast screens. A road near the cargo area offers limited views but it would be unwise to explore further because of high security in this area. The new Commuter Terminal has a huge mural of Lindbergh on its eastern wall, and up to eight aircraft may occupy the ramp at any one time. Views can be gained by passing through security.

At the intersection of North Harbor Drive and Laurel Avenue is the Coast Guard air station, which is home to a variety of rotary winged craft. There may also be a Guardian based, although this is now a very rare occurrence. Because the station is used mostly by helicopters, they coan take off over the harbour (where aircraft carriers can be seen). The fixed-wing Guardians, which visit occasionally, need a runway so a policeman stops the traffic on North Harbor Drive when they need to cross. Very convenient for the lucky photographer who is there on the right day!

Just beyond this crossing, Laurel Avenue begins. This is almost directly opposite the end of the short Runway 31 and very close to the threshold of 27. Blast screens block all views of this area, except for a tiny section of car park. This allows aircraft landings and take-offs to be observed but a double fence makes photography impossible. The general aviation ramp off Pacific Highway has become a very sensitive area and it would be wise not to stray from the sidewalk. The Windsock Restaurant has a terrace which offers an excellent view of this ramp but does not allow any form of notetaking or photography. Jimsair handles most of the movements on this ramp, with a wide variety of biz-jets and others filling it each day. Buildings along Pacific Highway block most views but as the road joins the San Diego Freeway an elevated section allows sight of several cargo carriers who spend their day parked on this side of the field.

It was the Ryan Aircraft Company of San Diego that built the Spirit of St Louis, used by Charles Lindbergh. His name is commemorated at the city's main airport. BROWN Municipal airport (SDM) some 18 miles south of town, keeps the tradition alive, too, in its way as it plays host to regular light aviation spectaculars. For the rest of the year, it is quiet with one or two executive aircraft among the light planes. Mexican visitors can be noted, just a few miles from home.

A visit to MONTGOMERY Field (MYF) could be essential as one of the few remaining Ford Trimotors is to be found there. There are no scheduled services, and the airfield is dedicated largely to general aviation but it makes an interesting detour for number crunchers.

SAN FRANCISCO CA
SFO   KSFO   International   13m/20km S (bus 30 minutes)

Generally, the only way to see what is on the stands is to walk from one end of the terminal area to the other, as many windows overlook the extensive aprons. The main problem is that whilst the longer runways, 10/28, are used for most movements, some smaller aircraft always use 1/19 so no vantage point is ideal, although the American Airlines terminal offers a good overall view. The shuffling around of various airlines operations to suit the completion of work in the terminals means that San Francisco may always be in a state of flux, and even recent reports may still be subject to regular updating.

United's presence at San Francisco is substantial, and its numbers are boosted by the Westair Jetstreams and Brasilias constantly on the move. USAirways, and to a lesser extent, Delta and American make up the rest of the movements, though Alaska Airlines are regular. The American Airlines presence is reducing, due to their development of the nearby San Jose as a regional hub.

Despite the upheavals in the centre of the airport, the perimeter has changed little and one of the best spots, adjacent to the threshold of 1R is still good for views of aircraft taking off. Photographers sometimes have a problem with the fence, because the ditch prevents close access to the chainlink. This is becoming quite a popular spot. It's used for short-term parking by buses and vans but, on the other hand, there are also toilets and a mobile snack bar. Maintenance areas to the north of the terminal area offer many different viewpoints and the best of these is probably the car park next to the Butler Air Terminal, where many executive movements can be seen at reasonably close range. The facilities at the north end of the field are not easily accessible, and anyone who penetrates this area will have obtained some written authority to pass through the security gate which guards it.

SAN JOSE CA
SJC   Municipal   3m/5km NW (bus 15 minutes)

The main entrance to the airport is off Coleman Avenue in the southeast corner, though a less

118

interesting entrance is off Guadeloupe Parkway from the north. Entering the complex off Coleman, it is possible to achieve some idea of the layout before reaching the passenger terminal. Airport Boulevard loops around the eastern, busiest, part of the field, passing the general aviation ramps and terminal, and the FBOs on the north side.

Despite being close to San Francisco, there is enough local demand for an alternative airport to justify a very wide variety of schedules here. International services are handled by SFO but San Jose is intent on capitalising on being a small and convenient airport. American Airlines plan to change things by the extension of hub operations to include their long-haul Pacific Rim flights. The new terminal, for American and Reno Air, is operational but has no internal viewpoints. The observation deck in the old one remains open and offers a limited view of the proceedings, being a little low, and set back behind the extended building to the right but scheduled airline movements do pass within range.

An alternative vantage point for the main apron is to the right of the tower, in the parking lot, though others are also available: a spot next to Fire Station 20 is close to the taxiway, and opposite the ramp where biz-jets are parked. San Jose University's 727 is usually parked on one of the ramps. Also, at the eastern end of the airport, the general aviation terminal usually contains a free parking space. From here, approaching and taxiing aircraft can be seen. In the southeast corner is Aris Helicopters. Their fleet contains a number of S-58s, and the friendly staff usually allow ramp access for photography.

SAN LUIS OBISPO CA
CSL   McChesney Field

If the confusion from having two airports serving such a small community were not enough, McChesney Field is also known as County Airport! The majority of scheduled services are commuter flights operated by American Eagle, Skywest and United Express, so most of the action is concentrated into the early morning and evening. During the day, there are still a few notable residents, up to Metro-size, so all the effort to leave San Luis Obispo with something to remember is not completely wasted. Wings West currently use the field as a store for their BAe 3201 Jetstreams. The restaurant, at the left hand edge of the apron, might be worth checking out. Watch out also for the MUNICIPAL Airport (SBP), though there is little of interest, apart from numbers, to be seen there.

SAN PEDRO CA
SPQ   Catalina Island Seaplane Base   3m/5km E

The road bridge sweeps high over the docks, and some very large ships are to be seen. From the highway, it is an interesting car journey to the ramp at the water's edge which was once Briles seaplane base. Grummans plied to and from Catalina Island, a few miles off shore. Briles, based at Long Beach, have moved with the times, and their operations now use a range of helicopters. One of them, parked on the dockside, can make an unusual photo for the collection.

SANTA ANA CA
SNA   KSNA   John Wayne International   5m/8km S

Officially Santa Ana John Wayne is still known as Orange County. An interest in general aviation, hardly the main topic of this book, makes this an attractive airport in theory as it houses countless light aircraft. Only the Pan Western GA Terminal is yet to post signs around its car parks, warning against spotters popping in for a good look. Lots of aircraft, and so few places to see them: expect to leave with only a small proportion, and Santa Ana won't be too frustrating.

The newer terminal, east of the old one, has no observation deck, but car parks at each end do overlook the commuter ramps. USAirways Express and United Express are at the western end, with American Eagle and Skywest at the other.

The afternoon is best enjoyed by taking a series of right turns from the terminal. Having taken a look at the occupants of the Million Air FBO, the road reaches, in the northeast corner, a spot close to the end of the runway. From the car park here, approach photos are easy to come by, but the construction of fuel tanks has stopped views of aircraft on the ground. Anyone in need of portraits of 757s in the colours of America West, American, Delta and especially TWA might spend some time here. East of the airport, and worth a detour for the military-minded, are Santa Ana and El Toro Marine bases, the former having helicopters easily seen from Barranca Road.

SANTA BARBARA CA
SBA   Goleta Municipal   10m/16km W

Most of the scheduled traffic is commuters, plus the occasional 737 or 146. An open terraced restaurant above the terminal offers an excellent viewpoint of scheduled traffic. On either side of the passenger terminal are mesh fences, where it is possible to see the parked aircraft. The car park to the left overlooks the ramp where commuter traffic stops, and photographs are no problem. Further left is a selection of general aviation, which makes up 90% of the movements.
  Tracor carry out modification work on a variety of airliners, and what can be seen on any visit is a matter of luck, although most visitors should find several 727's and MD-80's. Their hangars are reached from Highway 101 before the terminal area. The graveyard contains withdrawn Jetstreams, bearing a variety of colour schemes, and serving as a reminder of the days when the airport was served by Apollo and later Pacific Coast Airlines. Santa Barbara is a pleasant airport and usually has something present to justify the small diversion off the main road.

SANTA MONICA CA
SMO   Municipal   7m/11km NW of LAX

The desire to investigate Hughes Airport can be combined with a trip a little further up Lincoln Boulevard to Santa Monica. It is a general aviation field, with rather a lot of aircraft. The place oozes money, as it is the closest airport to fashionable Beverly Hills and Bel Air.
  Logging numbers from the fence is permitted but the far side of the field offers untold numbers, which elude the binoculars. The end product is between 100 and 150 light aircraft registrations, which might be the law of diminishing returns for anyone with only a limited amount of time. Apart from the biz-jets, the museum features six outdoor exhibits and, of all things in California, a Tornado simulator!

SANTA ROSA CA
STS   Sonoma County   8m/13km NNW

The small passenger terminal handles a few commuter airline movements, similar to Stockton (q.v.). Most aviation-minded visitors made the journey for one reason only: Macavia. The demise of that airline may mean that propliners are no longer in evidence. (Do note there is a small museum.) This is not the only airport north of San Francisco, so a journey by road will probably feature Santa Rosa on a day trip with visits also to Napa and Sacramento. Before including Chino on the itinerary, it's worth bearing in mind that it can make for a long day from San Francisco.

STOCKTON CA
SCK   KSCK   Metropolitan   6m/9km S

This is one of California's quieter airports, though hardly surprising when it is so close to San Jose and Oakland. Local scheduled services link it with the Bay, operators being American Eagle and United Express, with Wings West Jetstreams and West Air Brasilias respectively. The only reason it will receive visits from enthusiasts is the presence of the Hemet Valley base, which usually

120

contains a selection of aircraft, some of which are being serviced. The Trackers and Boxcars are now being augmented with more modern types, though the age of the C-130s hardly makes them young. A request at the office for a look at the ramp will probably meet with success, and the bonus of a couple of C-97s in storage.

ASPEN CO
ASE   Pitkin County   4m/6km

The playground of the rich in Colorado is, quite definitely, Aspen. In some parts of the world, it seems like only poor people take the bus, but in Aspen, it would appear that the poorer folk have to take scheduled flights. There is no shortage of executive transport at this airport.

Leaving Aspen on Hwy 82 to Glenwood Springs, the airport is next to the road, on the left. The airline terminal is immaculate, as the rich expect, and offers one of the few places to see an Aspen Air Do328. The apron to the north is where plenty of private transport is parked.

With the alpine scenery on the other side of the runway, most photographers will wish to leave with at least one record of their visit. Anyone heading west from here by car is strongly advised to ensure that the tank is full before tackling Independence Pass. At 12,000 feet above sea level, the drive is hard, and fuel goes quickly!

COLORADO SPRINGS CO
COS   KCOS   Peterson Field   7m/11km SE

The new passenger terminal, on the south side of the field, opened in 1994. The road from town is near-DIA proportions, and views from it of the airfield are good. Did somebody know something? It looks that way, because Denver's new airport is so far out of town (from the passenger's point of view) and so expensive for airline operators, that Colorado Springs has witnessed a major growth in traffic volume. Much of it was due to Western Pacific activities. If they go down, then what? The air cargo facilities remain unchanged, being just north of the old terminal. Across the field are the hangars and C-130s of Peterson AFB, which shares the runway.

DENVER CO
APA   Centennial   11m/17km SE

This field used to be called Arapahoe County, hence the code. When travelling on Highway 87 between Denver and Colorado Springs, there is an enormous airfield on the east side of the road. Whilst there is a reasonable amount of larger general aviation types at Stapleton, it's clear that there is more to be found elsewhere.

From I-70, take exit 295 and head north into the village of Watkins. From here signs give directions to AURORA (FRONT RANGE) Airport (FTG). The road north, numbered 25A, is paved as far as the turn-off, beyond which a dirt road leads to the airport. This is a general aviation airfield, built to replace Skyline Airport. It's very modern and open plan, with no fences (yet?). Continental Express Dash 7s are (were?) stored here, in the company of a Colorado ANG A-7E.

DENVER CO
DIA   KDIA   International   25m/40km E

On the day DIA opened, it became the eighth busiest airport in the world, which puts it on a par with Frankfurt. However, for a few years it will be surrounded by almost nothing, apart from prairie. They said that about what was known as *Stapleton's Folly* in 1929. It can safely be assumed that the price of the wide open spaces will be very high indeed, so that even the nearest house, some five miles away, will increase in value. Major airports attract business and DIA will be surrounded, for many years, by an enormous building site.

It takes between half an hour and forty five minutes to reach DIA from the city, along Pena Boulevard. What greets the eye, as it was meant to, are the thirty-four fibreglass peaks of the terminal roof, designed to mirror the Rockies on the skyline.

The control tower is, of course, the tallest in the world. It overlooks the five runways, none of which intersect and each of which is at least a mile from its neighbour. This is important, as it ensures the waves of United and Continental can arrive and depart without conflict.

The elevated bridge which links the terminal with the outside world offers views of the Rockies and of the aircraft which can taxi beneath. However it is not designed for spotters to stand on all day. A moving walkway sees to that.

The good news is that, unlike Atlanta, the three concourses have plenty of glass, albeit tinted. There is, however, a lot of space between the concourses, so it may be difficult to find a good spot which allows movement on all the runways to be monitored. The mutli-storey parking garage will certainly offer a view but the sheer size of the place means it will be distant. A fence next to the service road just north of the main terminal can be seen, together with the taxiway to/from the parallel Runways 17/35L/R. Frontier's gates, on Concourse A, gave them the best position for passengers and photographers alike.

The perimeter is enormous. The first exit off Pena Boulevard, when leaving the main terminal area, leads to the airport services and cargo area. UPS and FedEx are encountered first, after which comes AMR Combs FBO which will no doubt contain a fair quantity of biz-jets. Leaving this area westbound, past the rental car lots, there is a distant view of Runway 7/25. Back on Peña Boulevard, the next exit is Tower Road which leads in turn to 56th Street and a long drive, at the end of which is TRACON. Beyond here is the perimeter fence with a view of the taxiway and approaches to Runways 3L/R.

Tower Road also leads to 88th Street, where a public viewing point was created, but only for watching the construction. The opening of the airport and the closing of this facility will probably coincide, not that it would be much use: it's a very long way from any of the runways. Further north, however, is somewhere more promising. Take 96th Street. A long drive west eventually leads to the United and Continental maintenance hangars. The road ends, after passing under the approach for 16L, with a view of Concourse C and the outer parts of Concourse B. Several runways can be watched from this general area.

Nothing can be said as yet about what spotting and photography are like at DIA because, as yet no comprehensive reports have been received. Traffic is expected to be more varied than Stapleton's, with Markair, Vanguard and Frontier coming onto the scene, the latter with its colourful 737s each sporting unique schemes on the fin. Mesa and Air Wisconsin operations, from Concourse B, feature the usual array of colour schemes, ranging from pure United to almost anything else. GP Express, the Continental Connection, shares Concourse A with the host airline.

GRAND JUNCTION CO
GJT   Walker Field   6m/9km NE

A prosperous town on the Colorado River is served by a modern airport. There is a Sabre on a pole in front of the terminal, but action on the tarmac is confined largely to commuter flights in the morning and evening, with little action during the day. Hawkins & Powers have an operational base here, to the left of the terminal, and access to the ramp, to photograph the resident P-2V Neptune, or similar, is normally granted at the office.

HAYDEN CO
HDN   Yampa Valley   25m/40km W

This runway is long enough to allow 727s to land, usually en route, and so the community offers a gateway for the rich on their way to the ski slopes. It is probable that a close-up view of a Continental Express Dash Seven at the smaller airport may provide more excitement than a few American, America West and Northwest Boeings calling at Hayden. Variety is provided by smaller types which commute from Denver during the day.

STEAMBOAT SPRINGS CO
SBS   Municipal   3m/5km W

This winter resort has already split into two, the old town along the main street, and a separate upmarket village at the foot of the ski slopes. The airport barely qualifies for the description but the small terminal handles the occasional Continental Connection Dash Seven. The gate next to the terminal allows ideal photos to be taken as the aircraft taxis past. The almost compulsory FedEx Feeder Caravan is parked with a dozen or so light aircraft. The airport which serves as the resort's link with major centres of population is further west along I-40, at Hayden.

GROTON-NEW LONDON CT
GON   Trumbull   6m/9km S

Trumbull's terminal handles a number of movements, including some US Navy executives, associated with the submarine base. The Army Guard has its own facility, with a number of UH-1s and, rather more interesting, some AVCRAD C-7 Caribous. It is possible to stand next to the fence for photography but a request at the gate may result in closer inspection, during the week.

NEW HAVEN CT
HVN   Tweed   4m/6km SE

Tweed is small, by any standard. Fortunately it is also informal. Access to the ramp is usually available on request, but the casual visitor may not find anything to see. Always worth a detour from the highway, Tweed occasionally plays host to one or two (literally) interesting aircraft.

STRATFORD CT
BDR   KBDR   Sikorsky Memorial   2m/3km SW

Heading east by car from New York City, there are a few airports along Connecticut's southern shore. The first used to be known as Bridgeport but there is so much economic influence in Stratford, the name has been hi-jacked. Stratford really is one of the most important industrial centres on the aviation scene. Sikorsky Memorial airport offers a clue: it is here that production of S-76s and the various H-60 variants are assembled. What can be seen, at the edge of the field, are only massive buildings and car parks.

Near the small passenger terminal is a viewing area at ramp level. The Business Express Beech 1900s can be seen at close quarters, and good photographs of aircraft taxying on the ramp are easy to take. The southerly aspect towards the ramp can make sunny days a nuisance for the photographer.

WINDSOR LOCKS CT
BDL   KBDL   Bradley International   14m/22km N

Hartford, is quite close to Springfield, in Massachusetts so a location about halfway between the two was chosen for a joint airport. This is Bradley Field, at Windsor Locks, whose growth is testament to local prosperity. The passenger terminal is split into two: Terminal A is linked to the two halves of Terminal B by an elevated corridor, in front of the Sheraton Hotel.

The entrance to the airport is from Highway 20 (off I-91) and terminal facilities offer little of interest. Since there are so many alternative points from which to see the action at close quarters, this is no problem. To the left of Murphy Terminal B is the FedEx cargo building, and this gives access to large, under-used car park very close to the taxiway for Runway 6. No matter how small the aircraft using this taxiway, it is within reach of the camera. Beyond the runway, some of the ANG A-10s are visible, and the base attracts a small number of military visitors.

Leaving the terminal area via Schoephoester Road (instead of Highway 20), there is a left turn just before Route 75. It leads, ultimately, to the Aviation Museum, but passes some very interesting aprons on the way. A left turn at the 4-way stop sign leads to Corporate Air, a FBO with a car park close to one of the taxiways to Runway 33. The new taxiway on the other side of this runway has drastically reduced what can be seen passing close by, but it still good for executive movements. AMR Combs owns the other hangars and terminal, where more biz-jets are to be seen. The next left off the perimeter road leads to Business Express, whose movements dominate activity at Bradley.

The next ramp is used by the Army Guard, complete with UH-1s and (still?) CH-54 Tarhes. Most of the helicopters can be seen quite easily from the low fence, and a request at the office, on the far side of the building (off the car park) usually allows a stroll around the apron (at least). The road winds round the end of Runway 24 to the museum. It is one of the biggest in America, with some of the larger exhibits parked outside. There are twice-yearly open-cockpit days, when visitors can scramble around inside such aircraft as a B-29 or a B-47. The road terminates at the Connecticut ANG base but general access is barred, just beyond the museum.

Traffic is reasonably mixed, though there's a lot of Delta and USAirways/Express. The cargo terminal, next to Passenger Terminal A, also sees plenty of traffic but the evening package operations are when most of the aircraft move.

Not too far from Bradley is East Hartford, beside the Connecticut River, near the Pratt & Whitney division of United Technologies. It would be easy to dismiss HARTFORD BRAINARDas a small general aviation field without this item of information. Executive aircraft are always to be expected in number and variety,especially during the week.

WASHINGTON DC
IAD   KIAD   Dulles International   27m/42km W (bus 50 minutes)

Orange Line Metro trains serve West Falls Church Station, from where a shuttle bus operates to the airport, at a cost of $7 one way. The airport is becoming increasingly busy, and its highly-regarded (and completely open-fronted) observation deck on Concourse A can reward the patient with quality photos of taxiing aircraft. It should be noted that the observation deck is not necessarily open all year round. When the deck is closed, Concourses B and C allow views of all aircraft except those on the cargo and general aviation ramps.

Many airline visitors park well away from the main terminal, at the midfield concourse, primarily used by United and American. Although these movements are visible from the observation deck at the front of the main terminal, they are really too far away for good quality portraits. Nevertheless, aircraft on the taxiways closer to this deck do make for good photographs, though patience is needed. Prior reference to United's timetable is also useful. Arrival at the wrong time can mean seeing thirty or so United Express commuter-liners but nothing at all of United's own fleet. When in evidence, examples of just about every type of airliner that United operate can be seen, so a prolonged stay does have its rewards. Also visiting are Saudia, KLM, Swissair and ANA 747s, TACA and Transbrasil 767s and Valujet DC-9s. Daily Lufthansa and Air France A340s are also worth a mention, as is the fact that DCA is now the USA's fifth most important international airport.

Access to many of the boarding areas, even by the so-called moving lounges, is possible. Boarding cards have not been required for access to the midfield area, Concourse C/D, but the ongoing situation cannot be taken for granted.

The main terminal has doubled in length. The International Arrivals Building will eventually be demolished and a much larger replacement built elsewhere. Visitors should expect, for the next couple of years, that the observation deck might be the only place offering a view.

To the east of the terminal is a general aviation area (the other being in the northwest corner), which handles a fair amount of business traffic, with the occasional foreign official aircraft, RAF and Luftwaffe representatives being regular visitors. As long as smaller aircraft don't block the view, it is often possible to obtain fairly close-up shots of these aircraft through the fence. Airborne/FedEx aircraft, parked at the cargo terminal, are visible from the parking lot next to the Post Office.

124

WASHINGTON DC
DCA   KDCA   National   5m/8km S (train 20 minutes)

The new $450 million terminal has opened. Its three piers allow good views of all movements, and the slightly tinted windows give photographers a fighting chance. At the north and south ends of the terminal, outdoor terraces have been created, offering semi-obstructed views of aircraft taxying to and from Runway 18/36. From here a 300mm lens allows good photographs of aircraft on the runway. Best views are probably from the Center (American Airlines) Pier. Eagle ATRs, parked at the end, do not obstruct the view of moving aircraft.

Only 27 new gates are currently open with ten more scheduled for completion by the end of 1998.This means that changes will continue to take place at DCA. The US Airways/Delta terminal will return to its original use as a hangar, whilst much of the old landmark building in the old terminal will be converted into offices for the airports authority. Nine gates will remain in the old terminal, connected to the new terminal by shuttle buses. Just to the north of the new terminal, a 9-gate commuter terminal for USAirways Express is scheduled to open in 1999.

The quantity of movements is enormous, with influential companies having sufficient political clout to retain parking space and slot times, so that their own movements cause serious delays to scheduled traffic. It is not uncommon for airliners to wait at the holding point for over half an hour while half a dozen or so corporate jets land in a continuous procession.

Even the most ardent DCA supporter would concede that airline traffic is limited in variety - pretty much Delta and USAirways, but the general aviation ramps situated to the south of the new terminal offer a wide variety of biz jets. If Runway 36 is in use, take the free shuttle bus to the satellite parking area. An early stop is made near Signature Aviation, giving views of the biz-jet ramp but, for viewing arrivals and departures, get off at the farthest stop from the terminal. A short walk to an employee parking lot gives excellent views of all movements, although for high quality photographs, some means of elevation will be necessary.

Alternative locations at DCA are restricted in their nature: to the north is Daingerfield Park, with its wildfowl sanctuary and marina. The boat landing area offers extremely close up views of traffic landing on Runway 18, regarded by some as being as good as anywhere in the world for photographers. If the runway is in use, this location is certainly worth serious investigation. When Runway 36 is in use, photos of aircraft on take off are to be considered. For further information about the airport, its website is *www.metwashairports.com*. For the new passenger terminal, also check *www.washingtonpost.com* (presumably for a limited time only).

WASHINGTON Airfields

There are so many true major airports, the subject of this book, in the Washington area that the need to look for general aviation fields may be ruled out of the average itinerary, if only due to restrictions of time. To complete the picture, some fields may repay attention: COLLEGE PARK is north Washington's main g.a. field, with over 150 residents. The Metrorail isn't recommended on this occasion, as the station of the same name is nowhere near the airfield.

To the east of Washington is ANDREWS Air Force Base, where tours are arranged for visitors on a regular basis during the summer months. These are subject to cancellation and written details should be obtained prior to departure from home. In the event of the Public Affairs Department turning down an application for a visit, an alternative may be contact the Air National Guard Unit, located at the end of a road which passes the Naval facilities on the base.

Silver Hill is not a famous place in its own right but it deserves to be. Anyone visiting the Smithsonian Air and Space Museum in Washington should note there is an annex, served by a free shuttle bus. The annex, at Silver Hill, has some extremely impressive exhibits, including a YF-12 to complement the SR-71 housed in the downtown building. Silver Hill is southeast of the city, on the way to Camp Springs and Andrews.

Also close to Andrews is HYDE FIELD, with some items of vintage interest among the Pipers and Cessnas. Forty-five miles south is FREDERICKSBURG (SHANNON) which is well worth the mileage for its collection of pre-war aircraft, including Bellanca and Northrop airliners in flying condition.

GREATER WILMINGTON DE
ILG   KILG   6m/9km SSW

The city is the home of the du Pont Chemical Company, owned by about 1600 very wealthy adult family members, few of whom bear the surname. The extraordinary quantity of biz-jets to be found here is a tribute to their prosperity.
   Not far off Interstate 95, between Philadelphia and Baltimore, Highway 141 from the north gives a first, stunning impression of the airport and its well-heeled residents. Apart from two ramps and hangars of these private aircraft, there is very little activity. A quick foray onto the tiny roof deck will rarely reveal more than one airliner on the ramp, as most of the movements are used for commuting. Also visible on the far side of the field is the Delaware ANG base, with its own ramp of C-130s, their serials just readable through the average binoculars.

CLEARWATER FL
PIE   KPIE   Saint Petersburg   10m/16km ESE

The alternative airport for Tampa Bay comes a very distant second to the busy international field of Tampa. Airline traffic is mostly of a modest nature but the terminal does also handle occasional charters from Canada. Sun Jet International DC-9s, Canada 3000 A320s, American Trans Air 727s and Air South 737s are the most regular visitors. The amount of interest (or lack of it) in Clearwater as an active airport is evident from the total absence of any reports about what can be seen through the tinted windows of the passenger terminal.
   Off the main highway, the terminal and general aviation facilities are side by side, and one or two interesting smaller aircraft can be seen. There is normally a couple of UPS 727s parked all day but often too close to the fence for a photograph of any quality. Another access road leads to the business terminal and a few biz-jets park here, though often difficult to see from the fence. Close to this executive terminal are the US Coastguard base, with Hercules and HH-53s, and an aircraft museum with one or two interesting exhibits including an A-4 Skyhawk. Pemco carry out work on 727s mostly, and one or two can sometimes be seen.
   It is unlikely that anyone would visit this airport for more than a casual look around while passing, because of the lure of Tampa and more lively runway activity. The aviation enthusiasts' shop is worth a visit, specialising in all sorts of publications for the light aircraft flyer as well as a selection of T-shirts and suchlike.

DAYTONA BEACH FL
DAB   Regional   3m/5km W

Another small airport where not much happens, it is well worth the detour, if only to see what is present at Trans Florida Airlines. A couple of their CV-240s have been withdrawn from use for some time, and are unlikely to move in a hurry. If the gate is closed, ask at the FAA tower for access to take photos. The aircraft may have a slightly South American air to them but the immaculately cut grass gives a very different impression.

FORT LAUDERDALE FL
FLL   KFLL   Hollywood International   4m/6km S

Despite being so close to the northern edge of Greater Miami, Fort Lauderdale handles a prodigious amount of traffic, with surprising quantities of Delta TriStars and other widebodies. The traffic to the extremely busy terminal is similar to the domestic airliners visiting Miami, and Runway 9L/27R is used for the majority of it. Fortunately, both ends are accessible for the photographer, with SW 39th Street offering an impressively close vantage point at the western end, and Marriotts Catering car park at the east. There are two economy car parks, north and south, which cost only $3.50 a day, for anyone intending to spend time in the terminal.

Three passenger terminals are arranged in an arc. Delta's Terminal 1 is also used by Icelandair. Terminal 2 has been described, dismissively, as being used by the usual airlines and not very interesting. Few would disagree with that verdict. Terminal 3 offers variety, with Air Tran, Spirit and Laker. If photographs are not essential, this might be the place to spend a day. Between the terminals, the upper level road offers the chance to wield a camera to some effect.

A clockwise tour starts by leaving the passenger terminal and taking the first exit, marked for car rental returns. The employee parking lot, accessible from the perimeter road running parallel to Griffin Road, overlooks the threshold of 9R. The first ramp of note is that of Paradise Island.

A series of right turns leads to the FAA tower and, next to it, the Combs-Gates Lear Jet facility. The number of biz-jets handled here and at Hudson General is large, and there are gateways close by which allow good views of any traffic landing on the diagonal 13/31 Runway, which is used mainly by small aircraft. The old FedEx facility has been taken over by Carnival Airlines. Its ramp ususally holds a variety of interesting residents. The FBOs have, in the past, been quite accommodating to requests for a look around. This is no longer the case, as spotters have caused trouble, thereby spoiling the enjoyment for everyone else.

The next vantage point is at a gate by the threshold of the busy Runway 9L, on SW 39th Street, particularly useful when the sun is behind the camera, as it faces north. This corner of the field is extremely popular with photographers. Here the airport authority has conceded defeat, and made holes in the fence. Continuing past this point, watch out for a large viewing mound which is ideal for photographers, with the sun at their backs.

The elevated road along the northern boundary, above SW 34th Street, dominates the many ramps full of all sorts of airliners, many of which have been here for some years. The first ramp is occupied by FedEx. Beyond it lie a variety of aircraft ramps, several of which are accessible after a request at the offices. The main cargo ramp contains Kittyhawk, Airborne Express etc, whilst the Chalk's maintenance ramp may have a Catalina hidden amongst their Grummans.The Embraer apron may yield a 145 while the Walkers International ramp has a reputation for holding more than its fair share of interesting aircraft. DC-4s/6s are becoming a rarity, as are CV-440s, but Dave's Airplane Repairs can usually be relied upon to offer something out of the ordinary. Florida Air Transport is a resident operator, using a fleet of propliners such as DC-6's, CV-440's and a C-117. Access to their ramp is also normally granted, upon request.

To anyone who hasn't visited Fort Lauderdale for two or three years, the cargo terminal comes as a surprise. It has enjoyed much growth, and it isn't finished yet. The overnight parcels traffic operators spend the day here, with a couple of Burlington 727s being a regular feature, though usually parked too close to other aircraft to make good subjects for the camera. At the end of the northern perimeter is the Marriott car park but with the disadvantage that the prospect is southwards, into the sun.

FORT LAUDERDALE FL

| FXE | KFXE | Executive | 6m/9km N |

Continuing north along Interstate 95 from Fort Lauderdale-Hollywood, the next port of call is likely to be Fort Lauderdale Executive airport, accessible from NW 50th Street. Most of the facilities and aircraft are on the southern edge, with many ramps and hangars containing a good variety of general aviation. Apart from a huge number of light aircraft and a fair number of biz-jets (including one or two from Latin America) there are some specific items to note. A Mexican 125 and a Brazilian Sabre have been stored for several years but the Mexican Westwind appears to have been scrapped. The ramps most likely to hold something of special interest are probably World Jet Center and Renown Aviation.

FORT MYERS FL

| FMY | KFMY | Page Field | 4m/6km S |

Despite the rise of the regional airport, Page Field is still worth a visit. It achieved fame from the

Modern Air Transport DC-7 which ended its days here. With scheduled traffic using Southwest Florida, the accent is on general aviation. It is a strong accent. From occasional pistons up to DC-3 size and an array of biz-jets, the Fort Myers community needs a lot of aircraft. This is where to find them.

FORT MYERS FL
RSW   Southwest Florida Regional   14m/22km SE

Some miles away from Page Field is an impressive new airport with a very long access road. The darkened glass of the passenger terminals overlooks a quantity of stands but the operators are a rather mundane lot. There are a few vantage points, one reached by an emergency access road which ends very close to the runway, though a car parked at this point could attract attention, being easily seen across the expanse of flat grassland, when parked in what is, in all probability, a prohibited place. The alternative would be to walk to the spot, a long way on a warm day, and very likely to generate the interest of several thousand mosquitoes.

A grassy bank overlooks the commuter ramp, where Beech 1900s park within reach of any camera, though the sun can be a problem. Better views are to be enjoyed at NAPLES (q.v.). Also in the Fort Myers area, due east, is LEHIGH ACRES. The exit north from Highway 82 leads to the field. The main reason for visiting is probably the chance to see the DC-3s of Lee County Mosquito Control.

FORT PIERCE FL
FPR   Saint Lucie County   2m/3km NW

One of several stops on the road along Florida's east coast, St Lucie is only likely to reveal an occasional Aero Coach Cessna on the little ramp and, parked all day, a FedEx Caravan.

GAINESVILLE FL
GNV   KGNV   J R Alison Municipal   6m/9km NE

An indication of how busy this inland airport gets: seeing a Delta 737, a USAirways Fokker 100 and a USAirways Express Beech 1900 in the space of two hours is about average during the day. However, the detour might be worthwhile if only to see and photograph the Gators' F.27. Florida University's basketball team use it as their hack. The field is mostly surrounded by trees, so the apron is where to see whatever is present. Most people do so, and move on.

HOLLYWOOD FL
HWO   North Perry   6m/9km W

Only a short drive east from Opa Locka, to Highway 817/NW 27th Avenue, North Perry is easy to find, even without a map. It is also only a short distance east of Fort Lauderdale. Apart from a lacklustre selection of light aircraft, North Perry is the home territory of Pelican Express. One or two of their Hansas, or their DC-3s, might be present. For anyone who likes to fill a notebook, the Army National Guard offer a number of UH-1s.

JACKSONVILLE FL
JAX   KJAX   International   14m/22km N

Since the traffic which visits this average-sized regional airport is fairly ordinary, the military activity is likely to be of greater appeal. Identifying these movements from the passenger terminal's observation deck is difficult, usually due to the heat haze.

The ramps next to the approach road have an interesting selection of aircraft, up to DC-3 size, but the end of the runway may have to suffice for most of the photographers intent on capturing an Air National Guard aircraft on the move. Prior contact with the base is worth a try, for a tour of the flightline.

KENDALL-TAMIAMI FL

TMB	KTMB	Executive	8m/13km SW of MIA

West from Miami International is what used to be called New Tamiami. It is reached by following the South Dade Tollway/Highway 874. A turn at North Kendall Drive and a drive westwards leads to Lindgren Road/SW 137th Ave, the entrance being on the right. Fences appeared, spreading like weeds, preventing free access to the ramps. Requests are necessary, but usually granted. There are often as many as 300 light aircraft parked here.

The Kermit Weeks Museum has attracted a growing collection of rarities, some of the larger ones merely using cheap storage space. At the last count, there were two DC-3s and DC-6s plus a CV-240. The devastation of the 1992 hurricane has been repaired and the museum has re-opened, with an admission charge of a reasonable $6.50

KEY WEST FL

EYW	KEYW	International	3m/5km E

The customs facilities justify the International tag. Once the dawn flight of an ASA Brasilia has left for Freeport in the Bahamas, there is little else during the day to cause excitement. The rest of the traffic includes only the occasional foreign light aircraft to augment the types seen further to the north. For lovers of spectacular scenery (and Florida doesn't offer much) the drive to Key West may be worthwhile. It may also be nice to reach the tip of the country but the journey is of little value for the aviation enthusiast.

The airport is small and has adequate opportunities for taking photographs from the fence next to the apron. General aviation, to the left, occupies a crowded ramp, so that photos can only be taken with access. The right side of the apron is used for freight but little arrives or leaves during the day. The Naval Air Station is not renowned for giving casual tours and it is a long way to drive without confirmation, views of the field from the perimeter being impossible.

MARATHON FL

MTH			1m/1.5km NE

On the way from Miami to Key West is Marathon, still surviving as an airport with some scheduled commuter traffic, which can be easily seen. As befits a local airport of this size, activities are quite informal and photographers are satisfied. Apart from the occasional scheduled visitor, DC-3s of the Monroe County Mosquito Control can also be inspected at close quarters.

MELBOURNE FL

MLB	KMLB	Regional	3m/5km NW

The passenger terminal is tiny and very quiet. Melbourne's catchment area is limited, due to Orlando being only a short drive away. As is often the case with smaller airports, it is possible to get closer to the aircraft and this has certainly been the case at Melbourne. Airline traffic, though by no means busy, features surprisingly large aircraft for such a small region. The opportunity for one or two, at the most, photos will compensate the detour but a stay in excess of an hour will only be due to the wait for something interesting on the arrivals monitor. Grumman have a systems division base here, which is used for carrying out radar modifications to a variety of aircraft. Security precautions are inevitable around USAF E-8As, so expect the worst.

MIAMI FL

MIA   KMIA   International   7m/11km W (bus 40 minutes)

The sun deck on the international satellite is only available to passengers with a boarding card, and even then seems to be closed more often than not, though the windows in the terminal do offer reasonable views. Security has tightened considerably at Miami, and boarding passes are required for entry to all concourses. Because there are only restricted views from any concourse, keeping pace with the changing scene involves much physical activity.

There seems little doubt that the best vantage point at the airport itself can be found at the top of the hotel in the terminal. A lift at the Hotel MIA will take you to the 7th floor, where access is available - even if you are not a hotel guest. With drink and food available the sundeck here offers a chance to monitor most movements but for the photographer it offers little. When the sun becomes too fierce the perimeter of the health club on the 8th floor offers more shade, and a variety of bars. Should this facility be closed, the top level (7) of Car Park 2 or 4, which are linked to each other, also offer views but without the luxury of three essentials - food, drink and shade. To see the entire field, access is also required to Car Parks 3 and 5. This is where the fun starts. Level 7 is an island in these two car parks, offering direct connections nowhere else. Level 4 becomes that for all interchanging. If it all seems too complicated, or tiresome, hire a car!

Prolonged stays out in the hot Florida sunshine, like on a rooftop car park, can become very wearing. Without soft drinks, or water, dehydration and sunstroke are genuine health hazards. A large bottle of Diet Coke, no matter how warm it becomes, is much cheaper than a few minutes in an American hospital. Baseball caps, worn backwards, offer more than street cred. Red faces, no matter how uncomfortable, are less dangerous than red necks.

From inside the air-conditioned comfort of a rented car, the visitor will need to plan a tour of the boundary, starting at the main terminal. The huge car parking blocks are topped with a heliport, and the tunnel-like roads beneath can make it difficult to understand the road layout. A right hand exit leads away from the main road to the city and into some minor service roads. The ramp to be seen on the right is used by Delta, USAirways and for some charter flights, and an adjacent ramp has been used for storage in recent years.

Passing the thresholds of 27L and 30, the southern perimeter offers superb views of the aircraft using the southern runway (in one direction or another) with several parking places. The height of the fence is just enough to make photography difficult, and something to stand on will be of use. There may be signs of previous attempts to solve the problem, with a pile of stones, wood or even an old tyre being left for further use. The serious, and professionals, prefer a set of steps. These can be purchased from Home Depot on Flagler Street or rented from *Just Plane Crazy*.

Much of the international traffic uses this runway and it is only necessary to get into position at one end or the other to watch a procession of some extremely exotic airlines. Even movements on Runway 9R can be photographed at the eastern end, as they taxi a long way parallel to the runway before turning into the terminal complex. A 300mm lens may be necessary for good shots on the taxiway, however. The carriers normally using this runway include many Latin American airlines, ranging from TACA 767s to TAN Electras, Varig 767s to Aero Coast Rica 727s.

Parked at the old Airlift hangar are 707s and DC-8s of several operators, some American and some foreign, and all too close to each other. Runway 9R, Miami's longest, sees a lot of use and photographers may find themselves settling in the NW 72nd Avenue area. Keep an eye open for the excellent aviation enthusiast's shop, called *Just Plane Crazy* at 1200 NW 72nd Avenue, and the premises of Eddy Gual (Aviation Photography of Miami), who also rents out stepladders.

A drive around the western end of the runway gives closer views of these aircraft but photos are still difficult to obtain. For landings on 9R, a furniture store called *El Dorado* offers a car park which might make a good base. Cargo World looks a little long in the tooth these days but modern extensions are still being added, none of which make things better for the enthusiast. The various cargo ramps and hangars contain a huge variety of 707s and DC-8s along with more modern aircraft operated by cargo carriers from around the world. FLS and Commodore Aviation have facilities for aircraft maintenance which are always busy with constant conversions taking place. After the demise of propliners at Miami, even the 707 is now becoming a rarity with DC-8s far more strongly represented. Before leaving this area for other ramps to the north, note should be made of one vantage point off NW 25th Street which has given good service over the years, overlooking the thresholds of both Runways 9L and 12. The Department of Agriculture has a car park which seems to be freely available, but *do not leave your car unlocked or with any items of value on display inside.* With the sun behind, aircraft taking off from this corner are extremely photogenic, especially as exotic oldies are often best seen on the move from here. Aircraft landing on 9L also make good subject matter for the camera.

Passing the thresholds of 9L and 12, a right turn leads into a small cargo complex, used mostly by Latin American companies - Tampa Colombia are regular visitors.

Returning to the perimeter, and heading to the north eastern corner, those who remember *Cockroach Corner* will find it surrounded by a wall of blast ramps. Not much has changed for the better here and, along the northern perimeter road, thirty feet-high concrete walls have been erected, blocking most of the views. This wall is expected to extend around most of the perimeter, so reports of its progress will be gratefully received. All side roads of NW 36th Street have to be driven down for views of the ramps. Continuing along the northern perimeter road, the next right turn leads past the Trans Air Link ramp, with a chance of seeing their fleet of propliners, all of which are parked too close to the fence and buildings to be easy to photograph. At the end of this road is a small terminal used for customs clearance by cargo and executive flights arriving at the north side. Views from here are a matter of luck but the Aeromar and Pan Aviation presence can be enriched by the occasional sight of a parked TAN Carga Electra.

Miami was once synonymous with piston aircraft, but today Trans Airlink are the only active operators, using two DC-6s, a DC-7 and a C-118. Conner, Aerial Transit and Regal Air (all names associated with old airliners) have gone, to be replaced by others for a while, but most of the new operators have upgraded to jets. There may still be the odd DC-6 or Convair along the northside but most are unserviceable and being used for spares.

The next street offers closer views of Pan Aviation and a few derelict airliners, and the confined space of the Department of Commerce apron, often with an Electra and/or Hercules. Other aircraft to be seen here can include a Varig wide-body parked for the day before its evening departure. Leaving this street, the first real view of the general aviation activity is seen, with a ramp used by a good number of biz-jets. Often a good selection of Central American executive aircraft are present, and behind them is another enormous apron. The inhabitants of this stretch of tarmac can be the most exotic to be seen in Florida, featuring VIP aircraft of many Latin countries, some of them military, in the company of small airliners old and new. This is not always the case, however. The perimeter tour ends, effectively, at NW 57th Avenue, where a right turn at the lights leads ultimately to the northern taxiway. This road gives access to some large car parking areas and there should always be something of interest to be seen. Some folk have been known to make use of the hire car roof as a vantage point for good photos but it should be remembered that the police have quite a presence on this street, and this sort of activity arouses the wrong sort of interest. The Page Avjet terminal here is not always busy.

NW 36th Street is a divided highway and turns to the right are numerous. Only one or two are worthwhile, these being at either side of the former Pan Am Training Center. The huge car parks next door overlooked the Eastern maintenance facility, and still offer a good view of the threshold of 27R and executive aircraft taxying along to the holding point as a bonus.

A right turn at the end of NW 36th Street leads onto NW 42nd Avenue (also known as le Jeune Road) and under the approach to Runway 27R. A little further along the road is the entrance to the passenger terminals and the tour is complete.

Future expansion plans at Miami include the addition of the third parallel runway just north of the existing runway, which would considerably alter the face of the northern side of the airport. A concourse, being built to the northeast, will increase gate capacity and in turn allow for the closure and refurbishment of other concourses.

On the northbound side of le Jeune is the George T Baker Aviation School, which should be of interest to first-time visitors, with its ex-Belize 720 and other interesting types. Apart from the views of aircraft which are the reason for visiting, there are other buildings which may be worth noting. Breakfast in America is one of the joys of the holiday and The Grand Slam at Denny's is highly recommended: their local restaurants are just south of George T Baker and north of NW 57th Avenue. Lovers of fast food will find the Burger King just across the road from Page Avjet, and gourmets will find an excellent Chinese restaurant nearby. A good value lunch can be found at Jerry's Catering next to Cargo World. Hotels abound on all sides except the west but those on the north side are of variable quality. Comfortable and quiet is the Ramada Inn in the southwest corner, close to Dolphin Expressway.

Miami International enjoys a reputation as being one of the most interesting airports in the entire world. It is busy, it offers variety and there is no shortage of vantage points. To get the most from it, a car is essential, as most Florida itineraries require independent mobility.

MIAMI FL
OPF   Opa Locka   7m/11km N of MIA

Opa Locka is north of MIA, up le Jeune to NW 135th Street. Its inmates guarantee something interesting (if not outstanding). They include the US Coastguard, a varied selection of executive aircraft from several Latin American countries, DC-6s and other propliners, plus plenty of large jets, in storage or under restoration, and a lot of general aviation with exotic registrations.

The TPI ramp held a number of Electras for some time, one of which bore ALM Cargo titles. A book, written in late 1997, cannot offer reliable information on what may be seen there a year or so later. One visit can result in seeing a number of Beech 18s whilst another, six months later, can offer something else.

Taxiway activity is not brisk, so the possibility of a sensible spotter coming into conflict with aircraft on the move is improbable. The airport manager's office may grant permission for a look around, and it is unusual to have to get out of the car, once airside, except to take the photographs and check the contents of the hangars. The three large hangars near the control tower have a good variety of inmates, from the USCG at one end to Twin Otters and Latin American twins in the others. A request for access to the coastguard facility is best obtained by walking along the path between hangars and apron to the main office, thereby omitting the gatehouse, where negotiations can take a little longer.

Beechcraft and MAC are the FBO's and their ramps and hangars are guaranteed to contain some interesting types, ranging from American biz-jets to Latin American twins. Despite the amount of fencing around Opa Locka, there have been no reported instances of difficulty in gaining access to the aircraft. All that's normally needed is a polite request and sensible behaviour. Storage and scrapping areas can be found further around the field, and these usually contain a large number and variety of aircraft, ranging from TriStars, A300s and 707s to DC-3s.

MIAMI FL
MPB   Watson Island   2m/3km E

Heading east from Miami International, along Dolphin Expressway, the highway leads across the MacArthur Causeway, to Watson Island, with Chalk's Seaplane Base on the right immediately after the bridge.

NAPLES FL
APF   Municipal   2m/3km E

Situated at the western end of Alligator Alley, Naples is well worth the trip, if only to get close to a completely different set of aircraft from those seen at Miami. Renowned for its sunshine and, for many years, for its surprisingly large number of executive movements, Naples has, in recent years, acquired a new passenger terminal and a proportionate increase in scheduled services.

Close to the highway is the old terminal and its ramp crammed with bizjets. The informal attitude here should make access for photographs easy. Usually to be seen is the odd aircraft withdrawn from use, though others have been secreted elsewhere. The terminal is very pleasant indeed and features several operators, compared to the times when all scheduled action was dominated by PBA. Fierce competition at Naples means that commuter flights are regular, and the sight of two jets side by side on the small ramp is quite impressive. The enclosure which separates the terminal from the ramp is an ideal spot for any photographer and a short stay during the week should yield a good selection of portraits not easily obtained elsewhere.

There is another spot, just left of the terminal building which overlooks half of the apron and is also good for some different views, also at close quarters. The C-47s of Collier County Mosquito Control are based in their own secure compound, which is reached by continuing round the perimeter road, instead of turning right into the passenger terminal. Naples' most famous residents were the Martin 404s, access to which requires official permission.

ORLANDO FL
MCO   KMCO   International   10m/16km SSE

A central location is needed to overlook all the action. Above the main terminal is a multi-storey car park. This must not be confused, by people with cars, with Critters A or Critters B garages. Every level of each of the three multi-storey car parks has its own name. In Disney's make-believe world, leaving your car on Tropical Fish or Manatees is more user-friendly than trying to remember B1 or A2. Level 10 on the central garage is Eagles. It offers, instead of shade, a panoramic view of everything that moves. When it gets too hot, go down a level to Pelicans.

There is no shortage of action on the eastern side of the airport and yet it is just a fraction of what is to be seen at Orlando. Airside 4's main occupant are Delta Airlines and its associate Comair. Mickey Mouse and his friends are often to be seen in this modern terminal but they have yet to be seen boarding a plane. The terminal is reached from the central concourse by monorail, and allows good views of all aircraft on their stands and on Runway 17/35. As well as playing host to Delta, it is also used by some of Orlando's more interesting international visitors, which include TransBrasil, LACSA, and Saudia. Checking out the arrivals board is a necessity, given the time it takes to travel from this terminal to those on the western side of the field.

Returning to the main concourse it is time to explore Airside's 1 and 3 (Airside 2 is still a concrete base). Airside 1 is perhaps the most crowded terminal, featuring constant activity by a variety of US airlines including Western Pacific, Carnival and Vanguard. When you add to these American, America West, Continental, TWA, and the Canadian operators, things can get hectic at times. Photographers will feel frustrated by the poor views through windows which are often obscured by ground vehicles and cargo pallets. Airside 3 movements are dominated by United and USAirways. ANA is the only major international carrier using this terminal.

Away from the central area, the western side of the field is worthy of detailed exploration and care should be taken to avoid the Beeline Expressway as a link. Not only does it cost 75 cents each trip between the east and west sides, it is also time-consuming. Instead, it is best to watch out, on leaving the eastern terminal facilities, for Cargo Road and a left turn. This leads to the perimeter of the field and an anti-clockwise circuit passes close to some interesting features. Alternatively, drive under the Expressway and turn left at the lights next to Lee Vista Center. This is Semoran Blvd (SR436) which has a parking area opposite the threshold of 18R, where landing aircraft pass, at close quarters.

Reaching the northeast corner from Cargo Road, the cargo facilities occupy the site of the original airport complex. Normally parked here is a DC-8 of UPS and a Burlington 707 keeps it company in the early morning. On the other side of the road is a B-52D and a small car park. By following Ports of Call Street past the thresholds of the parallel runways, a left turn at Tradeport Drive is best followed by patience. Despite views of interesting ramps, it is sensible to head south to the far end, make a U turn and carry out the detailed investigations from the right side of the divided highway.

Freezone Street is the last accessible turn which, apart from giving access to the Citation maintenance hangar, is a dead end. The police are not too happy with long term parking near the fence in this area. When the runways in use are 36-oriented, this can be the best location on the airport for watching movements, although those on the far runway are distant. Page Avjet have a charter terminal served by a fair selection of US carriers, and the taxiway passes indecently close to this vantage point.

Returning north, past the charter terminal and the large Page hangar, the next ramp is used by a good variety of executive traffic, followed by a long low freight facility used most regularly by

Airborne Express. The maintenance base on the next ramp was occupied by Florida Express and subsequently Braniff. Ramps here, which otherwise remain empty, have been used for storage.

The F-101 is prominently displayed as a tribute to McCoy AFB, though in dilapidated condition, at the end of the street, with only a peek into what remains of the military base to complete the tour. Inmates are the RU-21s and UH-1s of the US Army, most of which can be readily identified.

Having seen all the residents at close quarters, the business of monitoring movements remains to be considered. When the 36-runways are in use Freezone Street is the best vantage point, though it can be an unpleasant experience, with a cool northerly wind. Fortunately, Florida is famous for its balmy (at least) climate when the wind is from the south. Orlando is at its best most of the time as the warm weather and prevailing winds also allow the use of the best parking place on the entire perimeter. A vast, though underused, customs car park takes up most of the space next to the holding point at the northern end of the field. From the roof of a hire car, classic portrait shots with no background clutter are easily achieved. The police patrols pass, without conflict.

The Park and Ride car park, at Cargo and Bear, allows traffic at the north side of the international terminal to be seen, and photographed though once again some artificial means of getting above fence level is needed. The southerly aspect of this location should be borne in mind by the photographer.

ORLANDO FL
ORL   KORL   Executive   4m/6km E

When the USAF quit McCoy AFB, Orlando acquired the site for the new civil airport which we know as Orlando International. This also explains the MCO code. Orlando's old airport, formerly known as Herndon, became used for executive traffic, being conveniently placed closer to town. Whilst there are no scheduled services, anyone seeking biz-jets to boost a day's log should consider the detour. It is only a few miles east of the centre of town, and can be reached by taking Ewell Ave, to the south of Colonial Drive (Hwy 50). The shopping mall car parks, off Interstate 4, offer good views across the field. What can be annoying is the sight of interesting airliners passing overhead on their way into MCO, almost all of which carry no under-wing registration markings.

PALM BEACH FL
LNA   KLNA   County (Lantana)   8m/13km W

Not to be confused with its big brother, Palm Beach International (which is actually WEST Palm Beach!), Palm Beach County is just west of Interstate 95 and is a busy little general aviation field whose main attraction is the maintenance base of Florida Airmotive and the ramp containing a pleasant selection of types.

PANAMA CITY FL
PFN   Bay County   3m/5km N

The airport is not busy by any stretch of the imagination, but it is worth a detour, if anyone wishes to find out what aircraft Bay Aviation are working on. The only guaranteed inmate is the DC-3 used by a spider-research unit.

SANFORD FL
SFB   6m/9km SE

Once just another quiet airfield on many a Florida itinerary, Sanford has over the past few years taken on the role of international gateway for many European charter flights. The huge expanse of tarmac which formerly saw little action now plays host to Britannia 767s, Monarch 757s and other charter traffic. Despite its location, operators have been attracted away from Orlando by the

134

speed of immigration and cheaper landing fees. It once provided a last resting place for Air Nevada's Beech 18s, in the company of some converted C-45s. One or two examples are still in reasonable condition. Starliner N974R started its life as D-ALAN with Lufthansa. It could end it here. Also to be seen here are numbers of S.55 helicopters, some restored for further action but most heaped unceremoniously in a storage compound.

SARASOTA FL
SRQ   Bradenton   5m/8km N

Not the easiest of airports to find from the average map but it is worth the effort. From Interstate 75, take exits 40 or 41 and head west. Whilst it is not busy, the observation deck is either (a) reasonably well placed or (b) a complete waste of time, depending on who is telling the story. It certainly does allow views of aircraft up to 727 size, as well as the occasional Delta 757, but there are other options which may be better. Photography is certainly hampered by plenty of ground handling equipment and some closely spaced lighting columns. The appeal of Sarasota is the relatively large number of executive aircraft on both sides of the field, and withdrawn airliners directly opposite (and distant) from the terminal. The question is: where to go?

Immediately to the right of the terminal, is an elevated grass bank complete with bench seats, right in front of the commuter ramp. For classic shots of such movements as USAirways Express Beech 1900s, American Eagle Jetstreams or Comair Brasilias, this is certainly the place. Photos of some taxying aircraft are also possible, depending on the runway in use.

For a different view of the proceedings, other than that to be seen from by the terminal, leave and turn onto University. After the cargo road entrance, take the first left, past the runway approach light towers. Look out for 15th Street, sometimes known as Old Route 301, where there is a very nice place to watch, only a few hundred feet from the runway.

Dolphin Aviation, half a mile to the north on I-41, is always worth checking out. It's close to the runway and allows good access close to the taxiway. A small selection of biz-jets and one or two Nomads might be enough reward but there is always the chance of something a little special.

STUART FL
SUA   Witham Field   2m/3km E

Driving around Florida, seeking saturation coverage of its aviation scene, means a car is essential. There is little to see between West Palm Beach and Melbourne, except possibly for the declining Vero Beach and Stuart. Witham Field is close to the highway, and possibly worth the short detour because the airport has a toilet.

TAMPA FL
TPA   KTPA   International   5m/8km W (bus 30 minutes)

Photographs taken from Tampa's multi-storey car park are always easy to spot and the results are less than ideal, as the subject matter can be upstaged by palm trees in the foreground. It should be noted that there are many other vantage points worthy of exploration. At the centre of things is a semi-circular concourse area, with six terminals. The approach road leads north from Spruce Street but it should be avoided unless seeking only an overall view from the car park.

Arrival at Tampa airport by car may be via the Memorial Highway or Interstate 92, both of which lead to Spruce Street and a link road on the southern edge of the field. Taking this link road and then turning left, the road follows the perimeter fence, past some stored rental cars, to the large Post Office building. On the right of the road is a car park, where overspill use is permitted. The right turn at the intersection gives access to the service road which runs parallel to the main approach road.

Once the staff car park is passed, the first terminal to be seen is Airside A, occupied by Continental and Southwest. Airside B, previously occupied by Eastern, was still vacant (Summer

97) for lack of a tenant. What can be noted, instead of aircraft here, is the occasional lay-by. They are very convenient for a quick photo. The tow-away warnings have more relevance to long-term parking. The stop-go tour continues past Airside C occupied by Delta, Airside D - the home of United and Northwest, with Airside E again lacking a tenant. Airside D is occupied by American and US Airways and is one of the few terminals to offer good ground level photographs from within. Aircraft parked at this terminal also offer good photographic opportunities from the roadway adjoining the ramp.

The inner perimeter road can be very useful for photographers arriving by air and therefore without a car. By setting up base under the monorail to Airside E, familiarisation with what parks where can result in extremely good photos, as the aircraft taxi onto their stands. It does require a certain amount of energy, especially when a couple of interesting aircraft arrive at more or less the same time. Inside the accessible Airside E, the glass really is far too dark for photography but the view of Runway 36L is excellent.

Leaving the central complex, the close proximity of the taxiway and runway on the right are to be noted before making a left exit for the Post Office car park. A short walk back across the main road, and the aircraft on the taxiway are at the perfect distance for any photographer. Since most of Tampa's traffic lands on 36L and more than half of it leaves the same way, this is the single best place to stand. Sitting has its problems, however: it only takes one fire ant to give you a bite and it's time to look for somewhere else!

Up until lunchtime, when the sun starts to shine down the centreline of the runway, good photos are easy to take but afternoon options aren't quite as clearly defined. Alternative vantage points of such quality are rare and more than one at any airport would be asking too much.

Returning around the southern perimeter, the Raytheon Executive Center screens many of its inhabitants from view but the ramp still has quite a few executive occupants, best seen from the patch of waste land off West Columbus Drive. Also to be seen from here are the Mosquito Control DC-3s on the far side, reached by way of Dale Mabry Highway (I-92) and Tampa Bay Boulevard.

The internal angle of the field is occupied by Suncoast, an FBO handling more biz-jets, but views along the West Shore Blvd are hard come by.

Hillsborough Avenue, at the north of West Shore Boulevard, forms the northern airfield boundary. Look out for the large blue sign for the bowling alley. The car park is almost directly under the flightpath, when traffic is landing on 18R. During the mornings, this is an ideal place to take approach shots, with the bonus of there being less ants than at the other end of the field. A left turn leads into the cargo complex, which is a dead end. Whilst none of the aircraft parked at the cargo centre are visible from the road, the southern edge of the car park overlooks the main terminal apron. It does offer a reasonably close (but not comprehensive) view of aircraft moving around the taxiways and apron.

Tampa's international movements aren't quite as common as one might hope. The majority of these are Air Canada A320s, with Air Aruba and Cayman Airlines also regular visitors. Condor 767s can be seen, three days a week, with British Airways making an equal number of visits. Interesting US charter visitors include Sun Pacific Airlines and Spirit.

TITUSVILLE-COCOA BEACH FL
TIX   Space Center Executive   2m/3km S

Known to old Florida hands as Tico, a visit is usually made because it isn't far from Patrick AFB or Cape Canaveral. The reason for the diversion used to be the presence of the ex-Danish Air Force Dakotas which might still be there. Apart from these, there is normally little or no traffic of note.

VERO BEACH FL
VRB   KVRB   Municipal   1m/1.5km W

This small airport was the home of Piper Aircraft's Cheyenne assembly plant. Today it is better known as a ghost town. The last report referred to the workforce numbering a mere twenty. All

136

the activity that remains to be seen, as a reminder of better days, is the big training school's fleet of Piper twins. The small airline passenger terminal building handles the occasional feederliner and the ramp is seen at close quarters from the grassed enclosure between the building and the apron. If the commuter flights are few and far between, the ramp does offer a small collection of executive aircraft as consolation.

WEST PALM BEACH FL
PBI   KPBI   International   3m/5km SW

The affluence of West Palm Beach is conspicuously displayed along the southern perimeter of the airport. While the terminal is quaint, with views of the ramp through the fence between the buildings, the presence of airliners is totally eclipsed by the prodigious quantity of biz-jets. The various Fixed Base Operators handle an astonishing array of aircraft and a log of fifty biz-jets was considered the norm, though this was before the deepening of America's recession.

Apart from a good selection of airline traffic, up to 767 size, the south side of the field has two enormous ramps, both offering much, and both worth exploration. Unique to West Palm Beach is the regular presence of the US Navy's C-27, which may be parked with little consideration for the photographic fraternity, close to the Jet Aviation FBO. Lovers of older aircraft are not usually disappointed, as Renown Aviation Convairs are usually to be seen.

ATLANTA GA
FTY   Fulton County   2m/3km N

A lengthy stay in the Atlanta area means that Hartsfield will not be the only airport visited. For a change from Delta's fleet, there are two other fields of note. The first is Fulton County, some ten miles north of Hartsfield. Though there is a general aviation terminal on the north side of ATL, clearly it does not accommodate anything like the number of aircraft likely to be used by such a prosperous community as Atlanta. A drive around the perimeter gives the impression that Fulton County contains most of Atlanta's (indeed Georgia's) general aviation. Not so . . .

ATLANTA GA
PDK   de Kalb-Peachtree   12m/19km NE

Situated to the northeast of Atlanta, off Interstate Highway 85, is a general aviation field much used by the business fraternity. Anyone with an interest in executive transport should ensure a visit here. The observation area is popular enough for a commentary on the public address system.

ATLANTA GA
ATL   KATL   William B Hartsfield   9m/15km S (train 15 minutes)

Hub operations are now a common way of operating airlines, with many airports in the United States being dominated by one or two carriers, just as they are in Europe. The main difference is that, in Europe, the hub is usually the base for the national airline, such as British Airways at Heathrow and Air France at Charles de Gaulle. Atlanta was very much a forerunner of this practice in America, with 75% of all movements (and there are a lot) operated by Delta and Eastern. ASA included, Delta's share of the movements at Atlanta currently stands at an astonishing 81%. Whether time spent at such an airport as Atlanta is an enjoyable experience is subjective, and reports suggest that it is highly regarded by many.

The concourses are served by an underground people-mover, and many visitors will choose to investigate the situation fully for themselves. There are now five to choose from, but only one is reserved for 'Other Airlines'. Other airlines now include Lufthansa A340s, Swissair 747-300s and newer operators like Kiwi and Valujet.

It will be apparent very quickly that comprehensive logging (if such a thing is possible at all) involves quite a lot of travelling, made worse by the fact that both sides of each concourse can't be seen at the same time. If any reader is tempted by the prospect of fleet-watching without recourse to touring North America, a visit to Concourses C and D at Atlanta will ensure the best chance, as they overlook the runways and the cargo area, thereby allowing much of the action to be monitored.

At each side of the concourses are pairs of parallel runways: 8/26 to the north and 9/27 to the south. The numbering of gates on each concourse is consistent, so that C1 and D1 are both at the same end though they do not necessarily offer the same facilities. C1 has windows at the end, offering good views of the taxiway and runways, as well as being over-run with commuter passengers. A1 does not have this window feature, so viewing is inferior. There is little, apart from aprons, taxiways and runways to be seen on the southern side, as Delta's base occupies a large area between the runways, with everything else to the north.

Because concourse-based locations for watching aircraft only offer limited possibilities, alternatives are bound to be sought. Since photographic subject matter is also limited, a central overview would be ideal. Multi-storey car parks are often suitable, and Atlanta offers a choice of two such elevated vantage points. The South Deck overlooks the thresholds of Runways 9L/R, but looks into the sun, and prevailing winds mean that the 27 direction is most used. The North economy parking lot offers a view of landing aircraft, suitable for many photographers. Riverdale Bridge, over I-85, offers an alternative view of aircraft landing on the southern runways. This spot is only for the fit and dedicated - it's a long walk, the nearest legal parking being half a mile away.

The northern perimeter contains substantial cargo facilities, the vacant Eastern maintenance base and Hangar One, though photographs are only possible at the executive facility, with a car park allowing a decent view of the inmates. Watching the aircraft at the thresholds of Runways 8L and 8R offers some variety to the day, but photographers will be disappointed by the elevated aspect of the runway's end. Delta's maintenance hangars are centrally placed at the eastern end of the field but portraits of aircraft parked here are rare.

The Stouffel Concourse Hotel overlooks Hangar One, and south facing rooms on the upper floors will prove attractive, though the cost of such rooms may be out of reach to some. West of the terminal complex is the MARTA railway station, which supplies the link with the city, some fifteen minutes away. Though the airport sits in the middle of three Interstate highways, I-85 is that which actually serves the passenger terminals.

Atlanta is a major transatlantic gateway to much of America and, as such, it ensures that vast quantities of registrations are collected at the start of a holiday. The return trip with Delta might entail the use of Cincinnati, thereby allowing two airports to be sampled en route.

AUGUSTA GA
AGS   Bush Field   10m/16km S

Though this is the city's main gateway, its traffic is mostly Jetstreams operating feeder services to Atlanta for Delta. Jet traffic is mostly restricted to DC-9s plus some USAir F.28s, whose SD3.60 feeders are also in evidence. Augusta is still quiet enough for the casual observer to be able to pursue his interest without problems being encountered.

Very much Augusta's 'other' airport, DANIEL FIELD (DNL) is small but densely packed with light aircraft. The passenger terminal is used mostly by executives travelling in corporate and chartered air taxi aircraft, a good proportion of them being jets. It's about five miles south of the city.

GRIFFIN GA
6AZ   Spalding County   2m/3km S

About halfway between Atlanta and Macon, the airfield is on Highway 155, and worth a detour. If it moves, it probably has only one engine: it's all Cessnas and Pipers - well, nearly all. A lot of trees were cleared to make the airfield possible, so open views aren't to be expected. The single runway is surrounded by light aircraft and trees but arrival here gives an altogether different impression. The first sight, to the right, is the Academy Airlines hangar beside which are a couple of Carvairs, N83FA and N89FA. The airfield reception area is housed in the hangar next door. Ask and it shall be given.

Only N83FA was operational, at the last report. Close attention to detail around here will reveal several component parts of another Carvair, N155243, the fin still bearing its Pacific Air Express titles. If future visits to Griffin reveal no sign of N83FA, it may have been relocated permanently to BEAR CREEK (q.v.). Before getting back in the car, photos safely in the camera, take a look down the far end of the airfield. At either side of the runway are a couple of grassed clearings. Half a dozen C-47s have been seen here, including two owned by Academy Airlines. A few Beech 18s can also be expected, parked around here.

LA GRANGE GA
LGC   Callaway

Not an airport at all, though no apologies are made for including La Grange. There aren't too many places in the world where a Carvair can be seen. Make the most of it while it lasts. Some way southwest of Atlanta, and quite a long way out of town, the road leads to a crossroads at the perimeter. Instead of turning left and heading for the general aviation terminal, go straight ahead. The road stops at a gate next to a hangar. Beyond the garages (in 1993) was N103, wearing Pacific Express colours but no titles. Since the parking fees were being paid, this aircraft is considered an asset by its owner. Whether it will remain at La Grange is another matter. It's been here since 1989 - so far so good.

MACON GA
MCN   KMCN   Lewis B Wilson   8m/13km S

Also known as Middle Georgia Regional, it shouldn't be confused with Herbert Smart Airport, at Wheeler Heights, some 6 miles east of town. Neither the map nor an airline timetable give any impression of what the airport is like, and it would be easy to underestimate its status.

An F-86 Sabre on a pole is displayed at the airport entrance, in recognition of the Air National Guard base, seen to the right. This is not Warner-Robins, which is further out. The passenger terminal handles a modest amount of feeder traffic, many of which are ASA Brasilias. The ASA maintenance hangar is in the southwest corner of the airfield.

SAVANNAH GA
SAV   KSAV   International   9m/15km W

The name of Savannah means only one thing to the biz-jet afficionado: Gulfstream Aerospace Corporation. The scheduled 727s and DC-9s may come and go, albeit thinly spread, but enthusiasts usually visit Savannah to see completed Gulfstream corporate jets. The facility is located, not surprisingly, on Gulfstream Road, so there can be no excuse for missing it. This is where the construction process is completed, and aircraft are rolled out.

The only other presence here is that of the Georgia Air National Guard. To be seen on the far side of the field from the passenger terminal, there are normally half a dozen or so C-130s on the ground.

HANA HI
HNM   PHHN   Municipal   4m/6km NW

Reports from the Hawaiian Islands are so infrequent, it took some time to confirm this was the only airport at the eastern tip of Maui. The confusion arose from the two designators: normally three-letter IATA designators in the Pacific are prefixed with a letter P, for the four letter ICAO code. This does not apply to several of the Hawaiian airports. Apart from a small number of light aircraft, the only visitors here are the regular Aloha Island Twin Otters. It is probably the least interesting of the three airports on the island, the others being Kahului and Kapalua.

HILO HI
ITO   PHTO   General Lyman   2m/3km SE

Hawaii Island's Hilo International (Lyman Field) used to handle a selection of long-haul traffic but this now uses Honolulu almost exclusively. Inter-island services are mostly a restricted range of DC-9s and 737s, operated by the competing Aloha and Hawaiian Air.

HONOLULU HI
HNL   PHNL   International   6m/9km NW

This extremely large airfield is to be found on the south coast of Oahu, between the evocative Waikiki Beach and Pearl Harbour. Runways 04/22L/R are placed diagonally to the main passenger terminal, whilst Runway 8L/26R is aligned roughly parallel with the terminal. Reclaimed land in the bay was used to construct Runway 8R/26L, totally remote from any vantage point.

The international terminal is very impressive, especially when its open-fronted first floor observation level is first seen. This main terminal has one central pier projecting into the apron and, at both ends, L-shaped piers pointing outwards. The prospect which is offered is considerably better than what can be seen, however, because the traffic is essentially the same wide-body movements at Los Angeles or San Francisco, the view is due south, and four of the stands are arranged for the aircraft to park nose-in. For much of the time the view can be restricted by at least one large aircraft in the foreground. To the right of the international terminal is the inter-island terminal which is fully enclosed and has air bridges. Aloha and Hawaiian maintenance areas are situated opposite. A six-storey car park is situated at the rear of these buildings from which the activity can be seen, though long lenses will be needed for photos. The cargo facilities offer a good range of aircraft, and the ramp immediately to the left/east of the terminal contains quite a number of smaller aircraft.

Leaving the terminal area, the enthusiast makes his way to Lagoon Drive, at the eastern end of the field, for the other ramps. These are on the far side of Runway 4R/22L, and it is here that most of the local operators will be found. The essential hire car will enable the considerable length of these ramps to be explored, with many interesting operators to be seen, though the fence obstructs the view, and use will have to be made of the car's mobile elevated vantage point. Quite frustrating at times, this is a very individual part of the world, and what is seen (and photographed) here will be a peculiar mixture of old and new types in strictly local colours.

The western portion of the field is occupied by military bases, Hickam AFB and the ANG, both having their taxiway access at the threshold of Runway 8L. Without authorised access to one or other of these bases, identification of military aircraft is difficult and photography almost impossible.

For the most spectacular view of the airport, a trip to the Aloha Tower is essential. This overlooks the harbour and Runway 8R/26L. Through a long focus lens, departing aircraft seem to be aiming for the tower. Admission is free.

KAHULUI HI
OGG   PHOG   Maui Island   5m/8km E

Kahului is becoming an airport of international status. In addition to the regular Hawaiian DC-9s and Aloha 737s, Kahului is being used as a destination port for aircraft routing both inward and outward from Honolulu International. Traffic includes various trijets belonging to American, Northwest, United, and Delta, with Canadian International also visiting. There is also a wide variety of light aviation.

KAPALUA HI
JHM   West Maui   4m/6km S

Until 1987, Maui was served only by Kahului airport but it is more than an hour's drive from the major resort area on the west coast of the island, considerably longer than the flying time. Hawaiian Airlines formed a subsidiary company to develop this rival airport, on the west side. The impact on local aviation was significant: Aloha bought Princeville Airways and Mid-Pacific did a deal with Reeves Aviation, to be sure of operating the short-field airliners which were needed.

The small terminal has views through glass, and space at either side from which to watch a restricted number of shuttles, but one of these is the colourful Mahalo Air with their ATRs.

LIHUE HI
LIH   PHLI   Municipal   2m/3km E

The island of Kauai is the only other, apart from Hawaii, to be served from Honolulu by jet traffic with any regularity, although the same DC-9s and 737s visit Hilo. These schedules are operated to Lihue Municipal Airport, whilst elsewhere on the island, the Twin Otters use Princeville (HPV) - a small coastal airport, carved out of some fairly dense forest.

MOLOKAI HI
MKK   PHMK   Hoolehua   10m/16km SW

Another island, for those hopping . Once again, the scheduled ATR-42 flight will cause the biggest stir until it leaves, and everything goes quiet again. The Hawaiian Islands are exotic but they don't offer excitement at every turn.

BOISE ID
BOI   Air Terminal   3m/5km S

A real reason is needed to visit Idaho. Nice scenery is not enough, as the Rocky Mountains offer plenty of attractions in neighbouring states. Boise is, however, an extremely memorable airport. Gowen Field, as it is still known locally, is obviously scenic and it does offer a variety, though not quantity, with Horizon Air supplying many of the movements. Larger jet traffic is modest but nice. There can be few better places in the USA to see an America West 737 at close quarters. The general aviation terminal also handles a few biz-jet movements.

The Idaho Air National Guard base sees little activity during the week but, at weekends, part-time fliers climb into their jets for a spot of fun at the tax-payer's expense. The Army National Guard also has a base here, and their helicopters can be seen from the adjacent car park.

COEUR D'ALENE ID
COE   10m/16km NW

Empire Airlines. That name sums up the airport. Twenty miles east of Spokane, just across the border in Washington State, Couer d'Alene is eclipsed by it bigger neighbour. The Empire base can be relied upon to provide close contact with their small fleet, especially at weekends, when their F.27 or one of the Metros are present. Some wear Federal Express colours, for whom services are operated.

IDAHO FALLS ID
IDA   Fanning Field   2m/3km NW

The smart, modern terminal offers no views of the apron and, for the greater part of the average day, this is quite appropriate, as there is little to see. Occasional movements by Skywest and Horizon Air link Idaho Falls with the outside world, and a FedEx feeder Caravan occupies a separate cargo apron, awaiting its evening flight to Salt Lake City.

CHICAGO IL
CGX   Merrill C Meigs   1m/1.5km E

This small airport is located on the shore of Lake Michigan, with Soldier Field (home of the Chicago Bears) behind it. Because this airport is so close to the business district, and because its (short) runway is quite remote from noise-sensitive areas, there is a fair selection of executive movements.
   Closely comparable to Toronto's Island airport, where the STOLport capability has been used to the best effect, Meigs still seems under-used but its charming little terminal does have an observation area, very close indeed to traffic parking at the terminal.

CHICAGO IL
MDW   KMDW   Midway   10m/16km SW

Midway is the home to many of the country's second level airlines. A map shows the field to be a square reservation bounded on all four sides by residential development. Because it is such an old airport, the layout is perimeter-oriented, which is quite good news for the enthusiast.
   Arrival by car at the passenger terminal can be followed by investigation of the terminals. After a security check Midway offers some excellent photographic opporunties as long as you can find your way around the general ground clutter. With arrivals and departures operating from ground level the airport takes on a different dimension. One of the best vantage points is at gate B14 where all movements can be seen, although traffic taking off from the right can come up rather quickly. A large floor-to-ceiling window here offers the best light for photographs in the morning. Because of congestion (and possibly landing fees) at O'Hare, Valujet, Amtran, Western Pacific and Air South are all regulars. The constant flow of Southwest aircraft may initially give the impression that Midway has little to offer, but a wait will be repaid by the variety of scheduled movements and a large number of bizjets, especially at the weekend. An alternative point for photographers exists at gate A17 although, depending on the time of day, results can be variable. For those without a hire car, these may represent the best locations to log, and photograph, a proportion of the traffic. A pedestrian bridge from the main terminal leads to the Midway CTA rapid transit station (Orange Line) which connects to downtown Chicago at a cost of $1.50.
   A clockwise tour of the perimeter ensures an easy access to each turning, road traffic being on the right, and the western side of the field is occupied mostly by hangars filled with executive aircraft. The ramps, too, contain a worthwhile assortment, though not all the aircraft are going to be seen. The north side is where most of Chicago's general aviation is to be found; considerable numbers of single-engined aircraft are present, though few are very interesting. In the southeast corner is another batch of executive and light aircraft but access to this FBO is difficult, since the majority of the eastern side is bordered by buildings.

CHICAGO IL
ORD   KORD   O'Hare   21m/33km NW

The central terminal area is surrounded by runways on all sides, and traffic lands and takes off on almost all of them, regardless of wind direction. Since there is no single point where the bewildering number of movements can all be seen, it is an extremely difficult business to gain a complete picture of what is going on. If ever the enthusiast needed a guide to an airport from his own point of view, O'Hare is a real example, since research and decisions should prove to be essential before arriving.
   The spotter, armed with binoculars, notebook and pen, can spend a day here and be certain that his log will be a considerable one. Selectivity as to what particular movements are most sought will determine a single vantage point, and a number of aircraft (and even a number of airlines) will not be seen at all. The notebook will be full but by no means complete, so the more discerning are advised to have a plan of action. Photographers who prefer taxiing and ramp shots, and who don't like taking photos through glass, need not bother coming to O'Hare as the many views of the aprons are all from the terminal windows, and close access to taxiways is rare. The multi-storey car park

shares centre stage with the Hilton Hotel, and arranged round them are the passenger terminals in a large semi-circle. Even from the windows of Terminals E, F, H and K, there is more to see than at most other airports in the world but it is still frustrating to think how much activity is missed.

Two of the terminals are Y-shaped, leading respectively to piers/terminals E/F and H/K. Thus the gates, and aircraft parking at them, in the fork of the Y can remain hidden from view. The plan of the central area shows the general disposition of the buildings and detailed notes of what can be seen are quite spurious: all the major operators in the USA have scheduled flights to O'Hare, so their aircraft are to be seen. By walking from one end of the complex to the other (often several times a day) all the various windows can be found, and many offer good views of the ramps.

Constant motion from one end of the terminals to the other makes for a long day, so a permanent base must be found. One candidate has to be a seat near Gate C2 in the United satellite terminal. It offers comprehensive coverage of all movements passing round the north side, including Air Canada's CRJs and A319s. Gates K17-19 in the American Terminal offer good views of passing traffic. From here landings and take-offs on 22L/4R 27L/9R and aircraft taxiing to 32R and 27R can all be seen - and it also affords the opportunity to monitor movements at the International Terminal. Traffic at the International Terminal (5) does not start to arrive until late afternoon, but it can provide an excellent showcase for many European airlines' premier aircraft. Access is by boarding card only but little is lost because views are limited.

Delta's Gate L10 serves a similar function for the observer, at the other end. L10 faces the International Terminal but possibly at the expense of missing some of the many United movements.

On the north side of the terminal area is a large limousine park, bigger than most airports' taxi ranks, and this offers a north facing view of one of the inner taxiways, where some good photographs can be obtained. To the east of the international terminal is a small general aviation ramp and a cargo area used by TWA and Continental. In the northeast corner of the airfield are bases for the USAF and Illinois ANG, who operate KC-135s, and there are a few locations in the airport where the serials can be read off. Closer inspection is impossible without having made prior arrangements for a visit.

The main cargo area, in the southwest corner, is occupied by UPS, FedEx, United, American and Northwest. Identification of aircraft, once they're in this area, can be difficult from the passenger terminals, although Gate 18 in the American terminal does offer a chance. Also visible, from some parts of the terminal area, are the various maintenance hangars, in the northwest corner of the field. The drive to this area is a long one, and the reward for the effort is nil. Few aircraft are normally present in the daylight hours, and the whole area is only accessible through a security gate.

CHICAGO IL
PWK   Pal-Waukee Municipal   7m/11km N of ORD

Midway is linked to O'Hare by helicopter services, and other fields may be worthy of a visit, since they are now profiting from downtown congestion with similar helicopter links. One of these is Pal-Waukee, seven miles north of O'Hare at the intersection of Highways 45 and 21, where a selection of the region's general aviation can be seen at reasonably close quarters.

A serious interest in airliners will probably mean that the drive north from O'Hare is not considered. Biz-jet buffs will need to make the trip, to be sure of the chance for another twenty or so for their logbooks. This is easy to achieve without taking the trouble to negotiate entry to any of the hangars.

DU PAGE IL
DPA   County   30m/48km W of Chicago

Time to spare in Chicago may also make a visit to Du Page possible. It is west of the city on Highway 64. Much like Pal-Waukee, this is a destination for the enthusiast anxious to visit all the local fields for quantity, regardless of the interest (or lack of it). This is by far the largest general aviation field in the Chicago area, though only half a dozen biz-jets are likely on the average visit. It is the scrap compound opposite the main field which invites some real scrutiny. Among many other wrecks are the mortal remains of Falcon 20 LN-FOE which was written off in 1973. Also present, ex-TWA 707 N742TW, the active life of which came to an abrupt halt at Cincinnati in 1967.

GARY IN
GYY   Municipal   2m/3km W

Accessbile from, and close to, I-90 is Gary Municipal Airport, just across the state border from Chicago and Illinois, in Indiana. It may be close to the highway but a river runs between the road and the airport. To get there, take the Hwy 12 exit north, along Columbus Drive and Industrial Highway. Scheduled traffic is minimal.

INDIANAPOLIS IN
IND   KIND   International   8m/13km SW

Exit 11 off I-74 leads to Airport Expressway. Arrival by car normally means leaving it in the Remote Lot, which only costs $5. The free shuttle bus takes you to the passenger terminal's upper level. The large, spacious terminal building is arranged in a twisted W shape, with two piers extending from the centre tip. The layout is so open that the moderate traffic seems very thinly spread. There isn't one single spot which allows all the aircraft to be seen at close quarters but there is no shortage of windows from which to see particular movements. Most of them are slightly tinted but many of the doors are clear glazed.

The observation deck is located where Concourses B and C meet, and almost everything can be seen, though much of it from rather a distance. In winter, only the indoor portion is accessible. The railings to the outdoor deck are just at the wrong height, making work with a camera difficult. Something to stand on, like a solid camera case, is an advantage. Whilst a 200mm zoom lens is good enough for most shots, some of the movements, particularly on Runway 5L/23R, need 300mm. Not far from the American Airlines gates, the deck allows most aircraft on the move to be witnessed though the sun can be a problem in the afternoon. Mornings are definitely best.

About half the traffic is USAirways, the remainder being thinly divided between the other domestic carriers. Daily scheduled departures total something like two hundred. For close-up views of American Trans Air, gates C7 and C10 can be worth the walk, though A1 to A3 are also used. Gate C6 is used by Valujet, and C8/9 are for Southwest Airlines. Concourse D, used by USAirways, overlooks the distant executive apron and cargo areas. American Trans Air's maintenance base and the general aviation ramps are visible from various parts of the terminal area. A tour of the perimeter will lead to two viewing areas. Viewing park S is situated near the tower with views of aircraft on the taxiway leading to 5R. Continuing around the perimeter will lead to viewing park N. The Indy 500, at the end of May, attracts a large number of biz-jets.

LIBERAL KS
LBL   George Welch Municipal 2m/3km W

The three runways form a triangle, and the facilities are positioned on the east side of the field. Only the bare minimum of scheduled operations, however: Mesa operate Beech 1900s during the week. To the south of the passenger terminal is a museum with exhibits inside and out, spaced to allow photography.

WICHITA KS
BEC   Beech   6m/9km E

Wichita is peppered with airports and airfields, all of which are worthy of exploration. BEECH FIELD is on the north side of Highway 54. Webb and Greenwich Roads are the western and eastern boundaries. The drive up Webb possibly as far as JABARA Airport (for general aviation) on 29th Street, then back down Greenwich. What can be seen will include King Airs, 1900s and BJ400s. Log them and go, as that's all there is to do at this field. It is not the end of Beech's presence in Wichita, however, because there are two maintenance areas at Mid-Continent.

A little further out of town, and a few miles south of Beech, is CESSNA AIRCRAFT. The Cessna finishing centre is close enough to the northern boundary of McConnell Air Force Base to be almost part of it. Because of this, the view from Cessna Finance is more interesting to military enthusiasts. The F-16s can be seen and their serials, or most of them, can be logged. From Beech Field, a few blocks towards town leads to Rock Road. A left turn (south) along Rock Road passes under the turnpike, Interstate 35. Cessna Aircraft is on the right, and can't be missed.

McCONNELL Air Force Base is the other enclave of the military base to the western end of the field. For views of the dozen or so B-1s and about twenty KC-135s, try the tower in the old terminal building, part of Kansas Aviation. There is a museum, open between 10:00 and 15:00 during the week (but only 13:00 to 16:00 on Saturdays), from which is a view of the Boeing ramp. To reach Boeing skirt round the perimeter or reach it direct from town by George Washington Blvd. Apart from leading to McConnell this road also passes the aptly named Planeview Park. Boeing is to the south.

WICHITA KS
ICT   KICT   Mid-Continent   6m/9km W

At the opposite end of town from Beech, the airport entrance is also off Highway 54. To the north of the road is Lear Jet Inc. For a view of what is out in the open, there are a few places on the perimeter. Weekends are definitely good for visiting and viewing. Much the same applies to Cessna's facility. The factory area is enormous, with several assembly plants. The road marked 'Shipping' off what is believed to be Tyler, has no security check. It offers the best view. The purpose of production lines is to complete aircraft for delivery. This means that they are not supposed to spend weeks parked outside on the tarmac. Numbers of pre-delivery aircraft at Lear Jet and Cessna are not great.

Jet traffic at this, the main airport, is a good mix though the pace during the day is only moderate. There are plenty of 737s and DC-9s plus an assortment of commuters serving Kansas City. What is to be seen needs exploration. Cargo carriers at Mid-Continent supply a range of aircraft but, once everything on the ground has been logged, it might be time to move on.

CINCINNATI KY
CVG   KCVG   Northern Kentucky International   12m/19km SW

The city may be in Ohio, but the airport is on the south side of the Ohio River, in Kentucky. Its scheduled traffic is brisk, though limited to mostly a mixture of Comair and Delta. The twin runways are aligned 18/36, with the terminal area facing south, towards Runway 9/27, directly into the midday sun. To the west of the passenger terminal is a large cargo ramp, and to the east is a small Delta hangar. The main Comair base is on the south side, though a long way from the passenger terminal.

There was once an observation deck but it has been closed for several years and the only chance to witness movements at close quarters is to pass through the security check and watch from one of the lounge areas. An early start is recommended, to witness the departure of Comair's rather large fleet of Brasilias, CRJs and SF340s on their first flights of the day. Some may not return before dark, which happens early, due to the strongly tinted windows. Comair has its own terminal but it has few windows and is not worth the trouble of getting there, only to find it's a waste of time.

For a general view of proceedings, the top level of the car park oppsite Terminal 3 is probably as good as anywhere. Two of the three runways and the cargo ramp can be seen. The international building, an island on the far side of the main apron, obscures much of the action.

LEXINGTON KY
LEX   KLEX   Blue Grass   6m/9km W

Don't be tempted to use the free 15-minute parking, as a visit here can take longer than seems likely. By road from town, take Versailles Road (US 60). The main passenger terminal is surprisingly good for anyone who wants to stick around all day, log and photograph a selection of aircraft, without demanding huge quantities in the logbook. Most of the traffic is Delta and USAirways 737s but there are lots of commuters to be seen. The upper level of the terminal is glazed, and the view from it is panoramic. Photography through the glass presents no problems yet there is more good news: not only are the gates on the floor below accessible for close-ups, there is also a staircase, to the right-hand side of the concourse, which leads up to an observation deck.

Movements on Runway 26 and its taxiway are seen at close quarters from the area around Gates C4 and C5 - everything else, including the Southern Jet Hangar and Island Creek, from the central area of the main concourse. Outside the Aviation Museum of Kentucky are a C-46, B-24 and B-29. Lexington might not be the busiest airport in the world but it is certainly one of the more enjoyable.

NEW ORLEANS LA
MSY   KMSY   International   13m/20km NW

A city that has more character and tourist attractions than many others, and the airport (known locally as Moisant) offers plenty to see for a limited amount of time. Interest wears off after a lengthy stay, and only photographers with patience enjoy stays of more than a day. Inside the passenger terminal, the Delta area is poor for photography but the large windows elsewhere make up for this. Miami, Carnival and American Airlines all come commendably close to the camera, with even a chance to get a photo of the elusive American Airlines F.100s. West of the terminal, but out of view, is Lafon Air Park. Used by general aviation, this apron is worth the walk for close-up views.

Outside the terminal area, the perimeter is at its most attractive to the east. Airport Access Road offers everything. Traffic on all three of the runways, subject to normal wind conditions, passes (or passes over) this road. For the photographer, this road is what Americans call a turkey-shoot. You can't go wrong, assuming you park your car in one of the side streets, rather than on the main road. The No Stopping signs are strictly enforced. In the mornings, something will be needed to stand clear above the perimeter fence, to allow high quality photos. In the afternoons, Washington Street, on the other side of the runway, is an ideal spot when Runway 19 is in (normal) use.

NEW ORLEANS LA
NEW   KNEW   Lakefront   6m/9km NE

A brief geography lesson might be in order: New Orleans actually faces north, onto Lake Pontchartrain. The Mississippi passes round the south side of the city in a loop, hence the term Crescent City. Lakefront Airport sits on a promontory, just north of I-10. Take exit 241. This is the old airport, where the majority of the region's biz-jet population is to be found in the company with plenty of other general aviation and an ANG detachment of UH-1s. Most of the action can be seen from the fence.

BOSTON MA
BOS   KBOS   Gen E L Logan International   4m/6km E (train 10 mins)

Almost completely surrounded by water, like Vancouver and San Francisco, Boston is similarly frustrating for the enthusiast in offering very little in the way of compensation. For someone without a camera, the multi-storey car parks offer panoramic views of the proceedings, though even a good pair of binoculars may be inadequate to read off every registration.

Where Boston once boasted one of the best overall views of any airport, from the top of the 17th Floor, recent reports suggest that this facility no longer exists. The value of alternative vantage points will be dependant on the runways in use but Terminal B has its own multi-storey car park, offering what is probably the best chance to get close to much of the action, as it is reasonably centrally located. All traffic can be seen, and most of it identified, the bonus being it is reasonably close to the executive terminals. Terminal A, formerly used by Eastern, is completely new, with fourteen-gates.

After discovering that none of the car parks allows close scrutiny of a fair proportion of all the movements, it may be worth considering walking through the terminals, the darkened glass of which allows reasonable views of most aprons.

On leaving the central terminal complex, look out for a right turn after the Hilton Hotel. This leads to the cargo area and often features a healthy selection of visitors, ranging from Electras to 727s. Since the small-package business is founded on departure times between 17:00 and 18:00, the aircraft which have been parked all day too close to the fence for photography, should move into a better position on the way out.

Highway 1A north leads to Bennington Street, where beaches overlook 4L/22R and 4R/22L. By subway train from the airport, the station is Orient Heights, followed by a walk. Alternatively, Route 45 in Winthrop passes the yacht club, where a car park allows a reasonable view of traffic on 9/27. None of these locations are ideal for a photographer, and what.s seen from here is at the expense of movements on other runways.

HYANNIS MA
HYA   Barnstable   1m/1.5km N

Barnstable is at the gateway to the Cape Cod peninsula and its airport handles considerable traffic in summer. Permission for a walk around the apron is normally granted at the control tower and there is a good selection of smaller types to be seen. PBA's ability to survive was under threat year after year, and only by moving to Florida for the winter did it keep two seasonal traffic peaks viable. Gull Air was an attempt to do the same. After their demise, operations became more diffuse, with a good range of commuters to be seen, including Nantucket Airlines with Cessna 402s and the locally-based Hyannis Air Service, which operates as Cape Air. Quiet enough for some great photos.

BALTIMORE MD
BWI   KBW   Washington International   10m/16km S

This airport continues to benefit from substantial investment, capitalising on the overcrowded nature of Washington National and the relative remoteness of Dulles. Being very modern in terms of planning and convenience to the traveller, it has much to offer, with road connections entailing a relatively short journey time to the cities of Baltimore and Washington.

Modernity is usually the last feature of an airport which best serves the enthusiast but Baltimore's brand new observation area represents a significant investment. Between 09.00 and 21:00, visitors to this area have a vantage point forty feet above the old south passenger lounge. It even includes an exhibition area, with the cockpit of a 737 (which allows visitors the chance to simulate a landing) and *Flightview*, the facility to pinpoint the exact location, flight number and arrival time of airline flights currently in the nation's airspace. The Smithsonian Air and Space Museum operate a gift shop stocking a wide variety of aviation ephemera. The three thousand square feet of glass (only slightly tinted) ensure a wide angle of view. Of the five piers, only the new Pier E is inaccessible, as it's the international departures area, used by Air Aruba, Air Jamaica, El Al, Icelandair, BA and charters.

The other piers offer close encounters with aircraft at their stands but the glass is heavily tinted. Even on sunny days, quality photographs are hard to come by. This, of course, is highly subjective. For many, it's some consolation that the majority of its traffic can be seen just as well elsewhere. Pier C, completed in 1995, is used mostly by American, Continental and Northwest and Southwest. Pier D between gates 30-47 provides a good spot to record the many US Airways and US Airways Express flights, along with the chance to photograph an Air Aruba DC-9 or an Icelandair 757.

Since the airport is close to the Baltimore-Washington Expressway (I-295), a small diversion will at least be rewarded by a good selection of executive aircraft parked at the terminal to the north of the main passenger buildings. Leaving the terminal on Elm Road, a car park allows views of most of the executive aircraft as well as a glimpse of the cargo facility immediately to the north. An access road, Aviation Boulevard (Hwy 170/162) leads around the northern perimeter of the cargo ramp, where parked aircraft can be seen easily. The new large Building F belongs to Emery Airfreight. This in turn leads to the extensive general aviation area, east of Runway 15L/33R. On the southern edge of the field is the Thomas A. Dixon Jr. Aircraft Observation Area, close to the threshold of Runway 33, (BWI's main runway) and with a fast food outlet nearby. Follow Aviation Boulevard until it joins Hollins Ferry, two right turns onto Dorsey Road (Hwy 176) and you can't miss it.

BALTIMORE MD
MTN   Glenn L Martin   11m/17km E

Without a road map it would be very difficult to find Baltimore's other significant airport: east of the city, off Eastern Avenue (Hwy 150) is Glenn L Martin State Airport which has historical connections with the production of Martin seaplanes. It is now a general aviation field, shared by a quantity of light aircraft and the Maryland Air National Guard's C-130s and A-10s, most of which can be seen at relatively close range from the road.

When travelling by car from Wilmington, and wishing to avoid the unlovely city of Baltimore, head east from I-95 on the Beltway (I-695) to Eastern Avenue. Care should be taken at Intersection 36 where the highway becomes No 702 for a short distance to its end. Also in the area, a few miles to the south, is Essex Skypark, on the shores of one of the Chesapeake Bay inlets.

COLLEGE PARK MD
CGS   1m/1.5km E

This is north Washington's main general aviation field, with about 200 residents. They include a good number of warbirds, antiques and homebuilts. The Metrorail station, which serves the community of College Park from Washington, is nowhere near the field. It is served by an Amtrak commuter service, however. On the map, the airport is inside Washington's Beltway northeast of the city, reached by going south from Intersections 23 and 25.

BATTLE CREEK MI
BTL   W K Kellogg

The road between Detroit and Chicago is not one of America's loveliest, and the journey needs a break. Battle Creek may be worth a detour. Very little happens, with only a moderate amount of general aviation to be seen but the ANG ramp can be seen from the car park. Many of the inmates can be read off, and more if they are on the move, but this needs more time.

DETROIT MI
DET   KDET   City   5m/8km NE

For many years, aviation enthusiasts who specialised in piston power extolled the virtues of Detroit as if the only airport was Willow Run (q.v.) but the Motor City has other attractions which should be borne in mind by the would-be visitor. Not least of these is the City Airport which handles quite a number of commuter flights, with ATR-42 sand ATR-72's being accompanied by SF340s.

The decline of Willow Run as a centre for piston-engined operations, and the closure of Metropolitan Airport's observation deck has thrust Detroit City Airport forward as worthy of more attention. The main centre of operations for most of the executive movements as well as the commuter operators is now well worth a visit in its own right.

Interstate 94 links Detroit with the north and the City Airport is reached from the Gratiot Avenue exit. Further directions are superfluous for anyone with a car, as all that is necessary is to circumnavigate the field clockwise to gain close access to a real selection of the Midwest's general aviation activity.

Continuing north along Interstate 94 leads to Mount Clemens and SELFRIDGE ANG Base, which shares the field with a Naval Air Station. A letter to the Air National Guard would be almost obligatory for any military-minded enthusiast, as the varied assortment of types present is matched by a very enthusiastic approach to the subject of aviation at the base. A good reason for visiting the base is the reasonably well stocked Military Air Museum.

Heading in the opposite direction from the centre of Detroit are the two airports which most enthusiasts know about, though both are a shadow of their former selves.

DETROIT MI
DTW   KDTW   Metropolitan   20m/32km WSW (bus 45 minutes)

The airport is known locally as Wayne. Terminals A and G are not accessible without boarding cards. American Airlines Gate B8 overlooks a busy taxiway and one active runway. FedEx can be seen, and a modest amount of Continental traffic, but the view is restricted. The end of Terminal C is probably the best place, as it allows almost all the airline traffic to be seen taxiing by. The glass is, in most cases, in rather smeared condition, making photos of any quality unlikely.

Try instead the open air swimming pool deck of the Marriott. The view is comprehensive, including the cargo ramps, most of the terminals and traffic on Runway 3L/21R. A 200mm lens is adequate. The only problem is that, if enough people take this advice, it becomes self-defeating. The sun is most helpful in the mornings and a positive nuisance late in the afternoon.

The adventurous may investigate the employee car parking lots but they are only accessible to vehicles by the driver placing a card in the machine slot, obviously not a problem to pedestrians, and the main lot is very close to the central runway and its taxiway.

A road leaving the airport parallel (and to the right of) the main thoroughfare, leads to maintenance facilities and, ultimately, to the general aviation hangars in the northeast corner. The cargo facilities to the west of the field usually contain the occasional aircraft but daytime operations are quiet.

DETROIT MI
YIP   KYIP   Willow Run   30m/48km W

Willow Run was once Detroit's most famous airport. It is some distance west, on I-94, on the edge of Ypsilanti. Its renown as one of the world's great airfields for piston airliners is historical but, as an airport devoted largely to cargo operations, there is still a few older types on view.

What remains is an eerie atmosphere, caused by the presence of the nearby GM Transmission Plant and by the fact that very little on the field moves during the daytime. The large passenger terminal still exists, though now occupied mostly by offices of varying sorts. The advantage is that the field is quiet enough for access to the apron to be possible, with little risk ofconflict with taxiing aircraft. When Zantop ceased operations in 1997, only Trans Continental with their fleet of DC-8's remain based here. The Yankee Air Museum is situated off Belleville Road, and might be worth investigating. Among its exhibits there are a B-17, B-52, C-47 and an F-101.

KALAMAZOO MI
AZO   County   5m/8km SSE

Take Portage Road, exit 78, from I-78. Little has yet been reported from this airport but it is known to house an increasing quantity of warbirds in a museum, aptly named Air Zoo. Not just short for Kalama-zoo, but also because of the "animals" on display: these are Wildcat, Hellcat, Tigercat and a Flying Tiger, which make up part of a display of about twenty aircraft. Also located there is the Guadalcanal Campaign Veterans Museum. To find the museum, take East Milham Road, a left off Portage hwhen heading east.

PONTIAC MI
PTK   KPTK   (Oakland-Pontiac)   7m/11km NW

Anyone staying in the Detroit area might want to cover the aviation scene to saturation point and, if so, Pontiac is worth the trip. Not much information about the facilities but there's more than a slack handful of executive aircraft. Add to them a very healthy selection of third level activity and the attraction becomes obvious. Contract Air's CV-580s and Corporate Express DC-3s are based here and there are also Roayl Air Lear Jets and EMB-110s to be seen.

MINNEAPOLIS/SAINT PAUL MN

MSP   KMSP   International   10m/16km SSE (bus 45 mins)

Just as Atlanta is dominated by Delta, the reputation of Minneapolis grew from its Northwest Airlines hub operations. A band of dedicated European enthusiasts pass through Minneapolis each year on their way to the biggest general aviation event on the calender, at Oshkosh. Close encounters with aircraft will have to wait until arrival in Wisconsin, as airliners are seen mostly from a distance here, and the multi-storey car park has to be used for the only panoramic view of proceedings on all three runways. In the centre of the runways is the Lindbergh Terminal. The Green Concourse has an indoor observation deck between Gates 62 and 68. Northwest Airlines dominates so variety is usually found on Gates 34-36 Red Concourse (Canadian Regional, Express One), Gates 44-48 Blue Concourse feature the rest of the American carriers, whilst the regional airlines congregate on Gates 78-90 on the Green Concourse.

From the elevated platform of the car park, the two main runways can be seen on either side, beyond the terminal buildings. From here all arrivals and departures should be easily seen. The cross runway, 4/22, to the west is no shorter than 11L/29R but is used mostly by commuter carriers, dominated by Northwest Airlink.

The general aviation hangars around the perimeter are easily seen, though not always their inmates, and the only other features worthy of mention are the AFRES base, the Northwest maintenance base and the Minnesota Air National Guard C-130s tucked away, inaccessibly, in the remote northeast corner of the field.

SAINT PAUL MN

STP   Downtown/Holman Field   3m/5km SE

To reach Holman from Minneapolis, cross the river south on Lafayette Freeway (Hwy 3) and the first exit leads there. It is compact, with the Mississippi along one edge. The general aviation includes many executive types, with no shortage of biz-jets. Remarkably for a downtown location, the Army Guard has a base here, where AH-1s, OH-58s and AH-54s are found.

The other general aviation is dispersed widely around the area. FLEMING FIELD is further down the same road. FLYING CLOUD is ten miles southwest and CRYSTAL is six miles northwest. Leaving town north on Central Avenue leads to BLAINE-ANOKA COUNTY, aka James Field.

KANSAS CITY MO

MKC   KMKC   Downtown   1m/1.5km N

On a loop of the Missouri River, the g.a. scene has mirrored the decline at the International Airport. However, there is still a good number of corporate aircraft to be seen during the week, but it would be wise not to expect too many biz-jets. There is competition for the business from several airports. All have a number of fixed base operators, and all are finding times to be tough.

Number crunchers will delight in Central Air Southwest's fleet of Aero Commander 500s but there are also items of individual worth: in addition to their L-1049H Super Constellation, the Save-a-Connie group owns a Martin 404 and a DC-3 which is being restored. There are occasional air shows on summer weekends, and a small museum which is open on weekdays between 10:00 and 14:00.

KANSAS CITY MO

MCI   KMCI   International   18m/30km NW

Because of the passenger terminal layout, a lot of walking is now needed to see the traffic. TWA's hub and spoke operations used to mean periods of absolute dead quiet were interspersed with chaos. Chaos has become little more than occasional bouts of activity.

Of the three round terminals, Terminal A is probably now the busiest, handling lots of Beech 1900s of USAirways Express. Just to the north is an employee parking lot, reasonably close to Runway 1/19. A long lens will be needed by photographers.

Some of TWA's redundant 727s and a 747 are stored at their maintenance base, which is not accessible by public roads, so permission for access will be required. Across the street from the post office is a garishly painted 727-100, used by the Trans World Technical School.

There are also a couple of general aviation fields, confusingly both called Johnson - Municipal (JCI) and Executive (OJC) - which are worth investigation for quantities of smaller aircraft.

SAINT LOUIS MO
STL   KSTL   Lambert-Saint Louis International   13m/20km NW

The terminal occupies the southern edge of the perimeter. Its eastern apron is expansive and can be seen by passing through a security check. A left turn at the Y-junction allows the runways to be seen, and the main apron behind. The airport authority might take the purpose of its own notices rather more seriously one day. Having allowed all the world and his dog through the security check, there is then a small sign saying "Ticketed Passengers Only". It was seen, quite by chance, on the the third visit. Clearly, there are not enough non-ticket holders using the concourses for there to be a problem but anyone travelling to STL should bear in mind that the situation can change. In the meantime, head for Gate 38 which provides a good vantage point.

Most of the airliners are easily seen, if not photographed, from Concourse C. Traffic using Runway 6/24 and parking at the conveniently placed Concourse A can remain a mystery to anyone who stays at Gate 36. It's worth walking around. Southwest use Gates 77-88 with a further eight gates under construction (in1997).

Across the field are various facilities: McDonnell-Douglas has an enormous plant on the north side, away from TWA's maintenance base and the general aviation aprons. Between these two hangar areas is the cargo ramp. To see them at close quarters a car is essential. There are one or two vantage points round here that overlook the field but the two main runways, 12R/30L especially, are somewhat distant.

Satellite parking lots B and C are quite close to the approach for Runway 12R, normally the main arrivals runway. Shuttle buses operate to these lots, so it is only a short walk for the dedicated photographer. McDonnell-Douglas has a gift shop on the corner of Lindbergh and McDonnell Streets, just to the north of the airport. Among the mainly military-oriented stock are a few items which may be of interest to the civil enthusiast.

Apart from the terminal and general aviation areas, there are one or two quiet roadside places to watch the perimeter. Care should be exercised when parking the car, as the police are vigilant for anyone who disobeys the 'No Stopping' signs. Rather than pull up at the roadside, wind down the window and point the binoculars at something, it's more sensible to find somewhere to park and do the job properly. It's certainly less hassle in the long run.

GULFPORT-BILOXI MS
GPT   Regional   3m/5km NNE

This is not a busy airport nor, it has to be admitted, a particularly interesting one. One or two Northwest DC-9s and Continental Express Brasilias comprise the only scheduled movements. The opening of gambling casinos on the coast continue to generate additional flights, from a variety of charter carriers. What the field does have to offer is the National Guard unit. The army presence is very large indeed. Their Mohawks are easy to find but identifying them is a different matter. The extremely rare AVCRAD Caribous can also be seen. An ex-PBA Martin 404, N40413 is stored here, having been moved from Naples. The military ramp on the east side of the field sometimes holds entire squadrons of Air National Guard aircraft, deployed here for their annual two-week drills. All park close to the fence, and can be logged and photographed with ease.

Nearby, Keesler Air Force Base sees relatively little action but of interest are the Air Force's hurricane-hunting WC-130s which are based. Spotting and photos require access to the base.

BILLINGS MT
BIL   Logan International   2m/3km NW

A quiet place, this Logan International bears no resemblance to Boston's airport of the same name. The Billings version is served by Continental, United, and Northwest as well as being the base of operations for Big Sky Airlines (Montana is Big Sky Country). Their Metros can be photographed with ease over the car park fence, just next to the terminal. Lynch Flying Service usually have some smart B-26 sprayers parked on the far side of Runway 9L/27R and access to them should not be a problem.

The terminal area sits compactly facing the intersection of 9L/27R and 4/22. This would be enough runways for most small airports but Billings also has 16/34 and, for general aviation only, the short 9R/27L. To the right of the terminal is the airport's fixed base operator, Lynch, with whom it is worth having a short discussion before driving around to the far side.

HELENA MT
HLN   KHLN   3m/5km NE

Apart from Hawkins & Powers, there is very little in the way of civil aviation to justify the mileage but that is not to say that Helena is not interesting. The Montana Army Guard's unit flies AH-1s, UH-1s and H-58s. Preserved here are some 1950s fighters and EC-121T N4257L, c/n 4335. With one or two Metros and the occasional Delta 737, scheduled traffic takes a distant second place to the other delights.

CHARLOTTE NC
CLT   KCLT   Douglas Municipal   8m/13km W

Anyone visiting the United States with USAirways will get to know Charlotte, as this is a very significant hub indeed. As with any hub and spoke operation, an enormous influx of traffic is followed by similar chaos as they all depart. The sight of fifteen USAirways-craft lined up at the holding point, awaiting take-off, is common at Charlotte. When they have departed, calm returns.

Across the diagonal runway, 5/23, from the old passenger terminal, the present one stands between two parallel runways, 18/36L/R, and walkways connect the various concourses. Concourse A is reserved for all airlines except USAirways. The others, B to D are almost the exclusive preserve of the one airline. USAirways Express is represented by CCAir, with SD3.60s, Jetstreams and Dash 8s; and Piedmont with Dash 8s; their ramps are around Concourse D.

This may be the best place to watch the action, though one runway is out of sight. Passengers flood the buildings, so anyone attempting to keep apace with what is moving will have an energetic time. Taking photos through the glass of the feederliners can be followed by a walk round the concourses, to and fro, just to keep track. The end of Concourse C has the advantage of being close to the cargo ramp, and photos from here of the Airborne Express YS-11s or UPS 757s do not need particularly sophisticated equipment. The end of Concourse B is also good for great views of aircraft using Runway 5. The general aviation apron, close to the dozen or so North Carolina Air National Guard C-130s, is out of sight from the terminal.

The present terminal, on the north side of the field, has its own access off Billy Graham Parkway. Leaving the parking area by car, instead of taking the main road, make a left, as if returning to the terminal. Go straight ahead to the T-junction and make a right turn. A left turn at the next T-junction onto Old Dowd Road leads round the end of 18R to the elevated viewing area. This offers a panorama of the airfield as well as a close-up of anything landing on the main (longest) runway.

The road meanders beyond this point and, after a few left turns, leads to the cargo area. Amongst the modern aircraft, Saber Airlines stand out as belonging to a different era: they operate C-47s and DC-3s, a few of which are normally present on the ramp. Next to cargo is what was once the main apron, now used by general aviation. The loop road to the old terminal also offers a glimpse of the main general aviation apron, on the the the side of 18L/36R.

A left onto West Boulevard passes the end of 36R before its junction with Airport Parkway. Another left gives access to the FBOs across the road. The apron just beyond, to the north, is used by the Air National Guard, whose C-130s spend most of their time doing nothing. Airport Drive continues to a junction, offering the choice of returning to the terminal or heading into town. Wilkinson Boulevard, at the end, is the easiest way to do so.

ELIZABETH CITY NC

ECG	KECG	Municipal	5m/8km SE

Take Highway 34 out of town, on the opposite side of the estuary from the road leading to Kitty Hawk and the Wright Brothers Monument. Traffic at the airport is negligible but Albatross 7247 guards the gate to the main attraction. The US Coast Guard's main base is here, and its facility is large. Maintenance hangars and aprons normally have examples of all types, but access cannot be guaranteed. A letter in advance might help, of course. Most of the C-130s can be logged from outside the gate but the various helicopters and Guardians are mostly hidden from view.

GASTONIA NC

0A6	Municipal	15m/24km W of Charlotte

An interest in propliners and a car are the two essential requisites for a trip to Gastonia. Patience doesn't come amiss, either, as it can be a difficult place to find. It's on the south side of town, farthest from I-85. Take New Hope Road and, if necessary, ask for directions. If you want to find Piedmont Air Cargo, it would be silly to give up when you're this close! Union Road passes the end of the small airfield. Past the terminal building are the hangars and apron, where a few C-47s and Beech 18s might be seen. A recent report gave only a Sikorsky AirCrane (N97AA) as present. Very little moves here during the day, so access to the ramp is relatively easy to obtain.

GREENSBORO NC

GSO	Piedmont Triad International	11m/17km W

Greensboro is quite a major regional capital, and its airport handles a fair amount of scheduled traffic. From town, take US 421 in the direction of Winston-Salem, and the airport is on the north side of the road. It's relatively quiet, and nobody would want to spend a day or so logging the movements, most of which are DC-9s and 727s, plus some commuters. The only aircraft to offer any interest are Eastwind 737s and the odd Airtran flight.

The main terminal consists of two piers but access is limited to those with a boarding pass. There is no shortage of general aviation, including some biz-jets.The general aviation area is located next to the control tower but also allows aircraft at the TIMCO facility to be seen at a distance. To see it, a car is needed. Take West Market Street past the Tradewinds facility, turn left at the second stoplight on West Friendly Avenue, then left on Old Friendly Avenue, followed by a right onto Radar Road. Triad International Maintenance Corp (TIMCO) works on a range of aircraft, and their centre is on the east side of the field, a long way from the terminal. DC-10s, DC-8s and 737s wait their turn for maintenance, and some of the aircraft appear to have been in storage for a while. Just past TIMCO is the USAirways maintenance hangar.

Also worth investigation is the GTCC Aviation Technical School, where a range of airframes can be seen, including T-39s and at least one Hansa. One of the more famous residents of Greensboro is Tradewinds International, whose CL-44s were amongst the last airworthy examples in the world.

Tradewinds' facility is close to the highway, next to the disused cargo shed, on the south side. The CL-44s gave been exchanged for L1011s, one of which may be parked on the apron. Here you will see what remains of the CL-44 fleet along with two ex-Korean DC-10's and an unmarked A310. Photographs of these residents are possible and, by moving to the small cargo buildings, another CL-44 becomes visible.

RALEIGH/DURHAM NC
RDU   KRDU   14m/22km NW

North Carolina is not flat country and, around this airport it's quite hilly. Arrival, from the main road, gives little impression of the airport. There is a choice: park the car and walk into either or both of the passenger terminals, or continue past the car parks, under the two taxiways, to a spectator's area next to the control tower. A grassy bank overlooks both runways, though only 5L/23R is close enough for photography. The majority of scheduled movements are American.

Close to the viewing park is the large general aviation apron with its many hangars and residents. The executive movements also pass within range of a good zoom lens, so that Raleigh-Durham does offer some variety in return for a long stay. What will be remembered here, though, is seeing an awful lot of American 727s and MD-80s.

A shuttle bus operates to the terminals from the satellite parking lot, for anyone intent on finding out that there is little to see from inside the buildings. The Army National Guard helicopters are parked, some distance away, beside Runway 14/32. There may be somewhere in Terminal A or B from where the serials can be read.

WINSTON-SALEM NC
INT   KINT   Smith Reynolds   3.5m/6km NNE

The airport, like everything else in town, depends on the prosperity of the Reynolds Tobacco Company. This is an enormous business concern, and it comes as no surprise to find that general aviation includes plenty of corporate aircraft. There is little else of any note.

MORRISTOWN NJ
MMU   Municipal   17m/27km W of Newark

There are no scheduled visitors, and probably very little reason to trek out into New Jersey to see this airport. A band of dedicated biz-jet fans will consider the trip worthwhile, as the g.a. activity includes some interesting aircraft including, it was reported some time ago, a Grumman Widgeon.

NEWARK NJ
EWR   KEWR   International   1m/1.5km S

None of Newark's three terminals possess observation decks. Despite a good variety of movements, Newark has generally been considered by enthusiasts as the poor relation in this part of the world. This may be due to the terminals facing east, and therefore only at their best in the afternoon. When faced with a choice of watching the world's wide-bodies land at JFK or getting good views of domestic airlines at Newark, most enthusiasts will choose JFK. However, the windows in Terminal C offer such sights as SAS 767s for those who choose this airport as an alternative. The lack of slots at JFK will force more airlines here, and operators and passengers alike will probably benefit. Terminals A and B are accessible only to passengers, most of whom fly with United, USAirways and Virgin Atlantic.

Through darkened glass, most of the aircraft can be seen at reasonably close quarters. Also good for photos are the emergency exit landings at the corners of the terminals, as they offer quite elevated views of aircraft pushing back or taxiing in. This additional height is useful as the walk between each terminal is at a level considerably below that of the blast screens.

Gates 85 and 86 in Terminal C offer a good view of the active runways, plus the ability to monitor movements on the taxiways. There is a good variety of food on offer here, though all at New York prices of course, and anyone who isn't intent on taking photos will find the only drawback is that the FedEx/UPS ramp is out of sight. Those without a car who wish to see this area will need to show a boarding pass to visit the United departure lounge in Terminal A.

154

Brewster Road leads from a very complex road layout (it can be missed easily) to the freight and general aviation areas. Passing close to the parcel cargo ramp, it is possible to make a quick stop for a photo of what may be on the apron, before taking the next right turn. This leads into the cargo complex proper where views of aircraft on the ramp are limited. The loop road leads back to the executive terminal and hangar, both of which can be relied upon for a good selection of biz-jets. The rest of this large ramp is used for parking, mostly by cargo aircraft. The Forbes Magazine 727 is a regular visitor, as is the Presidential 747, which parks next to the tower.

TETERBORO NJ
TEB   KTEB   15m/23km N of EWR

Most of the residents are to be seen along the western perimeter. In the southwest corner is the Falcon Jet Center, which overlooks an apron renowned for quantities of biz-jets. The museum on the western perimeter may not contain anything intrinsically thrilling but its presence does allow the casual visitor a valid reason to stroll onto the ramp. It occupies the lower two floors of the old control tower building. (There is incidentally another museum at Teterboro, on the opposite side of the field, by the new control tower.) Passing a large hangar full of executive wares, the apron beyond is laden with more visitors of interest.

TRENTON NJ
TTN   KTTN   Mercer County

One might think that as the capital of New Jersey, Trenton would be a busy airport but, with Newark to the north and Philadelphia to the south, Trenton has never developed much of a commercial market. The primary reason for a visit here would be to photograph the Eastwind Airlines 737s at their home base. This is easily done in the morning, from the grassy areas on either side of the terminal. Despite the lack of other movements a drive to the opposite side of the field will result in a variety of light aircraft and perhaps a few biz-jets parked on the general aviation ramp.

ALBUQUERQUE NM
ABQ   KABQ   International   9m/15km NW

Not a particularly busy airport but it is interesting for the variety of traffic to be seen here. The small observation deck in the original terminal building has been overtaken by progress, and is closed. America West, Southwest, TWA, American and United are the most frequent operators, while Mesa Air/United Express Beech 1900s dominate the commuter activity.

Extensions to the original terminal include one pier to the right and another projecting forward, linking it to a new terminal, closer to the intersection of two major runways. The link faces the USAF base and offers some restricted views of airliners on the apron, as does the terminal. It is now best to take advantage of one of the many places around the perimeter, if a stay of any length is planned.

Much of the field is occupied by Kirtland AFB, outside which is a preserved T-39 on a pole. The C-21As are parked quite close to the passenger terminal, together with any visiting military movements. The A-7s and C-130s are relatively inaccessible at the far end of the field, though landing shots of all movements are possible near the end of the main runway. Regular activity can be interrupted by the arrival of Air Force fighters, as well as F-14s and F-18s of the US Navy.

The general aviation area is situated directly opposite the passenger terminal, on the other side of the runway whilst Ross Aviation, who fly on government contract work, are to be found next to the military installation. The cargo sheds are to the right of the passenger terminal, on the same side of the runway. For more general aviation, in quantity, CORONADO Field should be investigated. It's northeast of town on the Pan American Freeway.

ALAMOGORDO NM
ALM   White Sands Regional   5m/8km SW

To the west of town is the vast White Sands National Monument. There are about 150,000 acres of pure white sand, drifted into dunes up to forty feet high. Ten times that area is occupied by the White Sands Missile Range, a playground for Holloman Air Force Base crews.

Based at White Sands is, rather inappropriately, Black Hills Aviation. Their many P-2V Neptunes have been joined by ex-Spanish P-3As. Commuter airline movements are few and far between, so there is little reason for Alamogordo to be more than a short stop between El Paso and Roswell. Some miles to the northeast is Hondo, New Mexico and the Mescalero Apache Reservation. However, the T-41 Mescaleros are based at Hondo, Texas.

ROSWELL NM
ROW   KROW   Industrial Air Center   3m/5km S

Once upon a time, Roswell was the home of Lufthansa's training school. Though some 737s are to be seen, they are not German. F-5s are also much in evidence, but the most memorable resident is probably JetStar N440RM, in its livid red colour scheme. In recent years the field has become a popular storage area and features a diversity of aircraft ranging from a Convair 580 to the Rich International TriStars. The rest amounts to a few Mesa Beech 1900s.

SANTA FE NM
SAF   KSAF   Municipal   9m/15km SW

This may be New Mexico's state capital, but the airport is extremely disappointing, especially if driving for a few hundred miles in expectation. What passes through is Mesa Beech 1900s, and even these are infrequent.

ELKO NV
EKO   Municipal   0.5m/1km W

Commercial gold-mining in northeast Nevada has led to the growth of this airport. Skywest, for example, now operate eleven daily flights to Reno and Salt Lake City. The big attraction is, however, the colourful Casino Express fleet of 737s operating regular charter flights from across the western states. Two are based at Elko. In the mornings, the accessible perimeter fence allows good photos of anything on the taxiway.

LAS VEGAS NV
LAS   KLAS   McCarran International   6m/9km SSE

The main passenger terminal are was never of real use for photography but all domestic concourses are accessible without boarding passes. Behind it is a multi-storey car park which offers the spotter a view of everything on the move. An awning offers much-needed shelter from the blistering (quite literally) sun, and a zoom lens allows some of the larger aircraft to be photographed with some success. The police however are not over tolerant, especially after dusk.

Access to Concourse C is by monorail, and the airlines here are mainly by Southwest, American, and United. Finding somewhere to sit between Gates C9 and C11, for example, allows all traffic on the busy parallel Runways 25L and 25R to be monitored. East of C, Concourse D was under construction in 1997, and will have no less than seventy additional gates.

There is a huge expansion programme in the southest corner, so any advice for that part of the field might be short-lived. Try Russell Road, for example, where the road to the cargo terminal ends in a dirt lot near the taxiway for the departure runway 25R. Earplugs might be a good idea.

This is pretty much opposite the spot on Sunset Road (see later).

Leaving the terminal, a left turn at the holding point of 19L onto Tropicana Boulevard leads to the Scenic Airlines and new Executive Air Terminals. The passenger waiting area at the Scenic terminal allows much of the ramp to be seen, with a variety of visiting biz-jets present. A left onto Koval Lane reveals the large general aviation apron, which is best visited in the early morning before many of the Eagle Canyon Air Cessnas depart for Grand Canyon duties. Next to the turning into Reno Avenue is the C-124 Globemaster, on its own ground. Passing the Quail Air Centre on the left, another left turn on Haven Avenue reveals the EG & G terminal. In the early morning up to six 737s can be parked here. At the end of Haven an enlarged storage area acts as home to a wide variety of widebodies, most belonging to United, and an assortment of smaller aircraft including several F.27s.

Returning to Las Vegas Boulevard and heading south, the area formerly occupied by the Hughes executive terminal has been redeveloped by Signature Aviation who have their own new terminal here. A ramp to its north side gives good views of the biz-jets, but security is tight and anything longer than general observation in passing would be viewed with suspicion. There is increasing resistance to photography of corporate aircraft, extending even to allegations of it being illegal. Whether or not this is the case may not be relevant: visitors to Las Vegas can be influential in one way or another, and they can be temperamental. Movie stars get upset about being photographed without make-up, and some of the businessmen here have a reputation for being single-minded! Any warnings should be treated politely, and taken seriously.

Storage areas on The Strip side of the field can all be seen, with a car, and it might be worth noting some of the hotels around here. They might not be luxurious but they are affordable, being away from the town's main action and close to a noisy airport. Higher level floors, facing the terminal area, should therefore be even cheaper but it doesn't actually work like that. Watch for a private terminal with a few red and white 737s next to it. This is EG & G who fly for the US Dept of Energy to the Tonopah Test Range in Nevada. Maybe they also fly people to Area 51 or Groom Lake - who knows?

A trip east on Sunset Road (not Sunset Boulevard) leads to a small shopping complex opposite the threshold of 25L, good for photography of landing aircraft, but fencing prohibits those on the ground becoming good portraits. The area to the north of Runways 25L/R has undergone massive development with a large new terminal building under construction and east of this is a large new cargo building whose apron is usually well stocked by a variety of carriers.

In the early Seventies, McCarran was still on the outskirts of town, but the huge growth of mega hotels has progressed steadily south, with the Excalibur and Luxor Hotels offering excellent views of the airport. From an upper storey room it is possible, with the aid of good binoculars or a telescope, to enjoy the comfort of air-conditioning whilst monitoring all movements on 19L and many of the movements at the main passengers terminal. One wing of the Tropicana hotel also offers similar views with the added attraction of overlooking the new executive ramp. The international charter terminal handles the more interesting movements at Las Vegas: Aeromexico, Air Atlantic, Air Transat, Condor, Meridian and Sobelair are all regular visitors.

The city's other field, apart from Nellis Air Force Base, is NORTH AIR TERMINAL. To find it, take Rancho Road (Highway 95) northwest out of town. Like Las Vegas/Henderson Sky Harbor, it is used mainly as a departure point for the many sightseeing flights over the Grand Canyon.

HENDERSON is on the road between Las Vegas and the Hoover Dam, and this is more than just another private field with lots of general aviation. Sky Harbour is a centre for Air Vegas who operate Grand Canyon tours with Beech 99's and Cessna 402's The two Toa Domestic YS-11s which are stored here will never fly again.

RENO NV

RNO   KRNO   Cannon International   4m/6km SE

For variety, Cannon is worth the long journey, especially if combined with a visit to Stead Airport. Scheduled traffic is reasonably varied, though not brisk during the week, except for the morning and evening peaks. Weekend gamblers provide more activity for the usual airlines: Delta, Southwest and America West are regulars. Locally-based Reno Air MD-83s are much in evidence. During the daytime, Cannon is an airport with a perimeter to explore. General aviation includes a fair amount of biz-jets and, for once, plenty of places from which to see them.

The passenger terminal is in the northwest corner of the field, facing Runway 16L/34R, with the shorter parallel runway beyond it. At each side of the terminal are large ramps and, to the south, the cross runway. Probably the best place inside the terminal is by Gate C6, which also overlooks the cargo apron. There is no problem finding somewhere around the remote g.a. facility and, during race week, it houses about four hundred aircraft, many of them twins. From here all runways can be seen, and most aircraft taxi by at close range. The Nevada Air National Guard ramp can be seen, to the right, from the passenger terminal with several C130's in evidence.

STEAD Airport is at its best in mid-September, when the Reno Air Races are held here. Plenty of visitors, and many of them are extremely exotic types and paintjobs. To get there from town, follow Highway 395 for about fifteen miles. What is to be seen all year round is of more than passing interest to many visitors. Aviation Classics have half a dozen Chinese MiG-15s and at least one An-2. The other notables include a couple of Il-14s and various older US military types.

Too close to Reno to generate any traffic of its own, CARSON CITY is only worth a detour if seeking a couple of Albatrosses, which are the only notable aircraft to be seen.

ALBANY NY

ALB   KALB   County   9m/15km NW

The appeal of this small airport lies in its pleasant little roof terrace which overlooks a fairly busy ramp. Despite the mesh which now surrounds it, photography is still possible. Apart from the regular airlines, like USAirways and Continental, there is a splendid amount of feeder airline traffic and this is one of the few airports in the north eastern states to feature such a variety of Beech 1900s, Shorts, Dash 7s/8s, Dornier 228s and ATR-42s in the company of DC-9s, F.28s and 737s, all visible at close quarters.

As befits feederliner traffic, a good part of it passes through in the morning and evening rush hours, the middle of the day being somewhat slower.

A car park next to the main road has been designated as an observation point, where close views of the threshold and holding point are on offer. The Army National Guard AH-1s and OH-58s can also be seen parked on the field, on the far side of the runway. There is also a separate lay-by on Albany-Shaker Road, close to where traffic using the shorter cross-runway lands.

BINGHAMPTON NY

BGM   Broome County   10m/16km N

Better known locally as Edwin A Link Field, it's easy to find from town. Drive north on Airport Road! Scheduled operations are busier than might be expected, with a number of commuter flights during the day. It is not, however, a place to settle down and watch the action. Worth a detour when passing through the area, Binghampton's residents include a few antiques, and biz-jets are regular visitors, though not in great numbers. Permission for ramp access should be sought from Broome County Aviation.

BUFFALO NY

BUF   KBUF   International   9m/15km ENE (bus 45 minutes)

The passenger terminal area is divided into two parts: the newly enlarged Western Terminal and its next door neighbour, solely for domestic use, the Eastern. Boarding cards are required in the Eastern Terminal.

Traffic, though busy, is generally lacklustre, being dominated by US Airways, whose acquisition of Piedmont included the hub of Empire Airlines. A name which lives on at Buffalo is Flying Tigers, though it refers to the wartime heroes, rather than the airline. This is the name of a restaurant,

158

located close to the intersection of Runways 5/23 and 14/32. To get there, a left turn onto Genesee Street is followed by another left turn at the lights by the Holiday Inn. Two more left turns lead to an underpass below Runway 5/23. Before the tunnel, the restaurant and its car park are on the left. Catering for the enthusiast, quite literally, in more ways than one, some of the tables have headphones tuned to the tower. Since meals start at lunchtime, the car park is usually empty in the mornings. A meal there would certainly repay them for their facilities!

ELMIRA NY
ELM   Corning Regional   7m/11km NW

Corning handles one or two jet airliners a day. Schweizer build Ag Cats here, so there is usually something to be seen. Crop sprayers find their way to some remote corners of the world, so exotic registrations are always a possibility, particularly in early spring before the seasonal delivery peak. Nearby is the Soaring Society of America, and the field has a strong accent on this activity, with rides and lessons on offer to the interested.

FARMINGDALE NY
FRG   Republic   2m/3km E

Finding Farmingdale on a map of New York State can be difficult. It's on Long Island, about twenty miles east of Kennedy. Exit 32 on Southern State Parkway leads north to the airport. Jetstreams do visit occasionally but the Lockheed Air Terminal handles mostly executive movements, including some jets. Considered as a general aviation field with a fair number of residents, Farmingdale is worth the trip, as almost everything can be seen.

ISLIP NY
ISP   KISP   Long Island MacArthur   8m/13km NE

The residents of Long Island may live close to New York City but they can avoid the traffic jams and check-in queues if they fly from Islip (pronounced eyes-lip). A few commuter airlines seized the opportunity to capitalise on this fact, and the airport witnessed some major growth in the mid-1980s. Unfortunately, investment in the airport failed to keep pace with demand, and travelling via Islip became as much trouble as anywhere else. Facilities were stretched beyond the limit, and the airport has settled back into a comfortable role of offering a limited alternative to New York's major airports.

Facilities for viewing are non-existent but the fence at the left side of the terminal does allow photographs to be taken of the movements. Islip's appeal has always been that it is possible to get close to feeder liners, and the varied selection includes Henson Dash 7s/8s, as well as many other types which have been around a bit longer.

Although Islip has two runways, neither are easily reached for close-up photos. The general aviation apron is located separately from the passenger terminal, and houses very little of real interest. However, next to it is the National Guard helicopter base, with numerous UH-1s and OH-6s, all easily seen from the fence at very close quarters without offending anyone, and a bonus here is the proximity to one of the taxiways. If the right runway is in use, the aircraft do pass very close. Success at Islip can be very much a matter of luck.

MONTICELLO NY
MSV   Sullivan County

Nestling in the Catskill Mountains, Monticello is quiet and pleasant. It is rarely troubled by the noise of jets or large aircraft of any kind. It is, however, on the road from New York City to Binghampton, Elmira and other larger cities, and may be worth a stop en route.

NEWBURGH NY
SWF   KSWF   Stewart International   4m/6km NW

Close to the West Point Military Academy, Newburgh is convenient for rich dads to visit their sons. The fathers use corporate aircraft and the sons use T-41 Mescaleros. Newburgh's long runway has been the basis for many plans for the field's future. Scheduled flights total about a hundred a day, up to 727 size, mostly related to American and USAirways. There is no shortage of feeder services, so that Stewart Field offers links to almost anywhere.

Probably the most impressive arrivals at Stewart were the dozen or so C-5s which are used by the New York Air National Guard. There is also a US Marines unit based here with, it is believed, KC-130s. The quantity of general aviation seems to be growing daily.

NEW YORK NY
JFK   KJFK   John F Kennedy International   14m/22km SE (bus 60 minutes)

When the very first edition of this book was written, a long, long time ago, New York was *the* transatlantic destination. It had everything . . . from the chance to see, at one airport, all the wide-bodies operated by Europe's national airlines to a phenomenal selection of domestic US carriers. Better still, both JFK and LGA had top-notch faclities from which to watch and photograph just about anything that moved. My word, how times have changed.

La Guardia is crammed beyond sensible limits with domestic traffic, none of which can be seen in Europe, while JFK still handles vast numbers of movements from across the Atlantic. Assuming that the decision is to sample the delights of JFK the first day after arrival, it is quite likely that an early start will be made, getting to the airport before the action starts. It will be a long wait. Apart from some extreme rarities which do pass through in the mornings, interest isn't generated until lunchtime when the first of the international flights start arriving.

Kennedy is a vast airport with all the passenger terminals at the middle, where further growth is just about impossible. Major airlines have their own terminals and there is a separate, large building for international arrivals. This is also stretched beyond the limit in the afternoons and evenings, and many transatlantic flights arrive at other terminals, which also have customs and immigration facilities. The Worldport also handles international flights including those from Central and Eastern Europe.

The centre of the airport is occupied by five separate car parks, and it is wise not to consider moving the car from one to another as the costs can be frightening. Before leaving the car out here, despite the fact that there aren't many others, a careful note should be made of its exact location. When returning at dusk the car park will be, literally, full so departure will need time and patience. The alternative was to park on the roof of the Worldport, once the best vantage point in the central terminal area. It is now completely spotter-proof.

Instead, the five-storey car park outside the International Arrivals Building is tall enough to offer a good overall view of proceedings. A security guard is always on duty so, sooner or later, he will become interested in anyone spotting. It is best to discuss intentions, and reach some agreement, as he merely contacts the local police who despatch a car with predictably tedious (though not disastrous) consequences.

A typical stay in New York needs a plan of action, the most common being to arrive at JFK from La Guardia at lunchtime, using the Van Wyck Expressway. The terminals will not contain anything significant yet, so a look around the maintenance areas will save a lot of time. On the right, what were Pan Am's hangars are where the occasional Saudia, Varig and Chinese 747 spend the day, parked quite close to the fence, and easily photographed from the roof of a car. Next is TWA, though there is normally little exciting here. Making a U-turn to get to the opposite carriageway, United and American hangars contain more aircraft and the use of an employees' car park allows closer inspection.

Continuing, after another U-turn towards the central area, the general aviation terminal is on the right but handles only a small amount of biz-jet traffic so a stop here isn't worthwhile. Faced with the prospect of nine terminals to visit, the advice is simple: assume nothing can be seen from any of them. This includes the Delta Worldport (including what was the Eastern Airlines Terminal), Northwest, American and British Airways, as they offer no facilities at all. The interior of the TWA terminal (including the National Airlines building which they acquired for domestic flights) offers a sight of part of their ramp, but nothing that would justify the trip. Terminal One has been completely rebuilt as a joint venture between Air France, JAL, Korean and Lufthansa. As their requirements called for four gates and T1 now has eleven, a variety of new subtenants can be expected here.

Security precautions meant that the Worldport rooftop car park had to be enclosed, and it has been done in an extremely effective manner. Around its perimeter, there are two fences, about five feet apart, one of which has the wooden slats - extraordinary precautions which cost money to erect. The number of parking spaces (and the income therefrom) has also been reduced, in order to be rid of spotters and, presumably, any threat of terrorist activity.

The balcony of the International Arrivals building is closed but, on the level below, glass allows good photography of a restricted number of wide-body movements. The authorities have been slow to appreciate that enthusiasts are being denied access to views of aircraft and that they use their imagination to compensate. This leads to unnecessary, but inevitable, conflict and such places as the 150th Street exit, so close to the BA ramp and the threshold of 13L, continue to get more attention, from both parties.

The taxiway between 13L/31R and the American terminals passes over the road next to the Post Office Building and an ample of provision of grassy bank can serve admirably for taking photographs of traffic as it lands on 13L (a regular feature, but not a continual one). Passing very close to this taxiway is another overbridge, used to transport cargo containers into the freight areas, and this vantage point allows ridiculously close views of taxiing aircraft as well as a good prospect of the British Airways and TWA ramps. It must be borne in mind that the police also use this bridge and they will not take kindly to anyone standing here.

Standing with camera in hand, awaiting the arrival of a Swissair 747, is taken to be loitering in the USA and there are penalties for this. Anyone tackled by the police should be aware of the fact that 'loitering' is a subjective word. Someone engaged in the legitimate business of aviation photography cannot, realistically, be accused of this, though the purpose is to deter. A positive approach to the situation, if it occurs, would be to inform them that, as a free-lance photographer, one is trying to earn a living.

The central cargo area, near the 150th Street exit, is difficult to see well but there is a major facility on the other side of Runway 13L, where aircraft can be seen more easily from the roof of a car, with photos possible over the fence. Like Lufthansa, JALCargo operate their 747F into JFK at night and these aircraft may be a rare sight unless a special trip is made, possibly at dawn. The second major turning to the right leads to an assortment of ramps, with Northwest Cargo at the end. An early morning visit may be rewarded by a shot of a Lufthansa 747F on the move and a Northwest example with its nose door open.

At the end of this cul-de-sac, the road turns to a large staff car park and, at the turning, it is possible to get high quality shots of aircraft landing on 22R, with the sun on the aircraft, instead of behind. Standing here, even when the runway is heavily used, will mean missing many movements arriving and departing on other runways.

Food and drink are not readily available at sensible prices in JFK and anyone spending any amount of time here should consider the need for nourishment. The 150th Street exit leads to Rockaway Boulevard. This road passes the thresholds of 22L and 22R, so many of the locals pull in here to watch the planes land. Continuing along Rockaway Boulevard, there is a shopping centre and a good selection of eating establishments, with something to suit most tastes. It is possible to read the underwing registrations of aircraft landing on 31L (not American, of course) from the comfort of a seat in Dunkin Donuts or Arthur Treachers.

Buses operate from Kennedy to the other airports: Carey Express to La Guardia and Princetown Express to Newark. Costs were last reported as $10 and $20.00 respectively. For more information and tickets, contact any ground transportation desk. Manhattan by bus costs $12, and the journey takes about an hour. The buses use either Grand Central Station or the Port Authority Bus Terminal. For a few dollars more (well, actually, quite a few dollars more) helicopters serve East 34th Street. The fare offers quite an experience but groups of travellers should bear in mind that reduced group fares can apply.

NEW YORK NY
LGA   KLGA   La Guardia   8m/13km E (bus 40 minutes)

La Guardia is reached, without a car, from Kennedy by the Carey bus which costs a maximum of $10 each way. Alternatively, buses also leave Grand Central Station, Rockefeller Center and Penn Station in Manhattan. The cost is, at most, $12 one way. There are alternative means of transportation: a ferry operates from Wall Street Pier, on the East River (11th and 34th) and the journey takes about 40 minutes. From the Marine Air Terminal a bus service, Q47, leaves every fifteen minutes or so, and serves local subway stations. $2.50 is a cheap way to get into Manhattan, though how long the journey takes will depend on the destination station. Anyone who is unfamiliar with New York (and New Yorkers) is strongly advised not to make use of the subway system after the evening rush hour. There are enough stories about muggings, and worse, for the situation to be taken seriously, and alternative travelling arrangements made. It's a tough town, and Brooklyn ain't no quiet suburb!

What readers no doubt want to know, more than anything else, if whether the journey is a waste of time. So, here is the wording on a sign, to be seen in LGA: "Public welcome at gates and Food Court". True, the fabulous rooftop observation deck has been closed for several years, but USAirways have shown imagination, largely because it is good business.

Always keen to be a user-friendly airline, USAirways has extended its terminal, more or less opposite the threshold of Runway 31. Lots of glass and lots of views. Admittedly most of the views are of USAirways' own planes, better than nothing, but anything using this runway passes very close. Wind direction is crucial. When Runway 31 sees heavy use, the situation is very good indeed. American and United might use Runway 4 but almost all the other carriers can be seen passing the USAir terminal.

The restaurant on the top floor is reported to be open again. Here, for the occasional Coke (albeit at New York prices) the aprons and runways can be seen.

The Butler Marine Air Terminal handles many executive aircraft each day. This building is a little piece of history and worthy of inspection for those interested in more than just registrations.

The fence around the Butler apron makes photos of the aircraft difficult, wide angle lenses suffering from vignetting caused by the chainlink being within the depth of field. A quick look from the roof of a hire car, parked in the taxi rank can reward camera users.

The cargo buildings close to the threshold of Runway 4 have a small car park from which the taxiway is but a small distance. Photography and viewing in the mornings can be particularly good from here if this runway is in use, though most photographers have to restrict themselves to landing aircraft as their subject matter. Most 'alternative' vantage points are now to be found around the threshold of Runway 4.

NEW YORK Heliports

The traffic on Manhattan's overcrowded and chaotic streets makes the use of helicopters essential for some businessmen with tight schedules, and many of the flights are included in the first class ticket to New York. Spotters will gain little by a visit to any of these locations, as the fleets are seen regularly at the three main airports.

For the photographer, the rewards are much greater, as rampside photos are possible at the heliports. The three most famous buildings in Manhattan are probably the Empire State Building, The World Trade Center and the United Nations, and each has a heliport close by. That at the WORLD TRADE CENTER was just to the southwest of the twin towers, on the bank of the Hudson River, and this may be the location of the DOWNTOWN MANHATTAN pad. The other two both overlook the East River. The EAST 34th STREET heliport is good in the afternoon, as the vantage point for the ramp looks northeast and the traffic handled is similar to EAST 60th STREET, known locally as Metroport, near the United Nations Building.

Anyone venturing into Manhattan with a car would do well to do so at the weekend, when the traffic is tolerable. On the west side of the island, at Pier 86, is the retired aircraft carrier USS Intrepid, and admission allows inspection of a good selection of airpower on the deck and below. The collection is no longer restricted to Naval types, as even an SR-71 has found its way here.

On Sunday mornings, Manhattan can be a sane place, and ideal for exploration.

NIAGARA FALLS NY
IAG   KIAG   International   12m/19km E

Since airline traffic to this scenic spot of New York State is handled through Buffalo, the airport is only used by general aviation, Bell Helicopters and some military units. Quite a drive out of the town, the airport is at the junctions of Highways 62 and 182, the latter being Porter Road. The terminal side of the field reveals nothing out of the ordinary for most enthusiasts but the southwest corner of the field is occupied by the Army National Guard, who have UH-1s and OH-6s on their ramp.

The Bell assembly plant, at the southeast corner of the field, rarely provides movements of any interest but the next left turn leads to the north side, where the New York ANG and an AFRES unit are based. A written request for a tour of the ramp may be rewarded but there will always be consolation in the camouflaged F-101 gate guardian.

Across the border, in Canada, there is another airport for Niagara Falls but this only has a collection of general aviation to be seen on the ramp.

PLATTSBURGH NY
PLB   Municipal   3m/5km SW

Plattsburgh is best known for its USAF base and the FB-111s which are found there. A lazy hour or two can be passed, sitting on the shore of Lake Champlain, as the swingers fly low overhead on final approach. The airport is not busy but it is pleasant. The apron in front of the tiny terminal often has at least one photogenic commuter. Permission to photograph is worth the request. Commutair have a maintenance base here, where weekends see work on their Beech 1900s. A few DC-3s are believed to have been added to the fleet for pleasure flights.

POUGHKEEPSIE NY
POU   Dutchess County   5m/8km SE

If a visit is planned to Plattsburgh, there is really little point in airliner enthusiasts trying to find Poughkeepsie. It is served by only a few Metro Beech 1900s each day. Corporate aircraft are to seen here, however, as IBM's headquarters are close by. Their business relations are enormous, meaning that large corporate customers also visit Dutchess County.

SYRACUSE NY
SYR   KSYR   Hancock Field   7m/11km NE (bus 15 minutes)

Leaving the city north on Highway 11, the airport is on the east of the road and its terminal has been substantially extended, so that it now looks rather more like a modern building. The old roof terrace was a casualty in these improvements but the multi-storey car park has always been the best vantage point anyway. A parking area, well signed from the main terminal, has been designated for public observation, where tuning your FM radio to 103.9 should produce the tower broadcasts. Scheduled traffic is a surprisingly good mixture, though USAirways dominates, and other airlines are represented with aircraft up to 727 size. This was, a long time ago, a hub for Empire Airlines, which was taken over by Piedmont, and now USAirways. The hub operations have been cut back drastically but the airline is still by far the biggest operator here.

The southern edge of the field has a number of general aviation facilities plus a resident Army detachment of UH-1s and OH-58s, whilst the northern side is home to the New York ANG, which operates F-16s. Various gates to this base are guarded by a selection of types which have previously seen service with the unit.

UTICA NY
UCA   Oneida County 11m/17km NW

Empire Airlines once used Oneida as their headquarters and maintenance facility, though the hub of their operations was Buffalo. With their absorption into Piedmont and then USAirways, the traffic at this small airport has been rationalised to mostly commuter flights which leave very early in the morning for destinations in upper New York State.

Only one or two, at the most, commuter-liners are seen at the small, neat terminal on a visit here, and it is probable that the reason for being in the area will be to take part in one of the guided tours of Griffiss Air Force Base. These are arranged for a 13:00 start on certain days but it would be worth checking before a long journey, as the tours are subject to annoying cancellation due to a lack of participants.

WESTHAMPTON BEACH NY
FOK KFOK Suffolk County 2m/3km NE

It's a long drive across Long Island to this airport, and not worth the effort without a specific purpose. Exit 63 off Sunrise Expressway (Hwy 27) leads south along Riverhead Road to the field. It was once an active military base but all that now remain are a few National Guard helicopters.

WHITE PLAINS NY
HPN KHPN Westchester County 7m/11km NW

This airport has a growing timetable of scheduled departures. It has capitalised, like Islip, on the difficulty of getting around New York City. No longer is it necessary to be troubled by the traffic and parking problems which a flight to another major city once entailed. Many cities in the northeastern states can be reached direct, with even Detroit and Chicago being served non-stop. Congestion at La Guardia, both landside and airside, is contributing to expansion here.

The new passenger terminal is open, with the good news that there is a well-signed observation deck on the third floor. The bad news is that it is enclosed with tight-knit chain link fencing, too small for a camera lens to fit through, making photography impossible. Whilst the area allows good views of all traffic on the move, the planners have obviously not thought that anyone would want to spend more than a little time here and have omitted seating.

Operations include jet services by United 737's and American F100's also visit. US Airways also have more than a dozen scheduled services. Whilst this is one airport where it may be possible to get close to commuter operations, SF340s and Jetstreams being a speciality here, the main attraction is the thirty to forty biz-jets which are based.

AKRON OH
CAK KAKR Akron-Canton Regional 10m/16km SSE of Akron

Easily reached by road, the airport is in North Canton, next to exit 115 off I-77. The long-term car park, which costs a couple of bucks, is a short walk from the terminal. On the roof is an open-air observation deck, overlooking Runway 5/23 and most (but not all) of the apron. Views to the sides are restricted but access to the boarding gates is possible, to see the others. There are only 35 weekday departures, over half of which are USAirways, so traffic can't be described as brisk. Comair, Northwest Airlink and United make up the rest, mostly with feeder-liners, though USAirways Fokker 100s make regular appearances.

Rather than stand on the observation deck all day, listening to its sweet music (!), a tour of the perimeter might be more rewarding. From the parking lot, a turn into Lauby Road leads to another right, resulting in views of the general aviation at the Goodyear, Laurence, Ohio Valley and Gordon Aviation facilities. Back on Lauby Road, look for a turning onto Mount Pleasant, which heads west. The 356th Fighter Group Restaurant has nothing on display outside but, by following Waywood, Wales and Massillon, the Military Aviation Preservation Society's C-47 and F-86 hulks can be seen.

Back on Massillon, the turn onto Koons Road brings more hangars and the Army Aviation Support facility into view, after which the next turn, Greensburg, heads east past the Goodrich Hangar alongside West Airport Road, after which Lauby Road heads back to the terminal.

There are plenty of FBOs, most of which handle executive traffic. References to BF Goodrich and Goodyear will indicate what you should know by now: this is where a lot of tyres are made!

CINCINNATI OH
LUK   KLUK   Lunken Municipal   6m/9km ENE

The international airport is located across the river, in Kentucky, so the city's only airfield in Ohio is used by general aviation. Take exit 9 off I-71 and head south. From Columbia Parkway, you can't miss it. Not just Cessnas and Pipers here - this is quite a busy airfield, with a reasonable selection of business aircraft to be seen.

CLEVELAND OH
CLE   KCLE   Hopkins International   12m/19km WSW

Berea Freeway links the city with its airport and the main terminal's small outdoor spectator deck, open from 07:00 and no charge, is to be found at the end of Concourse B. Early mornings are best for photographs and, by lunchtime, it's time to look for somewhere else. In winter, the open deck is inaccessible (to prevent juveniles throwing snowballs at the Southwest 737s!) but there is an indoor facility. All the concourses are accessible, and a close-up view of almost any airliner operating a scheduled service is possible. The window at TWA's Gate A5 is worth investigation, as are Delta's Gates B2 and B4. One window on the Connector to Concourse A offers a good view of USAirways activity.

Continental and its attendant feeder services, operated by Britt Brasilias, account for half the scheduled traffic, although the introduction by Continental of EMB 145s provides extra interest. The remainder consists of the usual American carriers plus Air Canada CRJs and one or two Air Ontario movements. In other words, Cleveland offers nothing that can't·be seen just as well at other airports. A tour of the perimeter is therefore in order but it isn't possible to drive right round the field. The road ends at Runway 5R where photos are possible.

All the various ramps are easily seen from the road, with a small number of executive aircraft bolstering the considerable quantity of single engined machinery. The Air Services FBO handles the occasional exotic visitor and is worth investigation. Beyond it are the cargo areas, with the usual Kitty Hawk Convairs, Airborne Express DC-9s and often two UPS DC-8s in evidence. The post office employees parking lot is useful for photographers. Fed Ex have their own apron, where several 727s and A310s normally spend the day. It's necessary to backtrack onto Berea Freeway, in order to get onto IX (International Exhibition) Center Drive. Beyond the IX Jet Center is the threshold of Runway 5R.

North of the field, Brookpark Road (SR17) passes the thresholds of Runways 23L/R. The 100th Bomb Group Restaurant has a P-51 Mustang and a car park. By standing on the car roof, it's easy to take good photos of aircraft turning onto 23L for take off, with the control tower in the background. Accessible from Brookpark Road, on West Hangar Road (the third set of lights after the restaurant) is NASA's Lewis Research Center. The road crosses the taxiway into the NASA ramp, where one or two aircraft can usually be seen. There is a visitors centre here with many exhibits. Beyond is 5K Flights and the airport's remaining stock of general aviation. Plans for a new runway, 23R to be constructed west of the current Runway 23R, may mean the closure or relocation of Brookpark Road.

Anyone interested in general aviation, and staying in the Cleveland area, will also investigate BURKE LAKEFRONT, once used by weekday Northcoast Executive Metros, but no longer. For those intent on taking a look, it's close to the stadium used by the Cleveland Browns and to the

Rock n Roll Hall of Fame. North Marginal Drive, leads past the coastguard base, to the airport. There is a small terminal, the main lobby of which allows the ramp to be seen.

A tour of the perimeter leads first to Million Air and Aircraft Companies, both ramps being behind a high fence which makes photography impossible, even when standing on the car roof. At the back of the Aviation High School is a DC-3 and a few other aircraft.

The best time to visit Burke Lakefront (if there is one) is in early September, when the Cleveland National Air Show is held. Traffic also increases in early July, when the Budweiser Grand Prix takes place.

CLEVELAND OH
CGF   Cuyahoga County   14m/22km ENE

Taking I-90 towards Richmond Heights, the airport is south of exit 182. It is a major general aviation field, handling a fair number of biz-jets among its many executive aircraft. For anyone with an interest in quantity, this is an airfield not to be missed. For saturation coverage of the area, a visit to LOST NATION Airport (LNN) in Willoughby will be essential. Its principal attraction is the United States Aviation Museum, which was relocated here in 1995.

COLUMBUS OH
CMH   KCMH   Port Columbus International   7m/11km NE

The city is not on many touring intineraries because it doesn't lie between two important centres. Like Cleveland, it is also served by several airports, spread out around the town. The international airport lacks volume of traffic to make it worth the detour in its own right but it's fine for America West A320s.

The passenger terminal sits at the end of its approach road, Stelzer Road off I-670, and good views of aircraft landing on both runways can be obtained from the top floor of the parking garage, with the parallel runways 10/28 on either side. Before reaching the terminal in a car, one of the general aviation facilities is on the right. The other, served by its own two short diagonal runways, is on the far side of the field, tucked in the southeast corner.

COLUMBUS OH
OSU   Ohio State University   11m/17km NNW

The airport's name says everything about its location. Much of the general aviation activity is generated by the university, which has its own Aerotechnology program. The number of residents is large though, in the main, somewhat lacklustre. For anyone who wants to log over a hundred light aircraft without trouble, this is a useful destination.

COLUMBUS OH
LCK   KLCK   Rickenbacker   11m/17km S

Highway 23 leads from exit 52 off I-270 to what is, for many, one of the more interesting airports in the area. It is not the exclusively a military field and its status is changing. A few C-141s and KC-135s are based, and the small museum could provide an excuse for seeking a short-term pass to get closer to the action.

DAYTON OH
DAY   KDAY   James M Cox International   12m/19km NNW

The airport is in Vandalia, easily reached from either exit 63 off I-75 or exit 32 from I-70. Terminal Drive leads to an impressive building, inside which things are rather good. There are two

166

piers/concourses, B and C (don't ask!) USAirways being on the left. The other is mostly for United and American flights. The concourse windows are not tinted, which is good news for photographers, and almost anything which uses the passenger terminal can be photographed from somewhere. If traffic gets slow, a game of pool next to the restaurant also allows one eye to be kept on events outside.

In 1992 USAirways stopped using Dayton as a hub, though they didn't pull out altogether. The effect on movements was instant and drastic. Daily jet departures fell overnight from seventy-three to twenty. Business is starting to get better. Including commuter traffic, there are now over a hundred scheduled passenger flights departing each weekday. USAirways accounts for more than a third of the movements, followed by Continental with a quarter. The rest is the usual mix but it must be said that variety of aircraft types is surprisingly good.

Dayton is regarded as synonymous with the major overnight parcels carrier, Emery Worldwide, and their Superhub. Anyone expecting to see large numbers of this airline's aircraft will be disappointed as they arrive from all over the country after midnight and leave again before dawn. Between these times, forty or so DC-8s and 727s are turned round. The apron is on the eastern side of the field, next to the threshold of Runway 24L, reached off Peters Pike. A large sign says (shouts?): AUTHORIZED PERSONNEL ONLY, which rather suggests Emery don't want to be bothered with casual visitors. Anyone with a serious interest in overnight parcels handling would be well advised to write to them at their headquarters: 3350 West Bayshore, Palo Alto, California 94303.

DAYTON OH
MGY   Montgomery County

Top Flight Air Service link Dayton with Cleveland, Toledo and Detroit. To keep services attractive to the businessman, they make use of smaller, and more convenient, airports. Their movements, mostly Aerostars and Navajo Chieftains, use this airport. General aviation is also to be found in quantity at MORAINE AIR PARK, some five miles south of the city.

DAYTON OH
FFO   KFFO   Wright-Patterson Air Force Base   9m/15km NE

West of Fairborn, this is the home of the United States Air Force Museum, which is open between 09:00 and 17:00. Arrival should be arranged early in the day as there is a lot to see. The museum now occupies two buildings, outside which a white B-1 bomber is parked. The first building is divided into two: the Early Years on the right and the Air Power Gallery to the left. A B-36 dominates this hall, though the B-29 at the other end also takes up a bit of space.

A walkway leads to the Modern Flight hangar, inside which you are greeted by an F-117. Behind it stands a B-52, with a B-47, SR-71, B-58 and the XB-70 Valkyrie at the back. On the right from the entrance door are, among many others, a C-46, C-47 and C-124. This is one very large building!

Not on show here are the Presidential aircraft, which form part of a separate display, found in the annex. To visit the annex, first get a parking pass from the main desk and drive to the area yourself. The shuttle bus service has been discontinued. Not to be missed is the IMAX movie theatre: what America does rather well. The usual - 80 feet high screen, six channel stereo that makes the floor move, that sort of thing!

Generally, it can be assumed that if the USAF flew it, the museum has it, and any military-minded enthusiast will find this museum to be exactly what it should be: the best in the world. It can take a whole day to enjoy this museum. Even the gift shop is worth an hour. For details, write to USAF Museum, Wright-Patterson ADB, Ohio 45433-6518, USA. Two telephone numbers which might be of use are the museum on (513) 255-3286 and the movies on (513) 253-IMAX.

An interest in the history of aviation makes Dayton a special place. It all started in a bicycle shop at 22 South Williams Street, where the Wright Brothers thought it might be possible to fly. The area has several attractions, and an information leaflet is avaiable at the museum for those wishing to investigate further.

MANSFIELD OH
MFD   Lahm Municipal   3m/5km N

Halfway between Akron and Columbus, Lahm handles most of mid-Ohio's general aviation as well as being the home of 179 Airlift Group's C-130s. It is worth the detour for anyone passing through.

SPRINGFIELD OH
SGH   Beckley Municipal   6m/9km SSW

Very little happens in the way of airline activity, as it's primarily a g.a. field. The civil aircraft share the runways, however, with the Ohio ANG F-16s. This may be enough reason for a visit.

TOLEDO OH
TOL   KTOL   Express   14m/22km W

It's wise to avoid the city, without good reason to visit. The airport is best reached from the Ohio Turnpike, I-80/90, off exit 3A. The long term car park is cheapest, and reasonably close to the terminal. Through the doors, go straight ahead to the security check point, after which an escalator leads to the upper level. Windows at either side allow views of the airliners, many of which are commuters, and those at the far end overlook the ANG ramp with its F-16s.

Scheduled traffic rarely exceeds 727-size (Delta, usually), the rest being a mixture of Comair SF340s, American Eagle ATR-42s, Chicago Express Jetstreams and the like. Photos in the afternoon are reasonable, though the glass is slightly tinted.

For views of the rest of the field, head east along Airport HIghway. An off-road car park allows a good view of the airfield (including the F-16s) but the company might be disturbing. It's a great place for whatever young couples do in cars. Wind down the window, breathe in and smell that pot! East Service Road leads to Express Aviation, for some general aviation, and is a dead end. Off Airport Highway in the opposite direction is Garden Road, which passes the gates of the ANG base. The next right, Eber Road, passes under the runway flightpath on the way to Burlington Express. Usually there is nothing to be seen during daylight hours.

WILMINGTON OH
ILN   Clinton/Airborne Airpark   6m/9km SE

Not to be confused with Greater Wilmington (ILG), this is the Airborne Express hub. Very little happens during the day but the evenings are most interesting, especially with an airband radio. The centre/approach frequency is officially 118.85, 24 hours a day, but the airline's own frequency (unknown) makes better listening, as the crews of the various YS-11s, DC-8s and DC-9s talk to each other. It has been reported that the tower offers no radio assistance at night. This, if confirmed, would make things very lively indeed!

YOUNGSTOWN OH
YNG   KYNG   Warren Regional   10m/16km NW

The observation deck is outdoors but the wire mesh is perfect for ensuring that photography is all but impossible. That said, the view is reasonable in the mornings. What is lacking is traffic. USAirways Express share the work with Northwest Airlink and United Express. Two commuter liners on the ramp at the same time is, at this airport, hectic. Visible are the AFRES C-130s, which rarely move, and a couple of FBOs, Cafaro and Am-Air, reached off State Road 193.

ARDMORE OK

ADM   KADM   Airpark   13m/20km E

This former Air Force Base is about halfway between Oklahoma City and Dallas. A signpost on the I-35 directs you to the Industrial Air Park. Its attraction has nothing to do with scheduled traffic, nor much with general aviation or military movements. Instead what it offers is a view over the fence of something that doesn't move at all. Lockheed's prototype L1011 came to rest here, in the company of an Eastern Airlines example, plus a Pan Am 747 and a Trump 727. They have been joined recently by a number of United 727s and DC-10s. If access is needed for photography, the fire/security department are likely to be of assistance.

OKLAHOMA CITY OK

OKC   KOKC   Will Rogers World   10m/16km SW

If this is truly a world airport, it must be due to the number of foreign-made aircraft which use it: American Airlines Fokker 100s and ASA ATR-72s being examples. Activity is, to be generous, modest. An observation tower, suitable for spotters, costs 20 cents admission and has speakers tuned to the control tower frequency. An open air observation deck in the passenger terminal faces south, so its popularity with serious photographers is limited. Without a car, afternoons are best, as the east employee parking lot, just north of the old air cargo building, faces the taxiway. The chain link fence has clearly proved problematical to preceding photographers but the problems seem to have been partially solved, judging by the state of the barbed wire.

Within walking distance (ish) from the terminal area are the north cargo ramp and AAR Oklahoma, the FBO. The cargo ramp can boast a good variety of air freighters and the FBO is partially an airliner repair station. Maybe it doesn't handle all that much business but few would turn down the opportunity to see such goodies as an Azerbaijan Airlines 727, a Southeast Pacific Airways (Chile) 737 or a Paradise Island Dash 7, all of which made their first appearances here. Discreet photography over the fence might yield better results than asking, as there is a policy of requiring the owner's permission to do so officially.

A car is required to visit the north end. The Oklahoma ANG C-130s are based here, as is the FAA's Mike Monroe Air Center. For access to the FAA ramp, which can't be seen from the road, contact with the public affairs office is obligatory. The other notable presence is a fleet of jets owned by the US Marshal. They are used for flying federal prisoners. Don't even think of asking! The third weekend in June is a good time to visit Will Rogers, when the west side of the field is taken over by the annual Aerospace America airshow. The line-up is impressive enough for it to be worth seeking written approval for access to the huge static display before the crowds arrive.

OKLAHOMA CITY OK

TIK   KTIK   Tinker Air Force Base   8m/13km SE

A visit to Oklahoma may mean more than passing through on an Airpass. If this be so, then Tinker is worth a look. It's home to the Air Logistics Center, though resident aircraft are few. The occasional B-1 or KC-135, undergoing or awaiting refurbishment, is consolation. TAFB has recently been designated as the overhaul centre for B-2 stealth bombers, so there's always hope of seeing something extraordinary in the pattern. More in evidence are the E-3A AWACS, the Oklahoma ANG F-16s and, most notably, the Navy's TACOMO E-6s. When aircraft land from the south, good approach photos are possible from an open field overlooking the end of Runway 18, just to the north of I-40. The police are used to enthusiasts and are unlikely to bother them but it must be remembered that activity is slow.

WILEY POST, the city's principal g.a. field. is also the home of the Commander Aircraft production line. Residents include a C-47 and an S-2F Tracker in full Navy colours. For spotters, the average weekday should yield a hundred or so light aircraft. Other general aviation fields in the area include STILLWATER Municipal), sometimes used by Oklahoma State University for college football charters, and NORMAN University Park which, if nothing else, is close to I-35.

TULSA OK
TUL   KTUL   International   9m/15km NE

The name is optimistic as there are no scheduled international flights. Traffic is mostly Comair Regional Jets, ASA ATR-72s and Northwest Airlink SF340s. The large, spacious passenger terminal faces northeast so photography through the concourse windows is relatively easy.

The perimeter invites exploration and a car is essential. A series of small streets leads round the end of Runway 1 to Sheridan Road. A turn to the north reveals the g.a. hangars and, possibly of interest, Nordam Industries, who make 737-200 hush kits. Their test bed is often present.

36th Street North is where the interest starts to grow. The first right leads to Tulsa Technology Center, where three ex-Alitalia DC-8-43s languish, now close to dereliction. The 727 wearing TTC titles is ex-Air France. Further along 36th Street North is the Oklahoma ANG unit, with its A-7Es. Look out also for a right turn to Mingo Road, where American Airlines have an enormous maintenance base. The hangars, unfortunately, block most of the view. The Rockwell and McDonnell Douglas plants, further south, are both closed.

Avid spotters should be aware that there are other, general aviation, fields in the area. R LLOYD JONES Airport is probably the most notable, southeast of the city. It has an An-2.

EUGENE OR
EUG   Mahlon Sweet Field   8m/13km NW

Anyone visiting Oregon will probably do so for its outstanding scenery, rather than to see this airport. It is a small, parochial field with a limited offering of flights, the links being to Seattle and Portland with Horizon Air, and elsewhere with United or Delta. The old fashioned terminal is on the east side of the runway and the airliners park in front of it, making photography difficult. The commuter types are easier to get at but the ground level access means that a lot of foreground clutter may spoil the view. The real view here is of the mountains and any would-be visitor would do well to remember the fact, rather than hope for close-ups with a scenic backdrop.

MEDFORD OR
MFR   Municipal   3m/5km N

Ramp access is essential for the photographer, as the more interesting residents are close to the fences. With thousands of square miles of forests all round, Medford makes an obvious base for a few fire fighters during the season. A Catalina, possibly resident, has been noted and one or two biz-jets can normally be expected.

ALLENTOWN PA
ABE   /Bethlehem/Easton   4m/6km NE of Allentown

Three industrial towns have grown into one conurbation. Their economic fortunes grew with the steel industry but the decline was abrupt and this became one of America's more depressed areas. A certain amount of regeneration is breathing new hope into the area but the airport, lacking its lifeblood of businessmen on the move, still functions at a fraction of its earlier hey-day. It is linked to all major hubs in the region, with a varied selection of operators and types, up to 727 size. Apart from being a good place to stop for a cheap snack and a good photo of one or two airliners on the ramp, the Bethlehem Steel fleet of biz-jets is based directly opposite the terminal, on the far side of the runway.

Heading northeast from Allentown, another airport rejoicing in the name of MIFFLINTOWN, is worth a visit, if only for its airworthy Lockheed Lodestar.

170

ERIE PA

ERI   International   6m/9km WSW

USAirways and Northwest Airlink serve this regional airport with 737s, DC-9s and Fokker 100s. It does not get busy. The apron can only be seen from the cafe and the restaurant, so buying a coffee and a donut seems to be the order of the day. What was the observation deck has now been turned into a break room for airport employees, though there is no report of what the view is/was like.

Given that airline operations are not particularly inspiring, a tour of the perimeter is likely. The general aviation is nothing special. The Erie Airways hangar and apron can be empty, not that it gets particularly full, and is reached on Kudlack, accessible off Ashbury Avenue.

HARRISBURG PA

MDT   KMDT   International   4m/6km SE

The airport shares a runway with Olmsted AFB and is located in Middletown, hence the MDT code. From Harrisburg, cross the river and turn right along Front Street, parallel to the river. After passing under the turnpike, keep straight on, along 2nd Street and the airport is on the north bank. It is hardly worth the effort for photography but the road from the terminal to Middletown reveals the Air Force Base on the right, in the distance. The Pennsylvania Air National Guard EC-130s rarely move and are normally lined up, within range of a 200mm lens.

Scheduled services for passengers are increasing, and there is a strong cargo presence here. Scheduled services are operated to all the region's hubs by a good range of aircraft, up to 727 size. The city's bizjet and King Air population are also in evidence, and access to the ramp isn't normally a problem. German Cargo are surprisingly regular visitors, and the local overhaul facility, Stambaugh's Aviation, services FedEx's F.27s as well as US Navy T-39s, A-4s and T-2s.

The new passenger terminal offers good views over the field from its observation deck on the elevated departure level, and reasonable photos can be taken through the glass.

HARRISBURG PA

HAR   KHAR   Skyport   3m/5km S

From Harrisburg International, backtrack to the Harris Bridge across the Susquehanna River and take Interstate 83 to New Cumberland. Harrisburg Skyport, previously known as Capital City, is easy to find from here. With all the scheduled traffic using the international airport, only general aviation is in evidence, though one or two antiques do make the trip worthwhile . . . but only if staying in the area, with time to kill.

JOHNSTOWN PA

JST   Cambria County   5m/8km E

Take Frankstown Road from town and a right turn leads south to the airport. Alternatively, it can be found just to the north of Highway 219. With only the occasional Beech 1900 commuter/ feeder during the day, traffic is light but, for anyone passing on the way across country to or from Pittsburgh, it may be worth a quick visit.

LATROBE PA

LBE   Westmoreland County   1m/1.5km

Once the home of Jetstream Airlines, Latrobe now receives the odd Twin Otter service. Most of these are bound for Pittsburgh and, unless there is a need to see all of Pennsylvania's airports, it might be sensible to do the same thing.

PHILADELPHIA PA

PHL   KPHL   International   8m/13km SSW (train 25 minutes)

Leaving the city southbound on Interstate 95, the airport is on the left with its eastern boundary being the Delaware River. Alternatively, the train costs $5 each way. There are no external viewing facilities (indeed there are no formal viewing facilities at all) but the main terminal is used almost exclusively by domestic traffic, and the fingers of the spread-eagled building all allow close inspection of airliners parked on the apron. Convenient for most purposes are Concourses B and C reached, as usual, via security checkpoints. Views of runway activity will depend on which direction traffic is landing. If it arrives from the west a viewpoint at the end of Concourse E is excellent but, if landings are being made from the east, Concourse A is the place to be.

An afternoon's patient viewing will be amply rewarded by a good selection of airlines, with a wide variety of local commuter carriers. USAirways dominate the proceedings however. The extremity of the piers is very close to one of the taxiways and there are few better locations for high quality photographs than this, after lunchtime.

Scheduled traffic does feature the occasional intercontinental arrival, which parks at the western end of the passenger terminal, and close views of these movements are a matter of luck.

To the north of the main terminal area, off Concourse E, is a ramp where USAirways Express carry out their Philadelphia operations. Those wishing to obtain some permanent detailed record of this will need to make the rather long journey between Concourses C and E, although the introduction of moving walkways has made this easier. It is worth the effort because there is also the biz-jet ramp, where up to ten aircraft are normally to be seen with, as an added bonus, aircraft on the cargo ramp, such as the occasional World Airways MD-11 and Capitol 727. At the opposite extreme, Concourse A might not be quite so rewarding: the parcels carriers can be seen from here but frustration can be in store, as only one or two of the aircraft can be logged.

Access to the Atlantic Aviation facility was once a matter of driving up to the gatehouse and being waved past by the guard. Security arrangements are now generally more stringent and a letter in advance could allow a good look at large numbers of executive jets and turbo-props, plus several Beech 18s operated by smaller cargo charter carriers. Another part of the field worthy of close attention is Cargo City, accessible by Island Road, to the south of the field. Opposite is the large UPS facility, with the occasional daytime movement.

Slightly further south, and visible from the highway, is Boeing Vertol's large hangar and apron. It is not renowned for having helicopter's on show.

PHILADELPHIA PA

PNE   KPNE   Northeast   12m/19km NE

Not an airport for scheduled traffic but the old terminal building remains to give an idea of what the place must have been like in its hey-day. The apron is often occupied during the week by a good number of executive aircraft whose operators benefit from the lower handling charges and relative proximity of the city. Ransome's base might be busiest at weekends, when maintenance work can be carried out on the Jetstreams, operating during the week in their TWExpress colours.

Visitors to this part of Pennsylvania may wish to consider a detour to one or two other locations of interest. Lovers of Constellations will take the trouble to locate the suburb of PENNDEL, a few miles northeast on Highway 1, where L-1049E N1005C was converted into Jim Flannery's Restaurant. Leaving the city on Highway 611, the WILLOW GROVE Naval Air Station can't be missed, being next to the road. A selection of museum pieces has been placed next to the road for the spectator's interest and, beyond these, a ramp of two squadrons of P-3s provides an excellent prospect. Because there are so many different types of military aircraft operated from this field, visitors will take advantage, no doubt, of the roads around the perimeter. A left turn off Hwy 611 at County Line Road leads to Keith Valley Road (small and easily missed) and the next left turn is Governor's Road, which peters out into a track before stopping at the fence, overlooking the ramp. By checking down every lane on the perimeter, views of the various naval/marines helicopters and other types will be possible.

Parallel to County Line Road is Highway 132 which gives access to the Turnpike and passes WARMINSTER Naval Air Development Center. The Turnpike (Interstate 276) crosses the Delaware River northeast of Philadelphia and just before the bridge is Exit 29 to 3M AIRPORT, where the Minnesota Mining & Manufacturing Company (3M) have a terminal.

PITTSBURGH PA

PIT   KPIT   Greater Pittsburgh International   16m/25km NW

Pittsburgh being a major hub for USAirways, the movements here are totally dominated by the one airline. The old terminal, like Stapleton airport, came to the end of its useful life overnight. From October 1992, the new Airside Terminal became operational. Without doubt, this is a very large airport indeed. According to one press statement, the field occupies over 12,000 acres - more than Atlanta and O'Hare combined.

The Airside Terminal lies between the parallel runways, accessible from the west. The main building forms a large diagonal cross and most of its gates are, not surprisingly, used by USAir. Commuter feeders have their own gates on a small apron in front of the check-in building. A people-mover gives access to the building and entry doesn't require boarding cards. Apart from the international wing, the rest is up to you. Each concourse has twenty-five gates, so there is a lot of walking to do. Concourse E, used by USAirways Express, is visible from C or D, so this cuts down the work. Walking to the extremity of Concourse A is essential, to log all the cargo aircraft, many of which park at very inconvenient angles. After that, it might be best to settle down at the end of D, which allows a view of 10L/28R.

A trip to USAirways maintenance base, in the centre of the field, also reveals the general aviation terminal, and a considerable number of business aircraft. Also seen from this part of the field are the Air National Guard movements, with A-7s in the circuit and the more static C-130s. The other general aviation is to be found at ALLEGHENY COUNTY.

READING PA

RDG   Regional (General Spaatz)   3m/5km NW

This is still the home of Allegheny Commuter Airlines,now a US Airways Express operator, and it is the only place to be reasonably sure of an Dash 8 portrait. For permission to look around the apron the fixed base operator, Reading Aviation (Suburban in disguise), should be contacted and the reward is seventy or so based aircraft, including some biz-jets and antiques.

STATE COLLEGE PA

SCE   University Park

This should not be confused with College Park, just north of Washington DC. Airline activity using the passenger terminal is restricted to Pennsylvania Airlines plus a couple of FedEx Caravans, but a half a dozen biz-jets and the Clark Motor Company's vintage and warbird collection make the field worth the visit. Since the museum is in a closed (and spotter-proof) hangar, permission for a look should be sought in writing prior to arrival: the company is welcoming on this basis.

WILKES-BARRE/SCRANTON PA

AVP   Avoca   12m/19km NE

The passenger terminal has a rooftop viewing area with free entry. Since it faces east, it is ideal for afternoon shots of USAirways jets and a range of dedicated commuters. With a 200mm lens, excellent landing shots of visitors are possible, with the bonus of picturesque mountain scenery in the background. The fleet of Pocono Airlines Nord 262s found its final resting place here.

WILLIAMSPORT PA
IPT   KIPT   Lycoming County   5m/8km E

This small regional airport is used solely by Pennsylvania Airlines, as USAirways Express, and the car park next to the passenger terminal is ideal for photography of these, and the odd collection of machines belonging to the Area Community College, including a T-29B. Inside the college hangar are more eccentric aircraft, and access is normally possible. A few of the other forty or so light aircraft on the main general aviation ramp, to the south, are also interesting.

ANDERSON SC
AND   KAND   County   3m/5km SW

The approach road, off Highway 24E, features an F-105 directly opposite the terminal. Mountain Air Cargo have a shed here, the first building of any size on the left when arriving. Whether anything is to be seen outside it is a matter of luck. At the far side of the passenger terminal are the FBOs, who normally grant ramp access if requested. At the far end of the ramp is a C-47, N3BA, which last saw service with Academy Airlines. The titles are still to be seen but the missing engine and the collapsed oleo suggest it won't be moving in a hurry.

GREENVILLE/SPARTANBURG SC
GSP   Municipal   11m/17km NE/SW

Busy it isn't but it's extremely popular with local enthusiasts. The authorities have created a park in the centre of the ramp, and it's freely open to all visitors. Probably unique in all the USA, this is more like it! The catch? Of course there's a catch. There are very few aircraft to see and something is needed on which to stand to see over the fence, in order to take good photos.

CHATTANOOGA TN
CHA   KCHA   Lovell Field   10m/16km E

The passenger terminal sits opposite the intersection of the two runways, 2/20 and one designated as 33 only. Everything can be seen from it, in theory, as no report has been received to confirm this. Our correspondent was more concerned with the FBOs and the cargo aircraft. Fed Ex use F.27s and Airborne Express station a YS-11 here during the day, both of which can be seen from the fence. The FBOs include the Chattanooga Jet Center and Signal Air Services, among others, where executive aircraft are normally to be seen. F-101 Voodoo 90412 is preserved with the ANG.

FAYETTEVILLE TN
FAY   Municipal   4m/6km S

Fayetteville Municipal handles a few United and American jet movements plus a regular procession of ASA Brasilias. Nearby is Fort Bragg, which generates some of the business. The 82nd Airborne Museum is at the base, and is probably of more interest, since its exhibits feature a number of transport aircraft.

KNOXVILLE TN
TYS   KTYS   McGhee Tyson   13m/20km S

US Highway 129 heads south from town and the airport is signposted. The passenger terminal handles an amount of commuters and up to DC-9 and 737-sized scheduled traffic. Next to the terminal is a car park, lower than the ramp so that nothing can be seen. On the right of the car park is the business terminal, which is accessible and, obviously, at apron level. A request for ramp access should meet with success. A C-47 is parked next to the garage hangars and on the far side of these is a Convair. The Cherokee Aviation hangar is at the end of the apron, where more general aviation is to be seen.

The Air National Guard base is on the far side of the parallel runways (4/22L/R). When leaving the terminal area, a side road to the left passes round the end of the runways, giving access to the cargo shed where an assortment of aircraft are parked, including the almost obligatory FedEx jet. For a general aviation field with a difference, travel into town. Cross the river on Alcoa and double back onto Riverside Drive. By heading east, the DOWNTOWN ISLAND Airport can be seen. It is, quite literally, what its name suggests.

MEMPHIS TN
MEM   KMEM   International   10m/16km SE

By day, a Northwest hub and by night Federal Express. These are the bare bones which need a little more meat. During daylight hours, the circular passenger terminal and car park offer the chance to see a reasonable number, but limited selection, of airliners. Among these are normally about thirty or so FedEx 727s. The cargo area also offers plenty to see. There are about three waves of Northwest flights a day - early morning, noon and early evening - and not much happeneing between. Unusually, this might be the ideal place to spend a Sunday because FedEx the late morning onwards sees plenty of activity. Expect about forty of their fleet, mainly DC-10s, MD-11s and Airbuses. Few pass the terminal area close enough for photos, though.

Major reconstruction of the terminal area looks likely, so it is possible that some of the favourite vantage points might be prejudiced, at least temporarily. Where have we heard that before? More likely they'll be gone for ever.

On the far side of the field is the Tennessee Air National Guard, usually with half a dozen C-130s and the odd C-141B on its ramp. Close to their base is Federal Express. A car is essential for close encounters, and these should be restricted to the road. Getting closer means conversation with security personnel. Real interest in the operation should be followed up. A phone call to FedEx reveals that a tour of the operation is available, starting at the wholly unreasonable, but highly appropriate, hour of 23:30.

Also to be seen at the airport is the Bomb Group Restaurant which, in this instance (there are plenty of others around the country), has an unmarked C-47. Memphis is more than a hub for Federal Express: it was the home of Elvis Presley. His home, Graceland, is west of the airport. The road which passes under the runways is Winchester. A few blocks west is Elvis Presley Boulevard. A left turn leads to the house and his two jet transports, the Jetstar and the CV-880. As good taste can be flushed down the toilet when discussing anything to do with the Elvis legacy, nothing else needs be said.

WEST MEMPHIS, across the river in Arkansas, is a quiet general aviation field but it does occasionally handle McNeeley's DC-3s, one of which still flies in RCAF colours.

MORRISTOWN TN
MOR   Moore-Murrell   6m/9km S

Signposts airport are difficult to find. Take US 11E, south from the town, and the airport is tucked away on the right, discreetly behind a housing estate. A memorial to the Reverend M M Murrell, an aviation pioneer, stands outside the entrance to the passenger terminal. One day, there may be a memorial to Morristown's more famous son, who became one of America's most famous drag-racing stars: Mr Conrad A Kalitta - or Connie, as he is better known. Having felt the need to fly his rods all over America, he developed a taste for aviation and the rest is history, as they say.

Off the approach road leading to the terminal is an insignificant turning on the left. Connie Kalitta Flying Services are to be found here. There is also a C-47 on display, visible en route to the passenger terminal. Behind it are the general aviation hangars and an FBO.

NASHVILLE TN
BNA   KBNA   Metropolitan   8m/13km SE

From Opryland, take I-40 east and Exit 216A to the airport. Next is Donelson Pike, effectively an approach road to the passenger terminal, though it also passes the threshold of the busiest runway, 31, on its way to Murfreesboro Road and a view of the two parallel cross runways.

Most of the movements are domestic, with a handful of flights to Toronto and Puerto Rico, so security checks allow access to gates. Perhaps the best views are at the end of North Concourse, Pier B, for the American Eagle movements which make up a large proportion of the traffic. Gates C22-24 (South) offer a view of the general aviation and cargo ramps but not of the runway.

Before arriving at Nashville, for a few hours' stay, it's essential to consult an American Airlines timetable. The waves of airline movements mean that two hours can pass with little or no movement. However, for a short period, things get very hectic. Between about noon and 15:30 (which might not always be a peak time) sixty or so American and American Eagle flights come and go. The monitors also reveal that, between 18:00 and 19:00, fifty arrivals can be expected. For a while, the situation is bewildering. At least two runways in use, and aircraft on the move in every direction. From Concourse C, the American/Eagle aircraft can be seen, plus some of the general aviation. The end of Concourse B allows a view of one of the busiest runways. Parked American Eagle commuters can be logged in passing, and anything bound for Concourse A can be seen from here.

A few stored Metros are also to be seen in the general aviation area, and there is a facility for preparation work on Dornier feederliners. The Air National Guard ramp normally contains about a dozen C-130s. As at Memphis, the Bomb Group restaurant has a C-47.

AMARILLO TX
AMA   KAMA   Air Terminal   9m/15km E

The large, spacious terminal has lots of clear glass through which to see the apron. Movements are, however, relatively few and feature mostly the occasional ASA ATR-72. Under-use of the facilities made Amarillo ideal for aircraft storage. In past years a notable array of aircraft have found their way here: USAirways' entire stock of ex-Piedmont 727-200s and the A300s of both Pan Am and Eastern. In 1997, mostly American Airlines DC-10s and 727s were present.

Outside DynAir's hangar are many stored aircraft, most of which can be seen from the fence. Across the field is a large aircraft scrapyard, also run by DynAir. Most of the airframes here, numbering another twenty, are 727s. Access for photography to either of DynAir's facilities is their decision. Only logging is believed to be permitted at the far side.

Hughes FBO, west of the passenger terminal, can play host to some interesting visitors including a few USAF T-38s and T-43s.

AUSTIN TX
AUS   KAUS   Robert Mueller Municipal   4m/6km NE

Austin is the state's capital city but its downtown airport is generally unremarkable, save for one fact: Conquest Airlines' hub means that their Metros visit four or five times a day. Photos can be taken through tinted glass in the rather cramped main concourse but serious photographers will consider the need for ramp access. It could be easier to walk a short distance from the terminal, to the weather service office, across from the municipal golf course parking lot. As long as departures are to the north, good photos of taxiing aircraft are easy to take in the afternoon.

This is a fairly large general aviation field, with no less than three runways, and the two Hughes FBOs (one on each side of the field) ensure it gets its fair share of traffic. Biz-jets bring a regular supply of VIPs to lobby the State legislature. A large cargo area can usually be found to contain six residents from FedEx, Kitty Hawk and Airborne Express. The best viewing is from the Signature Air Support Terminal on Airport Road, a long walk from the main passenger terminal.

To ensure saturation coverage of general aviation in the area a car is essential, enthusiasts will also need to visit EXECUTIVE AIRPARK, BIRD'S NEST and LAKEWAY AIRPARK.

BROWNSVILLE TX
BRO   KBRO   South Padre Island   5m/8km W

With no scheduled passenger services and only one or two parcels aircraft, it might be difficult to understand the appeal of Brownsville. For many people, there is none at all. A Confederate Air Force Museum is enough for some and T-2 Buckeyes (still?) suit others. In other words, Brownsville is a matter of personal taste and preference.

COLLEGE STATION TX
CLL   KCLL   Easterwood

For three seasons of the year, not much happens here: the usual trickle of Continental Express, American Eagle and ASA, so hardly worth a detour. Between September and Christmas, things get busier on Saturdays, when the college football season is in full swing. Plenty of rich Texas A&M University alumni fly into this airport in their private jets to support their team.

CORPUS CHRISTI TX
CRP   KCRP   International   5m/8km W

For anyone in need of ground level photographs of Continental or Southwest 737s, Corpus Christi is a good destination but the number of movements during the day is not great, and supplemented only by occasional United arrivals. Since it is possible to stand at the side of the apron, next to the passenger terminal, any camera with a standard lens will achieve the desired results. However, they will be very similar to those obtained at Houston Hobby or Dallas Love Field, where the majority of flights are bound. Perhaps the only movements that won't be seen elsewhere are the rig support helicopters, though not in great numbers.

DALLAS TX
ADS   Addison   11m/17km N

It's generally thought that a trip to Dallas means Love Field and Dallas-Fort Worth. When pursuing airliners, this is indeed true. Biz-jets are a bonus which, at Love Field, become a very big bonus. The wish to see more, or clean up the area, means that time must be made for a trip to Addison. It is a busy general aviation field with much to see. Hotels around here also tend to be slightly cheaper than near some of the better known locations.

DALLAS TX
DAL   KDAL   Love Field   4m/6km NNW

The home of Southwest Airlines, though some aircraft are based in Baltimore, St Louis, Midway, and San Antonio. The fleet operates point to point rather than hub and spoke services so some aircraft seen will disappear for the whole day. The passenger terminal contains some interest. Downstairs is an art gallery, specializing in aviation art and photography. Upstairs, across from the admin offices, a small museum offers something to justify the $2 entry: one of the exhibits is a model of a 727, used by James Calder to design Braniff's Flying Colours. The observation deck was scheduled to re-open some time in 1994 but most reports suggest this never happened. It overlooks some of the Southwest gates and the commuter ramp, but a re-opened deck represents serious progress in the USA.
    The south side of the central multi-storey car park offers a panoramic view, and excellent

photography in the mornings, when Southwest are at their busiest. The many hangar complexes and ramps can be relied upon to provide a sight of over a hundred biz-jets at any one time.

Between the runways are the passenger terminal and the facilities of Hughes (previously Jet East) and KC Aviation. Accessible from the perimeter is the Associated Air Center and, at the end of this road, a small circular parking area very close to one runway. From this spot, admittedly facing south, the whole field can be seen. To the left are Aviall, Citijet and one of the Associated Air Center hangars. To the right is another, plus Arco and Daljet. Anyone with a car will find these ramps worthy of the time and attention, but not so accessible are Rockwell and Associated Air Center, in whose hangars maintenance is carried out on electronic surveillance aircraft. Photography in the afternoon is probably at its best on Denton Road, next to the southern perimeter. In the southwest corner (where else?) is Southwest's corporate headquarters, quite close to the runway. From here, their aircraft can be photographed at their best. The airline staff are friendly, so it might be worth letting someone know your intentions before setting up for an afternoon's photo session.

Corporate attitudes to interest in their aircraft are now hardening. Anyone hearing a suggestion that photography might be unwise in any particular location would be well-advised to heed the advice given. The United States is the source of many stories about enthusiasts being given a hard time, including successful prosecution. Precautions relax in mid-September, when the NBAA biz-jet show is held. Access to the tarmac for casual visitors is generally easier if they wear something appropriate. Essential luggage should therefore include a pair of slacks and a drip dry short-sleeved shirt. A tie is useful and tie pins add a touch of local colour!

Having made the effort to go to Addison in pursuit of general aviation, DALLAS NORTH is the next logical step. A car is essential to get there and to cruise clockwise round the perimeter. REDBIRD completes the Dallas g.a. itinerary. If airliners are no more interesting than any other aircraft, then Dallas North, Addison, Love Field and Redbird will provide hours, perhaps days, of entertainment.

DALLAS-FORT WORTH TX
DFW   KDFW   International   15m/23km NW of Dallas

American Airlines' hub-and-spoke operations take on real meaning at DFW where huge numbers of the fleet come and go in waves, or 'banks', as they are known. Within a half-hour period there will be forty or so American flights arriving followed, half an hour later, by these aircraft departing. These banks of flights occur eight times a day and, since American/American Eagle's four hundred movements account for more than half the traffic, they leave a lasting impression.

Delta have also established a hub at DFW, making them the second largest operator, with nearly a quarter of the movements, many of which are 737s, operating a shuttle-type operation between Dallas and Atlanta. The other major presence here is the dedicated commuter carrier, Simmons. Their fleet can be seen sharing American Eagle commuter work with the Delta Connection, mostly ASA Brasilias and Bandeirantes, which are also conspicuous. DFW is, to put it simply, the second busiest commercial airport in the world.

American occupy two entire terminals: 2E and 3E. Delta and ASA use 4E, and everyone else use 2W, originally Braniff's facility.

The facilities don't cater for the needs of the aviation enthusiast but anyone in need of sample photographs should try Delta's new satellite off Terminal 4E. Regardless of which runway is being used, almost all the Delta and American movements pass within reach of even a standard lens. The tinted glass is, in east and west facing areas, wired to reduce sunlight penetration. The effect on photography becomes very subjective. At one extreme are the people who can live with it and, at the other, protests are loud. Windows facing north and south have no wiring,

Indoor vantage points can be desirable when the Texas sun makes the temperature soar. Those which could be checked include American Terminal 3E, where logging Delta and Delta Connection is good at Gate 38 . . . and Gate 35 for American. Gate 6 in Terminal 2E overlooks American Eagle arrivals and one of the holding points. Terminal 2W overlooks the general aviation terminal. For a closer inspection, leave the terminal at the southern end and follow the service road along the ramp perimeter. Traffic is brisk and most of it can be seen from the fence.

Nearby are long-stay airlines, mostly the locally based Express One. Charter action here includes Sun Country DC-10s and 727s plus American TransAir and Carnival arrivals. This is a good area for spotting in the mornings, particluarly as there is more to see than just AA and DL.

To reach the general aviation area by car, take one of the air cargo exits, before reaching the parking ticket booths. Continue north or south (depending on where you entered) and head towards 2W. Exploration of the rest of the field requires navigational skills of the highest order. West Cargo, out near American's huge maintenance base, has two small hangars used by Kitty Hawk Air Cargo and GTE's corporate fleet. Just beyond this is the UPS cargo area where 7 or 8 of their aircraft cann usually be found. At 6 am there can be as many as 20 aircraft present including Metros and Cessna's of Martinair and Merlin Express. Whatever is present can be photographed from the fence, by taking W. 18th St.

South of the AA maintenance base the fence (but not the road) is close to Runway 18R/36L. To reach it, park in the gravel lot next to the road and hike. On the southwest side of the field a viewing park, Founder's Plaza, has been constructed. Telescopes and seating are provided, toilets are not. A loudspeaker transmits what happens on the tower frequency and, when traffic is using 35L and R, it's good for landing shots.

The two employee parking lots off the north service road are great for spotting but not really for photography. WARNING: spending considerable periods of time out in the Texas sun is extremely hazardous. The heat can be extreme and large quantities of liquid, preferably non-alcoholic, are recommended. Beer is NOT a good idea as it actually helps cause dehydration.

American Airlines has opened the superb C E Smith Museum at their Learning Center, just south of the airport. Outside it is a beautifully restored DC-3 and, inside, the airline's history is presented as only the Americans know how (can afford). The movie theatre is equipped with first class airline seats, and shows "Dream of Flight" on a screen 25 metres high. Not 25 feet - 25 metres! To reach the museum, take the south exit from DFW and head west on Highway 360 southbound, in the direction of Arlington. The FAA Road exit leads to the Learning Center, open between 11:00am and 6:00pm Wednesday thru Sunday (as they say). Admission is free.

EL PASO TX

| ELP | KELP | International | 7m/11km NE |

Approaching this airport from town, the street names have a slight accent on aviation. From Airways Boulevard, a turn onto Convair Drive passes the freight terminal (used by FedEx), the passenger terminal and three hangars. Northrop Drive leads around the southern perimeter, where the general aviation hangars and terminal are found. The road continues past a biz-jet ramp of some size, and with plenty of occupants during the week. A UPS 757 awaits its evening work, and a NASA Guppy normally stands on the tarmac.

A request at the GA terminal for ramp access can result in the ability to photograph one or two visiting Mexican corporate aircraft, plus several older types, which have been known to include such diverse craft as YS-11s, an assortment of DC-3s and even an Il-18.

The Continental pier in the passenger terminal is also worthy of inspection, as it is close to the taxiways and most movements have to pass on their way in or out. Anyone visiting El Paso after lunchtime will find the sun is always in the right place, an unusual phenomenon!

FORT WORTH TX

| FTW | KFTW | Meacham Field | 6m/9km N |

With so many airfields around Dallas, plus DFW for quantities of airliners, it's easy to overlook Fort Worth itself. Meacham is a lively general aviation field and it has a few biz-jets and possibly still one or two other surprises in store. Literally in store were some old DC-8s and Convairs. Page Avjet had a repair facility at the north end of the field, where interesting aircraft were regularly seen. It was closed late in 1994. Some of the Page inmates were stored in front of the passenger terminal, in the company of several flight schools. If anything of interest remains, permission for ramp access should be sought at one of the schools, where someone may be able to assist.

CARSWELL was once famous as the home of B-52s and KC-135s. It was due to be realigned as a reserve centre for the air force, marines and navy in 1994. The access road to General Dynamics, on the west side of the field, has always been a fine spot to view the action and take photos with the help of a 200mm zoom lens. Afternoons are best.

GALVESTON TX
GLS   KGLS   Scholes Field

Galveston is so close to Houston, its own airport generates no scheduled traffic. But oil and gas rigs in the Gulf of Mexico mean some helicopter traffic. This is not Aberdeen, and expectations should not be too high. Possibly eight or nine Evergreen and Petroleum helicopters can be seen.

HARLINGEN TX
HRL   KHRL   Rio Grande Valley International   3m/5km NE

As an airport, there are Southwest and American Airlines scheduled services, both these airlines being seen readily in many other places, but Harlingen's reputation was founded on the Confederate Air Force collection. That was then; this is now. Most of the aircraft to be seen on the flying days were privately owned, and flown in for the occasion. For someone who is happy to stand by the fence and take a souvenir photo of one of the airliners visiting, Harlingen is pleasant enough, but the only warbirds to be seen are a Catalina, a Skyraider and the fuselage of a B-23.

HOUSTON TX
EFD   KEFD   Ellington Field   15m/24km SE

By taking Highway 13 south east from Hobby, Ellington offers variety to a Houston log. UPS and Continental Express offer airline interest but there are other delights, such an active Air Force Base bound to feature large numbers: mostly F-15s and F-16s, but there are a few T-43s. The proximity of the Space Center means that some NASA aircraft are always present.

HOUSTON TX
IAH   KIAH   Intercontinental   16m/25km N

The airport has all the features, including traffic, to justify the impressive name. The double bank of terminals are spread out and linked by an automatic People Mover, complete with recorded messages to tell travellers which terminal they are arriving at. They are now becoming accepted as the best means of ground transportation at many large airports.

   Each of the three terminals has island departure lounges attached and these are occupied by one or two airlines, though Terminal C is used by Continental, with the new Mickey LeLand Terminal reserved for international flights. Terminal B, now used by Delta, TWA and American, has seen its international arrivals area closed, when the new terminal was opened. The terminal at the north end, A, is shared by United, USAir and Northwest, plus a selection of less regular operators. At its centre is a multi-storey car park, the top level of which is the only place to get an impression of what is going on. Refurbishment work, involvng demoloition of two piers, has not seriously interfered with the view during 1997.

   The view from the car park is of the thresholds of Runways 8 and 14L/R and, in this respect, it is well placed. Sadly, wind directions can mean that aircraft land on Runway 26, which is long enough for the many Continental movements to stop and taxi to their stands, without having come into view. Assuming favourable winds/runways, a spell on the car park will result in a good quantity of interesting movements being logged and the quiet spells can be used to squint through binoculars at the more remote parts of the field. The terminal area, aligned east/west, has Runway 8/26 to the north and many of the more interesting stands are also on this side, making good photographs possible through the glass. The southern side has virtually no airlines of real interest to a seasoned traveller in the USA, but it does overlook the cargo ramp where a Burlington Express DC-8 is often parked.

Leaving the car park, with a collection of reasonable quality photos, a trip round the terminals can result in close-up views of some of the airlines and the only real opportunity to get shots of commuter carriers. Because the airport approach road, John Kennedy Boulevard, is more or less parallel to Runways 14/32, and because the majority of the executive terminals and hangars are lined up between the road and runway, these facilities are all but invisible from the car park. Only a small collection of hangars on the far side of 14L/32R are within sight and these are so far away that the LearJets parked outside Garrett's re-engine facility may be difficult to identify.

To appreciate the rest of the field, transport is really essential as the facilities are spread out. John Kennedy Boulevard leads to the terminals and turns east, as Will Clayton Boulevard, with a loop, Wright Road, allowing a view of The Delta hangar and the UPS freight apron. Major road works have been taking place on Will Clayton, meaning all sorts of diversions during 1997. Highway 145 might be the better access road if work continues to disrupt proceedings.

To the south of the terminal, leaving on Kennedy, two right turns lead to the various executive terminals, all of which can be seen at close quarters, and the FedEx terminal at the southern end, close to the threshold of 32R. Following the perimeter road, with its right angle turns, one corner reveals the Garrett apron and the threshold of 32L, both reasonably close but the latter unlikely to result in photographs. Another right turn leads to more executive hangars and the tour is complete. If the number of biz-jets logged is impressive, it should be borne in mind that there is another airport in the area where greater numbers are seen . . .

HOUSTON TX
HOU   KHOU   William P Hobby   12m/19km SE

The terminal area offers access to all security gates after the usual security check, and views of the field are reasonable with the added bonus of air-conditioning. The ability to drive around the perimeter and get very close to almost every aircraft is a feature at Hobby which few other airports in the world can match. A car is, however, absolutely essential. Air-conditioning is rarely an optional extra and it is needed. The range of airlines is limited but, for all that, Southwest and Delta 737s can be seen easier here than at most American airports. It's quite reasonable to expect at least fifty different Southwest 737s on an average weekday. Mesa's RJs, operating between here and Dallas (Ft Worth?), are also regular movements.

A tour of the perimeter is interspersed with stops to photograph passing airliners at ridiculously close quarters, and telephoto lenses are unnecessary. Parking remains a problem and stopping for any length of time on the perimeter is difficult. To the right of A.F.Fletcher Aviation there's a good vantage point, allowing all runways to be monitored. Biz-jets and props are numerous on the ramps in this area although tight security means that permission should be sought before approaching ramps or hangars. Don't take it personally if someone comes out of a building (not neceesarily Raytheon) and throws eggs at your car that's one of the ways they deter spotters in these parts!

Hobby may not handle TACA 737s or Aeromexico DC-9s, like its big brother, but it has many, many other delights for compensation, incuding fresh eggs. For those without a car, but determined to log some Southwest Airline(r)s, there is a bus service from Intercontinental. It costs $11.50 each way, and tickets are purchased in the terminals.

LAREDO TX
LRD   KLRD   International   8m/13km NE

Though there appears not to be much airline activity, the building of a new terminal signals expansion. TAESA's daily 737 spends most of the afternoon on the apron. Other operators include Conquest, Continental Express and American Eagle. Two Laredo Air Convairs were still present in May 1994, their colours fading, but propliner enthusiasts will keep to to date with the changing situation. The staff at American Air Cargo are friendly, and usually allow access to the ramp.

LUBBOCK TX
LBB   KLBB   Regional   6m/9km N

The terminal, now believed to be called Lubbock International, is on the east side of the field. It resembles a slice of DFW, being semi-circular with close kerbside access to the gates. Apart from the ASA ATR-72s, there isn't much of any interest to be seen here. The west side of the airport, the old Lubbock Regional, can play host to something worthy of inspection, one or two of Martinaire's air courier aircraft being the most likely.

McALLEN TX
MFE   KMFE   Miller International   2m/3km SW

The terminal is a splendid modern building that harkens back to the golden age of air transport. It faces south towards the runway but windows in the concourse allow reasonably good photos in the mornings. Metros, operated by Conquest and AeroLitoral, are part of the fare but DC-3s also fly cargo to/from Mexico. For an alternative perspective, the parking lot south of the tower, offers an excellent view of the runways, the general aviation hangars and the main terminal. Photographers will note that the morning sun favours the runway and terminal, while afternoons are best for the general aviation. A car is essential to reach the DC-3 apron. From the terminal, turn right onto Wichita Street, and right again on 10th Street South. You can't miss it.

PARIS TX
PRX   Cox Field   8m/13km W

Apart from three or four Lone Star Metro movements a day, there is just the general aviation, none of which is out of the ordinary. However, nearby Toco offers a sight to justify the journey, especially when travelling from the west. Rounding a bend, a Proair Martin 404 comes into sight, parked alongside the road. It's in full colours and in good condition, and shares a converted truck stop with a few warbirds, as Junior Burchenall's Flying Tiger air museum. The other aircraft include T-33s from Italy and Canada plus an A-26 and an F-86D.

SAN ANTONIO TX
SAT   KSAT   International   7m/11km N

The proximity of the Mexican border gives San Antonio its international status and two Mexicana Fokker 100s visit daily. Few aircraft exceed this size, and all movements can be enjoyed from the edge of the apron or from the glazed viewing deck. Other Mexican airlines include four or five AeroLitoral Metros, an occasional Aeromar ATR-42 and TAESA LearJets on package express services. There are few other American airports where these movements can be seen.

The perimeter road leads to West Cargo, where the TAESA LearJets can be seen early in the morning and it is also a fine vantage point for action shots on Runway 3/21, for anyone with a 300mm lens. This offers also the closest view of Fairchild's factory ramp, without official access. Merlins and Metros are assembled.

The far side really needs a car. Taking the road marked 'Car Rental Return' the Dee Howard hangars can be seen on both sides. The Sunjet terminal is sure to be of interest. Aircraft undergoing, and awaiting, conversion are numerous. Some of Dee Howard's cast-offs reach 707 size. They are found, in a compound, on Jones Maltsburger. To get there, turn left at the general aviation and then watch for a right turn.

The area around San Antonio has other attractions: Stinson Field has mostly light aircraft. The Marriott Riverside Hotel has a heliport on top of its car park, and Lackland Air Force Base has a museum. Many of the exhibits are out in the open but a large number of them are not. Official permission is possible for anyone who wants to see the lot.

182

About forty miles west is HONDO, Texas. The Municipal Airport is three miles west of town. It's here that some of the ex-Florida Express BAC 1-11s are stored. The airport's main user is the USAF's Officer Training School (OTS). Their T-41A Mescaleros, wearing civil registrations, are very much in evidence. An aircraft painting facility has been known to handle aircraft up to 747 size but what is to be seen is obviously a matter of luck.

SHERMAN-DENISON TX
F39   Grayson County   10m/16km NW of Sherman

Forty miles or so north of Dallas, this airfield might be of interest to enthusiasts staying in the area, even though it has no scheduled operations. Previously a military base, the terminal side was occupied by M & M Aircraft Services, whose Convairs and DC-4s/6s brought cheer to propliner enthusiasts' hearts. The other side of the field is, however, is another story . . .
    Express One operates the salvage centre on the west side of the field. Forests of tails can be seen from a distance, enough to quicken the heart of anyone, although most flyable aircraft have left, including the propliners formerly stored here. The facility is accessible from public roads. From Highway 82, take the Grayson County Airport exit (FM1417) and drive north for about a mile and a half. After the veterinary clinic, hang a left to go west on Plainview Road, (even the name sounds tempting!) as far as the first marked street, Hardenburg. A right here leads to the tails! Prior notice for a visit isn't necessary but the phone number, for those who need it, is (903) 786 9538.

WACO TX
CNW   KCNW   TSTI Airport

This used to be known as James Connally Airport and it is well-known to aviation specialists for a variety of reasons: Chrysler Technologies took over the former Elsinore Aircraft Support hangar, where a number of aircraft were stored. The Novair DC-10s, and almost everything else, have gone. What remains is the ex-Northwest CV-580 fleet. The airport manager should be contacted if access is required. Pointing a camera in the direction of Chrysler is not a good idea! The many security notices are necessitated by the work Chrysler does on EC-135s and NKC-135s.

WACO TX
ACT   KACT   Regional/Madison Cooper   8m/13km NW

This is Waco's main link with the rest of Texas, but its services are strictly limited to a few ASA Brasilias and American Eagle Jetstreams each day. There is little to keep someone on the move from heading for the other field, which has more on offer.

PRICE UT
PUC   Carbon Emery   3m/5km

The only scheduled passenger link with the outside world is by Alpine Air, whose fleet is best seen early in the morning at Provo. Apart from the chance of finding yet another FedEx Caravas sitting in a corner, there is little reason to call in. A short detour in Utah can mean a hundred miles or more!

PROVO UT
PVU   Municipal   3m/5km SW

Alpine Air's base of operations is the biggest thing on the airfield, and it's small. Arrival during the middle of the day can reveal nothing more than a handful of light aircraft, possibly including one or two Alpine Navajo Chieftains.

SAINT GEORGE UT
SGU   Municipal   1m/1.5km N

A tour of the West often includes the scenic splendours of Bryce Canyon, Zion National Park and Lake Powell. Travelling from Las Vegas, St George is a staging post on the road east. Interstate 5 runs north to Salt Lake City. The city nestles in the lee of the red bluffs, on the edge of a flat plain, its Mormon temple shining white and visible from miles away. With so much flat land around, it is strange that the airport wasn't built on some of it. It will be a long time before St George can boast a sophisticated, modern passenger terminal. What is there serves a number of Skywest movements.

SALT LAKE CITY UT
SLC   KSLC   International   5m/8km NW

The city straddles the north-south I-15, where it joins with I-80. This Interstate heads west to Reno and passes the airport, as do almost all roads west of town. 75% of all movements are Delta, so anyone in search of variety could be excused for disregarding Salt Lake City.

The terminal facilities may pass unrecorded, because there is an excellent observation facility at what is probably the best location, most of the time. In the southwest corner of the field, close by the approach road, is a reservation designed with the needs of enthusiasts in mind. By taking the road to the cargo terminals, and turning right at the two T-junctions, the car park is reached. Next to it is a grassy bank rising clear above the perimeter fence, with views of much of the airfield.

Directly in front are the runway thresholds with the general aviation on the far side, and the ANG base with its KC-135s at the far end. To the left is the holding point used by the majority of scheduled traffic and, further round to the left is the cargo apron with the main terminal area beyond. Use of the 34L/R runways is normal but not necessarily the rule, so there are days (or part thereof) when trying to make the most of Salt Lake City airport can be a waste of time. Sightseeing at Saltaire (flies permitting) or the excellent museum at Hill Air Force Base in Ogden are alternatives.

The constant stream of Delta movements through the day does comprise the complete range of types operated, and in good numbers. Skywest, the Delta Connection, offers the only variety apart from a handful of other flights. Photography is best after lunch, when the sun has passed the centreline of the runways, and anything of 737 size or larger makes portraits easy as it taxis to the hold. The evenings offer operators as varied as the aircraft: Ameriflight with Navajos and Beech 99s, half a dozen FedEx, UPS with DC-8s and 757s and, star attraction, a Union Flights Caribou.

The east side has its own runway, which sees much use during the average day and evening. There are several access roads to the individual fixed base operators, with Majestic Air occupying space close to I-80. Parked here are mostly Beech 18s and DC-3s, and the red T-33 in one of the hangars looks familiar to most British eyes. Views of the various ramps need patience but few of the executive aircraft go unrecorded. Parked on its own, next to waste ground, is a rather derelict Viscount, possibly N7411, ex-United. The road passes the Utah ANG base entrance, with an F-105 on display outside, and continues north where close views of the field are impossible. The rest of the g.a. is a few miles to the south at SALT LAKE CITY II.

By making left turns, Delta's maintenance base is reached, north of the passenger terminal. The road offers an unobstructed view of the ramp, though the quality of photos taken from here is moderate due to the busy background. Another left turn leads to the central terminal area.

HARRISONBURG/SHENANDOAH VA
          Regional   13m/21km S

For those travelling by car on Highway I81 this quaint airport may serve as a comfortable rest point. By the nearby Shenandoah mountains, as the name suggests, the small terminal has large windows overlooking the ramp. Movements are few with the occasional USAirways Express flight to Pittsburgh and a FedEx Caravan in the evening. Half a dozen ex-US Army and Navy C-12s sit idle, awaiting refurbishment. A polite request to the airport manager will almost certainly lead to ramp access.

LYNCHBURG VA
Preston Glen Regional   4m/6km SE

A new modern terminal offers good views of the ramp area. Commercial movements are few, averaging two per hour by USAirways, United Express, Continental Express and ASA with a variety of commuter aircraft. On the opposite side of the field is the old terminal and general aviation ramps where a few biz-jets may be parked.

MANASSAS VA
MNZ   Regional   4m/6km SW

The growth of commerical traffic at National and Dulles has meant that Manassas, located in the Washington DC suburban area, serves as one of the area's largest general aviation fields. Over 100 single-engined light aircraft and small twins are parked here with the occasional biz-jet visitor. Ramp access should not be difficult if one of the many FBOs is approached. The Colgan Air hangar serves as a maintenance base for the airline's Beech 1900s and SF340s, and a polite request usually results in some excellent ramp photographs. To the east of the main field a new general aviation terminal has been completed. Observation Road runs perpendicular to the two parallel runways, giving excellent views of all arriving and departing aircraft.

NEWPORT NEWS VA
PHF   KPHF   Patrick Henry   16m/25km NW

Virginia is a state quite remote from most itineraries but it receives a lot of aviation enthusiasts for the Oceana Open Day in autumn. The Chesapeake Bay metropolitan area is known as Tidewater, comprising Virginia Beach, Newport News, Norfolk, Portsmouth and Hampton.

Features in this part of the world are the F-15s at Langley and a small museum nearby, the guided tours of Norfolk Naval Base, to see which carriers are in port (their aircraft being at Oceana) and, not too far up Interstate 64, RICHMOND (q.v.) with a chance to see the Air National Guard A-7s.

Between Langley and Richmond, east of I-64, is Patrick Henry, almost on the edge of Williamsburg - hence the alternative name. Not quite in the same league as Norfolk, this is mostly a commuter airport, offering feeder links to most regional cities. Patrick Henry is a spoke in many systems. Occasional USAirways DC-9s visit but generally the largest aircraft are Henson Dash 8s. Photos around the terminal area present no problems and access to the airport is best from Morris Boulevard, intersection 9 on I-64. From here, the large amount of general aviation is apparent.

NORFOLK VA
ORF   KORF   International   9m/15km NE

The civil enthusiast is well catered for at Norfolk, though not in the passenger terminal which has no worthwhile views. The 'old' side of the field has some interesting aircraft with an occasional commuter airliner on extended stay. To keep a close watch on a varied selection of eastern seaboard airlines, a visit to the Norfolk Botanical Gardens is highly recommended. This quiet backwater has been separated from the noise of the airport, immediately adjacent, by a high grass bank or berm, from which the viewing and photography are very good.

Regardless of the runway direction, a 200mm lens will yield results which justify the small entrance fee into the gardens. The sun is at its best late in the afternoon. Anyone who intends to spend time here can find snacks and drinks at the cafeteria/shop, next to the parking lot, at the foot of the berm.

Photography in the morning requires a trip to the water's edge, at the other end of the field. Close to the naval base, north of the airfield, is a small parking lot favoured by anglers, with jetties to get them to deeper water. With a 200mm lens, good landing photos (of aircraft, not fish) are possible. If standing on dry land gets boring, you can always rent a canoe and row to a place which suits best.

RICHMOND VA
RIC   KRIC   Byrd International   8m/13km

Whilst not particularly busy, Richmond always seems to boast something of interest. The passenger terminal has been modernised and good close-ups of visiting airline traffic should be possible through the large windows overlooking the ramp. Most of the common American airlines serve the airport in reasonable quantities, along with an occasional Eastwind 737. Richmond is also well served by the overnight express companies, which means that the usual array of UPS, DHL and FedEx 727s etc can always be found in the sprawling cargo area.

There are surprisingly large quantities of executive aircraft and the spread-out nature of the field makes a car essential if they are to be seen. Just north of the main terminal, both the Virginia Department of Transportation and the food and tobacco giant R.J.Reynolds have hangars, but movements are slow and security fences make photography impossible. The most active general aviation ramp is that of Million Air which usually has several biz-jets or King Airs parked. The Virginia Museum of Aviaition is located just inside the main entrance to the airport, and boasts the only surviving Vultee V-1A (NC 16099), one of two known Standard E-1s and several other interesting vintage aircraft. The Virginia ANG is on the far side.

ROANOKE VA
ROA   Regional   6m/9km NE

Whilst this regional airport is unlikely to be on most itineraries, its growth in traffic volume is largely due to USAirway's activities, which in turn leads to competition from other carriers. The terminal has open car park areas next to the taxiway, from which movements can be witnessed. There is a reasonable amount of general aviation, though nothing exceptional has been reported.

BURLINGTON VT
BTV   KBTV   International   3m/5km

This small, but very attractive, airport has many points in its favour. The view from the terminal isn't one of them, however, as it is restricted to the darkened glass next to the gate onto the small apron. Jet airline traffic is minimal but there is compensation in the variety of commuters. Local airlines are Commutair, with Beech 1900s, and Metro Air Northeast, better known as Trans World Express, as their Metros and SF340s are seen widely throughout New England. Their maintenance base has a good sized hangar, and part of its apron is seen from the fence. When times are quiet (which is usual) it's worth asking for a look around.

The runway normally in use is served by a taxiway which passes very close to a chainlink fence, and open ground next to this allows a perfectly acceptable view of passing aircraft. The road which leads to the airport continues past the terminal, and a turning in the housing estate leads to this much-used observation point. Anything which passes is photogenic, especially in the mornings, when the sunlight is good. Even a King Air makes an excellent portrait without recourse to a long lens.

Not only is the taxiway close but the runway is near enough for reading off the serials of the active Vermont ANG aircraft, based on the other side of the field. Known as the Green Mountain Boys, they are friendly, and written permission for a visit may be worthwhile. It is quite a long drive round past the end of the runway to get to the base and there is no gate to define the entrance. Spontaneous visitors may find themselves in a car park right next to the apron, by mistake, if they aren't careful!

Another military operator to use the field, though not particularly actively, is the Army National Guard unit whose hangar is at the intersection of Highway 2 and the airport approach road. Some difficulty may be experienced in finding someone to give permission for a look around. This may involve entry into the hangar and walking through it, past the UH-1s and OH-6s, to find someone in authority. In the unlikely event that permission is not granted, it's then necessary to walk through the hangar again, on the way out.

BELLINGHAM WA
BLI   KBLI   1m/1.5km NW

The largest scheduled airliner to be seen here will probably be a Dash 8, in Horizon's colours. Apart from the occasional Air Pac Navajo, there isn't much else to make the detour worthwhile. The residents will only be of interest to number crunchers, and they won't crunch many.

EVERETT WA
PAE   KPAE   Paine Field   4m/6km SW

Also called Snohomish County, but not by the local population, a left turn off Interstate 5 leads there but, from Renton, it is easier to take I-405 and then Highway 525. The Boeing 747, 767 and now the 777 production facilities have very little to do with the rest of the airport, and the only problem about getting a free tour of the plant is the amount of time it will be necessary to wait. The two mid-morning tours are usually heavily over-subscribed but they do include a look into the assembly plant, normally the 747 side, and the ramp, passing aircraft on the flight line. Note that the bus doesn't stop on the ramp and that its windows are likely to be very dark. A feature of this part of the world is that the sky is either grey . . . or dark grey, so Kodak ASA25 will not be the best choice of film!

Tours are only offered during the week. That much is for sure and the fact that, officially, cameras are not allowed on Boeing proptery. Either there are two tours a day, at 10:00 and 14:00, or they leave on the hour every hour between 09:00 and 16:00 (with a break at lunchtime). Tours can only be arranged inadvance for parties of ten or more, and they include about half an hour of watching a promo video presentation. This is interactive and designed to assess how Boeing rates with the consumer against Airbus. A visit to the 747 production hall, which is very impressive, follows, after which there is a tour alog the flightline. To find out more (or the latest situation), contact The Boeing Aircraft Company at PO Box 3707 (OA-65), Seattle Washington 98124, or phone (206) 342 4801.

The rest of the airport is quite separate and the only aircraft guaranteed to be of interest is the BOAC Comet (4C!), though TRAMCO may be fitting hush kits to an interesting 707. Due west of the general aviation terminal, across the main runway, is an air tanker base. The only other feature of the field is an Army Reserve base with some helicopters.

FRIDAY HARBOR WA
FRD   0.5m/1km

Friday Harbor is on the south side of San Juan Island, between Victoria and Bellingham, and is part of the Natural History Park. Kenmore Air operate mostly Beavers but there are other aircraft to see. A remote spot to choose for a photo but there are few others to compare with it. Anyone flying from here into Seattle's Lake Union will remember the trip, and descent into the city, for a long time. Take lots of film but don't expect too much sunshine.

MOSES LAKE WA
MWH   Grant County   4m/6km NW

This is prairie land; open, dry and very hot in summer. The airport is north of I-90, on State Highway 282. The few commuter flights make little impression on what is clearly a rather major airfield. A distant hangar, bearing a Japan Air Lines logo offers one clue. Inside the fire station, numerous photographs of JAL 747s also suggest something. Clearly, most of the commuter aircraft have little need of a 13,500 feet long runway, one of the longest in Washington State.

Unless information is gleaned from Boeing, it would be unwise to travel such a long way in the hope of seeing half a dozen 747-400s doing circuits and bumps. Testing might take two or three days at the most, and nothing happens for another six months. Settle instead for the sight of SLAFCO's Catalinas, which are based here. There is also a B-23 Dragon and a stored C-97.

OLYMPIA WA
OLM   Municipal   3m/5km S

Lovers of Washington State scenery and its national park may find their way to Olympia, in the vain hope that a state capital may generate a reasonable amount of traffic. Disappointment awaits, with only a few aged UH-1s, operated (rarely) by the Fire Department.

OMAK WA
OMK   Municipal

A visit here at the wrong time of the year can give a completely wrong impression. The field is on a plateau between the mountains and the Okanogan River (not the Okanagan), and difficult to find. Persevere! Leave town on Highway 97 and look for Old Riverside Highway. For most of the year a dozen or so light aircraft await their owners flying around at weekends. In summer it becomes an operational, and often very busy, water bomber base. Wenatchee occasionally suffers from being smoked in when the fires are at their worst, and Omak is used instead.

A visit in August 1994 gives some idea of what can be seen: a couple of Skycranes, several C-130s, Neptunes, a C-54 and a DC-7. Activity can be intense, so a request for a look round might not be a good idea. Settle instead for watching the action from the terminal. Fully laden, these aircraft have a job getting airborne and make superb subjects for a camera.

Enthusiasts who pursue water bombers, smoke jumpers, air tankers and propliners in general, tend to know a thing or two which might not be common knowledge to the rest of us. The first rule is: Stick to the highway or dirt roads. Don't drive on grassland and NEVER park on it. Hot exhausts and dry grass don't mix. Well, they do, but it often ends in flames, one of the most common causes of fires.

PASCO WA
PSC   Tri-Cities Municipal 2m/3km NW

Together with Pasco, Richland and Kennewick make up the tri-cities, many miles inland on the Columbia River. Horizon Air provides the staple diet, including several F.28 movements during the day, though two or three Delta jets call. Photography, over the low fence next to the terminal, of taxiing aircraft is about as easy as it gets, especially on sunny afternoons. With an 80-200mm zoom lens, almost anything makes a good subject. General aviation activity is slow.

PORT ANGELES WA
CLM   William R Fairchild International   3m/5km W

The Strait of Juan de Fuca separates the relative sophistication of Victoria in Canada with the forests of the Olympic National Park. Port Angeles is on the American side. The sight of a 'Fairchild' sign can lead the unwary to the belief that bombers are close at hand, but this isn't the Air Force base.

SEATTLE/TACOMA WA
SEA   KSEA   International   14m/22km S (bus 50 minutes)

The busiest airport in a relatively small area reaching north to Vancouver, Sea/Tac has piers which are accessible with only a security check. Of the two piers which project out into the apron, the left hand offers extremely good views, especially from gates B5, B7 and B14 or the area around C10/C12. Assuming the movements land from the north, these two lounges are very well placed for the photographer, especially in the mornings. What can be seen from here are the two parallel runways and the taxiway, with all Alaska and United traffic doing a U-turn commendably close before heading back to the northern half of the terminal.

Until lunchtime, the sun is behind the viewer, so photography is at its best, and only the occasional Cessna Twin or Navajo pass outside the range of most lenses. Much of the glass through which everything is seen is tinted but some areas of glass are clear. Walking around the pleasant, modern terminal, there are chances to get close to some of the smaller types, Horizon's Dash 8s, Metros and F.28s for example. One of these is found by walking north to the end of the terminal buildings and then down a bank onto one of the approach roads. Being at the same height as the apron, with only an underpass between the viewer and the aircraft, some very close encounters can be had with the many United aircraft, and one or two of the Alaska fleet as they taxi, or park, very close.

The busy Pacific Highway (99) offers a good selection of moderately priced hotels and eating establishments. Old hands will not need an introduction to Denny's, one of which is just across the road here. Since it is just a short walk up South 160th Street to the perimeter road and the cargo area, it becomes apparent that a car is not essential to enjoy Sea/Tac.

Traffic is not at its peak in mid afternoon so it's a good time, if in possession of a car, to leave the terminal and seek an alternative vantage point. Having discovered that the very top level of the multi-storey car park only offers a limited view of proceedings, the car can be driven north along Perimeter Road, where some of the activity on the cargo ramps can be seen, though views are very restricted. Viewpoint Park still exists, having survived threats of redevelopment: to get there, take a left turn onto South 156th Way. After passing under the rather elevated thresholds of 16L/16R, the first permissible left turn is 12th Avenue South. The area is exceptionally hilly and climbing back to the top of a severe dip, a gated road on the left leads to Viewpoint Park. It is open between 08:00 and 20:00. Staying too late in the evening invites the interest of the police, who know it is used by local youngsters for purposes of which their parents would not approve and the law doesn't permit.

Vantage points south of the field are irrelevant if 16L/16R are in use but South 188th Street passes under the end of 34R and close to the threshold of 34L. Certainly a busy airport for scheduled passenger movements, Sea/Tac is not really noted for surprises but some traffic to watch out for includes Hawaiian Air DC-10s, departing quite early in the morning, and the rather elusive Weyerhaeuser Lumber Co Citations which live in the hangar on the west side of the field.

SEATTLE WA

BFI   KBFI   King County/Boeing Field   4m/6km S

Not too far south of downtown Seattle, King County (or Boeing Field) is under the flightpath to Sea/Tac's 16L/R runways, and much traffic flies overhead, most of which bears no registrations under the wings. There are two distinct sides to this long, narrow field: to the west, by Interstate 5, is a perimeter road with innumerable hangars and, between them, views across to Boeing's ramps. The terminal is of no use at all to the enthusiast but, just to the north of it is the Aviator's Store, an excellent bookshop with a vast selection of books, postcards and souvenirs. What will be seen *on* the east side is a fine assortment of aircraft but most visitors here will be more concerned with what can be seen *from* the east side. There is usually a selection of 737s and 757s in their full colours, and ready to go. All are seen from the tail end and many registrations are hidden by blast screens.

To get round to the west side, leave the perimeter road (which comes to a dead end in the southeastern corner) and head south on Airport Way to the aptly named Boeing Access Road. Another right onto East Marginal Way leads back up to Boeing. At the south end, the new museum has been opened around the Red Barn, where it all started. The Museum of Flight has a Great Gallery, from the roof of which is suspended a formation of interesting aircraft, led by DC-3 N138D. The large expanses of glass make photography easy, and the $4 admission is extremely good value. Opening hours are 10am to 5pm, and further details are available from the museum, 9404 E Marginal Way South, Seattle, Wa 98102, or telephone (206) 764 5720.

At weekends particularly, the vast car parks are empty and unattended. It is possible to get reasonably close to some of the aircraft but photographers will be extremely frustrated, especially if something really special is to be seen. There is absolutely no reason why all registrations can't be obtained by the patient, as there are a good few nooks and crannies. With luck, one of the aircraft will be airtested and it is only then that photos of any quality are likely . . . but probably taken from the eastern side of the field. For anyone without transport, but wishing to visit Boeing Field, there is a regular bus service which cost between 85 cents and $1.10, depending on the time of day.

SEATTLE WA
LKE   Lake Union Seaplane Base   3m/5km N

Just north of the city centre is Lake Union, with the seaplane base in the southwest corner. Access is by way of West Lake Avenue North, where Lake Union Air Service operate several Beavers and a Twin Otter, all on floats of course.

SEATTLE WA
RNT   Renton   10m/16km SSE

From Boeing Field/King County, Sunset Hiway (900) leads to Rainier Avenue North and a left turn here heads for Renton. At an intersection, the airport is suddenly visible on the right, with tantalising views of Boeings on the ramp. Behind the trees and a bank/berm is a very small airport with one or two Boeings nearing completion and, with luck, something exotic ready to go. Opposite the south-west corner of the field is a restaurant with a good-sized car park; a walk across Airport Way and up to the top of the bank, and one or two photographs should be possible.

Rainier Avenue (167) passes the west side of the field and offers good views of assorted general aviation, though there is nothing out of the ordinary. A turn onto the perimeter road leads back around the south side, and past the end of the short runway to the Boeing complex. By progressing up the east side, it is possible to get quite close to the new 737s and 757s but finding any on the apron, without clutter, is difficult. Halfway up the east side is a bridge over the creek and this is the link between Renton Field and the assembly plant.

On the other side of the bridge is an apron which normally contains half a dozen or so aircraft, all more or less complete with only their rudders painted, and all bearing the same registration. N1786B is easy to remember, and it has featured on many a 737. Careful notes of which rudders are seen followed by some research will usually reveal the identities of these aircraft.

SPOKANE WA
GEG KGEG   International   6m/9km SW

This airport handles the scheduled services, and the International tag derives from the services to Calgary and Vancouver. Jet traffic, up to 727 size, is regular and the array of commuter feeders makes Spokane an interesting destination. The views from the passenger terminal are not as good as from the rather neat little mutli-storey car park. Salair's base normally has one or two DC-3s in evidence, though Convairs are more so, and Federal Express colours are a familiar sight here.

WENATCHEE WA
EAT   Pangborn   5m/8km SE

Generally known as East Wenatchee, as it's on the same side of the Columbia River as that town. On the other side of the river is Wenatchee, its big brother. This small airport is only mentioned because it becomes an active fire-fighting base in summer. Those dedicated to the relentless pursuit of DC-7s, P-2Vs and C-130s will consider the journey to be worthwhile.

APPLETON WI
ATW   Outagamie County 3m/5km W

This small airport has a modern passenger terminal but views from it onto the apron are few. This is not a problem because there are plenty of adequate places around the terminal, and good enough for the photographer. The home of Air Wisconsin sees but a small proportion of the airline's movements, as they are concentrated elsewhere to match United Airlines' feeder traffic needs. Other traffic here is minimal, with a handful of competing commuter flights operated by Express/ Northwest Airlink. The FedEx resident is a 727, and at least one hangar-ful of biz-jets can be inspected.

MILWAUKEE WI
MKE   KMKE   General Mitchell International   10m/16km S

Most international visitors to the Oshkosh spectacular will be familiar with Mitchell Field. To be sure that travellers know it's Mitchell Field, there's a B-25 at the main entrance.

The passenger terminal is modern, offering from its windows enough views of aircraft parked on stands to satisfy the casual observer. The serious head north, to the public car park by the executive aircraft hangars. Taxiing aircraft pass close enough for good photos, but they do not include the 126ARS KC-135s which use their own runway, beyond the reach of most cameras. Note the AFRES base is on the opposite side of Runway 1L from the ANG facility.

Opposite the passenger terminal entrance, on South Howell Avenue, is a turning to the cargo area. The usual array of UPS, Emery and FedEx aircraft spend their daytime here, with Federal Express offering a decent selection. At the far end of the cargo area is a small Midwest maintenance base. Beside it is a car park and observation area, overlooking the cargo ramps. A 200mm lens should ensure a reasonable collection of photos. For anyone with a car, a perimeter tour involves taking a series of left turns from the cargo area. The road heads south, past the threshold of Runway 7R, to a T-junction. After a left turn, the AFRES base and the end of Runway 1L are passed, after which the road swings away from the perimeter, before returning to the northeast corner and the car park next to the end of Runway 19R.

Midwest Express and their commuter feeder, Skyway Airlines, offer pretty colour schemes, and there is also the usual assortment of airlines visiting. Commuter traffic is particularly good, with a fine selection of operators and types. Northwest and Northwest Airlink are, as to be expected in this part of the world, strongly represented.

OSHKOSH WI
OSH   Wittman Regional   3m/5km SW

The name is synonymous with one of the most famous events in the aviation calendar but, outside Convention time, the field reverts to its sleepy ways. A few commuter flights are operated by United Express F.27s, TWA Express Saab 340s and Beech 1900s, and Midway Commuter Do228s.

The main terminal is less use for photography than the car parks or the Basler ramp. Their DC-3s, of various types, are very much in evidence. Basler have two aprons, the old one being next to the terminal, and used as the executive ramp. The new hangar complex is on West 35th Avenue, reached via the perimeter road. Up to ten DC-3s can be accommodated inside the hangar (that's one extremely large hangar), where turbo conversions take place. With such customers as the Ecuador Air Force, Basler offer the chance to see something exotic. Whilst at Oshkosh it is worth looking out for the EAA museum, as it holds many interesting, and some unique, aircraft.

GREYBULL WY
GEY   South Big Horn County

The name of Greybull means only one thing to many enthusiasts: Hawkins and Powers. A visit here takes commitment, as it's very remote. Only a small portion of the large fleet can be seen, but it still amounts to a lot of aircraft. Work is carried out on an extremely interesting assortment: older C-118s and P-2Vs share the apron with KC-97s, C-130s and now P-3s. Some of the airframes will take to the skies on their fire-fighting missions, while others are there just to provide the spares.

The cannibalisation of large aircraft provides many interesting photographs, as well as the airworthy machines. Because it is so far off the beaten track, visitors to the field are small in number, and usually very keen. Enthusiasm counts for a lot, and a letter beforehand usually results in reasonable hospitality.

JACKSON WY
JAC   Jackson Hole   8m/13km N

This winter resort has become established as a year-round gateway to Grand Teton and Yellowstone National Parks, just to the north. The valley floor is almost perfectly flat, with spectacular mountains rising at the west. The airport is some way out of town, indicating forethought, and easily seen from a distance. The terminal is delightfully modern, though it offers no views, and handles some commuter traffic. For ramp access at this informal field, a request should be made at Jackson Hole Aviation, to the left. Apart from them being aware that photos showing tail numbers on biz-jets lead to sensitivity from their owners, there are no problems.

AGUADILLA PR
BQN   TJBQ   Rafael Hernandez   65m/104km W of San Juan

At the north west corner of the island is an airfield, generally known as Borinquen, that conjures up rather more nostalgia than can be gleaned at Luis Muñoz Marin. Along the north side of the runway, and facing the Ramey base, is a line of buildings with a distinctly Caribbean feel. The passenger terminal is a modest affair and to its left is a hangar used by Trans-Air-Link DC-6s. Beyond this is the US Coastguard base with a couple of C-130s and a Dauphin. At the right of the terminal are two disused hangars, adding greatly to the flavour, after which are buildings which see regular use.
    First is that used by the Police, where a couple of GAF Nomads might be present. A Blackhawk was also there, according to the last report. An Aerial Transit DC-6, standing outside the next hangar, usually keeps company with Salair Convair 440s. The last hangar in the line is occupied by Fed Ex.
    The road passes round the end of the field and returns to reveal a scrapyard and a general aviation facility. Nearby are parked Tradewinds CL-44 N100BB and L-1049 N1542CT. The airfield is far from inactive, as it is used by a variety of charter traffic. Tradewinds' TriStar is a regular visitor and 727s (anything from Fed Ex and American to Carnival) are not uncommon.
    Since Aguadilla is a holiday resort, hotels are reasonably plentiful and quite affordable. The nearest hotel, La Cima, charges about $60 for a room but others, slightly further away, cost less.

ARECIBO PR
ABO   36m/57m W of San Juan

West of San Juan, just off Route 2, along the north coast, is another airfield which offers a taste of how aviation used to be. It's small time and quiet and, if anything moves, it carries cargo rather than passengers. The action takes place at night, as the field is used mostly for mail and packages.

SAN JUAN PR
SJU   TJSJ   Luis Munoz Marin   9m/15km E

The major US airlines, operating scheduled services, make San Juan seem like an average American airport. American and American Eagle are, with TWA and Delta, now the standard fare. FedEx underline this impression by basing a couple of feeder Caravans. Propliner activity has stabilised at a moderately attractive level: Dodita and Tolair T-29s and a few Four Star DC-3s with the chance of an occasional DC-3, C-46 or Constellation from the Dominican Republic. More exotic traffic is supplied by Copa 737s, ACES and Royal 727s, Air Guadeloupe ATR-42s, Air BVI HS748s and LIAT Dash 8s.
    The terminal's superb terrace stays closed, with little chance of re-opening. There are, however, one or two spots on the approach road between the almost intersecting runways where photos of taxiing and landing aircraft are possible. The bus stop, to the right, outside the terminal is a good place for photography of non-US airlines, though a 300 mm lens is needed. The hire car is useful to get to the spot but disposing of it next to a busy highway then becomes the problem! Good photos can only be

taken clear of the fence on the busier northern, 8/26, runway and taxiway, so unobstructed shots need aid from one of the bunker-like structures, or the car bonnet/roof! For anyone wishing to park the car and walk somewhere for a view, there is a shopping mall and cinema car park on Laguna Avenue, just off the busy Highway 26. It is a short walk from the car to the bridge, from where Runway 10 is seen.

A car park faces the taxiway to, and the threshold of, Runway 10. The improved view is of less movements, and into the sun. Access to the central cargo area (and the ANG base) is via a road parallel to the southern runway. Also to be found here is a general aviation terminal, directly opposite the international pier, where photography is good in the afternoon. What stored aircraft remain are next to the Executive Air/American Eagle facility. Tolair and Dodita Air Cargo have C-47s and CV-240s, normally parked on the ramps next to American Eagle. Driving parallel to Runway 10, take the first slip road which leads down to a roundabout and the access road.

SAN JUAN PR

SIG	TJIG	Isla Grande	5m/8km NW

A real taste of the Caribbean is much easier to experience at Isla Grande, on the way to old San Juan town, by the docks. From Luis Munoz, follow Highway 26 (Baldorioty de Castro Avenue) towards Old San Juan, and the airport is on the left, just before crossing the bridge. It's here that Vieques Air Link and Sunaire Express can be seen. Islanders and Twin Otters evoke much more of the local feel than can be enjoyed at the busier main airport. The pace is more relaxed and casual. Photos present no problems, and ramp access is possible after a little nogotiation at quieter times. A few damaged and derelict aircraft litter the field: a couple of Islanders and a Piaggio won't fly again. Keeping them company is an engineless C-117, still in US military colours.

Flamenco Airways use their C-47s mostly for night-time cargo flights, so they are usually in evidence during the day, in the company of one or two Islanders.

OB = PERU

IQUIQUE

IQQ	Cavancha

There are two fields at Iquique, the other being General Diego Aracena (SCDA), so it's frustrating to receive a report which doesn't actually name the field. Scheduled traffic is mostly a mixture of 737s of Avant, LANChile, Ladeco and National but there are other aircraft to be seen on the field and, surprise, surprise, they tend to be slightly more interesting. Because airline traffic is not brisk, the terminal is not the place to spend any time. Mornings are busiest and the average afternoon is likely to yield not much more than a dozen movement before night falls.

The authorities are reasonably friendly, particularly since they don't see too many enthusiasts from one week to the next. Their attitude is common sense but assumes the guest will match like with like. If you want to take photographs, you can, but you are specifically asked not to take them of the military aircraft. These are a rather tempting collection, it must be said: probably something like a 707, trainers, fighters and an Orion or two. The Halcones Aerobatic Team might be expected here also, doing their training.

LIMA

LIM	SPIM	Jorge Chavez International	10m/16km NW

This is a fascinating airport, with a fine selection of international carriers. It would be a good idea to get as many photographs as possible from the taxiing aircraft. An important military presence here is the reason for the closure of the observation deck, though the smoked glass does allow views from the terminal. Cameras are definitely excess baggage. The report which best summed up Lima was, "stay in the terminal or get ready to answer questions." An honours degree in Spanish will be useful. The perimeter is enclosed by a high screen, and even the semi-derelict aircraft should be avoided. The remains of L-749s OBR-833 and N22CS may no longer be present at the end of the field. The naval and army facilities can be seen through gaps, with Mi-8s and S-2s being strange bedfellows.

By venturing from the terminal to some of the operators' aprons, it may be thought that photos are possible. Both AeroPeru and Aeronaves are known to be friendly enough to interested parties but the authorities are still watchful, and capable of confiscating film at the slightest provocation. The possibility of this trouble means that a trip can only be recorded in the notebook.

Municipal blue buses Nos 35 and 56 serve the airport from Plaza Dos de Mayo, but beware of colectivos buses, which only run once five people have boarded.

OD = LEBANON
BEIRUT
BEY   OLBA   International   10m/16km S

The city is gradually returning to something like normality after many years of strife. American readers can forget about visiting as entry visas are not granted. It is possible this might have something to do with the many pictures of the Syrian President, which are very much in evidence. The airport area goes one step further, being situated in a Hezbollah neighbourhood: pictures of Ayatollah Khomeni decorate most of the street lamps. Normality in Beirut is not like normality in Birmingham, however. Around the perimeter are anti-aircraft gun emplacements which are manned.

It's essential to make hotel reservations by fax or in writing before leaving for Beirut. Failure to pre-book means queueing to use the airport's one telephone! Worse, it could mean paying $130 for a night in the Carlton. The ABC Hotel & Travel Index offers details of other downtown hotels, where a single bed costs about $60. Ask your travel agent for a little assistance.

The passenger terminal is 1950s vintage, from the days when Air Liban Caravelles stood on its apron (pause for older readers to sigh) but there are two new piers. Neither have stood the test of time very well - and the Caravelles have been scrapped! Little by little, some modernisation is taking place. Security is still very tightly controlled. About half a kilometre from the terminal is a roundabout, where heavily armed militia man check points. Straight on, south, is the passenger terminal. To the left is MEA and to the right is TMA. In other words, whichever way you turn, there are going to be Boeing 707s. A thorough search of belongings is required before proceeding to any of the facilities, and it may be necessary to surrender the passport, if visiting either MEA or TMA. Aviation photographers are not discouraged. Within the terminal, there is no observation deck but the coffee shop on the second floor overlooks the main apron, between the two piers.

Outside the perimeter, the afternoon sun favours a walk along the coastal road, parallel to Runway 18/36, the north end of which is surrounded by shops and housing. To the south is the beach, still undeveloped, and at more or less the same level as the airfield.

As Lebanon strives to get back to normal, foreign visitors are made very welcome. Someone with a specialist interest might expect a warm welcome, if making himself known to officialdom. This is a nation famous for its politeness and hospitality. Anyone with an enduring passion for 707s would do well to consider a trip to Beirut before it's too late.

OE = AUSTRIA
GRAZ
GRZ   LOWG   Thalerhof   15m/24km S (bus 30 minutes)

A very small airport in the south of the country. Most of the scheduled movements are local but the occasional Lufthansa or Air Malta makes a change. In the car park is an An-2 and the passenger terminal overlooks the small apron and the main, surfaced, runway 17/35. To the left, seen from landside, is a general aviation apron with a few light aircraft and a glimpse of the military base, tastefully hidden in the trees, on the far side of the runway. There are plenty of locations around the perimeter where the movements can be seen and photographed with a variety of backgrounds. Until it's realized there are also a couple of grass strips, some of the light aircraft movements can cause some concern!

INNSBRUCK

INN   LOWI   Kranebitten   3m/5km W (bus 15 minutes)

Innsbruck is surrounded by the breathtaking scenery of the Tyrolean mountains, and the local operator is named after the region, its Dash Eights being equally photogenic.

The small terminal has a cafeteria but self service is only available on Saturdays in winter and spring, when charter flights are normally operated. Access to both the balcony and the cafe is related to the purchase of a coffee or a snack. Since quantities of each can be expensive in Austria, a prolonged stay here is rare. This is a pity, as the glass front of the cafeteria offers an excellent view of the apron, where most of the aircraft are parked. The balcony runs along the front of the entire terminal, faces north and therefore offers photographers an ideal and unobstructed view all day long.

Photos of aircraft on approach can be taken from the low hill at the eastern end of the apron, to the right of the terminal, thereby keeping the fence out of the picture. Since most landings take place on Runway 26, this is a very satisfactory location. If the wind changes direction in th afternoon (as it is prone to do) and Runway 08 is used, the levée beside the river offers an alternative, equally good vantage point. The restricted zone between the river and the fence is closely watched, and trespassers face the prospect of trouble. Construction work around the hangar area may have reduced the appeal of a good spot for taking photos of taxiing aircraft.

With careful planning of a visit, to coincide with a busy period, the terminal can be used to record a good variety of scheduled movements, before investigating the rest of the field. Winter weekends bring plenty of charter traffic mostly from Britain and Scandinavia but there are also visits by such airlines as Corsair and Eurocypria plus, of course, Lauda Air and Austrian. Even when traffic gets slow, as it can during the summer, there is always the chance of a good quality photo of a couple of Tyrolean Dash Eights. Occasional exotic Dash Eights call in at Innsbruck on their delivery flights.

KLAGENFURT

KLU   LOWK   Woerthesee   2m/3km NE (bus 10 minutes)

Anyone visiting this quiet little airport might consider doing so in the morning, when the sun is at its best. The bus service F leaves from Anabichl, in town. The passenger terminal sits at the western end of the field, to the north of the runway. The passenger terminal is modern and occupies the north side of the apron, with a couple of large general aviation hangars to the left.

Seen from the car park, a flight of steps at the left-hand end of the terminal leads to a small balcony where landing aircraft can be seen and photographed. On the roof a circular cafe opens onto a roof garden, where for the price of a nice beer (equivalent to the cost of a small house in Britain) the occasional Austrian Airlines Fokker 50, MD-87 or A320 can be seen sharing the apron with a dozen or so Cessnas.

LINZ

LNZ   LOWL   Horsching   9m/15km SW (bus 20 minutes)

The modern terminal building is served by only a handful of scheduled movements each day and, because the periods when nothing happens can be long, anyone paying a casual visit may see no activity whatsoever. Even the general aviation presence is minimal. The roof terrace is ideally placed, as is often the case with so little to witness, though it fulfills its intended purpose: friends and relatives do await arrivals there. Traffic peaks at weekends in summer, when charter movements to the sun are more frequent. Even so, Saturday's visitors are unlikely to exceed a dozen. Cargo operations are developing, which means a visit by the occasional Fred Olsen Electra or BAe 146 (or F.27) operating for TNT.

SALZBURG
SZG   LOWS   Maxglan   3m/5km SW (bus 15 minutes)

The view from the observation area is restricted. Entry used to cost 5 Schillings but it's possible that the cafeteria means the entry fee has been waived. Most of what can be seen are the 30 or so light aircraft. In summer, scheduled links are mainly Austrian Fokker 50s to Vienna and Zurich but there are also a few flights to London and Paris, most of which are operated for the businessman. Times of departure and arrival are therefore tailored to suit their needs, so the middle of the day, especially during the week, can be quiet which is unfortunate because that's when the sun is at its best.

A walk along the road by the perimeter reveals, on the other side, the rather scenic castle, Hohensalzburg. Aircraft on the runway are close enough to make good photos and, with the castle behind, they are undoubtedly rather special. Weekday visits in summer are good but the festival in August usually means many additional biz-jets can be seen. Traffic in winter is busiest at weekends, when the many charters arrive, mostly from Britain and Scandinavia. The road passes underneath the runway and, from the other side of the field, views and photos can be good. It's one of the best paces, for example, to take a perfect shot of an LTU A330.

VIENNA
VIE   LOWW   Schwechat   11m/18km SE (bus/train 30 minutes)

The layout of the airport is generally similar to Frankfurt, though scaled down to suit the needs here. The roof terrace (zuschaur) area, at the western end of the terminal complex, has been closed, largely because of the building that's gone up in front of it. There is also a lounge in the new building, next to the American Bar on the top level, which offers a good view of the apron and runway. Alternatively, try the top level of Car Park 3 which appears to be the accepted place for spotters to congregate. Security personnel make casual checks of who's doing what. Car Park 2 is, if you can read German, out of bounds to spotters. This is a problem because Car Park 2 is better for photographers. Photos are possible from Car Park 3, but distant. Also, runway patterns change with some regularity, so keeping up with events might be frustrating. The top floor is covered.

Movements on the runway are distant, needing at least a 300mm lens, and those on Runway 16/34 are virtually out of sight. To the right of the passenger terminal is the cargo centre and, beyond that, the general aviation hangars and ramp, very close indeed to the taxiway to Runway 12. The pleasure flight office has always been noted for its proximity to the action and this should be investigated by any photographer who wants some high quality portraits. At the end of the road, past the general aviation centre, is the Austrian Airlines maintenance base.

East meets west at Vienna; a good variety of carriers complements the various Austrian fleets. Asiana and Transbrasil 767s, Egyptair and Royal Jordanian A320s are all regular scheduled visitors, as are (have been) Samara, Air Moldova, Orbi Georgian and Kazakh Tupolevs. Timetables are important, as different days have different specialities. Air Malta RJs don't visit every day of the week. Charters can include tasty stuff from Russia - VAP Group Tu-134s and Russian State Transport Il-62s are among Vienna's visitors.

The railway service is the quickest and cheapest way of getting between the city and the airport, though trains only run hourly.

OH = FINLAND
HELSINKI
HEL   EFHK   Vantaa   12m/19km N (bus 35 minutes)

The Finnair coach from the city terminal costs 24 Markka and serves the airport's three passenger terminals. Cheaper (15 Markka), but slower, is service bus 615 from the railway station, which also stops at the aviation museum. The three terminals are housed in two buildings - the new "Middle Terminal" is actually part of the old international terminal and there are no formal viewing facilities in any of the buildings. The Fly-Inn restaurant/bar probably offers the best view, though not of

196

dommestic movements, because it's on the top floor of the international terminal. At the far end of this building, close to Finnair maintenance, traffic on the move can be seen. Photographers might need a long lens, even for an MD-11 on pushback. There is a similar place at the far end of the domestic terminal. This is definitely where to go for good photos of Finnaviation Saab 340s and Air Botnia Jetstreams, though the view can sometimes be restricted by parked aircraft.

None of the parking lots are of any use at all - well, except for parking cars, obviously. You can save yourself the walk unless, being intrepid, you intend walking to the TNT facility on the far side of Runway 15/33. Being close to the end of the runway, the view is good from here and there is usually at least one 727 to be seen on this ramp.

The aviation museum, close to car park P50, has many military exhibits as well as a Karair DC-3 and the ex-Finnair Convair Metropolitan OH-LRB. Opening hours are 12:00 to 18:00. Finnair's DC-3, OH-LCH, is kept in one of the small hangars to the left of the terminal area, which might be accessible if a request is made in writing prior to leaving for Finland.

If nothing else the passenger terminals are handy for one thing. At an information booth, copies of the Airport Area maps are available. On one side of the map is the central termianl area and, on the other, you can see (though not marked) where views of the field facing Runway 15/33 are possible - next to the domestic terminal, at the end of Rahtikuja beyond the cargo terminal, and at the far end next to the general aviation terminal. When you've walked that far, you can decide for yourself if you're going as far again, to TNT.

HELSINKI
HEM   EFHF   Malmi   4m/6km NE

Helsinki's other airport, being closer to the city, is now strictly for general aviation, and can be reached by taking the No 77 bus from the railway station. By car from the city centre, take Lahti Road, and the entrance to the field is on Nordostra Motorvagen. Most of the time, the largest inhabitant could be an Islander or Twin Otter used for para-dropping but Border Guard Do288s appear regularly. The fabulous old passenger terminal, painted white and dating from a time when beehives were the fashion, has a snack bar on the upper floor which offers a general view of the field. Do buy something - they don't get many visitors! For collectors of airport brochures, call in at the briefing office, on the next floor up. Also of note, possibly, is the Finnish Aviation Association (SIL) office and shop by the road. The two big hangars to the left of the terminal are worth inspection as they contain quite a few helicopters.

OK = CZECHIA
PRAGUE
PRG   LKPR   Ruzyne   17m/27km W (bus 30 minutes)

Prague is rapidly establishing a reputation as one of Europe's loveliest cities and one which has become increasingly attractive to tourists. What is less widely-publicised is the growth in street crime. This does not, apparently, include flogging half a kilo of decent-grade ganja in Namesti Republiky. Interesting city, interesting people. If you see someone smile, they're probably high on drugs. Everyone else is as miserable as sin. Trams are the cheapest way to get around. Get a three-day pass, write your name and date of birth on the back and, whatever else you do, punch it into a machine on the first tram you board. The ticket inspectors are all ex secret police, over two metres high with bad attitudes. They would like tourists to go home. The author, a tourist, would have loved to go home but somebody nicked his ticket, passport, money and photographic equipment.

The bus service to Ruzyne (pronounced Roozeeny) airport leaves every 30 minutes from the CSA office in Prague but is needlessly expensive. The Metro Green Line goes to Dejvicka, on a main road called Evropska. From here No 119 buses run regularly, inexpensively, and reasonably comfortably, to the airport. Get your tickets at any newstand. As for taxis, forget it, at the prices they charge.

As this book is written, Ruzyne is in the process of expanding to cope with future traffic. The main (North) Terminal area is likely to be something of a building site for a while, with a 20-gate pier extension being constructed out to the right of the main terminal. Observation facilities, if there are any, have been restricted to a balcony, some way back from the glass, in the international building. The view isn't very good and the chances of decent photos from here are minimal.

By walking away from the terminal, to the north, the fence (and particularly a fire access gate) by the taxiway offers an ideal location for photos, and on the far side is grassland which also allows close up views of traffic on Runway 24. On the far side, it is tempting, though perhaps unwise, to use some sort of aid such as a hard camera case to see over the fence.

Scheduled traffic is a reasonable, if thinly spread, mixture. Most of the main European airlines feature on the departures board, all with the usual aircraft: Alitalia MD-80s, Air France A320s, Swissair Fokker 100s, Lufthansa A320s and Fokker 50s. Every now and again there something a little bit different arrives, like a Listavia Yak-40 or one of Air Ostrava's feeder-liners

This is the active part of the airport. Arrival from the city by bus allows a view of the rest of the field, vast and quiet, including the South Terminal area. Most of the time, this looks a fairly desolate place but it does handle some charter flights as well as official and general aviation flights. At one side of the apron here is CSA's maintenance and training base, usually with a couple of Turbolets, and withdrawn Il-62s and Tu-154s to be seen. Access to the South Terminal is restricted and views from it are non-existent.

OM = SLOVAKIA

BRATISLAVA
BTS	LZIB	M R Stefanik	5m/8km N (bus 30 minutes)

The airport is still generally known as Ivanka. The passenger terminal's small terrace has, in the past, been quite adequate for watching and photographing the scheduled movements, but extensions and alterations to the terminal may have jeopardised its continued existence.

There is a choice of buses from the city centre. From the railway station, service No. 24 takes half an hour, whilst the airline bus from the City Air Terminal is a little quicker.

Ongoing political changes are bound to have consequences for the airport's traffic. The introduction of a western-style economy meant that many domestic services were no longer viable. The limited amount of services saw drastic reductions though, as compensation, there is a reasonable range of cargo flights and occasional charters.

KOSICE
KSC	LZKZ		5m/8km

Slovakia's easternmost airport is situated near a monster steel mill. For anyone who thinks he's seen everything, Kosice is somewhere to go - interesting, to say the least. The airport management usually has enough free time during the average day to offer a guided tour of the apron. Do not expect this to include the military base, however, which contains L-29s, L-39s and L-410s. A car is essential for a visit as the bus service only operates five times a day (and twice a day at weekends).

Tatra Air SF340s operate to Bratislava, and CSA ATRs to Prague. Tyrolean Dash Eights also visit, as do SK Air Jetstreams. Air Transport Europe Tupolevs operate charters to various places during summer. East of the passenger terminal are the Cassiovia Air Service crop sprayers, not to be confused with the Cassovia Air 125 and King Air which are often present.

POPRAD
TAT	LZTT	Tatry	3m/5km W

Visitors to the Slovak Republic will almost certainly want to see the Tatras, a range of splendidly picturesque mountains. Eight miles from the slopes is this small international airport, with a rather old-fashioned terminal, at least when seen from the outside. The interior is, however, modern but the enthusiast will probably settle for the view from gates at the side of it.

The apron rarely holds many aircraft but those which can be seen include Let 410s and the occasional charter from the Ukraine. In summer, the pace picks up, with increased general aviation activity, many of which are helicopters. This is the main base of Air Transport Europe, the country's biggest helicopter operator, so movements by Mi-2s, Mi-8s and Alouette IIIs are regular. The fleet also contains a number of fixed wing aircraft, used for charters. Summer weekends see increased activity but only with gliders and the odd Cessna 172 or helicopter, doing sight-seeing flights.

As Central Europe becomes an increasingly attractive summer destination for tourists, this airport is likely to get its fair share of visitors. Anyone touring by car will be able to spend at least a couple of hours beside the terminal, taking satisfactory photos with even the most basic equipment.

OO = BELGIUM

ANTWERP
ANR   EBAW   Deurne   3m/5km SSE (bus 20 minutes)

The proximity of Antwerp to major commercial centres has meant increased scheduled services, particularly with England. Since there are good road connections to Brussels, this is now a convenient gateway for the businessman. What was the Delta Air Transport hangar, close to the terminal, is now owned by Air Venture, whose Xingu and Zlins are kept inside, in company with some other business twins. Since DAT transferred maintenance to Brussels, only VLM is based here, with at least one Fokker 50 in evidence most of the time.

Antwerp is one of the centres of European enthusiasts (the Aviation Society of Antwerp has 600 members), so the authorities are used to dealing with requests to have a look around. The best way to achieve results is to write from home to the airport director (Paul Paridaens) - the postcode for Deurne airport is B-2100. To the left of the terminal building is the Stampe museum, the adjacent hangar containing nine of these biplanes. Of the other 120 or so resident aircraft, there are eight biz-jets and a Spitfire. There are hangars and workshops on both sides of the runway. Ibis and Travair are the most likely to contain something larger than a single-engined aircraft.

BRUSSELS
BRU   EBBR   National   8m/13km NE (bus/train 20 minutes)

Also known as Zaventem, enthusiasts generally find it most frustrating. Anyone without a car is restricted to the central terminal area. It is virtually impossible to follow all the movements, as there are three runways, and various spots may be selected to watch individual parts of the activity. The main passenger terminal has a glazed wall overlooking a part of the apron, with a dozen or so stands in view, but the glass is usually fingermarked and unsatisfactory for photographers' use. The cafeteria, to the right, offers a similar prospect but movements on the far side of the right-hand pier can also be seen, though the price of even a coffee here is outrageous.

The multi-storey car park is too low to overlook the terminal buildings but it does face Runway 07R/25L, the circular satellite and, to a limited extent, the Sabena wide-body hangar. What follows is a bit like a practical geography lesson. It is factually correct but it might be misleading, with the passage of time, because double fences have started to appear. Within in the next two years, photographers might therefore find that all their options have been pretty much closed.

Leaving the terminal area, the Sabena maintenance hangars on the right offer an impenetrable prospect but, just beyond, the general aviation terminal is very close to the taxiway to 07L and the view from the small car park will reward the patient, subject to wind direction, of course.

It can be a tricky business finding a way round to the Melsbroek side of the airport, and the use of main highways is the simplest, with first exits being used repeatedly. The north side houses the cargo complex, more general aviation and the inaccessible Belgian Air Force base.

The patient enthusiast can circumnavigate the field. On leaving the central terminal area, take a right marked "general aviation, Zaventem-Centrum". Look out for Sabena Technics and a (slightly restricted access to vehicles) road between a couple of civil aviation authority buildings. From here, the DHL facility is visible, as have been an ex-Nigerian A310 and an ex-Niger Herc. The journey continues for another 100 metres or so, when Abelag is reached. Logging and photos are possible, before continuing a little further to the Sabena House car park, where the rest of the apron is seen.

The JBA terminal comes next, one of the most common biz-jet inmates here being a Portuguese Falcon. This is about as far as people on foot can go. A car really is essential for the rest of the tour. Pass the end of Runway 07L and watch out for *de post* (the post office), as their car park is likely to be less hostile than any of the Brucargo staff car parks. When 25R is in use, there isn't much to see, as departures are usually too high for photos. From the roundabout, there is DAT maintenance with stored Xingus or, from a different exit, other views (including the wings of a Portuguese Ju-52).

Heading towards Haacht for about a kilometre, there is a Cessna dealer, whose car park allows some of the Air Force serials to be read off. After passing Melsbroek, continue along Hachtsesteenweg and take a right at the second set of lights. Signposts are for Steernokkerzeel, Nossegem and Waterloo. After a couple of hundred metres, there are more places to read of the Melsbroek inmates, plus chances to see movements on 25R (which isn't saying much). Next comes the tunnel under 25L, after which is a turn-off to the left. A bit restricted access, this one, but it's where to climb the embankment for movements on the runway, and with the sun behind.

For the end of Runway 02, directions are easiest from the terminal area. Take the g.a./Zaventem route again and turn LEFT at the roundabout. Watch out for the Peugeot garage on the right, and turn left at the crossroads, immediately after it. Don't go under the railway bridge but turn left before you get to it. Park after the level crossing (directions to building sites in 1997 can be misleading in 1999!) And it's a two or three hundred metre walk to the fence. Molenstraat is now called Zeven Tommen. Brilliant in the afternoon. In the moring, follow the road round a few bends until you come to the woods, and stop. This is where a bit of co-operation is essential, as the famer doesn't have to put up with deck chairs in his crops.

Brussels has developed as a European hub for distribution of overnight parcels delivery. From 20:00, over thirty aircraft arrive from various parts of the continent. A FedEx DC-10 and bizjets from Spain and Portugal are included, though many of the movements are British or Belgian. Anyone standing close to the general aviation area at night should be able to log these visitors.

CHARLEROI

CRL	EBCI	Brussels South	5m/8km N

Still generally known as Gosselies but it's now been marketed as a user-friendly alternative to Brussels International. At present, it's slightly under-capacity, to say the least. The passenger terminal is nice enough (though whether it offers views or not isn't known) but there are plenty of nooks and crannies to what's on the apron - if anything. Apart from some general aviation, it does seem to handle a few charter flights. The marketing blurb suggests Air Algerie, Royal Air Maroc and Sobelair use the airport. Movements, in reality, might be few and far between. Maybe it will be worth a detour for anyone touring this part of Europe. It's easy to find, just south of the intersection between the Paris - Luxembourg E42 motorway, exit 24 off the A54 (E19) heading towards Charleroi.

LIEGE

LGG	EBLG	Bierset	5m/8km W

Sabena now provides a regular link to just about anywhere else in the world from Liège, though from the town centre by bus to Brussels. It is also very close to Maastricht, in the Netherlands, so scheduled services have proved uneconomic. A visit may still form part of an itinerary, as the small number of light aircraft share the field with Belgian Air Force Mirages.

OSTEND

OST	EBOS		3m/5km SW (bus 20 minutes)

This airport depends on cargo traffic, which can include some interesting aircraft. The ramp usually contains something to justify the detour on the way past, but a protracted stay is unlikely to yield worthwhile results. Due to the quiet nature of the runway, Sabena use it frequently for Xingu training flights and these aircraft can be seen sharing the ramp with one or two unusual aircraft or, sometimes, very little. The roof terrace offers an elevated view of the field, with the occasional cargo carrier within range of the camera.

Almost the entire perimeter is accessible for the photographer, with the threshold and holding point for Runway 26 offering the best possibilities. From the terminal, Duinkerkseweg leads east to the end of the runway, and a turning to the right leads up the southern side, reached before the T-junction with Torhoutsesteenweg. The main road past the airport, Nieuwpoort-sesteenweg, passes close to the threshold of 08, and a left turn here on Kaklaertstraat offers a close view from the south side.

OY = DENMARK
AALBORG
AAL   EKYT   4m/6km NW (bus 15 minutes)

The peace of this quiet little airport is only occasionally shattered by the arrival of a SAS MD-80 from Copenhagen or (slightly less noisy) the competing Cimber Air ATR-42. The glazed front of the terminal overlooks a large apron, with a couple of dozen light aircraft parked. The runway is also used by air force fighters during the week. There are one or two charter flights, but nothing that can't be seen elsewhere. Some way north of Aalborg (75 km) is SINDAL, and 110 km west is THISTED. Both are served two or three times a day by Sunair/BA Express Jetstream services to Copenhagen.

AARHUS
AAR   EKAH   Tirstrup   25m/40km NE (bus 50 minutes)

Served mostly by a handful of Cimber Air ATR-42s, SAS MD-80s and Sunair Jetstreams, Tirstrup is a long way from anywhere else and hardly worth the effort. The passenger terminal, north of the runway, does have views of the ramp from the first floor, and some of the hangars can also be seen.

BILLUND
BLL   EKBI   1.5m/2km E

Few maps even show the town, situated in the middle of Jutland, but the location is important because it is so centrally placed. The road from Esbjerg to Vejle passes through Grindsted and a right turn in the town leads to Billund. Investment in the airport has been followed by regular scheduled services to Copenhagen by Maersk Air 737s and Fokker 50s.

Billund, a departure airport for charters to the sun, is now becoming established as a destination in its own right. Just next to the terminal is Legoland: the children can enjoy the park while dad watches the aircraft from behind the glass of the viewing gallery. Visible on the grass is what remains of an EAS Cargo DC-8. Activity is moderate, though much of it is generated by general aviation. Initial confusion by the vacant hangars (in aviation terms) next to the terminal is resolved by taking the access road to the west, which leads to the main hangar area. This may be Denmark's second busiest airport but it's a long way behind Copenhagen! Anyone touring central Jutland might also want to call in at SKIVE which handles the occasional Suniar Jetstream.

COPENHAGEN
CPH   EKCH   Kastrup   6m/9km SSE (bus 30 minutes)

The SAS bus from town costs Kr40 (£4) and the cheaper alternatives, only Kr15, are service buses Nos. 9 and 250S from Central Station and Raadhusplaadsen (Town Hall Square) in the city centre. A car is not essential but it does save a little time. Once at the airport, it saves a lot of time.

Denmark's premier airport, with nine hundred movements on some days, has one of the most frustrating terminal complexes in Europe for the enthusiast. Hall 6 in the domestic terminal offers the best chance for the spotter. By passing the security check, access to departure lounges has been possible without a boarding card. Most of the movements can be seen but powerful binoculars would be needed to log everything. Much of what is to be seen would be considered extremely rare in other parts of Europe, so quality information about Kastrup might be particularly important. The gap between the domestic and international terminals has been closed by a new building.

The only really useful location is still that at the end of Amager Landevej, overlooking Runway 22R, a couple of kilometres from the terminals. The place is generally known as Flyvergrillen, (there is a snack bar) and this is where a viewing platform has been built, especially for spotters. Most of the airport can be seen from here and many of the movements can be photographed quite easily. Access by public transport is possible. Catch the 250S service from the terminal area to Amager Landevej, and change to either a southbound 34 or 350S. The fare is about a pound (Kr 10). Not *all* bus drivers speak twenty four languages, so it might be worth writing the names on a piece of paper. Then they're only too pleased to help. For photographers, afternoons are best if the sun is shining. Officially, there is no charge for Flyvergrillen but the private enterprise snack bar might reasonably expect something in return for providing the facilities - prices, by Danish standards, are very reasonable indeed.

When the 04 runways are in use, departures from 04R are also within range of the camera. From Flyvergrillen, take Tommerupvej and Englandsvej towards Dragor. At the first set of lights after the tunnel beneath 04L/22R, turn left, and fence here offers good east-facing views. It's therefore at its best in the mornings. Nobody is welcome here for too long. There are security patrols, inside the fence, and somebody will ask you to leave. If you don't, your next encounter is with someone on *your* side of the fence, which is a slightly different matter.

Kastrup is SAS's main hub, so all their types (apart from the cargo 747 but including the Fokker 50s) can be seen. This does not mean that a stay of three or four days guarantees seeing the entire SAS fleet. Some of the domestic DC-9s don't visit Kastrup at all. Whilst SAS and Lufthansa account for about 60% of the movements, Maersk and Cimber are regular, plus a range of European carriers. DC-8 LN-PIP is reported to be more-or-less intact, by the cargo area.

The SAS maintenance base is east of the international terminal but there are no views of it. Also on the north eastern side of the field is the DHL facility. The road, which goes to Gate Gourmet, has signs in Danish saying the road is closed to the public, and the one or two 727s wich are parked during the day are out of sight. Kastrup South is the maintenance area used by Maersk, Muk Air, Sterling European and Premiair. It's a long way to find out that there's nothing to be seen.

COPENHAGEN
RKE   EKRK   Roskilde   21m/33km W (train/bus 35 minutes)

Roskilde specialises in air taxi, executive and commuter operations. Marketing blurb suggested that it was going to become Copenhagen West but, as is often the case, big ideas don't always work out. Scheduled services have not been attracted but there is steady traffic operating flights which are the next best thing. Fleet operators abound, including Ikarosfly, Jetair and Copenhagen Airtaxi, and it is fortunate that access to the aprons is easily achieved. Many hangars and aprons offer a range of aircraft, in a quantity unrivalled throughout Denmark. Any disappointment experienced at Kastrup is compensated by the packed ramps of Roskilde.

Bus services Nos. 210/212/213 from Roskilde railway station to within a kilometre of the airport (lufthavn). Before getting involved with aircraft, it is prudent to check the bus timetable. Timing the walk from the bus stop is also sensible. The service is infrequent, and lack of planning can result in a two-hour wait! Permission for ramp access should be sought at the airport's administrative office.

ESBJERG
EBJ   EKEB   5m/8km NE

The airport terminal is pleasant, and a parked Fokker 50 might be visible from the cafe, lounges etc but through glass, and the fence at each end of the terminal also offers limited views of the ramp. The Maersk hangar contains the company's Bell 212s, which operate to off-shore rigs, and other hangars are famous for their clean windows which allow the occupants to be identified with ease.

202

ODENSE
ODE   EKOD   Beldringe   8m/13km NW

Beldringe is the base of Falck Air, who operate ambulance services for the Danish Rescue Corps, and things are usually quiet enough for a visitor to be offered some hospitality, though the Islanders may be away on ambulance duties. The hangars can all be visited and it may be possible, on a pleasant afternoon, to enjoy the trip in one of Falck's golf buggies.

SOENDERBORG
SGD   EKSB   4m/6km NW

Soenderborg is best remembered for the presence of Cimber Air, and the chance to see an ATR-42 on its home ground. A few scheduled flights are operated from here to Kastrup but there are only a couple of dozen other residents to note.

GREENLAND

Greenland, a Danish dependency, occupies a similar area to Saudi Arabia, although its total population is a mere 50,000. A number of small communities exist on the coastline, often for reasons of exploration or NATO defence. They are linked, virtually exclusively, by Gronlandsfly (Greenlandair), as all other means of transportation are restricted by the weather or geography.

SONDRESTROM
SFJ   BGSF   Kangerlussuaq

Flights between Denmark and Greenland operate to Sondrestrom (correctly known as Sondre Stromfjord), with SAS staff being helpful to visitors. This is about as remote as you can get - with the reader's level of interest to match - the entry in the last edition caused one specialist to put pen to paper on the subject (at least *he* cares). The names by which the community and its airport are known in Official Flight Guides are not, apparently, *correct*. Rightly or wrongly, this book calls airports by the same names as other publications - nothing more, nothing less.

The airport used to share the runway with the USAF base (now abandoned) on the opposite side of the field. Action is strictly civilian which, in this part of the world, doesn't amount to much. The occasional transatlantic ferry flight either calls in here, or at NARSSASSUAQ, for fuel. Greenland has other fields, GODTHAAB Nuuk (GOH/BGGH) being a major one - relatively speaking.

PH = NETHERLANDS
AMSTERDAM
AMS   EHAM   Schiphol   19m/30km SW (bus/train 25 minutes)

This large airport has an extensive terminal area at its heart and the facilities attract much attention from foreign enthusiasts because of the selection of aircraft to be seen. Plans are under way to turn Schiphol into a major trading and transport centre, Mainport 2000, by the turn of the century.

Assuming first that the visitor will make use of the extensive roof terrace at some time, guidance notes are worthy of attention. The terrace, or Wandelpier, has been extended and is open (according to official information) between 08:45 and 18:00 and can get very busy throughout the summer. When the weather is not at its best, the cafeteria, open all day, offers an alternative. The commuter apron used to be out of sight from the terrace, as was all of the cargo area, but things have been improved, which isn't the same as saying they're perfect. Not bad, though!

Arrival by car, bus or rail might mean stocking up with sensibly-priced food and drink for the day, and Schiphol Plaza, on the ground floor, is the place to go. There is also an aviation hobby shop in the plaza. Another detour before going onto the roof may be worthwhile as the ground floor information desk has lists of the day's flights: the yellow Aankomsten sheet shows arrivals and the blue Vertrekken/ departures. Whilst the registrations are shown for Dutch aircraft, these should not be taken too literally as they have a habit of being unreliable. Really good photos are possible from the Wandelpier. This is one of the few places in Europe to see Transbrasil 767s, Cabo Verde 757s, Iran Air A300s, Northwest 747-400s and Armenian Tu-154s. There's also a few MD-11s worth watching out for, such as those of JAL, Mandarin and Thai International.

Among the facilities at Schiphol Oost are KLM Helicopters and KLM's maintenance base, plus Fokker's silent assembly plant. A close look at the aprons of Schiphol Oost also reveals a fair selection of general aviation, and often a cargo DC-8 or 707. Continuing southeast along the road from Schiphol Oost, past the threshold of Runway 01R, a right turn on Oude Meer Weg leads to a road very close to 06/24. In the last couple of years, reports from Amsterdam omit to mention this spot, so it has probably been screened off from the action in some permanent way. Instead, attention has been drawn to the McDonald's, close to Runway 09/27. Leaving the terminal area, by car or bus, and passing under this runway, Loevensteinserandweg passes car park P3 (also quite good for spotting as it's next to this runway) on its way to Schiphol Oost. After passing round the end of Runway 19L, you can't miss the golden arches. The platform is 2 metres off the ground, thus clearing the fence, so it's ideal for photographers when 09/27 is in use. Not only is there a reasonably good view of much of the terminal area, there are also monitors, showing the movements.

Few airports have done as much for the enthusiast as Schiphol. Authorities in Britain and the USA spend much money making things more difficult whilst, in Holland and Germany, they actively encourage spotters. While observation decks are being closed all over the world, Schiphol extends its Wandelpier in an imaginative way. It's as if they've thought about what people want to do and then made it possible. Don't forget the Aviodome Museum, at the main entrance, for complete coverage of everything that's to be seen.

EINDHOVEN
EIN   EHEH   5m/8km W (bus 20 minutes)

The single storey passenger terminal building has a roof garden which is open in the summer, and a ground level external viewing area at its left. From this terrace it is difficult to see the Philips aircraft unless on the move, their hangar being to the right of the terminal, but all visitors are reasonably close, many being photogenically so. The staple diet is Cityhoppers but there are other attractions. The military base has F-16s, F.27Ms and KC-10s. Throughout the year, the local Jetstreams of BASE Business Airlines are very much in evidence, their movements being complemented by the occasional Air Engiadina and Alsair service.

Aerofurn's painting and refurbishing shop means that one or two interesting arrivals can be expected during the year. Additional storage space is still used at WOENSDRECHT. Charter traffic in summer raises the tempo, with airlines such as Sun Express, Pegasus and, of course, Transavia.

ENSCHEDE
ENS   EHTW   Twente   4m/6km N

A tiny terminal is served by Twente Airlines Caravans, and the car park to the right overlooks the (empty usually) apron. The F-86 mounted on a pole indicates that this airport may have more relevance to the military minded. Whilst the runway is distant from the terminal, it can be seen from other dead-end roads around the perimeter, but the taxiway to the hangars passes close to the terminal car park, and good portraits of the F-5s or F-16s can be taken with ease. In summer, charter operations do liven things up.

Some 120 km from Twente is the SOESTERBERG Air Force Base: well worth a visit because there are good facilities for the large band of enthusiasts who congregate here. Quite close to the runway is an enclosure, where good portraits of F-15s can be taken as they take off and land. A visit here should include time for the museum, which houses some beautifully restored aircraft, though not necessarily with enough room around them.

GRONINGEN
GRQ   EHGG   Eelde   5m/8km S

Only the dedicated will consider a trip here to be worthwhile. On the southern edge of the town, just off the A28, is the home of the RLS and its fleet of Citations etc. A written request can result in a visit to RLS, during the week, but it should be noted that the airport is no longer served by scheduled flights. The area reserved for viewing is at the apron's edge, so good quality souvenir photos are a compensation, but it would take luck to be present in summer when a charter aircraft occupies the apron. Forty miles to the west is LEEUWARDEN, and its F-16s.

MAASTRICHT
MST   EHBK   Beek   4m/6km NNE (bus 20 minutes)

Maastricht is still really only a small regional airport, but it handles an increasingly interesting amount of traffic. Air Exel Brasilias, and BASE Jetstreams operate most of the commuter flights but there are charter services, mostly Transavia and Sultan Air, throughout the year. Between the terminal and the hotel is a terrace providing excellent viewing facilities for the taxiway and the runway. Almost any camera gets good results here, and above it is a cafeteria with an equally good view. Cargo charters are seen almost daily, frequently involving a Balkan An-12 or an Il-18 but various Russian operators have started to appear. GPA Expressions is the paintshop and refurbishment facility which guarantees an assortment of interesting visitors.

ROTTERDAM
RTM   EHRD   Zestienhoven   5m/8km NW (bus 20 minutes)

For anyone without a car, access to the airport is by bus from Rotterdam's Centraal Station. The passenger terminal is modern and features an open terrace at the apron's edge. Whilst it is ideally placed for many of the movements, traffic is increasing at Rotterdam and the most interesting aircraft may not occupy the most photogenic stands. There is a chainlink fence separating the terrace and the apron, though photographs are still possible. To the right of the terminal and the car park is another vantage point, but only used for seeing incoming aircraft taxiing to the apron. The expanse of apron to the left of the terminal is normally occupied by smaller aircraft, and it is often here that something out of the ordinary may be parked, usually within range of the average zoom lens.

KLM Aerocarto, whose Cessna 207 and Navajo are used for mapping and aerial photography, have a hangar at the side of the approach road, the other end of it used by Quick Airways. Without permission for access to these hangars and ramps, the presence of so much greenery can preclude an adequate view of the residents. Hamburg Airlines Dash 8s are regular visitors and it is always possible that some interesting, and unusual, visitor will arrive here.

PJ = NETHERLANDS ANTILLES

CURAÇAO
CUR   TMCC   Hato

Officially, this is Willemstad (Hato). It's a great place to visit but the airport is rather on the quiet side. The passenger terminal has everything any spotter (or photographer) could wish, apart from quantity of movements. Upstairs there is a bar and a cafe, both with views of the runway and apron, and there is also an external deck, the floor of which can be used for frying eggs at lunchtime. It will come as no surprise to read that most of the movements are ALM but there is a daily KLM 747 Combi.

There is no shortage of Dutch influence, much of it interesting. A couple of F.27Ms are based and one or two P-3s should also be in evidence. The rest of the visitors should suffice to raise the average pulse - an Aerosucre Caravelle visits, and DHL operate a Venezuelan-registered King Air.

With time to explore, it's worth having a look around the field. Beyond ALM Catering is a hangar, containing some light aircraft. The fire dump has the mortal remains of a blackened Neptune and a couple of F.27s.

SABA
SAB   TNCS   Juancho Yurausquin

The passenger terminal is reminiscent of a branch line railway station but maybe it's not quite as busy. Strangely, displayed inside, for all to see (as if to help passenger confidence) there is information about some of the less successful arrivals, such as the Winair Dornier Skyservant that didn't quite make it. The runway is 600 feet long. Yes, that's right, 200 yards. To put it another way, it's about the same as the average aircraft carrier. Fancy a try? If so, catch a Winair Twin Otter, about the only movements this field sees.

SINT MAARTEN
SXM   TNCM   Prinses Juliana   7m/11km W of Philipsburg

This is the Caribbean for real jet-setters: white sand, turquoise water and very expensive indeed. A jewel is Maho Beach, at the end of the runway, which must be classed as an enthusiast's paradise. With only a few hundred feet separating beach and runway, aircraft can taxi to the end, turn (when they are photographed) and then set off down the runway. One small catch is the combination of aviation fuel and sandblasting which comes next! Even aircraft using the runway from the opposite end are within reach of a telephoto lens as they come over the beach.

Information strictly for the rich (courtesy of Genie online services): the Beachside Villa Resort is located very close to the airport and on the beach. The rooms are soundproofed and, in addition to the great photo opportunities, the beach is clothing-optional.

Many visitors are small: Winair base their three Twin Otters in the hangar next to the terminal, LIAT's largest movements are HS748s, Air St Barthelemy Trislanders and Air Guadeloupe ATR-42s are common visitors. Trans Air Link DC-6s offer variety, and the well-heeled arrive for the sun in a wide range of chartered jets, from TriStars to Express One 727s, and scheduled wide-bodies once a week from Air France, KLM and Lufthansa. The busiest time is between January and April, when winter is at its deepest in Europe.

The airport is small enough for all its facilities to be within reach of the average photographer, and the Leeward Islands are small enough for other islands to be within reach of St Maarten. The French island of ST BARTHELEMY is nearby, only ten minutes away by Air Guadeloupe Do228. The airfield is small, and highly photogenic, being next to the beach. The Trislanders of Air St Barths and Winair's Twin Otters are frequent visitors, shuttling to and from St Maarten.

PK = INDONESIA

BALIKPAPAN
BPN   WRLL   Sepingan   5m/8km E

This is Indonesia's second-ranking airport for aviation interest. It is on the eastern seaboard of Kalimantan (Borneo), an island shared between Indonesia, Brunei, Sarawak and Sabah. This may not be a rich country but there is an active oil industry, much of which is found on the edge of Balikpapan and nearby Pasar Baru. Oil-related flights dominate the traffic, and lunchtime is hectic as people transit through this hub. Bouraq movements abound, though there is no shortage of Sempati, Merpati and Pelita traffic, up to A300 size. Garuda movements are, however, few. Apron space is limited, and peak time here is an experience never to be forgotten. The quantity of movements is more than adequate but the real interest lies in the frantic activity as passengers are transferred between flights. The viewing gallery is glazed but, if it lands or moves, it can be seen from here. Photographers will be pleased to note the glass is kept clean.

DENPASAR
DPS   WRRR   Ngurah Rai   8m/13km S

Bali seems to be a matter of taste. According to some, it's pretty close to being the Garden of Eden. Others reckon it's all about reputation - having paid handsomely to get there, nobody's prepared to ask what all the fuss is about. Palm-fringed beaches of white sand, and impossibly blue sea, might be run-of-the-mill these days, but at least the Aussies can get there without flying for what feels like three weeks.

The international terminal handles an increasing amount of traffic, though Garuda wide-bodies dominate the scene. This is not particularly long-haul from Australia, so 737s, A320s and even 146s can turn up. There's almost nothing to be seen from inside either of the terminals but the perimeter is worth exploration.

Arriving at the airport from Denpasar town on the dual carriageway, the bemo (cheap) bus passes a single storey cargo shed and the Merpati Nusantara hangar. Between these two buildings is a view of the taxiway through the chainlink fence. Photos of the Merpati CN235s are possible through the fence, as are their F.27s. To the left are normally a few helicopters and the occasional exotic visitor. Beyond the cargo shed are the domestic and international terminals.

Some time around 17:00, local people start to arrive, to pass the time watching the aircraft from the fence. What they don't realise is that many of the domestic movements aren't normally seen at Jakarta. There's no shortage of F.28s to be seen.

The Bali Beach Hotel at Sanur is where most airlines have a ticket office. The weekly roster of flights is shown there. Failure to book local flights there can sometimes be resolved by a visit to Garuda's office. Flights may not be as full as they say.

Bali may be an idyllic holiday spot but few other airports in Indonesia offer so little to the enthusiast. For an inexpensive change, the island of Lombok is less than a half-hour away by Merpati HS748, F.27 or CN235. The airport, MATARAM Selaparang, is served by these inter-island flights, most of which stop at Denpasar en route. The return fare is about £25.00.

JAKARTA
CGK   WIII   Soekarno Hatta   12m/19km NW (bus 45 minutes)

Jakarta is not the cheap destination it once was. Facilities aren't necessarily all that convenient either. So-called airport hotels involve a drive of at least half and hour. The new Sheraton will be the only hotel actually on the airport itself. Prices might make your eyes water. For US$50 a night, the Nelayan offers reasonable facilities and comfort, as well as transport to/from the airport. Taxis can work out quite expensive, so it's worth discussing money before getting inside. A trip to Halim might cost about £25, and unmetered cabs might offer the best value. Shop around, as they say.

Much of the traditional-style terminal area is open, with check-in desks on the plazas, though covered from the sun by splendid ornamental roofs. There is an air of bustle, especially in the morning, and everywhere is perfectly clean. Shade is important, and each observation deck has some, plus a welcome breeze (with luck).

European enthusiasts will be drawn initially to the complex on the south side, the domestic terminals, as it is here that the more interesting movements can be seen. The three original passenger terminals are now the domestic passenger terminals, used by anybody that isn't Garuda. Viewed from landside, Sempati (A) to the left, Merpati (B) in the middle and Bouraq/Merpati/Sempati (C) on the right. Redundant Viscounts, Electras, ATPs and HS748s occupied a ramp opposite Terminal C for a number of years but have been moved half a mile or so to a site on the opposite side of the link taxiway. Most of this is visible by walking from one side of the airport to the other. Garuda's stored DC-9s are dwindling in number and the F.28s have gone. Anyone actually using the international terminal (as a passenger, that is) would do well to take a look around Gate D3, normally used by MAS for flights to Kuala Lumpur, as it offers a good view of what's in storage

Mesh fencing encloses the domestic viewing decks, which makes photos difficult . . . but not impossible. What can be seen is an interesting (for a while) procession of airline movements but photographers will be frustrated. Morning and lunchtime witness a constant procession of domestic traffic, and the quantity of ex-Garuda (now Merpati) DC-9s and F.28s is still quite remarkable.

Things have been changing (for the worse, of course) on the international side of the complex. The observation area was taken over for use as a "transit hotel", and is therefore not accessible to landside folks. A shuttle bus operates between the terminals, the cost of which is a trifling 500 Rupyah, about 20 pence, as an alternative to walking in what can be very intense, and enervating, heat. Naturally, only one side of the airport can be monitored at any one time, so the shuttle bus might be used several times by anyone spending an entire day here.

Prior to leaving for Indonesia, it is wise to be familiar with the aircraft on the register. Busy though Soekarno-Hatta is, one must bear in mind that several airlines never visit. Merpati Nusantara, Bouraq, Sempati and Mandala are all present, plus the occasional Pelita movement but it becomes apparent that there must be a huge number of aircraft in Indonesia which only operate elsewhere. Pelita, for example, traditionally had a major presence at Halim.

JAKARTA
HLP   WIIH   Halim Perdana Kusuma   8m/13km SE

Because there are now so few scheduled movements, Halim is no longer regularly served by the Damri link bus from Soekarno Hatta. For those who feel a visit is essential, taxis are the only means of transport (see above). The viewing deck has been closed, and there are no views of aircraft from public areas of the terminal. What moves is almost certainly non-scheduled traffic. Indonesia is a muslim country, so it's worth remembering the Hadj season because things do get rather busy, with movements including plenty of Garuda wide-bodies.

With no viewing facilities, it may come as something of a relief to know that traffic is slow, with only Merpati CN235s operating regular flights. The balance is made up by Pelita, IAT and Eastindo, though access to see some of the helicopters at close range would be welcomed by most, if possible.

Hadj apart, normal traffic is as its peak, not saying much, in the early morning. A visit to Halim on the way to Soekarno-Hatta would be worthwhile, if only to ensure that an essential part of the national aviation scene is witnessed and that nothing is missed. For an indication of how frustrating Halim can be, this quote is from a well-travelled spotter: *"Been there three times - heard a lot, seen nothing."* Ideally, you should write a letter before leaving home. If you get a reply, you will find an official tour of the place costs getting on for 90,000 Rupiah, due to security arrangements. It's value for money, though, because you'll probably get someone who knows what he's talking about (even if you don't always know what he's talking about) and the tour is comprehensive. There's plenty of Indonesian Air Transport to be seen but Pelita sightings are relatively rare. The fleet operates all over Indonesia (which is a very large area indeed) - only their head office is at the airport.

On the far side of the field is a road leading to the nearby golf courses. It isn't marked on most maps but worth looking out for, if exploring with a car. At the eastern end of this raod is an Air Force (TNI-AU) college with a Mig-21 on display. Parked nearby are a few C-47s and an ex-Bayu CL-44. From time to time, there are visits by Hawks, F-5s and F-16s, so use of a camera would be unwise.

Having come this far, it might be tempting to seek out PONDOK CABE (PCB), an airfield some 20 miles south of Jakarta. This is a major base for Pelita and Indonesia Air Transport. Parked on the Pelita apron are usually some helicopters, F.28s, Transalls and Hercules, plus the VIP 146s. It's Skyvans and Gulfstreams mostly at IAT. Parallel with the runway is a rather busy road, from which can be seen pretty much everything. Stopping the car, to take photos, is not recommended. At one end of the field is a golf course, over which landing aircraft pass at absurdly low levels. Scary indeed. Close by is a small flying club with a few interesting residents. Note also the presence of aircraft (and therefore people) employed by the air force and the police.

KEMAYORAN is now the Jakarta Fairground and is scheduled to be developed with housing.

JOGYAKARTA
JOG   WIIJ   Adisucipto   6m/9km NE

Java's cultural capital is a major tourist centre, being close to a number of famous ruins, including Borobodur. Pronounced Joag-jah, Jogya is equivalent to Japan's Kyoto, the Kraton and Taman Sari palaces dominate the heart of the town. The mini-bus which serves Solo calls at the airport, leaving from Terminal Terban, in the town centre.

Traffic is limited mainly to tourist flights from Jakarta. The small, and perfectly adequate, terminal has a central viewing area where good photographs are possible, especially in the afternoon. Only a low boundary wall separates the viewer and traffic, though candidates for the camera are limited. DC-9s are the staple diet, though Bouraq HS748s and Merpati F.27s do visit.

MEDAN
MES   WIIM   Polonia   1.5m/2km

The international terminal at Medan only has windows for passengers, and these overlook the car park! Attention is therefore focussed on the domestic terminal, where the interesting aircraft arrive. Here is what is described officially as a "Waving Gallery". Access requires a modest payment and there are catering facilities on the deck . . . waving isn't compulsory, incidentally!

The exotic palm trees enhance the tropical feel but they do obstruct the view of the apron. A zoom lens and some skill are the two ingredients for a photographic record. As aircraft taxi across the apron, a well-timed click should produce more than just trees. Not only is the resident C-47 still used regularly but there is also a good selection of regional carriers. Fokker 100s and F.28s are much in evidence as well as the occasional Dash Seven.

Medan can't be mentioned, in September 1997, without reference to the ecological disaster that has swept over much of Indonesia. Tropical rain forest has always been burned, immediately before the monsoon but, in 1997, the rains didn't come and the fires got out of hand. The smoke became smog, affecting also the Philippines, Singapore and even Malaysia. Visibility was reduced such that the airport couldn't operate.

PADANG
PDG   WIMG   Tabing   5m/8km

This is an international airport but almost all its traffic is domestic. As with Medan, it is the domestic terminal (part of the only terminal, in fact) which offers a chance to see the aircraft. It is at the extreme southern end of the field, next to the runway threshold, so landing aircraft can normally be seen. Trees make photography of landings practically impossible.

The departure lounge is really the best place to be, and from here a few Sempati, Merpati and, of course, Garuda movements can be seen. Perhaps the most exotic visitor to be seen regularly is the Pelangi Air Do228, all the way from Kuala Lumpur. Telephoto lenses are essential without ramp access. Both require discretion. This is not Frankfurt, London or Los Angeles . . . the security forces are trained to be sceptical of sophisticated equipment. Talking to someone can ensure that problems don't occur and open up the possibility of a walk onto the ramp.

SURABAYA
SUB   WRSJ   Juanda   15m/24km S

According to official sources, this one of three airfields, the other two being Gedangan and Perak. There is, in the passenger terminal, a sign saying "Waving Gallery" and maybe there is one. If there is, either it takes a bit of finding or it's been closed for quite a while. Be advised, then, not to be in too much of a hurry when arriving by air. In fact, it's best not to leave the departure area prematurely because it's one of the best places to get an idea of what's on offer. The Sempati part of the departures lounge gives fleeting glimpses of aircraft on the move but that's about all. This is an airport to be explored.

Merpati maintains its prop fleet here, and its hangar, at the western end of the field, is big enough to house half a dozen aircraft at a time. There is a Fairey Gannet displayed outside. Next to the hangar is the airline's storage compound, containing at the end of 1996 two HS 748s and two F.27s as well as the hulk of an F.28 that skidded off the end of the runway at Semareng. Access to Merpati means turning right outside the terminal and walking about a mile. Getting airside might be possible but not in a hurry. Remember first that the European idea of getting a move on isn't necessarily understood in Indonesia. The think of negotiations procedding at *their* idea of a relaxed pace.

The miltary base, at the far end of the airport, has several navy CASA 212s and a couple of what look like airworthy army C-47s. Another five are in various stages of dereliction, like the nearby Bouraq 748. If all this sounds like fun, there are a few things to bear in mind. Here we go again - the bad news is . . . hotels are not quite up to western standards, though some have air-conditioning. Turn off the air-con, even for a few minutes, and the mosquitoes come to life. Go to sleep and you'll wake up itching, and short of a couple of pints of blood. What is quite satisfying, if you still have the energy, is to splatter the (literally) bloody things all over the walls. The resultant mess is *your* blood. Do leave a tip for the maid, who will have to clean up after you. The Airport Transit Hotel has a "sitting out area" area on the first floor, with excellent views of aircraft landing.

PP = BRAZIL

BELO HORIZONTE
PLU   SBBH   Pampulha   6m/9km N

When jet traffic moved to Confins, Pampulha became the airport for regional, prop-driven traffic. In Brazil both halves of the picture are interesting but, when traffic is split into two, the old airport takes on a desolate look for a while. The crowded, noisy, hectic days of Pampulha are over, and the pace is now more relaxed. It should not be assumed that, because Lider Air Taxi are based at Pampulha, there will be a ramp crammed with LearJets. They operate from satellites all over the country.

The last report suggested that even the regional carriers are being moved out of Pampulha. To what extent this is true remains to be seen. Few passengers are going to welcome the prospect of a thirty mile drive to the airport, on Brazil's crazy roads, for the privilege of a short commuter flight.

BELO HORIZONTE
CNF   SBCF   Tancredo Neves/Confins   28m/44km N

Beautiful new passenger terminals have sprung up almost as fast as the rain forest is being destroyed. Confins has all the right facilities that are expected in Brazil. The passenger's needs are not those of the enthusiast: pile it all onto one or two runways and fill the aprons to capacity. By splitting the traffic between two airports, life is more civilised but the pace at each airport is now very slow. For strangers, the name of the city is pronounced Bayo-orri-zonch.

BRASILIA
BSB   SBBR   International   7m/11km S

Like many federal capital cities, where the centre of commercial activity is elsewhere, Brasilia is not bustling with scheduled airline traffic. Like almost anywhere else in Brazil, the number of airlines to be seen is rather limited but Brasilia is one of the best places to see them. The terminal is set to one side of the runway, at a right angle, normally close enough for movements to be identified. The terminal faces east and good photos are possible almost any time except early morning. The roof of the entire building is an observation deck with a view of all the stands and the g.a. behind.

The general aviation and executive aprons can both be seen but the air force base is screened from view. However, the movements are plentiful during the week and, if Runway 09 is in use, they can also be inspected at very close quarters. A short walk from the terminal leads to the Transbrasil maintenance hangar and a right turn here passes the ramp, with a good view of any 727 which may be undergoing checks in the open air. The road ends at Lider Air Taxi's car park and this spot is very close to the taxiway. Any aircraft, no matter how small, can be photographed as it passes and photos of landing airliners are just distant enough to provide a side view as they flare out for touchdown.

Apart from Lider LearJets, there are several operators to be seen on the executive ramps, including those used by FUNAI, the indian development agency. Even though the traffic is limited, most of the Brazilian airlines are regular visitors and a couple of days in the warm sunshine should allow representative shots of each to be obtained.

CAMPINAS
VCP   SBKP   Viracopos   60m/92km NW of Sao Paulo

Viracopos was used for many years as Sao Paulo's main international gateway. This was where all the European flights arrived. The opening of Guarulhos meant that all flights could be transferred there, leaving Viracopos to lead a quiet existence as the regional airport for the city of Campinas. With so little traffic, it is improbable that anyone would tear themselves away from the bustle of Guarulhos, for the sake of a couple of Bandeirantes or F.27s.

CUIABA
CGB   SBCY   Marechal Rondon 5m/8km

Like so many other regional airports in Brazil, the verdict is the same: excellent but slow. With only twenty or so light aircraft on the ground, it takes more than six scheduled movements a day to make Cuiaba worth the journey.

CURITIBA
CWB   SBCT   Afonso Pena   12m/19km SE

Few visitors will stay here but it is a stop between Sao Paulo and Iguassu. The airport is small but, like most others in Brazil, it has been developed to the most modern standards. The apron is shared by airline visitors and a squadron of MB.339s which operate training flights. The short stop en route will allow time to get off the aircraft and take a few photographs of the other aircraft here. Purists will need to make a note of the different squadron markings, and the serials, which are quite small, also feature the 'last two', painted a little larger, on the nose.

FOZ DO IGUASSU
IGU   Cataratas   7m/11km NW

The name of the airport is Foz do Iguassu and should not be confused with Iguazu Cataratas, on the Argentine side of the border. What separates the two countries are the waterfalls, among the greatest sights in the world, comparable with the Grand Canyon, especially in the spring, when Niagara Falls pales into insignificance.

The airport, like most Brazilian examples, caters for waving off friends and there are actually two small observation decks here. Either allows a good view of the ramp and anything which uses the airport can be seen reasonably well. Airliners like TABA F.27s and Varig A300s are normal everyday traffic here but they do seem a little tame after seeing the spectacular waterfalls.

When at the falls, a pair of binoculars should always be kept close by, as one of the bonuses of a landing here is the chance to overfly, while turning onto approach. This could be the only chance to log something truly outstanding, as Austral 1-11s and Aerolineas Argentinas F.28s overfly, on approach to their destination, on the other side of the border.

Contrary to popular fears, Argentines have never been particularly hostile to Britons, and a day trip from Brazil is possible, even without a visa. Anyone who wants a passport stamp may encounter unexpected difficulties, as the bus does not normally stop at the border checkpoint! The short journey to Argentine Iguazu could result in a memorable souvenir photo.

MANAUS
MAO   SBEG   Eduardo Gomes   11m/17km NW

Signs of past glories abound in Manaus but the city is generally very run down now. The airport represents a major investment and is suitably modern, to attract tourists and investment into the area.

The passenger terminal faces the runway and has eight jetties for airliner use, though views from it are hard to find. Almost any other airport in Brazil offers better viewing facilities than Manaus, and the range of movements is fairly typical. Immediately left of the terminal area is a visitors ramp, where one or two executive aircraft park, all easily seen from the fence. Beyond this is a cargo ramp of some size, reflecting the proportion of cargo which arrives here by air, and its inmates range from Rico's fleet, largely redundant, to visiting aircraft of VASP and Varig.

Primarily a military base, PONTA PELADA is used mainly by the FAB Buffaloes, though the occasional TABA FH-227 can be seen from the main airport, while on approach to this field. It is located relatively close to the city centre, and might be worth exploration. The authorities may be reasonably welcoming to anyone who approaches the matter sensibly.

RECIFE
REC   SBRF   Guararapes   6m/9km SW

Photographs taken at Recife have a very distinct look to them because of the hill on the opposite side of the field from the terminal. A first floor open observation deck gives a perfect view of any traffic here and almost any airliner will make a fine subject for the camera as it taxis in to its stand. The international flights which refuel here do so during the night, though they are all generally airlines which are readily seen on many European trips. Outside the passenger terminal is a preserved B-17 in FAB markings and to the north is the general aviation area, with a hangar used by Western Air Taxi, and there are other facilities around the field, including a small military presence at the far end of Runway 36.

RIO DE JANEIRO
GIG   SBGL   Galeao   9m/15km NW (bus 40 minutes)

This is very much a major international airport in every sense of the word, being extremely modern and handling a varied range of airlines from different countries. Sadly, it doesn't offer any real quantity and, even more sadly, the superb open air observation deck which once fronted the semi-circular terminal, has also been a victim of progress.

What remains is a rather small room on the third level, occupying the right-hand corner of what was once the deck, now glazed and smeared so that photography of any quality requires more than good luck. Essential equipment for the photographer is now a bottle of Windowlene and and wash leather. What is most frustrating is that the deck doesn't really face in the right direction. It overlooks the threshold of Runway 15 and, to a certain extent that of Runway 09 also, but if 27 and 33 are in use, which is quite often, trying to see the action is extremely frustrating.

The airfield is shared by a substantial FAB base. C-130s can be seen from the terminal, identification being easiest from the road, and there are HS125s and HS748s, also. As the base is quite close to the causeway road, it is very tempting to stop and take a portrait shot of a military transport but the guards tend to keep an eye out for this activity, so it involves some risk.

The long runway, 27/09, behind the original main terminal, is used for many departures and the Varig maintenance base is next to it, accessible only via a security gate. Some arrangement to pass this should be sought by anyone wishing to acquire a photograph of the preserved DC-3 (PP-ANU) and possibly one or two of the wide-body fleet undergoing checks. Access might be easier by expressing an interest in the Rapide, PP-VAN, which is stored inside.

RIO DE JANEIRO
SDU   SBRJ   Santos Dumont   2m/3km E

Located downtown, Santos Dumont is on a peninsula, surrounded on three sides by Guanabara Bay (Rio Harbour), with the Sugar Loaf at the end of Runway 18L. The airport is, in fact, a collection of various facilities of which a passenger terminal is one. There is a small, upper level, observation deck with a cafe, and the Punta Aereas airliners park in front, offering themselves very photogenically. Activity is slow, though all movements are worthy of attention. The Punta Aerea, or Air Bridge, was once Varig's exclusive territory but is now operated by VASP and Varig 737s with additional competition from the F.100s of TAM.

Enthusiasts with some interest in military aviation will enjoy Santos Dumont as it handles a good number of FAB movements, with Bandeirantes being operated by many different squadrons, each with its own distinctive scheme. The military base is spread along the roadside and a walk reveals hangars/ramps containing HS125s and a selection of trainers, as well as a fair number of Bandeirantes. Closer to the terminal are the facilities of Lider Air Taxi and Cruzeiro Aerofoto, where a variety of aircraft can always be seen but rarely photographed, unless on the move.

Being downtown, Santos Dumont handles executive movements in some profusion and the field holds a variety, parked on the many stands in the middle of the field. Attempts to obtain a tour of the airside may involve some unofficial discussion regarding money, with large sums being considered reasonable. This is based on the assumption that photographs will be sold at a profit (to be shared), so the 'private collection' angle should be mentioned at a very early stage!

Some twenty-odd miles southwest of Rio, next to the old Grand Prix circuit is JACAREPAGUA airfield, one of the maintenance bases for Votec. Enthusiasts are not common here, and anyone showing an interest can expect to be shown round, for the purposes of taking a few photographs.

What is immediately apparent is that there is a distinct lack of S-61s as Votec operations are from MACAE, some miles north of Rio and Niteroi. Anyone with a hire car and some dedication would be advised to investigate, and obtain the name of a contact at Macae, to ensure some hospitality before making the journey. Other activity is varied and includes some locally built single-engined types used to train Air Force Reserve pilots, as well as Prospec Islanders and a selection of stored aircraft, both civil and military.

Apart from being an active military base, with Pumas, C-130s and Buffaloes, the museum at CAMPOS DOS AFONSOS houses an outstanding collection of aircraft each of which warrants a mention in its own right. The drive from Rio is horrendous, except for the brave, and approach from Jacarepagua is far more leisurely, with the aid of a good road map. A variety of these can be purchased in the shop at Santos Dumont, and the best value is the most expensive, as the cheaper ones are, effectively, useless.

SALVADOR
SSA   SBSV   Dois de Julho   22m/34km NE

Not one of Brazil's more interesting airports. Apart from the occasional Cruzeiro wide-body, most of the traffic is restricted to 737s. The heavies tend to pass through at unsociable hours on their way to Rio. The Nordeste apron, in front of their hangar, usually holds a few Bandeirantes.

SAO PAULO
CGH   SBSP   Congonhas   5m/8km S

Now very much a domestic airport, time has taken its toll on a downtown location and scheduled traffic has been moved to Guarulhos. Still worth a visit, even if the huge quantities of movements have been severely trimmed, the observation deck offers an adequate view of most of the Air Bridge traffic (even some of this now uses Guarulhos).

All that remains is a row of hangars along the taxiway, out of sight from the terminal. Rather than wait for the occasional movement, it's necessary to walk down to the hangars and see what's there. Congonhas may be a mere shadow of its former self but it still has some exotic machinery.

SAO PAULO
GRU   SBGR   Guarulhos   15m/23km (bus 50 minutes)

Guarulhos is now established as a very major airport, as is to be expected when it serves such an enormous city. All Sao Paulo's interesting scheduled movements, like Aerolineas Argentinas and Ladeco 727s, and Pluna 737s, use this airport. Transatlantic services, too, have been transferred here, so the pace and variety are enough to satisfy any enthusiast. The passenger terminal does have an open observation deck, with good views of the scheduled traffic. Cargo facilities are found at both sides of the terminal and the Varig/Cruzeiro maintenance base is on the far side of the runways. There are bus services between the city and the airport, and it is possible to catch the Metro to Bresser (on the Linha L'Este-Oueste/East West Line) and take a bus from there, which saves a little time. More important, it saves experiencing the awful downtown traffic . . . not much fun, even in a bus!

RA = RUSSIA

BRATSK
BTK   UIBB   Yurba

Mainly a military field, with lots of MiG-25s to be seen in the company of several An-2s and Yak-40s. A pair of Tu-154s, damaged after an accident, found their way here, and the rear portions of their fuselages can be seen. On the opposite side of the road is an enormous helicopter base.

MOSCOW
MOW

To reach the main airports from the city centre, public transport is reliable, if spartan. Buses leave from Leningradski Prospekt and trains to Vnukovo go from Kievski station. It might be possible to travel by taxi between a few of the airports in the south but, before parting company with your Lada and its driver, it is essential to ensure that means of leaving are available. There are no regulations for taxi drivers, so they charge whatever they can. When bargaining for any trip, expect negotiations to start at about US$100. Yes, really. Moscow just isn't the sort of place to visit alone. Ignore this advice and suffer the consequences. If you still have your passport, airline ticket and wallet by the end of your trip, you should feel unbelievably lucky. The best thing to come out of Moscow is the plane home.

MOSCOW
BKA   Bykovo   12m/19km E

The last few miles of the road to Bykovo give a constant impression that it must be the wrong way. Do not be fooled into thinking that just because the road looks like it must stop at any moment, it will. Bykovo is, to put it simply, out in the sticks. When the hovels and kiosks, the peddlers and the whores stand by the roadside, you're almost at the airport entrance.
    Bykovo has an Il-14, CCCP-91484, on display at the far end of the car park, at the right-hand end of the terminal. Directly behind are the Il-76s. The rampside spectators area has been converted into a building site, so go up to the first floor of the terminal where a glazed area overlooks the ramp. Predictably, the glass is dirty. Visible from here are assorted Antonov turboprops directly in front and Yak 40/42s to the right. The range of colour schemes now being applied to the Yaks is interesting but many of them are being stripped down for parts.
    To be blunt, Bykovo has seen better days, but we can't be sure if it actually took part in them. Weeds grow, in abundance, through the concrete and the hangars seem to be semi-derelict. This can also be said for many of the Il-76s, few of which are now fully intact. This is a major maintenance base for Il-76s, often used by foreign air forces. Russia has more than its share of problems and nowhere are they more evident than at Bykovo. It can be a shock to see such squalor, especially around an airport but that is a major part of what makes a visit to Bykovo so memorable. Two movements per hour is as busy as it gets.

ZHUKOVSKY is close to Bykovo but it's not for the intrepid solo traveller. No matter how much Russia is opening up to the west, and very much to market forces, this airfield is still used by the Flight Research Institute, so it can't be assumed that interest by foreigners is harmless. The Russians have to be fast learners, if they are survive and prosper. A little entrepreneurial skill is essential. They have discovered that the appeal of this airport has a high price on its head. Even if tours are promised, don't be surprised if the arrangements are not finalised. Zhukovsky offers lots more than Il-76s and, reportedly, stored Tu-144s.

Expect the price to be raised at the last minute. Even when it's agreed, it can still be raised. Getting to this airport will be a matter of luck, until the going rate is established. Charging so much that a visit is cancelled is in nobody's interest. It will all be sorted out, in the course of time.

MOSCOW

DME   Domodedovo   25m/ SE (bus 80 min)

A moderately active airport, dominated by Il-62s, Domodedovo still looks superficially modern. Closer inspection reveals things are otherwise, however. The passenger terminal has a huge glass frontage, overlooking the central apron where many aircraft (mostly parked Il-62s) can be seen. The car park offers an additional, and also partial, view. At first floor level is a snack bar - cough up, stand up and eat up (and, possibly, throw up). The windows are draped with very heavy net curtains and, if one of the old dears behind the counter doesn't like you, she calls one or two very heavy guys to have a chat with you. Time to go. Bloody country! All is not lost, however, because it's possible to log most of what's around by simply keeping on the move. Russians are starting to have the same terror of loiterers as Americans.

Displayed on a plinth, and in good condition, is Tu-114 CCCP-76464. This is the very large and impressive, four-engined, passenger propliner with contra-rotating propellors. It still makes a fine subject for the camera. Immediately behind the Tu-114 is the East Line cargo terminal, outside which are normally parked 80% of the Domodedovo Airlines fleet. Continue past East Line and the main hangar, and there's the fuselage of another Tu-114, used for cabin training, visible to the left. After another couple of hundreds or so, there's yet another.

To each side of the passenger terminal are runways, though only that on the left is used. Most of the movements are Tu-154s, rather than Il-62s, and many of them are operated by CIS airlines, so a welcome range of colour schemes passes through. Long fingers project from each side of the terminal, obscuring from sight anything parked on the far side, though registrations can be read off the Tu-154s. Be thankful that it is traditional to place the registrations on the central air intake, rather than below the cheat line. A few Il-76s and An-12s are parked on the far side of the central apron so that they appear nose-on. They are difficult, if not impossible, to identify.

The Aviatrans cargo ramp forms the remote left-hand corner of the main apron. To the left of the main terminal is another building, seen from the car park, behind which is a ramp. Before entering the passenger terminal, or certainly before leaving, it is worth investigating, because this ramp isn't visible from inside. A few hours spent in the terminal can give the impression that Domodedovo is an interesting airport. This would mean departing in complete ignorance of its star residents. Parked around the corner, to one side and completely out of sight, are several Il-96s. Without a ramp tour, they are inaccessible. Whether or not these aircraft are visible between the hangars is for others to discover. Caution is strongly advised.

MOSCOW

          Myatchkyvo

This airfield is strictly for tour groups. If you think Bykovo is out in the sticks, then Myatchkyvo is more so. It's down a dirt track, in the woods. Little can be seen, and nothing heard, from the perimeter fence and one would be foolish to try taking a look. Not much moves here, mostly because there is no longer any reason for it do so. The days when aerial reconnaissance were needed (or could be afforded) are long gone. Parked here are plenty of An-30s, the ones with the glazed noses. They wear Aeroflot colours but their primary purpose wasn't as civil airliners.

Access, by prior arrangement, allows close encounters of a rotary kind. Long rows of helicopters, many derelict, offer much of interest to lovers of wrecks and relics. Add an Il-14 on its last legs and a few rows of An-2 biplanes, many covered by tarpaulins for some reason, and it's like one of world's best car boot sales. For non-British readers, Americans call them yard sales or garage sales. Believed to be close to Myatchkyvo is another field, LYBERTSKI. Most of it is reported to be hidden behind a high wall. On the other side are Mi-26s and much, much more.

MOSCOW
SVO   UUEE   Sheremetyevo   18m/ NW (bus 50 min)

Sheremetyevo is effectively two airports, located on either side of the two parallel runways, only one of which appears to be in use. To the north is the domestic terminal, Sheremetyevo 1: a long low building with an upper floor level balcony along its front, and a circular satellite with a wide, overhanging roof. The balcony is closed but this is not much of a problem because movements at Terminal 1 are few and far between.

On the south side, Terminal 2 has an Il-18 outside and a restaurant on the fifth floor. This is not too high for phographers and it does ensure that many (but by no means all) of the distant aircraft parked on the north side, can be identified. About a hundred, in fact. The international movements dominate proceedings here, so Terminal 2 is the best place to be. Traffic is reasonably brisk, featuring a good assortment of ex-Soviet bloc and western types. What turns up might be a matter of luck because not all the goodies are daily - far from it - but it would be reasonable to expect the occasional MIAT 727 or Air Koryu Il-62 to vary the diet from Orient Avia and the other, less colourful Russian carriers. The restaurant has tinted glass, which can make life difficult for the photographer. The food is cheap enough but that's about all that can be said in its favour. The first sight, from these windows, is indeed impressive. On the far side are rows of Il-86s, Il-76s, Il-62s and Tu-154s. It is best to be contented with what is recorded, rather than be frustrated by what is not. After even half a day at Sheremetyevo, there will be plenty to remember. Subsequent visits, however, involve the law of diminishing returns.

MOSCOW
VKO   UUWW   Vnukovo   19m/ SW (train 75 min)

On arrival here by road, the Tu-104 at the entrance catches the eye. Stopping to take a photo is the last time the air is filled only by the sound of jackdaws. This is Moscow's main national airport, handling flights from all over Russia. It gets very busy indeed. Chaotic might be a better description. The upper floor has a cafeteria at the front of which is an open terrace. In fact, there are two open terraces, side by side. To be seen from here is pandemonium - people walking all over the apron between the many Tu-154s, yellow buses transporting passengers to and from their aircraft, and yellow tankers doing the refuelling. Rather than head off for Vnukovo, expecting one of the most fascinating days of your life, it might be better to brace yourself for the supreme disappointment that might lie in store. Not only might both terraces be closed but the windows of the cafeteria had, by summer 1996, been applied with almost floor-to-ceiling brown paper. Goodbye view . . . but why? Reading of movements from outside the terminal building is likely to result in being told, ever so politely, but ever so firmly: *niet*. Comparisons in the last edition between LGA and VKO could have meant somebody wanted to stay with the pace, and ruin everything here also, if they could. So far, they appear to have done a reasonably thorough job.

NOVOSIBIRSK
OVB   UNNN   Tolmachevo

Novoskibirsk is a major regional capital in eastern Russia. Scheduled airline activity here is best described as leisurely. A connection onwards might make a stop necessary. Anything seen on the field is unlikely to move during a short stay of an hour or two. The huge military base can be seen from the aircraft when taking off (or landing, if the wind is not in its prevailing direction). An Il-86 is to be seen, dumped, probably as the result of some landing accident. The selection of airliners is nothing exceptional, with a few examples of most types to be seen. The other field is called SEVERNIJ, which is used mostly by local traffic. Apart from a lot of helicopters, the other aircraft are Turbolets and An-24s.

SINT PETERSBURG

LED   ULLI   Pulkovo   11m/17km S (bus 45 minutes)

The LED code tells us that, until recently, this was Leningrad. The local spelling of Saint is Sint, so the title block is not a typographical error! Despite being Russia's second city, airline activity is decidedly slow. There are very few international flights, and these can only be seen from the terminal by passengers, after passport control.

To be seen on the right from the international area, some parked/stored An-12s rarely move. What interest is generated by a visit to St Petersburg will be found at the domestic terminal. For anyone who is prepared to walk, the best views are from the approach road. There is also an officially approved viewing park next to one runway but details about it are vague.

Another airfield, closer to the city, is RSHEVKA. It may be small but it houses a considerable number of helicopters and An-2s, many of which are present for maintenance.

ULYANOVSK

ULY   10m/16km

Until very recently, the city of Ulyanovsk was officially rather important: it was Lenin's birthplace. But times have changed! The old city of Ulyanovsk lies on the west bank of the River Volga and has recently come to our attention as being the site for Aviastar's assembly plant. The airport is an entirely separate location, and of interest not for the very few scheduled flights during the average day but for its Civil Air Training Centre. Aeroflot's jet pilots are trained on all fleet types here, from Yak-42s to Il-76s.

On the east bank of the river is Ulyanovsk new town, with the Aviastar plant on its outskirts. New towns in this part of the world are rarely beautiful. The Russians usually have good reasons for some of their seemingly strange decisions. Locating the assembly plant nine miles from the runway is an interesting example!

Visitors to the city are almost sure to be in a guided tour party, so the civil aviation museum might be on the itinerary. At different locations in the east bank new town are Tu-134 CCCP-65618 and Il-62 CCCP-86685. Financial resources to preserve them in good condition are non-existent.

RP = PHILIPPINES

MANILA

MNL   RPMM   Ninoy Aquino International   8m/13km S (bus 30 minutes)

Unless one has a definite objective, there is little incentive to spend time at the international terminal, where the activity is not particularly brisk. Likely exceptions are Continental 727s, Qantas 767s and 747 Combis, Cathay Pacific TriStars, and assorted A300s, any of which may be enough to encourage the average photographer. Visitors are fewer than at Hong Kong or Singapore and the opportunities for photography are limited. Visible from the international terminal is 707 RP-C911, previously used by President Marcos but now used as the very static *Club 707.* The airport is now named in memory of his political adversary, whose widow was subsequently elected to rule.

Heading towards Manila, on the Love Bus or in a (very cheap) taxi, the domestic terminal is seen, very shabby and overcrowded but which now hosts A300s on the Cebu flights as well as PAL Fokker 50s. Photography of these taxiing aircraft is possible from either side of the terminal but some care should be exercised: the police and military personnel can be unpredictable.

The terminal is located opposite the threshold of Runway 13. Next to it is the largest of the general aviation areas: that of the PADC (Philippine Aerospace Development Corporation), with the other general aviation area directly opposite. Access to the various facilities might be a thing of the past (surprise, surprise), reportedly because of what an FAA inspection revealed.

The PADC facility has a wide taxiway separating the rows of hangars. It is a reflection on the economic situation that many of the aircraft rarely leave their hangars but there are good numbers of locally-built Islanders, quite a few Beech 18s and most of the nation's biz-jets to be seen. The aprons feature a collection of derelict and (just) operational DC-3s, and a number of other types including a YS-11 and the T-29. There is a smaller general aviation ramp across the runway, next to which is PAL's domestic maintenance base. As well as Fokker 50s, the locally based US Embassy C-12 lives here, and a couple of PAF F.27s should also be in evidence. The sizeable PAL training fleet of Seminoles and Tomahawks, all in full airline scheme, is parked on the runway side of one of the hangars, close to a few derelict PAF C-47s minus their wings.

Air Force transports to be seen should normally include Maritime and ex-PAL F.27s, Islanders, the (civil) VIP F.28, the occasional Nomad, Hercules and even a C-123, plus numerous helicopters. Photography and conspicuous note-taking are definitely injudicious.

In summary, Manila offers probably as many as two hundred executive and light aircraft, with perhaps up to fifty military machines (if you can see them) plus the resident and visiting airline traffic. What is not certain is the extent to which accessibility has become something of the past. Before setting out on such a long journey, it might be prudent to write beforehand, stating intentions and seeking official permission for access to some of the facilities.

SE = SWEDEN

GÖTEBORG

GOT   ESGG   Landvetter   15m/23km E (bus 40 minutes)

The international traffic is probably the least attractive aspect. A handful of 737s and DC-9s from Europe's major capitals, none of which would warrant more than a passing glance at Frankfurt or Schiphol, are supplemented by SAS flights, several of which are operated by Fokker 50s.

The view of the apron is through the windows of the terminal's large observation deck, close to the threshold of Runway 21, but more than one visitor on the ramp at any time is an unusual event. Smaller aircraft provide occasional interest, Malmo 146s being the most regular. There are international flights (and charters at weekends), which might be best seen from the ground floor cafeteria. Gate 15 determines how things will go. If something parks at it, the chance of a photo will be superb. Once it's on stand, the view of the taxiway has gone for an hour or so. With so few movements during the average day, this is something of a disaster!

Landings on Runway 21 can be photographed from the Eurowings car park, and most departures taxi past here on their way to the hold. A 200 mm lens should suffice.

Any visitor with time to spare would do well to investigate SAEVE, as it is quite a busy little general aviation field. Several air taxi and other fleet operators base their operations here, and it's normal to see a number of Citations and King Airs.

JONKÖPING

JKG   ESGJ   Axamo

This is how most of us would imagine a Swedish regional airport. The single storey brick terminal, with three gates, is spotlessly clean. The cafeteria is also the news-stand and information desk - it closes at about tea-time. A small waiting area overlooks the tiny apron, with a northerly view, which should please photographers. To the right of the terminal, a state-of-the-art hangar houses a dozen or so residents and its apron regularly holds foreign visitors. So, what's the catch?

Well, obviously, it doesn't get very busy. Transwede Fokker 100s to Arlanda, SAS Fokker 50s to Kastrup and the occasional Flying Enterprise service to Bromma, with four five services a day by each. Oh, and one last thing . . . three times a week there's a TransEast Yak-40 from Riga. Monday mornings, Wed and Fri afternoons at the last count but check timetables before you go. There is no public transport as we know it, so a hire car is essential. The car park has benches on which people have been known to stand, so that their photos exclude the chainlink fence.

LINKÖPING
LPI   ESCF   Malmen

Linkoping, some hundred miles or so south of Stockholm, is fairly well known as the home of Saab. Hence there is inerest in the place, not matched unfortunately by quality information. Malmen is the airport which handles the ocasional scheduled service, and should not be confused with Saab's own airfield (ESSL). There are reports, possibly about Saab airfield, that there is an SF340 on a pole by the north gate and a Safir at the south gate. It would be nice to offer something more accurate than this but at least anyone, who is intent on making the journey, knows to look out for more than one field.

MALMÖ
MMX   ESMS   Sturup   20m/32km E (bus 35 minutes)

The majority of Sturup's flights are domestic and this has always been one of the best places to get a quality photo of a SAS domestic-only 737. Malmo Aviation is obviously based here, so sight of their 146s is to be expected. The observation deck has been closed but, for the best chance in Sweden of a Malmo 146, take a walk north from the terminal along the perimeter fence. Late afternoons are best and an MD-80 needs a 50 mm lens.

NORRKÖPING
NRK   ESSP   Kungsangen   3m/5km E (bus 10 minutes

The Syd Aero SD3.30 flights supplement the usual Fokker 50s, operating their regional schedules. The based Calibrator C-53 and Kungsair's modest base are other marginal attractions, though it will be a dedicated enthusiast who heads for Norrköping. The general aviation apron, on the far side of the runway, is accessible upon request.

STOCKHOLM
ARN   ESSA   Arlanda   25m/40km N (bus 45 minutes

The observation deck, above the international pier, is open but during the summer months only. When this is the case, Arlanda is a good airport to visit, and an early start is advised. Access to it is at the right hand side of Terminal 5, as seen from landside. There is no admission charge, and only photographers will be unhappy with the facilities, as the glass doesn't help. Apart from the apron, the threshold of Runway 26 can also be seen from here. Subject to the observation deck being open, Arlanda poses no problems. Being practical, and assuming it isn't, Arlanda can be treated as an American-style airport, with all terminals being linked landside. Try *Sky City*, effectively the link between T4 and T5, which offers one of the better views. Domestic terminals are T3 and T4, with *Sky City* giving direct access to the others. The best view, apart from the deck and *Sky City*, is at McDonald's on the upper floor of the international terminal T5.

As this is the main airport for the country, it handles much international traffic, and is Europe's fourth busiest airport. Of most interest are probably the Kar-Air ATR-72s, Finnaviation Saabs and Latavio Tu-134s. Estonian "only" use Yak-40s on Saturday mornings, 737s and Tu-134s being weekday fare. It's the local traffic, SAS, Air Hudik, Air Nordic and Skyways especially, which are of most interest but representative portraits will probably be restricted to landing shots taken beside Runways 01 and 26. For landing shots, on 01, 26 and 19, catch the 583 bus (it goes from Marsta railway station) which passes and stops directly under the approach to Runway 01. And finally, don't expect to clear your SAS MD-80s at one airport because it can't be done!

STOCKHOLM
BMA   ESSB   Bromma   5m/8km W (bus 20 minutes)

Closer to the city centre than Arlanda, Bromma's scheduled traffic is mostly Malmo Aviation 146 commuter flights but there are also occasional Golden Air, Sun-Air and Flying Enterprise services. The field is now mostly used for air taxi and general aviation operations, as well as much maintenance, so it is worth a visit. A written request for access to the ramps is normally successful, and a few hours spent here can compensate for any disappointment at Arlanda. Interesting residents include the derelict hulk of CV-440 SE-CCX, used by the fire crews (it last saw service with Linjeflyg) and C-47 SE-CFP. A couple of hundred metres left of the passenger terminal is an office block and a small terrace, overlooking activities, but facing south.

SP = POLAND

GDANSK
GDN   EPGD   Rebiechowo   9m/15km NW

Rather more like old Poland than Warsaw, Gdansk is an industrial city. It lacks charm! LOT ATR-72s operate there from Warsaw, as do occasional split-load flights to Heathrow. Traffic is extremely slow, and hardly worth the effort, when there is more to see and do in Warsaw.

WARSAW
WAW   EPWA   Okecie   6m/9km S (bus 30 minutes)

Poland has revalued its currency, so readers of the last edition might have been alarmed at some of the prices. Entrance to the observation deck used to be Zl15,000, which is now about £3,000. The view is good but not *that* good! In the new currency, it's Zl1.50 or about 30 pence. That's better. Okecie (pronounced Oh-ken-chi) has a passenger terminal to match the country's active interest in the rest of Europe. Scheduled traffic is still moderate but there is usually something to keep the mind occupied whilst waiting for something to taxi past.

Every effort has been made to encourage travellers to visit Warsaw. The prices, by western standards, are an incentive in themselves. There aren't too many ancient European capital city centres where a coke and a burger cost less than a pound. The airport has its own express bus service and the traveller can get his act together in the airport's main concourse. Hotels to suit all budgets can be booked at the travel agency, and tickets for the bus can be bought at the kiosk marked 'RUCH'. They are so cheap, it's worth buying a few, to save inconvenience later.

The new terminal, called Okecie II, is as modern as any in Europe, the only difference being that the pace is relaxed and civilised. Few passengers have said that about Heathrow. On the roof of this building is the observation deck, accessible by going outside, turning right and walking a few metres. It's open between 07:00 and 20:30.

Arrival by plane allows sight, normally while taxiing, of the extensive aprons to the north, which are bound to excite interest. For the best view of this area, the roof of the new multi-storey car park is good. From here the Yak-40s can be seen, usually in the company of both Polonia Il-18s. One or two Aeroflot Mi-8s are sometimes present, often in the company of a few Polish military examples of the same type.

The domestic terminal is the farthest building beyond the maintenance hangars and anyone who has visited the old Olympic terminal at Athens will see a similarity, though there are less passengers. The apron may contain one or two biz-jets. In front of it are parked the ATR-72s, awaiting duties. Most of the Tupolevs are to be seen in front of the hangars, whilst the Tu-154s which are ready for service have their own ramp. The Tu-134s in use are parked in front of the old terminal.

Some of the Yak-40s are painted in military colours, and others in a basic LOT scheme, without titles. They have three-digit serials, unlike SP-GEA which lurks in its own small hangar. At around 16:00, when scheduled traffic gets quiet, is when the Yaks and Turbolets tend to move. From the deck, a leisurely perusal of the perimeter reveals, sooner or later, a couple of Il-14s. One, SP-LNE, bears Aeropol titles and sits behind the fire station. the other, SP-LNB, is next to the control tower. At the northern edge of the field are some unsold PZL crop sprayers and, just to the right of them, a MiG-15 is derelict. The domestic terminal is barely visible from this new deck.

Airline traffic is interesting, and most European carriers visit during the week. The airport has been made inviting, and officials are friendly but efficient. It will take some time for westerners to be understood. After so many years, a young officer may be alarmed at the sight of a telephoto lens, as these are beyond the means of the average Pole. Covert activity is bound to raise attention. It is so much easier to make contact with someone beforehand and explain your presence, and the purpose of your activities.

The nearest hotel to the airport is the Novotel, on the main highway to town, called Zwirki i Wigury. It is more expensive, and less convenient, than those in town. The Metropol and Polonia are both very affordable, though the late night trams make a noise. Only a two-hour flight from London, Warsaw is within easy reach. The weather in summer will come a pleasant surprise, as will everything else, to anyone who thinks Warsaw is a cold and inhospitable city.

The bus into the city is No.175, though No.114 also goes there. Be sure to punch the ticket in the machine, as penalties for free-riding are severe. An express service into the city might now be operated. At the crossroads a few hundred metres from the airport is a road called 17 Styeznia. A left turn here leads past the hangars to the domestic terminal, and there is a bus service. The journey is hardly worth the effort. It might be possible to identify one or two visiting biz-jets, but everything will, sooner or later, pass the main terminal on its way to Runway 33.

The ability to watch, log and photograph aircraft at Okecie is one thing, but to be seen doing so at BABICE may arouse rather more unwanted interest. On one side of the runway is a military base with a couple of MiGs and several Mi-8s. The civilian operations are dominated by Aeropol, though activity is rare. The many An-2s and Mi-2s share the field with one or two Turbolets. If guidance can be offered in this book, it would be to treat Babice with some caution. Making contact with officials could prove better than allowing them to make the first move.

SU = EGYPT

CAIRO
CAI   HECA   International   14m/22km NE

Any opportunity to transit through Cairo should be welcomed, though a stay of any length is another matter. Take a flak-jacket, just in case. As the passenger terminal has no air jetties, everyone must take a bus between the aircraft and the terminal. Arrival by air always means a long taxi to the apron, so the opportunity to see a splendid array of aircraft is thus presented. Inactive and withdrawn aircraft used to include some An-12s but these have now gone. In their place are 707s, wearing the remains of Egyptair and Sudanair colours. Close by, Petroleum Air Services Twin Otters and a few DC-3s are also to be seen.

Commercial flights are interesting, though traffic is slow. Terminal One, for domestic flights, has a viewing gallery, and the International Terminal has a cafeteria, where most of the action can be also be witnessed. Security is strict in much of Africa and the Middle East. Cairo has been, during 1997, very much on the front line. Fundamentalists are prepared to say they're sorry when the bus-load of tourists they bomb into oblivion turns out to be Greek, and not Israeli.

The Movenpick Hotel is up-market, and its location so close to the airport allows prices to rise even further. Even if a stay there isn't planned, it is worth a look, for anyone with transport. The remains of a 707 are to be found outside it.

SHARJAH International – Air Cess An-12 EL-AKN on the ramp, a shopping trolley for a few hundred grand's worth of duty free goods, so it's worth waiting for a ramp pass   Steve Wilson

GUANGZHOU Baiyun – The low wall next to the perimeter fence makes an excellent place from which to take runway shots like Zhongyuan 737-300 B-2936.   Henry Tenby

CALGARY International – The viewing area next to the taxiway for Runway 28 is ideal for photos of smaller airliners, such as Canadian Regional Dash 8 C-GLTA   Lars-Inge Grundberg

SHANNON – Whatever shows up on the ramp, such as Belavia Tu-154 EW-85538, is usually close enough to the fence to be photographed with ease.   Michel Magalhaes

BOLOGNA Guglielmo Marconi – The perimeter fence offers a close-up view of Albanian's leased A320 SU-RAB on the taxiway. Marco Finelli

CORDOBA Pajas Biancas – Southern Winds Regional Jets are based, so shots like this of LV-WPF are easily taken from the fence by the security gate. Paul Chandler

FAIRBANKS International – More an airport for cargo operations than passengers, Lynden Air Cargo Hercules N402LC was seen from the terminal windows. Paul Chandler

PALM SPRINGS Regional – The Skywest maintenance facility, off Gene Autry Boulevard, usually contains something to photograph, mostly Brasilias like N190SW. Chris Walker

BURBANK Glendale Pasadena – The top of the parking garage is the place for aircraft on the runway, this being Southwest 737-500 N519SW on the move.   Chris Walker

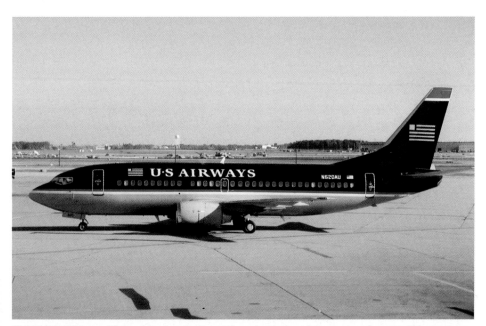

CHICAGO O'Hare – Many of the terminals are glass-fronted, and many aircraft pass within range, US Airways 737-300 N520AU being typical.   Alan Lord

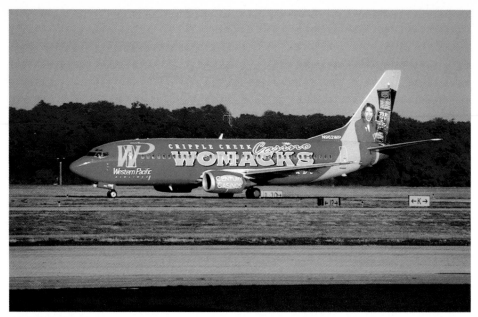

WASHINGTON Dulles International – Aircraft, such as Western Pacific flying billboard 737-300 N962WP, on Runway 19 are seen from the fence by Signature Aviation's ramp.   Chris Walker

HELSINKI Vantaa – Interesting visitors like Avroliner YL-BAK are regularly seen on the taxiways and there are vantage points outside the ends of the terminals.   Mikko Tolonen

LINZ – The terminal's rooftop deck offers a fine view but gems like (late lamented) Fred Olsen
Electra LN-FOI need a slice of luck.   Luca Dall'Olio

SAO PAULO Congonhas – Varig 737-200 PP-VPA on Air Bridge duty uses the old downtown airport
whose external deck is ideal for photography.   Paul Chandler

HONG KONG Kai Tak – For old times' sake, Qantas 747-400 VH-OJO turning onto short finals, seen from one of the many nearby apartment buildings. Paul Chandler

DAKAR Yoff – The view from the bar in the passenger terminal might be restricted but is still good enough to allow this shot of Air Mauretanie ATR-42 F-OKMS. Chris Walker

LUXOR
LXR   HELX   4m/6km

Islamic fundamentalists are doing their best to ruin the nation's tourist income but, in the main, Luxor has been well-protected from any signs of trouble. This is where to see most of the major sights and sites. On one side of the river are Karnak and Luxor temples, the Valley of the Kings etc is on the other. The airport is within a security cordon, with a check point half a mile before reaching the terminal. Strange, then, that so-called porters manage to get in. If anyone offers to pick up your suitcase, tell them (and tell them very firmly indeed) to bugger off. It's the only way.

The terminal is, to be polite, a tip. Dirty, hot, overcrowded much of the time with charter passengers, and prices that wouldn't raise an eyebrow in St Tropez. Most of the action is charter traffic, much of it from Britain, but the airport does handle some extremely interesting aircraft. What might look like an American Eagle reject at first sight turns out, on second glance, to be from Sudan. Anything might turn up here - anything from a Dutch Air Force KC-10 to a couple of Saudi Tornadoes. There are regular domestic flights to Cairo and, when times are quiet, an Egyptair 747 can put in a few circuits for an hour or two.

There are hardened shelters dotted about the field (which might contain aircraft) but there is normally only a Mi-8 to be seen on its own ramp. Landside of the terminal, some MiGs are displayed but it would be an over-statement to say they are preserved. If a coating of sand helps preservation, they're probably doing all right.

SX = GREECE

ATHENS
ATH   LGAT   Hellenikon   6m/9km S (bus 30 minutes)

The appeal of Athens has diminished little, in spite of the security precautions necessitated by terrorist activity, though the front portion of the observation deck is closed and the perimeter is closely monitored by the police. This can result in photographers being arrested for 'anti-tourist' activities, though all are released after some muscle-flexing. It should be borne in mind that using a camera at the edge of the airport is NOT an offence, though it is very unpopular with those who have to be seen to be coming to grips with present day security requirements. Most of what people in uniform do is harass, the intention (usually quite successful) is to deter.

Considering first the Olympic terminal and its viewing facilities, these can be dismissed as being virtually non-existent. There are no windows in the terminal, so the movements of the smaller Olympic aircraft cannot be seen. At the extreme northern end of the terminal, large windows offer some view of the Olympic training aircraft, Cessna 152s and Cherokee, and the air taxi Ecureuils. Reasonable photographs can only be obtained by negotiation with Olympic Aviation, on the other side of this small apron. It is necessary to walk across this apron to talk to the people who can give that permission! The Olympic Aviation hangar normally contains one or two Shorts or ATRs undergoing maintenance checks.

The International Terminal is split into two buildings, for departures and arrivals, and facilities are different at each. The arrivals building has a lounge fronting the apron, approached via a corridor at the right hand side, though the part of the ramp it overlooks only has a limited amount of traffic. The glass and the westerly aspect should be borne in mind in the afternoons.

The departures building was famous for the backpackers who slept on the roof overnight but the police have taken a negative stance on this activity as part of the clampdown. At the same time, they also sealed off the front of the deck, where photographs of all movements were quite easy to take. The remaining part of the roof looks down on the north ramp (quite busy) and diagonally across the stands in front of the arrivals building.

Photographers will be frustrated by these facilities at the terminal, especially when there are so many interesting movements. Consequently, the perimeter of the field will continue to be investigated, no matter how much it conflicts with officialdom. Since many of the airport workers

222

live in Glyfada, a gap in the fence at the edge of the coach park has been created, allowing them to take the short cut, and this has been used by enthusiasts for many years. The gate next to the 33R holding point has always yielded impressive results for the average photographer. The presence of El Al aircraft usually entails at least one Israeli security vehicle being somewhere in the vicinity and, since they can make life difficult, caution is advised if confronted. Sensible behaviour helps, of course.

The attraction of this corner of the field is increased by its proximity to two hotels much favoured by spotters: the Fenix roof is closed, and the only view is from inside the building, for residents. The Emmantina has better facilities to compensate for being a little further out. The roof here has a bar and a pool . . . and a very good view. Security personnel have paid visits, but nothing unpleasant has been reported. It must be borne in mind that the local weather pattern is changing, resulting the prevailing winds being increasingly from the south. This means that Runway 15L sees greater use, with a corresponding reduction in the amount of aircraft which approach over Glyfada. In other words, it can now be more a matter of luck.

Athens has much to offer the enthusiast, and the weather is probably best in May, June and September (mid summer being very hot); the attractions of the holiday resort of Glyfada on one side and historic Athens on the other, and aircraft in delightful profusion.

Intercontinental flights between Western Europe and the Far East make stops here (though many are at unsociable hours), European scheduled traffic is attracted by the world of commerce and holidaymakers, and charter flights are abundant from all over the rest of Europe. Airlines from all the Middle East countries fly here in quantity and executive movements are also plentiful throughout the year. To list the traffic in detail would take up unnecessary space but visitors can expect an assortment of movements unmatched by any other airport in Europe.

Military activity hasn't been completely curtailed: the Hellenic Air Force operate crew training sorties by C-130s, YS-11s (though both break off approach early) and there are occasional visits by C-47s, F-104s and T-33s.

Hellenikon isn't normally busy, by any stretch of the imagination, but the weekends see plenty of German charters, when scheduled traffic is quietest.

Car hire is expensive and unnecessary, as walking to Hellenikon from Glyfada is good exercise, buses are regular from the city and taxis are cheap. Most of the buses go to the Olympic side of the airport, though an irregular yellow bus service links both sides. From Athens, the Olympic buses are quick and comfortable, leaving from the terminal on Syngrou Avenue, while local buses leave from Syntagma Square, cost less but take longer.

Notable by its absence from Hellenikon is general aviation, though a few visiting (mostly foreign) light aircraft can be seen tucked in one corner. This is to be found at MARATHON, though the journey there by bus takes time . . . a lot of time, and a passport will be useful. A street map of Athens is also handy, to locate the bus stops before setting off. Most of Athens buses use Zappio (an official building in a large park) as the terminus. Tickets should be bought beforehand, and punched into the machine. False economy is running the risk for a few pennies, as the penalties are strict. The No.122 from Glyfada passes the coastal side of the airport. A brisk walk from Zappio along Vasilissis Sofias to Leoforos Alexandras, where the country bus for Kato Souli leaves, is followed by a pleasant journey to Marathon. Asking the driver to say when the bus reaches Aerodromo Marathon helps missing the stop. It's a fifteen minute walk to the field, where the passport can normally be exchanged for a walk around the ramp.

SPATA, Athens' new airport and it should be operational by 2000. Plans show a central highway, one both sides of which are terminals and a runway. There should be fourteen gates plus another ten at a satellite in Phase One, to be on one side of the road. In time, and rather like Jakarta, the other side will be developed. Clearly, it's rather early to be discussing much more than this.

HERAKLION
HER   LGIR   Nikos Kazantzakis 3m/5km S (bus 40 minutes)

Crete is a major tourist island in the Mediterranean and its airport handles a predictably large amount of charter traffic. Scheduled links with the rest of the world are via Athens, so the traffic is dominated by Olympic A300s. The terminal faces the runway, and the A-7 dispersals on the far side, with a few air jetties restricting the view of proceedings. The balcony is for departing passengers, though other views can be had from the restaurant. The road leading to Heraklion curves around the edge of the apron, with shuttle buses and ground handling equipment in the foreground, but it does allow quite a decent chance to see the movements on the apron and runway, sufficiently so for the authorities to have posted 'no photography' signs here.

The main car park overlooks a military apron where two or three C-130s are often noted, with the hardened A-7 shelters, on the far side of the runway, directly behind. The beach, to the east of the airport, is close enough for photographs of movements to be taken with a 200mm lens, except for the SD3.30s and Do228s, which are too small.

KERKYRA
CFU   LGKR   I Kapodistrias   1m/1.5km S (bus 10 minutes

British and Dutch charters make up a good proportion of the traffic but the passenger terminal is not the place to watch or photograph them. The delapidated little terminal has a coffee shop with a bit of a view - the windows can be opened - but it is neither the nicest nor the quietest of places. Try instead the Imperial Hotel, in Perama, opposite the threshold of Runway 35. Leave the terminal in the direction of the end of Runway 17, the only direction possible, then make a couple of right turns onto the road which passes the cemetery. There is a choice of roads, both of which lead to the hotel. Along the front of the building is a deck which faces west over the lagoon to the runway. A landing 757 needs about 100mm focal length. Photography from here is obviously best in the mornings.

The causeway across the lagoon can be used only by pedestrians, and is much favoured by the local population. On the far side of the causeway, beside the lagoon, is a cafe which offers a good view all afternoon, as it faces east. Photography here does require concentration. The beach here features large numbers of topless sunbathers which, if nothing else, mean that it shouldn't be necessary to take a book when airport movements go quiet.

KOS
KGS   LGKO   10m/km

Not all the Greek islands have short runways, necessitating night flights, and Kos is longer than most. However, charters do seem to peak in the middle of the night. Kos is, these days, about as Greek as the Eurovision Song Contest. It caters for the Dutch (who have their own restaurants), Germans, lots of Scandinavians and, of course, the Carling Black Label community. People who are prepared to fly Cattle Class, for the best part of four hours in the middle of the night, get pretty much what they deserve when they land here. To be fair, there are probably airports in the Back End of Russia that are worse.

For anyone over the age of thirty, the airport is disgusting. Since most travellers seem to be either retired Brits (who remember how lovely things used to be - and pretend they still are) or the Very Young, nobody cares much. To see and photograph the action there is, to the right of the terminal, a chapel on a hill. From up here, everything can be seen. During most of the day, it doesn't amount to much.

MYKONOS
JMK   LGMK

Mykonos is one of the more interesting islands, though its airport offers only one exciting moment: if arriving direct on a charter jet, the landing requires what is described as more rapid retardation than usual! A balcony to the left of the terminal is useful for the occasional portrait. Most of the movements, and there aren't many, tend to be small Olympic Aviation propliners doing their lifeline service to Athens. What can be seen at the airport comes a distant second to what can be seen on the beach.

224

RHODES
RHO   LGRP   Paradisi   10m/km SW (bus 30 minutes)

This tourist airport handles plenty of traffic, but the terminal has no viewing facilities. Anyone wanting to monitor every movement will stay at the hotels between the airport and Trianda: these are the Sunflower, Blue Bay and Sun Beach. An indication of the proximity of this area to the threshold of the runway may be gleaned from the fact that visual aids are sometimes not essential to note under-wing registrations! The mention of 'every movement' is a reminder that sleep can be interrupted by arrivals in the night. Light sleepers would do well to stay elsewhere on the island and catch the bus to the airport from Mandraki Square.

SANTORINI
JTR   LGSR   Thira

Crete's Minoan culture came to an abrupt end over two thousand years ago, when this volcano exploded. What remains is a crescent-shaped island which once formed part of the volcano's rim: civilisation steeped in tradition and culture. The airport's passenger terminal is modern but only compared with the island's history. It is primitive and enjoyable. The departure lounge is out in the open and the baggage reclaim is the trolley behind a tractor.
   The runway is shared by the small civil facility and an Air Force presence, mostly peaceful until the occasional commuter flight arrives. Anyone visiting will spend little time here, being content with three, at the most, photos of the Olympic Aviation island hoppers. Olympic 737s are not unknown, however. Charters from Scandinavia, Germany and Austria add to the occasional British aircraft. Military activity is, under normal circumstances, subdued but it can include anything from a C-130 to the pilot of an F-104 or F-5E showing off to the holidaymakers.

THESSALONIKI
SKG   LGTS   Makedonia   10m/16km S (bus 25 minutes)

In northern Greece, on the mainland, is where another military base shares the civilian runway. Enthusiasts who have visited for a day, taking advantage of the attractive air fares, have occasionally been allowed a tour of the base, though no photographs are allowed.

S2 = BANGLADESH
DHAKA
DAC   VGZR   Zia International

There are places you migth fancy going that turn out to be a disappointment. This is one where it's best not to fancy going in the first place. Zia International is not what you'd call spotter-friendly. It is, however, quite a useful stopover because the entire Biman fleet can be wrapped up in a few mid-morning hours on the average day. The passenger terminal faces the single runway with airline maintenance to the right and a military base to the left (on the far side of the runway).
   From the transit lounge (which sounds quite civilised until you get there) there is a perfect view of all movements but photography is totally out of the question. As you would expect I a Third World transit area, the duty free shop offers extremely good value and, if you get stuck there, the snack bar is sometimes open. There are Emirates A310s, Saudia 747s, Thai MD-11s and A330s, plus a few Russian visitors. If you don't see it on the apron, and it belongs to Biman, the odds are it's at the maintenance base and can be seen while taxiing past.

S7 = SEYCHELLES

MAHE
SEZ   FSSS   Seychelles International   6m/9km SE of Victoria

Without doubt a romantic destination but the airport is not going to be one of the main reasons for visiting. The runway is built on reclaimed land to be capable of taking 747-400s (which it does). British Airways and Air France are the operators but Kenya Airways, Air Europe (Italy), Condor and Air Seychelles also operate wide-bodies. The USAF operate the occasional 707 or C-130, related to a satellite tracking station on the island. Regular inter-island activity keeps the pace ticking over all day.

The international passenger terminal is a simple two-storey affair, offering no views of the aircraft until into the departure lounges. A few yards to the north is the more modest inter-island terminal. At either side of the main terminal are grassed areas where the apron can be seen but the fence can make some angles difficult for photography. This is not too much of a problem as there are other places to go at both ends of the field.

When Runway 31 is in use, try a shop called Butcher's, about a mile south of the terminal. Movements using the opposite direction runway, 13, can be seen from a similar spot, on reclaimed land to the north. It must be borne in mind that Seychelles is a socialist single-party state, which has its own ideas about security. The police appear to show no interest in spotting activity but it would be wise to be discreet when in the presence of someone wearing a military uniform.

PRASLIN
PRI   FSPP

If any reader ever dreams of taking the perfect photo of a Twin Otter or an Islander, this is the place to visit. The island is small and its airport handles the regular inter-island flights from Mahe, its only air-link with the outside world. The passenger terminal is as modest and delightful as the rest of the island, ideal for seeing the movements arrive every 45 minutes or so. Only four or five aircraft are involved, however. The Indian Ocean is a stunning crystal blue, over which the aircraft come in to land. If you can't take good pictures here, you can't take good pictures at all! Praslin is the sort of place to get away from aviation, and everything else associated with a normal way of life, so aviation could take a back seat for a couple of days.

TC = TURKEY

DALAMAN
DLM   LTBS

Security precautions in the Middle East are so well documented, anyone who gets into trouble is certain to have ignored several warnings. Turkey has a reputation, ill-deserved it must be said, because of the film 'Midnight Express'. If the West wants drug smuggling stopped, it must expect appropriate action closer to the source.

This is a modern airport, built to handle the tourist trade being developed along Turkey's beautiful coastline. Open scrubland surrounds the field, where views are possible. This is more than can be said for the passenger terminal, inside which the only windows onto the apron are from the departure area. An early check-in at peak charter times allows a few British aircraft to be seen, with the possibility of one or, at the most two, Turkish airliners.

Doubtless, other days see mostly arrivals from other countries, Germany and Scandinavia particularly. As Turkey continues to invest in its tourist trade, Dalaman will handle visitors in greater numbers and variety.

226

ISTANBUL
IST   LTBA   Ataturk   6m/9km SW

The Turkish way of doing things is difficult for westerners to understand. Everything seems very strict. Underneath, the locals take no notice and just get on with life. Thus, at Istanbul airport the army, who provide the security, appear very daunting. Stay there for two or three days, talk to a couple of these guys and they can be very friendly indeed, once they've sized you up.

Around the perimeter, every 200 metres or so, are watch towers, mostly because the field is shared with an active military base. Nothing more to be said there, then! In other words, it's a case of having to stick to the terminal area. Probably as good as anywhere is the cafeteria in the domestic terminal, which has been refurbished. By treating yourself to the occasional purchase (and prices are quite reasonable), this can be a good place to settle, largely because it gives the plain clothes men a chance to watch what you're doing without actually making contact until the feel like it. What they say, and how they handle things, is pretty much in your own hands.

To the left is the cargo apron with half a dozen stands. To the right is the international terminal, beyond the site for the new terminal (under construction late 1997). A walk towards the international terminal, which has no views at all, reveals much of the general aviation, parked on the far side of Runway 18/36.

Trains operate from the city to the nearby resort of Yesilkoy, where landing aircraft approach over the sea. Photos from here aren't bad at all.This is probably the only place anywhere near the airport that spotters aren't conscious of having an escort. The Polet Ramada is slightly upmarket but it does have rooms overlooking 06/24 and the domestic/cargo ramps. Rather less expensive (and very basic) is the Motel Yesilkoy - about £30 a night including breakfast. It's close to the town centre, the beach and it's virtually underneath the flightpath to Runway 36.

There is an interesting aviation museum with over thirty exhibits including a Viscount and a couple of C-47s. It receives few visitors, even at about 50 pence admission. Even in the museum, you will not be alone. As soon as you arrive, someone will appear and start to show an active interest in the exhibits. This seems to dry up the minute you leave.

Istanbul airport is not for the lone traveller. Two or three guys do better but, if they are to survive unmolested and unthreatened, they will be on their absolute best behaviour every minute. There are some parts of the world where one camera represents a greater threat to the Powers-That-Be than a couple of boxes of Kalashnikovs. Istabul airport might be one of them. It's stinking hot in summer, so much so that the arrivals hall in the domestic terminal is unbearable, and horribly cold in winter. So, a trip in spring or autumn then? Certainly, but three days would be plenty.

IZMIR
ADB   LTBJ   Cumaovasi-Adnan Menderes   16m/25km S

Izmir is taking its share of the tourist trade, and the airport handles a small amount of charters from Europe. Condor and EAS are seen from the terminal's glazed frontage, as is the military base. Caution and common sense could result in a photograph or two but plain clothes and armed patrols are meant to be taken seriously as a deterrant. Discreet noting of registrations and serials is wise, and the best opportunity to see the military aircraft is probably from the taxiway.

TF = ICELAND

AKUREYRI
AEY   BIAR   3m/5km SW

Outside Reykjavik, this is the next most probable destination for a foreign visitor. Akureyri is on the scenic north coast, and can be reached by regional services from Reykjavik. The cost of the air fare from Reykjavik may seem expensive compared with overland transport but a bus takes ten hours, compared with one hour by Flugfelag Nordurland Twin Otter. Their small fleet includes some Piper twins and they are based at the airport. The occasional visitor on the ramp can be seen with ease from the fence, and the pace is slow enough for ramp access to be possible after short negotiation. June is the best moth for visiting and, to a lesser extent, May and July.

REYKJAVIK
REK   BIRK   3m/5km S (bus 40 minutes)

The enthusiast who has been everywhere and seen everything may consider Iceland as a destination which offers something different. The capital city nestles in the warmer southwest corner, with an airport for domestic traffic and general aviation, and another for international flights. The domestic field is close to the city, with a small terminal building handling the F.27 flights. Views of these movements are more than adequate from inside the building. Variety is supplied, though not in quantity, by Norlandair Twin Otters, Eastair Navajos and Odin's Jetstreams. The Loftleidir Hotel overlooks the commuter apron, and the variety seen from its rooms is interesting. Movements are modest but unusual, by most standards. The coastguard base can also be seen.

KEFLAVIK
KEF   BIKF   32m/50km SW of Reykjavik

Some thirty miles southwest of the city, on a promontory, is Keflavik where Icelandair operate their international hub and spoke operations. 737s and 757s arrive in the afternoon, all visible from the approach road next to the modern terminal building. The 737s arrive from Europe, to connect with the 757s, mostly on their way between Luxembourg and a range of destinations on the USA's east coast. On the far side of the runway is the USAF base where C-130s and P-3s are most visible. Other movements are sporadic, featuring a few tech-stops and airline movements such as SAS MD-80/87s and Greenlandair Dash 7s.

TR = GABON

LIBREVILLE
LBV   FOOL   Leon M'ba

This is, without doubt, West Africa's most interesting airport, with a surprising collection of about eighty light aircraft, half of which are twins. A long apron on one side of the runway has the passenger terminal more or less in the middle. To the left is the civil side, with the National Guard hangar at the far end, occupied by an ATR-42 and a Bandeirante, several T-34Cs and a few immaculate Harvards. The Guard's next door neighbour is the general aviation area, shared by Air Service and Air Affaires, the latter operating a varied fleet of Bandeirante, Lear Jet, HS125, King Airs etc. With so many Frenchmen around this area, it is easy for a European to look part of the scene, and photos of some of the more unusual residents and visitors should present no problem, as access to the apron may be obtained.

The Air Gabon hangar is often empty, usually with an ATR-72 and 737 out on the ramp, in the company of the Air Service CASA 212s, and visible from the terrace, more or less opposite the domestic terminal building.

To the right/east of the terminal is the small cargo area and a large military compound. A selection of hangars spreads, seemingly at random, eastwards and the extensive transport fleet of the Gabon Air Force is parked here. A French Air Force KC-135 sits on the cargo apron, nearer to the terminal, on rotational detachment.

The excellent terrace above the main terminal is normally packed with plenty of Gabonese, awaiting the arrival of a 747 or a DC-10 from Europe, and the odd gendarme is on duty to enforce the 'no camera' warnings, posted everywhere. With permission, good standard lens shots of civil airliners are possible. Traffic at Libreville is generally always interesting, though some of the European movements will have a familiar look to them. Really exotic visitors include the likes of a Lina Congo F.28 or 737. Nigerian 737s appear most days but the Air Zaire 737 rarely keeps its schedule, and Cameroon 737s visit about three times a week. Regular appearances are made by many of the Port Gentil-based Air Inter Gabon fleet.

TU = IVORY COAST

ABIDJAN
ABJ	DIAP	Port Buet	13m/20km E

The passenger terminal sits at one side of the single runway. To its north are the six hangars used by Air Afrique and other carriers, and to the south is the parking area for general aviation. A few light aircraft are also parked at the front edge of the main apron. Most of Abidjan's visitors are making transit stops, which means restriction of movement once inside the terminal.

Normally there is little to see on the ramp, so most of it will be recorded when landing or taking off, as the airliner taxis by. Assuming the same runway direction is used for both landing and departure, a window seat offers one chance. Prior reference to a JP Airline Fleets list of Abidjan-based aircraft reveals that, apart from the governmental aircraft (TU-V..) almost everything carries TU-T.., so only the last two characters need to be recorded. With only one shot at a rather unusual array of machinery, it helps to be prepared beforehand.

UK = UZBEKISTAN

TASHKENT
TAS	UTTT	Yuzhny

When the Israeli Air Force paid their unexpected visit to Entebbe, they must have left it in a similar condition to Tashkent. The passenger terminal is now dirty, shabby, run-down and crumbling. The price of freedom and democracy can be seen here: once one of the greatest economic powers, this is now the Third World. It costs money to build runways but it costs more money to maintain them, hence the number of runways in the CIS states abandoned for lack of finance to make them operable.

Soviet jet airliners were built to keep people employed. Few of them flew much. Many of them now lie, like so much litter, around Yuzhny airport. Naturally, this makes it a number-cruncher's paradise. If an aviation enthusiast has to be stuck for four hours or so in a transit lounge, this would be the place to choose.

Binoculars can be used. Discretion might be wise. There is now such a general air of couldn't-care-less in the CIS that maybe nobody will take any notice of anyone writing down aircraft registrations. It seems more likely that you'd be offered a flight in one or, for a few dollars more, the chance to buy one. It must not be assumed that anybody actually owns anything. People here desperately need cash. If someone has an excuse to part a stranger from his passport, the motive could be money.

The quantity of ex-Aeroflot aircraft is extraordinary. Most of them sport hybrid Uzbekistan colour schemes and titles. There are Il-86s, Il-72s, Il-62s, Tu-134s and Tu-154s, plus an assortment of Antonovs. Aviation fuel (and possibly paint) seems to be more valuable than the aircraft, and certainly more difficult to get. Most of the aircraft at Yuzhny will disintegrate at an alarming pace, such is the climate. Parts will be stripped from most in order to keep some in flying condition. This, is must be added, does not necessarily mean airworthy as interpreted by western authorities.

Virtually the entire Uzbekistan fleet can be recorded in a single day. Turkmenistan and Kazakhstan Airways are frequent visitors, and Aeroflot can seen be seen in large numbers. Yuzhny, for all its faults, is still somewhere to make the pulse race.

229

UN = KAZAKHSTAN

AKTYUBINSK
AKX   UATT

Remote from almost everywhere, on the central Asian steppes, it seems like this is the end of the world. Ask the locals and they'll say it isn't . . . but you can see it from there! This large industrial city has an airport which possesses a military feel, despite there being no fighters in sight. The passenger terminal is small, and offers good views of the apron. Most of what is to be seen on the stands are passing Yak-40s.

Most of Kazakhstan's allocation of ex-Aeroflot aircraft is parked about a mile north of the terminal. There are rows and rows of Yak-40s, Tu-134s, Tu-154s and An-2 biplanes, all idle, and most of them unlikely to move ever again.

UR = UKRAINE

KIEV
KBP   UKBB   Borispol   24m/38km E (bus 55 minutes)

This is Kiev's main airport, with its passenger terminal between the two parallel runways which are aligned north/south. It would appear that only one runway is in regular use, but this could be an isolated report which coincided with maintenance work. More likely, they can't afford the repairs. The terminal's first floor windows offer a good view of the proceedings. Traffic is mostly Tu-134s and Tu-154s, as is to be expected, though there are plenty of inactive Il-76s to be seen.

On the far side of the unused runway is an apron where the Il-76s are parked, possibly up to twenty at one time.

KIEV
IEV   UKKK   Zhulyany   2m/3km S (bus 10 minutes)

Historically this was a domestic airport, where operations linked the regional capital with its surroundings. For this reason, the majority of aircraft to be seen are Antonovs (24s and 26s). It is possible to see some of the movements from the terminal but the facilities are not ideal, by any stretch of the imagination.

Kiev has two other airfields: GOSTOMEL, some 20 miles to the northwest, is used by Antonov for testing purposes. What can be seen is without doubt extremely interesting. To what extent it is wise to investigate in depth or take photos is another matter. The new way of doing things is fine in theory but it is in situations like this when the enthusiast realises that security will take a while to be relaxed. CHAIKA is also known as Kiev West, and is nothing more than a grass strip used for general aviation.

SIMFERAPOL
SIP   UKFF

This city is in the Crimea peninsula, so it attracts plenty of tourists heading for resorts along the Black Sea coast. Domestic flights, still operated mostly by Aeroflot, use one terminal and tourist traffic goes to the other. There are no viewing facilities in either, mainly because this is an active (a strange term, under the current circumstances) military airfield. The MiG-25s can be seen at a distance from the moving aircraft.

VH = AUSTRALIA

ADELAIDE
ADL   APAD   5m/8km W (bus 30 minutes)

Vickers Vimy G-EAOU arrived in Australia in 1919, when the journey from England was more of an adventure and travelling time was rather more than a day. Keith and Ross Smith left England on November 12 and arrived in Australia on December 10. Their Vimy is now housed in its own museum building in the terminal area.

Both international and domestic terminals are good for viewing and photography. Access is possible, through security, to the departure lounges. The international terminal is, by far, the least interesting part of this airport. A walk down the road to the old part of the field, towards the domestic terminal, reveals first the general aviation ramp. Beyond the domestic terminal are hangars and aprons, where some of the more interesting aircraft can be seen at close quarters. Among these smaller are operators: Air Charter, Sky-Link, Lloyd Aviation and Rossair have facilities, though there are few aircraft above Cessna 402 size.

PARAFIELD is home to most of Adelaide's general aviation, and there are some small fleet operators also. Because it is to be regarded as an airfield, there is little in the way of security measures which would prevent a sensible enthusiast from passing a useful half-hour here.

ALICE SPRINGS
ASP   7m/11km S

There are few places in the world as far in the Outback as Alice Springs. It would be easy to imagine a rickety old terminal, with old fashioned facilities, like the stage set for Crocodile Dundee's Walkabout Creek. That's Alice Springs! More remarkably, this airport is the *new* one. Whilst there is a garden in front of the terminal, it doesn't offer much of a view through the security screen. There is so much planting, vehicles and other paraphenalia to obscure the view, photography is practically impossible.

The old airport, Connellan, is now the Central Australian Aviation Museum, to be found on Memorial Avenue, off Larapinta Drive. On a pole outside is Flying Doctor Service Drover VH-FDC. Entry to the museum is free and the exhibits include aircraft up to DH Dove size. There is so little of interest at Alice Springs airport, mostly because the scheduled visitors can be seen just as easily, and certainly in greater comfort, at more accessible airports. Folks come here to see Ayers Rock, and there aren't too many reasons for prolonging the stay!

Any desire to imagine AYERS ROCK as an exotic location is best maintained by not visiting it. Most of the services are operated from Alice Springs, where there is just as little chance of seeing them well. To the left of the terminal is a general aviation facility which is used by the many sightseeing flights.

BRISBANE
BNE   ABBN   International   7m/11km NE (bus 40 minutes)

The airport occupies a large area of land at the edge of Moreton Bay, between a canal and the Brisbane River. The original runways and terminals occupy the southern corner of the field, close to Gateway Arterial Road. Arriving by road from the city, the road continues for several miles to the international terminal and passes on the left some hangars and a lay-by. This parking facility is officially recognized, and is ideal for watching and photographing the airliners as they taxi by. The general aviation ramp usually contains one or two Lloyd aircraft, and the general aviation ramp next to the Ansett terminal has the Flightwest and Jetcare hangars, which can be accessible, by negotiation. Don't forget the Southern Cross museum, because it is an integral part of Australia's aviation history.

Within the international terminal is an observation deck, offering close views of proceedings. However, there are only about eight stands, so close proximity to the aircraft can be a mixed blessing. When a Qantas 747 is parked, the view becomes severely restricted. A wide angle lens may be required - good news if present when one of the international visitors arrives, such as an Air Niugini A310, an Air New Zealand 767 - or not so bad if it's an Air Pacific 737.

Brisbane can be quite busy early in the morning, and an airband radio is particularly useful. It has been practice for pilots to use the aircraft's registration, rather than flight number, when talking to the tower. To many enthusiasts, this would represent paradise, as movements can be identified from a rather greater distance than usual! For those who find it too hot, standing beside the road, cooler close encounters can be obtained by visiting the domestic terminal, passing through the security check, and watching from a departure lounge.

Temperatures do rise quite alarmingly during the day, so spending too much time walking along perimeter fences is not a good idea. The end of Runway 01 is only about a fifteen minute walk from the domestic terminal but the comfort of an air conditioned car is safer. It also allows "proper" clothes to be worn, which are adviseable if seeking access to the various hangars.

The lack of significant quantities of general aviation at the international airport is explained by a visit to ARCHERFIELD. It would be reasonable to expect a hundred and fifty light aircraft. Some of these are genuinely interesting, like an RAAF Tiger Moth, Hawker Hunter fuselages, and Hempels Aviation have an An-2. Ipswich Road leads out of town, and a left turn after passing Rochlea at Granard Road reveals the field. The small terminal is to be found on the far side, on Beatty Road.

CAIRNS
CNS   ABCS   3m/5km

The Great Barrier Reef attracts large numbers of tourists. Because of the distances involved, most of them arrive by air, and Cairns is the airport they use. Across the road from the domestic terminal is a Bush Pilots Airways DC-3 on a pole, the only remaining link with the old days.

Everything else about Cairns is very modern and pleasant. The international terminal has an observation gallery, though the view is poor. However, it is from here around lunchtime that an Air Niugini F.28 or A310 can be seen. Qantas movements tend to be mostly 747s. A covered walkway links the two terminals, at the far side of which is the ramp used by the regional carriers, all visible from the fence. Twin Otters, Bandeirantes and Brasilias, operated by the local air services are usually in evidence. On the far side of the runway is quite a varied collection of general aviation. This includes Customs service Aero Commanders and Beech 99s, but the continued exisence of the two Kamov helicopters has not been confirmed. With scheduled activity so slow, any lengthy visit might be best spent near the Flightwest ramp, subject to the heat.

CANBERRA
CBR   ASCB   4m/6km

This small airport handles a fair amount of traffic, all seen from the bar inside the small passenger terminal. On the far side of the field is an air force base, where a few of the based Falcon 900s can usually be seen. Canberra, being a planned city, has a very definite layout: at the centre is Capitol Hill, surrounded by State Circle. Leaving this ring road to the northeast, on King's Avenue, the next intersection after crossing the water is Morshead Drive, which leads to the airport.

DARWIN
DRW   ADDN   5m/8km W

Technically, Darwin is closer to the real Crocodile Dundee country than Alice Springs. The movie, and its successor, have generated enough interest in the area for tourism to be growing. What they come to see is Kakadu National Park.

There are two runways, 11/29 and 18/36. Arriving by road, there is a roundabout ofering three options, all of which are worth pursuing. To the left is the cargo area, normally rather quiet, beyond which, at the far side of the shorter runway, 18/36, is a helipad used by Bristows and Lloyds. The hangar could contain something, if there's nothing on the ramp. Straight on from the roundabout is the passenger terminal, used mostly by Qantas and Ansett. Pass through a security check and there might be something to see or photograph. International traffic includes the occasional Garuda A300, Singapore A310, Malaysian A330 or Royal Brunei 767, so Darwin clearly offers quality as well as quantity.

The quantity is found by turning right at the roundabout. This is where the general aviation ramps are found. Cross over the next roundabout and park. In front, and to the left, are Pel Air, Ross Air and Skywest. At the far end of the street is a ramp used by coastwatch aircraft and, on the right are the aprons of Executive Air and Wimray Air Charter. The road to the right passes the ramp, at the far side of which are more hangars - for Arnhem Air, Phoenix Air, Hardy Aviation and Air Frontier. Air North's DC-3, VH-MMA, is probably the star resident.

DUNK ISLAND
DKI

Just off the coast, about halfway between Townsville and Cairns, this is becoming one of Australia's star tourist destinations. The airport, if it can be called that, is served by a couple of Australian Regional Twin Otters each day. Photographs present no problems, as long as you can guess which way they are going to taxi!

KALGOORLIE
KGI   APKG

This is not the sort of place anyone would drive to, because there's nowhere near it. Maybe it could be a stopover, between Adelaide and Perth, in which case it might be of interest. This is a modest airport with a small, modern terminal for domestic flights. Outside is a terrace from which the apron can be seen but the perspex glazing makes photos impossible. It does, however, ensure that anyone standing there doesn't get a face-ful of part-burned kerosene as something taxis out. Fortunately, at the sides are rather lower fences from which excellent photos are possible. Photos, that is, of Skywest Fokker 50s and Ansett F.28s and 146s. It's a few minutes walk to the general aviation apron, home to about thirty or so aircraft including one or two operated by the Flying Doctor Service.

MELBOURNE
MEL   AMML   Tullamarine   13m/20km NW (bus 30 minutes)

Approaching the airport from the city on the Sunbury road, the busy field of Essendon is passed en route. Little of Tullamarine is seen before arriving in the central complex, even from the elevated road. The car park has an Australian feel, with its many eucalyptus, or gum trees as they are known, but the pendant DC-3 which used to be here is flying again.

There are two observation decks, one of which is well signposted. The other, which still exists, takes more finding and offers better views (neither is brilliant for the photographer, the Qantas one being all but useless most of the day). Behind the Ansett Australian check-in area on the departures level is a staircase which leads to the deck. Because the right-hand deck faces only the threshold of Runway 09/27, it is the most remote from the intersecting main runway, 16/34. To the left/south of the now-Qantas deck are general aviation ramps, the cargo centre and, in the distance, the maintenance areas.

International movements feature mostly the regular range of European and Asian carriers, whose aircraft can be seen at almost any major airport, with Qantas dominating. Scheduled movements are busiest in the early morning and at tea time, though there is a small peak in the middle of the day. Between these times, the going is slow, only compensated by the occasional 737 of Air Nauru or Air Caledonie.

The maintenance areas of Ansett Australian are in a remote corner, a couple of kilometres away, and accessible via Melrose Drive and Links Road. Some out-of-service Fokkers can usually be photographed from the fence. By following the signs to Tullamarine Country Club on Operations Road, an official spectators' park has been made, right next to Runway 16/34. However, there is a wire fence to hamper photography, and Runway 09/27 is a long way off. Just a little further on is the fire station, which has a derelict F.27 behind it. Towards the end of 09 is a Bristol Freighter, rather derelict. Qantas keep a DC-3 at the rear of their maintenance area, easily seen from the Ansett deck, but too distant to photograph. General aviation activity is subdued, as much of the action takes place elsewhere . . .

MELBOURNE
MEB AMEN Essendon 7m/11km NW (tram 30 minutes)

Accessible by the No. 59 tram from the city, Essendon is only a few miles from Tullamarine. The Sunbury buses, Nos. 478 and 479, operate to Tullamarine, with the stop on Matthews Road, on the far side of Tullamarine Freeway. A walk over the bridge leads directly to the airport entrance on English Street, a few yards away. From Tullamarine, and assuming you have a rental car, backtrack to the second roundabout, by Ansett maintenance and, instead of heading along Links Road to the terminal, go straight on to the bottom and turn left towards Sharpes Drive. Go to the end and it joins the Freway to the city. The entrance, as above, is at English Street. The drive is only about five minutes.

The first impression is of a sprawling airfield, with lots of hangars. Even without ramp access, there are so many aircraft parked on the grass next to the various roads, the photographer with only an hour or two to spare can leave with an interesting selection. A car will undoubtedly save time, and Essendon needs time, more than anything else.

At the end of the street is the administrative building, well worth a call to let someone know what the visit is all about. Some help may then be available. In front is a large, crammed, apron with another to the right serving the passenger terminal. There are hangars to the left, on Wirraway Road, and more at the end of a short road, called Short Road. Nomad Road leads across English Street to the IPEC hangar and the rest of the main parking areas and hangars are on Bristol Street, facing one of the two runways.

A limited amount of Melbourne's third level traffic operates here. The small terminal handles it, and a few executive movements. A request for access to the ramps is normally successful, as the Australians are renowned for being fairly relaxed. Twin-engined aircraft are numerous, though the two hundred or so residents include only two or three dozen executive types. The largest inmates were IPEC's Argosies, but these were cut up in 1990. They also operate two DC-9s, which are normally seen at Tullamarine.

A serious interest in the smaller aircraft on the Australian register will also necessitate a visit to Melbourne's third airport, MOORABBIN. With two airports in such close proximity, it is inevitable that the third is on the other side of the city. The trip is worthwhile, however, as scheduled services are operated by Aus-Air Bandeirantes and Navajo Chieftains, and by Promair Navajos.

PERTH
PER APPH 6m/9km E (bus 45 minutes)

The passenger facilities at Perth are placed on opposite sides of the runway. The smart, modern International Terminal has a wonderful (though glazed) observation gallery, spanning all six of the air jetties. The view includes the domestic movements on the far side but distance and heat haze hinder identification of the traffic. International traffic has increased to about twenty flights a day, basically to be summed up as British Airways, South African and Air Mauritius plus plenty of carriers from south-east Asia. Malaysian and Cathay Pacific A330s are considered run of the mill.

From a separate approach road off Tonkin Highway, the domestic facilities offer a far better, and somewhat busier, prospect. There are two terminals, for Qantas and Ansett. From the Qantas building there are excellent views of their 767s, 737s and 146s, as well as Ansett's 767s, A320s, 146s, Fokker 50s and Jetstreams. Afternoons are definitely best and, every evening, an Air Transport International DC-8 does a Market Garden flight to Singapore.

Perth is the most isolated ciy in the world. Its next door neighbour is Adelaide, some 1500 miles away, so air links are quite important, to say the least. General aviation is fairly active, with Skipper Aviation making up the bulk of the fifty or so residents, all visible from the fence.

By far the greater majority of Perth's smaller aircraft are to be found at the busy JANDAKOT field, named after a suburb on the Fremantle side of the Swan River. Drive for a bout fifteen kilometres down Leach Highway (7), which joins Tonkin Highway (4) just south of Perth Airport, and there are signs for Jandakot. The 25 km journey, southeast from the city on Kwinana Freeway (2), is essential for anyone with an interest in Australian aviation. The Royal Flying Doctor Service has some aircraft based here, and there are other operators, such as Aerodata, Corpair and Central Air, to be seen. There is a raised, and very pleasant, viewing area. If in the vicinity, it's also worth looking out for the excellent aviation museum at BULL CREEK.

SYDNEY
SYD   ASSY   Kingsford Smith   5m/8km S (bus 30 minutes)

Despite its official name, the airport is still generally known as Mascot, after the suburb over which it spreads its noise and fumes. There are two viewing areas, one on each side of the central pier. What can be seen is limited and, since the sun is often directly ahead, photography is difficult. Large scale construction work has prepared the airport for its big event: the Olympics to be held there in 2000.

International traffic is steady, comprising representatives from most Asian airlines. The domestic scene is likely to be of greater interest. Because boarding cards aren't needed for access to the domestic gates, it is possible to get close enough for photos through the glass as airliners taxi onto their stands or when they are pushed back. Reflections, however, do make it hard work. Some of the best views are probably from the floor above departures, next to the airline lounges, with only the general aviation being out of sight. Heat haze can be a serious problem, though.

What was formerly the Ansett terminal is worth the visit, as it offers the best views. From the large lounge windows, aircraft landing on Runway 16/34 can be photographed taxiing to, parked at, or leaving their gates. The newer right-hand pier allows virtually all movements to be seen. At the opposite end, there are views of smaller operators, such as Hazelton's Metros and SF340s, as well as a limited view of the maintenance ramp. The Kendell SF340s operate in Qantas colours and Kendell titles.

Almost certain to be seen on such a trip is the enormous Qantas Jetbase. Anyone with a car will pass this maintenance facility on Airport Drive. Since work is carried out for the RAAF, some interesting aircraft are often seen. Behind the domestic terminal area is a multi-storey car park, from the top of which can be seen most of the movements and anything at the Jetbase. Anyone without a car, in need of a closer inspection of the Jetbase inmates must risk the scorn of the 'okkers' by reading the registrations through binoculars from a seat on the transfer bus which runs between Sydney and the international/domestic terminals.

There's not much point in renting a car in Australia, if you're not going to use it, so perimeter tours are bound to be tried. The map in this book is incomplete for such purposes but offers some of the main roads which are used. Arriving from Sydney means using Joyce Drive. Take Qantas Drive, pass the entrance to the domestic terminal, and the hangars come into sight, possibly drawing attention away from a left turn. After Sir Reginald Ansett Drive, the car park for the CAA offices could be good for a short stop, and a jog back to the hangar area, where a couple of biz-jets might be visible. There should also be some VIP and military transports.

Fromhere, it's only about thirty seconds to a small lay-by, opposite Gate 29, and a different view of the maintenance area. Unless in a hurry, forget the international terminal. Follow instead the Route 1 directions for Princes Highway. It gets tricky here - you have been warned - as you have to cross quite a bit of traffic to get into the left-hand lane. Follow directions for Huntsville and Sutherland on Route 1 and head west along West Botany Street. Left again onto Bestick (spelling?) Street, and left again at the busy junction onto General Holmes Drive. After crossing Cook's River, there is a parking area on the left with an ice cream van (usually), some seats, and quite a decent view.

Heading back towards Sydney, and following the signs for the airport, an important moment looms. There are signs for the city and the airport, only they look as if they're pointing in the wrong directions. Get this wrong and it could be a ten-mile detour. For the airport, it's the right-hand lanes. There is then a left turn into Roger Smith Avenue which is, effectively, the perimeter road. Which way to go?

To the right is the domestic terminal and a couple of hangars, containing some executive aircraft, possibly accessible by request. Alternatively, turn left and there are no problems stopping for a look at what's on display. It's rather good, actually. The road is a dead end after passing the helicopters, but there is a left turn towards the control tower, by which you can park. Here is a raised area, excellent for both spotting and photography. Whether it be taxiing, landing or departing, you can't really go wrong here. There is a security guard who is most likely to welcome you as someone to talk to, relieving the monotony of his job. It isn't too stimulating, spending eight hours a day, raising an lowering a barrier.

A car probably also means a trip to BANKSTOWN, as it handles much of the general aviation, with about three hundred residents, some of which are quite extraordinary. Air taxi, executive and commuter traffic is modest. This is a substantial field, 25 km west of Sydney on Canterbury Road (Highway 54). Ramp access is hardly necessary to see, and photograph, the majority of the residents but requests are normally successful. For a pleasure flight over the city, and the harbour, it may still be possible to take a ride in a Tiger Moth from here. The far side of the field has a separate entrance and it is here that four DC-3s are normally parked. Access is granted cheerfully to photographers.

On the south side of Sydney Harbour, AU ROSE BAY (RSE) is the arrival point for air taxi flights from Palm Beach. There is generally nothing else to see, and even the sight of one aircraft takes luck.

Some distance north of Sydney on Broken Bay, next to the Ku-Ring-Gai Chase National Park, PALM BEACH is becoming a select suburb. Vic Walton's Aquatic Air Beavers are based here. It is normal to see at least one sitting on the water, awaiting duties. Anyone intent on making the trip out to Palm Beach should consider relative costs. As Vic Walton points out, his air fare is cheaper than a taxi . . . but it's still a little pricy. However, for the chance to sample a take-off and landing on water, it's one of the cheapest.

VR-G = GIBRALTAR

GIBRALTAR

GIB	LXGB	North Front	2m/3km N (bus 10 minutes)

They say in Gibraltar that, when a Hercules lands, the whole town knows about it. This is primarily because it's a small community, close to the airport and because lots of reverse thrust is needed on landing, as the runway is short. A ten minute walk from town, this a local airport in every sense of the word, served by Yogi, as the local airline is known. Yogi Bear . . . Yo-Gibair.

Handling a few charters and scheduled movements, Gibraltar has for a long time been a small civil airport with airspace restricted by Spain's political posture on its territorial claim. Its existence is dependant upon Britain's strategic needs, no matter how small they are these days, and it is now mostly a staging post for Nimrods and Hercs on their way to the Falklands.

The runway crosses the road to La Linea and photos at the barrier, next to the Vulcan, can be taken but few would find the long wait between movements acceptable. The terminal is on the north, remote, side of the field but it is hardly the best place for photos with so many other vantage points. The Tangier pier is close to the western end of the runway and, at the other end, a footpath leads to the runway at Catalan Bay from Devil's Tower.

For elevated views, which are very photogenic, the Upper Galleries of the Rock itself are also worth considering. In reality, Gibraltar has little more than novelty value. After three or four hours with nothing to do, the novelty can wear off.

(VR-H) B = HONG KONG

HKG	VHHH	Kai Tak	4m/6km N of Kowloon (bus 40 minutes)

Just when the book looked finished, and the last check of the index was under way, the entry for Hong Kong was found to be missing. It had been deleted as a British Crown Colony (VR-H). . . but not pasted in as part of China (B). The same goes for Macau. This is a bit of a problem when the printer has started work on putting the book together. To make matters worse, all the reports that were supplied have been consigned to the rubbish bin because they were no longer needed. As the Chinese say: borrocks!

Kai Tak has been a favourite with spotters, and even more with photographers, for several years. Its days are numbered because, as everyone knows, work on Chep Lap Kok is well-advanced. Before most readers even buy this book, one well-loved airport will close (supposedly in April 1998) - and everything about it will become out of date overnight. The new one will open and fresh information will be needed. Details about bus services and their cost will require replacement, so there's little point in writing about how to get to and from Kai Tak.

Too many people got to like using the Aero Club so they closed it to spotters at weekends. It may still be available for use during the week, in exchange for an admission charge. The official observation deck was closed long ago, to make room for an executive lounge. On the airport's premises, this meant that only the multi-storey car park was left. There's no doubt that it was good for shots of aircraft passing very close indeed as they flared out on short finals.

A short way up the hillside is the famous Chequerboard Hill, used as a navigation aid. There is a park and a sports ground nearby, both of which offer good views of the arrivals passing more or less overhead, and both of which are within walking distance, even on a warm day. Around the perimeter of the field, there are no views at all.

The vast apron became too small so it was extended, with access for wide-bodies over a bridge to a newly-constructed area. The days of the Auxiliary Air Force were clearly numbered, as the seconds ticked by in Tiananmen Square. China's rule changed a few things but, it will be noted, there is still a small non-civilian presence at the far end of a new apron.

Good quality pictures, such as one of our illustrations, of aircraft on approach, have always been possible from some of the nearby apartment blocks. Many have access to the roofs but this is best achieved in the comany of a local who knows what he's doing.

The new airport, CHEP LAP KOK, is on the edge of Lantau island. It will open slightly before the Metro rail connection is complete, so transportation could be a bit of a nightmare for a while. The layout is similar to most new airports these days. It's like Singapore, Munich and Gardermoen, in other words. Parallel runways set wide apart with the terminal area in the middle. Do note the multi-storey car park in a similar position to that at Kai Tak, which will at least mean a good view of one runway.

MACAU (Taipa) is a 75-minute ferry ride from Hong Kong's China Ferry Terminal (on Kowloon). Bearing in mind that it's still Portuguese territory, passports are needed for the journey. The cheapest round trip costs about £25 but tickets are bought as singles - not returns. There are expensive alternative methods of transportation, ranging from hydrofoils and turbocats to helicopters, the latter leaving from a heliport close to the Star Ferry terminal on Hong Kong Island.

Taipa's runway is built on reclaimed land, out in the sea. The passenger terminal is somewhat under-used and, being brand new, has next to no views from landside, since the Food Court on the first floor is useless. The upper level (departures) approach road does give a good view of aircraft on the move, which are quite varied and interesting. Naturally, most of the stands - six in number - are out of sight from here, though.

Traffic is not what you'd call brisk, there being about fifty movements a day. Afternoons, however, are not without interest. Apart from the Air Macau fleet, there are TAP A340s, Transasia A320s, EVA 767s, Korean MD-80s and a reasonable variety of Chinese carriers. With Chinese airspace pretty much all around, aircraft have to land and take off from right to left (as seen from the terminal). Taipa doesn't have anything like Kai Tak's hurly-burly but it does offer a bit of a change.

VT = INDIA

BANGALORE
BLR   VOBG   Hindustan   5m/8km

The airport's name suggests something other than passenger services might be seen here. This is indeed the home of Hindustan Aeronautics Ltd (HAL). The single terminal building is divided into two: Indian Airlines in Terminal One and the rest of the domestic carriers in Terminal Two. They are separated by a snack bar! One gate serves all aircraft parked on the apron and, because passengers walk to their planes, they park as close as possible to the terminal.

Stairs at the back of "Terminal One", behind the Indian Airlines check-in desks, lead to an observation gallery on the upper level, where the view is excellent. A prominently-displayed notice might need a second reading. At first glance, it appears to say no spotting but, in fact the restriction is against SPITTING. Whilst there is no glass at the front of the gallery, there are two other drawbacks instead: mosquitoes and a heavy mesh screen. Another matter to bear in mind is the gallery also serves as the corridor leading to the security office so, despite this being a rather informal place, attempts to take photos could lead to difficulties.

Next to the terminal can be seen a small general aviation ramp, which can be expected to contain some interesting visitors. On the far side of the runway is HAL. What can be seen on the move to and from HAL is purely a matter of luck but of one thing we can be sure - it's all very interesting.

Anyone staying in Bangalore, with time to spare, might care to look out for the original airport, some twenty miles north of town. Precise location: Byatarayanapura Bangalore 560092. The passenger terminal is now used as offices but the runway is still active . . . and paved, unlike the taxiways. Apart from a few Cessnas, an Indian Geological survey Dash 8 uses the field and Indian Air Force C-130s are fairly regular visitors.

As a general note, which applies throughout India, exploration of airport perimeters means that special insurance is essential. This should take the form of something like a thousand rupees in cash, which usually suffices to extricate one's self from the occasional tight spot.

CALCUTTA
CCU   VECC   Netaji Subas Chandra Bose International   17m/27km

Historically, Calcutta has always been synonymous with poverty and it is very much in evidence, right up to the airport's perimeter fence. Whilst there is nothing to stop anyone taking a trip around the perimeter, it can be quite a frightening prospect: teeming millions, living in wooden shacks, with sewage systems that are best described as being below modern standards.

The passenger terminal is, however, clean and roomy. The one building handles both international and domestic traffic, though there is very little of the former. Whilst no viewing area has been reported, it is possible to see the aircraft from the departure lounge. Indian Airlines predominate, as is to be expected, but Jet, Sahara and Damania are also in evidence.

DELHI
DEL   VIDP   Indira Gandhi International   9m/14km

Without a valid ticket, the armed guards at the doors will not allow entry. New Delhi is the nation's capital city, so it can be expected that security precautions are strict and maintained at a high level. Photography is, of course, prohibited.

There are two separate terminals, international and domestic, a long way from each other. The international terminal is, predictably, secure and there are no viewing facilities. Most of the visiting airliners are operated by Air India and the usual European carriers. There is little to see here, in any quantity, that can't be seen elsewhere with greater ease. Close links with the CIS mean that a number of Aeroiflot (and ex-Aeroflot) aircraft visit.

The domestic terminal does have a viewing area. The corridor, leading to the restaurant, has ten or so narrow windows (all solidly locked) which overlook the apron. Most of what is to be seen are Indian Airlines Airbuses and 737s but the newer, privately owned, airlines are well represented. Beyond the domestic apron is a tempting line of Indian Air Force 707s, An-32s and some CIS cargo aircraft. Also stored here are several DC-3s.

Consider also SAFDIR JANG (or Safdarjung), the other airport, though nothing has been reported about it. This is likely to yield a quantity of helicopters, as Pawan Hans is based here. It used to be the Helicopter Corporation of India. A number of other small operators are also based but it would be wise to make contact by telephone to arrange a visit before turning up in a taxi, hoping to see something. To find Safdir Jang from the international airport, take the main road towards the city, as far as Delhi Cantonment. Here, take the ring road east, as far as a major road called Sri Aurobindo Marg. The airport is on the left.

GOA
GOI   VAGO   Dabolim   18m/29km SSE

Formerly a Portuguese protectorate, Goa is rapidly becoming a major tourist destination, causing all the associated problems: drunkenness and prostitution are extremely alien to the local culture. The beautiful tropical beaches and cheap alcohol are probably more attractive than the airport, mostly because of military activity. Mi-8s and Kamovs can be seen, though not always logged. Indian Navy Tu-95s are also usually visible. If things are tightly controlled at purely civil airports, it takes little imagination to work out what would happen if caught investigating what is to be seen here. A perimeter tour can result in one or two approach shots, since Jet, ModiLuft, Damania, East West and Indian Airlines operate 737s, plus the occasional A320. The bonus is an increasing amount of international charter traffic. Occasional references are made to stored Connies but reports received suggest they might not be there any more.

HYDERABAD
HYD   VOHY   Begumpet   4m/6km S

Towards the end of 1996, there was only one passenger terminal but another was scheduled to open early in 1997. Information is therefore only for the old terminal, which has an observation deck. Beyond the check-in desks and the shopping arcade, stairs lead to a restaurant, in front of which is an observation area. From here, everything that moves on the single runway can be clearly seen. Because there is no parallel taxiway, aircraft landing in either direction have to backtrack, s there's plenty of time to identify them. To the left of the field, as seen from the deck, are the twin facilities of the Indian Air Force and HAL's 748 maintenance area, both on the far side of the runway. Antonovs are usually to be seen, and all the Vayudoot 748s came here for storage.

MADRAS
MAA   VOMM

The terminals are about a quarter of a mile apart, and it's the domestic (equals interesting) terminal that has the deck . . . which may or may not be closed. The stairs take a bit of finding but they lead from between the check-in area and arrivals to a fine view of the apron and runway. To the right is a general purpose maintenance hangar, the doors of which are always open during the day, so aircraft can be logged with ease. Needless to say, they're rather interesting.

MUMBAI
BOM   VABB   Santa Cruz/Sahar International   23m/37km N

What happened to Bombay? It became Mumbai, that's what. Maybe, in the course of time, everyone will get used to the new name or maybe the novelty will ear off and we can all go back to calling the city what it's been called for quite a while. We'll see.

The Indian government, like that of Pakistan, treats security very seriously indeed. Naturally, this means that international airports are tightly controlled. Most airports are considered as special security areas, meaning that the public needs a good reason to gain access. Although New Delhi is the capital city, Bombay/Mumbai is the country's main international gateway and has been one of Asia's main seaports for many years.

Santa Cruz is, effectively, two entirely separate airports - Santa Cruz Domestic and Sahar International. This being India, nothing is wasted when it reaches the end of one useful life. The original passenger terminal still stands (but only just) and is used by private domestic airlines. Sahara India, Jet, Modiluf and East West Airlines are all regular movements. Note that Indian Airlines movements are fairly modest. Next to it is the second passenger terminal to be built, originally for international traffic, now used exclusively by Indian Airlines. A small cargo ramp completes this complex, which more or less faces Runway 09/27. A twenty minute journey away, the present international terminal is the newest, on the far side of Runway 14/32.

In other words, it's the domestic (non-Indian Airlines) terminal that's most interesting. The good news (fr spotters, if not photographers) is that the restaurant on the first floor has a view as good as any airport in the world, except that this one specialises in some fairly unusual airlines. From here, everything can be seen, including Airworks. With decent binoculars, even the biz-jets and stored aircraft on the far side can be logged. A square meal and a few judiciously-spaced cups of coffee should cost no more than £5.

Airworks India is directly opposite the international terminal, though some way off, but the hangars are only likely to be seen from a window seat in a moving aircraft. All the DC-3s bar one might have gone but there are Mil helicopters there instead. There is also a defunct DC-7, N71950 (c/n 45207/840), parked outside the old Air India hangars.

Making contact with Airworks can result in what sounds like good news. Propliner fans can be welcome but Airworks' approval is only half the story. Obtaining a security clearance is another matter, not so easily achieved without prior written notification. Anyone who considers a tour round the perimeter will be extremely disappointed by the high concrete wall that surrounds the field.

The port of Bombay/Mumbai was built on a peninsula which juts south into the Arabian Sea. To its east is the Harbour and slightly further north is Mahim Bay. Swami Vivekland Road heads north across the bay beyond which, another couple of miles away, is JUHU Airport. This is one of India's main general aviation fields with plenty of interesting aircraft to be seen, including Beech 18s, a couple of King Airs, about five Mi-8s, and the main base of Pawan Hans. Anyone venturing towards the government hangar can expect anything between unfriendliness and hostility.

V2 = ANTIGUA

SAINT JOHNS

ANU   TAPA   V C Bird - Antigua   4m/6km

It's easy to imagine, without visiting this part of the world, that life is informal and unhurried. Apart from important cricket matches, nothing really upsets the leisurely pace, and life is pretty good. VC Bird airport reflects this in every way. The passenger terminal has an open observation deck, and access is free. Wire mesh prevents security worries without making life particularly difficult for the photographer.

Much of the traffic is Caribbean-based general aviation, and an interesting selection it is. Scheduled traffic is mostly Leeward Islands Air Transport (LIAT) with mostly Dash 8s, HS748s and Twin Otters, and BWIA supply the MD-80s. Wide-bodies from Europe are regular without being frequent, and there are a few American arrivals on most days.

Most of what Antigua's airport has to offer can be seen just as well at Miami, but Miami isn't the West Indies, by any stretch of the imagination. A trip to this island is probably planned for relaxation, and a chance to get away from it all. One or two visits to the airport offer a nice change from drinking by the hotel pool . . . the best of both worlds.

V3 = BELIZE

BELIZE CITY
BZE   MZBZ   Phillip S W Goldson International   10m/16km

A sign of the country's recent history is displayed at the entrance to the airport: a Harrier GR.3. The British Army base, with its Gazelle helicopters, is on the far side of the field from the passenger terminal, but barely visible.

An open waving gallery offers a fine view of the airfield, with the sun usually in the right position. Traffic is reasonably varied, being a mixture of American Airlines services from Miami, Continental, TACA, Trans Jamaica and the local Tropic Air. Even a short stay at the airport should result in seeing a few Twin Otters, plus the Islanders of Maya and Island Air. There is only one hangar, containing a couple of local Cessnas but a few visitors from neighbouring countries make the ramp look more interesting. Any biz-jets in evidence are normally from the USA or Mexico.

The cargo area is used sporadically, one of Kalitta's DC-8s being the most likely visitor. For a complete picture of the city's aviation scene, a visit to the Municipal Airport (TZA), on the edge of town, is essential. This is where much of the maintenance is carried out but, in this part of the world, Islanders are considered to be quite large aircraft.

XA = MEXICO

ACAPULCO
ACA   MMAA   General Juan N Alvarez International   16m/25km SE

Few holiday destinations have as much charisma as Acapulco, though it is nothing like the place it used to be. It's America's answer to the Costa Brava. The small airport has managed to cope with traffic, though its facilities are rather modest. Wedged in between a lagoon and the sea, it's all white concrete and palm trees, so arrival here is a pleasant experience. The back edge of the apron is an unbelievable assortment of rampside clutter, so it is fortunate that the restaurant's observation area is on the upper floor of the terminal.

Scheduled traffic is minimal, almost half of it from the States, and 727s are the staple diet plus Aeromexico DC-9s/MD-88s/MD-82s. Winter is high season, when wide-bodies operate charters from Canada and other cooler climes. Generally speaking, there is little out of the ordinary. Acapulco's name is sure to impress friends but photos of airliners on the ramp are less likely to do so. It takes time and patience for the number of movements logged to reach double figures, and there are other pleasures to be enjoyed elsewhere.

CANCUN
CUN   MMUN   International   15m/23km SW

Cancun now reigns supreme as the resort for Americans to take their holidays, especially in winter. The rest of the world has followed, so that the airport has had to expand at the same rate as the resort. International services are generally similar to those to be seen at MIA, though also with smaller types operated by Ladeco, AeroPeru and Cubana's Yak-42s.

Domestic movements are plentiful and varied, with all jet-equipped carriers, except Aero California, making appearances on scheduled or charter flights. Saturdays are by far the busiest, though Wednesdays are not far behind. Opportunities for viewing are, however, rather limited and the chances of photography almost negligible. Travellers, both international and domestic, show their tickets and boarding passes to access the boarding concourses, after which only the international area offers any real panorama for an hour and a half or so before the plane leaves.

Non-travellers have a difficult time. The windows en route to the boarding area allow aircraft to be seen but only through the ornamental vegetation. There is a single glass door which is unobstructed but, even here, the view is restricted.

Photographers will need ingenuity, and probably a formal request to at least one of the airlines for ramp access (rather than the ASA). This has been possible in the past. Hints for those considering this approach: you'll need a white short-sleeved dress shirt, black or dark blue slacks and leather shoes, in order to blend in with everyone else. Goodwill is on the increase and it helps to thank your hosts profusely, thereby helping to ensure that the relaxed atmosphere continues to improve.

One of the cheapest ways to visit Cuba is to book through Divermex, a local travel agency, which does inexpensive 2, 3 and 7 day trips to Havana in Cubana Yak-42s.

CHICHEN ITZA
CZA

An airstrip, built on the Yucatan to serve tourists visiting the famous archaeological sites from Cancun and Cozumel, most of the movements occur in the week. They comprise mostly TAESA and AeroCaribe F.27s. Before making a trip to the airport, it would be wise to ring the airlines and ask for confirmation of their movements. The tarmac can be seen easily from the approach road, and it is only a short walk from the nicer hotels, near the ruins. Afternoons are definitley best for photography.

COZUMEL
CZM   MMCZ   International   2m/3km NE

Apart from a few Continental and Mexicana movements, this airport handles mostly regional types, operating from Cancun. The passenger terminal is, however, one of the country's typical examples, offering no views of the proceedings. The approach to the runway can be seen from the beach at San Miguel and satisfactory photos of aircraft can be taken, depending on the wind direction.

GUADALAJARA
GDL   MMGL   Don Miguel Hidalgo International   11m/17km SE

Though a considerable distance behind Mexico City, this is one of the country's busier airports, handling all sorts of scheduled traffic from DC-10s down to DC-3s. The Wings restaurant on the passenger terminal's upper floor overlooks the ramp. What can be seen is a lot of construction work and, beyond it, the main apron. The air jetties reduce the amount of passengers being bussed around the ramp, but they partially restrict the view.

The domestic stands are to the left and the international flights park in front. There are enough American carriers for Guadalajara to look like any airport in southern Texas. To the right, and almost out of sight, is the general aviation ramp. To see this at close quarters, it's necessary to walk out of the terminal past the control tower.

East of the passenger terminal are the cargo apron and Mexicana maintenance area. Most of the movements on the main runway can be seen from the terminal but there is another, away to the left. The road which serves the airport continues towards Chapala, passing the threshold of Runway 28. Photos from the road of aircraft on approach need a 200mm lens from here.

MERIDA
MID   MMMD   Lic. Manuel Crescencio Rejon   5m/8km S

The Yucutan Peninsula is famous for its Mayan remains which attract tourists, especially on charter flights from Canada and the United States in winter. Scheduled airliners are now mainly domestic, all of which are regular visitors to the USA. What little traffic there is can be seen adequately from around the terminal but most enthusiasts who visit will arrive for reasons other than the traffic.

242

MEXICO CITY
MEX   MMMX   Benito Juarez   8m/13km E (train 25 minutes)

The two parallel runways are used by airliners, with a shorter diagonal runway intended for smaller aircraft. Because of the Spanish words for left and right, the runways are known 5l (left) and 5D (right). Traffic is so brisk that, as predicted, general aviation has been forced out. The pressure on slots at Benito Juarez led to restrictions on general aviation there. Most prop-driven aircraft, with a cruising speed of less than 250 knots, were the first casualties. The various fleets of business aircarft are now based mostly at TOLUCA.

It would be sensible at Benito Juarez to expect official hostility to spotting activities, and more so to photography. What takes place in (or from) the privacy of a hotel room in the Marriott is unlikely to meet with opposition but it's too far away for *quality* photos. The three ground level viewing platforms really do exist but they are at present unaccessible. In other words, we won't get to use them again . . . ever. Security is becoming ever tighter at Mexico City, and not without reason. Crime, and drugs-related crime in particular, is a matter of grave concern to the authorities, who are taking all the necessary precautions. Step outside the airport terminal, walk along the highways next to the perimeter, and be prepared for the worst.

The main elevated viewpoint is multi-storey Car Park 2, though the power of a telescope may be essential to note the executive movements. Spotters are bound to take the top (sixth) floor, and that's where the guards look for them. The fifth floor is just as good, but there is shade from the very hot sun, and less hassle.

Hotels in the area are affordable, $15 being reasonable in Zocala, but what was the Hotel Fiesta Americana (now the Marriott) has more to offer in return for its higher prices. Its roof garden is close enough to the runways for photography of some sort to be possible, an important consideration when the multi-storey car park displays several signs prohibiting photos. Rooms on the 7th and 8th floors offer the best views. The hotel management is getting familiar with people asking for rooms overlooking the airport. The Marriott is just a walk over the link across the road from the terminal and its Eighth Floor facilities also offer a fine view.

What was the Aviacion General complex is busy, with its own terminal, busy apron and several hangars. It has its own Metro rail station, called Hangares. Based here are many operators, and traffic is brisk throughout the morning and early evening. This apron is directly opposite the main terminal area and no longer contains anything which would normally be considered general aviation. Aeromexico and TAESA have maintenance facilities here, as do Aeromar.

By leaving the terminal and turning left, the busy main roads around the perimeter are easy to follow but, as stated above, take sensible precautions against being mugged. Beyond what was the Aviacion General apron is the military ramp. On it sit a Convair and a couple of (rather famous) Caravelles, painted in military colours. They can be photographed from the perimeter but not without some of the fence intruding into the pictures.

From the terminal, a right turn leads to other areas of interest. The Mexicana maintenance base is to be found up the road, at the far side of the growing cargo ramp. US-based parcels carriers usually have a few 727s on the ground during the day. On the far side of the runway are two abandoned C-46s and, to justify the walk all the way to the end of Runway 26R, there is a playground with a DC-8 sitting in it. So, there's plenty to see, without doubt. Do bear in mind that, after two or three days, it all becomes rather repetitive so it would make a nice detour from the States but might not be the sort of place to fly to direct from Europe.

MONTERREY
MTY   MMMY   General Mariano Escobido International   15m/23km NE

An interesting airport, this is the home of AeroExo, SARO, Servicios Aerolineas Mexicanas (SAM) and VARSA, and is a major station for Mexicana's fleet of Fokker 100s. Add some Aeromonterrey FH-227s and AeroLitoral Metros, and a visit here is most enjoyable, mostly because the restaurant in the boarding concourse can be reached without a boarding pass. The passenger terminal lies to the south of the east-west runway, with a ten-gate concourse reached via a tunnel, similar to those at LAX. The restaurant at the other end of this tunnel offers a good view of the runway. There is another on the upper floor of the main terminal which overlooks part of the general aviation ramp, to the east. Outside, the considerable AeroLiteral fleet can be seen from the fence to the west of the terminal.

Travellers should remember that Monterrey isn't one of the world's cheapest cities. A taxi from downtown costs about 50 new pesos (about $17 and rising) and a modest hotel near the bus station, where most of them are, can be $50 a night. Consolation is that travelling from the airport is cheaper, by taking one of the colectivo buses. Bear in mind it can be a long wait if you are the first to get on board, as these buses only move when there are enough passengers.

The general aviation airfield is called Aeropuerto del Norte (codes: NTR MMAN) so care should be taken if driving out of town. As the name suggests, the field is to the north, reached by taking Av Alfonso Reyes (Hwy 58) but anyone heading for the international airport should head east along Av Miguel Aleman (Hwy 54).

TIJUANA
TIJ   MMTJ   General Abelardo Rodriguez   4m/6km S

There seems to be a rule in Mexico that, the smaller the airport, the longer is its name! Tijuana is the most easily reached of all Mexico's airports, being just across the border from San Diego. The culture shock of the crossing is enormous, as the town is squalid, but the airport is modern and quite pleasant. To the right of the terminal is an executive ramp, where half a dozen or so business twins are usually parked. Once inside the terminal, the only views are through windows but an early morning arrival can ensure photos of Mexicana DC-10s, as they taxi to their stands, very close indeed to the terminal.

YK = SYRIA

DAMASCUS
DAM   OSDI   International   18m/30km E (bus 30 minutes)

The excellent roof terrace has been kept open despite the mysterious nature of many of the visiting aircraft. There are, however, distinct warnings against photography. The passenger terminal and ramp are located at right angles to the axis of the main runway and a taxiway leads in both directions to runways, though that on the left appears to be generally out of use. The observation area provides a good, if elevated, view of the main apron and there is room for four aircraft to park at the terminal's jetties. To the left, Syrianair's seldom-used Tu-134s are parked, though some may be seen at the remote parking area at the other end of the main runway. To the right is the cargo terminal, where some general aviation movements also park. Other aircraft park out on the ramp but particularly sensitive visitors, like Libyan Il-76s, stay out of reach near the threshold of the runway. On the far side of the taxiway, opposite the terminal, disused Syrian DC-6 YK-AEC sits, decaying, in the sun.

At the far end of the runway is a military controlled parking area, where the Syrian Government Il-76s, An-26s, Yak-40s and Falcon 20s are to be found. Most carry Syrianair titles and can be clearly seen from the airport road. Enthusiasts visiting Damascus should ensure that they are sitting on the left side of the aircraft when they arrive, to content themselves with low-quality photos out of their (western) airliner rather than be tempted to try poking a telephoto lens through the fence. The Syrianair maintenance base is just around the corner from the terminal and successful negotiations at the security barrier, not easily achieved, result in meeting an extremely friendly airline staff who will be happy to show a visitor around one of their unwanted Tu-154Ms.

The extent of military activity at Damascus is unknown and detailed investigation is hardly encouraged. Hardened concrete shelters do exist next to the main runway but only (!) the occasional MiG has been seen overshooting. The inaccessible area behind the passenger terminal may be a military base and the runway beyond it may serve some purpose related to it, but details are sketchy.   Visiting airlines feature arab and mid-European carriers, though some visit at quite ridiculous hours. The demand to get to Budapest must be extreme if the only flight leaves at 0335 on Sunday mornings! The political status of Syria means that numbers of 'extra' flights are almost regular, both from Central Europe and arab countries. Swissair, Austrian and Air France come from the west and PIA pause on the way between New York and Karachi. Cyprus Airways also operate regular 1-11 flights from neighbouring Larnaca, though these may be classed as being some of the most mundane visitors in this part of the world.

YL = LATVIA
RIGA
RSC   EVRA   Skulte   10m/16km N (bus 30 minutes)

Traffic here is surprisingly brisk for an airport in one of the Baltic states. From inside the passenger terminal, there are views from windows on the second and third floors. One "air bridge" forms a link to a small departure gates satellite. It's round, built from breeze block and has a roof that looks like origami. Between the terminal and the control tower is a gate, closed of course, to the apron from which good quality ground level photos are possible. For a guided tour of everything, it's worth making contact with the Airport Authority, as these half-hour tours might still be possible for about US$25. They allow access to the most interesting aircraft, which are unlikely to move again from beside the active apron.

Taxis are a rip-off but buses are dirt-cheap. The No 22 service links the airport with the railway station. Also close to town is SPILVE, now supposedly being used for general aviation. To get there, take the No 3 bus and expect difficulties without some basic knowledge of the language. English is virtually unknown. Inside the fabulously ostentatious terminal building, the airport manager's office might be the place for limited dialogue. Suggest that photos are needed for a private collection and this might lead to being allowed access to an assortment of An-2s, Mi-8s and even Il-76s and Il-62s.

YR = ROMANIA
BUCHAREST
OTP   LROP   Otopeni   10m/16km

International traffic uses Otopeni airport, described as being inadequate to cope even in the bad years. The spectator's terrace has been closed for many years, and what could be witnessed was mostly a procession of airliners to be seen far easier at most other European airports. With negligible charter traffic, a day's movements are unlikely to exceed twenty or so arrivals.

A network of subsidised domestic flights was operated by Tarom's An-24s, to link the country with its capital, through BANEASA airport. The aircraft are now virtually unused and therefore so are most of the airport's facilities. The passenger terminal looks rather like a concrete mosque.

With so many Tarom Antonovs to be seen, in the company of Romavia's aircraft and a fair selection of older Soviet-built types, Baneasa is not without interest, and the short taxi ride from Otopeni should allow the logbook to be filled with plenty of aircraft at minimal risk. The terminal and apron are, like everything else, in the southwest corner of the field, by the threshold of 07.

CONSTANTA
COZ   MDCZ   M Kogalniceanu

This is a military airfield, used in summer by a handful of charter flights to the small civil passenger terminal. Spectators have never been encouraged because of the military presence and, now that the economy has slackened even more, there is even less reason to visit.

TIMISOARA
TSR   LRTR   Giarmata

Technically, Timisoara still survives as an international airport, though its movements were, at best, restricted to a BAC-111 to Frankfurt and an Il-62 or 707 to America. These weekly services are supplemented by two daily air links to Bucharest. If Romania is planned as a destination, only the military presence at Timisoara is likely to appeal.

YV = VENEZUELA
CARACAS
CCS   SVMI   Simon Bolivar International   13m/20km NW (bus 60 minutes)

To the north of the airport, behind a low hill, is the Caribbean Sea. There are, effectively, two separate airports whose facilities overlap, but an explanation is complicated: to the west of the field is Runway 09/27 which has, to the south of it, an international and domestic terminal. East of this, but slightly overlapping, is Runway 08/26 with its general aviation, military and cargo terminals. That much can be seen from a basic map.

The international and domestic terminals, both of which have outdoor spectator decks, face Runway 09/27 but are also close to the threshold of Runway 08. Both decks are closed. Windows (tinted and dirty) in both terminals allow aircraft to be seen but photographers will find this a frustrating airport. To make matters worse, many of the aircraft park so that they are either nose-on or tail-on to the viewer. The international terminal is passed by most departing airliners and taxiing international movements are seen at closer range than from the domestic terminal. There is, however, no view at all of Runway 08 or the other areas, and aircraft landing come into view so quickly as to make life difficult.

Windows in the domestic terminal overlook the general aviation and cargo areas. They also allow movements to be seen on Runway 08, which tends to be busy. The view is restricted and international movements are too distant for photography. In other words, it might be necessary to spend equal amounts of time at each terminal if a truly representative record of the airport's movements is to be made.

The Aeropostal and Avensa fleets can be seen in a day and there are plenty of other domestic airlines. International traffic is not particularly brisk, and many of the movements arrive at odd hours. Caracas does seem to specialise in one or two rather unusual visitors: Rentavion's Martin 404 is likely to please many enthusiasts, for example, but there are also one or two Servivensa and Aero Executive DC-3s and a good selection of biz-jets and governmental aircraft.

To the right of the terminals are the separate military, general aviation and cargo facilities, though it should be noted that cargo traffic is minimal and features no major indigenous carriers. There are multiple rows of hangars in the general aviation area where a vast array of biz-jets can be seen, including the government's Gulfstreams. Photographers might walk (a long way) west from the terminal area to where the perimeter allows views of landing aircraft. The best spots are much used by the locals, with whom close contact is not always a good thing. Note also that the use of long focus lenses can, and does, attract attention. With so many military and governmental aircraft around, careless photography can lead to misunderstanding and trouble.

Taxis are relatively expensive, so it might be necessary to sample the local buses. They stop on the highway, across the car park from the terminal area, and can be flagged down. The drivers speak little English but do their best to help.

CARACAS
SVCS   Charallave/O Machado Zuloaga International

This is the other airport for Caracas, some miles inland, and 2000 feet above sea level. With so much confusing information coming from one airport, it would be unwise to offer further

246

speculation about the other. However, whilst there are no scheduled operations, the general aviation does include a number of fleet operators who have maintenance facilities here. Apart from Cessna twins and one or two Trislanders or Metros of Viajes Expresos (CAVE), a few of Aeroejecutivos DC-3s can be seen. Some working Spanish is useful, to gain access to the ramps for a close-up look.

CARACAS
SVFM   Generalisimo Francisco Miranda   3m/5km E

This is Caracas' military air base, generally known as La Colota. To reach it, travel east from town, towards Parque del Este or along the Autopista. The adjacent general aviation terminal is, rather optimistically, called Metropolitano Internacional. They are side by side, separated by a fence. The domestic airport (or perhaps even the domestic terminal only) is known locally, to confuse matter even more, as Caracas Maiquetia.
Aircraft arriving do so much the same way as they do at Kai Tak: avoiding the hills before turning onto tight finals over the city. Accidents do happen, and have happened, so the field is no longer open to single-engined aircraft, which could make it an attraction to many enthusiasts! Biz-jets and other executive types are extremely well-represented at this field, including those operated by the Aero Club. On the north side of the field is the small passenger terminal, used by visiting aircraft, none of which operate commercial services. Photography from the terminal is good, with the sun seemingly always in a good position. Permission should be sought to take photos of civilian aircraft for two reasons: it is usually granted and it helps reduce any misunderstanding.
The western part of the field, occupied by the miltary base, holds Aravas, Skyvans, King Airs and a whole range of helicopters, from S-61s and Pumas to JetRangers and Bo105s. A walk along the perimeter fence might seem like a good idea but it will soon be discovered that very few aircraft can be seen, because of the hangars and other buildings which obstruct the view.
One of the most convenient local hotels is part of the nearby CCCT shopping mall/hotel complex, almost directly opposite the entrance to the National Guard base. For a good view, the top floor of the multi-storey car park is recommended. The Eurobuilding Hotel's swimming pool offers a reasonably good view of the runway, from where the movements can be logged in comfort. Most of the other hotels are located in the Macuto/Caribe area. Walking along the perimeter is not necessarily a good idea.

CIUDAD BOLIVAR
CBL   SVCB

Some way inland, on the Orinoco River, is the regional capital of Ciudad Bolivar. There are, literally, one or two domestic flights each day, operated by Avensa and Aeropostal but most interest is generated by the various hangars and aprons used by a variety of operators, all of which are something special to European eyes.
This is an informal airport in many ways, where Big City pressures have yet to reach. An-2s are not common anywhere in the world, and they are certainly distinctive aircraft. They are an unexpected delight here, sharing the aprons area with plenty of DC-3s, plus a truly wonderful assortment of other types and colour schemes. Ciudad Bolivar doesn't warrant a long stay, but a visit here will be memorable, for sure.

CUIDAD GUYANA
PZO   Puerto Ordiz   8m/11km SW

The provincial town of Ciudad Guyana sits at the junction of the Orinoco and Caroni Rivers, some distance east of Caracas. The airport is served by Avensa, Servivensa and Aerotuy which operate regular services to Palomar and Ciudad Bolivar as well as the capital.
The passenger terminal is, by European standards, rather basic but the upper floor does have a cafe/bar with a view of the apron. For a good photo of a Servivensa DC-3, this is the place to

be. Also visible are a couple of based CL-215s, several twins and a Polish-registered An-2. Next to the apron are two hangars containing mostly Cessnas. By leaving the passenger terminal and turning left, a walk beside the boundary fence and the National Guard Camp will probably allow most of the residents (of the airfield, rather than the camp) to be identified. For a closer inspection, some working knowledge of Spanish will be essential. Puerto Ordiz is an interesting little airport, if you need to travel there on business. It is not, however, worth a detour as the airline traffic can be seen elsewhere.

Z = ZIMBABWE

GWERU
FVTL   Thornhill

Whether or not Gweru has two airports is not certain. The codes GWE and FVGW are supposedly allocated to Gweru/Gweru! Anyone with a passion for propliners might be tempted to visit this part of the world because two of Air Zimbabwe's Viscounts are located here. Apart from the chance to see a modest number of light aircraft and a few airline movements, just as easily seen at Harare in all probability, there is no reason to make the trip. Propliner fans will, of course, insist that is reason enough!

HARARE
HRE   FVHA   International   7m/11km S

As is often the case in Africa, maximum use is made of expensive runways, meaning that civil and military traffic often share the one facility. This is indeed the case at Harare, with the base situated to the north side and the civil complex on the south.

Air Zimbabwe made use, for many years, of one of the world's last Viscount fleets. Whilst these have now been withdrawn from use, they are still very much in evidence. Two examples, 'B and 'C, have been moved to Chegutu. On the far side of the runway from the passenger terminal, is semi-derelict 707 Z-WKT.

The passenger terminal is much loved by those who have used it, despite offering only very basic facilities. Compensation is the observation deck which offers unrestricted views across the apron and the rest of the airfield. There is no glass to mar the view, so photography couldn't be better. Access to the deck costs a couple of Zimbabwe dollars (that is to say, almost nothing) and there is waiter service for the rather good food and beer.

The terminal is divided into two, domestic passengers using the left side, outside which is the small executive apron. Further round to the left are the Air Zimbabwe cargo and customs buildings, beyond which are the remains of a Beech Baron.

Clearly visible, on the far side of the field, is the military base, with at least ten or so C-47s out in the open. There are also Islanders, CASA 212s, Hawks and helicopters. Activity is not brisk, and it can be difficult to identify all the aircraft. One report states that, after six visits, only three of the CASAs have been identified. Compared with airports in other parts of the world, this can probably be considered an achievement.

An early start is recommended - 07:00 is about right, because Air Zimbabwe's 707s tend to arrive between 06:00 and 08:00. The rest of the traffic includes heavy metal from Europe: Swissair MD-11s and KLM 747-400s make stopovers here, arriving from Johannesburg and returning there in the evening. British Airways 747s, Air Mauritius A340s are also regular visitors. The smaller scheduled visitors, likely to be of more interest to western eyes, are BAe 146s from Botswana and Malawi, plus a few 737 movements operated by Kenya and Uganda Airlines.

Rather than spend all day on the deck, consuming large quantities of cheap beer, a wander around the airport can be a welcome change (depending on how much you like beer). All the hangars, apart from those of Air Zimbabwe, are accessible by negotiation. The Catalina, Z-CAT, is no longer present but there are plenty of King Airs, United Islanders and an assortment of other types, including HS 125 Z-VEC, as some consolation. Worth looking out for is Jetstream 9Q-CFI, normally to be found in the Fields hangar.

Almost all the cargo is handled by Affretair, whose hangar is at the head of the maintenance ramp, closest to the runway. Due to cargo movements being slightly less regular than passenger traffic, what can be seen outside Affretair's facility is largely a matter of luck.

Harare's other airfield is PRINCE CHARLES, still officially an airport, but used almost exclusively by general aviation. A taxi journey from the city centre takes about twenty minutes and costs about £3, one way. For this, you get to see over 150 light aircraft in somewhat relaxed fashion.

HWANGE
HWN   FVWN   National Park

Zimbabwe's economy is partly dependant on the tourist industry, and Hwange is a major centre of activity for anyone seeking wild life (big game). The airport is therefore closer to where the tourists want to go than it is to the town, which has its own airport (Hwange Town: WKI/FVWT). Most of the movements involve ferrying tourists in twin-engined comfort from either Bulawayo or Harare but there is nothing special to be seen, if locally registered Navajos and Aztecs can be considered ordinary, that is.

KARIBA
KAB   FVKB

Lake Kariba was formed when the dam was built. It is becoming a tourist attraction in its own right, mostly because people don't seem to realise how hot it is here until they arrive. Traffic is, by local standards, uninspiring as it comprises mostly a few commuters.

VICTORIA FALLS
VFA   FVFA

A single runway, with the apron and terminal placed to one side, is used by visitors to the spectacular water falls. Apart from the occasional South African or Air Zimbabwe movement, the airport comes a very distant second place for even the most ardent aviation enthusiast. It can hardly be expected to compete with one of the greatest sights on earth. There are no problems with either viewing or photography at the airport, apart from the fact that there is very little to see. It is usual to find at least one biz-jet, parked on the apron. When staying in the area for more than one day, some spare time might be spent also at Spray View, Victoria Falls' other airport. This is nothing more than an airstrip, used mostly for sight-seeing flights.

ZK = NEW ZEALAND

AUCKLAND
AMZ   NZAR   Ardmore   20m/32km SE of Auckland

To visit this airfield near Clevedon, time and a car are essential, and what's on offer is a matter of taste. A couple of hundred light aircraft, including helicopters, may be what some people want to see. The staff are certainly friendly enough, so taking a look around is rarely a problem. After all, a company called Captain Al's Fantasy Flights can't take life too seriously. The New Zealand Warbirds collection includes C-47 ZK-DAK plus a couple of Devons and a few Harvards etc.

The visit to Ardmore ideally requires a rental car, and might be something of a pilrimage, for a few years yet, for piston-power freaks. Easily missed by anyone not knowing what to look for, there is a company specialising in aircraft spares, where a couple of Bristol 170 Freighters (ZK-

EPE/G) are still stored. Don't expect them to be in good condition after all these years. The moving surfaces and the engines have gone but the airframes are still pretty much intact.

AUCKLAND
AKL   NZAA   International   14m/22km S (bus 50 minutes)

This is the country's main international gateway, known locally as Mangere, after the prominent mountain just across the water. Anyone contemplating a visit to New Zealand should bear in mind that it is unlike Australia for its climate. Being further from the equator it is cooler, and most of the country is quite close to the sea. Thus it is rather more like Britain for its weather.

For this reason the popular viewing deck on the Jean Batten International Terminal is enclosed by a glass screen. The winds blowing off Manakau Harbour can be quite chilly, though less so in summer, of course. From the deck, at first floor level, there are good views of the international activity and the runway. However its angle and close proximity to many of the arrivals mean it can make life difficult for the serious photographer. A good zoom lens is essential. Inside the international terminal is displayed the Gull Six G-ADPR.

Of the regular visitors here, it is the Air Niuguini, Air Nauru and Royal Tongan aircraft which are most likely to please, the rest being mostly a selection of British and American carriers. It should be remembered that Air New Zealand's 767s use this terminal, so a premature walk to the domestic terminal could cause consternation. Most of the unusual airlines seem to arive between 17:00 and 20:00. These include a couple of NZ Air Freight CV-580s. Before settling down to watch these, it's important to have a look around the freight terminal. The many NZ Post Metros get put to bed quite early.

The shuttle bus links the terminals, but on most days it's a pleasant stroll taking no more than ten minutes. There are bench seats which offer some view of proceedings but they are of no use to anyone wishing to use a camera. The domestic terminal is divided into two, with Air New Zealand and its subsidiaries occupying one part, and Ansett New Zealand the other. Ansett's facility is strictly functional, with no viewing area. The ANZ part has a bar and an external view of the apron. When Runway 23 is in use, this is definitely the place to be. There are stands immediately in front, and taxiing aircraft pass within range of a 70-200mm zoom lens. It is here that close-ups are taken of Bandeirantes, Saab 340s and Metroliners.

The chainlink perimeter fence is barely six feet high, so photos can be taken on tiptoe by taller people. Following the fence leads to the cargo terminal where action is slower. Normal visitors are Postal F.27s and Metroliners but Air Freight CV580s visit occasionally, as do larger international cargo aircraft, such as a Singapore Airlines 747 twice a week. Sightings of An-124s and Il-76s are not unknown but should be regarded as exceptional.

A bus runs between the airport and the city every half hour, at a cost of about £3.50. (Bear in mind that car hire in New Zealand is becoming rather expensive.) Most hotels operate courtesy buses to the airport, despite offering high standard accommodation from about £30 per night.

CHRISTCHURCH
CHC   NZCH   International   6m/9km NW (bus 15 minutes)

With only limited time to visit New Zealand, Christchurch would probably feature as the Number Three destination, after Auckland and Wellington. On the eastern coast of South Island, Christchurch has carved itself a niche as a tourist destination by becoming the gateway to the South Pole. The beautiful Canterbury Plains also attract tourists.

The domestic terminal has an observation deck. Access is on the first floor, but don't expect any direction signs. Scheduled traffic offers nothing which can't be seen just as well elsewhere but there is a USAF presence featuring the occasional C-5 and C-130. What is unique to Christchurch is Air New Zealand's storage area, where their F.27s await sale. From the passenger terminal, the compound is along Orchard Road. The ANZ maintenance base also carries out work for the RAAF, and sightings of C-130s are fairly common. Mount Cook also have a base here.

Christchurch has another attraction for aviation enthusiasts, to be found at WIGRAM aerodrome:

the New Zealand Air Force Museum. South of the city, on Riccarton or Blenheim Road, the entrance is on Main South Road. Buses (Nos 8 and 25) go from Cathedral Square. Open from 10:00 through the week, and from 13:00 on Sundays, the museum closes at 16:00.

HAMILTON
HLZ   NZHN   5m/8km (bus 15 minutes)

The town is on North Island, between Auckland and Rotorua. A detour, for anyone in a car, is essential, a once-in-a-lifetime opportunity. Eagle Airways base their Bandeirantes here, and their movements occasionally liven up the day, together with the odd Air New Zealand 737. Residents are unlikely to exceed two dozen, and the displayed Fletcher has no identification marks.

INVERCARGILL
IVC   NZNV   2m/3km(bus 30 minutes)

Served by a selection of scheduled airliners, Invercargill is the least likely holiday destination in New Zealand. What can be seen at the airport is no different from most other places, with the exception of Southern Air Islanders. The fence either side of the terminal offers the chance to get close to ANZ 737s and Ansett 146s, but it is an expensive and time-consuming way of doing so.

LAKE TEKAPO

Not much more than a small airfield, Lake Tekapo is only reached from the outside world by road! A car is therefore essential. Air Safaris operate excellent, and affordable, scenic flights over one of New Zealand's most extraordinarily beautiful areas, in their Nomads and Cessna 207s from this field. Photography is no problem and the staff, in this backwater, are predictably friendly. It is only a short distance (in miles) from the beautiful Lake Tekapo to Glentanner, though the terrain which separates them is rugged and mostly undeveloped. The journey takes about five hours each way! Car rental insurance can mean that some routes, such as this, are not allowed without special high risk cover. No designator has been found for this field, so it is possibly also known by another name which is officially recognized.

MILFORD SOUND
MFN   NZMF

Located on the west coast of South Island, this is the heart of New Zealand's fjordland. It is unbelievably scenic, and on a magnificent scale. The quickest way to Milford Sound is by air from Queenstown but coach services are operated. The airport is a very distant rival to the scenery, even for the most commited enthusiast.

For about one hour each day, Milford's airport goes crazy as Mount Cook's various aircraft, and Waterwings Nomads and Cessnas, scurry about. For the rest of the day scenic flights boost the airport's movements, mostly operated by Twin Otters or Islanders.

MOUNT COOK
GTN   Glentanner

Glentanner, down on the shore where the Tasman River enters Lake Pukaki, has a small amount of general aviation and the operations base for The Helicopter Line's Ecureuil scenic flights over the glaciers and around Mount Cook.

MOUNT COOK
MON   Hermitage

This is the more northerly of the two Mount Cook airfields, used by the Airline to ferry tourists into the spectacular mountain area, called the Southern Alps. For any aviation photographer, this is one of the most wonderful places on earth. Pilatus Porters, Cessna taildraggers and 748s can all be seen at close range, with glacial and mountainous backdrops.

NELSON
NSN   NZNS

As befits a small regional airport, the air is relaxed and informal. Not only are the movements, the biggest of which are SF340s, easily seen from the terminal area, there are also a few hangars which contain local rarities. The Air New Zealand Link maintenance facility usually has at least one Bandeirante or Metro in evidence and the Helicopters New Zealand base features half a dozen or so inmates. Even without access to the hangar, the helicopters can be seen through the windows. A few other hangars contain a fairly standard selection of light aircraft.

PICTON
PCN   Koromiko

At the head of Queen Charlotte Sound, in the northeast corner of South Island, Picton is only a 30 minute flight across Cook Strait from Wellington in the Flying Dolphin (Float Air) Beaver. Picton, as a destination, offers the chance of an economical floatplane flight and scenery at the other end.

QUEENSTOWN
ZQN   NZQN   Frankton   5m/8km NE

On the beautiful north shore of Lake Wakatipu, Queenstown is the touring base for the Southern Alps and Fjordland. From a lakeside hotel, the airport is to the east, on the far side of Frankton: a five minute drive or an hour's walk along the picturesque lakeside track. Queenstown needs time, though not a lot of money. A pleasant, friendly hotel, like the Esplanade, charges only £10 a night.

Spectacular all year round, Queenstown is at its best in winter, when the mountains are covered in snow. The airport is not a disappointment. It offers variety, with plenty of operators and aircraft types. There is nowhere around the perimeter where good photos can't be taken. The scheduled 737s, 146s, ATRs, Nomads and Cessnas are supplemented by the comings and goings of the flightscene helicopters, and a lot of general aviation. Possibly one of the more notable light aircraft to be found here is Mount Cook's Tiger Moth. Pleasure flights in Tiger Moths and Ag-Cats are big business in this part of the world.

ROTORUA
ROT   NZRO   Lakefront   1m/1.5km N (bus 5 minutes)

Very much one of New Zealand's most popular tourist attractions, Rotorua's volcanic activity is on North Island. Only domestic services operate into this municipal field, though they are Mount Cook ATR-72s, Air NZ Link Metros and SF340s, and Ansett Dash 8s, so they have some appeal. More important, they are readily seen and photographed at close quarters from inside the rather basic terminal and around it. Photos are very definitely better in the mornings.

The chainlink fence has mesh large enough for a lens to be poked through. By standing at either side of the terminal, all airliners can be photographed successfully with little trouble. There is also a certain amount of general aviation to be seen.

At the far side of the field is Lake Rotorua, at the edge of which normally sits the Cessna floatplane of Volcanic Air Safaris. Ecureuils carry visitors up to the hot springs and geysers, and there is even a helipad on top of the volcano, Mount Tarawera.

Just across the water from the airport is Rotorua town harbour, where Volcanic Air Services operate their Cessna flights.

STEWART ISLAND
SZS

Stewart Island is New Zealand's outpost, off the southern tip of South Island. It is reached from Invercargill by Southern Air's scheduled Islander flights. Pretty though the island is, there is little else to see in aviation terms apart from the occasional Islander.

WANAKA
WKA

At the south end of Lake Wanaka, this is one of New Zealand's most scenic areas. In New Zealand, that means a lot. The airfield is reachable by road or by scheduled flights, mostly from Queenstown. It is from here that Aspiring Air operate their flightscene Cessnas and Islanders. The name is explained by the presence, some miles to the northwest, of the 10,000 feet high Mount Aspiring.

This is very much a ski centre, which means ski and, worse still, après-ski people in large numbers. There is plenty of hotel accommodation which, outside the season, is very affordable.

A new hangar houses the Alpine Fighter Collection, which includes a Spitfire, Corsair, Mustang and Kittyhawk. It's possible that all are airworthy, as the Spitfire has been seen flying. The Tiger Moth and Chipmunk, which also form part of the collection, need a lot of imagination to be considered as fighters!

WELLINGTON
WLG   NZWN   International   5m/8km SE (bus 30 minutes)

The single runway has water at both ends: Evans Bay to the north and Cook Strait to the south. The aprons to the east and west serve different functions, and it is to the Eastern Apron that scheduled airliners taxi after landing. The two terminals are linked by a covered way. The ANZ facility handles some international services, though most of the traffic is domestic, as at the Ansett building. Unlike Auckland, it is Ansett's terminal which offers a view from its observation deck. Good photography needs a long lens, as the taxiway is a little distant. Afternoons are better for the sun's aspect. Further opportunities for taking photos are offered along the covered link between the terminals. The glass, in some places, can mean problems.

What can be seen from here, as well as from the deck, is the far side of the field. Used mostly by general aviation, it is worth looking out for the presence of the occasional military aircraft, as there is a small base at the left/south end of that ramp. Access to the Western Apron needs transport as it is a long walk. Not visible from the terminal, because it's tucked away in the southeast corner, is the Air New Zealand maintenance area. The variety of scheduled operators is good, though exactly what constitutes 'busy' is rather subjective. The approach road to the airport is called Calabar Road. For anyone with a car, it's perfect for photos. The fence is close enough to the taxiway for taking pictures of anything that approaches the holding point for 34.

Float Air operate a shuttle bus service from downtown for use by passengers. $NZ65 buys a single ticket on the Flying Dolphin Beaver to Picton, so it's good value. The flight takes only half an hour each way, and pre-booking is advised. The need to record all aspects of Wellington's aviation will involve a trip out to PORIRUA HARBOUR, and it should be noted that flights are infrequent. A general aviation field in the Wellington area called PARA PARA is also reported, though it offers little of interest to be seen.

ZS = SOUTH AFRICA

BLOEMFONTEIN
BFN   FABL

A very pleasant airport indeed: apart from huge quantities of movements, it would be difficult to ask for more. The passenger terminal is very modern and comfortable, the cafe on the upper level serves enjoyable cheese & tomato sandwiches with a cold beer, all at easily affordable prices, the staff are extremely friendly and they will open the patio door to the balcony if you wish.

From here, anything that moves can be seen: SAA 737s, Airlink Metros and BAe 146s, and South African Express Dash 8s. Some care must be exercised when taking photographs because of Bloemspruit, the air force base on the far side of the runway. As long as it's made clear that your interest is in civil aircraft, there should be no problem. If you are tempted to take the binoculars (telescopes really aren't a good idea) to the Impalas, Dakotas and other communications aircraft, the situation might become complicated. Life here is suffuciently informal for some agreement to be reached with the security office. Bloemfontein is the sort of place which deserves to be remembered fondly, rather than for some unnecessary altercation with authority, which could have been avoided with a little thought. Night-time activity is very much on the increase, as this is a cargo hub. When staying in the area, it might also be worth making enquiries about Bloemfontein's general aviation field, NEW TEMPE.

CAPE TOWN
CPT   FACT   14m/22km E (bus 20 minutes)

South African aviation centres upon Joburg but Cape Town supports its own operations, the airport being on the side of Table Mountain remote from the city. The Flitestar passenger terminal has the best facilities for viewing but lacks subject matter. The departure lounge for passengers travelling to Joburg is accessible, and there is a glazed terrace, where the movements can be seen. Apart from SAA traffic, which can be seen at Jan Smuts, National Airlines/ Namakwaland are based locally, and a couple of Comair CV-580s are normally in evidence.

The general aviation area is home to about seventy aircraft. On the far side of the field is a military area, where C-47s are housed. The storage area contains Super Frelons and Piaggio P.166s. Security in South Africa is tight, and applies particularly to their military aircraft. Any attempts at photography could prove counter-productive.

Colourful Court Helicopters moved their headquarters and maintenance base here from Grand Central. A number of the smaller helicopters can be seen being serviced but the S-61s are usually found at the coastal town of George, some distance to the east. In Cape Town, the two locations where Court helicopters are most likely to be seen are in dockland: Bay Road Base should have at least one S-61 and a few JetRangers, while the nearby Victoria & Albert Base often houses a JetRanger used for sightseeing flights. Ysterplaat, in downtown Cape Town, is a military facility which is accessible because of its museum.

DURBAN
DUR   FADN   12m/19km SSW (bus 20 minutes)

Anyone based in Johannesburg would not find the trip to Durban really worthwhile, as its movements are virtually all 737s of SAA. Court (ex-Republic) Helicopters and Magnum Metros are based here, but action is very slow compared with the rest of the country. Traffic has increased with the opening of the international terminal but it is still unlikely to offer quality prospects for the enthusiast. A short way up the coast,VIRGINIA is the main field in Durban for general aviation, which also features one or two local carriers. The large roof terrace allows excellent views of the ramp and runway. About one hundred aircaft are present.

EAST LONDON
ELS   FAEL

Slightly busier than Port Elizabeth but used by more-or-less the same airlines, East London has a selection of freighters, primarily the C-47s and Albatrosses of Speed Services. The passenger terminal is spacious and pleasant, with grassed areas at both sides from which good photos of aircraft on the ramp are possible. Extensions to the terminal might mean the temporary (or even permanent) closure of viewing facilities. There are *very* good reasons why photographers shouldn't try their hand anywhere around the perimeter at East London (*trust me!*).

JOHANNESBURG
JNB   FAJS   International   15m/24km ENE (bus 30 minutes)

South Africa is a very security-conscious country, and anyone wanting to be sure of being able to take photographs at airports, considered to be security areas, should write to the Directorate of Civil Aviation in Pretoria. There are no other airports in Africa which could be considered as anything like busy as Joburg, and it seems to be improving all the time, especially after dark.

The general view from the observation deck, above the international terminal, is very good indeed for the logger but a little too elevated to allow first class photos. Long focus lenses are essential if the aircraft are to be captured in anything approximating to a side view. Apart from the height, there are other reasons why this deck has not met with universal approval. The glass is normally dirty and a long stay means tired feet, as no seats are provided.

The apron in front of the observation deck is used by long-haul arrivals, with some long-stay aircraft being parked to the left. SAA 737s park at the far side of the apron, and most other 'local' movements have to be logged while they are on the taxiways. Comair passengers are taken by bus to the cargo apron, where the aircraft are parked, and Air Botswana park close to the domestic terminal, out of sight from the deck. There is a waving deck in the domestic terminal, essential for anyone wishing to record at close quarters some of the smaller aircraft. Joburg is one of the few airports in the world where spotters (and even photographers) really do have a better view of what's happening than the passengers do.

To the north is the cargo apron, which is visible from the SAA car park. Also to be seen from here are the Comair and Safair facilities, on the opposite side of the runway. The South African Government (DCA) apron is also visible from here, plus a small quantity of general aviation. The other two areas worthy of note are the Atlas aircraft plant, inaccessible on the far side of the field, and the South African Airways museum. The Constellation at the southern end of the ramp forms part of the collection, but the Dove, Viking and Ju-52 are out of sight. The Junckers makes regular forays into the air: weekend flights, between Rand and Lanseria, can be booked.

Whilst arrivals from Europe are increasing exponentially (four-fold in two years), it's the variety of local carriers that is bound to be the main focus of attention. These include Zambian and Zimbabwe Express 727s, Zambian ATRs and 737s, LAMocambique Fokker 100s from neighbouring countries plus an assortment of Airlink, Comair, Nationwide, Sun-Air, Inter-Air and SA Express. A pair of Zambian ATR-42s, 9J-AFC/D, have been parked in the central cargo area for some time. So there you have it - the ideal destination for a winter break - good weather, lots to see and reasonable prices.

Other local airports offer a good range of alternatives: RAND is a major executive and general aviation field, with several helicopter operators based. It should be remembered that many of the aircraft earn their keep on contract work, and South Africa is a very large country, so it would be optimistic to expect fleets lined up on the ramp. Nevertheless the average log for a day at Rand totals as many as three hundred light aircraft. Rand used to be Joburg's main airport, before Jan Smuts (note it's not called that any more) was opened. The terminal retains some of its old facilities, including the observation deck, at first floor level. The more interesting aircraft at Rand, such as the military C-47s, C-54s and AT-6s, are in the company of large numbers of rather ordinary Cessnas and Pipers. Viewing from the road presents no problems. One hangar worth watching out for contains up to eight Tiger Moths.

JOHANNESBURG
HLA   FALA   Lanseria   11m/17km NW

The Joburg/Pretoria area is definitely worth exploring, especially the two main general aviation fields. Lanseria is where several executive operators, and three hundred or so other aircraft, are based. A request at the gate for access to the museum collection allows an interesting variety to be seen, including three Vampires, a Lancashire Prospector and a Falcon 50. On the far side of the field is the air force base, whose resident aircraft are mostly Macchi 362/Atlas Impalas, used for training duties. The main terminal has a restaurant with an outside terrace. Of the huge numbers of aircraft to be logged, there are lots of 3D- registrations, from nearby Swaziland.

Though not an airport, GRAND CENTRAL is an important general aviation field, also with a viewing area beside the apron. It is normal to see about a hundred aircraft on a visit. One other item of aviation interest is Vic's Viking Garage, which became well-known because of the Viking on display. Vic's Viking Garage would now be better described as Vic's Shackleton Garage, for obvious reasons.

KIMBERLEY
KIM   FAKM

South African Express operate about eight Dash 8 services daily into Kimberley, which means this is not one of the country's most exciting airports. Whilst the passenger terminal is small and modern, it possesses no viewing facilities, apart from the chance to see what's happening on the apron and runway from inside the main hall. Close to the terminal area are some small hangars which contain military Pumas, some of which might be out on the ramp. Don't get your camera out of its bag.

NELSPRUIT
NLP   FANS   3m/5km E

En route through eastern Transvaal to the Kruger National Park is the town of Nelspruit. The airport is worth the detour, if g.a. and, in particular, South African Thrush Commanders, are of interest. Larger aircraft are not numerous but the total to be seen is about eighty.

PIETERMARITZBURG
PZB   Oribi

Pietermaritzburg is in Natal province, 30 miles or so northwest of Durban. To find the field, take King Edward Road, off the N3 highway. Whilst there are no scheduled airline operations, the general aviation scene offers good numbers as compensation.

PORT ELIZABETH
PLZ   FAPE   3m/5km S

Port Elizabeth is another airport which is experiencing a significant increase in movements. It sees about thirty commercial flights a day, so it still isn't what you'd call frenetic, and most are SAA 737s and A320s, Comair, Nationwide and SA Express. The Police Air Wing (Pilatus Porter and

Bolkow) offer additional interest as does the military base with mostly helicopter and communications aircraft. There are plenty of ex-military Albatrosses which have been converted for use as freighters.

The small passenger terminal offers some views, all behind glass, but there are plenty of places around the perimeter to compete. Try, for example, the town's King's Beach for great views of arrivals. Take binoculars and Factor 6 sun lotion for a really nice day.

PRETORIA

PRY   FAWB   Wonderboom   5m/8km

Pretoria is only forty miles north of Joburg, so the wealth of aviation facilities in the area are used by both cities. Wonderboom is Pretoria's own field, being located on the north side of the city, remote from Joburg, and it is here that the many DC-3s of Wonderair are based. For access to this facility, a request at the security point in the main terminal should result in being escorted to the ramp.

Take a look on the map and you'll see the small distance between Joburg and Pretoria. Definitely close enough for the two to be considered in a single day's pigging out on general aviation. There aren't many places in Europe to compare, and only a few in America. Look on it as South Africa's answer to Dallas and Fort Worth.

UMTATA

UTT   FAUT   K D Matanzima

Umtata was the old capital of Transkei (nominally an independent state) and this airport was named after the tribal king, so its name hasn't disappeared like many of the others. The terminal is delightful but generally empty. There are occasional arrivals by Nationwide 1-11s (less than one a day), so this is not an airport worth a detour.

3B = MAURITIUS

MAURITIUS

MRU   FIMP   International   30m/46km E

An idyllic tropical island in the Indian Ocean is sure to attract tourists and the airport (correct name Sir Seewoosagur Ramgoolam International!) is extremely pleasant. The viewing area offers a cafe and shade, overlooking the apron and the runway. Modest photographic equipment produces good results here but a 300mm zoom lens does help. The tinted glass is scratched, normally appallingly filthy, and only very tall people are able to take photos over the top. Rather than dismiss the airport as a waste of time, exploration will reveal an alternative viewpoint.

The old terminal is now used for cargo operations and served by a road, from which first class photos can be taken of jet aircraft about to touch down or turning before take off. The ATRs, needing less runway, have an unfortunate habit of turning and departing some distance away.

Movements are few but they are interesting. The shuttle to Réunion is operated normally by F.28s and ATR-42s. The Air Mauritius long-haul fleet of A340s, 767ERs and 747SPs call regularly, as is to be expected, and other schedules include an Air Zimbabwe 737. South African Airways make tech stops on their way to and from Asia, occasionally also visiting with 737s, and the French connection is served by a regular Air France flight from Paris.

The airport is remote from many of the resorts, in the southeast corner of the island, where the weather is occasionally not as pleasant as further north. As there are no regular bus services, the journey can be time-consuming, and disappointment at the weather is always a possibility. Worth watching for are the Air Mauritius JetRangers which ferry some of their first class passengers to the more exclusive and remote resorts.

4X = ISRAEL

EILAT

ETH   LLET   J Hozman   1m/1.5km N

Eilat is a resort at the north of the Red Sea, at the end of one of the two prongs which we see on the map, called the Gulf of Aqaba (or Gulf of Eilat, depending on one's political viewpoint). Where most towns might have a Main Street, Eilat has a runway. This is no STOLport: 757s land here, though Arkia Dash 7s provide most of the movements. General aviation does use the airport, ranging from light aircraft to biz-jets, and military Queen Airs visit occasionally.

The prevailing wind is from the north, off the desert, so aircraft make a fairly tight turn to approach on Runway 03, avoiding the airspace of Jordan, Saudi Arabia and Egypt in doing so. Final approach is low over the beach, with the threshold of the runway just across the road. The terminal is not worth investigating because of security restrictions and, anyway, viewing and photography are possible from almost anywhere around the perimeter, mostly through the fence but there are places where views over are possible. The Hotel Dalia is the place to stay. It's on the coast with seaviews on one side. Why pay the extra, when the other rooms overlook the end of the runway and the passenger terminal? The view from an upper floor balcony is superb. At the far end of the runway, a road to the right leads to the border with Jordan, half a kilometre away.

OVDA

ETH   LLET   30m/48km N of Eilat

Also spelt Ouvda and Uvda, this is a military airfield in the middle of the Negev Desert, but used also by some civil flights, both scheduled and charter, from Western Europe. It should come as no surprise to read that it isn't exactly user-friendly to spotters. Access to the small single-storey terminal building is via a security gate, for passengers only. Say goodbye to relatives and friends here. Anyone without a ticket turns round and goes back. Passengers enter the security interview area before proceeding to passport control.

As well as the departure lounge there is also a patio where passengers can await their flights. The view is good and photography, stricty in theory, would be fine. Airliners are turned round in reasonably quick time, so the number on the apron is always small. Military transports, mostly C-130s and 707s share the ramp. The subject of this book is civil airfields, rather than detailed coverage of military air bases in politically sensitive regions. The rest of the field is of no consequence, as there isn't much to see. What is of interest is that airliners, when they have landed, shut down their engines whilst on the runway and await a tug to take them to the ramp. Restart occurs on the runway, thereby avoiding blowing half the Negev Desert into the terminal.

Be'er Sheva, some miles to the northwest, is worth the drive for military enthusiasts, as there aren't many other ways they can enjoy themselves in Israel. At nearby HATZERIM is the Israeli Air Force Museum where, for about £2.50, there is access to aircraft from the earliest days up to the current F-4, A-4 and Kfir plus a number of captured aircraft. There are no barriers, so it's rather like being the only person to arrive at a big air show, and having access to the flight line in (usually) perfect weather conditions. Even the scrapyard is worth detailed investigation.

TEL AVIV

TLV LLBG   Ben Gurion   9m/15km SE (bus 35 minutes)

Security is tight at Israeli airports. Tel Aviv has two fields, Ben Gurion being the main gateway for international flights. The whole airport is in a security cordon and casual visitors are unlikely to gain access. It is not going to come as a surprise therefore to read that the viewing area has been closed for a long time. What vantage points there are should not be used for photography and, even if permission to take photos has been formally given, it could still lead to trouble. Ben Gurion can be considered as one airport which is definitely not for the enthusiast!

SDE DOV is a small field close to the city, with a military base sharing the runway. The majority of scheduled flights are Arkia Dash Sevens providing an air bridge to Eilat, though these are few in number. Arkia does have a maintenance base here, in the company of military helicopters and some army trainers. What general aviation there is in Israel can be seen as well here as anywhere else, and twenty or so light aircraft are visible from the perimeter. By asking permission of the security staff, registrations can be logged but, predictably, photography is out of the question.

JERUSALEM
JRS   LLJR   Atarot   5m/8km N

Another small field, a few miles north of the city, where a dozen or so light aircraft are based. By checking with security staff, watching and logging the movements is normally permitted but of course photography is not allowed. The Arkia Dash Sevens only provide one or two movements each day.

5B = CYPRUS

LARNACA
LCA   LCLK   5m/8km S

Larnaca is still the principal airport in Cyprus, despite the existence of Paphos. For the spotter, there are enough vantage points around the terminal to ensure that all movements are seen, but the photographer can find the going a bit tough. The terminal is protected from moving aircraft by large red blast screens, so there are no views from inside the building. Two viewing points remain around the terminal: to the right, the staff car park overlooks the ramp and, on the opposite side, a gate close to the police station allows the Cyprus Airways movements to be seen. This spot is close to the taxi rank and the Cyprus Airways catering buildings. For at least ten years, DC-6 N19CA decayed slowly nearby but its continued survival has not been confirmed.

Cyprus shares with Athens a hub status where European and arab traffic meets. The civil war in the Lebanon, only 150 miles away, also reflected Larnaca's importance. The Middle East is often politically unstable, so the changing pattern of events will continue to have an effect. Traffic using the airport is variable in quantity and consistency. Some reports note much military activity, and others almost nil. Aeroflot movements, too, range from a regular Tu-154 to a varied range of Il-76s and An-22s. Delivery flights, though irregular, do include a number of short-range airliners on their way from Europe to customers in the Far East. Scheduled arrivals are nonetheless an interesting mix with 727s and 737s of Alyemda, Libyan, Gulf Air, Egyptair, Royal Jordanian, Yemenia and Saudia all normally featuring amongst the arab visitors. Like Athens, Larnaca is often used for refuelling when long distance flights are adversely affected by winds.

Elsewhere around the perimeter, the southeastern corner is close to the beach. The Flamingo Beach Hotel, despite its rooftop pool and view of the airport, cannot be compared directly with Glyfada's Emmantina, as aircraft pass to the south, and too far away for photography or even reliable reading of registrations. Walking towards the airport along the beach road leads to a row of tavernas and the perimeter fence. From here the Cyprus Airways hangar is seen, and much of the airport. Reports of conflict with the authorities in this area have been variable, and it is likely that regular use of these local bars by enthusiasts will lead to an a gradual relaxation of security measures.

PAPHOS
PFO   LCPH   International   5m/8km SE

Because the name of Paphos features on a few departure boards, it might be assumed to be an airport worthy of a visit. This is definitely not the case, unless a handful of Cyprus Airways and charter movements are sought. Despite the heavy investment that Paphos airport represents, it still appears to handle a minimal quantity of flights. The terminal can remain closed for most of the day if no arrivals are due but, if viewing facilities exist, the combination of the sun in the right direction and a mountainous backdrop would please most photographers. A Caravelle, possibly ex-Air Afrique, has been rotting away at Paphos for some time.

AKROTIRI
AKT   LCRA

Akrotiri, to the south of Limassol, is a relatively busy field, used for practice sorties, trooping flights and technical stops en route to the Middle East, and a Wessex flight is based here. There is also a Vulcan on the dump.

LAKATAMIA, about six miles north of Nicosia, takes some finding as there are no road signs pointing to it. A dirt track leads to the short runway and the majority of the island's fixed wind residents, including the National Guard Islander.

The rest of aviation activity in Greek Cyprus is strictly military, and RAF dominated. In the eastern corner of the Greek part of the island is DHEKALIA, home of the Army Air Corps Alouettes. The strip is close to the UN buffer zone and is one of the few places where these helicopters can be seen.

5N = NIGERIA
LAGOS
LOS   DNMM   Murtala Muhammed   5m/8km NE

This is not one of Africa's most stable areas, so guidance on activities such as aircraft spotting must start with warnings. Attempting to log (photography being absolutely out of the question) must only be attempted with discretion, and preferably in the company of someone local who knows more than just the lie of the land.

The airport has two parallel runways, between which sit the international terminal and the cargo centre. One runway is used solely for international movements, and the other for military and domestic flights. Maybe they will get the observation deck open one day. Maybe they'll get the air-conditioning working too. Traffic is slow, and most of it uses the domestic terminals, on the far side of one runway, next to the air force apron. Military aircraft are mostly C-130s and there are other aircraft to be noted, none of which are likely to move. Close to the fire station, between the terminal and the cargo area, is a 125, 5N-AVZ, and a couple of Caravelles, both of whose tails sport Air France colours. They are believed to be F-BJTE and 5N-AWF. The Nigeria Airways A310, near the 125, is 5N-AUE.

KANO
KAN   DNKN   Mallam Aminu International   5m/8km NE

The main terminal overlooks the scheduled airline ramp, which is still a paradise for lovers of BAC 1-11s. Gas Air and Kabo Air examples share the tarmac with Nigerian 737s and A310s. The balcony offers a good view but the use of binoculars and cameras is strictly prohibited because of the military traffic which shares the runway. As with most other parts of Africa, the amount of movements which use the airport on an average day is small.

To the left of the balcony are a few biz-jets and other general aviation twins. This area contains one or two stored aircraft. To the right, and rather more remote, are the other light aircraft. Behind the terminal, a mile or so distant, is the military base where a number of MiG-17s can be seen in rather delapidated condition.

5X = UGANDA

ENTEBBE
EBB   HUEN   22m/34km

The Ugandan president said that its main airport creates a first, and lasting, impression. A face-lift followed, including a new (and perfectly clean) terminal with courteous and efficient immigration staff. The runways and taxiways ave also been refurbished. Times have changed at Entebbe, in more ways than one. At the time of writing (and this is stressed) there are no restrictions on the use of cameras. After clearing customs, visitors have a full view of all rampside activity. What's more the large windows are usually open and good photos are easy to take. Naturally, the ongoing security situation should be checked before using either a camera or binoculars. Aircraft to be seen include the Uganda Airways fleet of course, plus Iran Air and Air Tanzania 737s, the occasional Ethiopian 727, BA, Alliance or Sabena wide-body. Eagle Air Let 410 5Y-ENT seems to be a regular visitor (or maybe it doesn't leave), and there are other turboprop movements, especially in the mornings, like an Air Rwanda Dash 8.

The civil aviation ramp is to the right of the terminal, just outsie the business class lounge, making it easy for users to record the twenty or so registrations. Alongside the president's Gulfstream might be all sorts of foreign metal, from an Iranian 737 to a Russian Yak-42. Taking a stroll alongside the ramp, and taking a few dozen photos at the same time might lead to imprisonment (if things get bad), a light conversation with some official who will remind you that, officially, you're not supposed to do that or, possibly, the exchanging of pleasantries (hard currency pleasantries, such as US dollars, are preferred).

The old terminal area is now used to house the military personnel who run security and look after the president. Ex-British Airtours 707 (wearing 5X-CAU), and Caravelle 9Q-CRU, which used to live nearby, have been moved to a photogenic site on the shore of Lake Victoria but HS 748 VN-008 was still stored in early 1997. Uganda's military activity, such as it is, takes place at Entebbe: the hangar area at the north end of the field contains the remains of the air force and the Uganda Police Wing, also defunct. At least three MiG-21s have been stripped of most of their useful parts, and a pair of Mi-8s sit around, doing nothing.

Thirty-four kilometres doesn't sound far but it's a long way in Africa. The drive from Kampala is strictly for the fun-loving and the suicidal. The alternatives are to stay at the Sheraton, which has a free transfer bus, or at the Windsor Victoria with the air crew.

5Y = KENYA

MOMBASA
MBA   HKMO   Moi International   8m/13km SW (bus 25 minutes)

The best way to the airport is to catch the Kenya Airways or No.6 bus from downtown, and the reward is an excellent view from the rooftop observation deck, next to the cafe. The security staff use this cafe for their breaks, so they are used to people showing an active interest in aviation.

Traffic doesn't match the interest however. Most of the few movements are Kenya Airways flights to Nairobi. All types can be seen but the A310s, travelling to London, are rarely present in daylight hours. Most interest is generated by Air Tanzania F.27s, the only foreign carrier of regular note, and the F.27s and DC-9s of Kenya Airways, which are very much local to this part of the world.

NAIROBI
NBO   HKNA   Jomo Kenyatta International   8m/13km SE (bus 30 minutes

Also known as Embakasi, this is a quiet but interesting airport. A visit should be timed to coincide with the several unusual scheduled movements, as there can be long periods during the day, especially in the afternoons, when nothing happens except the occasional movement by the resident Kenya Airways fleet. Apart from sporadic European traffic, which normally passes through at unsociable hours, there is a good selection of airline traffic to be seen.

The main terminal is semi-circular, with nose-in parking for most of the visiting airliners which use the jetties, if they are working. There is a good waving gallery atop the building but opening hours are erratic, to say the least; on some days it doesn't open at all. Access is via a door at the front of the terminal complex, which opens to a stairway. Photography is only possible when aircraft are on the move, as the viewing area doesn't extend to edge of the roof. Thus, most of the aircraft are semi-hidden from view by the roof when they park at their stands.

When the police or military personnel are in evidence, photography should not be attempted. The consequences are usually protracted negotiations about what might be best described as on-the-spot fines, a.k.a. cash transactions (dash), or sampling the pleasures of a cell for a short while. Authority, in this part of the world, can be surprisingly unsophisticated. Do not assume that someone in uniform knows the difference between a camera and a pair of binoculars!

Small visiting aircraft park to the right-hand side of the terminal, near to any long-stay airliners up to 727 size, and the Aeroflot Tu-154, Royal Swazi F.28, Airstar Zanzibar YS-11 and Air Madagascar 737 are usually found here. Unfortunately, many of these aircraft are not very photogenic when parked but reasonable shots can be obtained from the fence, next to the terminal. The YS-11 arrives late in the day, possibly after the deck closes. In this event it is worth seeking out the restaurant which isn't in the terminal at all but in the administration block opposite. The view from here is excellent.

The cargo terminal has its own access road, some distance from the passenger facilities. There is often something of interest on the ramp, usually in the company of something like German Cargo DC-8-73Fs and Air France 747Fs, which are regular visitors.

Across from the passenger terminal (on the other side of the runway) lies the modest Kenya Airways maintenance base with a small military compound adjacent, containing about twenty Hughes 500s. The remains of the Tradewinds CL-44 have now gone but, as compensation, the fuselage of 720 5Y-BBX is used for crew-training. The derelict C-119 N3267U is parked near the terminal, and YS-11 JA8723 has been a long-term resident. DC-6 5Y-BKG has been in storage for some time on the old military ramp (on the far side) but the Caribou, outside Kenya Airways Engineering, has been carted away. Other mortal remains to watch for are the 707s, 5Y-BBI/AXM/AXW, which won't fly again, DC-3 5Y-BIL, and an F.27 from which most of the marking have been obliterated. The engineless Cessna 402, by the fence, is 5Y-PFK.

The assortment of visiting airlines is good, with 737s of Air Madagascar, Air Tanzania, Cameroon Airlines and Air Zaire (with luck!), Saudia A300-600s, Uganda Airlines F.27s plus Air Malawi and Royal Swazi F.28s. Smaller visitors are quite limited in number but the interest factor is a compensation: the Malawi Citation is a regular, and foreign military visitors are often seen. It can't be stressed too strongly that any attempts at photography should be discounted totally if any police or military personnel are nearby. In several parts of Africa, the political scene is volatile. When times are tense, often unkown to a foreigner, there can be heavy clampdowns.

NAIROBI

WIL   HKNW   Wilson   2m/3km S

Some ten miles across the small but excellent Nairobi National Park from Jomo Kenyatta, lies the much smaller Wilson Airport. Just before reaching the city, a winding lane leads off the main road, up to Wilson which is only two or three miles from the city centre. There are probably over two hundred aircraft based here, so it is a good field for the enthusiast in pursuit of general aviation.

Hangars run almost the entire length of the 4500 feet runway and, with Kenya's climate, they are almost always open during the day (except at weekends). Access to the apron is normally possible, and permission should be sought. Achieved one way or another (!), an escorted walk will reveal a hive of activity, but the Kenya Police Air Wing should be given a very wide berth, as the local security personnel can be unpredictable. The Geosurvey hangar, at the far end of the field, should also be treated with some care, with permission being necessary to walk inside. Up to ten specially configured Cessna Titans, a Twin Otter and sometimes their Challenger are to be seen.

Star attractions abound here: numerous Islanders and Beavers of the East African Locust Control and rarer types, such as a Dromader or a Turbolet, plus a wonderful selection of non-Kenyan residents undergoing major maintenance.

Wilson is worth half a day. Either be there by 06:45, to see everything depart and then take a walk around the field, or arrive in the early afternoon so that you've done all the hard work before 16:00, when everything returns home for the night.

6V = SENEGAL

DAKAR
DKY   GOOY   Yoff   11m/17km NW

Dakar boasts a sizeable airfield which gained some prominence and prestige when its runway was constructed to handle Air France Concordes on their way between Paris and Rio de Janeiro. This service is no more, but the runway remains, and is now the emergency landing strip for any Space Shuttle suffering problems a few minutes after lift-off from Florida!

The terminal is not very good for viewing, although a landside bar in the terminal offers a restricted view of the apron. A small light aviation area, with about twenty or so residents, is located just along from the terminal and is usually accessible. Any airliner taxiing to or from the terminal passes this area and can be photographed with the average zoom lens . . . in theory.

An excellent panoramic view of the field is possible from the Meridien Hotel complex, a mile away from the terminal. A stay here allows the latest arrivals to be checked before heading to the terminal for a closer look. Frequent movements from Ouagadougou are a lone F.28, plus one or two Nord 262s and HS748s. In this part of the world, frequent means about three times a week! F.28s of Air Mauretanie, Air Guinée Dash7s/An-24s/737s call about twice a week but the Air Zaire flight has a habit of being cancelled.

The Ghanaian DC-9 and Nigerian 737s are regular, and the Air Afrique fleet is, officially, resident here. In reality, it spends much of its time at Charles de Gaulle, though Air Senegal's resident fleet includes a couple of HS748s and Twin Otters.

Military activity comprises resident F.27s, Twin Otter and Magister movements, and the derelict Air Force C-47s are still present. Regular visits are made by USAF C-141s, and RAF VC-10s refuel on their way to the Falklands, while French Jaguars and Transalls are based.

6Y = JAMAICA

KINGSTON
KIN   MKJP   Norman Manley International 12m/19km SE

A spit of land stretches out into the bay, east of town, on which the airport has been built. The runway, 12/30, sits on reclaimed land and is almost entirely surrounded by water. At its northeast corner is the apron and terminal.

The view from the terminal's rooftop terrace is southerly. Scheduled airliners park at either side of the central single-storey finger which is built out into the centre of the ramp. The fencing which encloses the terrace is, however, something of a major problem. People are kept at a distance from it, so it's impossible to take photos. Having been disappointed by the roof, photographers are bound to seek vantage points elsewhere. To save time and energy, they would do best to get on a plane and fly somewhere else.

Outside the terminal, landside, a right turn leads past Air Jamaica's maintenance facility, where nothing is visible from the road. Beyond it, however, is the rest of the old apron which is now used to store impounded aircraft. Drug smugglers have been caught using DC-3 PT-KZM, Martin 404 N404PS, a couple of Queen Airs and some Cessna twins. Behind the compound is the Defence Force ramp, with a brace of Islanders and a Cessna 210, but not within range of a camera lens. Next to the fire station is DC-3 N238GB, showing distinct signs of old age. It will be tempting to follow the road to Nelson's old barracks at Fort Royal, since it looks promising. Airborne movements are visible but they are too distant for photos.

Kingston's traffic is mostly Air Jamaica obviously but American, TACA, BWIA and British Airways appear in fits and starts. In other words, anyone who wants photos of Caribbean aircraft in exotic surroundings, Manley Airport is definitely the wrong destination.

From downtown Kingston, head out towards Spanish Town and TINSON PEN is on the edge of Kingston, to the north side of the road. Of the sixty or so light aircraft on the field, many are US-registered. A dump contains half a dozen singles and a Beech 18. The passenger terminal offers the chance to see, at close quarters, the visiting Trans Jamaica Do228s. It is adviseable to seek permission before taking photos.

MONTEGO BAY
MBJ   MKJS   Sangster International

There can be more to see here than at Kingston since this is a tourist detsination in its own right. Lots of American airlines, of course, plus Air Canada. The terminal faces the single runway but there are so many nice beaches around the field, from which to see the arrivals, it's best to stay in the open and enjoy the sun. Local specialities are, unsurprisingly, Do228s and Trislanders but do watch out for the remains of DC-3 N717A, lurking in the bushes.

7O = YEMEN

ADEN
ADE   OYAA   Khormaksar   6m/9km NE

Obtaining a visa to visit the Yemen is a difficult business, and possession of one doesn't even guarantee entry into the country! There has been internal strife for a long time and it would be a hardy enthusiast who set off in search of Alyemda aircraft at home. The squalid old terminal has been replaced by a new one, with just as few facilities for viewing proceedings. Left of the new terminal is the old one and to the right the open fronted Alyemda hangar with a few aircraft parked beside it. Some derelict DC-3s and DC-6s would make ideal subjects for first-hand research, if conditions were friendlier. The VIP Tu-154 7O-ACT is usually parked outside on the main ramp.

The only chance of realistic viewing will be fleeting, by sitting on the left of the departing aircraft and hoping it takes off to the east. The taxiway leads past the derelict machines, then past the Air Force transport ramp (with a dozen An-12s/An-26s) and the MiGs etc which live in the large, old RAF hangars. At the other side of the runway threshold is the military dump, which must contain a fascinating collection, but the road which passes all these facilities and the end of the runway, with the sea on the other side, will remain uncharted territory for many years to come. The only hope is to put a 100-300mm zoom lens on the camera and snap away on departure.

SANA'A
SAH   OYSN   International

At 7,000 feet above sea level, Sana'a is higher than Denver and the Yemenia publicity material makes a big deal about Sana'a being the oldest capital city in the world. The airport's passenger terminal seems to be one of the oldest too! Squalid it may be, but it does have an observation deck, with a good view of most of the proceedings.

The title 'International' is misleading to the unwary as it suggests a greater emphasis on foreign traffic than is really the case. Visiting airlines are few and far between, with occasional visits by Air France A300s and Aeroflot plus a handful of flights per week from middle eastern airlines: Saudia A300s and Gulf Air 737s, Ethiopian and Kuwaiti 727s and Egyptair 707 or 767 flights take place but mostly the airport can be considered as handling domestic traffic with the odd international movement.

The deck overlooks the 'domestic' ramp where the Dash 7s park. The heavy-weight traffic (everything else) parks on the apron to the right and can be easily seen, although at a greater distance. The 'No photography' signs are placed at strategic points along the balcony and, with machine gun-equipped guards to enforce the rule, it seems wise to comply. It doesn't say that binoculars are also out of the question but their use may also lead to a misunderstanding.

The prime reason for the sensitivity is the airfield's role as headquarters for the Yemen Arab Republic Air Force. Assorted types bear small serials in arabic (if at all) so the military presence is a significant one. The base is close to the terminal but hidden from view by several large buildings. From outside the terminal, a high concrete wall maintains privacy. If flying with an airline whose flight attendants are not concerned with Yemeni security (e.g. Air France) a window seat on the left-hand side of the aircraft should guarantee a closer inspection while taxiing out. The Antonovs and C-130s are normally within range of a 135-200mm lens.

At the other end of the field lies the Yemenia hangar and the civilian dump, sealed off by a security barrier beyond which is a host of treats, such as the rare Yemenia VIP 727, the two immaculate DC-3s with Yemen Airways titles, three DC-6s, an Alyemda DC-3 and the semi-derelict 707. Anyone wandering around any part of the airport, including around the passenger terminal area, should exercise extreme caution. There are military personnel everywhere and they are particularly sensitive about Iraqi Il-76 flights, and others, which fly very mysterious missions into Sana'a. At the end of the runway lie the remains, almost complete, of an Il-18 which failed to approach in the correct manner!

TA'IZZ
TAI   OYTZ   Al-Janad (or Ganed)

Visitors to the Yemen should also remember that Ta'izz, to the south of the country, has another three DC-6s, two of which still bear Yemen Airlines titles and colours. In this part of the world it would be wasteful to build a runway without using it for military purposes. Apart from the hulks, the only aviation interest at Ta'izz would come from the air force, as almost all the airliners operate from Sana'a. As with anywhere else in this country, active interest in aircraft is best confined to the departure lounge or the window of the aircraft.

7P = LESOTHO
MASERU
MSU   FXMM   Moshoeshoe International

As long as quantities of aircraft are not the reason for visiting airports, the trip to Maseru can be very worthwhile indeed. The setting is quite idyllic: a splendidly modern terminal nestling among the beautiful Lesotho mountains. There is an open air viewing gallery upstairs, with a glazed screeen which is kept perfectly clean. There appears to be no problem using a camera but the reason could be that there are only four Lesotho Airways F.27 flights each day.

7Q = MALAWI
LILONGWE
LLW   Kamazu

Like many other African airports, only the supreme enthusiast would consider a visit here, as there isn't really enough activity to justify leaving home. The terminal is a beautiful building, modern in the extreme, with an open balcony at first floor level, though a little remote from the apron for really good photos. Traffic is extremely slow, and the Air Malawi aircraft visit South Africa and Zimbabwe, and so are better seen there.

8P = BARBADOS

CHRIST CHURCH

BGI   TBPB   Grantley Adams International   7m/11km E (bus 30 mins)

Barbados is located just east of the Windward Islands, and its neighbours are nations in their own right. Grantley Adams is normally referred to as Bridgetown, although official sources differ, preferring to call it Christ Church. Movements at the airport may not be numerous but they do feature a very interesting array of registrations. The Leeward Islands are only 150 miles or so to the north, so LIAT's fleet of island hoppers are regular visitors. HS748s, Islanders, Twin Otters and Dash 8s operate the majority of scheduled services, though Air St Vincent/Mustique Airways Islanders are also much in evidence. Charter traffic features several American and Canadian carriers, as well as Britannia 767s, though exotic visitors can be very special indeed. Cubana operate Il-18s or Tu-154s twice a week, Varig 737s appear (but usually at night) and such rarities as Aerosucre Caravelles and smaller aircraft of the Brazilian Air Force can be seen.

    The terminal offers few vantage points and the apron can be too cluttered for photography, but LIAT and general aviation can be seen through the fence, between the terminal and the cargo sheds. Fortunately, anyone with a car can enjoy the perimeter. From the highway, a left turn onto Wilcox Road (at the garage) passes the holding point at the end of the runway before leading to the Aero Services hangar.

    The ground next to the airport's solitary hangar offers trouble-free viewing and photography, though the runway alignment means that quality portraits are best obtained, using 135-200mm focal length, in the morning.

9G = GHANA

ACCRA

ACC   DGAA   Kotoka   6m/9km SW

A visit to Kotoka on a Monday, Wednesday or Friday evening reveals a fair number of European heavies passing through. They give the impression of a bustling international airport . . . it is misleading. At all other times, there is very little happening - twenty-five movements means a busy day. Even the home-based Ghana Airways fleet is small. The cost of access to the roof terrace is negligible and the view is excellent, but everything else is bad news. Binoculars and cameras are forbidden by law, as a means of giving its enforcement officers the chance to supplement their income. Bribery is known as 'dash' (best as 2000 Cedis notes - about £1) and care should be exercised when trying to reach agreement. It's best to listen for the word, rather than suggest it. A smooth tongue is also crucial to successful negotiations.

    With aircraft such as an Air Afrique Fokker100 landing on the runway, time may be at a premium. The reason for the tight restrictions is the military presence at the far side of the runway, with mostly transports in evidence, from Skyvans to Fokkers, plus a sprinkling of MB 326s.

9H = MALTA

MALTA

MLA   LMML   Luqa   3m/5km W (bus 20 minutes)

The old terminal has become the cargo and executive terminal, having been replaced by a new passenger building. This is light and airy, with fountains in the courtyard between the arrivals and departures sections. The top floor is occupied by the observation deck, and fronted with glass. Refreshments are cheap enough and the view is first class. So, what's the catch? Apart from there only being modest traffic, and the glass making life difficult for photographers, there is none.

One of the regular departures from the old terminal is the Mi-8, wet leased from Aeroflot (replacing LZ-CAP). It operates a ferry link with the nearby island of Gozo, and is also used for pleasure flights. The cost, starting at ten Maltese pounds, is extremely reasonable for a 25 minute flight.

Serious photographers make their way along the road to the underpass which leads to the far side of the runway. A left turn after the tunnel leads to a good location. Depending on aircraft size, 135-300mm focal length allows moving aircraft to be photographed. Further along this road ex-Mauretanian Super Constellation 5T-TAF has just about reached the end of its life, being in extremely poor condition.

Also on this side of the field, reached by turning in the opposite direction after passing through the tunnel, is the Maltese Defence Force with its rather strange collection: an Agusta-Bell 47, a JetRanger and Ecureuil are hardly a rationalised fleet of helicopters, and Cessna Bird Dogs provide fixed wing assistance in times of need.

The occasional visit to Luqa by an Italian Air Force G222 is connected with their Agusta-Bell 212s which carry out sonar-dipping sorties in Mellieha Bay, north of the island. At the side of Runway 06/24, reached by passing this area (part military base, part disusued quarry) are the remains of an Air Malta 720, used for fire crew training. The general aviation community is served by its own facility in the north eastern corner of the field, on the far side of Runway 06/24 from the other facilities.

SAFI is close to Luqa, just to the southeast. From the airport it is a short distance past the remains of the Super Connie. Whether one would wish to walk there from Luqa's rerminal is another matter. In one corner are the Caribous of MIACO. They are visible, but only just, from the airport's observation deck. At least two appear to be airworthy and can operate from Safi's short runway. The others are slowly being dismantled. Also to be seen are a few light aircraft, including three camouflaged Bulldogs.

HAL-FAR is now an industrial estate. The derelict DC-6 and three DC-3s from Safi are still present. At least two will be burnt but their remains will join those of Eisenhower's Beech 18 N946F, still to be seen. A scrapyard to the south of Hal-Far, known as Brolli-Lane, is the last resting place of two C-54s, a Beech 18 and the remains of Canberra WT482.

The War Museum, to complete the picture of Malta, is at Fort Saint Elmo, in Valletta. It houses the wreckage of a Spitfire and a BF109 plus 'Faith', one of the three famous Gladiators. It carries the serial N5520 but is also reported in some publications as N5519.

9K = KUWAIT
KUWAIT
KWI   OKBK   International   10m/16km S

No entry in this book for an airport illustrates more vividly the volatile nature of Middle Eastern affairs than Kuwait. Even before 1990/91 Kuwait was partly a military field, without observation facilities. Many of the scheduled flights pass through Kuwait mostly during the night. The only post-war report was succinct: the place is a dump!

9M = MALAYSIA
KUALA LUMPUR
KUL   WMKK   Subang International   14m/22km

Visitors to Singapore soon realise that the air bridge to Kuala Lumpur generates plenty of traffic and passengers. The distance between the two airports is relatively modest, by Asian standards, (the flight taking less than an hour) so this may be considered as a day trip from Singapore.

The larger Malaysian airliners which are to be seen at Singapore, A330s and 737s, are obviously also present on their home tarmac. The appeal lies more in the presence of Malaysian Air Charter Skyvans, Islanders and Do228s, and the colourful Pelangi Air Do228s/Fokker 50s.

Terminal 1, for international traffic, sits between the road and the runway, and beside it are Terminals 2 (mostly for the Air Bridge) and 3. Between Terminals 1 and 2 is a hangar used by MAS for 737s and Fokker 50s. Directly opposite the terminals, on the far side of the runway and partially obscured by trees, is the military base where C-130s are regularly seen.

All movements can be seen from the windows of the newly renovated domestic Terminal 3 but photography can sometimes be difficult when aircraft are parked at it. For example, a fine photo of a Pelangi Fokker 50 is possible but, once it is parked, the view of the runway is partially obscured. It may therefore be necessary to spend an equal amount of time in Terminal 3, which allows views and photos of all the other (larger) movements. A free shuttle bus operates between arrivals levels of the domestic and international terminals but walking allows a sight of the general aviation ramp, usually with a few biz-jets present. It should be remembered that it is over a mile between the two terminals, so walking can be hard work in the Malaysian heat.

Walking is, unfortunately, essential to see what Subang has to offer: the cargo apron and MAS maintenance facility are side by side, with a grassy bank handily placed for the photographer. The Airod Sendirian Berhad ramp should be treated with extreme caution, as some of their customers are military. C-130s are regular visitors (it's a Lockheed joint venture) as are exotic helicopters. Stop anywhere near it, show a bit of interest and listen for the whistle. Don't think that, just because you start walking (running is not advised!), they lose interest in you - they don't. Beyond the Airod area, the walk is parallel to the runway, with plenty of movements, though dominated by the MAS 737s. Watch out for a glimpse of Continental Heights Resorts 737.

To the south of the city is the old airport, now used as a helicopter field and the base for the Royal Flight. Close scrutiny is not recommended, as there is a significant military presence.

PENANG
PEN   WMKP   International

This is the third most popular holiday destination in Asia, (it's slightly bigger than Ibiza), the airport being at the southern end of the island and the resorts at the north. A cafeteria overlooks the apron, instead of formal observation facilities. The glass features, apart from the view, the usual smears that are associated with watching planes while eating a burger. Not the sort of place to spend an entire day but an afternoon yields good results. Half a dozen MAS 737s, two or three A330s and a Pelangi Fokker 50 or two. Singapore Airlines can visit, with anything from an A310 to a lear Jet (yes, really) and there are other wide-bodies from other parts of Asia. Sempait 737s and Asia Pacific Metros help introduce a little variety and a FedEx A310 is likely.

A rental car might be essential, if staying in Georgetown or Batu Ferrighi, at about £45 for a day. There are lots of local companies that might offer the same conditions but one of the internationally-known names is a safer bet. That way you know for certain your insurance is in order. This is a pretty informal corner of the world. Attitudes to matters of a legal nature are treated with casual disdain in these parts. Taxis might be operating legally, road conditions are not for the faint-hearted, and road signs (where they exist) are to be taken with a pinch of salt. Even using the dual carriageway to the airport, where good signs are to be expected, there is little to let you know you mustn't go up onto the elevated section because, that way, you get to see the airport on your way past to the next intersection. Allow at least two hours for the journey from one end of the island to the other.

One last piece of advice, better late than never: don't be in too much of a hurry to get airside after checking in for departure, as views there are non-existant. With a hire car, it might be tempting to take a look at BUTTERWORTH. Driving by slowly is okay. Stopping for a photo, even of something as innocuous as a Sea King, can lead to big trouble. You might be lucky, and get your camera back, but don't expect to see the film again.

TIOMAN
TOO

Another island that's increasing in appeal, Tioman is strictly for local traffic only. Being a small

268

airport, this means close encounters of a photographic kind. In other words, this is where to come for good shots of Pelangi and Turom Air - Twin Otters, Dash 7s and 8s, Dorniers and Shorts. The terminal is beside the runway, at one end of which is a quarry. In time, they might excavate the entire hill, so that aircraft can approach/take off from either end of the runway. Meanwhile, everything comes in from the left and goes out that way also. For a choice of viewpoints around the perimeter, cycle hire is highly recommended.

9V = SINGÅPORE

SINGAPORE

SIN   WSSS   Changi International   12m/19km E (bus 25 minutes)

Widely regarded as the most sophisticated and civilised airport in the world, Changi is without equal. Because it was designed from the start to be able to cope with future needs, the airport is already too big for the enthusiast to have a relaxing day. The rapid expansion of Changi has not stopped with the opening of Terminal 2. Already an additional seventeen gates are being added to this terminal. A third terminal will be needed by 1997/8, and the CAAS are renowned for matching need with investment. By the next century, Singapore will be a very large airport.

The Viewing Hall in Terminal 1 was originally designed to face in three directions, but pressure for office space caused the loss of the east wing. What remains faces north and west. An airband radio is, in theory, the only means of ensuring that some significant movements are seen during the day, but these are illegal. Being caught using one means (at least) having the batteries confiscated. You *could* just fit some new ones, but if you get caught a second time . . . This Viewing Hall is definitely not where to see anything land on Runway 02R before it taxis to a stand, usually at Terminal 2. If it moves on that side of the field, you're not going to see it.

As is common in the Far East, international traffic reaches its peak after dark. Qantas, for example, use Singapore as their Asian hub and there can be, in an average evening, two 747s and four 767s on the ground at once. A recipe for frustration is guaranteed, although the daytime movements should provide some exciting moments for even the hardened traveller. China Southwest Boeings, and 737s in the colours of Myanmar, Royal Air Cambodge and Yunnan, Vietnamese A320s and Silk Air Fokker 70s are just some of the regular movements here.

Some consolation for the restricted views of stands is offered by Singapore Airlines' maintenance base, the long stay north apron and the cargo aprons, all north of the main ramp. It must be stressed that daytime traffic is not brisk, so patience and time are needed to get the most from Singapore. At the perimeter, a turn off Airport Boulevard, the approach road, leads to Changi Coast Road. There are views of aircraft using runway 02R, and the road continues past Singapore Airlines' service base.

Terminal 2 is served by the Skytrain, a monorail link with the original Terminal 1. If the Viewing Hall stays open, what can be seen is, of course, restricted to just one side of the field, though photo-graphers will welcome the chance of some different views of taxiing aircraft, particularly when Runway 02R sees so much use. The two piers that project from Terminal 2 really do restrict the view from this deck - this might be as civilised as aiports get but it's extremely frustrating for spotters. Because the view faces east, traffic landing on 02L and using stands on the west apron cannot be seen. The remote stands are out of sight from all internal vantage points, and busiest after dark. As Changi International grows, so does the frustration for the enthusiast, but what can be seen and photographed is still worth the trip.

There have been occasional instances where security personnel have expressed disapproval of photography. This is due to the presence of the military base, containing . . . hardly front-line combat aircraft. In the northwest corner of the field, off Upper Changi Road, and screened from the terminal by trees, is a ramp which usually contains four or five Skyvans but independent means of transport is essential to get close. The cost of living, even for a tourist, need not be high in Singapore. Car hire, however, is not cheap. For anyone anxious to see as much of possible of the island, shopping around for a keen price is advisable. Bus service 390 from Orchard Road serves the airport, though the excellent rapid transit around town does not, as yet. The other 'civil' field of any note is located towards the north of the island . . .

SINGAPORE
QPG   Paya Lebar   11m/17km NE

The number 92 bus links Orchard Road with the community of Paya Lebar but the airfield is some way out, if on foot. The terminal facilities are closed, as are most of the associated buildings. It can be safely assumed that Paya Lebar is no longer an airport of any description.

Because there are several ramps used only, it would appear, for storing withdrawn aircraft, a pedestrian with a notebook, or worse, a camera and binoculars, would be bound to attract unwanted attention. The word 'bound' suggests a stronger treatment than may be the case, but it would be foolish to run risks, just to be able to log a handful of T-33s.

SINGAPORE
XSP   WSSL   Seletar   12m/19km N

To visit Seletar, a hire car is preferable. Arriving by taxi is not necessarily a good idea, largely because it will be difficult to find another taxi to take you out. Nominally under military control, it might be necessary to check in at the security hut. There are forms to fill in and, possibly, cameras to be handed over. In practice, the camera can be quietly retained but seeking out the military areas might be injudicious. Alternatively, if you know the arrival time of a Silk Air flight (about one a day at the last count), you could say you're meeting a friend. It speeds things up a bit.

There is usually little or no movement at Seletar but there is usually plenty to be seen. AirFast have a maintenance base here, with an assortment of aircraft parked outside their hangar. Between the two Dowty hangars is a security hut, and requests for access to the ramp have been successful. What can be seen is anyone's guess. It's purely a matter of luck. The Bell Helicopters concession usually has an assortment of 212s and 206s in crates and various stages of assembly.

The military presence includes C-130s and a few trainers, though the US forces use Seletar as their main point of access to Singapore. The fire dump still contains the remains of a Convair or a Martin 404, and an unmarked fuselage next to the tower might be an ex-AirFast Grumman HU-16B (PK-AOH?). Speculation about aircraft identities is, however, hardly the purpose of this book.

9XR = RWANDA

KIGALI
KGL   HRYR   Gregoire Kayibanda International 7m/10km N

Rwanda is known as the Land of a Thousand Hills and Kigali is built on a few dozen of them. The airport is one of the nearby plateaus. It's dank, grimy and not the sort of place to visit from choice. The recent civil war has done nothing to raise its appeal. The terminal still has the bullet holes and broken windows from 1994, when the genocide of one million people started.

There is an open-fronted observation deck on the third floor of the terminal, overlooking a small apron. Nobody wants to photograph a small apron, thereby avoiding one chance to get carted off by the military. If there is something on the ramp, it's registration will stay in the memory for a few hours, because there won't be anything else to remember. In fact, it's probably going to be 9XR-KD.

This is a former Belgian colony, so Belgian A340s call in a couple of nights a week. Traffic grew in intensity during the course of 1996 when aid flights were operated by the various humanitarian agencies. That has passed, and the occasional visit by a Kenyan or Ugandan 737, or an Ethiopian 757, is about all that is now to be expected.

On the far side are several small hangars where one or two Cessnas and Beechcrafts can be seen and a derelict C-119 is as near as things get to having a military aviation presence.

AIRPORT RADIO FREQUENCIES

The publication in this book of airband radio frequencies must, on no account, be taken to mean that the use of portable airband radios is sanctioned or even recommended. It must be emphasised that local restrictions in several parts of the world can be strict, with penalties to match. Extreme caution must be exercised in some countries where security is taken seriously. If in doubt, ask.

The tables show basic information about most of the airports referred to in this book. The airport's name is often abbreviated and is shown with its IATA (3-letter) and ICAO (4-letter) codes, where applicable. Wherever possible, the exact location of the airport is given. Available information is variable. For example, the location for Ushuaia in Argentina is correct to within five miles but a 747, parked on Stand 12 at Buenos Aires Ezeiza can be pinpointed to within a few feet. (It's actually 34º 48' 9"S 58º 32' 4"W!)

The runway information is limited for reasons of space. That shown refers only to the longest runway, though in many instances it might be the only runway. Headings and lengths (in feet) are shown.

Radio frequencies are given for Approach and Tower only, for two reasons, the more important being space restrictions. Landing aircraft are normally told to contact Ground on 121.8 or 121.9. These are widely used, throughout the world, with only a few airports using different frequencies. Those variations can be heard locally. The number of radio frequencies which change throughout the year is appreciable, especially when there are several hundred airports in this book. Strict accuracy for a two-year period is therefore impossible. Some American fields have separate frequencies for aircarft using the various sectors (and even flight levels). They can be far too numerous, when they occur, to be printed in full and, indeed, they could be quite misleading.

Every effort has been made to supply the most comprehensive range of information at the time of printing and readers who wish to keep it up to date will need to invest in a number of publications. An example is the British Airways Aerad supplement: this is available in four volumes for the Western Hemisphere, Europe & Middle East, Africa, and Asia/Australasia & Pacific. When purchased from anyone other than British Airways, they are much cheaper because they are no longer current. Many of the changes will inevitably include radio frequencies.

AMSTERDAM
Schiphol

05

AUCKLAND
International

NORTH

international

pkg

pkg

domestic

pkg

golf course

maint

23

170

15R

Elm Road

Aviation Boulevard

10

15L

cargo

parking

parking

gen avn

viewing

NORTH

22

Aviation Boulevard

4

33R

28

162

Hollins Ferry Road

BALTIMORE

Washington International

176

33L

viewing

Dorsey Road

maint

21R

21L

military apron

domestic

international

Sukhumvit Road

station

golf course

NORTH

cargo

03R

BANGKOK
Don Muang International

03L

NORTH

26R 26L

Phase 2 Terminal

pkg pkg

pkg

cargo

maint

08R

18L

BERLIN
Tegel

BOSTON
Logan International

13R

pkg

T1
international

maint

<< preferred departure

NORTH

13L

cargo

31L

<< preferred landing

T2
domestic

parking

BUDAPEST

Ferihegy

grass strip

31R

military ramp

maintenance

NORTH

17

cargo

parking

T2 international

buses and parking

T3 Aerolineas

T1 domestic

23

29

35

05

11

BUENOS AIRES

Ezeiza International

NORTH

viewing

18R

Old Dowd Boulevard

parking

18L

23

A   D

B   C

Air National
Guard

general
aviation

general
aviation

5

cargo

36R West Boulevard

36L

CHARLOTTE
Douglas Municipal

CHICAGO
O'Hare International

ORE SUND

22L

SAS maintenance

cargo

KASTRUP

30

international

domestic

12

KASTRUP SOUTH

maintenance

22R

NORTH

flyvergrillen

04R

COPENHAGEN

Kastrup

DRAGOR

04L

East Air Freight

31R

13L

17L

17R

2E = American/Eagle
3E = American
4E = Delta & British Airways
4W = others

viewing

35R
35L

2E   3E   4E

employee parking

2W

employee parking

NORTH

18L
18R

36R
36L

maint

West
Air Freight

31L

DALLAS - FORT WORTH

13R

DETROIT
Metropolitan

FT LAUDERDALE HOLLYWOOD

GENEVA
Cointrin International

23

cargo

×DC-7

stands 14-19

P33

H3

H2

gen avn

viewing

GRASS STRIP

20

30

40

stands 2-12

viewing

Swissair

stn

P2/3

P9

gen avn

gen avn

NORTH

charters

MEYRIN

hotel

Jet Avn

Aeroleasing

05

HARTFORD-SPRINGFIELD
Bradley International

museum

24

19

15

Army

maint

Ct ANG

North Street

Route 75

6

Terminal B

Terminal A

pkg

FBOs

hotel

cargo

23

Schoephoester Road

NORTH

Route 20
to I-91

HELSINKI
Vantaa

KOWLOON CITY

hotel

Aero Club
car park

13

MA TAU WAI

main terminal

and

apron

HAECO

cargo

MA TAU KOK

NORTH

KOWLOON
BAY

apron

HONG KONG
Kai Tak

GFS hangar

31

JOHANNESBURG
International

LISBON
Portela de Sacavem

NORTH

MADRID
Barajas

MANILA
International

NORTH

23L

23R

C-46s

Mexicana
maintenance

cargo

pkg

parking

maintenance hangars

military
apron

Caravelles

HANGARES
Metro station

Avenida Oceania

Marriott hotel

05R

05L

Calz Ignacio Zaragoza

MEXICO CITY
Benito Juarez International

MOSCOW

Sheremetievo

26R

to Erding

NORTH

26L

general
aviation

F

hotel

station

A B C D E

main apron

to Attaching

viewing

08L

water and tree screen

cargo

MUNICH

Franz-Josef Strauss

Central Avenue

S-Bahn

maintenance

08R

A92

NORTH

EAST RIVER

parking 6

Marine Air
Terminal

general
aviation

hangars

Grand Central Parkway

parking 1

parking 2

Finger 1
gates 1-10

Finger 2
gates 11-21

Finger 3
gates 22-29

parking 3

Finger 4
gates 30-36

FLUSHING BAY

hangars

parking 4

USAirways

NEW YORK
La Guardia

Delta
Northwest

13

22

31

OTTAWA
Macdonald Cartier International

27R

Island Avenue

NORTH APRON

35

general aviation

E

D

parking

C

27L

B

I-95

parking

A

parking

parking

9L

PHILADELPHIA

International

CARGO CITY

NORTH

parking

9R

ROME

Leonardo da Vinci

16L

34R

25

NORTH

maintenance

domestic

parking

station

international

to Fregene

cargo   maintenance

16R

to Focene

07

34L

SAN JUAN
Luis Muñoz Marin

518

99

RIVERTON
HEIGHTS

S 156th Way

16L   16R

cargo

N E Perimeter Way

S 160th Street

12th Avenue South

cemetery

Pacific Highway South

SW 168th St

NORTH

viewing

509

United

Alaska

S 176th Street

McMICKEN
HEIGHTS

Delta
charters

Northwest

Alaska
maint

S 188th Street

to I-5

34L

SEATTLE -
TACOMA

34R

99

golf course

NORTH

23

cargo

24

China Airlines
maintenance

parking

parking

tower

museum

hotel

TAIPEI
Chiang Kai Shek
International

05

to Taipei

06

TORONTO
Lester B Pearson International

VANCOUVER
International

hotel

Grant McConachie Way

Miller Road

Canadian maintenance

Airport Road S

26L

Hud-Gen

transport

Air Canada maint

Service road

cargo

cargo

Seaplane jetties

South Terminal

exec terminal

empl pkg

parking

empl pkg

Middle Arm Fraser River

30

to 26R

main terminal

coast guard

NORTH

WASHINGTON
Dulles International

NORTH

Page	IATA	ICAO	Town/city	Name	St/country	location	R/W	length	APPROACH	TOWER
200	AAL	EKYT	Aalborg		OY	5706N 0951E	08L/26R	8694	123.875 120.7	118.3 122.1
200	AAR	EKAH	Aarhus	Tirstrup	OY	5618N 1037E	10R/28L	8885	119.275	118.525
11	YXX	CYXX	Abbotsford		BC C	4901N 12222W	07/25	8000	132.7	119.4
66	ABZ	EGPD	ABERDEEN	Dyce	G	5712N 0212W	16/34	6001	120.4	118.1
228	ABJ	DIAP	Abidjan	Port Buet	TU	0515N 0356W	03/21	8858		118.1 121.1
5	AUH	OMAA	Abu Dhabi	International	A6	2426N 5439E	13/31	13451		119.2
240	ACA	MMAA	Acapulco	Juan Alvarez Intl	XA	1645N 9945W	10/28	10824	119.9	118.5
265	ACC	DGAA	Accra	Kotoka	9G	0536N 0010W	03/21	9800	119.1	118.6
51	ADD	HAAB	Addis Ababa	Bole International	ET	0859N 3848E	07/25	12139	119.7	118.1
230	ADL	YPAD	Adelaide		SA VH	3457S 13832E	05/23	8294	118.2 124.2	120.5
263	ADE	OYAA	Aden	Khormaksar	7O	1250N 4502E	08/26	10168	118.7	118.7
191	BQN	TJBQ	Aguadilla	Rafael Hernandez	PR N	1829N 6708W	08/26	11700	134.3 135.7	118.3
163	CAK	KAKR	Akron	Canton Regional	OH	4055N 8126W	05/23	7600	125.5	122.1
259	AKT	LCRA	Akrotiri		5B	3435N 3259E	10/28	8999	122.1	126.0 121.5
229	AKX	UATT	Aktyubinsk		UN	5015N 5711E			118.1	118.2
226	AEY	BIAR	Akureyri		TF	6539N 1805W	01/19	6365		119.85
6	AAN	OMAL	Al Ain	International	A6	2416N 5536E	01/19	13123	126.1	120.6
155	ALM		Alamogordo	White Sands	NM N	3250N 10559W		7005		
157	ALB	KALB	Albany	County	NY N	4244N 7348W		7200	125.0	118.3 120.3
154	ABQ	KABQ	Albuquerque	International	NM N	3503N 10637W	08/26	13375	123.9 127.4	125.35 126.3
69	ACI	EGJA	Alderney	The Blaye	G	4942N 0213W	08/26	2887		118.15
42	ALC	LEAL	Alicante		EC	3817N 0034W	10/28	9843	118.8	118.3 123.0
230	ASP	YBAS	Alice Springs		NT VH	2349S 13354E	12/30	8000		118.2
169	ABE		Allentown	BethlehemEaston	PA N	4039N 7527W		7600		118.35
42	LEI	LEAM	Almeria		EC	3651N 0222W	08/26	10449	118.35	119.5
175	AMA	KAMA	Amarillo	Air Terminal	TX N	3513N 10142W	04/22	13500		119.8
91	AMM	OJAI	Amman	Queen Alia	JY	3143N 3600E	08R/26L	12008	128.9	118.1
202	AMS	EHAM	AMSTERDAM	Schiphol	PH	5218N 0446E	06/24	11483	119.05 121.2	127.2 126.4
99	EDF	PAED	Anchorage	Elmendorf	AK N	6115N 14948W	05/23	10000	118.6 119.1 123.8	118.6
99	MRI	PAMR	Anchorage	Merrill	AK N	6112N 14950W		4000		118.6 126.4
97	ANC	PANC	ANCHORAGE	International	AK N	6110N 15000W	06R/24L	10900	118.6 119.1 123.8	118.3 126.4
81	AOI	LIPY	Ancona	Falconara	I	4337N 1322E	04/22	9816	118.15 122.1	119.8 122.1
173	AND		Anderson	County	SC N	3429N 8242W		5000	127.5	257.8

Page	IATA	ICAO	Town/city	Name	St/country	location	R/W	length	APPROACH	TOWER
198	ANR	EBAW	Antwerp	Deurne	OO	5111N 0428E	11/29	4954		121.4 119.7
189	ATW		Appleton	Outagamie County	WI N	4415N 8831W		7000	126.3	
168	ADM	KADM	Ardmore	Airpark	OK N	3418N 9701W		7200	128.1	
191	ABO		Arecibo		PR N	1827N 6640W		3975		
120	ASE		Aspen	Pitkin County	CO N	3913N 10652W		7000	128.5	
221	ATH	LGAT	ATHENS	Hellenikon	SX	3754N 2344E	15L/33R	11483	119.1 121.4	118.1 122.1
136	PDK		Atlanta	deKalb-Peachtree	GA N	3353N 8418W	02R/20L	5000	121.0	119.3
136	FTY		Atlanta	Fulton County	GA N	3347N 8431W	8R/26L	5800	118.35 126.9	119.1 127.9
136	ATL	KATL	ATLANTA	Wm B Hartsfield	GA N	3338N 8426W	09L/27R	11889	118.1 120.1	120.5
248	AMZ	NZAR	Auckland	Ardmore	ZK	3702S 17458E	07/25	4800	120.5 124.3	118.7 129.6
249	AKL	NZAA	AUCKLAND	International	ZK	3701S 17447E	05/23	11926		124.975
32	AGB	EDMA	Augsburg	Muhlhausen	D	4826N 1056E	07/25	4199	126.8	
137	AGS	KAGS	Augusta	Bush Field	GA N	3322N 8157W		8000	124.9	118.5
175	AUS	KAUS	Austin	Robert Mueller	TX N	3018N 9742W	13R/31L	7200	127.85	118.8
7	BAH	OBBI	Bahrain	Muharraq Intl	A9C	2616N 5038E	12/30	13002	120.4	118.1
108	BFL	KBFL	Bakersfield	Meadows Field	CA N	3526N 11903W		10857	119.0	121.3
205	BPN	WRLL	Balikpapan	Sepingan	PK	0116S 11654E	07/25	8202		
147	MTN		Baltimore	Glenn L Martin	MD N	3919N 7624W		7000	119.0	
146	BWI	KBWI	BALTIMORE	Washington Intl	MD N	3911N 7640W	10/28	10500	119.0 119.7	119.4 124.55
236	BLR	VOBG	Bangalore	Hindustan	VT	1257N 7740E	09/27	10850	122.7	123.5
78	BKK	VTBD	BANGKOK	Don Muang Intl	HS	1355N 10036E	03L/21R	12139	119.7 121.7	118.1 125.5
31	BJL	GBYD	Banjul	Yundum Intl	C5	1321N 1640W	14/32	11810	121.3	118.3
42	BCN	LEBL	BARCELONA		EC	4118N 0205E	07/25	10197	119.1 124.7	118.1
71	BSL	LFSB	Basel	EuroAirport	HB	4735N 0732E	16/34	12795	119.35 121.25	118.3
147	BTL		Battle Creek	W K Kellogg	MI N	4218N 8515W		10003	121.2	118.1 119.7
32	BYU	EDQD	Bayreuth	Bindlacher-Berg	D	4959N 1138E	06/24	2936		
7	BJS	ZBAA	BEIJING	Capital	B	4004N 11636E	18R/36L	12467	129.0	118.45
193	BEY	OLBA	Beirut	International	OD	3349N 3529E	18/36	10296	119.3 120.3	118.9
69	BHD	EGAC	Belfast	City	G	5437N 0552W	04/22	6000	130.85	130.75
68	BFS	EGAA	Belfast	International	G	5439N 0614W	07/25	9110	120.1	118.3
240	BZE	MZBZ	Belize City	PSW Goldson Intl	V3	1732N 8818W	07/25	7100	121.0	118.0

Page	IATA	ICAO	Town/city	Name	St/country	location	R/W	length	APPROACH			TOWER	
230	BNE	YBBN	Brisbane	International	QL VH	2223S 15307E	01/19	11483	124.7	125.6		120.5	
59	BRS	EGGD	Bristol	Lulsgate	G	5123N 0243W	09/27	6598	128.55			133.85	
59	BZZ	EGVN	Brize Norton		G	5145N 0135W	08/26	10007	119.0	133.75		126.5	
176	BRO	KBRO	Brownsville	South Padre Island	TX N	2554N 9726W	13R/31L	7400				119.5	
198	BRU	EBBR	BRUSSELS	National	OO	5054N 0429E	07L/25R	11936	112.5	118.25		118.6	
244	OTP	LROP	Bucharest	Otopeni	YR	4434N 2606E	08/26	11483	120.6			120.9	121.85
70	BUD	LHBP	BUDAPEST	Ferihegy	HA	4726N 1914E	13L/31R	12163	129.7			118.1	
93	AEP	SABE	Buenos Aires	Aeroparque	LV	3434S 5825W	13/31	6890	119.5			118.3	
94	EZE	SAEZ	BUENOS AIRES	Ezeiza	LV	3449S 5832W	11/29	10827	119.9			119.1	
157	BUF	KBUF	Buffalo	Intl	NY N	4256N 7844W	05/23	8100	123.8	126.5		120.5	
109	BUR	KBUR	Burbank	Glendale Pasadena	CA N	3412N 11821W		6902	135.05				
185	BTV	KBTV	Burlington	International	VT N	4428N 7309W	15/33	7807	121.1	126.3		118.3	
231	CNS	YBCS	Cairns		QL VH	1653S 14545E	15/33	10489	118.4			124.9	
220	CAI	HECA	CAIRO	International	SU	3007N 3124E	05L/23R	10827	119.05	119.55	120.7	118.1	119.05
236	CCU	VECC	Calcutta	NSCB International	VT	2239N 8827E	01R/19L	11900	119.3	127.9		118.1	
11	YYC	CYYC	CALGARY	International	AL C	5106N 11401W	16/34	12675	123.85	125.9		118.4	
59	CBG	EGSC	Cambridge		G	5212N 0011E	05/23	6447	123.6			122.2	
210	VCP	SBKP	Campinas	Viracopos	SP PP	2300S 4708W	15/33	10630	121.4			118.9	
231	CBR	YSCB	Canberra		AC VH	3519S 14912E	17/35	8800	124.5			118.7	
240	CUN	MMUN	Cancun		XA	2102N 8653W	12/30	11484	120.4			118.6	
253	CPT	FACT	Cape Town		ZS	3358S 1836E	01/19	10500	119.7			118.1	
245	SVCS		Caracas	Chavallare	YV	1017N 6649W	10/28	6562					
246	SVFM		Caracas	Francisco Miranda	YV	1030N 6655W							
245	SVMI		Caracas	Simon Bolivar Intl	YV	1036N 6659W	09/27	11483	120.1	120.4		118.1	118.4
68	CWL	EGFF	Cardiff	Wales	G	5124N 0321W	12/30	7723	125.85			125.0	
109	CLD	KCNM	Carlsbad	Palomar	CA N	3307N 11706W	6/24	4700	127.3				
12	YCG	CYCG	Castlegar	Ralph West	BC C	4917N 11737W		5300				118.9	
83	CTA	LICC	Catania	Fontana Rossa	I	3728N 1504E	08/26	8366	120.8	122.1	123.3	118.7	
103			Chandler	Memorial	AZ N	3500N 11200W							
199	CRL	EBCI	Charleroi	Brussels South	OO	5028N 0427E	07/25	8366	119.7			121.3	
151	CLT	KCLT	CHARLOTTE	Douglas Municipal	NC N	3531N 8056W	18R/36L	10000	120.05	134.75		118.1	
52	CHR	LFLX	Chateauroux	Deols	F	4652N 0143E	04/22	11483				133.8	126.4
173	CHA	KCHA	Chattanooga	Lovell Field	TN N	3502N 8512W	02/20	7400	119.2	125.1		118.3	121.2

Page	IATA	ICAO	Town/city	Name	St/country	location	R/W	length	APPROACH			TOWER		
77	CJU	RKPC	Cheju	International	HL	3330N 12630E	06/24	9843	119.0	121.2	124.05	118.1		126.2
68	CEG	EGNR	Chester	Hawarden	G	5311N 0259W	05/23	6673	123.35			124.95		
79	CNX	VTCC	Chiang Mai	Ban Du	HS	1846N 9858E	18/36	10171	129.6			118.1		
79	CEI	VTCR	Chiang Rai		HS	1953N 9950E	18/36	5035	126.2			122.3		
141	CGX		Chicago	Merrill C Meigs	IL N	4151N 8736W		3947	121.3			118.4		121.3
141	MDW	KMDW	Chicago	Midway	IL N	4147N 8748W		6519				118.4		
142	PWK		Chicago	Pal-Waukee	IL N	4207N 8754W		5137	125.0			119.9		
141	ORD	KORD	CHICAGO	O'Hare Intl	IL N	4159N 8754W	14R/32L	13000	119.0	125.7		120.75		126.9
241	CZA		Chichen Itza		XA	2040N 8800W								
109	CIC	KCIC	Chico	Municipal	CA	3945N 12154W								
109	CNO		Chino		CA	3358N 11738W		6222						
265	BGI	TBPB	Christ Church	Grantley Adams	8P	1304N 5930W	09/27	11000	135.4			118.5		
249	CHC	NZCH	Christchurch	International	ZK	4329S 17232E	02/20	10784	129.35			118.7		
144	CVG	KCVG	CINCINNATI	N Kentucky Int	KY N	3903N 8440W	18L/36R	11000	120.9	124.1	125.0	118.3		118.97
246	CBL	SVCB	Ciudad Bolivar		YV	0807N 6631W		6726	119.7	123.87		118.3		
246	PZO	SVPR	Ciudad Guyana	Puerto Ordaz	YV	0818N 6244W			130.6					
125	PIE	KPIE	Clearwater	St Petersburg	FL N	2754N 8241W	07/25	8500	125.3			118.3		
165	CGF		Cleveland	Cuyahoga Co	OH N	4133N 8129W	17L/35R	5101	125.35			118.5		
164	CLE	KCLE	CLEVELAND	Hopkins Intl	OH N	4125N 8151W	05/23	9000	123.85	124.0	126.55	120.9		124.5
27	CBB	SLCB	Cochabamba	Jorge Wisterman	CP	1726S 6610W	05R/23L	12467						
140	COE		Coeur d'Alene	Air Terminal	ID N	4746N 11649W	13/31	7400				125.8		
147	CGS		College Park		MD N	3850N 7655W		2740				119.85		
176	CLL	KCLL	College Station	Easterwood	TX N	3035N 9622W	16/34	7000	121.05			120.4		
34	CGN	EDDK	COLOGNE/BONN		D	5052N 0709E	14L/32R	12516	118.5	120.6	124.0	120.5	119.9	133.15
120	COS	KCOS	Colorado Springs	Peterson Field	CO N	3848N 10442W	17L/35R	13500	118.5	120.6		119.9		
165	OSU		Columbus	Ohio State Univ	OH N	4004N 8304W	9R/27L	5000	124.2			118.8		
165	CMH	KCMH	Columbus	Port Columbus	OH N	4000N 8253W	10R/28L	10700	124.2	132.3		120.5		
165	LCK	KLCK	Columbus	Rickenbacker	OH N	3957N 8301W	18/36	12255	119.15			120.05		
244	COZ	LRCK	Constanta	M Kogalniceanu	YR	4422N 2829E	11/29	11483	122.9			120.5		
201	RKE	EKRK	Copenhagen	Roskilde	OY	5535N 1208E	04L/22R	4921	131.0			118.9		
200	CPH	EKCH	COPENHAGEN	Kastrup	OY	5537N 1239E	18/36	11811	119.8	120.25		118.1		
94	COR	SACO	Cordoba	Pajas Biancas	LV	3119S 6413W	18/36	10499				118.1		121.7

Page	IATA	ICAO	Town/city	Name	St/country	location	R/W	length	APPROACH	TOWER
48	ORK	EICK	Cork	International	EI	5150N 0829W	17/35	7000	119.9	119.3 121.7
176	CRP	KCRP	Corpus Christi	International	TX N	2746N 9730W	13/31	7506	135.25	119.25
60	CVT	EGBE	Coventry	Baginton	G	5222N 0129W	05/23	5300		118.1
241	CZM	MMCZ	Cozumel	International	XA	2031N 8656W	11/29	8858	120.4	118.1
12	YXC	CYXC	Cranbrook	Kimberley	BC C	4936N 11546W		6000	122.2 126.7	
210	CGB	SBCY	Cuiaba	Marechal Rondon	MT PP	1539S 5607W	17/35	7546		
110	CVR		Culver City	Hughes	CA N	3358N 11824W			132.4	
204	CUR	ATCC	Curacao	Hato	PJ	1212N 6857W	11/29	11188	119.6	118.3
210	CWB	SBCT	Curitiba	Afonso Pena	PR PP	2531S 4910W	15/33	7267	119.95 129.55	118.55
262	DKR	GOOY	Dakar	Yoff	6V	1445N 1730W	18/36	11450		118.1
225	DLM	LTBS	Dalaman	Mugla	TC	3642N 2847E	01/19	9843	129.5	118.5
176	ADS		Dallas	Addison	TX N	3258N 9650W	15/33	7200	123.9	121.1
176	DAL	KDAL	Dallas	Love Field	TX N	3251N 9652W	13R/31L	8800	123.9	118.7
177	DFW	KDFW	DALLAS-Ft WORTH	International	TX N	3254N 9702W	17L/35R	13400	119.875 125.025	124.15 126.55
243	DAM	OSDI	Damascus	International	YK	3325N 3631E	05R/23L	11811	126.2 134.1	118.5
231	DRW	YPDN	Darwin	International	NT VH	1225S 13053E	11/29	10906	134.45	133.1
13	YDA	CYDA	Dawson City	Municipal	YT C	6401N 13909W		6000		
165	DAY	KDAY	Dayton	James M Cox	OH N	3954N 8413W	6L/24R	9500		119.9
166	MGY		Dayton	Montgomery	OH N	3945N 8410W				
166	FFO	KFFO	Dayton	Wright-Patterson	OH N	3900N 8400W				126.9
125	DAB		Daytona Beach	Regional	FL N	2911N 8103W		7500	123.9	
236	DEL	VIDP	Delhi	Indira Gandhi Intl	VT	2834N 7707E	10/28	12500	127.9	118.1
206	DPS	WRRR	Denpasar	Bali-Ngurah Rai	PK	0845S 11510E	09/27	9843	119.7	118.1
120	APA		Denver	Centennial	CO N	3925N 10451W	16L/34R	10002		118.9
120	DIA	KDIA	Denver	International	CO N	3951N 10440W	08/26	12000	124.3 132.35	135.3 133.3
147	DET	KDET	Detroit	City	MI N	4224N 8301W	05R/23L	7526	118.45	121.3
148	YIP	KYIP	Detroit	Willow Run	MI N	4214N 8331W	03L/31R	12000	124.05 125.15	120.0
148	DTW	KDTW	DETROIT	Metropolitan	MI N	4213N 8321W	16R/34L	12000	125.1 130.5	118.4 126.85
80	DHA	OEDR	Dhahran	International	HZ	2617N 5010E	14/32	12008	121.3	118.4 135.0
224	DAC	VGZR	Dhaka	Zia International	S2	2351N 9024E	16/34	10499	121.1	118.3 118.7
7	DOH	OTBD	Doha	International	A7	2516N 5134E	16/34	15000		118.9 121.1
34	DTM	EDLW	Dortmund	Wickede	D	5131N 0737E	06/24	3445		134.175

Page	IATA	ICAO	Town/city	Name	St/country	location	R/W	length	APPROACH	TOWER
102	DHN	KDHN	Dothan		AL N	3119N 8526W		8500	125.4	119.7
35	DRS	EDDC	Dresden	Klotzsche	D	5108N 1346E	04/22	8202	125.625	120.9
142	DPA		Du Page	County	IL N	4154N 8814W		4000	133.5	118.75
4	DXB	OMDB	DUBAI	International	A6	2512N 5521E	12/30	13123	124.9 / 128.85	118.6
49	DUB	EIDW	DUBLIN	Collinstown	EI	5326N 0615W	10/28	8652	118.5 / 121.1	122.9
72	DND	EGPN	Dundee	Riverside	G	5627N 0301W	10/28	4593		
232	DKI		Dunk Island		QL VH	1759S 14614E				
253	DUR	FADN	Durban		ZS	2958S 3057E	05/23	8015	119.1 / 120.7	118.7
35	DUS	EDDL	DUSSELDORF	Rhein-Ruhr	D	5117N 0645E	05L/23R	8858	119.4 / 120.05	118.3
254	ELS	FAEL	East London		ZS	3302S 2749E	10/28	6348	120.1	118.3
60	EMA	EGNX	East Midlands	Castle Donington	G	5250N 0119W	09/27	7480	119.65	124.0
67	EDI	EGPH	Edinburgh	Turnhouse	G	5557N 0322W	07/25	8400	121.2	118.7
13	YEG	CYEG	Edmonton	International	AL C	5319N 11335W	02/20	11000	120.5	118.3
257	ETH	LLET	Eilat	J Hozman	4X	2934N 3458E	03/21	6234		118.6 / 119.0
203	EIN	EHEH	Eindhoven		PH	5127N 0523E	04/22	9843		122.1 / 131.0
178	ELP	KELP	EL PASO	International	TX N	3151N 10619W	04/22	11012		118.3
152	ECG	KECG	Elizabeth City		NC N	3615N 7610W		7219	123.85	
155	EKO		Elko	Municipal	NV N	4040N 11550W				
158	ELM		Elmira	Corning Regional	NY N	4209N 7653W		7000	133.35	
203	ENS	EHTW	Enschede	Twenthe	PH	5217N 0653E	06/24	8599	119.7 / 122.1	119.95 / 122.1
260	EBB	HUEN	Entebbe	Dr I M Obote Intl	5X	0003N 3226E	17/35	12001	119.1	118.1
250	ECN		Ercan		TC	3530N 3355E				
36	ERF	EDDE	Erfurt		D	5059N 1058E	10/28	7218		
170	ERI		Erie	International	PA N	4205N 8010W	06/24	6500	119.7 / 132.3	121.15
201	EBJ	EKEB	Esbjerg		OY	5532N 0833E	08/26	8530	121.0	
169	EUG		Eugene	Mahlon Sweet	OR N	4407N 12313W	03/21	5251		120.15
186	PAE	KPAE	Everett	Paine Field	WA N	4754N 12217W	16R/34L	9010	128.5	119.6
100	FBK	PAFB	Fairbanks	Fort Wainright	AK N	6450N 14750W				120.2 / 121.3
99	FAI	PAFA	Fairbanks	International	AK N	6449N 15656W	01L/19R	10300	118.1 / 126.5	
158	FRG		Farmingdale	Republic	NY N	4043N 7324W	14/32	6827	127.4	118.3
28	FAO	LPFR	Faro		CS	3701N 0758W			119.4	
102	FYV	KFYV	Fayetteville	Drake Field	AR N	3600N 9410W	10/28	8169		118.2

Page	IATA	ICAO	Town/city	Name	St/country		location	R/W	length	APPROACH		TOWER	
173	FAY		Fayetteville	Municipal	TN	N	3503N 8633W	7000	4900	125.6			
103	FLG		Flagstaff	Pulliam	AZ	N	3508N 11140W	128.45					
83	FLR	LIRQ	Florence	Peretola/A Vespucci		I	4349N 1112E		5413			118.3	122.1
126	FXE	KFXE	Fort Lauderdale	Executive	FL	N	2612N 8010W	05/23	6000			120.9	
125	FLL	KFLL	FT LAUDERDALE	Hollywood Intl	FL	N	2604N 8009W	08/26	9000	118.1	128.6	119.3	
126	FMY	KFMY	Fort Myers	Page Field	FL	N	2635N 8152W	09L/27R	6400	126.8			
127	RSW		Fort Myers	SW Florida	FL	N	2632N 8145W	05/23	8400	126.8			
127	FPR		Fort Pierce	St Lucie County	FL	N	2729N 8022W		5000				
13	YFS	CYFS	Fort Simpson		NT	C	6145N 12114W	14/30	6000				
102	FSM	KFSM	Fort Smith	Municipal	AR	N	3520N 9422W		8000			122.2	
178	FTW	KFTW	Fort Worth	Meacham Field	TX	N	3249N 9721W		7500			119.25	
210	IGU	SBFI	Foz do Iguassu	Cataratas	PR	PP	2535S 5429W	14/32	7219			118.1	
36	FRA	EDDF	FRANKFURT	Main		D	5002N 0834E	07L/25R	13123	118.5	124.2	119.9	124.85
110	FAT	KFAT	Fresno	Air Terminal	CA	N	3647N 11943W	11L/29R	9222	119.6	132.35	118.2	
186	FRD		Friday Harbor		WA	N	4831N 12301N	01/19	3400	129.3		118.2	
43	FUE	GCFV	Fuertaventura	Puerto del Rosario		EC	2827N 1352W	16/34	7874	118.4		118.5	
86	FUK	RJFF	Fukuoka	Itazuke		JA	3335N 13027E	06/24	9186	119.2	126.2	119.1	120.7
29	FNC	LPFU	Funchal	Santa Cruz Madeira		CS	3241N 1646W		5906	134.4		118.1	119.65
127	GNV	KGNV	Gainesville	J R Alison	FL	N	2941N 8216W		7500	135.35			
179	GLS	KGLS	Galveston	Scholes Field	TX	N	2916N 9451W		6022				
49	GWY	EICM	Galway	Carnmore		EI	5318N 0856W	08/26	4429				
143	GYY		Gary	Municipal	IN	N	4137N 8725W	12/30	7000	133.1		122.5	
152	0A6		Gastonia	Municipal	NC	N	3512N 8109W		3500	125.35		126.3	
13	YND	CYND	Gatineau	Municipal	QU	C	4531N 7533W		6000	122.3			
219	GDN	EPGD	Gdansk	Rebiechowo		SP	5423N 1828E	11/29	9186	132.2		118.1	
72	GVA	LSGG	GENEVA	Cointrin		HB	4614N 0607E	05/23	12795	120.3	131.32	118.7	119.7
83	GOA	LIMJ	Genoa	Sestri		I	4425N 0850E	11/29	9925	119.6		118.6	
44	GRO	LEGE	Gerona	Costa Brava		EC	4154N 0246E	02/20	7874	120.9		118.5	
235	GIB	LXGB	Gibraltar	North Front		VR-G	3609N 0521W	09/27	6000	122.8		122.8	123.3
1	GIL	OPGT	Gilgit	International		AP	3555N 7420E	07/25	5440			119.1	
67	GLA	EGPF	GLASGOW			G	5552N 0426W	05/23	8720	119.1		118.8	
238	GOI	VAGO	Goa	Dabolim		VT	1523N 7350E	08/26	11253	119.7		118.1	130.4
104	GYR		Goodyear	Municipal	AZ	N	3325N 11222W		8500	134.1			

Page	IATA	ICAO	Town/city	Name	St/country	location	R/W	length	APPROACH	APPROACH	TOWER	TOWER
217	GOT	ESGG	Goteborg	Landvetter	SE	5740N 1217E	03/21	10827	124.2	124.675	118.6	123.3
44	LPA	GCLP	Gran Canaria	Las Palmas	EC	2756N 1523W	03L/21R	10170	124.3		118.3	
57	CFG		Grand Case	Esperance	F-O	1805N 6305W						
104	GCN		Grand Canyon	National Park	AZ N	3557N 11208W		9000	124.85		118.1	
121	GJT	KGJT	Grand Junction	Walker Field	CO N	3907N 10832W	11/29	10500	119.7	134.5	118.2	
193	GRZ	LOWG	Graz	Thalerhof	OE	4700N 1526E	17/35	9055	119.3			
152	GSO		Greensboro	Piedmont Triad	NC N	3606N 7956W		10000	120.9		118.8	
173	GSP		Greenville	Spartanburg	SC N	3453N 8213W		7600				
190	GEY	KGEY	Greybull	South Big Horn	WY N	4430N 10803W		6300	133.25		119.8	
137	6AZ		Griffin	Spalding County	GA N	3313N 8416W	14/32	3300			118.7	
204	GRQ	EHGG	Groningen	Eelde	PH	5308N 0635E	05/23	5906	120.3		119.45	
122	GON	KGON	Groton	New London	CT N	4119N 7203W		5000				
172	PIT	KPIT	GTR PITTSBURGH	International	PA N	4030N 8014W	10R/28L	11500	123.95	124.15	119.1	128.3
125	ILG	KILG	Gtr Wilmington		DE N	3945N 7532W		7165				
241	GDL	MMQL	Guadalajara	Manuel Hidalgo	XA	2031N 10319W	10/28	13120	119.3	120.8	125.0	
8	CAN	ZGGG	Guangzhou	Baiyun	B	2311N 11316E	03/21	11089	119.6	126.35	118.1	
69	GCI	EGJB	Guernsey		G	4926N 0236W	09/27	4800	128.65		118.1	124.3
9	KWL	ZGKL	Guilin		B	2512N 11019E	18/36	7546			119.95	
150	GPT	KGPT	Gulfport-Biloxi	Regional	MS N	3024N 8904W		9002	124.6		118.0	133.0
247		FVTL	Gweru	Thornhill	Z	1927S 2952E	13/31	7800	126.5		123.5	
14	YHZ	CYHZ	Halifax	International	NS C	4453N 6331W	06/24	8800	119.2		118.4	
38	XFW	EDHI	Hamburg	Finkenwerder	D	5332N 0950E	05/23	7615			123.25	
37	HAM	EDDH	HAMBURG	Fuhlsbuttel	D	5338N 0959E	15/33	12028	120.6		126.85	
250	HLZ	NZHN	Hamilton		ZK	3752S 17520E	18/36	5600	119.5	125.3	122.9	125.9
14	YHM	CYHM	Hamilton	Civic	OT C	4310N 7956W	12L/30R	8000	128.1		119.7	125.0
138	HNM	PHHN	Hana	Municipal	HI	2048N 15601W	08/26	3605			122.1	
38	HAJ	EDDV	Hannover		D	5228N 0941E	09L/27R	12467	118.15		123.55	
247	HRE	FVHA	Harare	International	Z	1756S 3106E	05/23	15509	119.1		118.1	
179	HRL	KHRL	Harlingen	Rio Grande Valley	TX N	2613N 9739W		8300			120.7	
170	MDT	KMDT	Harrisburg	International	PA N	4014N 7701W						
170	HAR	KHAR	Harrisburg	Skyport	PA N	4014N 7701W						
30	HAV	MUHA	Havana	Jose Marti Intl	CU	2300N 8225W	05/23	13123	120.3		118.1	

Page	IATA	ICAO	Town/city	Name	St	country	location	R/W	length	APPROACH	TOWER
110	HHR	KHHR	Hawthorne	Municipal	CA	N	3355N 11820W		4956	124.5 121.1	122.3 123.6
14	YHY	CYHY	Hay River		NT	C	6050N 11546W		10000		
121	HDN	KHDN	Hayden	Yampa Valley	CO	N	4031N 10718W	09/27	9000	128.5	118.3
151	HLN	KHLN	Helena	Regional	MT	N	4636N 11159W	18/36	4590	119.5	118.9 119.7
196	HEM	EFHF	Helsinki	Malmi		OH	6015N 2503E	04/22	11286	119.1	118.6 119.7
195	HEL	EFHK	**HELSINKI**	Vantaa		OH	6019N 2458E	09/27	8990	119.85 122.1	120.85 122.1
222	HER	LGIR	Heraklion	Nikos Kazantzakis		SX	3520N 2511E	08/26	9803	118.9 119.7	122.1 122.2
139	ITO	PHTO	Hilo	General Lyman	HI		1943N 15503W	13/31	11130	119.1	118.7
236	HKG	VHHH	**HONGKONG**	Kai Tak	VR-H		2219N 11412E	08L/26R	12360	118.3	118.1 123.9
139	HNL	PHNL	**HONOLULU**	International	HI		2120N 15756W	17R/35L	9000	127.25	118.1
179	EFD	KEFD	Houston	Ellington AFB	TX	N	2936N 9509W	14L/32R	12000	120.05 124.35 124.35	125.35 118.7
179	IAH	KIAH	**HOUSTON**	Intercontinental	TX	N	2959N 9520W	04/22	7602	120.05 120.8 120.8	118.55 119.9 127.3
180	HOU	KHOU	Houston	William P Hobby	TX	N	2939N 9517W	03/21	7218	124.675 124.35	118.2
60	HUY	EGNJ	Humberside	Humberside		G	5335N 0021W	08/26	14764		119.9
248	HWN	FVWN	Hwange	National Park		Z	1838S 2700E		5430		
146	HYA	KHYA	Hyannis	Barnstable	MA	N	4140N 7016W	09/27	9080	118.3	123.5
238	HYD	VOHY	Hyderabad	Begumpet		VT	1727N 7828E	06/24	9186	119.8	118.5
44	IBZ	LEIB	Ibiza			EC	3852N 0122E		9000	134.5	
140	IDA	KIDA	Idaho Falls	Fanning Field	ID	N	4330N 11204W	05L/23R	10005		120.9
143	IND	KIND	Indianapolis	International	IN	N	3944N 8617W	08/26	6562	124.65 127.15 127.15	120.1 123.95
194	INN	LOWI	Innsbruck	Kranebitten		OE	4716N 1121E	04/22	5997	119.275	122.4
250	IVC	NZNV	Invercargill			ZK	4625S 16819E		7337		
111	IYK	KIYK	Inyokern	Kern County	CA	N	3539N 11750W	12/30	10997		
1	ISB	OPRN	Islamabad	Chaklala		AP	3337N 7306E	08/26	5751	119.7 121.8	123.7
70	IOM	EGNS	Isle of Man	Ronaldsway		G	5404N 0438W		6020	120.85	118.9
158	ISP	KISP	Islip	Long I-MacArthur	NY	N	4047N 7306W		9843	120.05 124.9	125.5
226	IST	LTBA	Istanbul	Ataturk		TC	4059N 2849E	18/36	10630	121.1	118.1 121.8
226	ADB	LTBJ	Izmir	Adnan Menderes		TC	3818N 2710E	16/34	6300	120.1 129.3 132.9	118.1 121.9
191	JAC	KJAC	Jackson	Jackson Hole	WY	N	4336N 11044W	07/25	10000	133.25	118.3
127	JAX	KJAX	Jacksonville	International	FL	N	3029N 8141W		9843	sectors	118.3
207	HLP	WIIH	Jakarta	Halim P Kusama		PK	0616S 10653E	06/24		119.75 127.9	

Page	IATA	ICAO	Town/city	Name	St/country	location	R/W	length	APPROACH	TOWER
206	CGK	WIII	JAKARTA	Soekarno-Hatta Intl	PK	0608S 10639E	07R/25L	12008	119.75 127.95	118.2
217	JKG	ESGJ	JONKOPING	Axamo	SE	5746N 1404E	01/19	7218		118.25 123.3
80	JED	OEJN	Jeddah	King Abdulaziz	HZ	2141N 3909E	16R/34L	12467	119.1 124.0	118.2 124.3
69	JER	EGJJ	Jersey		G	4913N 0212W	09/27	5597	120.3	119.45
258	JRS	LLJR	Jerusalem	Atarot	4X	3152N 3513E	12/30	6447		118.8
207	JOG	WIIJ	Jogyarkarta	Adisucipto	PK	0747S 11026E	09/27	6070	120.2 123.4	118.1 122.4
255	HLA	FALA	Johannesburg	Lanseria	ZS	2555S 2756E	06L/24R	10000		124.0
254	JNB	FAJS	JOHANNESBURG	Jan Smuts Intl	ZS	2608S 2815E	03L/21R	14495	123.7 124.5 125.3	118.1 121.9
87	KOJ	RJFK	Kagoshima		JA	3148N 13043E	16/34	9843	119.4 120.8 126.0	118.2 126.2
139	OGG	PHOG	Kahului	Maui Island	HI N	2054N 15626W	02/20	7000	120.2	118.7
148	AZO		Kalamazoo	County	MI N	4214N 8533W		6500	121.2	
232	KGI	YPKG	Kalgoorlie		WA VH	3047S 12128E	11/29	6562		
259	KAN	DNKN	Kano	Aminu Mallam Intl	5N	1203N 0832E	06/24	10827		118.1
149	MKC	KMKC	Kansas City	Downtown	MO N	3907N 9436W			119.0	126.8
149	MCI	KMCI	Kansas City	International	MO N	3918N 9444W	01L/19R	10801	120.95 132.95	125.75 128.2
139	JHM		Kapalua	West Maui	HI N	2052N 14641W				
2	KHI	OPKC	Karachi	Quaid-e-Azam Intl	AP	2454N 6709E	07L/25R	10500	118.4 121.3 125.5	118.3 121.8
248	KAB	FVKB	Kariba		Z	1631S 2853E	09/27	5413		125.3
227	KEF	BIKF	Keflavik		TF	6359N 2237W	02/20	10056	119.3	118.3
14	YLW	CYLW	Kelowna	Ellison Field	BC C	4957N 11922W		5350		119.6
100	ENA	PAEN	Kenai	Municipal	AK N	6034N 15115W	01/19	7575	121.3	
128	TMB	KTMB	Kendall-Tamiami	Executive	FL N	2539N 8025W		5002	118.1 118.9	121.1
223	CFU	LGKR	Kerkyra	I Kapodistrias	SX	3936N 1955E	17/35	7792	122.35	120.85
128	EYW	KEYW	Key West	International	FL N	2433N 8145W		4800		118.7
229	KBP	UKBB	Kiev	Borispol	UR	5021N 3053E	18R/36L	11483	121.2 124.6 127.9	119.2 119.3
229	IEV	UKKK	Kiev	Zhulyany	UR	5024N 3027E	08/26	5906	124.3	122.5
269	KGL	HRYR	Kigali	Greg Kay Intl	9XR	0158S 3008E	10/28	11483		118.3
255	KIM	FAKM	Kimberley	B J Vorster	ZS	2848S 2446E	02/20	9843		123.8
104	IGM	KIGM	Kingman	Municipal	AZ N	3515N 11356W		6831		
262	KIN	MKJP	Kingston	Norman Manley Intl	6Y	1756N 7648W	12/30	8786	119.45	120.6
194	KLU	LOWK	Klagenfurt	Worthesee	OE	4639N 1420E	10/28	8924	118.0 123.9	118.1
173	TYS	KTYS	Knoxville	McGhee Tyson	TN N	3549N 8400W	05L/23R	9000		121.2
223	KGS	LGKO	Kos		SX	3648N 2706E	15/33	7874	119.95	121.05

Page	IATA	ICAO	Town/city	Name	St	country	location	R/W	length	APPROACH	TOWER
197	KSC	LZKZ	Kosice			OM	4840N 2115E	01/19	10171	119.85	120.4
266	KUL	WMKK	Kuala Lumpur	Subang Intl		9M	0308N 10133E	15/33	12400		118.2 124.2
87	KMJ	RJFT	Kumamoto	International		JA	3250N 13051E	07/25	9840	119.0 126.5	118.7 126.2
266	KWI	OKBK	Kuwait	International		9K	2913N 4758E	15L/33R	11483	121.3 124.8	118.3
138	LGC	SADL	La Grange	Callaway	GA		3300N 0504W		5600		119.25
27	LPB		La Paz	El Alto		CP	1631S 6811W				
259	LOS	DNMM	Lagos	Murtala Muhammed		5N	0635N 0319E	01L/19R	12795	124.7	118.1
2	LHE	OPLA	Lahore			AP	3131N 7424E	18/36	9000	121.3	118.1
250			Lake Tekapo			ZK	4400S 17030E				
111	WJF		Lancaster	Fox Field	CA	N	3444N 11813W		5000		
45	ACE	GCRR	Lanzarote			EC	2857N 1336W	04/22	7874	129.1	126.1
180	LRD	KLRD	Laredo	International	TX	N	2732N 9927W		8201	127.8	120.7
258	LCA	LCLK	Larnaca			5B	3453N 3338E	04/22	8858	121.2	119.4
44	LPA	GCLP	Las Palmas	Gran Canaria		EC	2756N 1523W	03L/21R	10170	124.3	118.3
155	LAS	KLAS	LAS VEGAS	McCarran Intl	NV	N	3605N 11509W	07L/25R	14505	127.15	119.9
170	LBE		Latrobe	Westmoreland	PA	N	4016N 7924W		7000		
61	LBA	EGNM	Leeds/Bradford			G	5352N 0140W	14/32	7382	123.75	121.2
38	LEJ	EDDP	Leipzig	Halle		D	5125N 1214E	10/28	8202		120.3
144	LEX	KLEX	Lexington	Blue Grass	KY	N	3802N 8436W	04/22	7000	120.75	121.1
143	LBL		Liberal	Geo Welch	KS	N	3702N 10057W		7100	134.0	
227	LBV	FOOL	Libreville	Leon M'ba		TR	0027N 0925E	16/24	9843	126.5	118.7
199	LGG	EBLG	Liege	Bierset		OO	5038N 0527E	05R/23L	10784	119.7 122.5	119.7 122.1
140	LIH	PHLI	Lihue	Municipal	HI	N	2159N 15920W	17/35	6500	126.5	118.9
264	LLW	FWLI	Lilongwe	Kamazu		7Q	1347S 3347E	14/32	11614	128.0	118.7
192	LIM	SPIM	Lima	Jorge Chavez Intl		OB	1201S 7707W	15/33	11506	119.7	118.1
218	LPI	ESCF	Linkoping	Malmen		SE	5824N 1532E	01/19	7382	119.75 129.625	129.8
194	LNZ	LOWL	Linz	Horsching		OE	4814N 1411E	09/27	9219	120.6	118.8 123.3
29	LIS	LPPT	LISBON	Portela de Sacavem		CS	3846N 0908W	03/21	12483		118.1 126.4
103	LIT	KLIT	Little Rock	Adams Field	AR	N	3443N 9214W		7173		124.2
61	LPL	EGGP	Liverpool	Speke		G	5321N 0253W	09/27	7500	119.85	118.1
15	YXU	CYXU	London		OT	C	4302N 8109W	15/33	8800		119.4
61	LCY	EGLC	London	City		G	5130N 0003E	10/28	3934		127.95
62	LGW	EGKK	LONDON	Gatwick		G	5109N 0011W	08R/26L	10364	126.825	124.225 129.25

Page	IATA	ICAO	Town/city	Name	St/country	location	R/W	length	APPROACH	TOWER
62	LHR	EGLL	**LONDON**	Heathrow	G	5129N 0028W	09L/27R	12802	120.4	118.7
63	LTN	EGGW	London	Luton	G	5153N 0022W	08/26	7087	128.75 129.55	132.55
64	STN	EGSS	London	Stansted	G	5153N 0014E	05/23	10000	125.55	123.8
111	LGB	KLGB	Long Beach	Daugherty Field	CA N	3349N 11809W	12/30	10000	124.65	119.4
113	VNY		Los Angeles	Van Nuys	CA N	3414N 11829W	16R/34L	8000	119.3	120.2
112	LAX	KLAX	**LOS ANGELES**	International	CA N	3356N 11824W	07L/25R	12090	124.5 124.3 128.5	120.95 133.9
181	LBB	KLBB	Lubbock	International	TX N	3340N 10149W		11500		119.9
73	LUG	LSZA	Lugano	Agno	HB	4600N 0855E	01/19	4429	118.9	118.25 122.55
95	LUX	ELLX	Luxembourg	Findel	LX	4937N 0612E	06/24	13123	124.3	118.1 119.9
221	LXR	HELX	Luxor		SU	2540N 3242E	02/20	9843	119.25 125.8	118.1
52	LYS	LFLL	Lyon	Satolas	F	4544N 0505E	18R/36L	13123	120.2	120.45
204	MST	EHBK	Maastricht	Beek	PH	5055N 0547E	04/22	8202		119.7
138	MCN	KMCN	Macon	Mid Georgia	GA N	3241N 8338W		6500		119.6
113	MAE		Madera	Municipal	CA N	3700N 12006W		4500		119.45
238	MAA	VOMM	Madras		VT	1300N 8011E	07/25	12001		
45	MAD	LEMD	**MADRID**	Barajas	EC	4029N 0334W	15/33	13450	119.9 127.5	118.15 120.15
225	SEZ	FSIA	Mahe	Seychelles Intl	S7	0440S 5531E	13/31	9800	119.7	118.3
46	MAH	LEMH	Mahon	Menorca	EC	3952N 0413E	01/19	7710		119.65
46	AGP	LEMG	Malaga		EC	3640N 0430W	14/32	10500	118.45	118.15
218	MMX	ESMS	Malmo	Sturup	SE	5533N 1322E	17/35	9186	123.95	118.8
265	MLA	LMML	**MALTA**	Luqa	9H	3552N 1429E	14/32	11627	121.0 127.1	118.9 121.7
210	MAO	SBEG	Manaus	Eduardo Gomes	AM PP	0302S 6002W	10/28	8858		
64	MAN	EGCC	**MANCHESTER**	International	G	5321N 0216W	06/24	10000	119.4	118.625 123.1
216	MNL	RPLL	**MANILA**	Ninoy Aquino Intl	RP	1430N 12100E	06/24	12261	119.7 121.1	118.1
39	MHG	EDFM	Mannheim	Neuostheim	D	4928N 0831E	09/27	3280	134.9	
167	MPD		Mansfield	Lahm Municipal	OH N	4049N 8231W	14/32	9000	119.25	119.8
31	MPM	FQMA	Maputo	International	C9	2556S 3234E	05/23	12008	121.3	118.1
104	MZJ		Marana	Pinal Air Park	AZ N	3230N 11119W		6860		
128	MTH		Marathon		FL N	2443N 8103W		5000		
52	MRS	LFML	Marseille	Provence Intl	F	4326N 0513E	14L/32R	11483	120.2	118.1 119.5
264	MSU	FXMM	Maseru	Moshoeshoe Intl	7P	2927S 2733E	04/22	10500	120.7	118.5
256	MRU	FIMP	Mauritius	International	3B	2026S 5741E	14/32	8500	119.1	118.1

Page	IATA	ICAO	Town/city	Name	St/country	location	R/W	length	APPROACH	TOWER
181	MFE	KMFE	McAllen	Miller International	TX N	2610N 9814W	13/31	7100	121.0	128.42
208	MES	WIMM	Medan	Polonia	PK	0334N 9841E	05/23	9514		
76	MDE	SKMD	Medellin	Olaya Herrera	HK	0613N 7536W	01/19	8028		
169	MFR		Medford	Jackson County	OR N	4222N 12252W		6700		
233	MEB	YMEN	Melbourne	Essendon	VI VH	3744S 14454E	08/26	6300	125.3	125.1
232	MEL	YMML	MELBOURNE	Tullamarine	VI VH	3741S 14451E	16/34	12000	124.7	120.5
128	MLB	KMLB	Melbourne	Regional	FL N	2806N 8038W	09R/27L	9481	124.7	
174	MEM	KMEM	Memphis	International	TN N	3504N 8958W	18R/36L	9319	125.1 125.8	118.3 119.7
241	MID	MMMD	Merida	Manuel Cresencio	XA	2056N 8940W	10/28	8858	119.1	118.3
105	FFZ		Mesa	Falcon Field	AZ N	3327N 11143W		5100	121.2	119.2
242	MEX	MMMX	MEXICO CITY	Benito Juarez	XA	1926N 9904W	05R/23L	12796	121.2	118.1 118.7
131	OPF	KOPF	Miami	Opa Locka	FL N	2554N 8017W	09L/27R	8002	118.6	120.7 125.6
131	MPB		Miami	Watson Island	FL N	2550N 8010W				
129	MIA	KMIA	MIAMI	International	FL N	2548N 8017W	09R/27L	13002	124.85	118.3 123.9
84	MXP	LIMC	MILAN	Malpensa	I	4538N 0843E	17L/35R	12844	126.3 132.7	119.0 128.35
83	LIN	LIML	MILAN	Linate	I	4527N 0917E	18L/36R	8005	126.3 132.7	118.1 119.25
250	MFN	NZMF	Milford Sound		ZK	4440S 16755E	11/29	2600		
190	MKE	KMKE	Milwaukee	General Mitchell	WI N	4257N 8754W	01L/19R	9690	118.0 126.5	119.1 125.35
149	MSP	KMSP	MINNEAPOLIS	St Paul Intl	MN N	4453N 9313W	04R/22L	11000	119.3 126.95	123.95 126.7
87	KMI	RJFM	Miyazaki		JA	3152N 13127E	09/27	8200	120.1 121.4	118.3 126.2
102	MOB	KMOB	Mobile	Regional	AL N	3041N 8814W		8527		
113	MOD		Modesto	Harry Sham	CA N	3737N 12057W		5911	120.95	
113	MHV		Mojave	Kern County	CA N	3503N 11809W		9600		
140	MKK	PHMK	Molokai	Hoolehua	HI N	2109N 15706W	05/23	4494		125.7
260	MBA	HKMO	Mombasa	Moi International	5Y	0402S 3936E	03/21	10991		118.6
39		EDLN	Monchengladbach	Düsseldorf Express	D	5114N 0630E	13/31	3937	120.3	118.125
263	MBJ	MKJS	Montego Bay	Sangster International	6Y	1830N 7755W	07/25	8705		120.8
114	MRY		Monterey	Peninsula	CA N	3635N 12157W	10R/28L	6597	133.5	
242	MTY	MMMY	Monterrey	Mariano Escobido	XA	2547N 10006W	11/29	9843	121.4	118.1
31	MVD	SUMU	Montevideo	Carrasco International	CX	3450S 5602W	06/24	8858	119.2	118.1
158	MSV		Monticello	Sullivan County	NY N	4142N 7447W		6300		120.2
16	YMX	CYMX	Montreal	Mirabel	PQ C	4541N 7402W	06/24	12000	125.15	119.1
16	YHU	CYHU	Montreal	St Hubert	PQ C	4503N 7325W		7840	125.15	

Page	IATA	ICAO	Town/city	Name	St/country	location	R/W	length	APPROACH	TOWER
153	EWR	KEWR	NEWARK	International	NJ N	4043N 7410W	04R/22L	9300	127.6 128.55 132.8	118.3
159	SWF	KSWF	Newburgh	Stewart Intl	NY N	4130N 7406W	09/27	11818	121.2 132.75	121.0
65	NCL	EGNT	Newcastle	International	G	5502N 0141W	07/25	7644	124.375	119.7
184	PHF	KPHF	Newport News	Patrick Henry	VA N	3708N 7629W	07/25	8003	125.7	118.7
162	IAG	KIAG	Niagara Falls	International	NY N	4306N 7857W	10L/28R	9125	126.15	118.5
53	NCE	LFMN	NICE	Cote d'Azur	F	4340N 0713E	05R/23L	9711	124.175	118.7 119.7
184	ORF	KORF	Norfolk	International	VA N	3653N 7612W	05/23	9000	118.9	120.8
218	NRK	ESSP	Norrkoping	Kungsangen	SE	5835N 1615E	09/27	7228		120.35
16	YYB	CYYB	North Bay		OT C	4622N 7925W	08/26	10000		118.3
65	NWI	EGSH	Norwich	Horsham St Faith	G	5241N 0117E	09/27	6043	127.25	124.25
215	OVB	UNNT	Novosibirsk	Tolmachevo	RA	5501N 8240E	07/25	11808	119.35	118.5 128.0
40	NUE	EDDN	Nurnberg		D	4930N 1105E	10/28	8858	127.1 128.5 133.8	118.3
114	OAK	KOAK	OAKLAND	International	CA N	3744N 12213W	11/29	10000	119.475 119.525 sectors	118.3 127.2
202	ODE	EKOD	Odense	Beldringe	OY	5529N 1020E	06/24	5397	121.1	119.525
88	OKA	ROAH	Okinawa	Naha	JA	2612N 12739E	18/36	9840	119.1 126.5	118.1 126.2
168	TIK	KTIK	Oklahoma City	Tinker AFB	OK N	3500N 9700W				
168	OKC	KOKC	Oklahoma City	Will Rogers World	OK N	3523N 9736W		9800	126.65	120.1
187	OLM		Olympia	Municipal	WA N	4658N 12254W		5419		
187	OMK		Omak	Municipal	WA N	4828N 11931W		4650		
115	ONT	KONT	Ontario	International	CA N	3403N 11736W	08L/26R	12200	sectors	120.6
30	OPO	LPPR	Oporto	Francisco da Carneiro	CS	4114N 0841W	17/35	11417	121.1	118.0
133	ORL	KORL	Orlando	Executive	FL N	2830N 8725W	07/25	6000		120.15
132	MCO	KMCO	ORLANDO	International	FL N	2826N 8119W	18L/36R	12004	sectors	118.45 124.3
89	OSA	RJOO	Osaka	Itami	JA	3447N 13527E	14R/32L	9840		118.1 126.2
88	KIX	RJBB	Osaka	Kansai Intl	JA	3425N 13515E	06/24	11483	120.25	118.2 126.2 127.5
17	YOO		Oshawa		OT C	4353N 7855W				
190	OSH	KOSH	Oshkosh	Wittman Field	WI N	4403N 8833W	18/36	8000	127.5	
93	GEN	ENGM	Oslo	Gardemoen	LN	6012N 1105E	01/19	10499	120.1	118.3 120.1 122.1
92	FBU	ENFB	OSLO	Fornebu	LN	5954N 1037E	06/24	7776	119.65 120.45 131.35	118.1 119.775
199	OST	EBOS	Ostend		OO	5112N 0252E	08/26	10499	120.6	118.7
17	YOW	CYOW	OTTAWA	M-C International	OT C	4519N 7540W	14/32	9646	135.15	118.8 119.6
257	VDA	LLOV	Ovda		4X	2956N 3456E	02R/20L	9843		
115	OXR		Oxnard	Ventura County	CA N	3412N 11912W		5950	124.7	129.9

Page	IATA	ICAO	Town/city	Name	St/country	location	R/W	length	APPROACH	TOWER
208	PDG	WIMG	Padang	Tabing	PK	0053S 10021E	16/34	7054	124.0	122.2
40	PAD	EDLP	Paderborn	Lippstadt	D	5137N 0837E	06/24	7152		118.275
105	PGA		Page	Municipal	AZ N	3655N 11126W		5500	124.2	
133	LNA	KLNA	Palm Beach	County/Lantana	FL N	2636N 8005W		3485	127.35	
115	PSP	KPSP	Palm Springs	Regional	CA N	3349N 11630W	13R/31L	8500	118.85 126.7	119.7 121.05
47	PMI	LEPA	Palma	Son San Juan	EC	3933N 0244E	06L/24R	10728	118.95 119.15	118.3 119.4
115	PMD	KPMD	Palmdale		CA N	3438N 11805W	07/25	12002	124.55	123.7
101	PAQ	PAAQ	Palmer	Municipal	AK N	6135N 14910W		6314		
133	PFN		Panama City	Bay County	FL N	3013N 8540W			120.8	119.1
258	PFO	LCPH	Paphos	International	5B	3443N 3229E	11/29	8858	124.8	119.9
181	PRX		Paris	Cox Field	TX N	3338N 9527W		6000		118.5
54	JDP	LFPI	Paris	Issy les Moulineaux	F	4850N 0220E				119.1
55	LBG	FLPB	Paris	Le Bourget	F	4858N 0227E	07/25	9843		118.5
54	CDG	LFPG	**PARIS**	Charles de Gaulle	F	4901N 0233E	10/28	11860	118.15 119.85 121.15	119.1 120.65
55	ORY	LFPO	**PARIS**	Orly	F	4843N 0223E	07/25	11975	118.85 124.45	119.25 120.5
3	PBH	VQPR	Paro		A5	2724N 9826E	15/33	6512		118.7
187	PSC		Pasco	Tri-Cities	WA N	4616N 11907W	04/22	7700	125.0	122.7
267	PEN	WMKP	Penang	International	9M	0518N 10017E		10000		121.1
18	YYF	CYYF	Penticton	Municpal	BC C	4927N 11936W	04/22	6000		118.5
233	PER	YPPH	Perth		WA VH	3156S 11558E	03/21	11300	118.7 123.7	120.5
2	PEW	OPPS	Peshawar		AP	3400N 7131E	17/35	9000	119.7 125.6	122.9
18	YPQ	CYPQ	Peterborough		OT C	4413N 7821W		5000		
171	PNE	KPNE	Philadelphia	Northeast	PA N	4004N 7500W		7000	123.8	
171	PHL	KPHL	**PHILADELPHIA**	International	PA N	3953N 7514W	09R/27L	10500	sectors	118.5 135.1
106	PHX	KPHX	**PHOENIX**	Sky Harbor	AZ N	3326N 11201W	08L/26R	11001	sectors	118.7 120.9
79	HKT	VTSP	Phuket	International	HS	0806S 9818E	09/27		126.7	118.1 122.7
251	PCN		Picton	Karamika	ZK	4118S 17403E		4840		
255	PZB	FAPM	Pietermaritzburg	Oribi	ZS	2939S 3024E	16/34	4200		122.0
84	PSA	LIRP	Pisa	Galileo Galilei	I	4341N 1024E	04R/22L	9820		119.1
162	PLB		Plattsburgh	Clinton County	NY N	4441N 7331W				121.1 122.1
148	PTK	KPTK	Pontiac	Oakland	MI N	4240N 8320W		5000		121.1

Page	IATA	ICAO	Town/city	Name	St	country	location	R/W	length	APPROACH	TOWER
197	TAT	LZTT	Poprad	Tatry		OM	4904N 2015E	09/27	8530	119.6 120.25	118.9
187	CLM		Port Angeles		WA	N	4807N 12330W	08/26	6349		
255	PLZ	FAPE	Port Elizabeth	Fairchild Intl		ZS	3359S 2537E		6496	119.7	118.1
162	POU		Poughkeepsie	Dutchess County	NY	N	4137N 7353W	08/26	5000		120.2
196	PRG	LKPR	**PRAGUE**	Ruzyne		OK	5006N 1416E	06/24	12188	119.0 120.05 121.4	118.1
225	PRI	FSPP	Praslin			S7	0419S 5542E	15/33	3993		
67	PIK	EGPK	Prestwick			G	5530N 0435W	13/31	9800	120.55	118.15 121.8
256	PRY	FAWB	Pretoria	Wonderboom		ZS	2539S 2813E	11/29	6000		120.6
182	PUC		Price	Carbon County	UT	N	3936N 11045W		7300	134.8	
182	PVU		Provo	Municipal	UT	N	4012N 11143W		7091	124.3	
75	POP	MDPP	Puerto Plata	La Union		HI	1946N 7034W	08/26	10102	119.0	118.0 121.9
26	PUQ	SCCI	Punta Arenas	C I del Campo		CC	5300S 7051W	07/25	9154		118.1
9	TAO	ZSQD	Qingdao			B	3616N 12023E	13/31	8530		120.3
18	YQB	CYQB	Quebec City		PQ	C	4648N 7123W	06/24	9000	124.0	118.1
251	ZQN	NZQN	Queenstown	Frankton		ZK	4501S 16844E	05/23	5000		126.9
75	UIO	SEQU	Quito	Mariscal Sucre		HC	0008S 7829W	17/35	10236		
153	RDU	KRDU	Raleigh-Durham	International	NC	N	3747N 8107W	05L/23R	10000	124.95 125.3 128.3	119.3 127.45
6	RKT	OMRK	Ras al Khaymah	International		A6	2537N 5556E	16/34	12336	124.0	118.25
172	RDG		Reading	General Spaatz	PA	N	4022N 7557W	18/36	6350		119.25
211	REC	SBRF	Recife	Guararapes	PE	PP	0807S 3455W	18/36	9846	119.1 119.5	118.35 122.8
18	YQF	CYQF	Red Deer	Industrial	AL	C	5210N 11353W	13/31	3450	120.1	118.5
18	YQR	CYQR	Regina	Municipal	SA	C	5026N 10440W		7900	119.2 126.3	118.6
156	RNO	KRNO	Reno	Cannon Intl	NV	N	3930N 11946W	16R/34L	11000	119.0	118.7
227	REK	BIRK	**REYKJAVIK**			TF	6408N 2157W	02/20	5987		118.0
224	RHO	LGRP	Rhodes	Paradisi		SX	3624N 2805E	07/25	10696	120.6	118.2
185	RIC	KRIC	Richmond	Byrd Field	VA	N	3730N 7720W	16/34	9000	119.9 126.3 126.4	121.1
244	RSC	EVRA	Riga	Skulte		YL	5655N 2358E	18/36	8366	127.3	118.1
211	SDU	SBRJ	Rio de Janeiro	Santos Dumont		PP	2252S 4309W				
211	GIG	SBGL	**RIO DE JANEIRO**	Galeao		PP	2249S 4315W	10/28	13123	sectors	118.0 118.2
76	MDE	SKRG	Rio Negro	J M Cordova		HK	0611N 7526W	18/36	11483	124.8	
116	HMT		Riverside	Hemet-Ryan	CA	N	3344N 11701W	18/36	4315		
81	RUH	OERK	Riyadh	King Khaled Intl		HZ	2458N 4643E	15L/23R	13780	120.0 126.0	118.6 118.8

Page	IATA	ICAO	Town/city	Name	St/country	location	R/W	length	APPROACH	TOWER
185	ROA		Roanoke	Regional	VA N	3720N 7958W		6802	124.5	
19	YRM	CYRM	Rocky Mtn House		AL C	5225N 11454W		6400		
85	CIA	LIRA	Rome	Ciampino	I	4148N 1236E	15/33	7208	119.2	120.5 122.1
85	FCO	LIRF	ROME	Fiumicino	I	4149N 1215E	16R/34L	12795	119.2	118.7 119.3
155	ROW	KRQW	Roswell	Industrial Air Ctr	NM N	3318N 10431W		13000		
251	ROT	NZRO	Rotorua	Lakefront	ZK	3807S 17619E	01/19	4500	119.5	121.2
204	RTM	EHRD	Rotterdam	Zestienhoven	PH	5157N 0426E	06/24	7218	127.025	118.2
40	SCN	EDDR	Saarbrucken	Ensheim	D	4913N 0707E	09/27	6562	129.675	118.35 119.7
116	SMF	KSMF	Sacramento	Metropolitan	CA N	3842N 12136W	16R/34L	8600	sectors	125.7 118.55
183	SGU		Saint George	Municipal	UT N	3705N 11335W		6100		
19	YJN	CYJN	Saint Jean		PQ C	4520N 7350W				
238	ANU	TAPA	Saint John's	V C Bird Antigua	V2	1708N 6147W	07/25	9000	119.1	118.2
150	STL	KSTL	Saint Louis	Lambert Intl	MO N	3844N 9021W	12R/30L	11019	126.5	118.5 120.05
149	STP		Saint Paul	Downtown	MN N	4456N 9304W		6550	121.2	119.1
183	SLC	KSLC	SALT LAKE CITY	International	UT N	4047N 11158W	16L/34R	12000	sectors	118.3 119.05 132.65
195	SZG	LOWS	Salzburg	Maxglan	OE	4748N 1300E	16/34	9022	123.725	118.1
212	SSA	SBSV	Salvador	Dois de Julho	BA PP	1254S 3819W	10/28	9859	119.35 119.8	118.3 120.8
181	SAT	KSAT	San Antonio	International	TX N	2932N 9828W	12R/30L	8500	sectors	119.8
116	SAN	KSAN	SAN DIEGO	Lindbergh Intl	CA N	3244N 11711W	09/27	9400	119.6 124.35	118.3
117	SFO	KSFO	SAN FRANCISCO	International	CA N	3737N 12223W	10L/28R	11870	120.35 134.5	120.5 125.6 135.65
117	SJC		San Jose	Municipal	CA N	3722N 12155W		8900	120.7	124.0
192	SIG	TJIG	San Juan	Isla Grande	PR N	1827N 6606W	09L/27R	5332		
191	SJU	TJSJ	SAN JUAN	Luis Munoz Marin	PR N	1826N 6600W	08/26	10000	119.4 120.9	118.3
118	CSL		San Luis Obispo	McChesney Field	CA N	3521N 12038W				
118	SPQ		San Pedro	Catalina	CA N	3346N 11814W				
263	SAH	OYSN	Sana'a	International	7O	1529N 4413E	18/36	10669	119.9 125.3	118.1 118.9
133	SFB	KNRJ	Sanford	Central Florida	FL N	2847N 8114W	03/21	8000		121.1
73	SMV	LSZS	Sankt Moritz	Samedan	HB	4630N 0950E		5600		119.42
118	SNA	KSNA	Santa Ana	John Wayne	CA N	3340N 11752W				119.9
119	SBA		Santa Barbara	Goleta	CA N	3425N 11950W			6049	123.85 126.8
28	SRZ	SLET	Santa Cruz	El Trompillo	CP	1748S 6311W	15/33	9144	125.4	
28	VVI	SLVR	Santa Cruz	Viru Viru Intl	CP	1738S 6308W	15/33	11482		
155	SAF	KSAF	Santa Fe	Municipal	NM N	3537N 10605W		8323	132.8	

Page	IATA	ICAO	Town/city	Name	St	country	location	R/W	length	APPROACH	TOWER
119	SMO		Santa Monica	Municipal	CA	N	3401N 11827W		4987	128.5	119.15 120.1
119	STS		Santa Rosa	Sonoma County	CA	N	3830N 12248W		5115	127.8	
26	SCL	SCEL	Santiago	A. Merino Benitez		CC	3323S 7047W	17/35	10499	119.4	118.1
30	SCU	MUCU	Santiago/Cuba	Antonio Maceo		CU	1958N 7550W	09/27	13123		118.1
75	STI	MDST	Santiago	Cibao		HI	1928N 7042W	12/30	5200		118.1
76	HEX	MDHE	Santo Domingo	Herrera		HI	1830N 7000W				
75	SDQ	MDSD	Santo Domingo	Las Americas		HI	1826N 6940W	17/35	11000	119.3	118.05 122.1
224	JTR	LGSR	Santorini	Thira		SX	3624N 2528E	16L/34R	6955		
212	CGH	SBSP	Sao Paulo	Congonhas	SP	PP	2337S 4639W	17R/35L	6362	sectors	118.1 118.4 126.4
212	GRU	SBGR	Sao Paulo	Guarulhos	SP	PP	2326S 4629W	09L/27R	12140	sectors	120.1
134	SRQ		Sarasota	Bradenton	FL	N	2724N 8233W	13/31	7003	119.9	118.3
19	YXE	CYXE	Saskatoon		SA	C	5210N 10642W	09/27	8300		
138	SAV	KSAV	Savannah	International	GA	N	3208N 8112W	09/27	9351	118.4 120.4	119.1
106	SDL		Scottsdale	Municipal	AZ	N	3337N 11154W	03/21	8251		119.2
188	BFI	KBFI	Seattle	King/Boeing	WA	N	4731N 12218W	13R/31L	10001		120.6
189	LKE		Seattle	Lake Union	WA	N	4741N 12215W				
189	RNT		Seattle	Renton	WA	N	4730N 12212W		5379		119.2
187	SEA	KSEA	SEATTLE	Tacoma Intl	WA	N	4727N 12218W	16L/34R	11900	sectors	119.9
106	SEZ		Sedona		AZ	N	3450N 11147W		5142		
77	SEL	RKSS	SEOUL	Kimpo Intl		HL	3733N 12648E	14R/32L	11811	sectors	118.1
50	SNN	EINN	Shannon			EI	5242N 0855W	06/24	10500	119.1 119.9	118.7
5	SHJ	OMSJ	Sharjah	International		A6	2520N 5531E	12/30	12336	120.2 121.4	118.6
182	F39		Sherman-Denison	Grayson County	TX	N	3343N 9640W	03/21	9000	134.15	123.15 125.4
65	ESH	EGKA	Shoreham-by-Sea			G	5050N 0018W		2703		
229	SIP	UKFF	Simferapol			UR	4502N 3359E	01L/19R	12159		118.1 120.8
269	QPG	WSAP	Singapore	Paya Lebar		9V	0121N 10354E	02/20	12402	124.7 125.2	118.05
269	XSP	WSSL	Singapore	Seletar		9V	0125N 10352E	03/21	5354	119.9 127.7	118.45 130.2
268	SIN	WSSS	SINGAPORE	Changi Intl		9V	0122N 10359E	02L/20R	13123	119.3	118.6
205	SXM	TNCM	Sint Maarten	Prinses Juliana		PJ	1802N 6307W	09/27	12408	128.95	118.7
216	LED	ULLI	Sint Petersburg	Pulkovo		RA	5948N 3016E	10R/28L	7053	125.2 129.8	118.1 118.7
73	SIR	LSGS	Sion			HB	4613N 0720E	08/26	6562	122.35	118.27
101	SGY		Skagway	Municipal	AK	N	5927N 13518W		3850		
2	KDU	OPSD	Skardu			AP	3521N 7532E	15/33	6500		119.7

Page	IATA	ICAO	Town/city	Name	St/country	location	R/W	length	APPROACH	TOWER
202	SGD	EKSB	Soenderborg		OY	5458N 0948E	14/32	4921	118.7	
96	SOF	LBSF	Sofia	International	LZ	4242N 2325E	09/27	9186	119.5, 123.7	118.1, 120.4, 121.6
101	SXQ		Soldotna		AK / N	6028N 15102W		4973	125.7	
202	SFJ	BGSF	Sondrestrom	Kangerlussuaq	OY	6701N 5042W	10/28	9236	118.3	126.2
65	SOU	EGHI	Southampton	Eastleigh	G	5057N 0121W	02/20	5653	120.225, 128.85	118.2
66	SEN	EGMC	Southend	Rochford	G	5134N 0042E	06/24	5265	128.95	127.725
189	GEG	KGEG	Spokane	International	WA / N	4738N 11732W	03/21	9000	123.75, 133.35	118.3
167	SGH		Springfield	Beckley	OH / N	3950N 8350W	06/24	9000	118.85, 126.5	120.7
264	ANU	TAPA	St John's	VCBird - Antigua	V2	1708N 6147W	07/25	9000	119.1	118.2
172	SCE		State College	University Park	PA / N	4050N 7751W	09/27	5000	134.8	
223	STA	EKVJ	Stauning		OY	5559N 0821E		4757	121.4	
93	SVG	ENZV	Stavanger	Sola	LN	5853N 0538E	18/36	8383	119.4, 119.6	118.35, 122.1
122	SBS		Steamboat Spr	Bob Adams	CO / N	4030N 10651W		3913		
251	SZS		Stewart Island		ZK	4658S 16754E				
218	ARN	ESSA	Stockholm	Arlanda	SE	5939N 1755E	01/19	10827	119.4, 120.5	118.5
219	BMA	ESSB	Stockholm	Bromma	SE	5921N 1757E	12/30	5472	119.4, 123.3	118.1, 119.4
119	SCK	KSCK	Stockton	Metropolitan	CA / N	3754N 12114W	11L/29R	8651	123.85, 125.1	120.3
122	BDR	KBDR	Stratford	Sikorsky Memorial	CT / N	4109N 7307W	11/29	4761	126.6, 127.75	126.95
134	SUA		Stuart	Witham Field	FL / N	2710N 8013W		5300		
40	STR	EDDS	**STUTTGART**	Echterdingen	D	4842N 0914E	07/25	10974	118.6, 119.2	118.8, 119.05
208	SUB	WRSJ	Surabaya	Juanda	PK	0722S 11246E	10/28	9843	119.1, 124.0	118.3
234	SYD	YSSY	**SYDNEY**	Kingsford Smith	NS / VH	3357S 15110E	16/34	13000	125.3, 126.1	120.5, 124.7
162	SYR	KSYR	Syracuse	Hancock Field	NY / N	4307N 7606W	10/28	9005	124.2, 124.6	120.3
264	TAI	OYTZ	Ta'izz	Ganed	7O	1341N 4408E	01/19	9843	119.6	118.5
10	TPE	RCTP	**TAIPEI**	Chiang Kai Shek	B	2505N 12113E	05L/23R	12008	119.7	118.7, 125.1, 126.18
11	TSA	RCSS	Taipei	Sung Shan	B	2504N 12133E	10/28	8547	127.9	118.1, 126.18
50	TLL	EETT	Tallinn	Ulemiste	ES	5925N 2450E	09/27	10072	118.15	120.6
134	TPA	KTPA	**TAMPA**	International	FL / N	2758N 8232W	18R/36L	11002	125.2, 118.5	119.05, 119.5
228	TAS	UTTT	Tashkent	Yuzhny	UK	4115N 6917E	08L/26R	13123	118.85	120.4
66	MME	EGNV	Teesside		G	5431N 0125W	05/23	7516	120.5	119.8
257	TLV	LLBG	Tel Aviv	Ben Gurion	4X	3201N 3453E	08/26	11998	119.7	118.3
48	TFN	GCXO	Tenerife	Norte/Los Rodeos	EC	2829N 1620W	12/30	11155	120.3	118.7
47	TFS	GCTS	Tenerife	Sur/Reina Sofia	EC	2803N 1634W	08/26	10500		119.0, 120.3

Page	IATA	ICAO	Town/city	Name	St/country	location	R/W	length	APPROACH	TOWER
154	TEB	KTEB	Teterboro		NJ N	4051N 7403W	10/28	7000	127.6	118.1 122.1
224	SKG	LGTS	Thessaloniki	Makedonia	SX	4031N 2258E	10/28	8005	120.8 122.1	119.3
221	TED	EKTS	Thisted		OY	5704N 0842E	10/28	5249		118.1
243	TIJ	MMTJ	Tijuana	Abelardo Rodriguez	XA	3232N 11659W	09/27	9711	119.5	120.1
245	TSR	LRTR	Timisoara	Giarmata	YR	4549N 2120E	11/29	11483	120.3	119.25
135	TIX		Titusville	Space Center Ex	FL N	2830N 8047W		6000		120.1
89		RJTF	Tokyo	Chofu	JA	3540N 13932E	17/35	3280		118.0 126.2
90	HND	RJTT	TOKYO	Haneda	JA	3533N 13946E	16L/34R	9843	119.1	118.1 118.8
90	NRT	RJAA	TOKYO	Narita	JA	3546N 14023E	16/34	13123	124.4 125.8	118.2 122.7 124.35
167	TOL	KTOL	Toledo	Express	OH N	4135N 8348W	07/25	8700	128.0 123.9	118.1
21	YKZ	CYKZ	Toronto	Buttonville	OT C	4356N 7919W				
21	YZD	CYZD	Toronto	Downsview	OT C	4345N 7928W				
21	YTZ	CYTZ	Toronto	City Centre	OT C	4337N 7923W		4000		
19	YYZ	CYYZ	TORONTO	Lester B Pearson	OT C	4341N 7938W	15L/33R	11050	125.4 124.3	118.35 118.7
130	TOA		Torrance		CA N	3348N 11820W		5000	118.9	124.0
56	TLS	LFBO	Toulouse	Blagnac	F	4337N 0123E	15R/33L	11483	121.1	118.1
21	YTR	CYTR	Trenton		OT C	4407N 7731W				
107	E14		Tucson	Avra Valley	AZ N	3224N 11113W		4200		
107	TUS	KTUS	Tucson	International	AZ N	3207N 11056W	11L/29R	11000	118.5 125.1	118.3
169	TUL	KTUL	Tulsa	International	OK N	3612N 9553W	18/36	10000	120.15 121.1	120.7
85	TRN	LIMF	Turin	Caselle	I	4512N 0739E	18/36	10827		118.5
216	ULY		Ulyanovsk		RA	5425N 4825E				
256	UTT	FAUT	Umtata	K D Matanzima	ZS	3133S 2840E	14/32	6562		121.3
94	USH	SAWH	Ushuaia		LV	5450S 6818W	07/25	8071		118.1
163	UCA		Utica	Oneida County	NY N	4308N 7523W	12/30	6000	126.65	118.1 122.1
48	VLC	LEVC	Valencia	Menitses	EC	3929N 0029W	12/30	8858	121.0 120.4 124.75	118.55
23	CXH		Vancouver	Harbor Heliport	BC C	4920N 12310W				
22	YVR	CYVR	VANCOUVER	International	BC C	4911N 12310W	08R/26L	11000	120.8 133.1	118.7 119.55 124.0
31	VRA	MUVR	Varadero	J G Gomez	CU	2308N 8118W	06/24	11483	119.6	118.4
96	VAR	LBWN	Varna	International	LZ	4314N 2749E	09/27	8202	121.0 124.6	118.9 119.5
86	VCE	LIPZ	Venice	Tessera	I	4530N 1221E	04R/22L	10827	120.4 121.15	120.2
135	VRB	KVRB	Vero Beach	Municipal	FL N	2704N 8026W	11R/29L	7296	120.4	119.65
86	VRN	LIPX	Verona	Villafranca Veronesa	I	4524N 1053E	05/23	9797	124.25 124.45	118.65 124.5

Page	IATA	ICAO	Town/city	Name	St/country	location	R/W	length	APPROACH	TOWER
23	YYJ	CYYJ	Victoria	International	BC C	4838N 12324W	12/30	7500	127.8	119.7
248	VFA	FVFA	Victoria Falls		Z	1806S 2550E				121.1
195	VIE	LOWW	VIENNA	Schwechat	OE	4807N 1633E	16/34	11811	119.8 124.55 128.2	119.4 121.2
77	VVC	SKVV	Villavicencio	La Vanguardia	HK	0404N 7323W				127.3
95	VNO	EYVI	Vilnius		LY	5438N 2517E	02/20	8202	120.7 128.0	118.2 128.0
182	ACT	KACT	Waco	Madison Cooper	TX N	3136N 9713W	11/29	6600		119.3
252	WKA	NZWF	Wanaka		ZK	4444S 16915E	15/33	3937		
219	WAW	EPWA	WARSAW	Okecie	SP	5210N 2058E	15/33	12106	128.8	118.3
123	IAD	KIAD	WASHINGTON	Dulles Intl	VA N	3857N 7727W	01R/19L	11500	sectors	120.1
124	DCA	KDCA	WASHINGTON	National	DC N	3851N 7702W	18/36	6869	124.2 124.7	119.1 120.75
50	WAT	EIWF	Waterford		EI	5211N 0705W	03/21	4701		129.85
252	WLG	NZWN	Wellington	International	ZK	4119S 17448E	16/34	6348	119.3 121.1 122.3	118.8 120.0
189	EAT		Wenatchee	Pangborn	WA N	4724N 12012W		5500		
136	PBI	KPBI W	West Palm Beach	International	FL N	2641N 8005W	09L/27R	7989	124.6	119.1
163	FOK	KFOK	Westhampton	Suffolk County	NY N	4050N 7237W		9000		120.5
163	HPN	KHPN	White Plains	Westchester Co	NY N	4104N 7342W		6548	126.4	119.7
24	YXY	CYXY	Whitehorse		YT C	6042N 13504W	13R/31L	7200	132.1	118.3
144	ICT	KICT	Wichita	Mid-Continent	KS N	3740N 9726W	01L/19R	10300	125.5 134.8	118.2
172	AVP		Wilkes Barre	Scranton	PA N	4120N 7543W	04/22	7500	124.5	
173	IPT	KIPT	Williamsport	Lycoming County	PA N	4120N 7646W		6450	124.9	
167	ILN		Wilmington	Airborne Park	OH N	3925N 8348W	04/22	9000	118.5	118.85
24	YQG	CYQG	Windsor		OT C	4216N 8258W	07/25	7900	126.85	124.7
122	BDL	KBDL	WINDSOR LOCKS	Bradley Intl	CT N	4156N 7241W	06/24	9501	125.8	120.3 125.65
24	YWG	CYWG	WINNIPEG	International	MN C	4955N 9714W	18/36	11000	119.5	118.3 125.4
153	INT	KINT	Winston-Salem	Smith-Reynolds	NC N	3607N 8015W	18/36	6655		120.9
9	WUH	ZHHH	Wuhan	Nanhu	B	3030N 11400E	18/36	5945		
9		ZHWT	Wuhan	Wangjiaddun	B	3030N 11400E				
10	XIY	ZLXY	Xi'an	Xianyang	B	3426N 10845E	05/23	9843		123.0
25	YZF	CYZF	Yellowknife		NT C	6227N 11426W	14/32	7500	135.8	118.5
167	YNG	KYNG	Youngstown	Warren Regional	OH N	4116N 8041W	14/32	7500	120.2 127.5	119.5
108	YUM	KYUM	Yuma	International	AZ N	3239N 11436W		13299		120.0
74	ZRH	LSZH	ZURICH	Kloten	HB	4728N 0833E	16/34	12140	118.0 120.75	118.1 119.7 127.75

Just Planes Videos

USA Domestic Series

1.	BOS	Boston/Logan, MA '92
2.	BOS	Boston/Logan, MA '92/3
3.	JFK	New York, NY '93 (No longer Available)
4.	BOS	Boston/Logan, MA '93
5.	ORD	Chicago/O'Hare, IL '93
6.	BOS	Boston/Logan, MA '93
7.	MIA	Miami, FL '93 Pt.1
8.	MIA	Miami, FL '93 Pt.2
9.	BOS	Boston/Logan, MA '93/4
10.	MCO	Orlando, FL '94
11.	FLL	Fort Lauderdale, FL '94
12.	JFK	New York / John F Kennedy, NY '94
13.	BOS	Boston, MA '94
14.	ATL	Atlanta/Harts Field, GA '94
15.	LAX	Los Angeles, CA '94
16.	SFO	San Fransisco, CA '95
17.	FAI	Fairbanks, AK '95
18.	JFK	New York / John F Kennedy, NY '95
19.	EWR	Newark International, NJ '95
20.	LAS	Las Vegas, NV
21.	ANC	Anchorage, AK
22.	*LAX*	*Los Angeles, CA '96*
23.	DFW	Dallas F.Worth/Love, TX '96
24.	MIA	Denver / Colorado Springs, CO
25.	DEN	Denvers, CO
	COS	Colorado Springs, CO
26.	DTW	Detroit/Metropolitan, MI
	DTL	Detroit Lake/Municipal, MI
	YIP	Detroit/Willow Run, MI
27.	IAD	Washington/Dulles International, DC
	BWI	Baltimore/Washington International, DC
	DCA	Washington/National, DC

all around 120 minutes long

View from the Cockpit series

1. Antalya, Istanbul, New York
2. Brussels, Lagos, Liege, Yaounde

Just Planes Specials

1. Amazing Flying Colours
2. DC-3 in the Caribbean
3. Airlines Flying the Boeing 747
4. Just 737s [due .97]

At least one new title added every month !

Flight in the Cockpit series

1.	Carnival Airlines Boeing 727-200 (55 min)
2.	Lufthansa Fleet
3.	Crossair Avro RJ85, Saab 2000
4.	Cargolux Boeing 747-200 (90 min)
5.	Sobelair Boeing 737-300
6.	Sobelair Boeing 767-300
7.	Cargolux Boeing 747-400
8.	Turkish Airlines Airbus A340-300
9.	VASP Fleet (A300, B737-200, N737-300, MD-11)
10.	VASP McDonnell-Douglas MD-11
11.	Sabena Airbus A310-200
12.	Sabena Airbus A340-200
13.	Transbrazil Boeing 767-200 and -300
14.	Fine Air Douglas DC-8-50 Miami - Caribbean
15.	Fine Air Douglas DC-8-50 Miami - South America

all 60 minutes long except as shown

International Series

1.	FRA	Frankfurt, Germany '95
2.	HKG	Hong Kong '95
3.	SJU	San Juan, Puerto Rico '95
4.	ORY	Paris/Orly, France '95
5.	CDG	Paris/Charles de Gaulle, France '95
6.	PRG	Prague/Ruzyne, Czech Republic '95
7.	ZRH	Zurich/Kloten, Switzerland '95
8.	PEK	Bejing/Capitol & Xiamen, China '95
9.	SGN	Ho Chi Min City, Vietnam '96
10.	BKK	Bangkok/Don Muang, Thailand '96
11.	CCS	Caracas/S Bolivar Int, Venezeula '96
12.	AMS	Amsterdam/Schiphol, Netherlands '96
13.	MEX	Mexico City, Mexico '96
14.	HKG	Hong Kong '96 Pt 1
15.	HKG	Hong Kong '96 Pt.2
16.	YYZ	Toronto, Canada '96
17.	JED	Jeddah, Saudi Arabia '96
18.	MXP	Milan/Malpensa, Italy
	LIN	Milan/Linate, Italy
19.	DUS	Dusseldorf, Germany
20.	ACE	Lanzarote, Spain
21.	MRS	Marseilles, France
22.	DXB	Dubai, UAE
	SHJ	Sharjah, UAE
23.	CHC	Christchurch, New Zealand
	WLG	Wellington, New Zealand
24.	HND	Tokyo/Haneda, Japan

all around 120 minutes long

BUCHair (U.K.) Ltd

PO Box 89, Reigate, Surrey, RH2 7FG, UK

Tel: +44 (0)1737 224 747   Fax: +44 (0)1737 226 777

email: buchair_uk@compuserve.com

www: http://www.buchair.rotor.com

Notes